FOR REFERENCE

Do Not Take From This Room

MILESTONE DOCUMENTS
IN WORLD HISTORY

Exploring the Primary Sources
That Shaped the World

MILESTONE DOCUMENTS
IN WORLD HISTORY

Exploring the Primary Sources
That Shaped the World

Volume 3
1839 – 1941

Brian Bonhomme
Editor in Chief

Cathleen Boivin
Consulting Editor

Schlager Group

Dallas, Texas

Schlager Group Inc.
2501 Oak Lawn Avenue, Suite 440
Dallas, Tex. 75219
USA

You can find Schlager Group on the World Wide Web at
http://www.schlagergroup.com
Text and cover design by Patricia Moritz

Printed in the United States of America

10 9 8 7 6 5 4 3 2 1

ISBN: 978-0-9797758-6-4

This book is printed on acid-free paper.

CONTENTS

MILESTONE DOCUMENTS IN WORLD HISTORY

Exploring the Primary Sources
That Shaped the World

LIN ZEXU'S "MORAL ADVICE TO QUEEN VICTORIA"

"The wealth of China is used to profit the barbarians."

Overview

In 1839, in light of the growing level of opium addiction in China under the Qing Dynasty, Emperor Daoguang sent Commissioner Lin Zexu to Guangzhou (also called Canton), Guangdong Province, and ordered him to stop the smuggling and sale of opium in China by Western, especially British, merchants. While negotiating with Charles Elliot, the British superintendent of trade, for his cooperation, Lin wrote a letter in the traditional "memorial" form to the ruler of Britain expressing China's desire for peaceful resolution of the opium trade. He used what limited—even mistaken—knowledge he had newly acquired about his adversary in the hope of evoking the latter's sympathy and understanding. Drawing on Confucian precepts as well as historical events, he also reasoned forcefully on moral ground, trying to persuade the English monarch that he naturally would not wish to ask of others what he himself did not want. The letter was, in effect, an ultimatum made by Commissioner Lin on behalf of the Qing emperor to the English monarch, delivering the unmistakable message that he and the Qing government were determined to ban the selling and smoking of opium once and for all and at any cost.

After drafting and revising the letter, Commissioner Lin asked his assistant and English missionaries and merchants to translate it into English and present it to the British king—who was actually Queen Victoria, whose reign had begun in 1837. Lin also circulated the letter as a public announcement to the Western merchants in Guangzhou. In the end, the letter was not delivered to the queen as he had intended, nor was his hope for a peaceful solution to the opium problem realized. Instead, the so-called First Opium War broke out in 1840, which ended in the Qing Dynasty's defeat and Lin's dismissal.

Context

From the late seventeenth century onward, international trade and commerce gained more and more importance in the West. The demand for tea and porcelain from China and for spices and indigo from India motivated many Europeans, especially the Dutch, Portuguese, and English, to establish trade depots or factories in Asia. The success of the emergent Industrial Revolution in England also fueled the English ambition to sell manufactured products in Asia in exchange for Asian goods. But most Asians, especially the Chinese, were simply uninterested in reciprocating trade with Western Europe. In 1793 Lord George Macartney, the first British ambassador to China, approached Emperor Qianlong and presented King George III's wish to establish diplomatic relations and expand trade between Britain and China. The emperor, however, firmly rejected all the requests made by the British embassy on the grounds that China had always been a self-sufficient country and that it had neither need for nor interest in foreign goods. At the time, any foreign trade with the West was administered through the Canton System, in which Western merchants were allowed to sell their goods in Guangzhou only through the Cohong (or Gonghang) merchants, who were the Chinese middlemen. Hoping to change the system and expand trade, Europeans continued to send embassies to China—the Dutch in 1795, the Russians in 1806, and the British again in 1816—all to no avail.

The Europeans repeatedly sent emissaries to China because they wanted to sell more goods to the Chinese in order to balance the growing trade deficit incurred through the purchase of Chinese goods, especially tea. Through the eighteenth century, tea imports in Britain had risen sharply; from 1784 to 1785 they grew to over fifteen million pounds, from just over two pounds a century or so earlier. The British East India Company, which handled the nation's trade with China, began to grow tea in India in the 1820s but would not ship tea to Britain until 1858. Therefore, through the mid-nineteenth century almost all tea had to be imported from China. Between 1811 and 1819, British imports from China totaled over £72 million, of which tea was worth £70 million.

Aside from diplomatic efforts, the British also searched for and found an alternative to the currency of silver for the purchase of tea and other Chinese goods: opium. Just as Lord Macartney was pleading with Emperor Qianlong for the establishment of trade relations, British merchants discovered this different and illicit way to address the mount-

1600
- **December 31**
  The British East India Company is founded.

1760
- The Canton System is established, forbidding direct access to trade in China by foreign merchants.

1820
- **October 3**
  Emperor Daoguang ascends to the Qing dynastic throne in China.

1834
- The monopoly of the British East India Company on trade with the Far East ends.

1837
- **June 20**
  Queen Victoria ascends to the British throne.

1838
- Commissioner Lin Zexu is sent by Emperor Daoguang to Guangdong to halt the sale of opium.

1839
- Lin Zexu writes an open letter to Queen Victoria, urging a peaceful resolution to the opium trade.
- The First Opium War breaks out.

ing trade deficit with China. They began selling opium to the Chinese even though it had been banned by Emperor Yongzheng, Emperor Qianlong's father, as early as 1729. Thanks to opium sales, the silver inflow to China dropped from over 26.6 million taels between 1801 and 1810 to under 10 million taels between 1811 and 1820, or by about 63 percent. Later, as opium addiction spread rapidly in China, silver began to flow out of the country to the West, especially Britain; between 1821 and 1830 China paid out 2.3 million taels. And from 1831 to 1833, a period of merely three years, China paid an astonishing 9.9 million taels.

During the 1830s, therefore, Qing China began to suffer seriously from the trade deficit with the West. The economic toll of the growing opium sales and addiction in China was twofold. First, as opium sales grew, sales in other areas of trade dropped as a result. In his early career as governor of Jiangsu Province, Lin Zexu observed that Chinese merchants could sell only half of what they used to sell a decade or two earlier. Second, the outflow of silver caused a financial crisis in the country by altering the exchange rate between silver and copper, which was used in people's daily transactions. The shortage of silver caused its value to appreciate, which aggravated the tax burden on the people, because in paying tax they had to exchange copper cash for silver. In the eighteenth century a string of 1,000 copper cash was equal to 1 tael of silver. By the early nineteenth century 1 tael of silver was worth 1,500 copper cash, and in the mid–nineteenth century it was worth 2,700 copper cash.

While opium does have medicinal use, relieving pain and allaying emotional distress, it is an addictive drug. Once the habit is formed, the withdrawal symptoms can include "extreme restlessness, chills, hot flushes, sneezing, sweating, salivation, running nose, and gastrointestinal disturbances such as nausea, vomiting, and diarrhea." Furthermore, "there are severe cramps in the abdomen, legs, and back; the bones ache; the muscles twitch; and the nerves are on edge. Every symptom is in combat with another. The addict is hungry, but he cannot eat; he is sleepy, but he cannot sleep" (Chang, p. 17). There can be little wonder, then, that ever since Emperor Yongzheng banned its consumption in the early eighteenth century, opium has remained contraband in China. During the early nineteenth century, when opium smoking spread across social strata and addicts numbered in the millions, many observers grew alarmed, especially scholar-officials, who presented a number of "memorials" to Emperor Daoguang, urging him to adopt harsh measures against the smuggling and selling of the drug. Lin Zexu was one, and arguably the most eloquent, among these scholar-officials. In one of his memorials, he argued vehemently that "if we continue to pamper it [opium smoking], a few decades from now we shall not only be without soldiers to resist the enemy, but also in want of silver to provide an army" (Chang, p. 96). Others suggested legalizing the drug to curb its abuse, but the proposal was rejected by the emperor, who regarded opium as an evil poison.

There is no source directly explaining why opium smoking—which entails first heating opium paste over a flame and then smoking it through a long-stemmed pipe—became so popular among the Chinese beginning in the late eighteenth century. Speculation holds that it might have had something to do with tobacco smoking, imported from Latin America in the previous century. When tobacco smoking was first introduced to mainland China by soldiers who returned from a campaign in Taiwan, opium and tobacco were mixed and smoked together. As opium's therapeutic effects were revealed, it gained in popularity, especially among people who struggled with boredom or stress, such as eunuchs, wealthy women, petty clerks, and examination takers. As time went on, the habit of opium smoking spread to the leisure and working classes alike for social relaxation. To abet sales, merchants prepared detailed accounts of means of consumption in simple language, available to anyone who could read.

Nor has a convincing explanation been put forth for why, despite the repeated edicts from the emperor and the government, opium smoking became so unstoppable in China. Aside from the persistence of Western merchants in selling the drug, it was generally believed that the Qing government had by then become corrupt and hence ineffective in executing imperial orders. When a new imperial edict was issued in 1813 banning opium smoking altogether, it was actually quite harsh in punishing both smokers and sellers. If caught, a smoker could be sentenced to one hundred blows of the bamboo stick and forced to wear a heavy wooden collar in public for a month. Afraid of the severe consequences, the Cohong merchants who had monopolized the trade with the Europeans ceased involvement, at least in public. But small dealers quickly took their place, approaching European merchants directly in swift boats and then distributing the drug through networks of local trade. Apparently, this was a risky practice; to ensure its success, both European merchants and Chinese dealers bribed officials for their connivance. Some officials even exploited the trade by enforcing a fee per chest of opium. Whenever a new anti-opium edict was issued from the central government, local officials, rather than carry it out, would increase the fee for enriching themselves.

The British East India Company also played a dubious role in the opium trade, to say the least. Some of its officials did have qualms about smuggling the drug into China; the company stopped sales at one point, only to allow their resumption shortly after. For the company, the establishment of a long-standing opium monopoly in the Bengal region was a major success of the British conquest of India. In the 1780s the British East India Company took control of opium sales and production in the English-controlled areas of India. Shortly thereafter, the company also monopolized the trade with China. Hence, the company's opium production in India coincided with its intensified trade with China. In light of the huge deficits it had incurred in buying tea from China, the company clearly had major incentive to engage in opium production, if not directly in its selling. In fact, thanks to the company's excellent management of its opium monopoly in India, Indian opium was regarded by both dealers and smokers as representing high quality. The profits made by the company through opium sales would be directly used to purchase tea. A triangular trade

Time Line

1842	■ **August 29** The Treaty of Nanjing is signed, ending the First Opium War as well as the Canton System.
1850	■ **February 25** Emperor Daoguang dies. ■ **March 9** Emperor Xianfeng ascends to the Qing throne.
1856	■ The Second Opium War breaks out, to last for four years.
1858	■ **August 2** Under the Act for the Better Government of India, the British East India Company's functions are transferred to the Crown.
1874	■ **January 1** The British East India Company closes its business operations.

network, from Britain to India, India to China, and China to Britain, thus formed. The company first bought (nominally) opium in India, selling it to private merchants, or "country traders," for smuggling into China; the merchants then used the silver gained to buy tea, porcelain, and other goods to sell back in Britain. This network helped to support the entire British position in the Far East, especially the ruling of India. Thanks to opium, the company and the British government not only corrected the earlier deficits in their China trade but also reaped a good fortune.

The success of the British East India Company in monopolizing and profiting from the trade with China caused envy

The East India Company ruled British India from East India House until 1858. (© Museum of London)

among others. By 1834 the company's monopoly of the trade came to an end, and the trade's being open to all comers resulted in the rise of opium sales. In 1832 China imported more than twenty-three thousand chests of opium (with each chest containing between 130 and 160 pounds); the figure rose to thirty thousand chests in 1835 and to forty thousand chests in 1838. These increases drove Western merchants to chafe more blatantly at the Canton System, the Qing government's means of control of foreign trade, in the hope of prying open China's door to the West, and merchants' actions were broadly sanctioned by the British government. After the end of the British East India Company's monopoly, British merchants in China were represented by the superintendent of trade. A government official, the superintendent often refused to deal with the Cohong merchants, demanding instead that he communicate directly with Qing officials. The clash over opium sales thus became not simply a matter between the Qing government and Western merchants but rather one between Qing China and Great Britain.

About the Author

Born in Fuzhou, Fujian Province, in 1785, Lin Zexu excelled in his study of the Chinese classics and in the civil service examinations; he earned the *jinshi* ("presented scholar") degree in 1811 and subsequently became a member of the Hanlin Academy, a prestigious institution of Confucian learning in Beijing, the dynasty capital. Lin then launched a successful career in government, serving in a range of posts in various provinces. His commitment to high moral standards and integrity earned him the epithet of "Lin the Blue Sky." Prior to becoming the imperial commissioner, Lin was the governor-general of Hunan and Hubei in 1837; in this post he launched a vigorous campaign against opium smoking. He also repeatedly memorialized the emperor for taking tough measures against opium sales. As commissioner, Lin assembled scholars to compile the book *Sizhouzhi* (Treatise on Four Continents), an effort to establish and disseminate knowledge about Europe and the world. After Western merchants refused to obey his orders to surrender illicit opium, he blockaded their enclave and eventually confiscated and destroyed 2.6 million pounds of opium. The British government retaliated by sending a fleet to China, and the British prevailed in battle. Angry over Lin's action for its leading to military conflict and defeat, Emperor Daoguang dismissed him and exiled him to Xinjiang. Lin was later reinstated, however, and ordered to deal with other difficult situations. He died while traveling to Guangxi to administer a campaign against the Taiping Rebellion in 1850.

Explanation and Analysis of the Document

Lin Zexu's letter to the British Crown starts by singing praises to the Qing emperor for his grace and benevolence. These praises reflect the long-entrenched Chinese notion that China was the center of the world, or the "Zhongguo" (Central Country/Middle Kingdom) in the cosmos. Out of courtesy, Lin acknowledges in the second paragraph that Britain is also a historical country with an honorable tradition. Yet this acknowledgment, too, builds on the Sinocentric conception of the world; he commends the "politeness and submissiveness" of the British in delivering tributes and offering "tributary memorials" to the ruler of the Celestial Empire—China. He also deems that the British have benefited considerably from these activities, a point he will stress again later in the letter.

Paragraphs 3–5 directly address the problem that prompted Lin to seek communication with the ruler of Britain: the smuggling and selling of opium in China by British merchants. Lin describes how his emperor is enraged by the harm to the Chinese people caused by opium smoking and how he has been dispatched by the emperor to put an end to the practice. He explains the punishment for the Chinese who smoke and sell opium and notes that were his emperor not so graceful, the same punishment could be extended to British sellers. Lin had recently confiscated a large amount of opium through the help of Charles Elliot, the British superintendent of trade; his reporting this serves as a warning because, as he reveals, the Qing Dynasty had, in fact, promulgated new regulations, whereby if any Briton was found selling opium, he would receive the same punishment as would a Chinese. Indeed, a major reason for Lin's writing and circulating this letter was to inform and warn the British and other foreign merchants about the new regulations. In order to carry them out, he needed the help of the British ruler, who "must be able to instruct the various barbarians to observe the law with care."

In seeking to secure the aid of the British ruler, Lin resorts to moral suasion in paragraphs 6–8. This is consistent with the teaching of Confucianism and Lin's own character. His central argument draws on the Confucian precept that, as phrased in paragraph 8, "naturally you would not wish to give unto others what you yourself do not want." But in exercising this moral exhortation, Lin shows his limited as well as mistaken knowledge about his adversary, and his mistakes invariably undercut the effect of his argument. He first assumes that the sale and smoking of opium are forbidden in Britain, which was erroneous, for most British then considered opium no more harmful to humans than alcohol. Second, he believes tea and rhubarb to be indispensable to the health of the British, which was wrong, even though tea drinking had become a national habit in Britain. Third, he states that without Chinese silk, other textiles could not be woven; this was clearly inaccurate. But even with these seemingly egregious mistakes, Lin makes a strong point: The British needed Chinese goods more than the Chinese did British goods, so how could the British repay the benefits from and benevolence of the Chinese by selling them the poisonous drug? In paragraph 6 he asks passionately, "Where is your conscience?" It would have been hard for the British Crown to counter this line of argument.

After asking such acute questions, Lin softens his tone in paragraph 9. He writes that perhaps the British ruler was unaware that some wicked British subjects have been involved in opium smuggling in China, since in the British homeland, because of the king's (that is, the queen's) "honorable rule," no opium is produced. He thus asks the British ruler to extend the edict against planting opium from Britain to India and to grow the "five grains" in its stead. This plea is also made on the moral ground that for such a virtuous course of action, "heaven must support you and the spirits must bring you good fortune." Lin's notion that the "five grains" are essential to humans and his belief in both "Heaven" and "spirits" are distinctly Chinese.

Paragraphs 10–12 offer further explanation of the new regulations from the imperial court by which the same punishments will be extended to the British if they continue ignoring Lin's anti-opium orders and policy. Central to these explanations is an idea of jurisdiction that Lin takes for granted (as do many sovereign nations today): A foreigner who lives in another country must obey the laws of that country rather than the laws of his own. That is, Lin repudiates the extraterritorial rights that the British then demanded from the Qing Dynasty—and which they later obtained through the First Opium War. Lin's refusal of such privilege in this letter does not draw on international law but follows the same Confucian principle that you would not do unto others what you yourself do not want done unto you, the line of reasoning he used before. He asks the English ruler, "Suppose a man of another country comes to England to trade, he still has to obey the English laws; how much more should he obey in China the laws of the Celestial Dynasty?"

Before he actually carried out the new orders—to punish opium sellers with "decapitation or strangulation"—Lin wanted to exercise caution, which was why he decided to write the letter in the first place. In paragraph 12, he again reminds the reader of the kindness of his emperor. When informed of the new regulations, Charles Elliot requested an extension, Lin writes. After Lin forwarded the request to the emperor, the emperor, out of "consideration and compassion," actually agreed to grant the extension with additional months of leeway. Lin thus hails his ruler's "extraordinary Celestial grace." Yet with the benefit of hindsight, historians may also interpret this "grace" as a sort of reluctance on the part of the Qing ruler to confront the British militarily. In other words, although the emperor ordered Lin to halt opium sales in Guangzhou and Guangdong, he was not ready to risk war with the British. If Lin's letter amounted to a last-ditch effort to solve the opium problem peacefully, this approach was indeed favored and sanctioned by the emperor. It was said that Lin memorialized Emperor Daoguang sometime in July 1839, enclosing in the memorial the letter that he had drafted for the English ruler. On August 27, Emperor Daoguang approved it. Lin then asked others to translate it into English, publicized it around Guangzhou, and looked for messengers to deliver it to Britain.

Illustration of an opium den in London (© Museum of London)

Milestone Documents in World History

> "The wealth of China is used to profit the barbarians. That is to say, the great profit made by barbarians is all taken from the rightful share of China. By what right do they then in return use the poisonous drug to injure the Chinese people? ... Let us ask, where is your conscience?"
>
> (Paragraph 6)

> "To digest clearly the legal penalties as an aid to instruction has been a valid principle in all ages. Suppose a man of another country comes to England to trade, he still has to obey the English laws; how much more should he obey in China the laws of the Celestial Dynasty?"
>
> (Paragraph 10)

> "The fact is that the wicked barbarians beguile the Chinese people into a death trap.... He who takes the life of even one person still has to atone for it with his own life; yet is the harm done by opium limited to the taking of one life only? Therefore in the new regulations, in regard to those barbarians who bring opium to China, the penalty is fixed at decapitation or strangulation. This is what is called getting rid of a harmful thing on behalf of mankind."
>
> (Paragraph 11)

In concluding his letter, Lin makes another—perhaps the strongest—request to the English monarch, asking the latter to take the responsibility of urging British subjects to observe Chinese laws and mores and cease the opium trade. Lin demands that the monarch, after receiving the letter, inform him and the Qing government of the means by which the trade will be stopped. Since Queen Victoria (most likely) did not even see the letter, Lin's request/demand went completely ignored.

Audience

The intended recipient of this letter was Queen Victoria, who was crowned monarch of the United Kingdom in 1837; she would also become the first Empress of India under the British Raj in 1876, and she retained both of these royal titles until her death in 1901. The last monarch of the House of Hanover, the queen was brought up speaking German, French, and English. She married off all of her nine children throughout Europe. During her reign, Great Britain saw the success of the Industrial Revolution and the establishment of the British Empire around the world. The Victorian era was marked by progress, prosperity, and power for Great Britain, which became one of the most formidable global empires in modern history.

Since the letter, before it made its way to Britain and appeared in the London *Times*, was first circulated and publicized in Guangzhou among the Westerners there, they were hence also its targeted audience. These Westerners included officials such as the British superintendent of trade, Charles Elliot, and his assistants; most, however, were merchants from Europe and America, with the British apparently constituting the majority. As "country traders," they at first obtained licenses for purchasing and selling Indian opium from the British East India Company on a select basis. After 1834, when the company's monopoly on trade in China ended, the countries where the traders came from multiplied, and the sources where they acquired the opium also diversified. Both of these factors exacerbated the opium problem on the eve of the First Opium War.

Impact

Since Lin Zexu failed to accomplish the delivery of the letter to the British ruler and thus failed to secure the latter's cooperation in ceasing opium sales, he stepped up his anti-opium campaign. After the British merchants refused to pledge not to sell opium, he expelled them from Macao, as they had been from Guangzhou. The British retreated to Hong Kong, then a small fishing island, where they were harried by the local Chinese. Having lost their opium and fearing for their lives, the merchants lobbied the British parliament for compensation and protection. Lord Palmerston, the foreign minister, dispatched a fleet of sixteen warships carrying four thousand mariners and over five hundred guns to China. Instead of engaging the Qing forces commanded by Lin in Guangdong, the fleet sailed north, where they

seized Zhoushan. This led Emperor Daoguang to dismiss Lin and replace him with Qishan, a trusted Manchu official who negotiated an agreement with Charles Elliot in January 1841. Through the agreement the Chinese were to, among other provisions, cede Hong Kong and pay six million taels of silver as indemnity to the British. The British fleet consequently returned to the south.

However, the war was not over. Dissatisfied with the agreement, Lord Palmerston fired Charles Elliot, and Henry Pottinger, the new superintendent of trade, resumed war. After losing several cities to the British, the Qing Dynasty pursued peace, which resulted in the signing of the Treaty of Nanjing on August 29, 1842. Ratified ten months later by Queen Victoria and Emperor Daoguang, the treaty stipulated that the Qing Dynasty open five port cities for trade, cede Hong Kong, and pay a total of thirty-nine million taels of silver to the British. It also officially ended the Canton System. Ironically, the opium trade is not mentioned in the treaty, except in the statement that of the total indemnity amount, six million taels were to com-

Questions for Further Study

1. For many years, the United States has been engaged in a "war on drugs," attempting both to curtail demand for illegal drugs and to interdict smuggling of illegal drugs into the United States. The limited successes of this war have prompted many Americans to call for the legalization of certain drugs, yet exporting nations show little interest in stopping drug production. In what ways does the drug situation in the contemporary United States parallel that of China in the nineteenth century?

2. Lin Zexu's letter never reached the hands of its intended audience, the British monarch, Queen Victoria. In what way, then, can the letter be regarded as a "milestone" document? Put differently, in what ways did Lin Zexu's letter represent a crucial turning point in relations between the West and Asia, specifically China?

3. During the eighteenth and nineteenth centuries, business enterprises such as the British East India Company were often instruments of both commerce and a nation's foreign policy. In what sense did British merchants in China represent British foreign policy with regard to China as well as India? Why did England dispatch its navy to China in response to the actions and policies of the Chinese on their own soil?

4. The dissension between the Chinese and the British that led to the First Opium War was in part the result of a failure of diplomacy. In the early nineteenth century, the history, culture, religion, language, politics, and traditions of Britain and China were so different that the two nations found it difficult to find common ground for communication. In what ways does Lin Zexu's letter—and, indeed, the entire controversy surrounding it—demonstrate this failure of understanding and diplomacy? What could either side have done, if anything, to preserve its interests and yet reduce the possibility of armed conflict? Do you see any conflicts in the modern world that parallel this conflict between East and West in the nineteenth century?

5. In the nineteenth century, Asians, especially the Chinese, showed little interest in trade relations with the West, despite the efforts of several European countries to establish such relations. Why were the Chinese so resistant to trade with the West?

pensate the losses of the opium sellers. Other Western nations followed suit in seeking such agreements. As they concluded similar and sometimes more-detailed treaties with the Qing, the benefits and privileges granted were also extended to the British, including the contested "extraterritorial rights." Thus, after the First Opium War, the Qing Dynasty lost most of its control of China's commercial, social, and foreign policies. As such, the war ushered in a new era of Chinese history, to be marked by the further intrusion of Western powers and by the continuous Chinese struggle against colonialism and imperialism.

Further Reading

■ Articles

Kwong, Luke S. K. "The Chinese Myth of Universal Kinship and Commissioner Lin Zexu's Anti-Opium Campaign of 1839." *English Historical Review* 123, no. 505 (December 2008): 1470–1503.

Newman, R. K. "Opium Smoking in Late Imperial China: A Reconsideration." *Modern Asian Studies* 29, no. 4 (October 1995): 765–794.

Wang, Dong. "The Discourse of Unequal Treaties in Modern China." *Pacific Affairs* 76, no. 3 (Fall 2003): 399–425.

■ Books

Chang, Hsin-pao. *Commissioner Lin and the Opium War*. Cambridge, Mass.: Harvard University Press, 1964.

Gelber, Harry G. *Opium, Soldiers and Evangelicals: Britain's 1840–42 War with China, and Its Aftermath*. Houndmills, Basingstoke, U.K.: Palgrave Macmillan, 2004.

Madancy, Joyce A. *The Troublesome Legacy of Commissioner Lin: The Opium Trade and Opium Suppression in Fujian Province, 1820s to 1920s*. Cambridge, Mass.: Harvard University Press, 2004.

Polachek, James M. *The Inner Opium War*. Cambridge, Mass.: Harvard University Press, 1992.

Zheng, Yangwen. *The Social Life of Opium in China*. Cambridge, U.K.: Cambridge University Press, 2005.

■ Web Sites

Chrastina, Paul. "Emperor of China Declares War on Drugs." Future Opioids Web site.
    http://www.opioids.com/opium/opiumwar.html.

"The Opium War and the Opening of China."
    http://historyliterature.homestead.com/files/extended.html.

—Q. Edward Wang

Lin Zexu's "Moral Advice to Queen Victoria"

A communication: magnificently our great Emperor soothes and pacifies China and the foreign countries, regarding all with the same kindness. If there is profit, then he shares it with the peoples of the world; if there is harm, then he removes it on behalf of the world. This is because he takes the mind of heaven and earth as his mind.

The kings of your honorable country by a tradition handed down from generation to generation have always been noted for their politeness and submissiveness. We have read your successive tributary memorials saying, "In general our countrymen who go to trade in China have always received His Majesty the Emperor's gracious treatment and equal justice," and so on. Privately we are delighted with the way in which the honorable rulers of your country deeply understand the grand principles and are grateful for the Celestial grace. For this reason the Celestial Court in soothing those from afar has redoubled its polite and kind treatment. The profit from trade has been enjoyed by them continuously for two hundred years. This is the source from which your country has become known for its wealth.

But after a long period of commercial intercourse, there appear among the crowd of barbarians both good persons and bad, unevenly. Consequently there are those who smuggle opium to seduce the Chinese people and so cause the spread of the poison to all provinces. Such persons who only care to profit themselves, and disregard their harm to others, are not tolerated by the laws of heaven and are unanimously hated by human beings. His Majesty the Emperor upon hearing of this is in a towering rage. He has especially sent me, his commissioner, to come to Kwangtung, and together with the governor-general and governor jointly to investigate and settle this matter.

All those people in China who sell opium or smoke opium should receive the death penalty. If we trace the crime of those barbarians who through the years have been selling opium, then the deep harm they have wrought and the great profit they have usurped should fundamentally justify their execution according to law. We take into consideration, however, the fact that the various barbarians have still known how to repent their crimes and return to their allegiance to us by taking the 20,183 chests of opium from their store ships and petitioning us, through their consular officer [Charles] Elliot, to receive it. It has been entirely destroyed and this has been faithfully reported to the Throne in several memorials by this commissioner and his colleagues.

Fortunately we have received a specially extended favor from His Majesty the Emperor, who considers that for those who voluntarily surrender there are still some circumstances to palliate their crime and so for the time being he has magnanimously excused them from punishment. But as for those who again violate the opium prohibition, it is difficult for the law to pardon them repeatedly. Having established new regulations, we presume that the ruler of your honorable country, who takes delight in our culture and whose disposition is inclined towards us, must be able to instruct the various barbarians to observe the law with care. It is only necessary to explain to them the advantages and disadvantages and then they will know that the legal code of the Celestial Court must be absolutely obeyed with awe.

We find that your country is sixty or seventy thousand *li* from China. Yet there are barbarian ships that strive to come here for trade for the purpose of making a great profit. The wealth of China is used to profit the barbarians. That is to say, the great profit made by barbarians is all taken from the rightful share of China. By what right do they then in return use the poisonous drug to injure the Chinese people? Even though the barbarians may not necessarily intend to do us harm, yet in coveting profit to an extreme, they have no regard for injuring others. Let us ask, where is your conscience? I have heard that the smoking of opium is very strictly forbidden by your country; that is because the harm caused by opium is clearly understood. Since it is not permitted to do harm to your own country, then even less should you let it be passed on to the harm of other countries—how much less to China! Of all that China exports to foreign countries, there is not a single thing which is not beneficial to people: they are of benefit when eaten, or of benefit when used, or of benefit when resold: all are beneficial. Is there a single article from China which has done any harm to foreign countries? Take tea and rhubarb, for example: the foreign countries cannot get along for a single day without them. If China cuts off these benefits with no sympathy for those who are to suffer, then what can the barbarians rely upon to keep themselves alive? Moreover the woolens, camlets, and longells of foreign countries cannot be woven unless they obtain Chinese silk. If China, again, cuts off this beneficial export, what profit can the barbarians expect to make? As for other food stuffs, beginning with candy, ginger, cinnamon, and so forth, and articles for use, beginning with silk, satin, chinaware, and so on, all the things that must be had by foreign countries are innumerable. On the other hand, articles coming from the outside to China can only be used as toys. We can take them or get along without them. Since they are not needed by China, what difficulty would there be if we closed the frontier and stopped the trade? Nevertheless our Celestial Court lets tea, silk, and other goods be shipped without limit and circulated everywhere without begrudging it in the slightest. This is for no other reason but to share the benefit with the people of the whole world.

The goods from China carried away by your country not only supply your own consumption and use, but also can be divided up and sold to other countries, producing a triple profit. Even if you do not sell opium, you still have this threefold profit. How can you bear to go further, selling products injurious to others in order to fulfill your insatiable desire?

Suppose there were people from another country who carried opium for sale to England and seduced your people into buying and smoking it; certainly your honorable ruler would deeply hate it and be bitterly aroused. We have heard heretofore that your honorable ruler is kind and benevolent. Naturally you would not wish to give unto others what you yourself do not want. We have also heard that the ships corning to Canton have all had regulations promulgated and given to them in which it is stated that it is not permitted to carry contraband goods. This indicates that the administrative orders of your honorable rule have been originally strict and clear. Only because the trading ships are numerous, heretofore perhaps they have not been examined with care. Now after this communication has been dispatched and you have clearly understood the strictness of the prohibitory laws of the Celestial Court, certainly you will not let your subjects dare again to violate the law.

We have further learned that in London, the capital of your honorable rule, and in Scotland (Su-ko-lan), Ireland (Ai-lan), and other places, originally no opium has been produced. Only in several places of India under your control such as Bengal, Madras, Bombay, Patna, Benares, and Malwa has opium been planted from hill to hill and ponds have been opened for its manufacture. For months and years work is continued in order to accumulate the poison. The obnoxious odor ascends, irritating heaven and frightening the spirits. Indeed you, O King, can eradicate the opium plant in these places, hoe over the fields entirely, and sow in its stead the five grains. Anyone who dares again attempt to plant and manufacture opium should be severely punished. This will really be a great, benevolent government policy that will increase the common weal and get rid of evil. For this, Heaven must support you and the spirits must bring you good fortune, prolonging your old age and extending your descendants. All will depend on this act.

As for the barbarian merchants who come to China, their food and drink and habitation are all received by the gracious favor of our Celestial Court. Their accumulated wealth is all benefit given with pleasure by our Celestial Court. They spend rather few days in their own country but more time in Canton. To digest clearly the legal penalties as an aid to instruction has been a valid principle in all ages. Suppose a man of another country comes to England to trade, he still has to obey the English laws; how much more should he obey in China the laws of the Celestial Dynasty?

Now we have set up regulations governing the Chinese people. He who sells opium shall receive the death penalty and he who smokes it also the death penalty. Now consider this: if the barbarians do not bring opium, then how can the Chinese people resell it, and how can they smoke it? The fact is that the wicked barbarians beguile the Chinese people into a death trap. How then can we grant life only to these barbarians? He who takes the life of even one person still has to atone for it with his own life; yet is the harm done by opium limited to the taking of one life only? Therefore in the new regulations, in regard to those barbarians who bring opium to China, the penalty is fixed at decapitation or strangulation. This is what is called getting rid of a harmful thing on behalf of mankind.

Moreover we have found that in the middle of the second month of this year Consul Elliot of your nation, because the opium prohibition law was very stem and severe, petitioned for an extension of the time limit. He requested a limit of five months for India and its adjacent harbors and related territories, and ten months for England proper, after which they would act in conformity with the new regulations.

Now we, the commissioner and others, have memorialized and have received the extraordinary Celestial grace of His Majesty the Emperor who has redoubled his consideration and compassion. All these who within the period of the coming one year (from England) or six months (from India) bring opium to China by mistake, but who voluntarily confess and completely surrender their opium, shall be exempt from their punishment. After this limit of time, if there are still those who bring opium to China then they will plainly have committed a wilful violation and shall at once be executed according to law, with absolutely no clemency or pardon. This may be called the height of kindness and the perfection of justice.

Our Celestial Dynasty rules over and supervises the myriad states, and surely possesses unfathomable spiritual dignity. Yet the Emperor cannot bear to execute people without having first tried to reform them by instruction. Therefore he especially promulgates these fixed regulations. The barbarian merchants of your country, if they wish to do business for a prolonged period, are required to obey our statutes respectfully and to cut off permanently the source of opium. They must by no means try to test the effectiveness of the law with their lives. May you, O King, check your wicked and sift your vicious people before they come to China, in order to guarantee the peace of your nation, to show further the sincerity of your politeness and submissiveness, and to let the two countries enjoy together the blessings of peace. How fortunate, how fortunate indeed! After receiving this dispatch will you immediately give us a prompt reply regarding the details and circumstances of your cutting off the opium traffic. Be sure not to put this off. The above is what has to be communicated. This is appropriately worded and quite comprehensive.

Glossary

camlets	fabrics made of silk and wool
Canton	Guangzhou
Kwangtung	Guangdong
li	a Chinese unit of measure for distance, which has varied over the course of history but is now considered to be 1,640 feet.
longells	often spelled "long ells," twilled woolen fabrics woven in long pieces
memorials	statements made to a government, often accompanied by petitions for action

TREATY OF NANJING

"The Emperor of China agrees to pay the sum of Six Millions of Dollars as the value of Opium which was delivered up at Canton."

Overview

The Treaty of Nanjing ended the Opium War of 1839–1842 and created the framework for a new commercial and diplomatic relationship between Great Britain and the Qing Empire of China. By demanding that China open new ports, fix regular tariffs on imports and exports, and abolish the merchant guild, or "Cohong," system of commerce, the treaty rectified for the British what they considered to be long-standing problems in their dealings with the Chinese. In the immediate sense, then, the Treaty of Nanjing provided a legal and enforceable means of maintaining a "harmonious" relationship between China and Great Britain.

In a larger sense the 1842 treaty did far more than settle a trade dispute. It opened a new chapter in the history of global power and provided a template for the dominance of Western trading nations in East Asia for roughly a century. As the first of many "unequal" treaties between modern mercantile nations and traditional East Asian societies, the Treaty of Nanjing ushered in an era of "treaty diplomacy," a euphemism for economic and political exploitation that defined the contours of Western imperialism in East Asia and confirmed the supremacy of the modern commercial state worldwide. In general, the unequal treaties were characterized by the imposition of demands for treaty ports in the host country; the creation of zones in the host country where foreign nationals could live, work, and worship; the establishment of consulates in the treaty cities; the control over tariffs; and extraterritoriality, which refers to the right claimed by foreign nationals to remain under the legal jurisdiction of their home countries, even while living and working abroad. In cases in which military operations were required to enforce a treaty, indemnities paid by the host country to the dominant power were also commonly included.

The historical irony of the unequal treaty concept is that the Western powers invariably used the rhetoric of "equality" to seek greater economic opportunities in Asia. However, for the Asian powers involved, these treaties were signed under duress and often without full knowledge of the complex mechanisms of modern economics, trade, and finance that formed the basis of these treaties and that had become

the operating assumptions of Western maritime powers since the early modern period. In seeking fair and equal treatment from the Qing Empire (1644–1911), the British wound up using the terms of the Treaty of Nanjing to control Chinese economic life and, by extension, to determine the course of Chinese political life as well. The practice of influencing the politics of a dependent nation by controlling its economy, commonly referred to by historians as "indirect imperialism" or "semicolonialism," was arguably born with the Treaty of Nanjing.

Context

At the end of the seventeenth century, China's contact with Europeans was limited mostly to waterfront trade with British, Dutch, and Portuguese merchants in a few cities on China's southeastern coast. The port cities of Canton (Guangzhou), Amoy (Xiamen) and Zhoushan had been open to foreign trade since 1683 and were fairly independent in the way they conducted their affairs. Foreign trade was managed by a guild of merchant brokerage firms called the Cohong. The individual firms, or Hong, were licensed by the Qing Empire to buy and sell merchandise and worked through an imperial trade supervisor (the Hoppo) to ensure that the court received its revenues. The enforcement of commercial regulations and tariff payments by the Hong was irregular and usually self-serving, frustrating Western traders.

At the turn of the eighteenth century, Great Britain was the dominant European trading power in China, and its merchants became strident in their demands for greater access to Chinese markets and regulation of the arbitrary practices of the Cohong. The British East India Company, which owned the British monopoly on Asian trade, asked repeatedly for standardized tariffs and tried to secure for its employees the right to reside in China and to receive treatment equal to their Chinese counterparts. The Chinese government refused such petitions and generally showed little willingness to cooperate with foreigners. In 1741 HMS *Centurion*, commanded by George Anson, put into Canton after sustaining damage at sea. Anson's efforts to get his ship repaired turned into a bureaucratic nightmare.

1683

- The Qing Empire lifts restrictions on maritime trade, allowing foreigners to trade in selected ports on the southeastern coast of China.

1720

- Merchants in Canton form trade guilds called Cohong. The Cohong, supervised by Hoppo (imperial trade superintendents), are licensed to conduct commerce with foreign powers.

- The British begin to export Indian opium to China on a small scale.

1729

- Opium is declared contraband by the Yongzheng Emperor, with exceptions for medicinal use.

1741

- Commodore George Anson of the British navy sails into Canton for repairs after a storm at sea, only to suffer a series of delays, frustrations, and refusals. Anson's report to the British government generates awareness of the problems encountered by British ships in China.

In 1759 an East India Company trader named James Flint asked the Chinese government to reform corrupt Hong practices and to open additional ports in northern China. In response, Qing officials sentenced Flint to three years in prison and placed even greater constraints on maritime trade. After 1760 the Chinese rigidly enforced the "Canton system," which restricted all foreign trade to the port of Canton and then allowed it only during the "trading season" between October and March.

As prodigious consumers of Chinese porcelains, silks, and tea—especially tea—and as proponents of the modern ideal of free trade, the British came to consider the Canton system intolerably restrictive. Besides being shackled by managed trade, the British were also being bled by Hong brokers of their precious silver reserves. By 1800 British merchants were paying £3.6 million in silver for Chinese tea. The great imbalance of silver payments represented an enormous burden to a treasury already strapped with the administration of a growing empire.

With the hope of stopping the silver drain and fixing the structural problems of the Canton system, the British government sent Lord George Macartney to China in 1793 to negotiate a comprehensive trade agreement. The British hoped to persuade the Chinese to purchase more British manufactured goods and to open an embassy in Beijing. The Macartney mission turned out to be a colossal failure. Macartney violated protocol by refusing to kowtow (bow down) before Emperor Qianlong, and the Chinese made clear that they had no particular desire for British manufactured goods. In what has become one of the most famous rejections in history, Qianlong refused Macartney all his requests and sent the British delegation home. Nevertheless, the relationship between Great Britain and China would change quickly and dramatically. Fewer than fifty years after Macartney was rebuffed by the Qing court, British ships were attacking Chinese cities at will and dictating the terms of surrender. The opium trade would bring about this radical reversal in power.

Undaunted by Qianlong's refusal, the British decided that if the Chinese did not want British products, they would find a suitable replacement. As an alternative to manufactured goods, the British turned to opium. Because the British East India Company was governing India by 1800, it also controlled India's poppy fields and could produce as much opium as it needed. Opium use had been illegal in China since 1729, but in the 1760s the British began smuggling small amounts of the drug into Canton. After the Macartney mission, the British began to increase their shipments. Between 1760 and 1830 the number of chests sold in China went from fewer than one thousand to more than twenty thousand per year, and it is estimated that by 1838, there were nearly two million Chinese addicts. When the Hong were ordered by Qing officials to ban all opium transactions in Canton, the British simply moved the enterprise offshore to Lintin Island. In time, besides creating a public health crisis, the opium trade created an economic crisis as well. Not only were the British able to redress the imbalance of payments, but they also had forced the Chinese into circumstances in which they were the ones bleeding silver. This situation worsened after 1834, when the British government lifted the East India Company's monopoly and new British "entrepreneurs," competing with Americans, brought even more opium into China. By 1836 the Daoguang Emperor was desperate for a solution.

In 1838 the emperor appointed an imperial commissioner, Lin Zexu, to "fix" the opium problem. Commissioner Lin employed a number of tactics: moral exhortations, stiff punishments, confiscations of opium and pipes, and even a letter to Queen Victoria asking her to bring moral pressure to bear upon the scourge of opium selling. None of these measures was completely successful. Finally, Lin went after the source of the problem: the British traders in Canton, who were known to have stockpiled opium chests in their waterfront factories. When the British refused to turn over an opium merchant named Lancelot Dent to Commissioner Lin, Lin ordered the confiscation and destruction of three million pounds of opium, shut down the waterfront entirely, and ordered the British out of Canton.

Lin's actions were interpreted by the merchants as an affront to free trade, a theft of private property, and an insult to the British Crown. So incensed were the British that they sent a punitive expedition of sixteen warships to China in the summer of 1840. In a series of one-sided engagements along the Chinese coast between 1840 and 1842, British naval and amphibious forces overwhelmed the Chinese defenses. In 1842, as steam-powered warships anchored in the Chang River threatened to destroy the city of Nanjing, the Qing accepted the British terms of surrender.

About the Author

Henry John Temple, 3rd Viscount Palmerston, was the foreign secretary of Great Britain during the Opium War. In this capacity he directed foreign policy for Queen Victoria, whose signature ratified the treaty, and he was the immediate superior of Sir Henry Pottinger, who signed as the British plenipotentiary. Lord Palmerston was, in a practical sense, the "author" of this document, if not the architect of the Opium War itself. A living emblem of British imperialism, Palmerston spent nearly sixty years in public life promoting the cause of British imperial power. He began his career as a conservative Tory, but coming of age in post-Napoleonic Europe, a time of dynamic political change, he came to embrace the spirit of nineteenth-century modernity, including its assumptions that economic efficiency and political reform were the keys to modern state power. At the height of his career, his thinking was more classically liberal than traditionally conservative, and his approach to the cultivation of Great Britain's strength was both rational and practical. Palmerston's reformist sentiments occasionally came into conflict with his imperial aspirations. In the 1830s, as the conflict between the Qing court and British trade merchants began to escalate over the issue of opium trading, Palmerston was less than enthusiastic about supporting merchants who violated Chinese laws. This position

Time Line

1759
- James Flint of the British East India Company asks the Qing imperial court to address the extortion, bribes, and other corrupt practices of the Canton Hong and for an expansion of trading rights.

1760
- The Canton system is formalized, restricting all foreign trade to the waterfront of Canton (Guangzhou) during the "trading season" between October and March.

1770s
- British sales of opium in China surpass one thousand chests per year.

1780s
- The British East India Company suffers huge deficits in the silver-for-tea trade in China.

1793
- **September** Lord George Macartney meets with Emperor Qianlong to try to expand trading and diplomatic rights with China. Macartney's efforts to persuade the Chinese to purchase more manufactured goods are unsuccessful.

Time Line

1800
- The Qing court passes an edict against the import and the domestic production of opium.

1821
- The Qing court again attempts to stop opium trade by refusing to let the Hong handle the product. As a result, bulk transactions of opium are moved offshore to Lintin Island.

1834
- The British East India Company loses its monopoly on Asian trade, and more private merchants enter the illicit opium trade.
- The British East India Company replaces company officials with royal officials, putting more pressure on China to open diplomatic relations.

1839
- **March–May** Commissioner Lin Zexu, appointed to remedy the opium problem, begins to rail publicly against opium use and orders punishments for users and sellers of the drug. Calling for an end to the opium trade, he confiscates three million pounds of opium from British merchants and bans all foreign trade.

changed quickly when Commissioner Lin began arresting British subjects and confiscating British property in 1839. Palmerston made the decision to deploy a naval task force against China and was persistent in pressing for a settlement that optimized Britain's interests.

Explanation and Analysis of the Document

The Treaty of Nanjing was signed on August 29, 1842. It opens with a standard diplomatic preamble from the dominant signatory, Queen Victoria, who, along with her "Good Brother the Emperor of China," presented this treaty to posterity. This verbiage, while fairly common according to the standards of the day, is remarkable considering that fewer than fifty years earlier, Victoria's predecessor, King George III, had been dismissed as a minor "barbarian" king by Daoguang's predecessor, Qianlong. That the signing took place aboard HMS *Cornwallis*, a British warship anchored in the Chang River, only added to the ponderous symbolism of the dramatic reversal in power between the British and Chinese empires in the previous half century. The preamble names the Chinese plenipotentiaries Qiying and Yilibu (called Keying and Elepoo in the document and spelled a variety of ways in historical writings) of the Qing court and Pottinger of Great Britain. An additional participant in the treaty was England's Queen Victoria, who signed the treaty and added above her signature and seal a passage in which she pledged that Great Britain would "sincerely and faithfully perform and observe all and singular the things which are contained and expressed in the Treaty."

◆ Article I

Article I presents the formulaic pledges of peace and friendship between the rival nations that are standard in modern treaties but that strike the contemporary reader as ironic if not hypocritical, knowing that the British would have razed Nanjing had their friends, the Chinese, not accepted the terms. It is important to realize that the British, operating from their own standpoint of Enlightenment rationalism, did not insist on "peace and friendship" with any sense of irony. It was an accepted truth that no society remaining in a "barbarous" state could hope to attain any long-term historical satisfaction, and the British believed that they were bringing enlightenment to a backward civilization.

◆ Article II

Article II names the five treaty ports—Canton (Guangzhou), Amoy (Xiamen), Foochow-fu (Fuzhou), Ningpo (Ningbo), and Shanghai—and it provided for the establishment of foreign quarters and consulates in each city. This article is significant because it ended, for the British, one of the more irksome practices of the Canton system. It allowed foreign citizens and their families to live in China legally for the first time in history. It also demanded that British royal trade representatives serve as intermediaries between the merchants and Chinese trade officials. This situation had been a source of confusion after the British East India Company lost its monopoly. When the customary lines of communication between British company men and Hong merchants became unavailable, the Qing court experienced unwelcome pressure to deal equally with British officials.

◆ Article III

Article III provided for the cession of Hong Kong to the British Crown. By 1842 Hong Kong had already been occupied by the British for several years. With the closing of Canton and Lintin Island by Commissioner Lin, British traders established a haven on the sparsely populated island. During an abortive peace attempt made in 1841 by the British trade superintendent Charles Elliot and the Qing official Qishan, Hong Kong had been offered as part of the settlement. That agreement was vetoed by both the Qing emperor, who thought it too generous, and Lord Palmerston, who thought it insufficient. Palmerston was especially dismayed that Elliot had agreed to accept such a worthless island. In retrospect, the acquisition of Hong Kong was one of the greatest triumphs in British imperial history. Within several decades the island was transformed into a bustling entrepôt, and in the twentieth century it became an international center for manufacturing, transportation, finance, and culture. Although the treaty gave Hong Kong to Britain "in perpetuity," the legal status of the Crown colony would change over the years. In 1860 the British acquired additional territory in neighboring Kowloon and in 1898 even more land; these lands became designated as the "New Territories." In 1898 the New Territories were leased to Great Britain for ninety-nine years. All of this territory, including Hong Kong itself, was returned to China in 1997.

◆ Article IV

Article IV called for China to reimburse Britain for opium that had been confiscated and destroyed in 1839 by Commissioner Lin. Aside from this article, there are no other direct references to opium anywhere in the treaty, which is unusual considering the fact that the treaty ended an "opium" war. The problem was that opium trade was not legal before or after the war, and the war did not end the trade. Neither the British nor the Chinese were willing to treat opium as legitimate commerce, and contraband opium trafficking would continue until the Chinese Communist Party put an end to it in the early 1950s. This article reiterates that what was really at stake in this war was commercial and diplomatic power. It also indicates that the British possessed the extraordinary leverage to demand reimbursement for a product that was not legal in China or Great Britain. The reimbursement was assessed at $6 million, payment of which was rendered in Mexican dollars, a silver coin of reliable quality that was recognized as world currency in the 1800s.

◆ Article V

Article V ended the traditional Hong system that had vexed the British for so many years. The Cohong, or merchant guild, was now powerless to interfere with free trade in the treaty ports. British merchants operating in these cities claimed the right to do business with anybody they

Time Line

1839

■ **May**
The British trade superintendent Charles Elliot seeks help from his government on how to respond to Commissioner Lin. The decision is made to send a punitive naval expedition to obtain "satisfaction" from China.

1842

■ **August 29**
The Treaty of Nanjing ends the two-year-long Opium War between China and Great Britain.

chose. The article also required the Chinese government to pay an additional $3 million to cover the debts of Hong merchants who were in arrears to British merchants. The reason for this stipulation was that while the Canton system was in practice, the Qing court often used Cohong assets as an imperial cash reserve. When the Hong were required to make "contributions" to the court, they were often unable to purchase the commodities that the British had contracted to export. It was not uncommon for the British merchants themselves to cover the Hong on their wholesale purchases so that they could leave with their cargoes.

◆ Article VI

Article VI demanded indemnities for the costs Britain had incurred fighting the Opium War. From the perspective of the post–World War II warfare, in which the victor generally pays for the reconstruction of defeated nations, it seems difficult to imagine a day in which the conquering nation "sent the bill" to the conquered. Nevertheless, this practice was usual in nineteenth-century diplomacy. With thinking rooted firmly in the old mercantilist imperialism of the eighteenth century, it seemed prudent to keep a vanquished people poor; saddling them with war costs and punitive indemnities made it possible to retain them as captive markets. The ultimate folly of burdening the defeated nation with the costs for the war seems to have been one of the great lessons of the World War I, when a global depression made it impossible for nations to make their monetary reparations without causing hyperinflation or when forcing them to do so inadvertently triggered international lawlessness. The present-day practice of having

Illustration of an attack by the Chinese on a British boat in Canton River during the Opium War (Library of Congress)

A tea warehouse in Canton (© British Library Board. All Rights Reserved 10977)

nations rebuild conquered enemies for the purpose of drawing them back into an allied economic bloc may also be an ultimately self-serving strategy, but it is undeniably more humane.

◆ Articles VII–IX

Article VII established the repayment schedule and interest for the $21 million total in indemnities and reimbursements that China had to pay. Article VIII demanded the release of all British prisoners. This clause refers not only to British and Indian military personnel who may have been captured during the war but also to those traders who were incarcerated in the Canton factories during Commissioner Lin's initial shutdown of the contraband trade. Article IX required amnesty for all Chinese who may have collaborated or done business with the British during the Opium War. The British factories employed large numbers of Chinese subjects, many of whom were persecuted as contraband traders during the seizure.

◆ Article X

Article X provided for the publication of fixed tariffs ("duties" or "customs" fees) on imports and exports. The control of tariffs was a vital element of nineteenth-century diplomacy; what made these treaties unequal was the fact that they ensured that tariffs favored the winner. For states

that measured their national power in terms of balances of trade, the motive behind imperialism was to secure markets for their domestic manufactured products while reducing the costs of goods purchased abroad. Under the Canton system, it was impossible to predict how Hong brokers might have manipulated customs duties on imports (British goods) or inflated the price of products intended for export (Chinese goods). Requiring the Chinese to adhere to published tariff rates (and in the decades to come, dictating those tariff rates) was the signal achievement of the unequal treaties. It guaranteed the British easy and predictable access to foreign markets.

On the matter of transit duties, which were the fees paid by secondary merchants to bring goods from the port city into the interior, the British demanded here that the Chinese set an upper limit on these fees to keep British goods competitive outside the port cities. The final sentence of Article X contains the words "which shall not exceed." To make sense, this passage has to be supplemented with the "Declaration respecting Transit Duties," which is added near the end of the document, after the signature of the Chinese officials. The declaration states that British merchants are obligated to pay "fair and regular tariff of export and import customs and other dues." It goes on to say that after those customs and dues have been paid, goods could be transferred to Chinese merchants, who

"The Emperor of China agrees to pay the sum of Six Millions of Dollars as the value of Opium which was delivered up at Canton in the Month of March 1839."

(Article IV)

"The Government of China having compelled the British Merchants trading at Canton to deal exclusively with certain Chinese Merchants called Hong Merchants (or Cohong) ... agrees to abolish that practice in future at all Ports where British Merchants may reside, and to permit them to carry on their mercantile transactions with whatever persons they please."

(Article V)

"The Government of Her Britannic Majesty having been obliged to send out an Expedition to demand and obtain redress for the violent and unjust Proceedings of the Chinese High Authorities towards her Britannic Majesty's Officer and Subjects, the Emperor of China agrees to pay the sum of Twelve Millions of Dollars."

(Article VI)

again have to pay transit duties to transport the goods. Article X left open the amount of those duties. The added declaration simply concludes that duties "shall not exceed the present rates, which are upon a moderate scale."

◆ Article XI

Article XI required that British and Chinese officials communicate as equals, avoiding derogatory terms and according due respect to each other's offices. Under the Canton system, British East India officers had had no access to Chinese officials, and as the diplomatic exchanges between Britain and China from the Macartney mission forward show, British officials were treated as tributary barbarians. The historical irony of the insistence on "equality" is that the treaty was manifestly unequal. The lesson of power is vividly clear: As long as one possesses the firepower to destroy an enemy, one can claim as much respect as one demands, suggesting that equality is the last thing a nation employing superior force is actually seeking.

◆ Articles XII and XIII

Article XII states that once Great Britain received its first installment of indemnities, it would withdraw forces from

Nanjing but would leave a token force until all payments were made and the treaty ports were operational. Article XIII activated the treaty immediately on the authority of the signing plenipotentiaries, recognizing that it would take time for each nation's sovereign to ratify the treaty personally.

Audience

The audience for this treaty was the Chinese officials, merchants, and city magistrates whose lives would be altered forever by the presence of newly enfranchised foreign traders in their midst. It took some time before the reality of the treaty diplomacy sank into the urban populations of the treaty cities, and several skirmishes were fought even after the treaty was signed. The reality, though, was that the foreigners were in China to stay and that resistance against them would be answered by force. Of course, the treaty was also addressed to posterity and world opinion, and the commercial powers of the West paid very close attention, using the Treaty of Nanjing as their own model for unequal treaties that would be imposed on East Asian nations until the end of World War II.

Impact

The Treaty of Nanjing redefined world diplomacy and helped set the stage for the emergence of the "new imperialism" of the late nineteenth century. It is not the case that the terms, or even the categories of terms, were new to the world or to China. As recently as 1835, the Chinese had voluntarily granted extraterritoriality, a consulate, and rights to control tariffs to Quqon (Kokand), a central Asian tributary state that sought these privileges in its dealings with the Chinese-controlled city of Kashgar (Kashi). The substantive difference between this famous settlement and the unequal treaties after 1842 was the degree to which China granted or was forced to grant these particular rights. While only the most pessimistic of Chinese would have believed that China was surrendering its autonomy to the maritime states of the West, the Western powers had no doubt that they were, and should be, controlling the conversation. Officials from the United States, France, and Russia studied the Treaty of Nanjing carefully and rushed to present their own versions to the Chinese government for signing soon after the treaty was ratified. The American-sponsored Treaty of Wangxia and the French-sponsored Treaty of Huangpu (Whampoa), both signed in 1844, were based on the Treaty of Nanjing and were even more complete in their demands. Not only did each of these treaties specify terms for extraterritoriality, which the Nanjing Treaty did not, but they also demanded "most favored nation" status, meaning that the United States and France would automatically receive any trade privileges granted by China to other nations in the future.

Great Britain received extraterritoriality and most-favored-nation status in the supplementary Treaty of the Bogue, signed in 1843.

For the rest of the nineteenth century, all Western powers operating in East Asia would impose unequal treaties on their new "friends" in the Pacific. The 1858 Treaty of Tianjin (Tientsin), among Great Britain, the United States, Russia, France, and China; the 1861 Commercial Treaty, between Prussia and China; and the 1896 Li-Lobanov Treaty (also called the Sino-Russian Secret Treaty), between Russia and China are only three in a long list of treaties that systematically reduced the Qing Empire to the status of semicolonialism. Perhaps the most humiliating of all was the 1895 Treaty of Shimonoseki (also known as the Treaty of Maguan), in which a modernized Japan adopted the role of the Western power, imposing its own unequal terms on China after its victory in the Sino-Japanese War.

In the domain of domestic politics, the Treaty of Nanjing demonstrated the weakness of the Manchu Qing rulers and precipitated a permanent legitimacy crisis for the Qing Dynasty. Less than a decade after the signing, the Taiping Rebellion would shake China to its foundations. This massive insurrection, informed by explosive antiforeign and anti-Qing sentiment, ended only with the help of foreign intervention, strengthening the hands of the treaty powers. Subsequent treaties would sap China of its sovereignty, and rebellions would plague the dynasty for the next sixty years. In many ways the Treaty of Nanjing marked the beginning of the end of imperial China, destroying the legitimacy of the Qing Dynasty and sending it into a downward spiral from which it would never recover.

Questions for Further Study

1. Trace the history of Great Britain's relationship with China using the Treaty of Nanjing, Qianlong's Letter to George III, and Lin Zexu's "Moral Advice to Queen Victoria."

2. Treaties such as the Treaty of Nanjing are generally accounted as unequal, allowing commercial nations such as Great Britain to dominate colonies in Asia, Africa, and the Middle East. How was Great Britain—and other European powers—able to achieve such dominance? If the treaty was unequal, why did China not simply expel the British?

3. During the eighteenth and nineteenth centuries, the British East India Company, a private, commercial enterprise, assumed what could almost be characterized as governmental control in countries such as China and India. Using the Treaty of Nanjing and Queen Victoria's Proclamation concerning India, explain how the East India Company was able to achieve this position.

4. How did the Treaty of Nanjing contribute to the implosion of imperial China?

5. In one sentence, explain to an interested listener what the Opium War was. In one more sentence, explain why the war was important.

Further Reading

■ Articles

Downs, Jacques M. "American Merchants and the China Opium Trade, 1800–1840." *Business History Review* 42 (Winter 1968): 418–442.

Wang, Dong. "The Discourse of Unequal Treaties in Modern China." *Pacific Affairs* 76, no. 3 (Fall 2003): 399–425.

Zheng, Yangwen. "The Social Life of Opium in China, 1483–1999." *Modern Asian Studies* 37, no. 1 (February 2003): 1–39.

■ Books

Fairbank, John King. *Trade and Diplomacy on the China Coast: The Opening of the Treaty Ports, 1842–1854.* 2 vols. Cambridge, Mass.: Harvard University Press, 1953.

Fairbank, John King, and Merle Goldman. *China: A New History*, 2nd ed. Cambridge, Mass.: Belknap Press of Harvard University Press, 2006.

Spence, Jonathan. *The Search for Modern China*, 2nd ed. New York: W. W. Norton, 1999.

Waley-Cohen, Joanna. *The Sextants of Beijing: Global Currents in Chinese History.* New York: W. W. Norton, 1999.

■ Web Sites

"The Opium War and Foreign Encroachment." Columbia University Web site.
 http://afe.easia.columbia.edu/china/modern/opium.htm.

—Eric Cunningham

TREATY OF NANJING

Victoria, by the Grace of God, Queen of the United Kingdom of Great Britain and Ireland, Defender of the Faith, etc., etc., etc. To All and Singular to whom these Presents shall come, Greeting!

Whereas a Treaty between Us and Our Good Brother the Emperor of China, was concluded and signed, in the English and Chinese Languages, on board Our Ship the Cornwallis, at Nanking, on the Twenty-ninth day of August, in the Year of Our Lord One Thousand Eight Hundred and Forty-two, by the Plenipotentiaries of Us and of Our said Good Brother, duly and respectively authorized for that purpose; which Treaty is hereunto annexed in Original.

Treaty

Her Majesty the Queen of the United Kingdom of Great Britain and Ireland, and His Majesty the Emperor of China, being desirous of putting an end to the misunderstandings and consequent hostilities which have arisen between the two Countries, have resolved to conclude a Treaty for that purpose, and have therefore named as their Plenipotentiaries, that is to say: Her Majesty the Queen of Great Britain and Ireland, Henry Pottinger, Bart., a Major General in the Service of the East India Company, etc., etc.; And His Imperial Majesty the Emperor of China, the High Commissioners Keying, a Member of the Imperial House, a Guardian of the Crown Prince and General of the Garrison of Canton; and Elepoo, of Imperial Kindred, graciously permitted to wear the insignia of the first rank, and the distinction of Peacock's feather, lately Minister and Governor General etc., and now Lieutenant-General Commanding at Chapoo: Who, after having communicated to each other their respective Full Powers and found them to be in good and due form, have agreed upon, and concluded, the following Articles:

◆ Article I.

There shall henceforward be Peace and Friendship between Her Majesty the Queen of the United Kingdom of Great Britain and Ireland, and His Majesty the Emperor of China, and between their respective Subjects, who shall enjoy full security and protection for their persons and property within the Dominions of the other.

◆ Article II.

His Majesty the Emperor of China agrees that British Subjects, with their families and establishments, shall be allowed to reside, for the purpose of carrying on their Mercantile pursuits, without molestation or restraint at the Cities and Towns of Canton, Amoy, Foochow-fu, Ningpo, and Shanghai, and Her Majesty the Queen of Great Britain, etc., will appoint Superintendents or Consular Officers, to reside at each of the above-named Cities or Towns, to be the medium of communication between the Chinese Authorities and the said Merchants, and to see that the just Duties and other Dues of the Chinese Government as hereafter provided for, are duly discharged by Her Britannic Majesty's Subjects.

◆ Article III.

It being obviously necessary and desirable, that British Subjects should have some Port whereat they may careen and refit their Ships, when required, and keep Stores for that purpose, His Majesty the Emperor of China cedes to Her Majesty the Queen of Great Britain, etc., the Island of Hongkong, to be possessed in perpetuity by Her Britannic Majesty, Her Heirs and Successors, and to be governed by such Laws and Regulations as Her Majesty the Queen of Great Britain, etc., shall see fit to direct.

◆ Article IV.

The Emperor of China agrees to pay the sum of Six Millions of Dollars as the value of Opium which was delivered up at Canton in the month of March 1839, as a Ransom for the lives of Her Britannic Majesty's Superintendent and Subjects, who had been imprisoned and threatened with death by the Chinese High Officers.

◆ Article V.

The Government of China having compelled the British Merchants trading at Canton to deal exclusively with certain Chinese Merchants called Hong Merchants (or Cohong) who had been licensed by the Chinese Government for that purpose, the

Emperor of China agrees to abolish that practice in future at all Ports where British Merchants may reside, and to permit them to carry on their mercantile transactions with whatever persons they please, and His Imperial Majesty further agrees to pay to the British Government the sum of Three Millions of Dollars, on account of Debts due to British Subjects by some of the said Hong Merchants (or Cohong), who have become insolvent, and who owe very large sums of money to Subjects of Her Britannic Majesty.

◆ Article VI.

The Government of Her Britannic Majesty having been obliged to send out an Expedition to demand and obtain redress for the violent and unjust Proceedings of the Chinese High Authorities towards Her Britannic Majesty's Officer and Subjects, the Emperor of China agrees to pay the sum of Twelve Millions of Dollars on account of the Expenses incurred, and Her Britannic Majesty's Plenipotentiary voluntarily agrees, on behalf of Her Majesty, to deduct from the said amount of Twelve Millions of Dollars, any sums which may have been received by Her Majesty's combined Forces as Ransom for Cities and Towns in China, subsequent to the 1st day of August 1841.

◆ Article VII.

It is agreed that the Total amount of Twenty-one Millions of Dollars, described in the three preceding Articles, shall be paid as follows:

Six Millions immediately.

Six Millions in 1843. That is: Three Millions on or before the 30th of the month of June, and Three Millions on or before the 31st of December.

Five Millions in 1844. That is: Two Millions and a Half on or before the 30th of June, and Two Millions and a half on or before the 31st of December.

Four Millions in 1845. That is: Two Millions on or before the 30th of June, and Two Millions on or before the 31st of December; and it is further stipulated that Interest at the rate of 5 per cent per annum shall be paid by the Government of China on any portions of the above sums that are not punctually discharged at the periods fixed.

◆ Article VIII.

The Emperor of China agrees to release unconditionally all Subjects of her Britannic Majesty (whether Natives of Europe or India) who may be in confinement at this moment, in any part of the Chinese Empire.

◆ Article IX.

The Emperor of China agrees to publish and promulgate, under His Imperial Sign Manual and Seal, a full and entire amnesty and act of indemnity, to all Subjects of China on account of their having resided under, or having had dealings and intercourse with, or having entered the Service of Her Britannic Majesty, or of Her Majesty's Officers, and His Imperial Majesty further engages to release all Chinese Subjects who may be at this moment in confinement for similar reasons.

◆ Article X.

His Majesty the Emperor of China agrees to establish at all the Ports which are by the 2nd Article of this Treaty to be thrown open for the resort of British Merchants, a fair and regular Tariff of Export and Import Customs and other Dues, which Tariff shall be publicly notified and promulgated for general information, and the Emperor further engages, that when British Merchandise shall have once been paid at any of the said Ports the regulated Customs and Dues agreeable to the Tariff, to be hereafter fixed, such Merchandise may be conveyed by Chinese Merchants, to any Province or City in the interior of the Empire of China on paying a further amount as Transit Duties which shall not exceed [see Declaration respecting Transit Duties below] on the tariff value of such goods.

◆ Article XI.

It is agreed that Her Britannic Majesty's Chief High Officer in China shall correspond with the Chinese High Officers, both at the Capital and in the Provinces, under the term "Communication." The Subordinate British Officers and Chinese High Officers in the Provinces under the terms "Statement" on the part of the former, and on the part of the latter "Declaration" and the Subordinates of both Countries on a footing of perfect equality. Merchants and others not holding official situations and, therefore, not included in the above, on both sides, to use the term "Representation" in all Papers addressed to, or intended for the notice of the respective Governments.

◆ Article XII.

On the assent of the Emperor of China to this Treaty being received and the discharge of the first installment of money, Her Britannic Majesty's Forces will retire from Nanking and the Grand Canal, and will no longer molest or stop the Trade of China. The Military Post at Chinhai will also be withdrawn, but the Islands of Koolangsoo and that of Chusan will continue to be held by Her Majesty's Forces until the money payments, and the arrangements for opening the Ports to British Merchants be completed.

◆ **Article XIII.**

The Ratification of the Treaty by Her Majesty the Queen of Great Britain, etc., and His Majesty the Emperor of China shall be exchanged as soon as the great distance which separates England from China will admit; but in the meantime counterpart copies of it, signed and sealed by the Plenipotentiaries on behalf of their respective Sovereigns, shall be mutually delivered, and all its provisions and arrangements shall take effect.

Done at Nanking and Signed and Sealed by the Plenipotentiaries on board Her Britannic Majesty's ship Cornwallis, this twenty-ninth day of August, 1842, corresponding with the Chinese date, twenty-fourth day of the seventh month in the twenty-second Year of Taou Kwang.

(L.S.) Henry Pottinger, Her Majesty's Plenipotentiary

[Signatures of Chinese Plenipotentiaries]

Declaration respecting Transit Duties.

Whereas by the Xth Article of the Treaty between Her Majesty the Queen of the United Kingdom of Great Britain and Ireland, and His Majesty the Emperor of China, concluded and signed on board Her Britannic Majesty's ship Cornwallis, at Nanking, on the 29th day of August, 1842. ... it is stipulated and agreed, that His Majesty the Emperor of China shall establish at all the ports which, by the 2nd Article of the said Treaty, are to be thrown open for the resort of British merchants, a fair and regular tariff of export and import customs and other dues, which tariff shall be publicly notified and promulgated for general information; and further, that when British merchandise shall have once paid, at any of the said ports, the regulated customs and dues, agreeable to the tariff to be hereafter fixed, such merchandise may be conveyed by Chinese merchants to any province or city in the interior of the Empire of China, on paying a further amount of duty as transit duty; And whereas the rate of transit duty to be so levied was not fixed by the said Treaty; Now, therefore, the undersigned Plenipotentiaries of Her Britannic Majesty, and of His Majesty the Emperor of China, do hereby, on proceeding to the exchange of the Ratifications of the said Treaty, agree and declare, that the further amount of duty to be so levied on British merchandise, as transit duty, shall not exceed the present rates, which are upon a moderate scale; and the Ratifications of the said Treaty are exchanged subject to the express declaration and stipulation herein contained.

In witness whereof the respective Plenipotentiaries have signed the present declaration, and have affixed thereto their respective seals.

Done at Hong-Kong, the 26th day of June, 1843

(L.S.) Henry Pottinger

[Seal and signature of Chinese Plenipotentiary]

We, having seen and considered the Treaty aforesaid, have approved, accepted, and confirmed the same in all and every one of its Articles and Clauses, as We do by these Presents approve, accept, confirm, and ratify it for Ourselves, Our Heirs, and Successors: Engaging and Promising upon Our Royal Word, that We will sincerely and faithfully perform and observe all and singular the things which are contained and expressed in the Treaty aforesaid, and that We will never suffer the same to be violated by any one, or transgressed in any manner, as far as it lies in Our Power.

For the greater Testimony and Validity of all which, We have caused the Great Seal of Our United Kingdom of Great Britain and Ireland to be affixed to these Presents, which We have signed with Our Royal Hand.

Given at Our Court at Windsor Castle, the Twenty-eighth day of December, in the Year of Our Lord One Thousand Eight Hundred and Forty-two, and in the Sixth Year of Our Reign.

(Signed) Victoria R.

Glossary

Chapoo	a seaport in present-day Zhejiang Province
Chinhai	a port in present-day South Korea
Sign Manual	the handwritten signature of the emperor of China

TREATY OF GUADALUPE HIDALGO

"There shall be firm and universal peace between the United States of America and the Mexican Republic."

Overview

The Treaty of Guadalupe Hidalgo officially ended the Mexican-American War. The terms of peace set forth in the treaty were a catastrophe for Mexico and a triumph for the expanding United States. After a decisive military defeat, Mexico was forced to sell over half its national territory to the United States for the price of $15 million. The United States obtained clear legal title to more than 850,000 square miles of land, including territory that would eventually make up all or part of Arizona, California, Colorado, New Mexico, Nevada, Utah, and Wyoming.

The treaty had far-reaching consequences for both countries and set in motion a series of events that would lead to civil wars in both Mexico and the United States during the 1860s. In the United States the acquisition of the vast new territory exacerbated the conflict over slavery and led to the outbreak of the Civil War in 1861. In Mexico the sense of national humiliation inflicted by the treaty polarized Mexican politics and plunged the country into civil strife that endured throughout the 1850s and 1860s. The unequal terms of the treaty also called attention to the rising power of the United States. The territorial acquisition paved the way for rapid economic growth that would soon transform the United States into the dominant power in the Western Hemisphere. For Mexicans and other Latin Americans, the treaty would become an enduring symbol of U.S. territorial ambition and arrogance.

Context

When Mexico achieved independence from Spain in 1821, it inherited a long-standing border conflict with the United States. The conflict originated during the First Seminole War that began in December 1817, when U.S. forces under the command of Andrew Jackson occupied eastern Florida in defiance of Spain's claims to the area. Already fighting several wars and dealing with rebellion throughout its American colonies, Spain decided to bargain with the United States rather than fight. The result of these deliberations was the 1819 Adams-Onís Treaty, ratified by Spain in 1820 and the United States shortly thereafter and ratified again in 1831 after Mexican independence. In this agreement, Spain sold Florida to the United States and renounced its claims to the Pacific Northwest. In exchange, Spain received financial compensation and the promise that the United States would abandon its claim to Texas.

The Adams-Onís Treaty did not ultimately resolve the border dispute, however. Instead, it heightened tensions that would lead to war. The issue of who owned Texas continued to be a major source of contention. After independence, Mexicans pointed to the treaty as clear evidence of their right to Texas. Many Americans, however, continued to insist that Texas was rightfully part of the United States. In response to armed incursions into Texas by expansionist U.S. settlers, the Mexican government realized that the only way to substantiate its claim was to settle the area with people loyal to Mexico. Unable to entice Mexican citizens to migrate to a sparsely inhabited region, much of which was not well suited to agriculture, the Mexican government eventually handed out generous land grants to a group of U.S. settlers willing to relocate to the area and in effect colonize it. In return, Mexico required the settlers to respect Mexican sovereignty. Initially, men like Stephen F. Austin were willing to cooperate with the government in Mexico City, but during the 1820s and 1830s Texans found themselves increasingly at odds with Mexican policies. They revolted, prompting Mexico to send an army to restore order. After several skirmishes, the decisive battle took place on April 21, 1836, when soldiers under the command of Sam Houston defeated the Mexican army at the Battle of San Jacinto, thus forcing Mexican general Antonio López de Santa Anna to sign an agreement that put a temporary end to the fighting. Although Mexico never formally accepted this agreement, for all intents and purposes the victory made Texas an independent country.

Texas independence put the United States and Mexico on a collision course toward war. In the 1830s and 1840s the idea of Manifest Destiny had become widespread in the United States. Originating in a belief in racial, religious, and political superiority, Manifest Destiny was an ideology that insisted the United States was destined to extend its borders. In fact, many Texans wanted and expected that the

1819

- **February 22**
Adams-Onís
Treaty is signed,
granting Texas
to Spain.

1836

- **April 21**
Sam Houston
leads a Texas
army that defeats
Santa Anna at
the Battle of
San Jacinto,
forcing him to
sign a treaty
granting Texas
independence.
Mexico rejects
this treaty.

1845

- **March 1**
Joint resolution
is signed by
President John
Tyler three days
before leaving
office, which
paves the way
for Texas to be
admitted to the
United States as
a state.

- **May 1**
Congress passes a
joint resolution that
authorizes the
annexation of
Texas.

- **December 29**
President James
Polk signs the act
that makes Texas
part of the United
States.

1846

- **April 25**
Skirmish takes
place in disputed
territory between
U.S. and Mexican
forces.

- **May 13**
Act proclaiming the
declaration of war
with Mexico is
signed by President
Polk.

United States would annex Texas after it became independent. The issue of annexation became a major political issue in the United States, however, as it quickly became the centerpiece in the battle between pro-slavery Southerners and antislavery Northerners. Slavery was important to the Texas economy, and Northerners worried that the admission of another slave state into the Union would upset the U.S. Congress's delicate political balance. At the same time, Mexico refused to recognize Texas independence, and Mexican leaders stated unequivocally that U.S. annexation would be considered an act of war. These tensions finally boiled over in 1845 and 1846. On March 1, 1845, just a few days before leaving office, President John Tyler signed a joint resolution that paved the way for Texas to be admitted to the United States. On December 29, 1845, President James Polk completed the process by signing the act that made Texas part of the United States. A determined expansionist, Polk sent U.S. troops into the disputed territory of the Texas-Mexico border in the spring of 1846, an act which provoked a skirmish between Mexican and U.S. forces on April 25, 1846. On May 13, 1846, the U.S. Congress declared Mexico and the United States to be at war.

From the start, the war did not go well for Mexico. As U.S. forces pushed south into central Mexico, an invasion force was deployed to the Gulf of Mexico port of Veracruz. In March 1847, Veracruz was subjected to heavy bombardment and seized by U.S. soldiers. On September 13, 1847, U.S. soldiers won a decisive victory at the Battle of Chapultepec and entered Mexico City the following day. In addition to military defeats, the war unleashed rebellions and revolts directed against the Mexican government that threatened its legitimacy.

In early 1847, President James Polk sent Nicholas Trist to Mexico to negotiate a peace treaty. Trist was given specific instructions about the terms that would be acceptable to the United States. Following several failed efforts to work out a treaty in 1847, Polk sent a letter instructing Trist to abandon his mission and return to the United States. Trist prepared to leave Mexico, but at the last moment he decided that the time was right for negotiating and chose to ignore Polk's recall order. On January 2, 1848, Trist and three Mexican representatives began peace negotiations that culminated on February 2, 1848 with the signing of the Treaty of Guadalupe Hidalgo. The treaty was ratified by the U.S. Congress on March 10, 1848 and the Mexican Congress on May 30, 1848, and it was proclaimed on July 4, 1848.

About the Author

The Treaty of Guadalupe Hidalgo was negotiated entirely by four men. On the Mexican side were José Bernardo Couto, Miguel Atristain, and Luis G. Cuevas. Couto and Atristain were prominent lawyers who had been involved with earlier rounds of peace negotiations. Cuevas was also a well-known political figure and fluent in both English and Spanish. All three men were civilians and represented the political faction in Mexico that favored peace. The sole U.S.

negotiator was Nicholas Trist. Then serving as the undersecretary of state, Trist had worked during the 1830s in the U.S. consul's office in Cuba, where he learned Spanish and became familiar with Latin America. A fervent supporter of slavery, Trist had been involved, while he was in Cuba, in various illegal schemes to sell Africans as slaves—schemes that alarmed many Northerners. In Latin America, however, he was generally seen as sympathetic and well intentioned.

The U.S. Congress also played a role in authoring the final version of the treaty. Most members of Congress did not support the comprehensive guarantees of Mexicans' rights that were included in Articles IX and X. These men believed that the U.S. judicial system would provide adequate legal protection for Mexicans living in the ceded territory, and their beliefs guided their decision to amend Article IX and to strike Article X altogether from the final version of the treaty.

Explanation and Analysis of the Document

The Treaty of Guadalupe Hidalgo put an official end to the Mexican-American War. Many of the treaty's twenty-three articles are still in effect today. The introductory paragraph lists the treaty's authors, states their credentials, and proclaims their authority to negotiate on behalf of their respective countries. Although the document states that each of the negotiators has "full powers" to act on behalf of their government, the truth was not so simple. In fact, the U.S. negotiator, Nicholas Trist, had been recalled by President Polk in a letter Trist received in November 1847. Trist ignored his instructions to return to the United States and negotiated the treaty in direct defiance of Polk's orders. The preamble also describes the treaty's scope by declaring it a treaty of "Peace, Friendship, Limits, and Settlement." Thus, the treaty was intended not only to end the war but also to resolve the long-standing question of Mexico's borders with the United States and to lay out a blueprint for a sustained and lasting peace between the two countries.

◆ Article I
This article declares an immediate end to the war and calls for a "firm and lasting peace" between the two countries. Despite many tensions, flare-ups, and even the occasional incursion of U.S. soldiers into Mexico since the signing of the treaty, Mexico and the United States have never again entered into a state of war with each other.

◆ Articles II–IV
These three articles lay out the details of the transition from war to peace. Article II calls for a cease-fire between the two countries and proclaims the reestablishment of "constitutional order" in Mexico. However, since the evacuation of U.S. troops from Mexico would take several months, the article asserts that the reestablishment of Mexican sovereignty would be limited by the "circumstances of military occupation." Article III requires the United States to end its blockade of Veracruz, which it had occupied since March 1847. It also restores control to

Time Line	
1847	**September 13** U.S. troops capture Mexico City.
1848	**January 2** Peace negotiations open between U.S. representative Nicholas Trist and Mexican negotiators José Bernardo Couto, Miguel Atristain, and Luis G. Cuevas.
	February 2 Treaty of Guadalupe Hidalgo is signed.
	March 10 Treaty is ratified by U.S. Congress.
	May 30 Treaty is ratified by Mexican Congress.
	July 4 President Polk declares ratification process complete.
1854	**April 25** Gadsden Treaty is ratified by the U.S. Senate.

Mexican authorities over the customhouse at the port and contains stipulations to return all taxes collected during the blockade and to remove all U.S. troops from Mexico City within one month. Article IV requires the return to Mexico of all military equipment and forts captured by U.S. forces during the war and the mutual exchange of all prisoners of war. It also states that the United States would remove its military personnel from Mexico within three months from the ratification of the treaty.

◆ Article V
This important article defines the new boundaries of the United States and Mexico as a result of the treaty. The treaty cedes approximately 850,000 square miles of territory to the United States, including land that would eventually contain all or part of Arizona, California, Colorado,

Nicholas Trist (Library of Congress)

New Mexico, Nevada, Utah, and Wyoming. The beginning of the article settles the issue of the Texas-Mexico boundary that was the pretext for war by leaving no doubt that the southern border of Texas would be the Rio Grande, instead of the Rio Nueces, as Mexico had insisted. The California border with Mexico is also definitively settled. Despite Mexico's wish to retain the port of San Diego, the treaty states that the new border would be located one marine league south of the southernmost point of San Diego and run directly east in a straight line until meeting the point where the Colorado and Gila rivers intersect.

The southern border of the states that would become Arizona and New Mexico was more problematic. The treaty calls for a surveying team appointed by both countries to map the southern border within one year of the treaty's ratification. It states that the new border runs up the Rio Grande until it "strikes the southern boundary of New Mexico." The problem was that no one knew the exact boundaries of New Mexico. Trist wanted the Mesilla Valley to be included in the ceded territory, because he suspected it was the only feasible railroad route through the region. The authors of the treaty used a map made by John Disturnell, according to which the Mesilla Valley was north of the new boundary. However, when the surveyors mapped the area, they found that the Disturnell map was inaccurate, and they were subsequently unable to agree on the correct border. This dispute led to the Gadsden purchase in 1854, in which the United States paid the Mexican government $10 million in exchange for territory that included the Mesilla Valley.

◆ Article VI and VII

These two articles demonstrate the growing importance of new transportation technologies, especially railroads and steam-powered ships. Article VI gives the United States the right of passage on the entire length of the Colorado River, which according to the terms of the new treaty begins in the United States but passes through Mexico before emptying into the Gulf of California. The article also paves the way for both countries to cooperate on the construction of a future transcontinental railroad. If the route needed to pass through Mexico, the article requires an agreement that the railroad would "serve equally for the use and advantage of both countries." Article VII grants both countries equal rights to the Rio Grande and Gila River for both navigation and commerce. It also states that neither country could collect taxes on the commerce of either river without the permission of the other.

◆ Articles VIII and IX

These two articles provide rules for determining citizenship and affirm the protection of the civil and property rights of people living in the annexed territories. These articles were extremely important to the Mexican negotiators. Article VIII first clarifies that all those living in the annexed territories would be "free to continue where they now reside" or to "remove at any time to the Mexican Republic." In other words, people in the annexed lands could choose to remain in the territory that had become part of the United States, or they could return to Mexico. The article states that their property rights would be respected if they chose to leave and that they would not be subject to any tax if they kept or sold their property. According to Article VIII, those who chose to remain in newly acquired U.S. territory would be free to decide if they wanted to retain their Mexican citizenship or renounce it and become citizens of the United States. However, the default position was the loss of Mexican citizenship; the treaty gave individuals one year from ratification to announce their decision to remain Mexican or else forfeit their rights to Mexican citizenship. The article also states that the property rights of people who chose to remain Mexicans would be respected as if the property "belonged to citizens of the United States."

Article IX extends these guarantees to people who chose to become U.S. citizens but had not yet become so under U.S. law. This was especially important because the article is vague about when and how these people would gain U.S. citizenship. Rather than becoming citizens right away, the article explains that they would "be admitted at the proper time" to be decided by the U.S. Congress. In practice, this process was slow; many states, such as California, did not grant full citizenship under the terms of the treaty until the 1870s. The Mexican negotiators of the treaty tried to protect the rights of former Mexicans in this state of legal limbo by means of a long article that spelled out the precise protections they would be afforded. However, during the ratification process, the U.S. Congress voted to amend the article, replacing much of the text with subtler language promising that former Mexicans would be "protected in the free enjoyment of their liberty and property, and secured in the free exercise of their religion without restriction."

◆ Article X

This article asserts that all land claims made by the Mexican government in the annexed territories were valid. During the ratification process, it was stricken by the U.S. Congress and was not included in the final version of the treaty. Members of Congress believed that the article would revive old land claims, especially in Texas, and lead to conflict and confusion about property rights.

◆ Article XI

Article XI commits the United States to protecting Mexico from attacks and raids by Native Americans living in the annexed territory. Thousands of Native Americans inhabited the ceded area, many of whom had been in a prolonged state of conflict with U.S. and Mexican communities on both sides of the border. Mexican negotiators insisted that the United States bear the burden of forcibly controlling these groups. However, neither side during the negotiations appreciated the size of the Native American population and its determination to resist incursions into what they claimed as their territory. As a result, the article was a source of great tension in the years after the treaty's ratification, as Mexican leaders accused the United States of not fulfilling its obligations. The article was eventually canceled by the terms of the Gadsden Purchase in 1854.

Storming of Chapultapec (Library of Congress)

◆ **Article XII**

This article determines the final price of $15 million that the United States was to pay Mexico in exchange for the ceded territory. This figure is equivalent to approximately $300 million in today's money. Trist had originally been authorized by President Polk to offer $20 million for similar territorial concessions, but he lowered the price to offset the cost in American lives and money spent by the United States during the war.

◆ **Articles XIII–XV**

These three articles lay out the terms by which the United States agrees to pay the financial claims of its own citizens against the Mexican government, up to the amount of $3.25 million. This resolved one of the outstanding disputes between the two countries. For decades, many U.S. citizens had sought money from the Mexican government for property damage, confiscation, or outstanding loans. The United States agreed to pay these claims itself to resolve the issue, essentially adding $3 million to the price the United States offered Mexico in exchange for the annexed territories.

◆ **Articles XVI and XVII**

Article XVI authorizes both countries to establish defensive fortifications anywhere within their respective territories. Article XVII makes it clear that the Adams-Onís Treaty, ratified in 1831, is still in effect. However, the article also states that all the terms of the Treaty of Guadalupe Hidalgo, once ratified, would overrule any from the previous treaty if at any point there should be a conflict between the two.

◆ **Articles XVIII–XX**

These three articles lay out the process by which taxes would be assessed during the time it took for all U.S. troops to leave Mexico. They also outline the procedure for the restoration of Mexican authority over its customhouses. The articles were written to ensure that the United States would not owe Mexico any taxes for equipment and materials brought into the country to supply its occupying army.

◆ **Articles XXI and XXII**

These two articles concern the resolution of any future conflicts that might arise between both countries. According to Article XXI, both Mexico and the United States pledged to arbitrate any disputes over the terms of the treaty or with respect to the "political or commercial relations of the two nations." In essence, this article attempts to prevent future wars by a mutual promise from both countries that they would use a third party to mediate disputes. Article XXII lays out two rules in the event of a future war. The first commits each country to respect the rights of civilians, and the second calls for fair and tolerable treatment of all prisoners of war. In the years since the treaty's ratification, there have been a number of disagree-

"There shall be firm and universal peace between the United States of America and the Mexican Republic, and between their respective countries, territories, cities, towns, and people, without exception of places or persons."

(Article I)

"The boundary line [between Mexico and the United States] established by this article shall be religiously respected by each of the two republics, and no change shall ever be made therein, except by the express and free consent of both nations, lawfully given by the General Government of each, in conformity with its own constitution."

(Article V)

"The Mexicans who ... shall not preserve the character of citizens of the Mexican Republic ... shall be incorporated into the Union of the United States, and be admitted at the proper time ... to the enjoyment of all the rights of citizens of the United States ... and in the mean time, shall be maintained and protected in the free enjoyment of their liberty and property, and secured in the free exercise of their religion without restriction."

(Article IX)

"If unhappily any disagreement should hereafter arise between the Governments of the two republics, whether with respect to ... any stipulation in this treaty, or ... any other particular concerning the political or commercial relations of the two nations, the said Governments ... will endeavour ... to settle the differences ... and to preserve the state of peace and friendship in which the two countries are now placing themselves, using ... mutual representations and pacific negotiations."

(Article XXI)

ments submitted to arbitration. The decisions of arbitrators have not always been respected, but Mexico and the United States have remained at peace.

◆ **Article XXIII**

This article clarifies that the treaty must be ratified by the Congresses of both countries before it goes into effect. It also states that ratification should occur no more than four months from the signing of the treaty. The U.S. Con-gress ratified the treaty on March 10, 1848 and the Mexi-can Congress did so on May 30, 1848, three days shy of the required four months.

Audience

In the first place, the audiences for the treaty were the congresses of Mexico and the United States. Legislators in both counties were divided into several factions over the terms. In the United States, Northern members of the Whig Party led by Daniel Webster opposed the treaty, because they feared the addition of so much new territory would encourage the spread of slavery. Some Southern legislators, on the other hand, such as Jefferson Davis and Sam Houston, opposed the treaty because it did not annex enough of Mexico. The terms negotiated by Trist were a compromise between these extreme positions that made ratification by the U.S. Congress possible. Persuading Mexico's Congress to approve the treaty was more difficult. Mexican political factions were even more contentious than their counterparts in the United States regarding the end of the war. One faction, led by Manuel Crescencio Rejón, was convinced that the treaty would mean permanent economic subservience to the United States. Rejón and his supporters believed that Mexico could win a guerrilla war against the United States, and they recommended continuing the war. Another faction, under the leadership of Manuel de la Peña y Peña, who was serving as acting president of Mexico, viewed the treaty as the only way to prevent the loss of more territory or even the total annexation of Mexico by the United States. After a heated debate, the Mexican Congress agreed with Peña y Peña and ratified the treaty on May 30, 1848.

The treaty was also intended for the citizens of Mexico and the United States, especially those who lived in the newly annexed territories and border regions. It proclaimed an immediate end to all hostilities and the establishment of a permanent and lasting peace. For Texans, in particular, the treaty finally settled the question of the border between Texas and Mexico. It also provided information to the people living in the newly annexed territory about their rights and obligations and instructions regarding how to establish their U.S. citizenship.

Impact

The most obvious impact of the treaty was that Mexico lost over half of its national territory to the United States. Although it was sparsely inhabited at the time, the ceded territory would grow in economic importance in the future. For example, the discovery of gold in California in 1848 set off a gold rush that transformed the region into an important economic center. Although much of the newly acquired land was arid, new technology and investment in irrigation would allow agriculture to flourish during the twentieth century. The acquisition of so much new territory made possible the rise of the United States as a world power.

The treaty also had important consequences for Native Americans and the approximately 100,000 Spanish-speaking inhabitants of the ceded territory. The westward expansion of the United States prompted a series of conflicts

Questions for Further Study

1. In what ways did the Treaty of Guadalupe Hidalgo permanently change the relationship between the United States and Mexico? How would that relationship be different if the treaty—and the events that led to its signing—never occurred?

2. Most Americans "Remember the Alamo," a reference to the fort in San Antonio, Texas, that was defended by a small contingent of American troops in 1836. The battle for the Alamo, as well as other events that preceded the signing of the Treaty of Guadalupe Hidalgo, has become part of American lore, where larger-than-life heroes tamed the American West. Comment on whether or not you believe this view of American history is fair.

3. A troublesome issue in contemporary American life is immigration, particularly illegal immigration. Many legal and illegal immigrants to the United States come from Mexico. To what extent has the Treaty of Guadalupe Hidalgo and the events surrounding it contributed to the modern immigration problem?

4. The doctrine of Manifest Destiny was popular in the United States in the nineteenth century. Explain the meaning of the term and explain how the doctrine influenced American thinking with regard to Texas, the Southwest, and Mexico.

5. Some Mexicans continue to believe that Mexico was essentially cheated out of territory that is now part of the U.S. Southwest, and based on this belief they believe that Mexico should reclaim this territory. On what ground can this claim be made? Do you agree or disagree with this position?

with Native American groups, including the Sioux, Apache, and Navajo nations. These groups were decimated by disease and defeated militarily. Despite the efforts of the Mexican government to encourage people to relocate, most of the former Mexicans who lived in the annexed territory chose to stay. Although the terms of the treaty legally protected their civil and property rights, in actuality many lost their land and struggled against racism and persecution. The importance of the treaty was resurrected in the 1960s and 1970s by Mexican Americans who participated in the Chicano movement. Chicanos invoked the treaty's legal protection of the rights of Mexicans and Mexican-Americans living in the United States in order to advance claims for social and economic justice.

Further Reading

■ Articles

Curti, Merle. "Pacifist Propaganda and the Treaty of Guadalupe Hidalgo." *American Historical Review* 33, no. 3 (1928): 596–598.

Hale, Charles. "The War with the United States and the Crisis in Mexican Thought." *Americas* 14, no. 2 (October 1957), 153–173.

■ Books

Griswold del Castillo, Richard. *The Treaty of Guadalupe Hidalgo: A Legacy of Conflict*. Norman: University of Oklahoma Press, 1990.

Henderson, Timothy J. *A Glorious Defeat: Mexico and Its War with the United States*. New York: Hill and Wang, 2007.

Mahin, Dean B. *Olive Branch and Sword: The United States and Mexico, 1845–1848*. London: McFarland & Company, 1997.

Miller, David Hunter. "Treaty of Guadalupe Hidalgo." In *Treaties and Other International Acts of the United States of America*, vol. 5. Washington, D.C.: Government Printing Office, 1937.

Pletcher, David M. *The Diplomacy of Annexation: Texas, Oregon, and the Mexican War*. Columbia: University of Missouri Press, 1973.

■ Web Sites

"The Treaty of Guadalupe Hidalgo." Hispanic Reading Room, Hispanic Division Area Studies, Library of Congress Web site.
   http://www.loc.gov/rr/hispanic/ghtreaty/.

"The U.S.-Mexican War: 1846–1848." Public Broadcasting Service Web site.
   http://www.pbs.org/kera/usmexicanwar/index_flash.html.

—Ben Fulwider

TREATY OF GUADALUPE HIDALGO

In the Name of Almighty God

The United States of America and the United Mexican States animated by a sincere desire to put an end to the calamities of the war which unhappily exists between the two Republics and to establish Upon a solid basis relations of peace and friendship, which shall confer reciprocal benefits upon the citizens of both, and assure the concord, harmony, and mutual confidence wherein the two people should live, as good neighbors have for that purpose appointed their respective plenipotentiaries, that is to say: The President of the United States has appointed Nicholas P Trist, a citizen of the United States, and the President of the Mexican Republic has appointed Don Luis Gonzaga Cuevas, Don Bernardo Couto, and Don Miguel Atristain, citizens of the said Republic; Who, after a reciprocal communication of their respective full powers, have, under the protection of Almighty God, the author of peace, arranged, agreed upon, and signed the following:

Treaty of Peace, Friendship, Limits, and Settlement between the United States of America and the Mexican Republic.

◆ Article I

There shall be firm and universal peace between the United States of America and the Mexican Republic, and between their respective countries, territories, cities, towns, and people, without exception of places or persons.

◆ Article II

Immediately upon the signature of this treaty, a convention shall be entered into between a commissioner or commissioners appointed by the General-in-Chief of the forces of the United States, and such as may be appointed by the Mexican Government, to the end that a provisional suspension of hostilities shall take place, and that, in the places occupied by the said forces, constitutional order may be reestablished, as regards the political, administrative, and judicial branches, so far as this shall be permitted by the circumstances of military occupation.

◆ Article III

Immediately upon the ratification of the present treaty by the Government of the United States, orders shall be transmitted to the commanders of their land and naval forces, requiring the latter (provided this treaty shall then have been ratified by the Government of the Mexican Republic, and the ratifications exchanged) immediately to desist from blockading any Mexican ports and requiring the former (under the same condition) to commence, at the earliest moment practicable, withdrawing all troops of the United State then in the interior of the Mexican Republic, to points that shall be selected by common agreement, at a distance from the seaports not exceeding thirty leagues; and such evacuation of the interior of the Republic shall be completed with the least possible delay; the Mexican Government hereby binding itself to afford every facility in its power for rendering the same convenient to the troops, on their march and in their new positions, and for promoting a good understanding between them and the inhabitants. In like manner orders shall be dispatched to the persons in charge of the custom houses at all ports occupied by the forces of the United States, requiring them (under the same condition) immediately to deliver possession of the same to the persons authorized by the Mexican Government to receive it, together with all bonds and evidences of debt for duties on importations and on exportations, not yet fallen due. Moreover, a faithful and exact account shall be made out, showing the entire amount of all duties on imports and on exports, collected at such customhouses, or elsewhere in Mexico, by authority of the United States, from and after the day of ratification of this treaty by the Government of the Mexican Republic; and also an account of the cost of collection; and such entire amount, deducting only the cost of collection, shall be delivered to the Mexican Government, at the city of Mexico, within three months after the exchange of ratifications.

The evacuation of the capital of the Mexican Republic by the troops of the United States, in virtue of the above stipulation, shall be completed in one month after the orders there stipulated for shall have been received by the commander of said troops, or sooner if possible.

◆ **Article IV**

Immediately after the exchange of ratifications of the present treaty all castles, forts, territories, places, and possessions, which have been taken or occupied by the forces of the United States during the present war, within the limits of the Mexican Republic, as about to be established by the following article, shall be definitely restored to the said Republic, together with all the artillery, arms, apparatus of war, munitions, and other public property, which were in the said castles and forts when captured, and which shall remain there at the time when this treaty shall be duly ratified by the Government of the Mexican Republic. To this end, immediately upon the signature of this treaty, orders shall be dispatched to the American officers commanding such castles and forts, securing against the removal or destruction of any such artillery, arms, apparatus of war, munitions, or other public property. The city of Mexico, within the inner line of intrenchments surrounding the said city, is comprehended in the above stipulation, as regards the restoration of artillery, apparatus of war, & c.

The final evacuation of the territory of the Mexican Republic, by the forces of the United States, shall be completed in three months from the said exchange of ratifications, or sooner if possible; the Mexican Government hereby engaging, as in the foregoing article to use all means in its power for facilitating such evacuation, and rendering it convenient to the troops, and for promoting a good understanding between them and the inhabitants.

If, however, the ratification of this treaty by both parties should not take place in time to allow the embarcation of the troops of the United States to be completed before the commencement of the sickly season, at the Mexican ports on the Gulf of Mexico, in such case a friendly arrangement shall be entered into between the General-in-Chief of the said troops and the Mexican Government, whereby healthy and otherwise suitable places, at a distance from the ports not exceeding thirty leagues, shall be designated for the residence of such troops as may not yet have embarked, until the return of the healthy season. And the space of time here referred to as, comprehending the sickly season shall be understood to extend from the first day of May to the first day of November.

All prisoners of war taken on either side, on land or on sea, shall be restored as soon as practicable after the exchange of ratifications of this treaty. It is also agreed that if any Mexicans should now be held as captives by any savage tribe within the limits of the United States, as about to be established by the following article, the Government of the said United States will exact the release of such captives and cause them to be restored to their country.

◆ **Article V**

The boundary line between the two Republics shall commence in the Gulf of Mexico, three leagues from land, opposite the mouth of the Rio Grande, otherwise called Rio Bravo del Norte, or Opposite the mouth of its deepest branch, if it should have more than one branch emptying directly into the sea; from thence up the middle of that river, following the deepest channel, where it has more than one, to the point where it strikes the southern boundary of New Mexico; thence, westwardly, along the whole southern boundary of New Mexico (which runs north of the town called Paso) to its western termination; thence, northward, along the western line of New Mexico, until it intersects the first branch of the river Gila; (or if it should not intersect any branch of that river, then to the point on the said line nearest to such branch, and thence in a direct line to the same); thence down the middle of the said branch and of the said river, until it empties into the Rio Colorado; thence across the Rio Colorado, following the division line between Upper and Lower California, to the Pacific Ocean.

The southern and western limits of New Mexico, mentioned in the article, are those laid down in the map entitled "Map of the United Mexican States, as organized and defined by various acts of the Congress of said republic, and constructed according to the best authorities. Revised edition. Published at New York, in 1847, by J. Disturnell," of which map a copy is added to this treaty, bearing the signatures and seals of the undersigned Plenipotentiaries. And, in order to preclude all difficulty in tracing upon the ground the limit separating Upper from Lower California, it is agreed that the said limit shall consist of a straight line drawn from the middle of the Rio Gila, where it unites with the Colorado, to a point on the coast of the Pacific Ocean, distant one marine league due south of the southernmost point of the port of San Diego, according to the plan of said port made in the year 1782 by Don Juan Pantoja, second sailing-master of the Spanish fleet, and published at Madrid in the year 1802, in the atlas to the voyage of the schooners Sutil and Mexicana; of which plan a copy is hereunto added, signed and sealed by the respective Plenipotentiaries.

In order to designate the boundary line with due precision, upon authoritative maps, and to establish upon the ground land-marks which shall show the limits of both republics, as described in the present article, the two Governments shall each appoint a commissioner and a surveyor, who, before the expiration of one year from the date of the exchange of ratifications of this treaty, shall meet at the port of San Diego, and proceed to run and mark the said boundary in its whole course to the mouth of the Rio Bravo del Norte. They shall keep journals and make out plans of their operations; and the result agreed upon by them shall be deemed a part of this treaty, and shall have the same force as if it were inserted therein. The two Governments will amicably agree regarding what may be necessary to these persons, and also as to their respective escorts, should such be necessary.

The boundary line established by this article shall be religiously respected by each of the two republics, and no change shall ever be made therein, except by the express and free consent of both nations, lawfully given by the General Government of each, in conformity with its own constitution.

◆ Article VI

The vessels and citizens of the United States shall, in all time, have a free and uninterrupted passage by the Gulf of California, and by the river Colorado below its confluence with the Gila, to and from their possessions situated north of the boundary line defined in the preceding article; it being understood that this passage is to be by navigating the Gulf of California and the river Colorado, and not by land, without the express consent of the Mexican Government.

If, by the examinations which may be made, it should be ascertained to be practicable and advantageous to construct a road, canal, or railway, which should in whole or in part run upon the river Gila, or upon its right or its left bank, within the space of one marine league from either margin of the river, the Governments of both republics will form an agreement regarding its construction, in order that it may serve equally for the use and advantage of both countries.

◆ Article VII

The river Gila, and the part of the Rio Bravo del Norte lying below the southern boundary of New Mexico, being, agreeably to the fifth article, divided in the middle between the two republics, the navigation of the Gila and of the Bravo below said boundary shall be free and common to the vessels and citizens of both countries; and neither shall, without the consent of the other, construct any work that may impede or interrupt, in whole or in part, the exercise of this right; not even for the purpose of favoring new methods of navigation. Nor shall any tax or contribution, under any denomination or title, be levied upon vessels or persons navigating the same or upon merchandise or effects transported thereon, except in the case of landing upon one of their shores. If, for the purpose of making the said rivers navigable, or for maintaining them in such state, it should be necessary or advantageous to establish any tax or contribution, this shall not be done without the consent of both Governments.

The stipulations contained in the present article shall not impair the territorial rights of either republic within its established limits.

◆ Article VIII

Mexicans now established in territories previously belonging to Mexico, and which remain for the future within the limits of the United States, as defined by the present treaty, shall be free to continue where they now reside, or to remove at any time to the Mexican Republic, retaining the property which they possess in the said territories, or disposing thereof, and removing the proceeds wherever they please, without their being subjected, on this account, to any contribution, tax, or charge whatever.

Those who shall prefer to remain in the said territories may either retain the title and rights of Mexican citizens, or acquire those of citizens of the United States. But they shall be under the obligation to make their election within one year from the date of the exchange of ratifications of this treaty; and those who shall remain in the said territories after the expiration of that year, without having declared their intention to retain the character of Mexicans, shall be considered to have elected to become citizens of the United States.

In the said territories, property of every kind, now belonging to Mexicans not established there, shall be inviolably respected. The present owners, the heirs of these, and all Mexicans who may hereafter acquire said property by contract, shall enjoy with respect to it guarantees equally ample as if the same belonged to citizens of the United States.

◆ Article IX

The Mexicans who, in the territories aforesaid, shall not preserve the character of citizens of the Mexican Republic, conformably with what is stipulated in the preceding article, shall be incorporated into the Union of the United States. and be admitted at the proper time (to be judged of by the Congress of the United States) to the enjoyment of all the rights of citizens of the United States, according to the principles of the Constitution; and in the mean time, shall be maintained and protected in the free enjoyment of their liberty and property, and secured in the free exercise of their religion without restriction.

◆ **Article X**

[Stricken out by the United States Amendments]

◆ **Article XI**

Considering that a great part of the territories, which, by the present treaty, are to be comprehended for the future within the limits of the United States, is now occupied by savage tribes, who will hereafter be under the exclusive control of the Government of the United States, and whose incursions within the territory of Mexico would be prejudicial in the extreme, it is solemnly agreed that all such incursions shall be forcibly restrained by the Government of the United States whensoever this may be necessary; and that when they cannot be prevented, they shall be punished by the said Government, and satisfaction for the same shall be exacted all in the same way, and with equal diligence and energy, as if the same incursions were meditated or committed within its own territory, against its own citizens.

It shall not be lawful, under any pretext whatever, for any inhabitant of the United States to purchase or acquire any Mexican, or any foreigner residing in Mexico, who may have been captured by Indians inhabiting the territory of either of the two republics; nor to purchase or acquire horses, mules, cattle, or property of any kind, stolen within Mexican territory by such Indians.

And in the event of any person or persons, captured within Mexican territory by Indians, being carried into the territory of the United States, the Government of the latter engages and binds itself, in the most solemn manner, so soon as it shall know of such captives being within its territory, and shall be able so to do, through the faithful exercise of its influence and power, to rescue them and return them to their country or deliver them to the agent or representative of the Mexican Government. The Mexican authorities will, as far as practicable, give to the Government of the United States notice of such captures; and its agents shall pay the expenses incurred in the maintenance and transmission of the rescued captives; who, in the mean time, shall be treated with the utmost hospitality by the American authorities at the place where they may be. But if the Government of the United States, before receiving such notice from Mexico, should obtain intelligence, through any other channel, of the existence of Mexican captives within its territory, it will proceed forthwith to effect their release and delivery to the Mexican agent, as above stipulated.

For the purpose of giving to these stipulations the fullest possible efficacy, thereby affording the security and redress demanded by their true spirit and intent, the Government of the United States will now and hereafter pass, without unnecessary delay, and always vigilantly enforce, such laws as the nature of the subject may require. And, finally, the sacredness of this obligation shall never be lost sight of by the said Government, when providing for the removal of the Indians from any portion of the said territories, or for its being settled by citizens of the United States; but, on the contrary, special care shall then be taken not to place its Indian occupants under the necessity of seeking new homes, by committing those invasions which the United States have solemnly obliged themselves to restrain.

◆ **Article XII**

In consideration of the extension acquired by the boundaries of the United States, as defined in the fifth article of the present treaty, the Government of the United States engages to pay to that of the Mexican Republic the sum of fifteen millions of dollars.

Immediately after the treaty shall have been duly ratified by the Government of the Mexican Republic, the sum of three millions of dollars shall be paid to the said Government by that of the United States, at the city of Mexico, in the gold or silver coin of Mexico The remaining twelve millions of dollars shall be paid at the same place, and in the same coin, in annual installments of three millions of dollars each, together with interest on the same at the rate of six per centum per annum. This interest shall begin to run upon the whole sum of twelve millions from the day of the ratification of the present treaty by the Mexican Government, and the first of the installments shall be paid at the expiration of one year from the same day. Together with each annual installment, as it falls due, the whole interest accruing on such installment from the beginning shall also be paid.

◆ **Article XIII**

The United States engage, moreover, to assume and pay to the claimants all the amounts now due them, and those hereafter to become due, by reason of the claims already liquidated and decided against the Mexican Republic, under the conventions between the two republics severally concluded on the eleventh day of April, eighteen hundred and thirty-nine, and on the thirtieth day of January, eighteen hundred and forty-three; so that the Mexican Republic shall be absolutely exempt, for the future, from all expense whatever on account of the said claims.

◆ Article XIV

The United States do furthermore discharge the Mexican Republic from all claims of citizens of the United States, not heretofore decided against the Mexican Government, which may have arisen previously to the date of the signature of this treaty; which discharge shall be final and perpetual, whether the said claims be rejected or be allowed by the board of commissioners provided for in the following article, and whatever shall be the total amount of those allowed.

◆ Article XV

The United States, exonerating Mexico from all demands on account of the claims of their citizens mentioned in the preceding article, and considering them entirely and forever canceled, whatever their amount may be, undertake to make satisfaction for the same, to an amount not exceeding three and one-quarter millions of dollars. To ascertain the validity and amount of those claims, a board of commissioners shall be established by the Government of the United States, whose awards shall be final and conclusive; provided that, in deciding upon the validity of each claim, the board shall be guided and governed by the principles and rules of decision prescribed by the first and fifth articles of the unratified convention, concluded at the city of Mexico on the twentieth day of November, one thousand eight hundred and forty-three; and in no case shall an award be made in favour of any claim not embraced by these principles and rules.

If, in the opinion of the said board of commissioners or of the claimants, any books, records, or documents, in the possession or power of the Government of the Mexican Republic, shall be deemed necessary to the just decision of any claim, the commissioners, or the claimants through them, shall, within such period as Congress may designate, make an application in writing for the same, addressed to the Mexican Minister of Foreign Affairs, to be transmitted by the Secretary of State of the United States; and the Mexican Government engages, at the earliest possible moment after the receipt of such

demand, to cause any of the books, records, or documents so specified, which shall be in their possession or power (or authenticated copies or extracts of the same), to be transmitted to the said Secretary of State, who shall immediately deliver them over to the said board of commissioners; provided that no such application shall be made by or at the instance of any claimant, until the facts which it is expected to prove by such books, records, or documents, shall have been stated under oath or affirmation.

◆ Article XVI

Each of the contracting parties reserves to itself the entire right to fortify whatever point within its territory it may judge proper so to fortify for its security.

◆ Article XVII

The treaty of amity, commerce, and navigation, concluded at the city of Mexico, on the fifth day of April, A.D. 1831, between the United States of America and the United Mexican States, except the additional article, and except so far as the stipulations of the said treaty may be incompatible with any stipulation contained in the present treaty, is hereby revived for the period of eight years from the day of the exchange of ratifications of this treaty, with the same force and virtue as if incorporated therein; it being understood that each of the contracting parties reserves to itself the right, at any time after the said period of eight years shall have expired, to terminate the same by giving one year's notice of such intention to the other party.

◆ Article XVIII

All supplies whatever for troops of the United States in Mexico, arriving at ports in the occupation of such troops previous to the final evacuation thereof, although subsequently to the restoration of the custom-houses at such ports, shall be entirely exempt from duties and charges of any kind; the Government of the United States hereby engaging and pledging its faith to establish and vigilantly to enforce, all possible guards for securing the revenue of Mexico, by preventing the importation, under cover of this stipulation, of any articles other than such, both in kind and in quantity, as shall really be wanted for the use and consumption of the forces of the United States during the time they may remain in Mexico. To this end it shall be the duty of all officers and agents of the United States to denounce to the Mexican authorities at the respective ports any attempts at a fraudulent abuse of this stipulation, which they may know of, or may have reason to suspect, and to give to such authorities all the aid in their power with regard thereto; and every such attempt, when duly proved and established by sentence of a competent tribunal, They shall be punished by the confiscation of the property so attempted to be fraudulently introduced.

◆ Article XIX

With respect to all merchandise, effects, and property whatsoever, imported into ports of Mexico, whilst in the occupation of the forces of the United States, whether by citizens of either republic, or by citizens or subjects of any neutral nation, the following rules shall be observed:

(1) All such merchandise, effects, and property, if imported previously to the restoration of the custom-houses to the Mexican authorities, as stipulated for in the third article of this treaty, shall be exempt from confiscation, although the importation of the same be prohibited by the Mexican tariff.

(2) The same perfect exemption shall be enjoyed by all such merchandise, effects, and property, imported subsequently to the restoration of the custom-houses, and previously to the sixty days fixed in the following article for the coming into force of the Mexican tariff at such ports respectively; the said merchandise, effects, and property being, however, at the time of their importation, subject to the payment of duties, as provided for in the said following article.

(3) All merchandise, effects, and property described in the two rules foregoing shall, during their continuance at the place of importation, and upon their leaving such place for the interior, be exempt from all duty, tax, or imposts of every kind, under whatsoever title or denomination. Nor shall they be there subject to any charge whatsoever upon the sale thereof.

(4) All merchandise, effects, and property, described in the first and second rules, which shall have been removed to any place in the interior, whilst such place was in the occupation of the forces of the United States, shall, during their continuance therein, be exempt from all tax upon the sale or consumption thereof, and from every kind of impost or contribution, under whatsoever title or denomination.

(5) But if any merchandise, effects, or property, described in the first and second rules, shall be removed to any place not occupied at the time by the forces of the United States, they shall, upon their introduction into such place, or upon their sale or consumption there, be subject to the same duties which, under the Mexican laws, they would be required to pay in such cases if they had been imported in time of peace, through the maritime custom-houses, and had there paid the duties conformably with the Mexican tariff.

(6) The owners of all merchandise, effects, or property, described in the first and second rules, and existing in any port of Mexico, shall have the right to reship the same, exempt from all tax, impost, or contribution whatever.

With respect to the metals, or other property, exported from any Mexican port whilst in the occupation of the forces of the United States, and previously to the restoration of the custom-house at such port, no person shall be required by the Mexican authorities, whether general or state, to pay any tax, duty, or contribution upon any such exportation, or in any manner to account for the same to the said authorities.

◆ Article XX

Through consideration for the interests of commerce generally, it is agreed, that if less than sixty days should elapse between the date of the signature of this treaty and the restoration of the custom houses, conformably with the stipulation in the third article, in such case all merchandise, effects and property whatsoever, arriving at the Mexican ports after the restoration of the said custom-houses, and previously to the expiration of sixty days after the day of signature of this treaty, shall be admitted to entry; and no other duties shall be levied thereon than the duties established by the tariff found in force at such custom-houses at the time of the restoration of the same. And to all such merchandise, effects, and property, the rules established by the preceding article shall apply.

◆ Article XXI

If unhappily any disagreement should hereafter arise between the Governments of the two republics, whether with respect to the interpretation of any stipulation in this treaty, or with respect to any other particular concerning the political or commercial relations of the two nations, the said Governments, in the name of those nations, do promise to each other that they will endeavour, in the most sincere and earnest manner, to settle the differences so arising, and to preserve the state of peace and friendship in which the two countries are now placing themselves, using, for this end, mutual representations and pacific negotiations. And if, by these means, they should not be enabled to come to an agreement, a resort shall not, on this account, be had to reprisals, aggression, or hostility of any kind, by the one republic against the other, until the Government of that which deems itself aggrieved shall have maturely considered, in the spirit of peace and good neighbourship, whether it would not be better that such difference should be settled by the arbitration of commissioners appointed on each side, or by that of a friendly nation. And should such course be proposed by either party, it shall be acceded to by the other, unless deemed by it altogether incompatible with the nature of the difference, or the circumstances of the case.

◆ Article XXII

If (which is not to be expected, and which God forbid) war should unhappily break out between the two republics, they do now, with a view to such calamity, solemnly pledge themselves to each other and to the world to observe the following rules; absolutely where the nature of the subject permits, and as closely as possible in all cases where such absolute observance shall be impossible:

(1) The merchants of either republic then residing in the other shall be allowed to remain twelve months (for those dwelling in the interior), and six months (for those dwelling at the seaports) to collect their debts and settle their affairs; during which periods they shall enjoy the same protection, and be on the same footing, in all respects, as the citizens or subjects of the most friendly nations; and, at the expiration thereof, or at any time before, they shall have full liberty to depart, carrying off all their effects without molestation or hindrance, conforming therein to the same laws which the citizens or subjects of the most friendly nations are required to conform to. Upon the entrance of the armies of either nation into the territories of the other, women and children, ecclesiastics, scholars of every faculty, cultivators of the earth, merchants, artisans, manufacturers, and fishermen, unarmed and inhabiting unfortified towns, villages, or places, and in general all persons whose occupations are for the common subsistence and benefit of mankind, shall be allowed to continue their respective employments, unmolested in their persons. Nor shall their houses or goods be burnt or otherwise destroyed, nor their cattle taken, nor their fields wasted, by the armed force into whose power, by the events of war, they may happen to fall; but if the necessity arise to take anything from them for the use of such armed force, the same shall be paid for at an equitable price. All churches, hospitals, schools, colleges, libraries, and other establishments for charitable and beneficent purposes, shall be respected, and all persons connected with the same protected in the discharge of their duties, and the pursuit of their vocations.

(2) In order that the fate of prisoners of war may be alleviated all such practices as those of sending them into distant, inclement or unwholesome districts, or crowding them into close and noxious places, shall be studiously avoided. They shall not be confined in dungeons, prison ships, or prisons; nor be put in irons, or bound or otherwise restrained in the use of their limbs. The officers shall enjoy liberty on their paroles, within convenient districts, and have comfortable quarters; and the common soldiers shall be disposed in cantonments, open and extensive enough for air and exercise and lodged in barracks as roomy and good as are provided by the party in whose power they are for its own troops. But if any office shall break his parole by leaving the district so assigned him, or any other prisoner shall escape from the limits of his cantonment after they shall have been designated to him, such individual, officer, or other prisoner, shall forfeit so much of the benefit of this article as provides for his liberty on parole or in cantonment. And if any officer so breaking his parole or any common soldier so escaping from the limits assigned him, shall afterwards be found in arms previously to his being regularly exchanged, the person so offending shall be dealt with according to the established laws of war. The officers shall be daily furnished, by the party in whose power they are, with as many rations, and of the same articles, as are allowed either in kind or by commutation, to officers of equal rank in its own army; and all others shall be daily furnished with such ration as is allowed to a common soldier in its own service; the value of all which supplies shall, at the close of the war, or at periods to be agreed upon between the respective commanders, be paid by the other party, on a mutual adjustment of accounts for the subsistence of prisoners; and such accounts shall not be mingled with or set off against any others, nor the balance due on them withheld, as a compensation or reprisal for any cause whatever, real or pretended. Each party shall be allowed to keep a commissary of prisoners, appointed by itself, with every cantonment of prisoners, in possession of the other; which commissary shall see the prisoners as often a he pleases; shall be allowed to receive, exempt from all duties or taxes, and to distribute, whatever comforts may be sent to them by their friends; and shall be free to transmit his reports in open letters to the party by whom he is employed.

And it is declared that neither the pretense that war dissolves all treaties, nor any other whatever, shall be considered as annulling or suspending the solemn covenant contained in this article. On the contrary, the state of war is precisely that for which it is provided; and, during which, its stipulations are to be as sacredly observed as the most acknowledged obligations under the law of nature or nations.

◆ **Article XXIII**

This treaty shall be ratified by the President of the United States of America, by and with the advice and consent of the Senate thereof; and by the President of the Mexican Republic, with the previous approbation of its general Congress; and the ratifications shall be exchanged in the City of Washington, or at the seat of Government of Mexico, in four months from the date of the signature hereof, or sooner if practicable.

In faith whereof we, the respective Plenipotentiaries, have signed this treaty of peace, friendship, limits, and settlement, and have hereunto affixed our seals respectively. Done in quintuplicate, at the city of Guadalupe Hidalgo, on the second day of February, in the year of our Lord one thousand eight hundred and forty-eight.

N. P. Trist
Luis P. Cuevas
Bernadro Cuoto
Migl. Atristain

Glossary

30 leagues	90 statute miles (1,449 kilometers)
cantonment	temporary quarters for military troops
plenipotentiaries	persons empowered by their respective governments to sign a treaty
sickly season	May through October, the period during which malaria was rampant in the treaty area
three millions of dollars	about 75 million dollars in today's dollars

Portrait of Karl Marx (Library of Congress)

COMMUNIST MANIFESTO

" Let the ruling classes tremble at a Communist revolution."

Overview

The *Manifesto of the Communist Party*, commonly referred to simply as the *Communist Manifesto*, was published on February 21, 1848, to summarize the political standpoint of the Communist League, a small group of mostly German radicals. The German philosopher Karl Marx wrote the document in collaboration with Friedrich Engels, another young German critic of the social and political systems that prevailed in Europe at that time. *Communist* and *Socialist* were interchangeable terms in 1848, referring to an arrangement in which workers would own and control the places where they worked instead of selling their labor to factory owners ("capitalists"). Eventually, the term *Communist* became identified with the brand of Socialism that came to be called "Marxism."

Marxism differs from other varieties of Socialism by attempting to put into historical context the rapid and confusing changes that took place during what is now called the Industrial Revolution. By the early nineteenth century the rise of steam-powered factory production created cheap goods, new wealth, and new varieties of poverty. The factory system did not create social injustice, a state of affairs in which some people live in luxury from the work of other people, but it concentrated misery in unsightly, ill-smelling factory towns. The factory workers were more conspicuous than the more dispersed, similarly wretched agricultural laborers, and their misery could not be dismissed as something that had always been that way. Marx and Engels argued that the new class of factory workers could end the long, ugly history of exploitation; as soon as factory workers caught on to their potential strength, a workers' revolution would abolish the ability of some people to live off the work of other people. A world of decency, fairness, justice, and contentment would arrive.

Marxism's ability to present a Socialist society as not only more equitable than capitalism but indeed achievable, even inevitable, made it the dominant variety of revolutionary thinking in the late nineteenth and twentieth centuries. It affected the thinking of millions; highly modified mutant variations flavored revolutionary regimes, notably in Russia and China, and a major twentieth-century movement—Fascism—emerged as an antidote to it.

Context

After the defeat of the French Revolution and Napoléon Bonapart in 1815, European governments concentrated on preserving order and preventing a new and terrifying wave of revolution. For example, in 1819 the German government enacted the Carlsbad Decrees, which outlawed nationalist groups, established press censorship, and blacklisted radicals. Advocates of liberalism and political democracy campaigned for constitutional limits on monarchs' power. Liberals also demanded that more people be allowed to vote but were generally reluctant to extend suffrage to the poorest (and presumably most ignorant) citizens. Democrats wanted the vote extended to *all* men, even the poorest. ("Universal" suffrage meant "men" until late in the nineteenth century.) In economically developing regions, the rise of factories raised the possibility that political change might accompany spectacular economic change.

In large areas of Europe, most of the population was ruled by governments run by people of an alien culture, language, and sometimes religion, such as the assorted Slavs, Hungarians, northern Italians, and others under the German-speaking Habsburg ruling family in the Austrian Empire. In such areas, increasing calls for national liberation threatened the existing order. Where people who shared (more or less) the same culture and language were divided into many small states, as in Italy and Germany, nationalists called for unification, which would change the map and drive from their thrones most if not all of the small-state rulers within the newly united countries. The fungus that ruined potato crops in the 1840s starved people in Ireland and Germany and raised food prices for all. Costly food made the poorest workers desperate; both advocates and enemies of change expected something major to happen soon.

Liberals, democrats, and nationalists had many supporters, and Europe's rulers regarded them, correctly, as immediate threats to the existing order. A more radical but more remote threat was presented by Communists or Socialists,

1815

- **June 9**
  Final Act of the Congress of Vienna arranges Europe's borders, attempting to restore order after the disturbances of the French Revolution and Napoleonic era.

1818

- **May 5**
  Karl Marx is born in Trier, Prussia.

1819

- **September 20**
  The German government enacts the Carlsbad Decrees, outlawing nationalist groups, establishing press censorship, and blacklisting radicals.

1820

- **November 28**
  Friedrich Engels is born in Barmen, Germany.

1844

- **August**
  Marx and Engels begin working together on writing projects.

1846

- **January**
  Marx and Engels begin organizing a Communist Correspondence Society in Brussels, attempting to connect fellow radicals.

who regarded political democracy and nationalism as transient issues that would have to be resolved along the way to the *real* issue: eliminating the inherent injustice of the capitalist system. A pair of Communist groups, made up almost entirely of Germans, merged in June 1847 as the Communist League. The league met in London and in Brussels, Belgium, to avoid German police. It published the *Communist Manifesto* in London because of censorship in Germany. Friedrich Engels drafted a question-and-answer summary of the group's views ("Principles of Communism") but suggested that Marx compose a manifesto to present the position more fully and forcefully. After prodding by the group's council, Marx finished his assignment at the beginning of February 1848, and it was published (in German, in London) later that month.

The revolutions of 1848 spread across Europe after liberal demonstrations in Paris, calling for a modest increase in the number of voters, led to bloody riots that drove King Louis-Philippe from the country. Since everyone (those who wanted change and those who did not) assumed that a revolution in Paris meant revolution everywhere, as had happened after the French Revolution of 1789, changes erupted almost everywhere in Europe. In countries that already existed, like France, people struggled over liberal and democratic issues such as who could vote; in countries that did not yet exist, national liberation and unification were more prominent. All the revolutionary efforts of 1848 were crushed; as political refugees in England, Marx and Engels had plenty of company. Marx and Engels recognized that Communism would have to wait its turn; they published a radical newspaper in Germany (June 1848–May 1849) with the logo "Organ of Democracy," and it concentrated on Germany's unification under a democratic constitution as well as commenting on revolutionary events throughout Europe. Copies of the *Communist Manifesto* were seized by police in various countries, but except for a public discussion of the work that led to a riot in Amsterdam in March 1848, the document had little impact until later, as Marxism attracted wide interest and the manifesto provided a convenient introduction to the theory and movement. An 1850 English translation was little noticed; the 1888 translation by Sam Moore, edited by Engels, has remained the standard English text.

About the Author

Karl Marx and Friedrich Engels, born in 1818 and 1820, respectively, were from different parts of western Germany and from different levels of the middle class, or bourgeoisie—"a small section of the ruling class cuts itself adrift, and joins the revolutionary class," as the *Communist Manifesto* proclaims. Marx's father was trained as a lawyer and worked for the Prussian government. When Prussia took over the region after the fall of Napóleon, he converted from Judaism to Prussia's official Protestant Christian religion because Prussia allowed no Jews in its civil service, although the family was secular. Karl Marx married Jenny von Westphalen, the daughter of Trier's most prominent family, and for some time in the 1850s Marx's brother-in-law was a prominent Prussian police official who caught and prosecuted radicals like Marx.

Marx attended the University of Berlin and associated with radical philosophical thinkers. His ideas were perceived as a danger to the authority of the monarchy and the official church, so he was blacklisted and banned from any potential university job anywhere in Germany. His doctorate (in philosophy) led to no academic employment, and he spent his life in ill-paid radical journalism, scholarly research, and political organization, all devoted to the overthrow of capitalism. For most of his life he lived chiefly on subsidies from his friend Engels.

Engels's father was a cotton-mill-owning capitalist. The family took its Protestant religion seriously, but Engels found his way to a secular outlook in his teens. He was expected to serve in the family business, so he was not sent to university; he sat in on classes in Berlin but was largely self-educated. Engels wrote critical articles on politics, religion, and economics, some of them in a paper that Marx edited. He spent twenty months in England (1842–1844), where he was trained in management at the Manchester branch of his father's business and observed all he could in the world's greatest center of textile production, one of the key sites of the Industrial Revolution. His own observations and his reading of available sources were combined in *The Condition of the Working Class in England* (1845), a tirade against the mistreatment of factory workers.

After the revolutions of 1848 were stamped out in Europe, Marx and Engels became political fugitives because of their published opposition to Prussia's crackdown on the democratically elected assembly that had tried to unite Germany. (Engels was also wanted for treason, having failed to report for duty in the Prussian army and having fought in the last-ditch resistance of German democratic nationalism in the spring of 1849.) As refugees in England, Engels went to work for his father's firm in Manchester while Marx settled in London. They wrote, analyzed capitalist society, and planned for the proletarian revolution that the *Communist Manifesto* had promised. Engels's father died in 1870, and he sold his share of the inheritance to his siblings. He was able to move to London, and he and the Marx family lived off his well-managed investments, existing within the capitalist system they had not been able to abolish. Marx died in 1883 and Engels in 1895, both convinced that the revolution would soon arrive.

Explanation and Analysis of the Document

The manifesto begins with a somewhat optimistic opening declaration that Communism loomed over Europe, terrifying the authorities of the time (who were interested enough to spy on and harass Communists but more preoccupied with the dangers of liberal democracy and nationalism). Among those authorities are the pope (at the time, Pius IX), the czar of Russia (at the time, Nicholas I), the

Time Line

1847

■ **June 2**
The First Congress of the Communist League opens in London; the formation of the league includes the establishment of a Correspondence Society.

■ **November 9**
The Second Congress of the Communist League opens in London; on Engels's suggestion, the league designates Marx to write the *Communist Manifesto*.

1848

■ **February 21**
The *Communist Manifesto* is published in German in London.

■ **February 22**
Demonstrations in Paris about widening voting rights lead to riots that set off upheavals all over Europe.

■ **June 1**
Marx and Engels begin publishing the *New Rhineland Gazette*, a newspaper dedicated to a democratic unification of Germany, until the paper is shut down by the Prussian government. Publication continues to May 19, 1849.

1864

■ **September 28**
The First International Workingmen's Association is founded.

1867

■ **September 14**
Marx's *Capital*
(volume 1) is
published in
Leipzig.

1883

■ **March 14**
Marx dies.

1895

■ **August 5**
Engels dies.

German diplomat Prince von Metternich, and the French statesman François Guizot. The manifesto goes on to analyze the historical roots of mid-nineteenth-century society. This is where Marx differentiates his version of Socialism from other advocates' approaches and begins the argument that inspired hope and fear in so many people.

◆ **"Bourgeois and Proletarians"**

Marx's chapter heading "Bourgeois and Proletarians" identifies the two social classes that would fight out the coming class struggle: "Bourgeois" refers to the middle class, with implications of narrow material concerns and obsession with respectability, while "proletarians" are members of the industrial working class. The declaration that all history has been "the story of class struggles" summarizes the essence of the Marxist view of history. Marx cites examples of how a rigid class structure existed in the past, such as in ancient Rome, during the feudal Middle Ages with their trade guilds, and even in the Americas. The difference between the struggle between classes in these earlier eras and that taking place in the nineteenth century is that the modern class struggle is simpler, pitting just two social classes—the bourgeoisie and the proletariat—against each another.

Marx explains how this state of affairs evolved. The modern struggle arose because of new economic realities, including the growth of the population and therefore of markets, improvements in navigation and communication, and the emergence of organized industrial production—of "Modern Industry." The modern bourgeoisie emerged from the historical development of the consolidation of the means of production. As the bourgeoisie gained economic power, it also gained political power. As Marx puts it, "The executive of the modern State is but a committee for managing the common affairs of the whole bourgeoisie." Marx seems to see the modern bourgeoisie as worse than earlier aristocratic feudal overlords, for the bourgeoisie has converted the relationship between worker and employer into one based entirely on wage labor: It has "left remaining no other nexus between man and man than naked self-inter-

est, than callous 'cash payment.'" He goes on to note that modern industry in the hands of the bourgeoisie has effectively eliminated any chivalry or "sentimentalism" in favor of "egotistical calculation." The bourgeoisie's interest in freedom is restricted to a single "unconscionable" freedom, "Free Trade." Marx regards this relationship between worker and employer as one based entirely on exploitation, though this exploitation is masked by "religious and political illusions." Meanwhile, the bourgeoisie has reduced all occupations to mere paid labor, in the process damaging the ties that formerly bound families.

Marx goes on to specify some of the ways in which the modern bourgeoisie has disrupted traditional patterns of life. The bourgeoisie is constantly changing the means of production. It creates new industries to satisfy new wants, in the process destroying old industries. It travels the world in search of new markets. It replaces locally made products with products from around the globe. Nations and regions are no longer self-sufficient. It has subjugated nature. Marx acknowledges that the new means and methods of production have drawn "barbarian" nations into the community of civilized nations. Yet the cost of this development in Marx's eyes is heavy: "It compels all nations, on pain of extinction, to adopt the bourgeois mode of production; it compels them to introduce what it calls civilisation into their midst, i.e., to become bourgeois themselves. In one word, it creates a world after its own image."

Marx argues that the very successes of the bourgeoisie contribute to its own instability. Because of "too much civilisation, too much means of subsistence, too much industry, too much commerce"—in a word, because of overproduction—"the history of industry and commerce is but the history of the revolt of modern productive forces against modern conditions of production, against the property relations that are the conditions for the existence of the bourgeoisie and of its rule." Put simply, the bourgeoisie has created conditions that potentially lead to its own destruction, and that destruction will come at the hands of the proletariat. The process Marx describes is often referred to as the "dialectic" or "dialectical materialism." This is a philosophical view that states that any "thesis" creates its own "antithesis" and that the clash between the two gives rise to a new "synthesis." In Marx's view, the clash was between labor and the new industrial realities. The synthesis would be Communism.

Marx details the condition of the proletariat. In his view, workers are "commodities." They sell their labor piecemeal. They are victims of changes in markets. They become appendages of the machine. Their work is monotonous. They become like soldiers in an industrial army. They become slaves, men and women alike, and even tradespeople become part of the proletariat because they lack the capital—money—to take part in modern industry. The proletariat, though, is not without power. At first, individual laborers fight the bourgeoisie; then the workers in a plant resist. Ultimately, if competing workers are able to transform themselves from an "incoherent mass scattered over the whole country," they can organize into trade unions. Collectively, they can protect their interests, keep wages up, and resist

Russian Revolution: Peasant workers (AP/Wide World Photos)

their exploitation at the hands of capitalists. This resistance will often take a violent turn, but this violence is a necessary and inevitable part of the class struggle. It is the essence of revolution, and Marx sees the industrial class, in contrast with more conservative shopkeepers, tradesmen, artisans, and peasants, as the only truly revolutionary class.

◆ "Proletarians and Communists"

In this section of the manifesto, Marx details the relationship between proletarians and Communists. He sees the Communist Party not as a "separate party opposed to other working-class parties." He views it, rather, as an international movement, one that focuses on the "common interests of the entire proletariat, independently of all nationality." He sees Communists as the "most advanced and resolute section of the working-class parties of every country" and states the aim of Communism succinctly: "The immediate aim of the Communist is the same as that of all the other proletarian parties: formation of the proletariat into a class, overthrow of the bourgeois supremacy, conquest of political power by the proletariat."

Marx takes up the issue of private property. On the one hand he states that "the distinguishing feature of Communism is not the abolition of property generally, but the abolition of bourgeois property." He goes on to say, though, that because private property is essentially in the hands of

the bourgeoisie, and because the bourgeoisie uses that property to exploit workers, in essence the aim of Communism is "abolition of private property." He addresses the objection that people should be able to keep the fruits of their labor. However, the only people who are not bourgeoisie and who might have been able to do so, such as artisans, have already lost their private property to the bourgeoisie. If, however, "private property" means the property of the bourgeoisie, the problem in Marx's view is that such property is used only to create more capital put to use for the exploitation of labor. Capital is not really private property, for capital "is a collective product," something that can be used "only by the united action of many members" of a class. Capital is not money or property. Capital is social and political power. Meanwhile, he writes, "Private property is already done away with for nine-tenths of the population," so claims that Communists want to eliminate everyone's private property miss the point.

Marx addresses family relationships and the education of children. He argues that modern wage labor turns the family into purely an economic unit, one that takes subsistence wages for its own brute survival. Marx is especially critical of the modern education system, writing that

the bourgeois clap-trap about the family and education, about the hallowed co-relation of parent and child, becomes all the more disgusting, the more, by the action of Modern Industry, all family ties among the proletarians are torn asunder, and their children transformed into simple articles of commerce and instruments of labour.

This exploitation extends to women, who are similarly exploited by bourgeois values; he suggests that the bourgeois system has reduced women to the status of prostitutes.

Marx then addresses the issue of whether Communism wants to abolish nationalities. Marx argues that under current conditions, the working man has no country. He goes on to say that the conditions created by the bourgeoisie have stripped people of any real attachment to a nation or culture, substituting instead a need on the part of working people to engage in a quest for mere survival. In effect, the bourgeoisie has already eliminated nationality.

Marx specifies the steps that are necessary to wrest control over property from the bourgeoisie and turn the proletariat into an organized class that will usher in a new, more productive economic system. Some of these steps include abolition of land rents, a progressive income tax (that is, a tax system that taxes the rich at a higher rate than those of lesser means), elimination of inheritances, centralization of credit and transportation, state-owned factories, and free public education. When these and other steps are taken, class distinctions will disappear.

◆ "Position of the Communists in Relation to the Various Existing Opposition Parties"

In this brief section, Marx tries to reassure other democratic movements that Communism is not an opponent. He writes, "Communists everywhere support every revolutionary movement against the existing social and political order of things" and wants to see "the union and agreement of the democratic parties of all countries." The section concludes with perhaps the most famous quotation from the *Communist Manifesto*: "Working Men of all Countries, Unite!"

Audience

The *Communist Manifesto* was aimed at two groups. It spoke to the working class or proletariat to explain their situation, provide hope, and prod them toward revolutionary action. It warned the owners and beneficiaries of capitalism, the bourgeoisie, that their domination of the world was not only unjust but doomed. The intent was to energize the workers and demoralize their class enemies.

Impact

At first only a few radicals and police authorities paid attention to this mission statement of a small activist group. The 1848 revolutions swirled around nationalism and liberal democracy, not Communism. But the harsh repressions that subdued the rebels of 1848 suggested that moving beyond liberal, democratic, and national issues to the remoter problem of undoing capitalism's hold over the workers was unlikely to be accomplished by persuasion. The Marxist interpretation of society and the Marxist promise of revolutionary transformation attracted attention from people interested in improving their world, including many of the proletarians who were indeed increasing their numbers as industrialization advanced. Anyone wishing to know what the issues were was directed toward the *Communist Manifesto* for a reasonably concise, comprehensible summary. When rival variations on Marxism emerged after the founders' deaths, most leftist sects put out their own editions of the manifesto, providing introductions to persuade the reader that their own peculiar movements represented what Marx and Engels had really meant. Anticommunists also produced editions with know-your-enemy introductions. The fact that many people read the manifesto and absorbed Marxist views of the world did not mean that the prophecies came true.

Although few people paid attention to the *Communist Manifesto* when it was first published, Marx's views ultimately had a profound impact in Europe. By the end of the nineteenth century, Marxist concepts had been accepted by the trade union movement, and Socialist parties throughout Europe absorbed Marxist principles. However, a split began to emerge. Many Europeans accepted Marx's view that violent revolution and the overthrow of the capitalist state were necessary and inevitable. In contrast, others believed that some of the goals of Marxism, particularly the improvement of the condition of the working class, could be achieved through existing governmental structures. Until this time, the terms *Communism* and *Socialism* were used interchangeably. As the movements split, the words came to have different meanings. Communism was applied to a more-or-less pure form of revolutionary Marxism; Socialism came to refer to an economic and political system in which the existing state owned the means of production and distribution. In effect, Socialism was regarded as a less radical form of Communism. Even today, the words *Communism*, *Socialism*, and *Marxism* tend to be used without precise meaning or clear distinctions, but all represent a critique of the capitalist system. Further, pure capitalism, many would argue, does not really exist, and even in capitalist states such as the United States, governments try to correct market imperfections by providing benefits—tax breaks, agricultural subsidies, food stamps, welfare—and by imposing regulations that have a slightly Marxist flavor in that they try to curb the excesses of capitalism.

Marxism play a key role in the Russian Revolution of 1917 that gave rise to the Communist Soviet Union. Soviet leaders such as Vladimir Lenin and Joseph Stalin claimed to base their political views on Marxism, and the Soviets' numerous satellite states, principally those in Eastern Europe, asserted that they were Marxist states. At various times, numerous other nations have adopted Marxism as their ruling orthodoxy, including Albania, Angola, Benin, Bulgaria, Chile, the Republic of Congo, Ethiopia, Grenada, Laos, Mongolia, Mozambique, Nepal, Nicaragua, South

"*A spectre is haunting Europe—the spectre of Communism.*"

(Introduction)

"*The history of all hitherto existing societies is the history of class struggles.*"

("Bourgeois and Proletarians")

"*Society as a whole is more and more splitting up into two great hostile camps, into two great classes, directly facing each other: Bourgeoisie and Proletariat.*"

("Bourgeois and Proletarians")

"*What the bourgeoisie, therefore, produces, above all, is its own grave-diggers. Its fall and the victory of the proletariat are equally inevitable.*"

("Bourgeois and Proletarians")

"*Let the ruling classes tremble at a Communistic revolution. The proletarians have nothing to lose but their chains. They have a world to win. Working Men of all Countries, Unite!*"

("Position of the Communists in Relation to the Various Existing Opposition Parties")

Yemen, Venezuela, and Vietnam. In the wake of the collapse of the Soviet Union, the Eastern European nations and others throughout the world, including Russia, have adopted capitalism, sometimes in modified form, as their governing political and economic orthodoxy. In the early twenty-first century, only North Korea, Cuba, and China claim to be purely Communist states, although China and, to a lesser extent Cuba, have adopted some capitalist practices. The worldwide revolution that Marx predicted did not come about, and his views were corrupted by monolithic single-party states that were, in effect, dictatorships. In the twentieth century and into the new millennium, "Communism" evolved from a set of political, historical, and economic viewpoints into a hated ideology that, most would argue, has been thoroughly discredited.

Marxism, though, had and still has important social and philosophical impacts. The social view that people too often are alienated from their employers and source of income owes its origins to Marxist principles. Liberal and Socialist political parties continue their critique of capital-

ism in an effort to eliminate the extremes of class and economic distinctions. In the arts, novelists, playwrights, and poets espouse Marxist principles, even if they do not refer explicitly to Karl Marx. Marxist thought has influenced literary scholarship, with Marxist theories applied to the interpretation of fictional worlds and class structures depicted by such writers as Charles Dickens, Bertolt Brecht, and many others; indeed, it is possible to apply Marxist criticism to any literary work. The German sociologist Max Weber led a school that examined, for example, the relationship of Protestantism to the emergence of the modern capitalist system, using some of the principles of Marxism; the so-called Frankfurt School, based at the University of Frankfurt am Main in Germany, is a loose gathering of neo-Marxists whose critique of capitalism is based on Marxist principles. Numerous liberation groups throughout the world, including Catholic proponents of "liberation theology," advocates of "black Marxism," and feminists, still appeal to Marx's underlying views in their quest for political and social justice.

Further Reading

■ Books

Berger, Martin. "Revolutionary Tactics and the Importance of Engels." In *Crucible of Socialism*, ed. Louis Patsouras. Atlantic Highlands, N.J.: Humanities Press International, 1987.

Engels, Friedrich. *The Condition of the Working Class in England*, trans. W. O. Henderson and W. H. Chaloner. Stanford, Calif.: Stanford University Press, 1968.

Heilbroner, Robert L. *The Worldly Philosophers: The Lives, Times, and Ideas of the Great Economic Thinkers*, 7th ed. New York: Simon & Schuster, 1999.

Hunt, Richard N. *The Political Ideas of Marx and Engels*. 2 vols. Pittsburgh: University of Pittsburgh Press, 1974–1984.

Lichtheim, George. *Marxism: An Historical and Critical Study*, 2nd ed. New York: Praeger, 1965.

McLellan, David. *Friedrich Engels*. New York: Penguin, 1978.

Singer, Peter. *Karl Marx: A Very Short Introduction*. Oxford, U.K.: Oxford University Press, 1981.

Tucker, Robert R., ed. *The Marx-Engels Reader*, 2nd ed. New York: W. W. Norton, 1978.

■ Web Sites

Stanovsky, Derek. The MarX-Files Web site. http://www.appstate.edu/~stanovskydj/marxfiles.html.

—Martin Berger

Questions for Further Study

1. What impact did the Industrial Revolution have on the development of Communist and Socialist thought in the nineteenth century?

2. Why were regimes and government authorities frightened of Communism or at least wanted to suppress it? What surrounding historical events made Communism a more immediate threat?

3. Similarly, in the 1940s and 1950s, in particular, fear of Communists in the United States was rampant. Such organizations as the House Un-American Activities Committee investigated charges of Communist infiltration of government, education, and the entertainment industry. To what extent were the actions of American authorities similar to those of European authorities at the time Karl Marx wrote?

4. In modern political debate, reference is sometimes made to "class warfare" as politicians, it is thought, try to pit rich against poor for the purpose of winning votes. Do you think this is true in contemporary America? If it is, to what extent do you believe this debate parallels ideas presented in the *Communist Manifesto*?

5. In modern life, the very word *Communism* continues to strike a kind of fear. People in the West have been conditioned to regard Communism as perhaps little better than the Nazism of World War II Germany under Adolf Hitler. Do you believe that this is a fair judgment? Make the argument that the Communism of Karl Marx was different from the version of Communism practiced in repressive regimes such as the former Soviet Union and that Communism is simply a set of political and economic theories that help explain historical events.

COMMUNIST MANIFESTO

A spectre is haunting Europe—the spectre of Communism. All the Powers of old Europe have entered into a holy alliance to exorcise this spectre: Pope and Czar, Metternich and Guizot, French Radicals and German police-spies.... Two things result from this fact.

I. Communism is already acknowledged by all European Powers to be itself a Power.

II. It is high time that Communists should openly, in the face of the whole world, publish their views, their aims, their tendencies, and meet this nursery tale of the Spectre of Communism with a Manifesto of the party itself.

To this end, Communists of various nationalities have assembled in London, and sketched the following Manifesto, to be published in the English, French, German, Italian, Flemish and Danish languages.

I. Bourgeois and Proletarians

The history of all hitherto existing societies is the history of class struggles.

Freeman and slave, patrician and plebeian, lord and serf, guild-master and journeyman, in a word, oppressor and oppressed, stood in constant opposition to one another, carried on an uninterrupted, now hidden, now open fight, a fight that each time ended, either in a revolutionary re-constitution of society at large, or in the common ruin of the contending classes.

In the earlier epochs of history, we find almost everywhere a complicated arrangement of society into various orders, a manifold gradation of social rank. In ancient Rome we have patricians, knights, plebeians, slaves; in the Middle Ages, feudal lords, vassals, guild-masters, journeymen, apprentices, serfs; in almost all of these classes, again, subordinate gradations.

The modern bourgeois society that has sprouted from the ruins of feudal society has not done away with class antagonisms. It has but established new classes, new conditions of oppression, new forms of struggle in place of the old ones. Our epoch, the epoch of the bourgeoisie, possesses, however, this distinctive feature: it has simplified the class antagonisms. Society as a whole is more and more splitting up into two great hostile camps, into two great classes, directly facing each other: Bourgeoisie and Proletariat.

From the serfs of the Middle Ages sprang the chartered burghers of the earliest towns. From these burgesses the first elements of the bourgeoisie were developed.

The discovery of America, the rounding of the Cape, opened up fresh ground for the rising bourgeoisie. The East-Indian and Chinese markets, the colonisation of America, trade with the colonies, the increase in the means of exchange and in commodities generally, gave to commerce, to navigation, to industry, an impulse never before known, and thereby, to the revolutionary element in the tottering feudal society, a rapid development.

The feudal system of industry, under which industrial production was monopolised by closed guilds, now no longer sufficed for the growing wants of the new markets. The manufacturing system took its place. The guild-masters were pushed on one side by the manufacturing middle class; division of labour between the different corporate guilds vanished in the face of division of labour in each single workshop.

Meantime the markets kept ever growing, the demand ever rising. Even manufacture no longer sufficed. Thereupon, steam and machinery revolutionised industrial production. The place of manufacture was taken by the giant, Modern Industry, the place of the industrial middle class, by industrial millionaires, the leaders of whole industrial armies, the modern bourgeois.

Modern industry has established the world-market, for which the discovery of America paved the way. This market has given an immense development to commerce, to navigation, to communication by land. This development has, in its time, reacted on the extension of industry; and in proportion as industry, commerce, navigation, railways extended, in the same proportion the bourgeoisie developed, increased its capital, and pushed into the background every class handed down from the Middle Ages.

We see, therefore, how the modern bourgeoisie is itself the product of a long course of development, of a series of revolutions in the modes of production and of exchange.

Each step in the development of the bourgeoisie was accompanied by a corresponding political advance of that class....

The bourgeoisie has at last, since the establishment of Modern Industry and of the world-market, conquered for itself, in the modern representative State, exclusive political sway. The executive of the modern State is but a committee for managing the common affairs of the whole bourgeoisie.

The bourgeoisie, historically, has played a most revolutionary part.

The bourgeoisie, wherever it has got the upper hand, has put an end to all feudal, patriarchal, idyllic relations. It has pitilessly torn asunder the motley feudal ties that bound man to his "natural superiors," and has left remaining no other nexus between man and man than naked self-interest, than callous "cash payment." It has drowned the most heavenly ecstasies of religious fervour, of chivalrous enthusiasm, of philistine sentimentalism, in the icy water of egotistical calculation. It has resolved personal worth into exchange value, and in place of the numberless and feasible chartered freedoms, has set up that single, unconscionable freedom—Free Trade. In one word, for exploitation, veiled by religious and political illusions, naked, shameless, direct, brutal exploitation.

The bourgeoisie has stripped of its halo every occupation hitherto honoured and looked up to with reverent awe. It has converted the physician, the lawyer, the priest, the poet, the man of science, into its paid wage labourers.

The bourgeoisie has torn away from the family its sentimental veil, and has reduced the family relation to a mere money relation.

The bourgeoisie has disclosed how it came to pass that the brutal display of vigour in the Middle Ages, which Reactionists so much admire, found its fitting complement in the most slothful indolence. It has been the first to show what man's activity can bring about. It has accomplished wonders far surpassing Egyptian pyramids, Roman aqueducts, and Gothic cathedrals; it has conducted expeditions that put in the shade all former Exoduses of nations and crusades.

The bourgeoisie cannot exist without constantly revolutionizing the instruments of production, and thereby the relations of production, and with them the whole relations of society. Conservation of the old modes of production in unaltered form, was, on the contrary, the first condition of existence for all earlier industrial classes. Constant revolutionising of production, uninterrupted disturbance of all social conditions, everlasting uncertainty and agitation distinguish the bourgeois epoch from all earlier ones. All fixed, fast-frozen relations, with their train of ancient and venerable prejudices and opinions, are swept away, all new-formed ones become antiquated before they can ossify. All that is solid melts into air, all that is holy is profaned, and man is at last compelled to face with sober senses, his real conditions of life, and his relations with his kind.

The need of a constantly expanding market for its products chases the bourgeoisie over the whole surface of the globe. It must nestle everywhere, settle everywhere, establish connexions everywhere.

The bourgeoisie has through its exploitation of the world-market given a cosmopolitan character to production and consumption in every country. To the great chagrin of Reactionists, it has drawn from under the feet of industry the national ground on which it stood. All old-established national industries have been destroyed or are daily being destroyed. They are dislodged by new industries, whose introduction becomes a life and death question for all civilised nations, by industries that no longer work up indigenous raw material, but raw material drawn from the remotest zones; industries whose products are consumed, not only at home, but in every quarter of the globe. In place of the old wants, satisfied by the productions of the country, we find new wants, requiring for their satisfaction the products of distant lands and climes. In place of the old local and national seclusion and self-sufficiency, we have intercourse in every direction, universal inter-dependence of nations. And as in material, so also in intellectual production. The intellectual creations of individual nations become common property. National one-sidedness and narrow-mindedness become more and more impossible, and from the numerous national and local literatures, there arises a world literature.

The bourgeoisie, by the rapid improvement of all instruments of production, by the immensely facilitated means of communication, draws all, even the most barbarian, nations into civilisation. The cheap prices of its commodities are the heavy artillery with which it batters down all Chinese walls, with which it forces the barbarians' intensely obstinate hatred of foreigners to capitulate. It compels all nations, on pain of extinction, to adopt the bourgeois mode of production; it compels them to introduce what it calls civilisation into their midst, i.e., to become bourgeois themselves. In one word, it creates a world after its own image....

The bourgeoisie, during its rule of scarce one hundred years, has created more massive and more colossal productive forces than have all preceding generations together. Subjection of Nature's forces to man, machinery, application of chemistry to industry and agriculture, steam-navigation, railways, electric telegraphs, clearing of whole continents for cultivation, canalisation of rivers, whole populations conjured out of the ground—what earlier century had even a presentiment that such productive forces slumbered in the lap of social labour?

We see then: the means of production and of exchange, on whose foundation the bourgeoisie built itself up, were generated in feudal society. At a certain stage in the development of these means of production and of exchange, the conditions under which feudal society produced and exchanged, the feudal organisation of agriculture and manufacturing industry, in one word, the feudal relations of property became no longer compatible with the already developed productive forces; they became so many fetters. They had to be burst asunder; they were burst asunder.

Into their place stepped free competition, accompanied by a social and political constitution adapted to it, and by the economical and political sway of the bourgeois class.

A similar movement is going on before our own eyes. Modern bourgeois society with its relations of production, of exchange and of property, a society that has conjured up such gigantic means of production and of exchange, is like the sorcerer, who is no longer able to control the powers of the nether world whom he has called up by his spells. For many a decade past the history of industry and commerce is but the history of the revolt of modern productive forces against modern conditions of production, against the property relations that are the conditions for the existence of the bourgeoisie and of its rule. It is enough to mention the commercial crises that by their periodical return put on its trial, each time more threateningly, the existence of the entire bourgeois society. In these crises a great part not only of the existing products, but also of the previously created productive forces, are periodically destroyed. In these crises there breaks out an epidemic that, in all earlier epochs, would have seemed an absurdity—the epidemic of over-production.

Society suddenly finds itself put back into a state of momentary barbarism; it appears as if a famine, a universal war of devastation had cut off the supply of every means of subsistence; industry and commerce seem to be destroyed; and why? Because there is too much civilisation, too much means of subsistence, too much industry, too much commerce. The productive forces at the disposal of society no longer tend to further the development of the conditions of bourgeois property; on the contrary, they have become too powerful for these conditions, by which they are fettered, and so soon as they overcome these fetters, they bring disorder into the whole of bourgeois society, endanger the existence of bourgeois property. The conditions of bourgeois society are too narrow to comprise the wealth created by them. And how does the bourgeoisie get over these crises? On the one hand inforced destruction of a mass of productive forces; on the other, by the conquest of new markets, and by the more thorough exploitation of the old ones. That is to say, by paving the way for more extensive and more destructive crises, and by diminishing the means whereby crises are prevented.

The weapons with which the bourgeoisie felled feudalism to the ground are now turned against the bourgeoisie itself.

But not only has the bourgeoisie forged the weapons that bring death to itself; it has also called into existence the men who are to wield those weapons—the modern working class—the proletarians.

In proportion as the bourgeoisie, i.e., capital, is developed, in the same proportion is the proletariat, the modern working class, developed—a class of labourers, who live only so long as they find work, and who find work only so long as their labour increases capital. These labourers, who must sell themselves piece-meal, are a commodity, like every other article of commerce, and are consequently exposed to all the vicissitudes of competition, to all the fluctuations of the market.

Owing to the extensive use of machinery and to division of labour, the work of the proletarians has lost all individual character, and consequently, all charm for the workman. He becomes an appendage of the machine, and it is only the most simple, most monotonous, and most easily acquired knack, that is required of him. Hence, the cost of production of a workman is restricted, almost entirely, to the means of subsistence that he requires for his maintenance, and for the propagation of his race. But the price of a commodity, and therefore also of labour, is equal to its cost of production. In proportion therefore, as the repulsiveness of the work increases, the wage decreases. Nay more, in proportion as the use of machinery and division of labour increases, in the same proportion the burden of toil also increases, whether by prolongation of the working hours, by increase of the work exacted in a given time or by increased speed of the machinery, etc.

Modern industry has converted the little workshop of the patriarchal master into the great factory of the industrial capitalist. Masses of labourers, crowded into the factory, are organised like soldiers. As privates of the industrial army they are placed under the command of a perfect hierarchy of officers and sergeants. Not only are they slaves of the bourgeois class, and of the bourgeois State; they are daily and hourly enslaved by the machine, by the over-looker, and, above all, by the individual bourgeois manufacturer himself. The more openly this despotism proclaims gain to be its end and aim, the more petty, the more hateful and the more embittering it is.

The less the skill and exertion of strength implied in manual labour, in other words, the more modern industry becomes developed, the more is the labour of men superseded by that of women. Differences of age and sex have no longer any distinctive social validity for the working class. All are instruments of labour, more or less expensive to use, according to their age and sex....

The lower strata of the middle class—the small tradespeople, shopkeepers, retired tradesmen generally, the handicraftsmen and peasants—all these sink gradually into the proletariat, partly because their diminutive capital does not suffice for the scale on which Modern Industry is carried on, and is swamped in the competition with the large capitalists, partly because their specialized skill is rendered worthless by the new methods of production. Thus the proletariat is recruited from all classes of the population.

The proletariat goes through various stages of development. With its birth begins its struggle with the bourgeoisie. At first the contest is carried on by individual labourers, then by the workpeople of a factory, then by the operatives of one trade, in one locality, against the individual bourgeois who directly exploits them. They direct their attacks not against the bourgeois conditions of production, but against the instruments of production themselves; they destroy imported wares that compete with their labour, they smash to pieces machinery, they set factories ablaze, they seek to restore by force the vanished status of the workman of the Middle Ages.

At this stage the labourers still form an incoherent mass scattered over the whole country, and broken up by their mutual competition. If anywhere they unite to form more compact bodies, this is not yet the consequence of their own active union, but of the union of the bourgeoisie, which class, in order to attain its own political ends, is compelled to set the whole proletariat in motion, and is moreover yet, for a time, able to do so. At this stage, therefore, the proletarians do not fight their enemies, but the enemies of their enemies, the remnants of absolute monarchy, the landowners, the non-industrial bourgeois, the petty bourgeoisie. Thus the whole historical movement is concentrated in the hands of the bourgeoisie; every victory so obtained is a victory for the bourgeoisie.

But with the development of industry the proletariat not only increases in number; it becomes concentrated in greater masses, its strength grows, and it feels that strength more. The various interests and conditions of life within the ranks of the proletariat are more and more equalised, in proportion as machinery obliterates all distinctions of labour, and nearly everywhere reduces wages to the same low level. The growing competition among the bourgeois, and the resulting commercial crises, make the wages of the workers ever more fluctuating. The unceasing improvement of machinery, ever more rapidly developing, makes their livelihood more and more precarious; the collisions between individual workmen and individual bourgeois take more and more the character of collisions between two classes. Thereupon the workers begin to form combinations (Trades Unions) against the bourgeois; they club together in order to keep up the rate of wages; they found permanent associations in order to make provision beforehand for these occasional revolts. Here and there the contest breaks out into riots.

Now and then the workers are victorious, but only for a time. The real fruit of their battles lies, not in the immediate result, but in the ever-expanding union of the workers. This union is helped on by the improved means of communication that are created by modern industry and that place the workers of different localities in contact with one another. It was just this contact that was needed to centralise the numerous local struggles, all of the same character, into one national struggle between classes. But every class struggle is a political struggle. And that union, to attain which the burghers of the Middle Ages, with their miserable highways, required centuries, the modern proletarians, thanks to railways, achieve in a few years.

This organisation of the proletarians into a class, and consequently into a political party, is continually being upset again by the competition between the workers themselves. But it ever rises up again, stronger, firmer, mightier. It compels legislative recognition of particular interests of the workers, by taking advantage of the divisions among the bourgeoisie itself. Thus the ten-hours' bill in England was carried.

Altogether collisions between the classes of the old society further, in many ways, the course of development of the proletariat. The bourgeoisie finds itself involved in a constant battle. At first with the aristocracy; later on, with those portions of the bourgeoisie itself, whose interests have become antagonistic to the progress of industry; at all times, with the bourgeoisie of foreign countries. In all these battles it sees itself compelled to appeal to the proletariat, to ask for its help, and thus, to drag it into the political arena. The bourgeoisie itself, therefore, supplies the proletariat with its own instruments of political and general education, in other words, it furnishes the proletariat with weapons for fighting the bourgeoisie.

Further, as we have already seen, entire sections of the ruling classes are, by the advance of industry, precipitated into the proletariat, or are at least threatened in their conditions of existence. These also supply the proletariat with fresh elements of enlightenment and progress.

Finally, in times when the class struggle nears the decisive hour, the process of dissolution going on within the ruling class, in fact within the whole range of society, assumes such a violent, glaring character, that a small section of the ruling class cuts itself adrift, and joins the revolutionary class, the class that holds the future in its hands. Just as, therefore, at an earlier period, a section of the nobility went over to the bourgeoisie, so now a portion of the bourgeoisie goes over to the proletariat, and in particular, a portion of the bourgeois ideologists, who have raised themselves to the level of comprehending theoretically the historical movement as a whole.

Of all the classes that stand face to face with the bourgeoisie today, the proletariat alone is a really revolutionary class. The other classes decay and finally disappear in the face of Modern Industry; the proletariat is its special and essential product. The lower middle class, the small manufacturer, the shopkeeper, the artisan, the peasant, all these fight against the bourgeoisie, to save from extinction their existence as fractions of the middle class. They are therefore not revolutionary, but conservative. Nay more, they are reactionary, for they try to roll back the wheel of history. If by chance they are revolutionary, they are so only in view of their impending transfer into the proletariat, they thus defend not their present, but their future interests, they desert their own standpoint to place themselves at that of the proletariat....

All previous historical movements were movements of minorities, or in the interests of minorities. The proletarian movement is the self-conscious, independent movement of the immense majority, in the interests of the immense majority. The proletariat, the lowest stratum of our present society, cannot stir, cannot raise itself up, without the whole superincumbent strata of official society being sprung into the air....

The essential condition for the existence, and for the sway of the bourgeois class, is the formation and augmentation of capital; the condition for capital is wage-labour. Wage-labour rests exclusively on competition between the laborers. The advance of industry, whose involuntary promoter is the bourgeoisie, replaces the isolation of the labourers, due to competition, by their revolutionary combination, due to association. The development of Modern Industry, therefore, cuts from under its feet the very foundation on which the bourgeoisie produces and appropriates products. What the bourgeoisie, therefore, produces, above all, is its own grave-diggers. Its fall and the victory of the proletariat are equally inevitable.

II. Proletarians and Communists

In what relation do the Communists stand to the proletarians as a whole?

The Communists do not form a separate party opposed to other working-class parties.

They have no interests separate and apart from those of the proletariat as a whole.

They do not set up any sectarian principles of their own, by which to shape and mould the proletarian movement.

The Communists are distinguished from the other working-class parties by this only: (1) In the national struggles of the proletarians of the different countries, they point out and bring to the front the common interests of the entire proletariat, independently of all nationality. (2) In the various stages of development which the struggle of the working class against the bourgeoisie has to pass through, they always and everywhere represent the interests of the movement as a whole.

The Communists, therefore, are on the one hand, practically, the most advanced and resolute section of the working-class parties of every country, that section which pushes forward all others; on the other hand, theoretically, they have over the great mass of the proletariat the advantage of clearly understanding the line of march, the conditions, and the ultimate general results of the proletarian movement.

The immediate aim of the Communist is the same as that of all the other proletarian parties: formation of the proletariat into a class, overthrow of the bourgeois supremacy, conquest of political power by the proletariat.

The theoretical conclusions of the Communists are in no way based on ideas or principles that have been invented, or discovered, by this or that would-be universal reformer. They merely express, in general terms, actual relations springing from an existing class struggle, from a historical movement going on under our very eyes. The abolition of existing property relations is not at all a distinctive feature of Communism....

The distinguishing feature of Communism is not the abolition of property generally, but the abolition of bourgeois property. But modern bourgeois private property is the final and most complete expression of the system of producing and appropriating products, that is based on class antagonisms, on the exploitation of the many by the few.

In this sense, the theory of the Communists may be summed up in the single sentence: Abolition of private property.

We Communists have been reproached with the desire of abolishing the right of personally acquiring property as the fruit of a man's own labour, which property is alleged to be the groundwork of all personal freedom, activity and independence.

Hard-won, self-acquired, self-earned property! Do you mean the property of the petty artisan and of the small peasant, a form of property that preceded the bourgeois form? There is no need to abolish that; the development of industry has to a great extent already destroyed it, and is still destroying it daily.

Or do you mean modern bourgeois private property?

But does wage-labour create any property for the labourer? Not a bit. It creates capital, i.e., that kind of property which exploits wage-labour, and which cannot increase except upon condition of begetting a new supply of wage-labour for fresh exploitation. Property, in its present form, is based on the antagonism of capital and wage-labour. Let us examine both sides of this antagonism.

To be a capitalist, is to have not only a purely personal, but a social status in production. Capital is a collective product, and only by the united action of many members, nay, in the last resort, only by the united action of all members of society, can it be set in motion.

Capital is, therefore, not a personal, it is a social power.

When, therefore, capital is converted into common property, into the property of all members of society, personal property is not thereby transformed into social property. It is only the social character of the property that is changed. It loses its class-character.

Let us now take wage-labour.

The average price of wage-labour is the minimum wage, i.e., that quantum of the means of subsistence, which is absolutely requisite in bare existence as a labourer. What, therefore, the wage-labourer appropriates by means of his labour, merely suffices to prolong and reproduce a bare existence. We by no means intend to abolish this personal appropriation of the products of labour, an appropriation that is made for the maintenance and reproduction of human life, and that leaves no surplus wherewith to command the labour of others. All that we want to do away with, is the miserable character of this appropriation, under which the labourer lives merely to increase capital, and is allowed to live only in so far as the interest of the ruling class requires it....

You are horrified at our intending to do away with private property. But in your existing society, private property is already done away with for nine-tenths of the population; its existence for the few is solely due to its non-existence in the hands of those nine-tenths. You reproach us, therefore, with intending to do away with a form of property, the necessary condition for whose existence is the non-existence of any property for the immense majority of society.

In one word, you reproach us with intending to do away with your property. Precisely so; that is just what we intend....

Communism deprives no man of the power to appropriate the products of society; all that it does is to deprive him of the power to subjugate the labour of others by means of such appropriation.

It has been objected that upon the abolition of private property all work will cease, and universal laziness will overtake us.

According to this, bourgeois society ought long ago to have gone to the dogs through sheer idleness; for those of its members who work, acquire nothing, and those who acquire anything, do not work. The whole of this objection is but another expression of the tautology: that there can no longer be any wage-labour when there is no longer any capital.... Abolition of the family! Even the most radical flare up at this infamous proposal of the Communists.

On what foundation is the present family, the bourgeois family, based? On capital, on private gain. In its completely developed form this family exists only among the bourgeoisie. But this state of things finds its complement in the practical absence of the family among the proletarians, and in public prostitution.

The bourgeois family will vanish as a matter of course when its complement vanishes, and both will vanish with the vanishing of capital.

Do you charge us with wanting to stop the exploitation of children by their parents? To this crime we plead guilty.

But, you will say, we destroy the most hallowed of relations, when we replace home education by social.

And your education! Is not that also social, and determined by the social conditions under which you educate, by the intervention, direct or indirect, of society, by means of schools, etc.? The Communists have not invented the intervention of society in education; they do but seek to alter the character of that intervention, and to rescue education from the influence of the ruling class.

The bourgeois clap-trap about the family and education, about the hallowed co-relation of parent and child, becomes all the more disgusting, the more, by the action of Modern Industry, all family ties among the proletarians are torn asunder, and their children transformed into simple articles of commerce and instruments of labour.

But you Communists would introduce community of women, screams the whole bourgeoisie in chorus.

The bourgeois sees in his wife a mere instrument of production. He hears that the instruments of production are to be exploited in common, and, naturally, can come to no other conclusion than that the lot of being common to all will likewise fall to the women.

He has not even a suspicion that the real point is to do away with the status of women as mere instruments of production.

For the rest, nothing is more ridiculous than the virtuous indignation of our bourgeois at the community of women which, they pretend, is to be openly and officially established by the Communists. The Communists have no need to introduce community of women; it has existed almost from time immemorial.

Our bourgeois, not content with having the wives and daughters of their proletarians at their disposal, not to speak of common prostitutes, take the greatest pleasure in seducing each other's wives.

Bourgeois marriage is in reality a system of wives in common and thus, at the most, what the Communists might possibly be reproached with, is that they desire to introduce, in substitution for a hypocritically concealed, an openly legalized community of women. For the rest, it is self-evident that the abolition of the present system of production must bring with it the abolition of the community of women springing from that system, i.e., of prostitution both public and private.

The Communists are further reproached with desiring to abolish countries and nationality.

The working men have no country. We cannot take from them what they have not got. Since the proletariat must first of all acquire political supremacy, must rise to be the leading class of the nation, must constitute itself the nation, it is, so far, itself national, though not in the bourgeois sense of the word.

National differences and antagonisms between peoples are daily more and more vanishing, owing to the development of the bourgeoisie, to freedom of commerce, to the world-market, to uniformity in the mode of production and in the conditions of life corresponding thereto.

The supremacy of the proletariat will cause them to vanish still faster. United action, of the leading civilised countries at least, is one of the first conditions for the emancipation of the proletariat.

In proportion as the exploitation of one individual by another is put an end to, the exploitation of one nation by another will also be put an end to. In proportion as the antagonism between classes within the nation vanishes, the hostility of one nation to another will come to an end....

We have seen above, that the first step in the revolution by the working class, is to raise the proletariat to the position of ruling as to win the battle of democracy.

The proletariat will use its political supremacy to wrest, by degrees, all capital from the bourgeoisie, to centralise all instruments of production in the hands of the State, i.e., of the proletariat organised as the ruling class; and to increase the total of productive forces as rapidly as possible.

Of course, in the beginning, this cannot be effected except by means of despotic inroads on the rights of property, and on the conditions of bourgeois production; by means of measures, therefore, which appear economically insufficient and untenable, but which, in the course of the movement, outstrip themselves, necessitate further inroads upon the old social order, and are unavoidable as a means of entirely revolutionising the mode of production.

These measures will of course be different in different countries.

Nevertheless in the most advanced countries, the following will be pretty generally applicable.

1. Abolition of property in land and application of all rents of land to public purposes.

2. A heavy progressive or graduated income tax.

3. Abolition of all right of inheritance.

4. Confiscation of the property of all emigrants and rebels.

5. Centralisation of credit in the hands of the State, by means of a national bank with State capital and an exclusive monopoly.

6. Centralisation of the means of communication and transport in the hands of the State.

7. Extension of factories and instruments of production owned by the State; the bringing into cultivation of waste-lands, and the improvement of the soil generally in accordance with common plan.

8. Equal liability of all to labour. Establishment of industrial armies, especially for agriculture.

9. Combination of agriculture with manufacturing industries; gradual abolition of the distinction between town and country, by a more equable distribution of the population over the country.

10. Free education for all children in public schools. Abolition of children's factory labour in its present form. Combination of education with industrial production, &c., &c.

When, in the course of development, class distinctions have disappeared, and all production has been concentrated in the hands of a vast association of the whole nation, the public power will lose its political character. Political power, properly so called, is merely the organised power of one class for oppressing another. If the proletariat during its contest with the bourgeoisie is compelled, by the force of circumstances, to organise itself as a class, if, by means of a revolution, it makes itself the ruling class, and, as such, sweeps away by force the old conditions of production, then it will, along with these conditions, have swept away the conditions for the existence of class antagonisms and of classes generally, and will thereby have abolished its own supremacy as a class.

In place of the old bourgeois society, with its classes and class antagonisms, we shall have an association, in which the free development of each is the condition for the free development of all....

IV. Position of the Communists in Relation to the Various Existing Opposition Parties

In short, the Communists everywhere support every revolutionary movement against the existing social and political order of things.

In all these movements they bring to the front, as the leading question in each, the property question, no matter what its degree of development at the time.

Finally, they labour everywhere for the union and agreement of the democratic parties of all countries.

The Communists disdain to conceal their views and aims. They openly declare that their ends can be attained only by the forcible overthrow of all existing social conditions. Let the ruling classes tremble at a Communistic revolution. The proletarians have nothing to lose but their chains. They have a world to win.

Working Men Of All Countries, Unite!

Glossary

Cape	Cape of Good Hope
chartered burghers	middle-class professional guilds
complement	in this context, the typical proletarian family
Reactionists	in this context, people who wanted to maintain feudalism and intellectual privilege and hence were opposed to nineteenth-century liberal and Socialist thought
sectarian	in this context, favoring the proletariat
ten-hours' bill in England	the Factory Act of 1847, which limited the working day of children to 10 hours

Portrait of Queen Victoria as Empress of India (© Museum of London)

QUEEN VICTORIA'S PROCLAMATION CONCERNING INDIA

" It is Our earnest Desire to stimulate the peaceful Industry of India."

Overview

The purpose of Queen Victoria's Proclamation concerning India, issued in 1858, was to announce that England was assuming control of its Indian colonies, removing them from the administration of the British East India Company. A secondary purpose was to reassure the people of India that Britain intended to respect and preserve the culture of India, particularly the right of Indians to practice their traditional religions. The proclamation was issued in the name of Victoria, the queen of the United Kingdom of Great Britain and Ireland. It was actually written, though, by Edward Stanley, the 14th Earl of Derby. Queen Victoria placed her stamp on most of the nineteenth century in England, for after she assumed the throne in 1837, she ruled for an astonishing sixty-three years and seven months until her death in 1901. She presided over the expansion of a British Empire that spanned the globe, giving rise to the expression that "the sun never sets on the British Empire." Chief among Britain's colonies was India, which came to be known as "the jewel in the crown" of the British Empire and continued under British administration until it achieved independence in 1947.

The proclamation represented the end point of a process of colonization of India that began in the early sixteenth century, although the British presence began in the early seventeenth century. For more than two centuries, India had been in effect a series of trading outposts under the administration of the British East India Company—at least from the perspective of the British. The Indian subcontinent was fractured by the activities of competing local rulers, some of whom allied themselves with the British colonizers for their own gain and to preserve their own power. Greed and corruption, however, when combined with efforts to westernize India, undermined the authority of the British East India Company, leading in 1857 to an armed rebellion called the Sepoy Revolt. In response to the revolt, the British Parliament passed the Government of India Act (more formally, An Act for the Better Government of India), which transferred authority of India to the Crown. The queen's proclamation two months later announced the changes that were taking place in British-controlled India.

Context

The European powers gained their first toehold in India and the broader Indonesian archipelago in 1502, when the Portuguese established the first European trading post in India. Throughout the sixteenth century the Portuguese enjoyed a virtual monopoly in India, but that changed in the seventeenth century as the British, Dutch, and French established their own trading centers. Leading to the British colonization of India—and of the Indonesian archipelago—was the establishment of the British East India Company, a private enterprise that was chartered as a joint-stock company by the Crown on the last day of 1600. (A joint-stock company is similar to a corporation in that shares are issued to investors, but it has characteristics of a partnership in that the investors are personally liable for the acts of the company.) Two years later the Dutch formed the Dutch East India Company, and in 1664 the French established a similar enterprise.

Throughout the seventeenth century, rivalry between the English and Dutch was intense, both in India and in Europe, where the two nations fought a series of wars that are collectively called the Anglo-Dutch Wars. That state of hostility between England and Holland changed in 1688, when the so-called Glorious Revolution brought William of Orange, a Dutchman, to the throne of England, restoring peace between the two nations. England and Holland then struck a deal: England would have control over the textile trade in India, while Holland would control the spice trade in the Indonesian archipelago. In time, textiles proved to be more lucrative, and the British eclipsed the Dutch as a colonial power in India, controlling trading centers in Surat, Madras, Bombay, and Calcutta.

Beginning in 1526, the Indian subcontinent had been ruled by the Muslim Mughal Empire, which imposed some measure of unity on India's various regions and city-states. Early in the eighteenth century the empire began to crumble, principally because of religious intolerance, agrarian revolts, and wars of succession among the emperors. The

Time Line

1600

- **December 31**
  Queen Elizabeth I of England charters the British East India Company as a joint-stock company.

1609

- The British East India Company is granted perpetual trading rights in India.

1751

- **September 12**
  British forces under the command of Robert Clive deal a decisive defeat to the forces of the French East India Company at Arcot, which the British had seized in August.

1757

- **June 23**
  Forces under the command of the British East India Company defeat Sirāj-ud-Dawlah at the Battle of Plassey, gaining control of Bengal.

1773

- The British Parliament passes the Regulating Act to define the responsibilities and powers of the East India Company.

1784

- The British Parliament passes Pitt's India Act to strengthen the 1773 Regulating Act and end corrupt practices by the East India Company.

decline of the Mughal Empire, which remained an empire in name only until 1857, created a power vacuum that the British East India Company filled. In addition to trading in silk, cotton, indigo dye, tea, saltpeter, and opium, the company began to assume governmental and administrative functions in large parts of India and was the de facto ruling power in India, though that power was challenged by the French in a series of wars, called the Carnatic Wars, that began in 1746. (The name is a corruption of the name of the coastal region that was the site of the wars, Karnataka.) Accelerating the process of British ascendancy were two events. The first occurred in 1751, when British and Indian troops under the command of a young captain, Robert Clive, dealt the French East India Company's garrison a decisive defeat at the city of Arcot, some sixty miles west of Madras.

The second event was the Battle of Plassey, when forces again under the command of Robert Clive defeated the combined forces of the nabob (governor) of Bengal, Sirāj-ud-Dawlah, and the French. This battle, which took place in 1757, was a proxy battle during the Seven Years' War (1756–1763), which was fought in Europe and North America between the British and the French (and their respective allies). The company was able to win the battle by bribing a number of Indian military leaders. Among them was Mīr Ja'far, who was resentful because he had been stripped of his position as commander of the army. Although Sirāj-ud-Dawlah enjoyed vastly superior numbers, when the time came to fight, troops led by the bribed commanders stood their ground and did not fight. Accordingly, Sirāj-ud-Dawlah fled, but he was eventually caught and executed. Bengal, one of the largest and most lucrative regions in India, was now in the hands of the company. Mīr Ja'far was appointed puppet nabob.

In the years that followed, the British East India Company expanded its control over some two-thirds of India, often by striking alliances with local rulers. Its pattern of government and administration would survive for another hundred years. Clive returned to England and was replaced by Warren Hastings, the first governor-general of India. Hastings returned to England in 1784, where impeachment proceedings were begun against him in Parliament. Although he was eventually acquitted, Hastings's administration was, in fact, marked by corruption, bribery, and excessive use of force, creating a series of scandals that prompted Parliament to take steps to rein in the East India Company. One step was the passage of the Regulating Act of 1773, which defined the responsibilities and powers of the company. The Regulating Act, however, did not accomplish its purpose, so in 1784 Parliament passed the India Act, usually called Pitt's India Act after Prime Minister William Pitt (the Younger). This legislation established a board of governors for the company consisting of members of the British cabinet and the privy council. The act essentially brought the civil, economic, administrative, and military activities of the company under governmental control. A final step in the process of gaining control over the company's activities occurred in 1813 with the passage of the Charter Act. This act ended the East India Company's

MILESTONE DOCUMENTS IN WORLD HISTORY

trade monopoly in India, though the company, under the control of Parliament, remained as an administrative body (and retained its trade monopoly in China).

The events that led directly to the passage of the Government of India Act and the queen's proclamation began in 1857. Discontent with British rule had festered for years, but matters came to a head when the sepoys, or Indian soldiers serving under the British, revolted in what is variously called the Sepoy Mutiny, the Sepoy Rebellion, the Great Mutiny, and, among Indians, the First War of Indian Independence. The sepoys received low pay. Recruits were taken from lower castes rather than just from the traditional warrior caste. Sepoys were required to serve overseas, causing them to lose caste. In general, Indians were dissatisfied with the heavy-handedness of British rule. If a landowner died without a male heir, his property reverted to the British Crown. Various other traditional customs, such as suttee, the act of a widow's immolating herself on her dead husband's grave, were proscribed. Particularly nettlesome was the elimination of local rulers and perceived efforts to westernize Indians and convert them to Christianity. Despite all these real grievances, it was a rumor that gave the revolt momentum. At the time, a soldier had to break a rifle cartridge with his teeth before loading it. The rumor was that British cartridges were treated with cow and pig fat; tasting the fat of these animals was a violation of Indian religious beliefs. Accordingly, the sepoys refused to use the cartridges. The British, for their part, denied the rumor and encouraged the sepoys to make their own cartridges using beeswax or vegetable oils rather than animal fat. The rumors, though, refused to go away, and on May 9, 1857, a sepoy cavalry troop openly refused to use its British-supplied cartridges.

Revolt erupted on May 10, 1857, near Bengal. In the weeks that followed, sepoy garrisons in several cities, notably Delhi and Kanpur, mutinied. In some instances, civilians joined in the revolt, but in other instances local rulers were not dissatisfied with British administration and refused to join the revolt. In time, British forces regrouped, gained control of the cities where the sepoys had revolted, and reasserted the authority of the East India Company. The last of the mutineers were put down on June 20, 1858. The conflict was bloody, and British forces felt justified in retaliating. Entire villages were wiped out, and mutineers were put to death; in many instances, they were executed by the traditional Mughal method of strapping them to the mouths of cannons and blowing them to bits.

Debate emerged about the question of how England should respond to the bloody conflict and its aftermath. Ultimately, Queen Victoria came down on the side of clemency. In a letter to Edward Stanley, Lord Derby, who drafted the proclamation, she requested that he

> bear in mind that it is a female Sovereign who speaks to more than a hundred millions of Eastern people, on assuming the direct Government over them, and after a bloody war, giving them pledges, which her future reign is to redeem, and explaining the principles of her Government. Such a document should

Time Line

1813
- The Charter Act abolishes the East India Company's monopoly in India and makes it a purely administrative body under the authority of the Crown.

1857
- **May 10** The Sepoy Revolt begins.

1858
- **June 20** The last mutineers in the Sepoy Revolt are subdued.
- **August 2** The British Parliament passes the Government of India Act, which transfers power in India from the British East India Company to the Crown and abolishes the East India Company.
- **November 1** Queen Victoria's Proclamation concerning India is issued.

1869
- **October 2** Mohandas Karamchand Gandhi is born. He will eventually lead India to independence.

1876
- **May 1** "Empress of India" is added to Queen Victoria's titles.

1947
- **August 15** The independent Union of India is created.

breathe feelings of generosity, benevolence, and religious toleration, and point out the privileges which the Indians will receive in being placed on an equality with the subjects of the Crown, and the prosperity following in the train of civilization. (qtd. in Anderson and Subedar, p. 193)

That spirit of benevolence, generosity, and toleration pervades the proclamation.

About the Author

The proclamation was issued in the name of Queen Victoria, who was born on May 24, 1819. She ascended the throne of England on June 20, 1837, and reigned until her death on January 22, 1901—the longest reign in British history. In 1840 she married her first cousin, Prince Albert, and the marriage proved to be a happy one. When Albert died in 1861, Victoria went into mourning and never really emerged from it. She dressed in black for the remainder of her life and lived almost entirely in seclusion. Although she was popular, particularly in the early decades of her reign and in her final years, she survived several assassination attempts. On May 1, 1876, the title Empress of India was added to her many royal titles. She took the role seriously, for in the late 1860s she had begun to learn the Hindi and Punjabi languages.

By the nineteenth century the British monarch lacked the power that kings and queens in earlier centuries had wielded. Victoria, though, was a dominating figure, to the extent that the era in which she reigned is still referred to as the Victorian era. Her uprightness and that of her family elevated middle-class values and is responsible in part for the age's reputation for prudishness and middle-class conformity. Under her reign, England evolved into a constitutional monarchy, and with her reign and that of her successors the British monarch retained the rights only to advise and, in some instances, warn. At her death, flags in the United States were lowered to half staff, the first time in U.S. history that this honor had been given to a foreign ruler (and one that the British reciprocated later that year when the U.S. president, William McKinley was assassinated).

The actual author of Queen Victoria's proclamation was Edward Stanley, the fourteenth Earl of Derby. Lord Derby, who served as British prime minister three times (1852, 1858–1859, and 1866–1868), was born in 1799. He attended Oxford University but never took a degree. His career in politics began in 1822, when he became a member of Parliament. Throughout his political career, Lord Derby advocated positions that were remarkably tolerant for the times and in some instances unpopular. For example, as chief secretary of Ireland, he tried to improve education in Catholic Ireland and to make religious affiliation irrelevant in admission to state-run schools. Later, he introduced legislation calling for the emancipation of all slaves in the British Empire, and during his second stint as prime minister his ministry ended the practice of excluding Jews

from Parliament. The chief accomplishment of his second term as prime minister, though, was passage of the Government of India Act. During his third term he supported a reform bill that extended the franchise to a greater number of voters. He died on October 23, 1869.

Explanation and Analysis of the Document

Queen Victoria's Proclamation concerning India was essentially a diplomatic document, couched as it was in the formal language of diplomacy. It announced the results of the Government of India Act, which the British Parliament had passed two months earlier, in August 1858. Its purpose was to announce that the British government was assuming control of India from the British East India Company. It was addressed to the people of India, announcing the change and assuring the Indian people that the British government would not interfere with their rights and traditional practices, including religious beliefs.

The document begins with a formal salutation to the Indian people, including India's princes and chiefs, from Queen Victoria. It goes on to note that for "weighty reasons," the government of Great Britain, including the House of Lords and House of Commons of Parliament, is assuming control of India from the East India Company. The queen calls upon the people of India to bear allegiance to "Us" (it was and still is customary for monarchs to refer to themselves in the first-person plural) and to submit themselves to British authority.

The next paragraph announces the appointment of Charles John Canning, first Earl Canning, as viceroy and governor-general of India. Canning had already occupied the post of governor-general of India; Prime Minister Henry John Temple, third Viscount Palmerston, had appointed him to the post in 1855, though at that point he was part of the East India Company administration of the colony. In a letter to Queen Victoria dated September 25, 1857, Canning wrote of the Sepoy Revolt:

One of the greatest difficulties that lies ahead—and Lord Canning, grieves to say so to your Majesty—will be the violent rancour of a very large proportion of the English community against every native Indian of every class. There is a rabid and indiscriminate vindictiveness abroad, even amongst many who ought to set a better example, which it is impossible to contemplate without something like a feeling of shame for one's fellow-countrymen. (Anderson and Subedar, p. 189)

Although Canning suppressed the revolt, he tried to mitigate some of the worst acts of vengeance, earning the nickname "Clemency Canning." From the queen's perspective, Canning was already in place, and his attitude made him suitable for the position. Because other East India Company officials were experienced and on the scene, they were retained in their positions.

After assuring the Indian people that Great Britain would adhere to the treaties it had signed with various regions, the queen takes up the issue of religion. One of the chief objections to British administration in India was the belief that the British were trying to impose Christianity on the population. The queen assures the people of India that the Crown "disclaim[s] alike the Right and the Desire to impose our Convictions on any of Our Subjects." No one is to be "molested or disquieted by reason of their Religious Faith or Observances." People of all religious faiths would be subject equally to the same laws, and anyone who interfered with Indians' religious beliefs would be threatened with the queen's "highest Displeasure." All civil service positions were to be open to qualified people of any religion. The queen goes on to assure Indians that their ancestral lands would be respected, as would their "Rights, Usages, and Customs."

The proclamation then turns to the issue of the recent revolt. In diplomatic language, the queen blames the revolt on "ambitious Men, who have deceived their Countrymen, by false reports, and led them into open Rebellion." She chooses to see many of the rebels as having been misled and therefore deserving of the queen's clemency, as long as they return to the "path of Duty." She notes that Canning has already offered clemency to many of those who took part in the "late unhappy Disturbances," reserving punishment only for those "whose Crimes place them beyond the reach of forgiveness." She approves of this course but goes on to impose conditions. First, punishment would be meted out to anyone who took part in the murder of British citizens. Second, she states that anyone who has given sanctuary to murderers or who instigated the revolt was to be punished, though they would not be subject to capital punishment. Again she offers the hope of clemency to those "whose Crimes may appear to have originated in too credulous acceptance of the false reports circulated by designing Men." Finally, she offers full clemency to those who took up arms against the British but who returned to their homes and "peaceful pursuits."

The queen concludes with expressions of hope for the future. She states that when tranquility is restored, it is Britain's desire to promote industry, improvements, and "Works of Public Utility." She further expresses the hope that British administration of India would work toward the good of the nation's people.

Audience

The document itself, which begins with the words "Proclamation by the Queen in Council to the Princes, Chiefs, and People of India," announces its chief audience. The purpose of the document was to announce to the people of India that the British government was assuming control of the nation's Indian colonies, removing them from the administration of the British East India Company. A secondary audience included those members of the British administration who urged that harsh measures be taken against those who had taken part in the Sepoy Revolt. The queen made it clear that harsh measures would not be taken and that Indians who returned to their duty would be treated with clemency. The document also made it clear to interested parties throughout the world that Indian matters would now fall under the purview of the Crown and Parliament rather than the British East India Company.

Impact

The impact of British administration of India—which encompassed modern-day India, Pakistan, and Bangladesh and at various times included other territories, such as Burma, Ceylon, and Singapore—was profound. Britain established a complex governmental and administrative structure that came to be called the British Raj (a Hindustani word meaning "reign"). Indian affairs were overseen by a secretary of state for India and a Council of India whose members had to have spent at least ten years in India. Additionally, India was governed by a viceroy, though numerous other governmental officials were charged with overseeing affairs in India's various regions. Assisting them in their efforts were Indian officials who served in an advisory capacity. Additionally, a number of so-called princely states were recognized. These were smaller regions in India that remained under the rule of Indian princes, although the princes were answerable to the viceroy.

In the twenty-first century the very notion of one country's colonizing another is objectionable, for it implies a sense of superiority on the part of the colonizer. In the context of the times, however, when European powers were establishing colonies throughout Africa, Asia, and the Middle East, British rule of India was relatively enlightened and benign. The Sepoy Revolt, which precipitated the Government of India Act and the queen's proclamation, induced a period of introspection on the part of the British. They realized that the East India Company's administration of India had been harsh. Accordingly, efforts were made to establish a sense of partnership between Indians, particularly Indian civilians, and British people living in India. The army was restructured to include more Indians. No serious efforts were made to impose Christianity on Indians or to interfere with traditional religious beliefs and social practices. Most important, the Indian economy developed rapidly as the British built schools, railroads, ports—an entire economic infrastructure—to the point that "the Raj" was sometimes spoken of satirically to refer to the licenses, taxes, permits, and general red tape that became part of Indian affairs. The English language became a lingua franca that facilitated communication among India's four hundred or more language groups, and today English is spoken fluently by even moderately educated Indians.

Perhaps most important, the British Raj laid the foundations for the emergence of a democratic government. In 1869 Mohandas Karamchand Gandhi, more widely known as Mahatma Gandhi, was born in India. He would emerge as the leader and spiritual force behind the Indian inde-

"We have resolved, by and with the advice and consent of the Lords Spiritual and Temporal, and Commons, in Parliament assembled, to take upon Ourselves the Government of the Territories in India heretofore administered in trust for Us by the Honorable East India Company."

(Paragraph 3)

"We hereby announce to the Native Princes of India that all Treaties and Engagements made with them by or under the authority of the Honorable East India Company are by Us accepted, and will be scrupulously maintained."

(Paragraph 7)

"We shall respect the Rights, Dignity, and Honour of Native Princes as Our own."

(Paragraph 8)

"We declare it to be Our Royal Will and Pleasure that none be in any wise favored, none molested or disquieted by reason of their Religious Faith or Observances; but that all shall alike enjoy the equal and impartial protection of the Law."

(Paragraph 10)

"Our Power has been shewn by the Suppression of that Rebellion in the field; We desire to shew Our Mercy, by pardoning the Offences of those who have been thus misled, but who desire to return to the path of Duty."

(Paragraph 13)

"When, by the Blessing of Providence, internal Tranquillity shall be restored, it is Our earnest Desire to stimulate the peaceful Industry of India, to promote Works of Public Utility and Improvement, and to administer its Government for the benefit of all Our Subjects resident therein."

(Paragraph 19)

pendence movement. He also became a symbol of nonviolent opposition to colonization. Throughout the first half of the twentieth century, authority in India was gradually transferred to Indians, and by the end of World War II, India was largely self-governing. The process of Indian independence was completed in 1947, when British India was partitioned into two independent states, India and Pakistan (which included Bangladesh, which seceded from Pakistan in 1971). India, with more than 1.1 billion people, remains the world's largest democratic nation.

Further Reading

■ Books

Anderson, Clare. *Indian Uprising of 1857–8: Prisons, Prisoners and Rebellion*. New York: Anthem Press, 2007.

Anderson, George, and Manilal Bhagwandas Subedar. *The Expansion of British India (1818–1858)*. New York: Macmillan, 1918.

Bayly, C. A. *Indian Society and the Making of the British Empire*. Cambridge, U.K.: Cambridge University Press, 1995.

James, Lawrence. *Raj: The Making and Unmaking of British India*. New York: St. Martin's Press, 1998.

Kulke, Hermann, and Dietmar Rothermund. *A History of India*, 3rd ed. New York: Routledge, 1998.

Lawson, Philip. *The East India Company: A History*. New York: Longman, 1993.

Metcalf, Thomas R. *The Aftermath of Revolt: India, 1857–1870*. Princeton, N.J.: Princeton University Press, 1964.

Moorhouse, Geoffrey. *India Britannica*. New York: Harper & Row, 1983.

Porter, Andrew, and Alaine M. Low, eds. *The Oxford History of the British Empire*. Vol. 3: *The Nineteenth Century*. Oxford, U.K.: Oxford University Press, 1999.

Rothermund, Dietmar. *An Economic History of India: From the Pre-Colonial Period to 1986*. New York: Croom Helm, 1987.

Wolpert, Stanley. *A New History of India*, 8th ed. New York: Oxford University Press, 2008.

■ Web Sites

Marshall, Peter. "Empire and Sea Power: The British Presence in India in the Eighteenth Century." BBC Web site.
  http://www.bbc.co.uk/history/british/empire_seapower/east_india_01.shtml.

—Michael J. O'Neal

Questions for Further Study

1. Explain the extent to which the queen's proclamation and the Government of India Act sowed the seeds of eventual Indian independence.

2. What were the circumstances that allowed the British East India Company to assume many of the functions of government in India?

3. How did events in India illustrate the effects of "big power" colonialism in the seventeenth and eighteenth centuries?

4. What role did religion play in the queen's proclamation? Why would an administration run by a business enterprise such as the East India Company have attempted to impose religious beliefs in a colony?

5. It is sometimes argued that British colonialism in India, all things considered, was actually good for the country in the long run. On what considerations would such an argument be based? How would you respond?

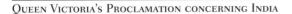

QUEEN VICTORIA'S PROCLAMATION CONCERNING INDIA

Proclamation by the Queen in Council to the Princes, Chiefs, and People of India (Published by the Governor-General at Allahabad, November 1st, 1858).

Victoria, by the Grace of God of the United Kingdom of Great Britain and Ireland, and of the Colonies and Dependencies thereof in Europe, Asia, Africa, America, and Australasia, Queen, Defender of the Faith.

Whereas, for divers weighty reasons, We have resolved, by and with the advice and consent of the Lords Spiritual and Temporal, and Commons, in Parliament assembled, to take upon Ourselves the Government of the Territories in India heretofore administered in trust for Us by the Honorable East India Company:

Now, therefore, We do by these Presents notify and declare that, by the advice and consent aforesaid, We have taken upon Ourselves the said Government; and We hereby call upon all Our Subjects within the said Territories to be faithful, and to bear true Allegiance to Us, Our Heirs, and Successors, and to submit themselves to the authority of those whom We may hereafter, from time to time, see fit to appoint to administer the Government of Our said Territories, in Our name and on Our behalf:

And We, reposing especial trust and confidence in the loyalty, ability, and judgment of Our right trusty and well beloved Cousin and Councillor, Charles John Viscount Canning, do hereby constitute and appoint him, the said Viscount Canning, to be Our first Viceroy and Governor-General in and over Our said Territories, and to administer the Government thereof in Our name, and generally to act in Our name and on Our behalf, subject to such Orders and Regulations as he shall, from time to time, receive from Us through one of Our Principal Secretaries of State:

And We do hereby confirm in their several Offices, Civil and Military, all Persons now employed in the Service of the Honorable East India Company, subject to Our future pleasure, and to such Laws and Regulations as may hereafter be enacted.

We hereby announce to the Native Princes of India that all Treaties and Engagements made with them by or under the authority of the Honorable East India Company are by Us accepted, and will be scrupulously maintained; and We look for the like observance on their part.

We desire no extension of Our present territorial Possessions; and while We will permit no aggression upon Our Dominions or Our Rights, to be attempted with impunity, We shall sanction no encroachment on those of others. We shall respect the Rights, Dignity, and Honour of Native Princes as Our own; and We desire that they, as well as Our own Subjects, should enjoy that Prosperity and that social Advancement which can only be secured by internal Peace and good Government.

We hold Ourselves bound to the Natives of Our Indian Territories by the same obligations of Duty which bind Us to all Our other Subjects; and those Obligations, by the Blessing of Almighty God, We shall faithfully and conscientiously fulfil.

Firmly relying Ourselves on the truth of Christianity, and acknowledging with gratitude the solace of Religion, We disclaim alike the Right and the Desire to impose our Convictions on any of Our Subjects. We declare it to be Our Royal Will and Pleasure that none be in any wise favored, none molested or disquieted by reason of their Religious Faith or Observances; but that all shall alike enjoy the equal and impartial protection of the Law: and We do strictly charge and enjoin all those who may be in authority under Us, that they abstain from all interference with the Religious Belief or Worship of any of Our Subjects, on pain of Our highest Displeasure.

And it is Our further Will that, so far as may be, Our Subjects, of whatever Race or Creed, be freely and impartially admitted to Offices in Our Service, the Duties of which they may be qualified, by their education, ability, and integrity, duly to discharge.

We know, and respect, the feelings of attachment with which the Natives of India regard the Lands inherited by them from their Ancestors; and We desire to protect them in all Rights connected therewith, subject to the equitable demands of the State; and We will that generally, in framing and administering the Law, due regard be paid to the ancient Rights, Usages, and Customs of India.

We deeply lament the evils and misery which have been brought upon India by the acts of ambitious Men, who have deceived their Countrymen, by false reports, and led them into open Rebellion. Our Power has been shewn by the Suppression of that Rebellion in the field; We desire to shew Our Mercy, by pardoning the Offences of those who have been thus misled, but who desire to return to the path of Duty.

Already in one Province, with a view to stop the further effusion of blood, and to hasten the Pacification of Our Indian Dominions, Our Viceroy and Governor-General has held out the expectation of Pardon, on certain terms, to the great majority of those who, in the late unhappy Disturbances, have been guilty of Offences against our Government, and has declared the Punishment which will be inflicted on those whose Crimes place them beyond the reach of forgiveness. We approve and confirm the said act of Our Viceroy and Governor-General, and do further announce and proclaim as follows:—

Our Clemency will be extended to all Offenders, save and except those who have been, or shall be, convicted of having directly taken part in the Murder of British Subjects. With regard to such, the Demands of Justice forbid the exercise of mercy.

To those who have willingly given asylum to Murderers, knowing them to be such, or who may have acted as leaders or instigators in Revolt, their lives alone can be guaranteed; but in apportioning the Penalty due to such Persons, full consideration will be given to the circumstances under which they have been induced to throw off their allegiance; and large indulgence will be shewn to those whose Crimes may appear to have originated in too credulous acceptance of the false reports circulated by designing Men.

To all others in Arms against the Government, We hereby promise unconditional Pardon, Amnesty, and Oblivion of all Offence against Ourselves, Our Crown and Dignity, on their return to their homes and peaceful pursuits.

It is Our Royal Pleasure that these Terms of Grace and Amnesty should be extended to all those who comply with their Conditions before the First Day of January next.

When, by the Blessing of Providence, internal Tranquillity shall be restored, it is Our earnest Desire to stimulate the peaceful Industry of India, to promote Works of Public Utility and Improvement, and to administer its Government for the benefit of all Our Subjects resident therein. In their Prosperity will be Our Strength; in their Contentment Our Security; and in their Gratitude Our best Reward. And may the God of all Power grant to Us, and to those in authority under Us, Strength to carry out these Our Wishes for the good of Our people.

Glossary

Lords Spiritual and Temporal	members of the British House of Lords; in Victoria's time these were, respectively, men belonging to the five highest ranks of the clergy of the Church of England and hereditary and life peers
open Rebellion	the Sepoy Revolt of 1857

John A. Macdonald (Library of Congress)

CONSTITUTION ACT OF CANADA

"The Provinces of Canada, Nova Scotia, and New Brunswick shall form and be One Dominion under the Name of Canada."

Overview

The Constitution Act of Canada of 1867, at the time called the British North America Act and still informally called the BNA Act, created the federal dominion of Canada and, in conjunction with other documents, continues to form the essence of that nation's constitution, defining Canada's governmental structure, legislature, justice system, and system of taxation. Because the provinces of Canada were British colonies, the Constitution Act was, in effect, a petition to the British Parliament, which originally enacted the document as law; until 1982 any change in the Canadian constitution had to be made by the British Parliament. In 1982, however, the Constitution Act was "patriated," a term used in Canadian law, along with "patriation," to mean that it was made part of Canadian as opposed to British law. In effect, the Canadian constitution was "brought home." The Constitution Act represented the coalescence of Britain's North American colonies into a sovereign nation, although Canada remained part of the British Empire and England's monarch—as of 2010, Queen Elizabeth II—is the country's ceremonial head of state.

Context

The history of North America in the seventeenth and eighteenth centuries was the history of colonization, with Great Britain and France competing in North America as they did on the European continent. This competition often led to armed conflict, including the Seven Years' War (1756–1763), which pitted England and its allies, principally Prussia, against France and its allies, principally Spain, Austria, and Russia. The French and Indian War (1754–1763, though hostilities largely ceased in 1760) was the name given to the North American theater of the Seven Years' War. The name "French and Indian War" followed the British practice of sometimes naming wars for one's opponents, in this case a coalition of the French and Native Americans.

The war on both continents ended in 1763 with the signing of the Treaty of Paris. Under the terms of the treaty,

France ceded large portions of its North American holdings to Britain and Spain. Those holdings, referred to as the Viceroyalty of New France, had been extensive, encompassing five huge provinces: Louisiana, Acadia, Hudson Bay, Newfoundland (which the French called Plaisance), and Canada—though not "Canada" as the word is understood today but instead a swath of land roughly coterminous with today's Quebec. Among these regions, Louisiana was ceded to Spain. France had already relinquished North American territory to Britain under the terms of the Treaty of Utrecht in 1713, so the end of the French and Indian War and the Treaty of Paris effectively curtailed French colonialism in North America.

The French and Indian War prompted Great Britain to prepare for the administration of its North American holdings. Thus, shortly after the Treaty of Paris was signed, King George III issued the Royal Proclamation of 1763 on October 7 of that year. The purpose of the proclamation was to organize Britain's North American holdings, including Canada (again, not modern-day Canada but essentially Quebec) and the colonies that would become the United States. In particular, the proclamation established a boundary line, called the proclamation line, between the colonies and Indian lands to the west. The proclamation provided for the orderly expansion of British territory to the west and outlined trade and other relationships with Native American tribes. Of course, the Royal Proclamation became null in the thirteen colonies that formed the United States after the American Revolution.

The next step in the emergence of Canada as a sovereign nation and the passage of the Constitution Act was the Quebec Act of 1774, which established procedures for the governance of England's colony of Quebec and which some historians mark as the beginning of an independent Canada. The Quebec Act expanded the province's territory to the west and south, encompassing portions of modern-day Ontario as well as territories that would become Ohio, Indiana, Illinois, Wisconsin, Michigan, and parts of Minnesota. From the standpoint of American Revolutionaries, the Quebec Act was one of the so-called Intolerable Acts, or Coercive Acts, passed to punish the American colonies for the Boston Tea Party. In Quebec, the act was generally well received and cemented the relationship between

1763

- **February 10**
  The Treaty of Paris ending the French and Indian and Seven Years' War is signed.

- **October 7**
  England's King George III issues the Royal Proclamation of 1763.

1775

- **May 1**
  The Quebec Act takes effect.

1791

- **December 26**
  The Constitutional Act dividing Quebec into Upper Canada and Lower Canada takes effect.

1837

- Armed revolts break out in both Upper and Lower Canada, lasting until the following year.

1841

- **February 10**
  The Act of Union of 1840 is proclaimed, uniting Upper and Lower Canada.

1848

- Responsible government is granted in the Province of Canada and Nova Scotia.

colonists and the Crown, though to the south the act helped foment the American Revolution.

Another step in Canadian constitutional history was taken when the British Parliament passed the Constitutional Act of 1791, written to amend the Quebec Act. The purpose of the act was to alter the government of Quebec in a way that would accommodate the interests of "United Empire Loyalists" who had fled the American Revolution in the soon-to-be United States. The act divided Quebec into two parts: Upper Canada, which is now southern Ontario; and Lower Canada, which is now southern Quebec. (The words *upper* and *lower* refer to locations on the Saint Lawrence River, so Upper Canada was south of Lower Canada.) The act established English common law in Upper Canada and French civil law in Lower Canada. Most significant, the act provided for representative assemblies in both colonies; it also made Lower Canada, in effect, a Catholic colony, in contrast to the Protestant Upper Canada. The result of the Constitutional Act was not what Parliament had hoped, however, for it increased rivalry and tension between the two Quebecs. *Canadiens* in the French-speaking Catholic Lower Canada came to believe that they were being dominated by English-speaking Protestants in Upper Canada; ironically, the latter believed that they were being dominated by French Catholics. The tension between the two eventually led to the Rebellions of 1837. These were simultaneous revolts in Upper and Lower Canada. In Upper Canada, rebels engaged in armed skirmishes with the oligarchy of wealthy Anglican elites that essentially ran the colony. The revolt in Lower Canada was more sustained and was launched by both French-speaking and English-speaking colonists against the inept British colonial administration.

In the aftermath of hostilities, Britain investigated the causes of the unrest. The result of this investigation was the Act of Union of 1840. The act abolished Upper and Lower Canada and merged the two into the Province of Canada. The act allowed for the future emergence of "responsible government," a term used in British legislative history to refer to the practice of colonial administration bowing to the will of the electorate in a colony. This development was pivotal in Canadian constitutional history. The concept of responsible government was first realized in the Province of Canada and Nova Scotia in early 1848, followed by Prince Edward Island in 1851, New Brunswick in 1854, and Newfoundland in 1855. In the ensuing years the Province of Canada became more and more autonomous from Great Britain until it led the push for the Constitution Act of 1867. Canada joined with New Brunswick and Nova Scotia in petitioning the British Parliament to create the Dominion of Canada; Prince Edward Island was part of the original discussions, but it declined to join the confederation until 1873 after almost becoming part of the United States. Newfoundland, too, took part in early discussions but did not join the confederation until 1949. Under the terms of the act, the Province of Canada was again divided, with the western portion becoming Ontario and the eastern portion becoming Quebec. Thus, Canada, as the name is understood today, was formed of Ontario, Quebec, New Brunswick, and Nova Scotia by the Constitution Act of 1867.

A number of factors influenced Canadians in their quest for greater unity and autonomy. One of the chief factors was political deadlock and a perceived need to reform the political structure of Canada. But various outside pressures played a role, too. One of these pressures was economic, the result of the United States' cancellation of its free-trade agreement with the Canadian provinces in 1865, partly because of Canadian unwillingness to back the Union in the Civil War; indeed, the Confederate "Gray Underground" freely conducted espionage operations in the North out of Canada during the war. The flight of many American slaves to Canada via the Underground Railroad also contributed to Canadians' sense that the provinces had to unite and firm up their borders. The U.S. doctrine of Manifest Destiny—the notion that expansion of the United States westward to the Pacific Ocean was inevitable—left many citizens in the provinces fearful of U.S. interference in their affairs. Additionally, the Fenian raids, conducted by the Fenian Brotherhood, spilled over from the United States into Canada. These were raids conducted by Irish nationalists to pressure the British government into withdrawing from Ireland. These raids, in conjunction with Britain's expressed unwillingness to maintain troops in its colonies anymore, led to the growth of Canadian nationalism and the passage of the Constitution Act.

About the Author

Like any complex piece of legislation, the Constitution Act was the work of many hands. The chief author and the motive power behind Canadian federation, though, was Canada's first prime minister, John Alexander Macdonald. Macdonald was born in Glasgow, Scotland, on January 11, 1815. His family immigrated to Kingston, Upper Canada, in 1820. From 1830 to 1836 Macdonald studied and apprenticed at the law, and after he was admitted to the bar he earned a reputation as a capable lawyer in his defense of eight men charged with treason in the wake of the Rebellions of 1837. He entered politics in 1843, first as an alderman and then as a representative to the legislature. Over the next two decades he was an energetic member of the legislature and a party leader.

During these years, however, the legislature was frequently deadlocked as a result of party disputes. Liberals and conservatives warred with each other, and the French-speaking eastern portion of the Province of Canada proved to be a thorn in the government's side. It was in about 1864 that Macdonald began to formulate the idea of a Canadian confederation. He formed a coalition of liberals and conservatives, and over the next three years he conceived the legislation that would become the Constitution Act. He presented his ideas to the Maritime colonies (Nova Scotia, New Brunswick, and Prince Edward Island) and Newfoundland at a conference in Charlottetown, Prince Edward Island, in 1864. This conference was attended by

Time Line	
1851	■ Responsible government is granted on Prince Edward Island.
1854	■ Responsible government is granted in New Brunswick.
1855	■ Responsible government is granted in Newfoundland.
1867	■ **July 1** The Canadian Confederation is formed under the terms of the Constitution Act.
1931	■ **December 11** The Statute of Westminster establishes legislative equality between Great Britain and the nations of the British Commonwealth, including Canada.
1949	■ The second of two British North America Acts of 1949 enlarges Canada's ability to amend its constitution.
1982	■ **April 17** England's Queen Elizabeth II signs the Canada Act, by which Great Britain relinquishes virtually all legislative authority over Canada, thus "patriating" the Constitution Act of 1867.

thirty-six representatives who are often regarded as the "Fathers of the Confederation." Later that year, delegates who supported confederation met in Quebec City to draft the legislation. The agreement was completed at a conference in London in 1866 and passed by the British Parliament the following year.

Macdonald went on to become Canada's second-longest-serving prime minister, holding office from 1867 to 1873 and then from 1878 until his death on June 6, 1891. He remains an iconic figure in Canadian history despite a life that was marked by tragedy, including the twelve years of his first wife's illness ending with her death, the sudden death of his infant son, and the physical and mental disabilities of his daughter by a second marriage. Macdonald himself gambled heavily, was often in debt, and was sometimes given to using law practice funds to pay personal expenses. He had a vicious temper, once physically attacking a fellow legislator on the floor of the legislature. He was also a binge drinker, and at times he was so drunk that he became sick during debates, both in the legislature and on the campaign trail. Nevertheless, he can be said to be the founder of Canada, and he worked tirelessly to impose unity on a nation of diverse interests, nationalities, and ethnicities.

Explanation and Analysis of the Document

The Constitution Act of 1867 (or the British North America Act) begins with a preamble in which the Province of Canada, New Brunswick, and Nova Scotia propose to form a united Dominion of Canada. Under the article titled "Union," the act specifies the provinces that shall make up the Dominion of Canada and notes that what formerly had been called Upper Canada and Lower Canada, joined by the Act of Union of 1840, were now severed into the provinces of Ontario and Quebec. The preamble also states that the dominion would have a constitution "similar in Principle to that of the United Kingdom." This was an important phrase, for in the ensuing decades it established a constitutional basis for Canadians to enjoy the same civil rights that citizens of the United Kingdom enjoyed. Throughout the Constitution Act, civil rights are implied, but they are not expressly stated in passages that would be analogous to the Bill of Rights of the U.S. Constitution. Canadians eventually made civil rights more explicit in the Canadian Charter of Rights and Freedoms, signed into law by England's Queen Elizabeth II in 1982. This charter extended the 1960 Canadian Bill of Rights, which was regarded as inadequate because it was a statute (and thus could be changed) and not a part of the constitution. The 1982 charter made the bill of rights part of the Canadian constitution.

The chief feature of Article III, "Executive Power," is that it vests executive authority in Canada in the monarch of England—at the time, Queen Victoria. Canada would have a governor general appointed by the queen, along with the queen's privy council, whose members would advise the governor general. A privy council is roughly equivalent to a cabinet, but the word *privy* implies that the deliberations

and advice of this body of close advisers are secret or private. This section of the act vests the authority to appoint advisers with the queen. It also notes that the queen remains the commander in chief of the armed forces. In sum, the Constitution Act by no means represented a complete severance from Great Britain. Canada would occupy a middle ground between complete independence and membership in the British Commonwealth, with the monarch as its head of state.

Perhaps the core of the Constitution Act is that portion that deals with legislative authority. The act proposes a single parliament whose powers cannot exceed those of the British Parliament. The parliament would consist of a senate and a house of commons, and the act specifies the number of representatives each province would have as well as qualifications for becoming a senator. Interestingly, a number of these qualifications have to do with the prospective senator's finances. To be eligible, a prospective senator must be "seised as of Freehold," which means simply that he has to own property. "Socage" refers to agricultural lands. Alternatively, he could occupy lands in "Franc-alleu," a rare form of property ownership that is free of any kind of mortgage, tax, or any other obligation (the English equivalent is called allodial lands), or he could occupy lands in "Roture," which in French-Canadian law means essentially that a person can discharge duties to the owner of the land by payment of rent (as opposed to providing services, as would have been the case under feudalism in the Middle Ages). A prospective senator also had to have a net worth (assets minus debts) of at least $4,000, a significant sum of money in 1867. This provision was seen to lessen the likelihood that a senator would use his position for financial gain out of desperation or be subject to bribery from special interests. This article goes on to specify the details pertaining to increasing or decreasing the number of senators and to replacing senators in the case of a vacancy. It also provides for the formation of electoral districts. It should be noted that senators were to be appointed, not elected, and the tenure of a senator was for life; thus, the Canadian Senate was conceived as analogous to the British House of Lords, an upper chamber of men of means who would provide continuity in legislative government and who, presumably, could vote without regard to short-term political considerations.

The House of Commons was the lower chamber of representatives elected by males who were twenty-one years old or older. This portion of the act specifies in detail such matters as voting, the election of a speaker, and the like. It further specifies the number of elected representatives in the House of Commons and details procedures to be followed for increasing the number of representatives, presumably as the population of Canada grew. One interesting feature is that the representation of Quebec would be used as a fixed reference point. The number of representatives in that province is fixed at sixty-five; this number would not change. In each of the other provinces, the number of its representatives would bear the same proportion to its population as Quebec's sixty-five bore to its population. The House of Commons would sit for a five-year period. The

Fenian Brotherhood troops charge the retreating Queen's Own Rifles of Canada in Ridgeway, Ontario, during a Fenian raid into Canada (Library of Congress)

requirement that a period of no more than a year pass between the closing of one session of the legislature and the opening of another was designed to help ensure the civil rights of Canadians. It eliminated the possibility that the monarch simply would not convene the legislature, as British monarchs had done in the past when they expected opposition from the people's representatives. Later, in section 128, the act specifies that members of the legislature must take an oath of allegiance.

Article VI, "Distribution of Legislative Powers," is quite particular in delineating the powers of the national, or federal, parliament and the parliaments of the individual provinces. Thus, for example, the national parliament was to have authority over the public debt, regulation of trade and commerce, borrowing, the postal system, the navigation system, coinage, and copyright law. The legislatures of the individual provinces were to have authority over direct taxation to raise revenue for provincial purposes. Later, section 102 specifies the division of revenues between the provinces and the federal government. In this sense, Canada was to operate in a manner similar to the United States at the time. Until the ratification of the Sixteenth Amendment to the U.S. Constitution in 1913, the federal govern-

ment raised money from the states through indirect taxation; money was collected in the states and then paid by each state to the federal government. The Sixteenth Amendment imposed a system of direct income taxation whereby citizens pay tax directly to the federal government. The Constitution Act elsewhere specifies the amount of money each province was to pay to the federal government to fund its operations, but individual provinces could directly tax their citizens to raise revenues for provincial purposes.

Additionally, the provincial governments were given authority over such matters as prisons, licenses, incorporation of businesses, marriage, and management of public lands and their timber in the provinces. A significant modern amendment to the Constitution Act is a section titled "Non-renewable Natural Resources, Forestry Resources and Electrical Energy." Canada is a huge, relatively sparsely populated nation with abundant natural resources, including timber, oil, hydroelectric power, and oil sands. As the world has focused more of its attention on such resources, Canada has had to wrestle with the question of how to manage them. The amendment specifically gives the provinces authority over exploration and development of nonrenewable natural resources.

"It shall be lawful for the Queen, by and with the Advice of Her Majesty's Most Honourable Privy Council, to declare by Proclamation that, on and after a Day therein appointed, not being more than Six Months after the passing of this Act, the Provinces of Canada, Nova Scotia, and New Brunswick shall form and be One Dominion under the Name of Canada."

(Article II: Union)

"The Executive Government and Authority of and over Canada is hereby declared to continue and be vested in the Queen."

(Article III: Executive Power)

"There shall be One Parliament for Canada, consisting of the Queen, an Upper House styled the Senate, and the House of Commons."

(Article IV: Legislative Power)

"It shall be lawful for the Queen, by and with the Advice and Consent of the Senate and House of Commons, to make Laws for the Peace, Order, and good Government of Canada, in relation to all Matters not coming within the Classes of Subjects by this Act assigned exclusively to the Legislatures of the Provinces."

(Article VI: Distribution of Legislative Powers)

The section titled "Education" is a good example of the inclusion of civil rights by implication. The act turns education over to the provinces. However, it also asserts that "Nothing in any such Law shall prejudicially affect any Right or Privilege with respect to Denominational Schools." The act goes on to say that

all the Powers, Privileges, and Duties at the Union by Law conferred and imposed in Upper Canada on the Separate Schools and School Trustees of the Queen's Roman Catholic Subjects shall be and the same are hereby extended to the Dissentient Schools of the Queen's Protestant and Roman Catholic Subjects in Quebec.

Thus, the Constitution Act recognized the religious tension that existed between the largely Catholic French-speaking people of Quebec and the largely Anglican English-speaking people of the other provinces. The Constitution Act protects the civil rights of both populations. Later, section 133 notes that either English or French could be used in the legislature and records were to be kept in both languages. To this day, the principal—and official—language of Quebec is French, and Canada is officially a bilingual nation. Buyers of products made or traded in Canada will note that labels, owner's manuals, and the like are all printed in both French and English. This recognition of Quebec as in some sense unique, enjoying what its people call *statut particulier,* or "special status," in the Canadian body politic, has been a source of tension in that nation. As recently as 1995 the people of Quebec voted on whether to become a separate, sovereign nation. The bill was defeated by a margin of just 1 percent, but a majority of French speakers (about 79 percent of Quebec's population) voted in favor of the proposal.

Audience

In common with nearly any piece of legislation, the Constitution Act had several audiences. One important audience was the British Crown and the British Parliament. Because the Canadian provinces were all British colonies, they could form a federation only with the consent of Parliament; the only other option was armed rebellion, similar to the American Revolution. The legislation that was submitted to Parliament was, in effect, a petition, so it contains no ringing rhetoric declaring independence from Great Britain or denouncing Parliament. Rather, the Constitution Act is a sober, straightforward document outlining the structure and governmental functions of the proposed new federation. A second audience, of course, was the Canadian people. The document informed the citizens of the four original provinces of the provinces' intentions and the complexion of their new government. It was intended to be a unifying document that would enable the provinces, with their differing political views, nationalities, and ethnicities, to put aside differences for the common welfare. A third audience was future Canadians, for the document specifically provided for the admission of additional provinces and territories to the federation, including the latest addition, Nunavut, in 1999.

Impact

The Constitution Act of 1867 was the final step in a century-long process of unifying Britain's remaining North American colonies into an autonomous, self-governing nation. Over the course of the next century, numerous acts titled British North America Act, each with a date appended, continued the process of settling Canada's relationship with Great Britain and of amending the original act. Interestingly, the delegates to the various conferences that forged the Constitution Act wrestled with the question of what to call Canada. They readily agreed on "Canada," but they debated whether to call it the "Federation of Canada" or the "Kingdom of Canada." John Macdonald argued for "kingdom" and wanted the new nation to retain features of a monarchical form of government. He argued that the presidential system of the United States was unsuitable for Canada, for it failed to provide an ongoing unifying figure in the nation's culture and politics. Many of the delegates, though, rejected the notion of a kingdom. Ultimately, the delegates settled on calling the nation the "Dominion of Canada."

While the Constitution Act gave the Canadian provinces more autonomy, Canada did not become entirely independent as a result of the act. Great Britain retained authority over foreign policy, and the Judicial Committee of the Privy Council in England remained Canada's highest appeals court. Further, the act could be amended only by the action of the British Parliament. Nevertheless, over the ensuing decades Canada became more and more autonomous, and in 1931 the British Parliament passed the Statute of Westminster, which established full legislative equality between the British Parliament and the parliaments of the nations of the British Commonwealth, including Canada. (The others were Australia, New Zealand, Newfoundland, the Union of South Africa, and the Irish

Questions for Further Study

1. Why do you think events in Britain's North American colonies proceeded so differently in Canada and in the thirteen colonies that became the United States? What impact, if any, did the American Revolution have on events in Canada? What impact did future events in the United States have on the drive for Canadian independence?

2. What tensions in Canadian society that date back to the eighteenth century continue to be issues in Canada? Why do you think these tensions continue to exist?

3. When Canada amends its constitution, it actually changes it, in contrast to the United States, where the Constitution as originally written is retained but amendments are added at the end and specifically identified as amendments. Examine the 1867 document. What provisions in the document do you think have likely been amended or repealed? What historical, economic, or social developments do you think would have led to the amendment?

4. Through the 1867 Constitution Act, Canadians did not try to "revolt" against Great Britain and sever all ties. How did the act maintain ties with Great Britain? Why do you think Canadians wanted at that time to maintain those ties?

5. Respond to the following statement: Canada, unlike the United States, does not have a constitutional bill of rights for its citizens.

Free State.) The process was completed with the Canada Act of 1892, which patriated the Constitution Act of 1867 and subsequent acts, turning them over to Canada. The process of Canadian separation from Great Britain was complete, with the exception that the monarch of England remains Canada's ceremonial head of state.

In the years following passage of the Constitution Act, the Dominion of Canada grew, eventually extending across North America from the Atlantic to the Pacific Ocean. Manitoba and the Northwest Territories joined the confederation in 1870, British Columbia in 1871, Prince Edward Island in 1873, and the Yukon Territory in 1898. In the twentieth century, Saskatchewan and Alberta joined in 1905 and Newfoundland in 1949 (and in 2001 the name of the latter province was officially changed to Newfoundland and Labrador, though Canadians still refer to it informally as just Newfoundland). The latest addition to the Canadian confederation was Nunavut, in 1999. With a land area of 3.85 million square miles, Canada is the world's second-largest country in area (following Russia) and is home to some 33 million people.

Further Reading

▪ Books

Conrad, Margaret, and Alvin Finkel. *Canada: A National History*. Toronto, Canada: Longman, 2003.

Francis, R. Douglas, and Donald B. Smith, eds. *Readings in Canadian History*, 2 vols., 5th ed. Toronto, Canada: Harcourt Brace Canada, 1998.

Hallowell, Gerald. *The Oxford Companion to Canadian History*. Don Mills, Ontario, Canada: Oxford University Press, 2004.

Morton, Desmond. *A Short History of Canada*, 5th ed. Toronto, Canada: McClelland and Stewart, 2001.

Taylor, M. Brook. *Canadian History: A Reader's Guide*. Vol. 1: *Beginnings to Confederation*. Toronto, Canada: University of Toronto Press, 1994.

Taylor, M. Brook, and Doug Owram. *Canadian History: A Reader's Guide*. Vol. 2: *Confederation to the Present*. Toronto, Canada: University of Toronto Press, 1994.

▪ Web Sites

"Constitutional History." Canada in the Making Web site. http://www.canadiana.org/citm/themes/constitution1_e.html.

—Michael J. O'Neal

Constitution Act of Canada

An Act for the Union of Canada, Nova Scotia, and New Brunswick, and the Government thereof; and for Purposes connected therewith

Whereas the Provinces of Canada, Nova Scotia, and New Brunswick have expressed their Desire to be federally united into One Dominion under the Crown of the United Kingdom of Great Britain and Ireland, with a Constitution similar in Principle to that of the United Kingdom:

And whereas such a Union would conduce to the Welfare of the Provinces and promote the Interests of the British Empire:

And whereas on the Establishment of the Union by Authority of Parliament it is expedient, not only that the Constitution of the Legislative Authority in the Dominion be provided for, but also that the Nature of the Executive Government therein be declared:

And whereas it is expedient that Provision be made for the eventual Admission into the Union of other Parts of British North America:

Be it therefore enacted and declared by the Queen's most Excellent Majesty, by and with the Advice and Consent of the Lords Spiritual and Temporal, and Commons, in this present Parliament assembled, and by the Authority of the same, as follows:—

I. Preliminary

1. This Act may be cited as the *The British North America Act, 1867.*

2. The Provisions of this Act referring to Her Majesty the Queen extend also to the Heirs and Successors of Her Majesty, Kings and Queens of the United Kingdom of Great Britain and Ireland.

II. Union

3. It shall be lawful for the Queen, by and with the Advice of Her Majesty's Most Honourable Privy Council, to declare by Proclamation that, on and after a Day therein appointed, not being more than Six Months after the passing of this Act, the Provinces of Canada, Nova Scotia, and New Brunswick shall form and be One Dominion under the Name of Canada; and on and after that Day those Three Provinces shall form and be One Dominion under that Name accordingly.

4. The subsequent Provisions of this Act shall, unless it is otherwise expressed or implied, commence and have effect on and after the Union, that is to say, on and after the Day appointed for the Union taking effect in the Queen's Proclamation; and in the same Provisions, unless it is otherwise expressed or implied, the Name Canada shall be taken to mean Canada as constituted under this Act.

5. Canada shall be divided into Four Provinces, named Ontario, Quebec, Nova Scotia, and New Brunswick.

6. The Parts of the Province of Canada (as it exists at the passing of this Act) which formerly constituted respectively the Provinces of Upper Canada and Lower Canada shall be deemed to be severed, and shall form two separate Provinces. The Part which formerly constituted the Province of Upper Canada shall constitute the Province of Ontario; and the Part which formerly constituted the Province of Lower Canada shall constitute the Province of Quebec.

7. The Provinces of Nova Scotia and New Brunswick shall have the same Limits as at the passing of this Act.

8. In the general Census of the Population of Canada which is hereby required to be taken in the Year One thousand eight hundred and seventy-one, and in every Tenth Year thereafter, the respective Populations of the Four Provinces shall be distinguished.

III. Executive Power

9. The Executive Government and Authority of and over Canada is hereby declared to continue and be vested in the Queen.

10. The Provisions of this Act referring to the Governor General extend and apply to the Governor General for the Time being of Canada, or other the Chief Executive Officer or Administrator for the Time being carrying on the Government of Canada on behalf and in the Name of the Queen, by whatever Title he is designated.

11. There shall be a Council to aid and advise in the Government of Canada, to be styled the Queen's Privy Council for Canada; and the Persons who are to be Members of that Council shall be from Time to Time chosen and summoned by the Governor General and sworn in as Privy Councillors, and Members thereof may be from Time to Time removed by the Governor General.

12. All Powers, Authorities, and Functions which under any Act of the Parliament of Great Britain, or of the Parliament of the United Kingdom of Great Britain and Ireland, or of the Legislature of Upper Canada, Lower Canada, Canada, Nova Scotia, or New Brunswick, are at the Union vested in or exerciseable by the respective Governors or Lieutenant Governors of those Provinces, with the Advice, or with the Advice and Consent, of the respective Executive Councils thereof, or in conjunction with those Councils, or with any Number of Members thereof, or by those Governors or Lieutenant Governors individually, shall, as far as the same continue in existence and capable of being exercised after the Union in relation to the Government of Canada, be vested in and exerciseable by the Governor General, with the Advice or with the Advice and Consent of or in conjunction with the Queen's Privy Council for Canada, or any Members thereof, or by the Governor General individually, as the Case requires, subject nevertheless (except with respect to such as exist under Acts of the Parliament of Great Britain or of the Parliament of the United Kingdom of Great Britain and Ireland) to be abolished or altered by the Parliament of Canada.

13. The Provisions of this Act referring to the Governor General in Council shall be construed as referring to the Governor General acting by and with the Advice of the Queen's Privy Council for Canada.

14. It shall be lawful for the Queen, if Her Majesty thinks fit, to authorize the Governor General from Time to Time to appoint any Person or any Persons jointly or severally to be his Deputy or Deputies within any Part or Parts of Canada, and in that Capacity to exercise during the Pleasure of the Governor General such of the Powers, Authorities, and Functions of the Governor General as the Governor General deems it necessary or expedient to assign to him or them, subject to any Limitations or Directions expressed or given by the Queen; but the Appointment of such a Deputy or Deputies shall not affect the Exercise by the Governor General himself of any Power, Authority, or Function.

15. The Command-in-Chief of the Land and Naval Militia, and of all Naval and Military Forces, of and in Canada, is hereby declared to continue and be vested in the Queen.

16. Until the Queen otherwise directs, the Seat of Government of Canada shall be Ottawa.

IV. Legislative Power

17. There shall be One Parliament for Canada, consisting of the Queen, an Upper House styled the Senate, and the House of Commons.

18. The Privileges, Immunities, and Powers to be held, enjoyed, and exercised by the Senate and by the House of Commons and by the Members thereof respectively shall be such as are from Time to Time defined by Act of the Parliament of Canada, but so that the same shall never exceed those at the passing of this Act held, enjoyed, and exercised by the Commons House of Parliament of the United Kingdom of Great Britain and Ireland and by the Members thereof.

19. The Parliament of Canada shall be called together not later than Six Months after the Union.

20. There shall be a Session of the Parliament of Canada once at least in every Year, so that Twelve Months shall not intervene between the last Sitting of the Parliament in one Session and its first Sitting in the next Session.

◆ Senate

21. The Senate shall, subject to the Provisions of this Act, consist of One Hundred and five Members, who shall be styled Senators.

22. In relation to the Constitution of the Senate, Canada shall be deemed to consist of Three Divisions: 1. Ontario; 2. Quebec; 3. The Maritime Provinces, Nova Scotia and New Brunswick; which Three Divisions shall (subject to the Provisions of this Act) be equally represented in the Senate as follows: Ontario by Twenty-four Senators; Quebec by Twenty-four Senators; and the Maritime Provinces by Twenty-four Senators, Twelve thereof representing Nova Scotia, and Twelve thereof representing New Brunswick.

In the Case of Quebec each of the Twenty-four Senators representing that Province shall be appointed for One of the Twenty-four Electoral Divisions of Lower Canada specified in Schedule A. to Chapter One of the Consolidated Statutes of Canada.

23. The Qualifications of a Senator shall be as follows:

(1) He shall be of the full age of Thirty Years:

(2) He shall be either a natural-born Subject of the Queen, or a Subject of the Queen naturalized

by an Act of the Parliament of Great Britain, or of the Parliament of the United Kingdom of Great Britain and Ireland, or of the Legislature of One of the Provinces of Upper Canada, Lower Canada, Canada, Nova Scotia, or New Brunswick, before the Union, or of the Parliament of Canada after the Union:

(3) He shall be legally or equitably seised as of Freehold for his own Use and Benefit of Lands or Tenements held in Free and Common Socage, or seised or possessed for his own Use and Benefit of Lands or Tenements held in Franc-alleu or in Roture, within the Province for which he is appointed, of the Value of Four thousand Dollars, over and above all Rents, Dues, Debts, Charges, Mortgages, and Incumbrances due or payable out of or charged on or affecting the same:

(4) His Real and Personal Property shall be together worth Four thousand Dollars over and above his Debts and Liabilities:

(5) He shall be resident in the Province for which he is appointed:

(6) In the Case of Quebec he shall have his Real Property Qualification in the Electoral Division for which he is appointed, or shall be resident in that Division.

24. The Governor General shall from Time to Time, in the Queen's Name, by Instrument under the Great Seal of Canada, summon qualified Persons to the Senate; and, subject to the Provisions of this Act, every Person so summoned shall become and be a Member of the Senate and a Senator.

25. Such Persons shall be first summoned to the Senate as the Queen by Warrant under Her Majesty's Royal Sign Manual thinks fit to approve, and their Names shall be inserted in the Queen's Proclamation of Union.

26. If at any Time on the Recommendation of the Governor General the Queen thinks fit to direct that Three or Six Members be added to the Senate, the Governor General may by Summons to Three or Six qualified Persons (as the Case may be), representing equally the Three Divisions of Canada, add to the Senate accordingly.

27. In case of such Addition being at any Time made the Governor General shall not summon any Person to the Senate except on a further like Direction by the Queen on the like Recommendation, until each of the Three Divisions of Canada is represented by Twenty-four Senators and no more.

28. The Number of Senators shall not at any Time exceed Seventy-eight.

29. A Senator shall, subject to the Provisions of this Act, hold his Place in the Senate for Life.

30. A Senator may by Writing under his Hand addressed to the Governor General resign his Place in the Senate, and thereupon the same shall be vacant.

31. The Place of a Senator shall become vacant in any of the following Cases:

(1) If for Two consecutive Sessions of the Parliament he fails to give his Attendance in the Senate:

(2) If he takes an Oath or makes a Declaration or Acknowledgment of Allegiance, Obedience, or Adherence to a Foreign Power, or does an Act whereby he becomes a Subject or Citizen, or entitled to the Rights or Privileges of a Subject or Citizen, of a Foreign Power:

(3) If he is adjudged Bankrupt or Insolvent, or applies for the Benefit of any Law relating to Insolvent Debtors, or becomes a public Defaulter:

(4) If he is attainted of Treason or convicted of Felony or of any infamous Crime:

(5) If he ceases to be qualified in respect of Property or of Residence; provided, that a Senator shall not be deemed to have ceased to be qualified in respect of Residence by reason only of his residing at the Seat of the Government of Canada while holding an Office under that Government requiring his Presence there.

32. When a Vacancy happens in the Senate by Resignation, Death, or otherwise, the Governor General shall by Summons to a fit and qualified Person fill the Vacancy.

33. If any Question arises respecting the Qualification of a Senator or a Vacancy in the Senate the same shall be heard and determined by the Senate.

34. The Governor General may from Time to Time, by Instrument under the Great Seal of Canada, appoint a Senator to be Speaker of the Senate, and may remove him and appoint another in his Stead.

35. Until the Parliament of Canada otherwise provides, the Presence of at least Fifteen Senators, including the Speaker, shall be necessary to constitute a Meeting of the Senate for the Exercise of its Powers.

36. Questions arising in the Senate shall be decided by a Majority of Voices, and the Speaker shall in all Cases have a Vote, and when the Voices are equal the Decision shall be deemed to be in the Negative.

◆ The House of Commons

37. The House of Commons shall, subject to the Provisions of this Act, consist of one hundred and

eighty-one members, of whom Eighty-two shall be elected for Ontario, Sixty-five for Quebec, Nineteen for Nova Scotia, and Fifteen for New Brunswick.

38. The Governor General shall from Time to Time, in the Queen's Name, by Instrument under the Great Seal of Canada, summon and call together the House of Commons.

39. A Senator shall not be capable of being elected or of sitting or voting as a Member of the House of Commons.

40. Until the Parliament of Canada otherwise provides, Ontario, Quebec, Nova Scotia, and New Brunswick shall, for the Purposes of the Election of Members to serve in the House of Commons, be divided into Electoral Districts as follows:

(1) Ontario. Ontario shall be divided into the Counties, Ridings of Counties, Cities, Parts of Cities, and Towns enumerated in the First Schedule to this Act, each whereof shall be an Electoral District, each such District as numbered in that Schedule being entitled to return One Member.

(2) Quebec. Quebec shall be divided into Sixty-five Electoral Districts, composed of the Sixty-five Electoral Divisions into which Lower Canada is at the passing of this Act divided under Chapter Two of the Consolidated Statutes of Canada, Chapter Seventy-five of the Consolidated Statutes for Lower Canada, and the Act of the Province of Canada of the Twenty-third Year of the Queen, Chapter One, or any other Act amending the same in force at the Union, so that each such Electoral Division shall be for the Purposes of this Act an Electoral District entitled to return One Member.

(3) Nova Scotia. Each of the Eighteen Counties of Nova Scotia shall be an Electoral District. The County of Halifax shall be entitled to return Two Members, and each of the other Counties One Member.

(4) New Brunswick. Each of the Fourteen Counties into which New Brunswick is divided, including the City and County of St. John, shall be an Electoral District. The City of St. John shall also be a separate Electoral District. Each of those Fifteen Electoral Districts shall be entitled to return One Member.

41. Until the Parliament of Canada otherwise provides, all Laws in force in the several Provinces at the Union relative to the following Matters or any of them, namely,—the Qualifications and Disqualifications of Persons to be elected or to sit or vote as Members of the House of Assembly or Legislative Assembly in the several Provinces, the Voters at Elections of such Members, the Oaths to be taken by Voters, the Returning Officers, their Powers and Duties, the Proceedings at Elections, the Periods during which Elections may be continued, the Trial of controverted Elections, and Proceedings incident thereto, the vacating of Seats of Members, and the Execution of new Writs in case of Seats vacated otherwise than by Dissolution,—shall respectively apply to Elections of Members to serve in the House of Commons for the same several Provinces.

Provided that, until the Parliament of Canada otherwise provides, at any Election for a Member of the House of Commons for the District of Algoma, in addition to Persons qualified by the Law of the Province of Canada to vote, every Male British Subject, aged Twenty-one Years or upwards, being a Householder, shall have a Vote.

42. For the First Election of Members to serve in the House of Commons the Governor General shall cause Writs to be issued by such Person, in such Form, and addressed to such Returning Officers as he thinks fit.

The Person issuing Writs under this Section shall have the like Powers as are possessed at the Union by the Officers charged with the issuing of Writs for the Election of Members to serve in the respective House of Assembly or Legislative Assembly of the Province of Canada, Nova Scotia, or New Brunswick; and the Returning Officers to whom Writs are directed under this Section shall have the like Powers as are possessed at the Union by the Officers charged with the returning of Writs for the Election of Members to serve in the same respective House of Assembly or Legislative Assembly.

43. In case a Vacancy in the Representation in the House of Commons of any Electoral District happens before the Meeting of the Parliament, or after the Meeting of the Parliament before Provision is made by the Parliament in this Behalf, the Provisions of the last foregoing Section of this Act shall extend and apply to the issuing and returning of a Writ in respect of such Vacant District.

44. The House of Commons on its first assembling after a General Election shall proceed with all practicable Speed to elect One of its Members to be Speaker.

45. In case of a Vacancy happening in the Office of Speaker by Death, Resignation, or otherwise, the House of Commons shall with all practicable Speed proceed to elect another of its Members to be Speaker.

46. The Speaker shall preside at all Meetings of the House of Commons.

47. Until the Parliament of Canada otherwise provides, in case of the Absence for any Reason of

the Speaker from the Chair of the House of Commons for a Period of Forty-eight consecutive Hours, the House may elect another of its Members to act as Speaker, and the Member so elected shall during the Continuance of such Absence of the Speaker have and execute all the Powers, Privileges, and Duties of Speaker.

48. The Presence of at least Twenty Members of the House of Commons shall be necessary to constitute a Meeting of the House for the Exercise of its Powers, and for that Purpose the Speaker shall be reckoned as a Member.

49. Questions arising in the House of Commons shall be decided by a Majority of Voices other than that of the Speaker, and when the Voices are equal, but not otherwise, the Speaker shall have a Vote.

50. Every House of Commons shall continue for Five Years from the Day of the Return of the Writs for choosing the House (subject to be sooner dissolved by the Governor General), and no longer.

51. On the Completion of the Census in the Year One Thousand eight hundred and seventy-one, and of each subsequent decennial Census, the Representation of the Four Provinces shall be readjusted by such Authority, in such Manner, and from such Time, as the Parliament of Canada from Time to Time provides, subject and according to the following Rules:

(1) Quebec shall have the fixed Number of Sixty-five Members:

(2) There shall be assigned to each of the other Provinces such a Number of Members as will bear the same Proportion to the Number of its Population (ascertained at such Census) as the Number Sixty-five bears to the Number of the Population of Quebec (so ascertained):

(3) In the Computation of the Number of Members for a Province a fractional Part not exceeding One Half of the whole Number requisite for entitling the Province to a Member shall be disregarded; but a fractional Part exceeding One Half of that Number shall be equivalent to the whole Number:

(4) On any such Re-adjustment the Number of Members for a Province shall not be reduced unless the Proportion which the Number of the Population of the Province bore to the Number of the aggregate Population of Canada at the then last preceding Re-adjustment of the Number of Members for the Province is ascertained at the then latest Census to be diminished by One Twentieth Part or upwards:

(5) Such Re-adjustment shall not take effect until the Termination of the then existing Parliament.

52. The Number of Members of the House of Commons may be from Time to Time increased by the Parliament of Canada, provided the proportionate Representation of the Provinces prescribed by this Act is not thereby disturbed....

VI. Distribution of Legislative Powers

◆ Powers of the Parliament

91. It shall be lawful for the Queen, by and with the Advice and Consent of the Senate and House of Commons, to make Laws for the Peace, Order, and good Government of Canada, in relation to all Matters not coming within the Classes of Subjects by this Act assigned exclusively to the Legislatures of the Provinces; and for greater Certainty, but not so as to restrict the Generality of the foregoing Terms of this Section, it is hereby declared that (notwithstanding anything in this Act) the exclusive Legislative Authority of the Parliament of Canada extends to all Matters coming within the Classes of Subjects next hereinafter enumerated; that is to say,

1. The Public Debt and Property.
2. The Regulation of Trade and Commerce.
3. The raising of Money by any Mode or System of Taxation.
4. The borrowing of Money on the Public Credit.
5. Postal Service.
6. The Census and Statistics.
7. Militia, Military and Naval Service, and Defence.
8. The fixing of and providing for the Salaries and Allowances of Civil and other Officers of the Government of Canada.
9. Beacons, Buoys, Lighthouses, and Sable Island.
10. Navigation and Shipping.
11. Quarantine and the Establishment and Maintenance of Marine Hospitals.
12. Sea Coast and Inland Fisheries.
13. Ferries between a Province and any British or Foreign Country or between Two Provinces.
14. Currency and Coinage.
15. Issue of Paper Money.
16. Savings Banks.
17. Weights and Measures.
18. Bills of Exchange and Promissory Notes.
19. Interest.
20. Legal Tender.
21. Bankruptcy and Insolvency.

22. Patents of Invention and Discovery.
23. Copyrights.
24. Indians, and Lands reserved for the Indians.
25. Naturalization and Aliens.
26. Marriage and Divorce.
27. The Criminal Law, except the Constitution of Courts of Criminal Jurisdiction, but including the Procedure in Criminal Matters.
28. The Establishment, Maintenance, and Management of Penitentiaries.
29. Such Classes of Subjects as are expressly excepted in the Enumeration of the Classes of Subjects by this Act assigned exclusively to the Legislatures of the Provinces.

And any Matter coming within any of the Classes of Subjects enumerated in this Section shall not be deemed to come within the Class of Matters of a local or private Nature comprised in the Enumeration of the Classes of Subjects by this Act assigned exclusively to the Legislatures of the Provinces.

◆ **Exclusive Powers of Provincial Legislatures**

92. In each Province the Legislature may exclusively make Laws in relation to Matters coming within the Classes of Subjects next hereinafter enumerated; that is to say,

1. The Amendment from Time to Time, notwithstanding anything in this Act, of the Constitution of the Province, except as regards the Office of Lieutenant Governor.
2. Direct Taxation within the Province in order to the raising of a Revenue for Provincial Purposes.
3. The borrowing of Money on the sole Credit of the Province
4. The Establishment and Tenure of Provincial Offices and the Appointment and Payment of Provincial Officers.
5. The Management and Sale of the Public Lands belonging to the Province and of the Timber and Wood thereon.
6. The Establishment, Maintenance, and Management of Public and Reformatory Prisons in and for the Province.
7. The Establishment, Maintenance, and Management of Hospitals, Asylums, Charities, and Eleemosynary Institutions in and for the Province, other than Marine Hospitals.
8. Municipal Institutions in the Province.
9. Shop, Saloon, Tavern, Auctioneer, and other Licences in order to the raising of a Revenue for Provincial, Local, or Municipal Purposes.

10. Local Works and Undertakings other than such as are of the following Classes:
    (a) Lines of Steam or other Ships, Railways, Canals, Telegraphs, and other Works and Undertakings connecting the Province with any other or others of the Provinces, or extending beyond the Limits of the Province:
    (b) of Steam Ships between the Province and any British or Foreign Country:
    (c) Such Works as, although wholly situate within the Province, are before or after their Execution declared by the Parliament of Canada to be for the general Advantage of Canada or for the Advantage of Two or more of the Provinces.
11. The Incorporation of Companies with Provincial Objects.
12. The Solemnization of Marriage in the Province.
13. Property and Civil Rights in the Province.
14. The Administration of Justice in the Province, including the Constitution, Maintenance, and Organization of Provincial Courts, both of Civil and of Criminal Jurisdiction, and including Procedure in Civil Matters in those Courts.
15. The Imposition of Punishment by Fine, Penalty, or Imprisonment for enforcing any Law of the Province made in relation to any Matter coming within any of the Classes of Subjects enumerated in this Section.
16. Generally all Matters of a merely local or private Nature in the Province.

◆ **Education**

93. In and for each Province the Legislature may exclusively make Laws in relation to Education, subject and according to the following Provisions:

(1) Nothing in any such Law shall prejudicially affect any Right or Privilege with respect to Denominational Schools which any Class of Persons have by Law in the Province at the Union:

(2) All the Powers, Privileges, and Duties at the Union by Law conferred and imposed in Upper Canada on the Separate Schools and School Trustees of the Queen's Roman Catholic Subjects shall be and the same are hereby extended to the Dissentient Schools of the Queen's Protestant and Roman Catholic Subjects in Quebec:

(3) Where in any Province a System of Separate or Dissentient Schools exists by Law at the Union or

is thereafter established by the Legislature of the Province, an Appeal shall lie to the Governor General in Council from any Act or Decision of any Provincial Authority affecting any Right or Privilege of the Protestant or Roman Catholic Minority of the Queen's Subjects in relation to Education:

(4) In case any such Provincial Law as from Time to Time seems to the Governor General in Council requisite for the due Execution of the Provisions of this Section is not made, or in case any Decision of the Governor General in Council on any Appeal under this Section is not duly executed by the proper Provincial Authority in that Behalf, then and in every such Case, and as far only as the Circumstances of each Case require, the Parliament of Canada may make remedial Laws for the due Execution of the Provisions of this Section and of any Decision of the Governor General in Council under this Section....

IX. Miscellaneous Provisions

◆ General ...

128. Every Member of the Senate or House of Commons of Canada shall before taking his Seat therein take and subscribe before the Governor General or some Person authorized by him, and every Member of a Legislative Council or Legislative Assembly of any Province shall before taking his Seat therein take and subscribe before the Lieutenant Governor of the Province or some Person authorized by him, the Oath of Allegiance contained in the Fifth Schedule to this Act; and every Member of the Senate of Canada and every Member of the Legislative Council of Quebec shall also, before taking his Seat therein, take and subscribe before the Governor General, or some Person authorized by him, the Declaration of Qualification contained in the same Schedule.

129. Except as otherwise provided by this Act, all Laws in force in Canada, Nova Scotia, or New Brunswick at the Union, and all Courts of Civil and Criminal Jurisdiction, and all legal Commissions, Powers, and Authorities, and all Officers, Judicial, Administrative, and Ministerial, existing therein at the Union, shall continue in Ontario, Quebec, Nova Scotia, and New Brunswick respectively, as if the Union had not been made; subject nevertheless (except with respect to such as are enacted by or exist under Acts of the Parliament of Great Britain or of the Parliament of the United Kingdom of Great Britain and Ireland), to be repealed, abolished, or altered by the Parliament of Canada, or by the Legislature of the respective Province, according to the Authority of the Parliament or of that Legislature under this Act.

130. Until the Parliament of Canada otherwise provides, all Officers of the several Provinces having Duties to discharge in relation to Matters other than those coming within the Classes of Subjects by this Act assigned exclusively to the Legislatures of the Provinces shall be Officers of Canada, and shall continue to discharge the Duties of their respective Offices under the same Liabilities, Responsibilities, and Penalties as if the Union had not been made.

131. Until the Parliament of Canada otherwise provides, the Governor General in Council may from Time to Time appoint such Officers as the Governor General in Council deems necessary or proper for the effectual Execution of this Act.

132. The Parliament and Government of Canada shall have all Powers necessary or proper for performing the Obligations of Canada or of any Province thereof, as Part of the British Empire, towards Foreign Countries, arising under Treaties between the Empire and such Foreign Countries.

133. Either the English or the French Language may be used by any Person in the Debates of the Houses of the Parliament of Canada and of the Houses of the Legislature of Quebec; and both those Languages shall be used in the respective Records and Journals of those Houses; and either of those Languages may be used by any Person or in any Pleading or Process in or issuing from any Court of Canada established under this Act, and in or from all or any of the Courts of Quebec.

The Acts of the Parliament of Canada and of the Legislature of Quebec shall be printed and published in both those Languages....

XI. Admission of Other Colonies

146. It shall be lawful for the Queen, by and with the Advice of Her Majesty's Most Honourable Privy Council, on Addresses from the Houses of the Parliament of Canada, and from the Houses of the respective Legislatures of the Colonies or Provinces of Newfoundland, Prince Edward Island, and British Columbia, to admit those Colonies or Provinces, or any of them, into the Union, and on Address from the Houses of the Parliament of Canada to admit Rupert's Land and the North-western Territory, or either of them, into the Union, on such Terms and Conditions

in each Case as are in the Addresses expressed and as the Queen thinks fit to approve, subject to the Provisions of this Act; and the Provisions of any Order in Council in that Behalf shall have effect as if they had been enacted by the Parliament of the United Kingdom of Great Britain and Ireland.

147. In case of the Admission of Newfoundland and Prince Edward Island, or either of them, each shall be entitled to a Representation in the Senate of Canada of Four Members, and (notwithstanding anything in this Act) in case of the Admission of Newfoundland the normal Number of Senators shall be Seventy-six and their maximum Number shall be Eighty-two; but Prince Edward Island when admit-

ted shall be deemed to be comprised in the third of the Three Divisions into which Canada is, in relation to the Constitution of the Senate, divided by this Act, and accordingly, after the Admission of Prince Edward Island, whether Newfoundland is admitted or not, the Representation of Nova Scotia and New Brunswick in the Senate shall, as Vacancies occur, be reduced from Twelve to Ten Members respectively, and the Representation of each of those Provinces shall not be increased at any Time beyond Ten, except under the Provisions of this Act for the Appointment of Three or Six additional Senators under the Direction of the Queen.

Glossary

Lords Spiritual and Temporal, and Commons	members of Parliament. At the time of the act, the lords spiritual were bishops. and the lords temporal were members of the hereditary peerage; they comprised the House of Lords. "Commons," representatives of the towns and cities, sat in the House of Commons, as they do today.
Ridings	electoral districts in Canada
Royal Sign Manual	the queen's handwritten signature
Sable Island	a sparsely populated island off Nova Scotia; protected under the Canada Shipping Act

CONSTITUTION OF THE FANTE CONFEDERACY

"We, the undersigned kings and chiefs of Fanti, have taken into consideration the deplorable state of our peoples."

Overview

In 1868 a group of chiefs of the Fante people, an ethnic group largely from the coastal region of modern-day Ghana, met at the town of Mankessim and founded the Fante Confederacy, often called the Fante Confederation. Then, in 1871, Fante leaders and members of the nascent educated class in the region wrote a new constitution designed to create the framework for Fante self-government; this constitution is sometimes referred to as the Mankessim Constitution. The Fante Confederacy was the product of several closely related factors, notably the growing threat of Europeans on the African coast, the need to check the centrifugal forces that fragmented the Fante states, and the ever-present fear of imperialism from the Ashanti (also spelled Asante) Empire in western Africa.

The period from the 1750s to the early nineteenth century was the great age of Ashanti expansion. The burgeoning Ashanti Empire had incorporated much of the area of modern-day Ghana, including the states of Gonja, Dagomba, Gyaman, Sefwi, and Anlo. The Fante states, however, had held their own in the face of the Ashanti peoples' remarkable war machine. The bone of contention between the two Akan powers ("Akan" referring to the larger ethnic group to which the two peoples belonged) was their relationship with the Europeans on the coast. The Ashanti Empire was landlocked and sought to enhance its economic position by gaining direct access to the coastal markets. The Fante states, in contrast, were unwilling to relinquish their strategic intermediary position in the lucrative trade with the Europeans. Ultimately, the Fante came together and created a confederacy with a written constitution that was intended to solidify their resistance to the Ashanti and gain the acceptance of the Europeans on the coast.

Context

The Fante are members of the Akan-speaking group of people. The historical evidence suggests that the Fante migrated from their homeland in the West African savanna to the West African coastal areas in the fifteenth century, whereupon they created self-contained farming communities. Agricultural production engendered population growth that increased the size of the Fante clans. These clans later coalesced into small states. The increased demand for gold, which newly arrived Europeans found in commercial quantities in the equatorial forests, would facilitate the growth of the Fante states. The Fante states were thus incorporated into the framework of international trade, which included the Portuguese and itinerant Dyula long-distance traders. (The Dyula, a caste of merchant-traders, were part of the larger Mandé ethnic group.) The Portuguese had embarked on voyages of exploration, in part to gain access to the rich gold-producing areas of the West African forests and also for the more distant objective of finding a direct sea route to the Far Eastern markets. The Dyula traders were the veritable intermediaries in the emerging trade, as they provided slaves to the Akan miners in exchange for gold. The slaves were deployed to the crucial task of clearing the forest for agricultural production.

The leaders of the Akan communities apportioned the newly opened arable land to immigrants in exchange for certain obligations. International trade took on a new dimension with the arrival of new European powers such as the Dutch, French, and British. The northern European powers, with their more advanced technology, not only began to supplant Portuguese power on the West African coast but also offered the Akan chiefs a wider range of manufactured goods, the most important one being firearms.

The acquisition of firearms bolstered the military power of the Akan states and facilitated the process of territorial expansion, especially by the Fante and the great inland Akan state, Ashanti. The wide-ranging opportunities created by international trade would exacerbate intra-Akan rivalry and pit one Akan state against the other. The Fante expansion was in part a consequence of their ability to capitalize on their strategic location by becoming middlemen in the productive trade between the Europeans and the states in the hinterland. In the closing years of the seventeenth century, the Fante expanded at the expense of the Etsii, who were earlier settlers in the area. Between 1700 and 1730, the Fante embarked upon wars of conquest against the non-Fante states in the coastal areas, including

1750s

- The Fante are in control of independent states along the coast of West Africa.

1800

- The Ashanti emerge as the most powerful of the Akan-speaking people.

1808

- Britain establishes a colony in Sierra Leone, which serves as a base from which to carry on a campaign against the slave trade.

1824

- An Ashanti offensive leads to the defeat of several Fante states as well as a British contingent led by Sir Charles MacCarthy.

1831

- George Maclean negotiates a treaty providing for Fante independence and Ashanti use of trade routes to the coast.

1843

- Britain takes over control of some forts on the coast of Ghana.

1850

- Britain buys out the Danes in Africa.

Asebu, Fetu, Aguafo, and Agona. The historical evidence suggests that up to the 1730s, the Fante created a cohesive group under the authority of the *braffo*, who also doubled as the king of Mankessim. The king of Mankessim also served as the chief priest of their deity.

The dominant themes in the history of the Fante from the mid-seventeenth century onward were the rivalry with the Ashanti from the powerful Akan state in the north and relations with the northern Europeans on the coast, especially the Danes, the Dutch, and the British. By the end of the eighteenth century, the Ashanti kingdom had emerged as the most powerful Akan state. The primary objective of the Ashanti was to annex the Fante states that blocked the path to direct access to the coastal markets. This was compounded by the Ashantis' accusations of flagrant malpractices by Fante merchants, including adulterating products such as gold and rum by mixing them with other substances. Further, the incessant closing of trade routes at the slightest rift exacerbated the dangerous tensions between the two Akan states. The Ashanti instigated three attacks on the Fante between 1727 and 1776, which all ended in a stalemate.

The stalemate that existed between the Ashanti and the Fante in the eighteenth century was to give way to a more aggressive, forward-looking policy by the Ashanti under the aegis of the indomitable Osei Bonsu. Asantehene ("king of the Ashanti") Osei Bonsu was determined to maintain the territorial integrity of the empire he had inherited from his illustrious predecessors. He was also committed to bringing to fruition the constitutional changes that they had begun. The reforms were intended to find a balance between the immense powers of the king and the demands of the provinces for political voice within the empire. The Fante, on the other hand, inserted themselves into the precarious politics of the Ashanti Empire by supporting provincial states, including Wassa, Akyem, and Akwapim, as they rose in protest against Ashanti overlordship.

The Fante kings sought to create a buffer zone of friendly states that would provide a bulwark against Ashanti imperialism and allow them to retain their middleman position. For Osei Bonsu, this position was untenable. In the early nineteenth century, he launched a series of attacks against the southern Akan states, including the Fante. In February 1824 the Ashanti defeated an army comprising the Wassa, Denkyira, Fante, and a British contingent under the leadership of Sir Charles MacCarthy. Shortly after this victory, Osei Bonsu died, but this was the Ashanti Empire's finest hour; it had reached the zenith of its power. This key moment in Ashanti's history was short-lived, as it put the empire on a collision course with the rising current of British imperialism.

The British had long been apprehensive of Ashanti dominance of the southern Akan states. The Ashantis' political control meant that they now held the forts and trading settlements along the coast and ultimately had the upper hand in international trade. This was a position that British trading companies on the coast and Christian missionaries who were on a proselytizing mission in African were unwilling to accept. These groups put pressure on the British government for a more aggressive policy toward Ashanti, which would allow them access to the interior. To this end, the British created an administrative system that gave a committee of merchants the authority over the forts. In addition, a governing council was created with executive functions. Captain George Maclean, who was the leader of the governing council from the mid-1820s to 1843, was able to fortify British control of the coastal areas primarily through skillful diplomatic relations with the Ashanti. In 1831, Maclean negotiated a treaty that provided for Fante independence but gave the Ashanti use of trade routes to the coast. Maclean's conciliatory leadership took the edge off Ashanti's imperial ambitions. Meanwhile, Maclean was behind a massive increase in trade: Exports from British forts increased from 90,000 pounds in 1830 to more than 325,000 pounds in 1840, while imports grew from 131,000 pounds to more than 422,000 pounds.

Nevertheless, some elements in the British community on the West African coast believed that Maclean's approach was not adequately advancing the interests of the trading companies and missionaries. He was replaced by the British Crown in 1843 but was retained as an official in the judiciary. Shortly afterward, the Crown signed treaties known as "bonds" with Fante chiefs. These treaties made the Fante states de facto British protectorates. In 1863 the Ashanti launched a massive offensive against the so-called protectorates. This invasion had two important consequences. First, it strengthened the resolve of the British government to conquer Ashanti. To this end, the British bought out the Dutch in February 1871 after the two nations agreed to exchange forts in 1869 in an effort to get out of each other's way. This exchange had led the king of the Ashanti to restate rather aggressively his claims to the former Dutch forts. Second, it set the stage for the emergence of the Fante Confederacy.

In the aftermath of the Ashanti offensive of 1863, great uncertainty grew regarding the future of the British presence on the West African coast. Although the Fante Confederacy was formed in 1868, the movement to bring the Fante states together in a union dates back to the 1830s. The movement, which comprised states such as Wassa, Denkyira, Assin, and Twifo (often spelled Twifu and Twifa) began, in part, in response to the expansion of British power and influence on the Gold Coast and also because of the ever-present fear of Ashanti control of the coast. This movement was galvanized by the nascent educated class that had been created by the tremendous economic gains made by the Fante states in the early nineteenth century and the social changes engendered by missionary activity on the Gold Coast.

The ascendancy of British power on the coast had led to the attenuation of the power of the traditional Fante chiefs and a diminution of the independence that the Fante had won from the Ashanti. In reaction to the curtailment of their power, various Fante states began to protest as early as the 1830s. First it was the king of Denkyira and then the king of Nzima. These protests were against the imposition of British law in the Fante states, the implementation of a poll tax, the enactment of an annual license fee of £2 sterling to be paid by sellers of alcoholic beverages, and the proposed plan to abolish domestic slavery.

The Fante Confederacy movement was also designed to rally a concerted effort against renewed Ashanti imperialism. This fear reached its apogee in the 1860s in the wake of the Ashanti invasion of 1863 and the tepid support given to the Fante by the British. The movement toward confederation of the coastal and inland Akan states gained a new sense of urgency with the Anglo-Dutch exchange of forts of March 1869. The exchange of forts between the British and the Dutch alarmed not only the Fante but also the Denkyira, Wassa, and Tonfu. The wishes of the southern Akan states were not taken into consideration before the exchange was made. Moreover, they feared that the areas that were controlled by the Dutch would be the weak link in the chain of resistance against Ashanti imperialism, for the Dutch were allies of the Ashanti. The Fante chiefs and members of the educated elite began making plans for educational, economic, and political reform. These plans would eventuate in the creation of the Fante Confederacy in 1868 and the writing of a new constitution in 1871.

Time Line

1863	■ The Ashanti launch a massive offensive against the British Fante protectorates.
1868	■ Fante chiefs create the Fante Confederacy.
1871	■ Britain buys out the Dutch in Africa. ■ Fante leaders and the educated elite create the Constitution of the Fante Confederacy.
1873	■ The Fante Confederacy ceases to exist.
1874	■ Britain annexes the Fante states.

About the Author

The Constitution of the Fante Confederacy was the brainchild of members of the emergent educated class. This class included such men as Joseph Smith, Henry Barnes, T. Hughes, Charles Bannerman, Africanus Horton, R. J. Ghartey, James F. Amissah, James Hutton Brew, and F. C. Grant (the first treasurer of the confederacy). Both Grant and Ghartey were respected parishioners in the Methodist Church, where they were receiving instruction to become ministers, and Ghartey was elected president of the confederacy shortly after it was formed (but before the constitution was written). These men were beneficiaries of the introduction of Western education by missionaries and the prosperity engendered by the expansion of international trade. The constitution they helped produce bears the imprint of their familiarity with Western political ideas.

The most prominent African who contributed to the drafting of the constitution was Africanus Horton, who was born James Beale Horton in 1835. Horton, from Sierra Leone, was an army surgeon who was educated at King's College in London and at Edinburgh University. As a medical student he took the name Africanus to reflect his pride in his African origins. He served as an officer in the British army and later worked as a banker and in the mining industry. His book titled *West African Countries and People* (1867) outlined the prerequisites for a self-governing Fante state. The book's subtitle, *Vindication of the African Race*, indicates that his other purpose in writing the book was to counter theories of racial supremacy that were growing more prevalent. Because of his writings, Horton is sometimes considered one of the fathers of African nationalism. After the chiefs met to form the confederacy, he wrote a series of letters to the British Colonial Office urging Great Britain officially to recognize the confederacy. These letters were published in 1870 as *Letters on the Political Condition of the Gold Coast*. After the confederacy was formed, Horton abandoned political writing. He retired from the army and devoted the remainder of his life to his business interests. He died in Freetown, Sierra Leone, on October 15, 1883.

Explanation and Analysis of the Document

The main objectives of the Constitution of the Fante Confederacy, as stated in the letter to the secretary of state for the colonies, were to enhance the economic, political, and social development of the Fante (called "Fanti" in the document). The constitution sought to improve the living standards of the people through the implementation of educational and industrial projects. The architects of the constitution were members of the growing educated class, who were familiar with the advances made by the Western European powers. They clearly saw in industrialized European countries examples of what their societies could achieve. The constitution, which is excerpted here, has forty-three articles, covering a broad range of issues. The most impor-tant of these issues are unity; economic, political and social development; and the creation of a legal system.

◆ Preamble and Articles 1–8

The constitution's preamble and Articles 1 through 8 focus on the issue of unity. The Fante states, for a large part of their history, were fragmented. This made them vulnerable to the incursions of the Ashanti kings. The constitution demonstrates that the kings and chiefs of the Fante states understood that only by creating a united front could they hope to maintain their independence. They recognized, moreover, that they could pursue their goals only if they had a politically stable environment. To this end, the constitution created an administrative system for the confederacy with certain key offices, namely, a president, vice president, secretary, undersecretary, treasurer, and assistant treasurer.

Article 8 spells out the goals of the confederation. The goals included but were not limited to fostering amicable relations among the various kings and chiefs of the Fante, creating an education system that would produce an informed and well-qualified group of public officials, opening up the hinterland to trade through the establishment of infrastructures such as roads, and ensuring economic development through industrialization and research into improved crop yields.

◆ Articles 9–20

In articles 9 through 20, the constitution created additional offices that were designed to facilitate the implementation of the policies of the Fante Confederacy. First, the constitution created an executive council. The articles also introduced the principle of representation into the system. For example, the kings and chiefs were each to have two representatives, "one educated, the other a chief or head-man of the district of such king and principal chief." All of the representatives would form a legislative council, which would be responsible for enacting laws. The assembly was to give a report of its activities at the end of every year.

Three aspects of articles 9 through 20 are particularly fascinating. First, the constitution provided for collaboration between members of the educated elite and the traditional political elite, as representatives of the people. It was clear that only through collaboration could the needs of the people be met. Second, the Representative Assembly was expected to present an annual report of its activities every October. The presentation of an annual report was considered important because it would ensure accountability. Third, and perhaps most important, the constitution imposed limits on the powers of the king. For example, article 18 states "that the king-president shall not have the power to pass any, or originate any laws … nor create any office or appointment, excepting by and under the advice of the ministry." Furthermore, article 20 stipulates that "members of the Ministry and Executive Council hold office for three years" and that the National Assembly could re-elect all or any of them or appoint others in their place.

Fort Prinzenstein on the coast of Ghana, built by the Dutch and ceded to the British (AP/Wide World Photos)

◆ **Articles 29–43**

Articles 29–43 provide the framework for a judicial system. For example, article 29 states that "provincial assessors" were to be appointed in "each province or district, who shall perform certain judicial functions." The constitution goes on to say in article 34 that it would be up to the undersecretary "to hear and determine, with an assistant appointed by the Secretary, cases which may be brought from the provincial courts" and "to arrange important appeal cases for the hearing of the Executive Council, which shall constitute the final court of appeal of the Confederation." Article 38 stipulates that the "Ministry and Executive Council" were to "hear, try and determine all important appeal cases brought before it by the under-secretary, option being allowed to any party or parties dissatisfied with the decision thereof to appeal to the British Courts." There is no question that the framers of the constitution recognized the importance of a legal system to the smooth running of any society. This probably explains why they established not only courts in the provincial states but also a system of appeals. It is also interesting to note that the constitution still recognized the British courts as the final arbiter in all judicial matters. As is stated in article 43:

"The officers of the Confederation shall render assistance as directed by the executive in carrying out the wishes of the British government."

Audience

The constitution of the new Fante Confederacy that was published in 1871 was truly a landmark document. It was intended for two main audiences. Clearly, it was designed to provide a rallying point for Fante nationalism. The Fante leaders and members of the educated class were the arrowhead of this incipient movement. The provisions of the constitution reflect a grand vision for the advancement of the economic, social, and political interests of the larger population of the Fante states. Additionally, since the constitution was addressed to the British secretary of state for the colonies, one can assume that the framers of the constitution were attempting to prove to the British authorities that they had the capacity not only to govern themselves but also to form modern political institutions that would create the conditions for political stability and economic development. Unfortunately for the Fante, the British government largely ignored it.

"We, the undersigned kings and chiefs of Fanti, have taken into consideration the deplorable state of our peoples and subjects,... and ... we are of opinion that unity and concord among ourselves would conduce to our mutual well-being, and promote and advance the social and political condition of our peoples and subjects, who are in a state of degradation, without the means of education and of carrying on proper industry."

(Preamble)

"That it be the object of the Confederation: To promote friendly intercourse between all the kings and chiefs of Fanti, and to unite them for offensive and defensive purposes against their common enemy."

(Article 8)

"That it be the duty of the Ministry and Executive Council: ...To hear, try and determine all important appeal cases brought before it by the under-secretary, option being allowed to any party or parties dissatisfied with the decision thereof to appeal to the British Courts."

(Article 38)

Impact

The 1871 Constitution of the Fante Confederacy is significant for a variety of reasons. First, it is a constitution that has all the hallmarks of a modern political document. It is important to remember that the constitution was written in the 1870s, during the early stages of the European conquest of Africa. This was a period that witnessed a heightened sense of the notion of African inferiority. Yet a group of educated Africans, with the support of traditional rulers, was able to fashion a document that reflected the enlightenment ideas of the rule of law; economic, political and social progress; and improved educational opportunities. Perhaps somewhat ironically, it was the very education that the British provided many of these men that enabled them to turn around and use British ideas to mount a self-determination movement.

Second, the constitution is a document that has a blueprint for economic development. For the framers of this constitution, economic development was not an end in itself but a means to enhance the social and economic well-being of the Fante people. They recognized the key role of good infrastructure and industrial projects in sustaining economic growth. Finally, the Constitution of the Fante Confederacy was a nationalist document. It was a document that sought to create the institutional framework for Fante unity, prosperity, and patriotism.

The Fante Confederacy, however, did not last, and a rapid succession of events led to its undoing. After it was formed, the confederacy created an army of some fifteen thousand soldiers. Under the leadership of King Otoo of Abura, the army marched to the coastal town of Komenda in an effort to prevent the Dutch from taking control of a fort that had been abandoned by the British. Otoo then tried to seize the coastal city of Elmina, the main center of Dutch influence, but this effort failed, and Otoo's forces became mired in a lengthy war. After the constitution was promulgated, it became apparent that the war was exhausting the confederacy's resources; efforts to collect a poll tax were unavailing, and the British resisted any attempt to tax trade in the area. Ghartey (along with his brother) tried to support the confederacy out of their own resources, but that money, too, was soon exhausted. The British were of little help in supporting the confederacy. While some in Britain welcomed the notion of a self-governing state in Africa, others saw it as a dangerous, anti-British development. Chief among these opponents was Charles Spencer Salomon, the British governor of the Gold Coast, who saw the confederacy as a treasonous conspiracy at a time when the "scramble for Africa"—a phrase often used to describe European competition for colonies in Africa and treaties designed to carve out spheres of influence—was at its height. Accordingly, he had various participants in the formation of the confederacy arrested.

Meanwhile, the Dutch were finding that the war was too costly and abandoned the Gold Coast, giving the British a free hand. The British agreed to help defend the Fante against the Ashanti in exchange for annexation of the Fante into Britain's Gold Coast colony. Accordingly, the confederacy dissolved in 1873, though both the confederacy and its constitution continue to serve as a rallying point. In the decades that followed, the Fante Confederacy and its constitution provided a model for other efforts toward self-determination in Africa. In 2007 the people of Ghana began celebrating the fiftieth anniversary of the confederacy's formation, and that nation's National Commission on Culture used the anniversary to call for formation of a new confederacy whose aims— the fight against colonialism, exploitation, poverty, illiteracy, disease and underdevelopment—would remain the same.

Further Reading

■ Articles

Fyfe, C. "Africanus Horton as a Constitution-Maker." *Journal of Commonwealth and Comparative Politics* 26, no. 2 (1988): 173–184.

Sanders, James. "The Expansion of the Fante and the Emergence of Asante in the Eighteenth Century." *Journal of African History* 20, no. 3 (1979): 349–364.

■ Books

Boahen, Adu. *African Perspective on Colonialism.* Baltimore, Md.: Johns Hopkins University Press, 1987.

Crowder, Michael. *West Africa under Colonial Rule.* Evanston, Ill.: Northwestern University Press. 1968.

Fage, J. D. *History of West Africa: An Introductory Survey,* 4th ed. London: Cambridge University Press, 1969.

Gocking, Roger S. *The History of Ghana.* Westport, Conn.: Greenwood Press, 2005.

Isichei, Elizabeth. *History of West Africa since 1800.* New York: Africana Publishing Company, 1977.

McCarthy, Mary. *Social Change and the Growth of British Power in the Gold Coast: The Fante States, 1807–1874.* Lanham, Md.: University Press of America, 1983.

—Ezekiel Walker and Michael J. O'Neal

Questions for Further Study

1. Describe how the Fante Confederacy became a first step toward African unity, as represented later by the Constitutive Act of the African Union.

2. Describe the role of economics and trade in the rivalry between the Ashanti and the Fante Confederacy.

3. Compare the role of the British in Ashanti-Fante relations with its role in India as reflected in such documents as the British Regulating Act and Queen Victoria's Proclamation concerning India.

4. Imperialism is often regarded derisively as characteristic of the European nations, which maintained colonies in Africa, Asia, the Americas, and the Middle East. To what extent did the imperialism of the Ashanti resemble the European imperialism that provided the context for such documents as Columbus's Letter to Raphael Sanxis on the Discovery of America, the D'Arcy Concession, or the Proclamation of the Algerian National Liberation Front?

5. How was the confederation of Fante states similar to and different from the confederation of Dutch states that formed the Dutch Republic at around the time of the Dutch Declaration of Independence? What cultural and historical factors would account for the differences? What common human aspirations would account for any similarities?

CONSTITUTION OF THE FANTE CONFEDERACY

To all whom it may concern.

Whereas we, the undersigned kings and chiefs of Fanti, have taken into consideration the deplorable state of our peoples and subjects in the interior of the Gold Coast, and whereas we are of opinion that unity and concord among ourselves would conduce to our mutual well-being, and promote and advance the social and political condition of our peoples and subjects, who are in a state of degradation, without the means of education and of carrying on proper industry; we, the said kings and chiefs, after having fully discussed and considered the subject at meetings held at Mankessim on the 16th day of October last and following days, have unanimously resolved and agreed upon the articles hereinafter named.

Article 1. That we, the kings and chiefs of Fanti here present, form ourselves into a committee with the view of effecting unity of purpose and of action between the kings and chiefs of the Fanti territory.

2. That we, the kings and chiefs here assembled, now form ourselves into a compact body for the purpose of more effectually bringing about certain improvements (hereinafter to be considered) in the country.

3. That this compact body shall be recognised under the title and designation of the "Fanti Confederation."

4. That there shall be elected a president, vice-president, secretary, under-secretary, treasurer and assistant-treasurer.

5. That the president be elected from the body of kings, and be proclaimed king-president of the Fanti Confederation.

6. That the vice-president, secretary and under-secretary, treasurer and assistant-treasurer, who shall constitute the ministry, be men of education and position.

7. That it be competent to the Fanti Confederation thus constituted to receive into its body politic any other king or kings, chief or chiefs, who may not now be present.

8. That it be the object of the Confederation:

i. To promote friendly intercourse between all the kings and chiefs of Fanti, and to unite them for offensive and defensive purposes against their common enemy.

ii. To direct the labours of the Confederation towards the improvement of the country at large.

iii. To make good and substantial roads throughout all the interior districts included in the Confederation.

iv. To erect school-houses and establish schools for the education of all children within the Confederation, and to obtain the service of efficient school-masters.

v. To promote agricultural and industrial pursuits, and to endeavour to introduce such new plants as may hereafter become sources of profitable commerce to the country.

vi. To develop and facilitate the working of the mineral and other resources of the country.

9. That an executive council be formed, composed of [the ministry] ... who shall be ex-officio members thereof, together with such others as may be hereafter from time to time appointed.

10. That in order that the business of the Confederation be properly carried on during the course of the year, each king and principal chief shall appoint two representatives, one educated, the other a chief or headman of the district of such king and principal chief, who shall attend the meetings which the secretary may deem necessary to convene for the deliberation of state matters.

11. That the representatives of the kings and chiefs assembled in council shall be known under the designation of the "Representative Assembly of the Fanti Confederation" and that this assembly be called together by the secretary as state exigency may require.

12. That this representative assembly shall have the power ... of exercising all the functions of a legislative body.

13. That the representatives of each king and chief be responsible to the nation for the effectual carrying out of the bills, resolutions &c passed at such meetings and approved of by the king-president....

15. That the National Assembly shall appoint an educated man to represent the king-president, and act as vice-president of the Confederation; and that the vice-president shall preside over all meetings convened by the secretary.

16. That there shall be in the month of October of each year, a gathering of the kings, principal chiefs, and others within the Confederation, when a recapitulation of the business done by the Representative Assembly shall be read, and the programme of the ensuing year discussed.

17. That at such meetings the king-president shall preside, and that it be the duty of the king-president to sanction all laws &c passed by the Representative Assembly, so far as they are compatible with the interests of the country.

18. That the king-president shall not have the power to pass any, or originate any laws … &c nor create any office or appointment, excepting by and under the advice of the ministry.

19. That the representatives of the kings and principal chiefs hold office as members of the Representative Assembly for three years, at the expiration of which it shall be competent for the kings and chiefs to reelect the same or appoint other representatives.

20. That the members of the Ministry and Executive Council hold office for three years, and that it be competent to the National Assembly to re-elect all or any of them and appoint others.…

[Articles 21–27. Details of school and road-building programme.]

28. That a site or town, unanimously agreed upon, be chosen as the nominal capital of the Confederation, where the principal business of the State should be conducted.

29. That provincial assessors be appointed in each province or district, who shall perform certain judicial functions and attend to the internal management thereof.…

[Articles 30–33. Duties of Secretary and Treasurer.]

34. That it be the duty of the undersecretary …

To hear and determine, with an assistant appointed by the Secretary, cases which may be brought from the provincial courts.

To arrange important appeal cases for the hearing of the Executive Council, which shall constitute the final court of appeal of the Confederation.…

[Articles 35–36. Duties of assistant-treasurer and provincial assessors.]

37. That in each province or district, provincial courts be established to be presided over by the provincial assessors.

38. That it be the duty of the Ministry and Executive Council:

To advise the King-President in all state matters.…

To hear, try and determine all important appeal cases brought before it by the under-secretary, option being allowed to any party or parties dissatisfied with the decision thereof to appeal to the British Courts.…

39. That three of the "ex-officio" members of the Executive Council, or two ex-officio and two non-official members of the Executive Council shall form a quorum of said Council.…

40. That one-third of the members composing the Representative Assembly shall form a quorum.

41. That all laws … &c be carried by the majority of votes in the Representative Assembly or Executive Council, in the latter the Vice-President possessing a casting vote.

42. That it be the duty of the National Assembly, held in October of each year …

To elect from the body of kings the President for the ensuing year.…

To consider all programmes laid before it by the Executive Council.…

To place on the "stool" in cases of disputed succession thereto, the person elected by the Executive Council, with the concurrence of the principal inhabitants of the town, croom or district.

43. That the officers of the Confederation shall render assistance as directed by the executive in carrying out the wishes of the British Government.

Glossary

croom	a municipal division between town and district
on the "stool"	in power in a given administrative division; an allusion to the Golden Stool, the symbol of the nationhood of the Ashanti people

Porfirio Díaz (Library of Congress)

TREATY OF LIMITS BETWEEN MEXICO AND GUATEMALA

"The Mexican Republic duly appreciates the conduct of Guatemala."

Overview

The Treaty of Limits between Mexico and Guatemala settled a long-standing controversy over the border between the two countries. According to the terms of the treaty, Guatemala renounced forever its claims to the Mexican state of Chiapas, including the District of Soconusco. From the time the region declared its independence from Spain in 1821, both Mexico and Guatemala had claimed Chiapas. The treaty decisively established the present-day location of the Mexico-Guatemala border and made most of the disputed territory a part of Mexico.

In addition to establishing the boundaries of modern-day Mexico and Guatemala, the treaty had important consequences for the future of both countries. Most directly, the signing of the treaty helped avert war between the two nations. Also, the easing of tensions with Mexico encouraged Guatemala to launch a disastrous military campaign to unify all of Central America under Guatemalan leadership. Over the long term, the treaty led to economic growth and a flood of foreign investment in agricultural products, especially coffee. The establishment of a clear border signaled to European and U.S. investors that their property rights would be secure, which ushered in a coffee boom and a period of rapid population growth and integrated Chiapas into the world economy.

Context

The border conflict between Mexico and Guatemala stretched back to the independence period. Under Spanish colonial rule, both present-day Mexico and Guatemala were part of the Viceroyalty of New Spain. When Mexico achieved independence in 1821, Central America stayed connected to Mexico. Both were a part of the short-lived Mexican Empire ruled by Agustín Iturbide. When Iturbide's empire collapsed in 1823, elites in Guatemala City announced the independence of Central America from Mexico and proclaimed the United Provinces of Central America. Beset by political and economic conflict, the United Provinces lasted only fifteen years before fracturing

into the five Central American nations of Guatemala, Honduras, Costa Rica, Nicaragua, and El Salvador in 1838.

Throughout these political transformations, the region known as Chiapas, and especially the southwestern portion that was known as Soconusco, was a constant source of conflict for Mexico and Central America. The primary reason was geographic. People living in the highlands, especially in the city of San Cristóbol de las Casas, had much in common with Mexico both economically and culturally. In the central valley and the lowlands of the Pacific coast, however, local elites had stronger economic and political ties to Guatemala than to the government in Mexico City. During the independence wars and the conflicts over Central American independence, Mexico and Guatemala fought for control of Chiapas. Finally, after several military invasions and a series of elections, the region was incorporated into Mexico as the state of Chiapas in 1824. However, many people in the region continued to feel closer ties to Guatemala than to Mexico, and Guatemala's leaders never gave up the idea that Chiapas was rightfully part of Guatemala. Throughout the first six decades of the nineteenth century, Chiapas remained a sparsely inhabited frontier region, and so finding a solution to the boundary conflict was not urgent.

However, the introduction and early success of large-scale commercial agriculture in the last third of the nineteenth century transformed the border controversy into a major problem for both countries. Throughout Central America, the lack of clear borders gave rise to instability that inhibited foreign investment. Central American nations fought wars over potentially lucrative border regions. In the 1860s and 1870s, Guatemala encouraged the establishment of coffee plantations in the border area, mostly by inviting German capitalists to purchase land and establish businesses. Mexican leaders sought to emulate this in Soconusco, yet both countries found that there was limited interest from U.S. and European investors while uncertainty over the exact location of the border persisted and war remained possible.

In addition, political changes during the 1870s in both countries brought the border question to a head. In Mexico, Porfirio Díaz became Mexico's president on November 29, 1876. With the exception of the period from 1880 to 1884, when Manuel González, a close associate of Díaz's, ruled in his stead, Díaz remained Mexico's president until 1911.

1873

■ **June 4**
Justo Rufino
Barrios becomes
president of
Guatemala.

1876

■ **November 29**
Porfirio Díaz
becomes
president of
Mexico.

1881

■ **July 9**
U.S. secretary of
state James G.
Blaine offers
U.S. arbitration
in Mexico and
Guatemala's
territorial
dispute. Mexico
refuses.

■ **December 19**
Blaine resigns from
his position as
secretary of state
and is replaced
by Frederick
Frelinghuysen, who
is less interested in
helping Guatemala
secure Chiapas.

1882

■ **July 10**
Barrios arrives in
the United States to
negotiate with
Mexican and U.S.
officials about the
border controversy.

■ **August 12**
A preliminary
agreement on the
border between
Mexico and
Guatemala,
negotiated primarily
by President Barrios
of Guatemala
and Mexican
representative Matías
Romero, is signed in
New York City.

■ **September 27**
The final treaty is
signed in Mexico
City.

One of the prime goals of the Díaz administration was to increase the power of the central government over Mexico's many regions in order to strengthen the unity of the country. After the Mexican-American War (1846–1848), in which Mexico lost over half its territory to the United States, Mexican leaders were especially keen on protecting the sovereignty of their country. The controversy over the border with Guatemala thus gained new urgency. Likewise, in Guatemala, a revolution led by Justo Rufino Barrios and Miguel García Granados in 1871 brought a new government with new priorities to power. For Barrios, who became president on June 4, 1873, a key goal was to reunify Central America under his leadership. The idea of a unified Central America appealed to the United States but worried Mexico.

Knowing the U.S. attitude, Guatemala attempted to involve the United States in the border dispute. In November 1881, after several attempts to persuade Mexico to agree to U.S. arbitration, Guatemala sent Lorenzo Montufar to the United States in one last effort to gain U.S. support for a favorable settlement of the border controversy. U.S. secretary of state James G. Blaine was highly receptive to the idea that the United States should arbitrate the conflict and determine the boundary. Guatemala hoped that U.S. support would result in Guatemala's gaining some or all of Chiapas. Mexico, however, remained solidly opposed to the idea of U.S. arbitration, seeing U.S. involvement as an attempt to meddle in Mexico's affairs. These maneuverings increased the tension between Mexico and Guatemala throughout 1881 and had the potential to erupt into war. However, Blaine left his position as secretary of state on December 19, 1881, and was replaced by Frederick Frelinghuysen. Frelinghuysen was much less supportive of Guatemala's claim to Chiapas. President Barrios, sensing a major shift in U.S. policy regarding the border issue, decided to travel to the United States personally to investigate the situation. Barrios knew that without U.S. support, Guatemala would have no chance of realizing its claims to Chiapas. Meanwhile, there was his larger aim of unifying Central America. Barrios decided that the larger goal would best be served by diffusing tensions with Mexico by giving in to Mexican demands and putting an end to the border controversy. On July 10, 1882, Barrios arrived in the United States. For the next several weeks, Barrios negotiated with Mexican minister Matías Romero over the terms of a treaty. On August 12, 1882, the same day Barrios was leaving the United States for Europe, the two men signed a preliminary agreement that affirmed Mexico's rights to Chiapas. Barrios appointed Manuel Herrera to be his special envoy and left the drafting of the treaty's language to him. Herrera and Mexican foreign secretary Ignacio Mariscal then crafted the final version of the treaty (formally titled Treaty on the Delimitation of the Frontier between Mexico and Guatemala) and signed it in Mexico City on September 27, 1882.

About the Author

Many people played a role in the discussions that led to the Treaty of Limits. During the negotiations of 1881,

Guatemala sent Lorenzo Montufar to the United States to persuade the United States to intervene in the boundary dispute. Montufar was a career diplomat and a close associate of Barrios's. He had served for several years as Guatemala's secretary of state and was well respected by many U.S. officials as a man who knew and understood the politics and culture of the United States. Montufar's appeals were made to the U.S. secretary of state, James Blaine. Blaine was a well-known politician who had been elected to both the House of Representatives and the Senate before becoming secretary of state. He adamantly believed that the United States could help prevent wars in the hemisphere by mediating disputes between nations. For this reason, he was receptive to Montufar's suggestions that the United States should try to arbitrate the border controversy and persuade Mexico to submit to U.S. arbitration.

With these events of 1881 as the background, the second round of negotiations over the treaty were carried out in the United States by President Barrios himself and by Matías Romero, who was then serving as Mexico's minister to the United States. Barrios was a general and a staunch nationalist. Upon his ascent to power in 1873, it became immediately clear that Barrios believed Guatemala had rights to territory in Mexico and Belize. It was also clear that he dreamed of uniting Central America under his leadership. Barrios was willing to engage in warfare to achieve his goals, as demonstrated by the short war he provoked in 1876 with El Salvador. Romero, in contrast, was a civilian who had worked loyally on behalf of various Mexican governments since 1857. He had served as the secretary of the treasury and had held various appointments in which he represented Mexico in the United States. Romero was a true diplomat, but he, too, was a strident nationalist who placed a high value on defending Mexico's sovereignty and its independence. Interestingly, Romero and Barrios despised each other. Both owned property in the disputed border area. Barrios believed that during the 1870s Romero was acting as a spy for Mexico while living in Chiapas. For his part, Romero thought Barrios had tried to have him killed.

Despite these resentments, Barrios and Romero agreed in principle to a treaty that would give Mexico unquestioned rights over Chiapas and Soconusco. They signed a preliminary agreement on August 12, 1882, which formed the basis of the final version of the treaty. The closing round of negotiations was undertaken by Manuel Herrera, whom Barrios appointed to finalize the treaty, and Ignacio Mariscal, who was Mexico's foreign minister. Like Romero, Mariscal was a determined nationalist who distrusted both Guatemala and the United States. Herrera was a close confidant of President Barrios's and was instructed to act on his behalf to finalize the treaty.

Explanation and Analysis of the Document

The treaty's introductory paragraph outlines its purpose and goals. It states that the treaty would resolve the con-

Time Line

1883

■ **May 1**
The treaty enters into force after ratifications are exchanged in Mexico City.

1885

■ **February 28**
Barrios proclaims the unification of Central America under his leadership. He meets resistance to this decree, especially from Rafael Zaldívar, president of El Salvador and so begins preparing his army for war.

■ **April 2**
Barrios is killed in the Battle of Chalchuapa while leading Guatemalan forces against El Salvadoran forces led by Rafael Zaldívar.

1895

■ **April 1**
A convention signed in Mexico City concludes the work of two scientific commissions and finalizes the Treaty of Limits between Mexico and Guatemala by clarifying the last details of the border.

flicts between the two countries "amicably." In the months before the signing of the treaty, tensions between Mexico and Guatemala over the definition of the border had reached a point where war seemed possible. The treaty was thus intended to prevent war by settling the boundary conflict. The introductory paragraph also establishes the official credentials of the treaty's negotiators and authorizes them to act on behalf of their respective governments.

Frederick Frelinghuysen (Library of Congress)

Most important, the introductory paragraph makes reference to the preliminary agreement that was signed in New York City on August 12, 1882. The treaty states that the negotiators have written the treaty while "bearing in mind" the preliminary agreement. This vague language did not do much to clarify how the treaty's authors were supposed to treat the preliminary agreement. In fact, there were important differences between the preliminary agreement and the final version of the treaty. Most significant, the preliminary agreement included an article that stipulated that in the case of any dispute over the border, both countries agreed to submit the matter to U.S. arbitration, whereas the final version of the treaty did not. During the original negotiations of July and August 1882, Barrios had insisted on including the arbitration article as a condition of signing the agreement. His Mexican counterpart, Matías Romero, eventually agreed to the article despite not having received permission from the government in Mexico City.

The issue of arbitration was contentious for both sides. From Barrios's perspective, excluding arbitration would have made it seem to many of his countrymen that he had simply voluntarily given up parts of Guatemala. For Mexico, agreeing to U.S. arbitration was undesirable because it gave the appearance that the United States was meddling in Mexico's internal affairs. Although Barrios had insisted that arbitration was a necessary condition for the treaty, during the drafting of the final document, Mexican foreign secretary Ignacio Mariscal demanded that it be left out. Barrios was not present for the drafting of the treaty in Mexico City, and Manuel Herrera, acting as Barrios's representative, agreed to the removal of arbitration from the final version. Thus, although U.S. arbitration of the boundary dispute was included in the preliminary agreement, it was excluded from the final version of the treaty, causing considerable embarrassment and political difficulty for President Barrios.

◆ Article I

This article states that Guatemala renounces all its rights to the territory of Chiapas, including the District of Soconusco. Although it is brief, this article was the result of considerable bargaining. During the original round of negotiations in New York, Barrios did not want to agree to an article that made it appear as if Guatemala never had any rights to the disputed territory, since for several decades successive Guatemalan governments had loudly insisted that Chiapas belonged to Guatemala. The original language submitted by the Mexican side stated that Guatemala "renounces the rights which until now she has had or believed to have had, upon the territory of the State of Chiapas." The Guatemalan negotiators wanted language that would affirm that Guatemala did have a legitimate claim to the territory. Since the result was the same either way, Romero was persuaded to phrase the article more in line with Guatemala's desires.

◆ Article II

In Article II, Guatemala promises not to seek any money from Mexico in exchange for renouncing its rights to the disputed territory. As in Article I, the key issue was the legitimacy of Guatemala's claims to Chiapas. In this article, by agreeing not to seek compensation, Guatemala was bolstering Mexico's claims that the territory had always belonged to Mexico. During negotiations that took place in 1881 and early 1882, Guatemala had presented to Mexican officials an offer that ceded all of Chiapas in exchange for $4 million. This offer was rejected quickly, not only because Mexico did not want to pay for land it already considered part of Mexico but also because agreeing to compensation would give more weight to Guatemala's claims to the territory.

◆ Article III

This very important article establishes the exact border between the two countries. The treaty was a validation of all Mexico's claims to the region. In exchange for small portions of the Mexican states of Tabasco and Campeche, Mexico gained clear title to the entire state of Chiapas, including the district of Soconusco. The border was fixed by referring to both astronomical calculations of latitude lines and geographic locations such as the summits of hills and town squares. This method was necessary because there was considerable confusion about the geography of the region being surveyed. The preliminary agreement signed in New York discussed only the border between Guatemala and the Mexican state of Chiapas. However, during the drafting of the actual treaty, the Mexican side insisted that the treaty establish the entire length of the Mexico-Guatemala border. This proved to be difficult because of the lack of accurate maps of northern Guatemala and the Mexican state of Campeche.

◆ Article IV

This article paved the way for the establishment of two scientific commissions to survey the dividing line between the two countries, produce accurate maps of the region, and place markers on the ground that clearly delineated the border. The article requires both commissions to convene no later than six months from the treaty's ratification. It also states that the work should take no more than two years. It makes clear that if either country failed to send its commission within the allotted time, the other country would be authorized to proceed with surveying and mapmaking, and the results were to be legally binding. Mexican negotiators inserted these phrases because they worried that if Barrios left office, future Guatemalan presidents would drag their feet about finalizing the treaty by delaying the work of surveying. The treaty was extremely unpopular in Guatemala, and although Barrios had agreed to renounce his country's rights to the territory, Mexico feared that future leaders would find a way to invalidate the terms of the treaty. In fact, after the death of Barrios on April 2, 1885, Guatemalan leaders did try to obstruct the finalization of the border by disputing many of the Mexican commission's findings. Eventually, however, both countries were able to agree on an exact boundary that could be affixed on maps. On April 1, 1895, both nations signed a convention that ratified the work of the two scientific commissions and determined the present-day boundary line.

◆ Article V

This article laid out the rights of people living in the ceded territory. First, it established a process for determining citizenship. People who lived in areas affected by the treaty could choose to be either Mexican or Guatemalan citizens. The treaty gave them one year from the date of ratification to announce their choice. Those who after one year had taken no action would automatically become citizens of the country in which, according to the terms of the treaty, they now lived. The treaty is vague about the precise steps required in order to achieve citizenship. In practice, few people changed their citizenship as a result of the treaty. In addition to citizenship rights, Article V guaranteed the property of people affected by the treaty. It assured property holders that their rights would be respected, that they were free to retain or sell their property, and that they would be exempt from any kind of special taxation if they sold their land or passed it to an heir. This provision had special importance for the negotiators of the treaty, since both Romero and Barrios owned large plantations in Chiapas. Neither man trusted the other one, and each of them worried that his property would be threatened if it suddenly became part of the other country. In any event, Barrios negotiated the boundary line defining the district of Soconusco so that his plantation would remain in Guatemala.

◆ Article VI

This article required that the commissions of both countries submit, within six months from the time they began their work, a list of the "villages, estates, and farms" that were "beyond any doubt" in either Mexico or Guatemala. The article's primary intention was to give clear authority to the governments of both Mexico and Guatemala to begin asserting their sovereignty, primarily by collecting taxes, as soon as possible. By agreeing on the list, both countries could govern their territories without having to wait for the completion of the commissions' work.

◆ Article VII

The last article of the treaty calls for the ratification of the treaty as soon as possible. In Mexico this was essentially guaranteed to happen without much debate. President Díaz controlled the Mexican Congress and was easily able to secure ratification. In addition, the treaty was well received in Mexico and considered by many Mexicans to be a vindication of long-held claims. The situation in Guatemala was more complex. Barrios held substantial power over the Guatemalan Congress, but the treaty's renunciation of Guatemala's rights made many angry. Barrios felt compelled to address these concerns in a carefully worded messaged he sent to the Guatemalan Congress on December 1, 1882, along with the request for ratification. Despite the opposition to the treaty, Barrios exercised enough control over Congress to secure the treaty's ratification on May 1, 1883.

Audience

The treaty was written with several audiences in mind. From Mexico's perspective, the treaty was intended in part as a message to the United States that Mexico would stand up to U.S. interference in its affairs. Throughout the period of bargaining during 1881 and 1882, Mexico consistently rejected offers of U.S. arbitration. By achieving its territorial aims without direct U.S. involvement, Mexico hoped to send a message to the United States that it was a major power capable of achieving its foreign policy goals. The leaders of the four other Central American nations were another important audience for the treaty. Before those nations, too, Mexico intended the treaty to be a sign that Mexico was a leader in the region and able to act independently of the United States in pursuit of its own interests. From Guatemala's perspective, the resolution of the border conflict with Mexico signaled to the rest of Central America that Barrios's plans for uniting the region under his leadership would no longer be impeded by the possibility of a war with Mexico. Finally, both countries wrote the treaty in large measure for foreign investors. As export crops such as coffee gained importance, both Mexico and Guatemala wanted to send a message to European and U.S. investors that the region was safe, secure, and a good place in which to invest. By putting to rest a long-standing source of conflict in the region, the treaty was meant as an invitation to foreigners to buy land and develop the region's agriculture.

Impact

The most immediate impact of the treaty was that it led to war in Central America. By ending the conflict with Mexico over the border, Barrios gained confidence that he could pursue the unification of Central America without having to worry about a possible conflict with Mexico over Chiapas. On February 28, 1885, Barrios announced the unification of Central America and proclaimed himself supreme military commander. Although it seemed at first that Barrios had enough support to achieve his goal, his displays of aggression alienated many of his initial supporters. When Salvadoran president Rafael Zaldívar refused to agree to the union, Barrios prepared his armies to attack El Salvador. This willingness to use force provoked the other Central American countries into a military alliance. Mexico and even the United States, which generally looked favorably upon the idea of unification, also opposed Barrios. Despite the opposition, Barrios proceeded to invade El Salvador, where he met his death at the Battle of Chalchuapa, putting an end to his plans.

The treaty also had long-term impacts. As intended, the settlement of the boundary question prompted a wave of foreign investment into Chiapas. As world demand for coffee continued to grow, foreigners rushed to invest in coffee plantations in the region. German investors were the most successful; by 1909 three-quarters of the coffee planta-

"*The Republic of Guatemala renounces for ever the rights which it deems it has to the territory of the State of Chiapas and its district of Soconusco, and consequently considers that territory an integral part of the United Mexican States.*"

(Article I)

"*The Mexican Republic duly appreciates the conduct of Guatemala, acknowledging that the ends which have prompted it to make the above renunciation are as worthy as they are honourable, and declares that in the same circumstances Mexico would have agreed to a similar disclaimer. Guatemala, being for its part satisfied with this acknowledgement and this solemn declaration, shall seek no compensation of any kind on account of the foregoing stipulation.*"

(Article II)

"*Each of the two Governments shall appoint a Scientific Commission to draw the dividing line with due precision on reliable maps and to erect markers on the ground clearly specifying the boundaries of the two Republics as described in the preceding article. The two Commissions shall meet at Union Juarez, six months at the latest from the date on which the instruments of ratification of this Treaty are exchanged and shall immediately begin work on the operations indicated.*"

(Article IV)

"*Property of any kind situated in the ceded territories shall be deemed inviolable; and the present owners, their heirs, and persons who may in future legally acquire such property shall enjoy the same guarantees in respect of the property as if it belonged to nationals of the country in which it is situated.*"

(Article V)

tions in Chiapas were in the hands of families of German descent. These businessmen received considerable funding from German banks. This economic development led to the doubling of Chiapas's population between 1877 and 1910. Thus, Chiapas became a good example of the increasing globalization of the world economy in the late nineteenth century. World demand for coffee encouraged Mexico and Guatemala to codify the boundaries of Chiapas. By accomplishing this goal, the Treaty of Limits prompted investment by German firms using German money. These changes transformed Chiapas from a frontier area into an important part of the world economy.

Further Reading

■ Articles

Palmer, Stephen. "Central American Union or Guatemalan Republic? The National Question in Liberal Guatemala." *Americas* 49, no. 4 (April 1993): 513–530.

Romero, Matías. "Settlement of the Mexico-Guatemala Boundary Question." *Journal of the American Geographical Society of New York* 29, no. 2 (1897): 123–159.

———. "Mr. Blaine and the Boundary Question between Mexico and Guatemala." *Journal of the American Geographical Society of New York* 29, no. 3 (1897): 281–330.

■ Books

Benjamin, Thomas. *A Rich Land, a Poor People: Politics and Society in Modern Chiapas.* Albuquerque: University of New Mexico Press, 1996.

Buchenau, Jürgen. *In the Shadow of the Giant: The Making of Mexico's Central America Policy, 1876–1930.* Tuscaloosa: University of Alabama Press, 1996.

Coerver, Don M. *The Porfirian Interregnum: The Presidency of Manuel González of Mexico, 1880–1884.* Fort Worth: Texas Christian University Press, 1979.

Woodward, Ralph Lee. *Central America: A Nation Divided.* Oxford, U.K.: Oxford University Press, 1999.

■ Web Sites

"History: Guatemala." Library of Congress "Portals to the World" Web site.

   http://www.loc.gov/rr/international/hispanic/guatemala/resources/guatemala-history.html.

"History: Mexico." Library of Congress "Portals to the World" Web site.

   http://www.loc.gov/rr/international/hispanic/mexico/resources/mexico-history.html.

—Ben Fulwider

Questions for Further Study

1. Why do you think this region of the world, encompassing Mexico and the Central American states, fractured as it did in the wake of Spanish withdrawal from the region? What insights would the Treaty of Córdoba provide in response to this question?

2. In what ways might the content of Columbus's Letter to Raphael Sanxis on the Discovery of America have prefigured the disputes that would arise more than three centuries later and that led to the Treaty of Limits?

3. Mexico also had border disputes to the north, with the United States. How might the terms of the 1848 Treaty of Guadalupe Hidalgo have influenced Mexican attitudes toward U.S. intervention in Mexico's dispute with Guatemala?

4. Often, particular commodities have played an important role in world affairs: silk and spices in Asia, sugar in the early Spanish colonies of the New World, oil in the Middle East, and coffee in Central America. What commodity do you think might come to dominate world affairs over the twenty-first century? Why?

5. What interests did the United States have in effecting a peaceful settlement of the Mexico-Guatemala border dispute? Where any of those interests economic?

Treaty of Limits between Mexico and Guatemala

The Governments of Mexico and Guatemala, seeking to resolve amicably the difficulties existing between the two Republics, have decided to conclude a treaty to achieve such a desirable objective; and to that end have appointed their respective plenipotentiaries; namely, the President of the Mexican Republic: Mr. Ignacio Mariscal, Secretary of the Office of Foreign Affairs; and the President of the Republic of Guatemala: Mr. Manuel Herrera, Jr., Envoy Extraordinary and Minister Plenipotentiary to the Government of Mexico; who, having exchanged their respective powers, found in due form, and bearing in mind the preliminary arrangements signed by the representatives of the two nations in New York City, United States of America, on 12 August 1882, have agreed as follows:

◆ Article I

The Republic of Guatemala renounces for ever the rights which it deems it has to the territory of the State of Chiapas and its district of Soconusco, and consequently considers that territory an integral part of the United Mexican States.

◆ Article II

The Mexican Republic duly appreciates the conduct of Guatemala, acknowledging that the ends which have prompted it to make the above renunciation are as worthy as they are honourable, and declares that in the same circumstances Mexico would have agreed to a similar disclaimer. Guatemala, being for its part satisfied with this acknowledgement and this solemn declaration, shall seek no compensation of any kind on account of the foregoing stipulation.

◆ Article III

The frontier between the two nations shall for ever be as follows: (1) the line running along the centre of the River Suchiate from a point situated in the sea three leagues from the mouth of the river, upstream through its deepest channel, so far as the point at which the river intersects the vertical plane passing through the highest point of the volcano of Tacana, 25 metres from the southernmost pier of the customs booth at Talquian, leaving the booth in Guatemalan territory; (2) the line formed by the vertical plane described above, from the point at which the plane meets the River Suchiate to its intersection with the vertical plane passing through the summits of Buenavista hill and Ixbul hill; (3) the line formed by the vertical plane passing through the summit of Buenavista hill, previously determined astronomically by the Mexican Scientific Commission, and through the summit of Ixbul hill, from its intersection with the preceding line up to a point four kilometres beyond Ixbul; (4) the parallel of latitude running through the latter point and thence eastwards until it meets the deepest channel of the River Usumacinta, or of the River Chixoy should the said parallel not meet the first-mentioned river; (5) the median line of the deepest channel, either of the Usumacinta in the one case, or of the Chixoy and then of the Usumacinta and continuing along the latter in the other case, from the point at which either river meets the aforesaid parallel so far as the point at which the deepest channel of the Usumacinta meets the parallel situated 25 kilometres south of Tenosique, in the State of Tabasco, as measured from the centre of the town square; (6) the last-mentioned parallel of latitude, from its intersection with the deepest channel of the Usumacinta so far as the point at which it meets the meridian passing at one third of the distance between the centres of the squares of Tenosique and Sacluc, as reckoned from Tenosique; (7) this meridian, from its intersection with the aforesaid parallel so far as latitude seventeen degrees forty-nine minutes (17° 49'); (8) the parallel of seventeen degrees forty-nine minutes (17° 49'), running indefinitely eastwards from its intersection with the aforesaid meridian.

◆ Article IV

Each of the two Governments shall appoint a Scientific Commission to draw the dividing line with due precision on reliable maps and to erect markers on the ground clearly specifying the boundaries of the two Republics as described in the preceding article. The two Commissions shall meet at Union Juarez, six months at the latest from the date on which the instruments of ratification of this Treaty are exchanged and shall immediately begin work on the operations indicated. They shall keep daily records and establish schedules; and the result of their work, mutually approved, shall be considered part of this Treaty and shall have the same force as the provisions thereof. The deadline for completing the said operations shall be two years from the date on which the Commissions meet. If either of the two fails to appear within the six-month period established above, the other shall begin its work notwithstanding; and the work it carries out separately shall have the same force and validity as if it had been done by both Commissions. The two Governments shall conclude as soon as possible an arrangement for determining the details relating to these Commissions and their work.

◆ **Article V**

Nationals of either of the two Contracting Parties who, by virtue of the provisions of this Treaty, shall henceforth be residing in territories of the other may remain there or move at any time elsewhere as they prefer, either keeping any property they may possess in the former territories or disposing of it and transferring its value wherever they may wish, such transfer being exempt from all levies, charges or taxes. Persons who prefer to remain in the ceded territories may either retain the status and rights of nationals of the country to which the said territories previously belonged or acquire the nationality of the country to which they shall henceforth belong. However, they must opt for one nationality or the other within one year from the date on which the instruments of ratification of this Treaty are exchanged; and persons who remain in the said territories after the year has elapsed without having declared their intention of retaining their former nationality shall be deemed to be nationals of the other Contracting Party.

Property of any kind situated in the ceded territories shall be deemed inviolable; and the present owners, their heirs, and persons who may in future legally acquire such property shall enjoy the same guarantees in respect of the property as if it belonged to nationals of the country in which it is situated.

◆ **Article VI**

It being the objective of the two Governments in concluding this Treaty not only to put an end to the difficulties existing between them but also to resolve or avoid any which arise or may arise between neighbouring towns in either country because of uncertainty as to what is now the dividing line, it is stipulated that, within their first six months of meetings, the Scientific Commissions referred to in article IV shall send to their respective Governments an agreed list of those villages, estates and farms which are situated beyond any doubt on a particular side of the dividing line agreed upon in article III. Upon receipt of this list, each of the two Governments shall have the right to issue forthwith appropriate orders establishing its authority in those localities which are situated within its national territory.

◆ **Article VII**

This Treaty shall be ratified in accordance with the Constitution of each of the two Republics; and the instruments of ratification shall be exchanged at Mexico City as soon as possible.

In Witness Whereof, the Plenipotentiaries have signed this Treaty and affixed their seals thereto. Done at Mexico City, in two originals on 27 September 1882.

[Ignacio Mariscal]
[Manuel Herrera]

Emperor Meiji (Library of Congress)

Meiji Constitution of Japan

"The Emperor is sacred and inviolable."

Overview

Towns across Japan celebrated with fireworks and feasts when Emperor Meiji promulgated the country's first constitution on February 11, 1889, while journalists around the globe recorded the popular joy. The exuberance was prompted as much by the constitution's symbolism as by its contents. The result of a decade of preparation, the document represented an era of modernization, when Japan had moved quickly from premodern authoritarianism to monarchical constitutionalism, from the clip-clops of horse travel to the clickety-clack of rickshaws and the roar of trains. With the emperor's pronouncement, Japan became the first Asian nation to operate under a modern, democratic constitution.

Among constitutions of the nineteenth century this document took a center-right approach, balancing imperial sovereignty with the elective powers of the people. The Meiji Constitution made the rule of law foundational; gave citizens limited freedom of speech, property, and religion; granted the legislature veto power over budgets; and set up an independent judiciary. At the same time, it created a powerful executive branch that was aloof from the legislature and placed final power for almost everything in the emperor. The Meiji Constitution would serve as the country's fundamental law until 1947, when the Shōwa Constitution replaced it following Japan's defeat in World War II.

Context

The Meiji Constitution was the culmination of two generations of national transformation. The changes had begun in earnest in 1854, when the ruling Tokugawa shogunate signed the Kanagawa Treaty with U.S. Commodore Matthew Perry, ending two centuries of Japanese isolation from most Western nations by opening two ports to American ships and providing for an American consulate in Japan. Four years later the 1858 Harris Treaty opened four more ports and initiated trade. Although the treaties were criticized by the Japanese as "unequal" because of the tariff and legal restrictions that they imposed on the coun-

try, they played an important role in bringing Japan into the global trade and diplomatic system.

Tokugawa officials put a great deal of energy into managing successful relations with the Western nations after Perry's incursion, but their rule was plagued by a spiraling set of problems: cumbersome administrative structures, serious financial crises, and rising opposition from a number of regional lords. Tradition-bound officials also found it difficult to conceive of the new approaches to governance that were demanded by the imperialist threat. As a result, when an ad hoc group of samurai staged an uprising—called the Meiji Restoration—in January 1868, the Tokugawa quickly fell. The coup leaders, whose youngest member was the twenty-seven-year-old Itō Hirobumi from the western domain of Chōshū, quickly set out to move the nation in new directions. Acting in the name of the teenaged Emperor Meiji (whose birth name was Mutsuhito) but with little of his input, they moved the emperor from his ancient Kyoto palace to Edo (today's Tokyo), announced their determination to broaden the base of government, and set out to make Japan an international power.

Within a generation, change had forced its way into every mountain valley and urban alley of Japan. Modern prefectures replaced feudal daimyo domains. Japanese silks were being produced for Europe's trade centers. The world's first nationwide compulsory education system was adopted, along with a military draft and a standardized land-tax system. City streets displayed newspaper offices, brick buildings, beer halls, and a twelve-story tourist tower in Tokyo replete with an elevator and foreign gift shops. And officials worked endlessly on creating a government structure that would help them centralize power and make Japan strong. They also began talking, almost from the first, about the need for a constitutional system of government, partly to enable Japan to emulate Western political systems and partly to satisfy domestic critics.

Two events sped up the movement toward constitutionalism. In 1874 several men who had left the Meiji government in a dispute over policies submitted a petition to the throne, recommending the creation of a national legislature, on the ground that "the people whose duty it is to pay taxes to the government have the right of sharing in their government's affairs" (de Bary, p. 54). The memorial

1854

- The Kanagawa Treaty opens Japan to American ships and diplomats.

1858

- The Harris Treaty, initiating trade, limits Japan's right to levy tariffs or exercise legal control over foreigners.

1868

- The Meiji Restoration overthrows the Tokugawa regime, ushering in an era of change meant to make Japan a great power.

1874

- A petition written to the throne by several men who left the Meiji government in a dispute over policies calls for forming a legislature and sparks constitutional debates.

- The "freedom and popular rights" movement begins to demand the formation of a legislature and the creation of a constitution.

1881

- An imperial edict promises preparations for a constitution and the convening of legislature by 1890.

sparked Japan's first newspaper editorial debates, with writers on all sides calling for the creation of a national assembly but arguing over the assembly's makeup and the kind of constitution needed to make an assembly government effective. Those debates inspired a "freedom and popular rights" movement that involved thousands of petitioners and speakers who demanded a voice in government. The second event was a corruption crisis in 1881, prompted by the secret sale of public properties to government insiders. When the press learned of the sale, uproar ensued, with critics complaining loudly that without a constitution or legislature they had no way to make officials accountable. To quiet the uproar, the emperor announced in October that a constitution would be drafted and a legislature would be convened by 1890.

For the next seven years beginning in 1881, officials devoted themselves to laying the groundwork for constitutional governance. When Japan's first political parties emerged in response to the promise of a legislature, officials encouraged the formation of a pro-government counterpart. In 1882, Itō Hirobumi, who had been given responsibility for drafting the constitution, left on a trip to Europe, where he would spend more than a year studying governing systems, primarily in Germany and Austria. Upon his return, he worked with several advisers to develop a document that would make the emperor supreme yet provide a modicum of popular political input. In preparation for constitutional government, officials created a peerage (1884) that was designed as a pool for the upper house of a bicameral legislature, initiated a cabinet (1885) that would stand between the emperor and the legislature (with Itō as the first prime minister), and formed a civil service system (1887). They also enacted laws regulating speech and publication in a sometimes draconian effort to assure public tranquility under constitutional rule. Once the constitutional draft was completed in April 1888, forty-four secret discussion sessions of the Privy Council, a small body created in 1888 to advise the emperor, allowed cabinet members and a few other top officials to suggest changes. A draft then was approved, and the constitution was promulgated on February 11, 1889.

About the Author

The Meiji Constitution was drafted by a team led by Itō Hirobumi. Although he was only forty, Itō was already highly experienced in national affairs when the imperial edict was issued in 1881. Studies in England before the Meiji Restoration had convinced him that Japan must modernize along Western lines. They also had given him the expertise to earn appointment as the overseer of foreign affairs in the new Meiji government. By the end of the 1870s, after taking a series of top-level posts in a variety of governmental divisions, he generally was regarded as one of the country's two or three most powerful men—an intimate of the Meiji Emperor, equally at home with foreign affairs and domestic administration.

To draft the constitution, Itō chose a team of men even younger than he: his protégé Itō Miyoji, who was twenty-four when the edict was issued; Inoue Kowashi, age thirty-seven, who had studied European constitutions in the 1870s; and Kaneko Kentarō, age twenty-eight, who had studied law at Harvard University. Youth did not make these men liberal, however. All of them had a strong traditionalist bent, and all were determined to create a strong, emperor-centered state.

Assisting the constitutional team were several German scholars, foremost among them Hermann Roesler, a former professor at the University of Rostock. Brought to Japan as part of a broader government policy of hiring foreigners to give advice on modernizing the country, he had been giving legal advice to the foreign ministry since 1878. Roesler took part in all of the constitutional drafting discussions and played a key role in the decision to create a "social monarchy" that placed the emperor at the center but balanced his authority by ensuring the rights of citizens through elections and the rule of law. The Emperor Meiji attended all of the review sessions once the initial draft was completed, but as in other governmental matters, he had little impact on the content.

Explanation and Analysis of the Document

Journalists and patriots universally praised the Meiji Constitution in 1889 as a sign of Japan's modernity. Scholars since then have been more nuanced, asking endless questions about the document's philosophy, balance, and impact. Was the constitution conservative or progressive? Did it better serve the sovereignty of emperors or the rights of citizens? Was it conducive to the development of genuine democracy? Had it led to the militarism that engulfed Japan in the 1930s?

One reason for the debates about the document lay in the many opinions stimulated by the drafting process itself. When Itō and his colleagues began their work, they already had a host of written materials from which to draw, many of them quite contradictory in nature. In 1878, for example, the quasi-legislative, nonelective Genrōin (Senate) had prepared a draft of a constitution that provided for power to be shared by the emperor and the people. Over the next few years, other constitutional opinions were written by the country's junior councilors (including Itō); most of those opinions favored a system with a strong emperor. Private groups and individuals, ranging from mountain villagers to newspaper editors, also drew up prospective drafts, most of which advocated a strong popular voice in the government. The result was a profusion of visions of what the constitution *should* mean and thus great differences in interpretations of what it meant in actual fact.

Another reason for these scholarly debates lies in the ambiguous nature of the constitution. The historian Marius B. Jansen says of the document's form: "Modernity and change were presented as a renewal of antiquity" (p. 395). In the constitution, classical symbols lend authority to its

Time Line	
1881–1882	■ Japan's first political parties form.
1882–1883	■ Itō Hirobumi travels to Europe to study constitutional systems.
1884	■ A peerage, designed as a pool for the upper house of a bicameral legislature, is created.
1885	■ Itō and his associates begin work on a constitutional draft. ■ A cabinet is formed to stand between the emperor and the legislature.
1887	■ A civil service system is initiated.
1889	■ **February 11** The Meiji Constitution is promulgated.
1890	■ Japan's first elections are held to elect representatives to the new national legislature, the Diet.

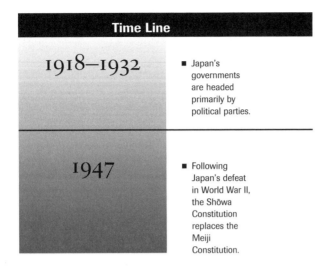

1918–1932
- Japan's governments are headed primarily by political parties.

1947
- Following Japan's defeat in World War II, the Shōwa Constitution replaces the Meiji Constitution.

modern content. Even more important, it is a carefully balanced document, reflecting the drafters' often contradictory goals. All the members of Itō Hirobumi's commission agreed, for example, that the document must reflect Japan's *kokutai* (national essence) and that imperial rule was the central pillar of that *kokutai*. But at the same time, they were determined to establish the rule of law, to create a legislature, to make the judiciary independent, and to guarantee certain personal rights—all of which, at a fundamental level, ran contrary to absolute imperial sovereignty. From that contradiction has sprung much of the debate about the constitution's nature. A look the document's major sections should make this clear.

◆ Chapter I: "The Emperor"

Itō Hirobumi wrote in 1882 that he could "die a happy man" because his study in Germany had shown him "how we can achieve the great objective of establishing Imperial authority" (qtd. in Ike, pp. 175–176). It should be no surprise, then, that the emperor's centrality permeates the constitution's preamble and serves as the focus of its first chapter. The language of the preamble is ancient, evoking a line "unbroken for ages eternal," a man who is sovereign and benevolent, who will make his "beloved subjects" prosperous, moral, and secure. (It bears noting that the original preamble mistakenly said that the imperial rescript promising a constitution was issued on October 14 of Meiji 14 (1881), two days after the actual date of the rescript. Most of the later versions changed the date to October 12.)

Chapter I states that the emperor is eternal (Article I), sacred (III), and sovereign (IV), with responsibility for supervising the country's administration (X) and making laws in times of "urgent necessity" when the Diet is not in session (VIII). The emperor is also placed in charge of the military (XI) and given sole responsibility for declaring war and peace (XIII). Of particular note is the fact that only males could reign (II), even though ancient emperors had included numerous women, among them, Suiko, who was on the throne when the famous Seventeen-Article Constitution was written in 604, and Jito, who oversaw the drafting

of Japan's first comprehensive set of penal and administrative regulations in the late seventh century—a point that Itō ignored in his *Commentaries* on the constitution (Ito, p. 6).

The chapter about the emperor also has a populist side. Roesler had argued that an emperor's power should not be made absolute in a modern society, where it was important to guard the interests of all classes, including business people and farmers. It is in this spirit that the constitution's first chapter circumscribes the emperor's prerogatives in important ways, making him subject to the constitution itself (IV) and rendering his legislative powers dependent on the Diet's consent (V). The drafters ignored Roesler's advice that the emperor's role should be wholly secular, however, and instead declared him to be "sacred and inviolable" (III). Emperors thus would reign as both political sovereign and spiritual fountain, providing a connection to the mythical Sun Goddess, from whom Japan's imperial line was held to have descended. The divinity clause would help to inspire loyalty to the state; it also would make the imperial symbol easy to manipulate during the militarist 1930s in order to justify propagation of ancient mythologies and support for foreign aggression.

◆ Chapter II: "Rights and Duties of Subjects"

While the first chapter undergirds central governmental control, the second addresses popular initiatives. Although the people are referred to as "subjects" rather than citizens, the section's overriding theme is the rule of law, under provisions that make "law" the basis of citizenship (XVIII) and speak about rights more than duties. Some articles prohibit authorities from overextending their reach, whether from taxing without a legal basis (XXI) or from making extralegal searches (XXV) or arrests (XXIII). Others provide for laws that limit freedoms. But in every case (with the sole exception of wartime or periods of national emergency), citizens are required to follow the legal system; even the emperor is not exempt. In Meiji Japan the idea of rule by law was hardly new; the Tokugawa era had produced detailed, sophisticated sets of legal codes. It was new, however, to have a central set of laws approved by a publicly elected legislature and available for all to read.

This chapter has much to say about freedoms, though often in ambiguous language. The two duties that it demands are military service (XX) and the payment of taxes (XXI). Freedoms and rights, on the other hand, include property holding (XXVII), privacy (XXV, XXVI), freedom of religious belief (XXVIII), and freedom of speech (XXIX). These freedoms are not absolute, though. In most cases, the drafters—worried that unfettered speech could raise "the temperature of politics ... to fever level" and "lead the nation into weakness and disorder" (Banno, p. 14)—included provisions for limiting freedoms through specific legislation. Such provisions, the 1920s and 1930s would show, carried with them the potential for thought police and the destruction of the very concept of free speech. That the Meiji drafters devoted so much space to subjects' rights, however, indicated how deeply they were committed to the welfare of the entire society.

◆ Chapter III: "The Imperial Diet"

The constitution's third chapter creates Japan's first national legislature, the Diet. Made up of twenty-two articles, this section gives flesh to the demands of freedom-and-rights campaigners that the public have a share in governmental decisions. Included in the chapter are articles creating a bicameral legislature (XXXIII), with an upper house selected from the imperial family and the national peerage (XXXIV) and a lower house "elected by the people" (XXXV). The Diet was to meet once a year for three months, unless the emperor prolonged the legislative session or called the Diet into an extraordinary session. Passage of bills would require an absolute majority (XLVII).

This chapter clearly addressed the drafters' worries about radical populism. It grants the Diet responsibility only for consenting to laws, leaving it little recourse when the government might refuse to accept its actions (XL). Nonetheless, the gains for citizens were immense. "Every law" has to be approved by the Diet (XXXVII); legislative discussions are to "be held in public" (XLVIII); and through the provisions of a later chapter, the Diet holds ultimate power over national budgets (LXIV). The people now had a formal role in the state; officials no longer could make laws without their input. Bureaucrats might have tried to mute the popular voice; they might have gotten the emperor to suspend a contentious Diet. But now that the populace had been given a legislative voice, the Japanese government never would be the same.

◆ Chapter IV: "The Ministers of State and the Privy Council"

The constitution's shortest chapter, which creates a cabinet of ministers (LV) and a privy council (LVI), is also one of its most important. While the privy council (intended to mediate cabinet-Diet disputes) seldom would play a crucial role in actual governance, the cabinet would operate at the heart of power. And the constitution's failure to create any connection between the cabinet and the Diet meant that the ministers of state could act on their own, without answering directly to the public. The omission was intentional. Fearful once more that popular passions might turn the Diet into a radical body, the constitutional drafters had decided to make the cabinet transcendent. Yamagata Aritomo, the prime minister during the first Diet session, expressed the drafters' view when he remarked, "The executive power is of the Imperial prerogative and those delegated to wield it should stand aloof from political parties" (qtd. in Hackett, p. 127). While the constitution's sections on the Diet and subjects' rights would make this aloofness increasingly difficult as the decades progressed, Chapter IV assured that cabinets would retain considerable initiative in setting national policies until after the Meiji era ended in 1912.

◆ Chapter V: "The Judicature"

This short chapter, which establishes the judiciary, continues the balancing act between authority and "social" governance with the creation of an independent judiciary free even from imperial constraints. Judicial decisions are to be rendered "in the name of the Emperor" but without input or influence from him or any other branch of government (LVII). Decisions are to be made in open sessions (LIX). The article on public trials contains caveats that would allow occasional breaches in later years—as in 1911, for example, when a group of conspirators against the Emperor Meiji were tried and sentenced to death in complete secrecy. But the independence of the courts was hailed as one of the triumphs of the constitution, a victory that would be confirmed just two years later when judges defied heavy government pressure and refused to use laws intended for Japan's own imperial family in the trial of a police officer who had stabbed Russia's visiting crown prince.

◆ Chapter VI: "Finance"

The chapter on finance is particularly important to the Diet's powers. Not only does it give the Diet primary responsibility for a host of financial matters, including the creation of taxes (LXII) and the approval of the imperial household's spending increases (LXVI), but it also provides that the legislature establish the annual budget (LXIV), with budget proposals beginning in the lower house. The drafters added a provision that the previous year's budget would be used if the Diet failed to pass a budget—to avoid what Itō Hirobumi feared would be the "paralyzation of the machinery of the administration" or "the destruction of the national existence" (Ito, p. 149). However, as the early 1890s would later prove, inflation and wartime costs could make a previous year's budget grossly inadequate. As a result, the Diet's budgetary power soon made the legislature almost as powerful as the oligarchs had feared that it might become.

Audience

The activities and ceremonies designed to mark the promulgation of the constitution made it clear that the document was aimed at two audiences. During the weeks before the big day, officials spread the word that the whole country should celebrate with festivals, sake drinking, and time off work. On the morning of the ceremony, Emperor Meiji dressed first in ancient court robes to secretly inform his departed ancestors of what was happening and then changed into Western military attire to issue the constitution in a new palace before an audience that included many Americans and Europeans. The empress wore a rose-colored gown and a diamond-studded crown in the European fashion. The aim of the ceremony—and of the document itself—was to convince both the Japanese public and the leaders of the imperial powers that Japan had become a powerful, "civilized" nation.

The attention to foreigners had its roots in the first years of the Meiji era. Threatened by Western imperialism, the early Meiji leaders had set out to create a strong state—and to convince the foreign powers that they had done so. On the one hand, they saw movement toward constitutionalism as essential to their efforts to revise unequal treaties that since the 1850s had deprived Japan of tariff autonomy and restricted its ability to try foreign residents in Japanese courts. Without a constitutional system, Japanese foreign

Commodore Matthew Perry (Library of Congress)

"*Having, by virtue of the glories of Our Ancestors, ascended the throne of a lineal succession unbroken for ages eternal; desiring to promote the welfare of, and to give development to the moral and intellectual faculties of Our beloved subjects ... and hoping to maintain the prosperity of the State, in concert with Our people and with their support, We hereby promulgate ... a fundamental law of State.*"

(Preamble)

"*The Emperor is sacred and inviolable.*"

(Article III)

"*Japanese subjects shall, within the limits of law, enjoy the liberty of speech, writing, publication, public meetings, and associations.*"

(Article XXIX)

"*Every law requires the consent of the Imperial Diet.*"

(Article XXXVII)

"*The respective Ministers of State shall give their advice to the Emperor, and be responsible for it. All Laws, Imperial Ordinances, and Imperial Rescripts of whatever kind, that relate to the affairs of the State, require the countersignature of a Minister of State.*"

(Article LV)

"*The expenditure and revenue of the State require the consent of the Imperial Diet by means of an annual Budget.*"

(Article LXIV)

diplomats maintained, treaty revision was unthinkable. On the other hand, Meiji leaders were convinced that without respect as a modern state Japan never would be taken seriously in imperialist circles. The constitution thus was proclaimed to the world as ultimate proof that Japan had become a modern state.

The focus on Japanese citizens sprang from more varied motives. For the intellectuals, the constitution was intended to demonstrate modernity and to prove the government's seriousness about instituting the rule of law and including a popular voice in governance. For the general populace, many of whom had been apathetic about the constitutional process, it was intended to stimulate loyalty to the state and expand engagement in public processes. While the campaign to engage the populace in promulgation festivities was quite successful, many observers found townspeople more interested in watching fireworks and consuming alcohol than in what the constitution said.

Impact

Contemporary press accounts praised the Meiji Constitution as a seminal document. And they were right in many ways. Scholars have since agreed, for example, that the constitution paved the way for new treaties with the Western powers that were signed five years later, which marked the beginning of the end of the unequal treaty system. The constitution also created a new governmental structure that was rooted in the rule of law and to some extent engaged average citizens in the nation's decision-making processes. The document also gained Japan worldwide recognition as the new leader of Asia. However, those who trace the constitution's impact over the long term usually write in more nuanced ways, often discussing one of two issues: the constitution's impact on the development of democracy or its role in nurturing the twentieth-century authoritarianism and militarism that ended in World War II.

Regarding the latter, there is no question that the constitution played into the hands of the militarists. Few, if any, doubt that the document's definition of the emperor as both sovereign and sacred undergirded the suppression of left-wing thought and the emergence of military cabinets in the years leading up to World War II. From the early 1900s onward, conservative officials worked hard at creating an emperor-system ideology, partly as an antidote to the corrupting impact of modern institutions and partly as a way to maintain a strong state. They revised textbooks repeatedly to emphasize the emperor's role as oracle and sovereign, they discouraged individualistic literature, and they supported the activities of patriotic societies—all in the name of loyalty to the emperor, whom the constitution described as "sacred and inviolable." Authoritarianism also was encouraged by the constitution's chapters on "subjects" (which made room for laws that circumscribed "dangerous" speech) and on the ministers of state (who were exempted from having to answer to the Diet). But even those chapters were grounded in the emperor's constitutional role, both in the provisions that gave him and his ministers such overriding authority and in the loyalist mindset that imperial sovereignty encouraged.

None of this made authoritarianism or militarism inevitable, however. Constitutions reflect the milieu in which they operate, and for two generations following the promulgation Japanese politics made it clear that democracy was highly feasible under the Meiji Constitution. Certainly, the constitution contains numerous provisions that encourage popular participation in an open, responsive system: the affirmation of rule by law, an independent judiciary, the creation of a popularly elected Diet, the assertion of fundamental rights, and the legislature's control over budgets, among other things. Even the emperor was subject to the constitution, and his legislative powers required the Diet's consent.

What is more, Japan experienced steady movement toward full-fledged democracy during the constitution's first four decades, with the document itself at the heart of democratic developments. By the early 1890s, Diet members were using their budgetary power to control cabinets. And they fought constantly for expansion of the electorate. While in 1890 the nation's electoral ordinance kept all but large landowners from voting, voting laws were continually changed in response to public demands, and by 1925 Japan had adopted universal male suffrage. In the late 1920s bills were being introduced in the Diet to give voting rights to women, as well. Moreover, political parties eventually took control of the cabinets, further expanding the country's democratic base. Itō Hirobumi had warned in 1889 that Japan "must avoid the quite dangerous temptation of hastily organizing a ... cabinet formed by political parties" (Takii, p. 105). By 1918, however, public pressure had become so great that even the most authoritarian oligarchs had to accept a system in which most cabinets would be headed by the leader of the dominant party in the Diet. At the theoretical level, scholars like Minobe Tatsukichi lent credence to these developments. Minobe dominated mainstream Japanese political theory in the 1920s with his "organ theory," which maintained that the nation's political body was composed of several political organs, the most important of which were the emperor and the Diet. The constitution, he maintained, called for them to rule jointly.

A mix of domestic and international forces undermined these democratic trends after the late 1920s. But the triumph of militarism and ultranationalism after the mid-1930s cannot hide the fact that democratic tendencies flourished for nearly forty years under the Meiji Constitution. The U.S.-dominated occupation government, which ran Japan after World War II, demanded that Japan adopt a new fundamental law in 1947, the Shōwa Constitution, which made the people sovereign and the emperor a mere state "symbol." While there is no question that the new constitution cut the heart from Japan's military and expanded suffrage to women, the occupying forces who had thought they were giving democracy to Japan simply exposed their own historical ignorance. Democracy had come first under that document that so vividly captured the "'shape of the nation' of Meiji Japan" (Takii, p. vii): the Meiji Constitution.

Further Reading

■ Books

Akita, George. *Foundations of Constitutional Government in Modern Japan: 1868–1900.* Cambridge, Mass.: Harvard University Press, 1967.

Banno, Junji. *The Establishment of the Japanese Constitutional System,* trans. J. A. A. Stockwin. New York: Routledge, 1992.

De Bary, William Theodore, et al., eds. *Sources of Japanese Tradition.* Vol. 2, part 2: *1868 to 2000,* 2nd ed. New York: Columbia University Press, 2006.

Hackett, Roger F. *Yamagata Aritomo in the Rise of Modern Japan, 1838–1922.* Cambridge, Mass.: Harvard University Press, 1971.

Ike, Nobutaka. *The Beginnings of Political Democracy in Japan.* Baltimore: Johns Hopkins University Press, 1950.

Irokawa, Daikichi. *The Culture of the Meiji Period*, trans. and ed. Marius B. Jansen. Princeton, N.J.: Princeton University Press, 1985.

Ito, Hirobumi. *Commentaries on the Constitution of the Empire of Japan*, trans. Miyoji Ito. 2nd ed. Tokyo: Chūō Daigaku, 1906.

Jansen, Marius B. *The Making of Modern Japan.* Cambridge, Mass.: Belknap Press of Harvard University Press, 2000.

Pittau, Joseph. *Political Thought in Early Meiji Japan: 1868–1889.* Cambridge, Mass.: Harvard University Press, 1967.

Siemes, Johannes. *Hermann Roesler and the Making of the Meiji State.* Rutland, Vt.: Sophia University, 1968.

Takii, Kazuhiro. *The Meiji Constitution: The Japanese Experience of the West and the Shaping of the Modern State*, trans. David Noble. Tokyo: I-House of Japan Press, 2007.

■ **Web Sites**
"Birth of the Constitution of Japan." National Diet Library Web site.
   http://www.ndl.go.jp/constitution/e/index.html.

—James Huffman

Questions for Further Study

1. Compare this document with Prince Shōtoku's Seventeen-Article Constitution. Although almost thirteen hundred years separate the two constitutions, does the modern document preserve any of the cultural or religious values of the earlier constitution? If so, what does this tell you about the continuity of Japanese culture through the centuries?

2. How did the Meiji Constitution in effect overturn, at least in part, the Japanese Closed Country Edict of 1635? What political, social, and economic changes might account for this "about-face" in Japan's relationship with the modern world?

3. The Meiji Constitution created a constitutional monarchy that gave the Japanese people much more say in their government. Why do you think that in the decades that followed, Japan became increasingly militaristic and authoritarian—a development that led to World War II in the Pacific?

4. Numerous important documents in world history, particularly over the past millennium, have been constitutions. Select one other constitution—possibilities include the Constitutions of Clarendon, the Constitution of Haiti, the Constitution Act of Canada, the Constitution of the People's Republic of China, and even the English Bill of Rights (which, strictly speaking, is not a constitution but functions as part of England's constitutional tradition)—and compare it with the Meiji Constitution. How do the two documents reflect similar or differing cultural and political values?

5. Article III of the Meiji Constitution states that "the Emperor is sacred and inviolable." Yet for the previous century, if not longer, the nations of Europe were rejecting the notion of the divine right of monarchs to rule, and the concept of divine right would unravel in China in the early twentieth century. Why do you think this viewpoint persisted in Japan into the twentieth century?

Meiji Constitution of Japan

Having, by virtue of the glories of Our Ancestors, ascended the throne of a lineal succession unbroken for ages eternal; desiring to promote the welfare of, and to give development to the moral and intellectual faculties of Our beloved subjects, the very same that have been favoured with the benevolent care and affectionate vigilance of Our Ancestors; and hoping to maintain the prosperity of the State, in concert with Our people and with their support, We hereby promulgate, in pursance of Our Imperial Rescript of the 14th day of the 10th month of the 14th year of Meiji, a fundamental law of State, to exhibit the principles, by which We are to be guided in Our conduct, and to point out to what Our descendants and Our subjects and their descendants are forever to conform.

The rights of sovereignty of the State, We have inherited from Our Ancestors, and We shall bequeath them to Our descendants. Neither We nor they shall in future fail to wield them, in accordance with the provisions of the Constitution hereby granted.

We now declare to respect and protect the security of the rights and of the property of Our people, and to secure to them the complete enjoyment of the same, within the extent of the provision of the present Constitution and of the law.

The Imperial Diet shall first be convoked for the 23d year of Meiji, and the time of its opening shall be the date, when the present Constitution comes into force.

When in the future it may become necessary to amend any of the provision of the present Constitution, We or Our successors shall assume the initiative right, and submit a project for the same to the Imperial Diet. The Imperial Diet shall pass its vote upon it, according to the condition imposed by the present Constitution, and in no otherwise shall Our descendants or Our subjects be permitted to attempt any alteration thereof.

Our Ministers of State, on Our behalf, shall be held responsible for the carrying out of the present Constitution, and Our present and future subjects shall forever assume the duty of allegiance to the present Constitution.

[His Imperial Majesty's Sign-Manual.]

[Privy Seal.]

The 11th day of the 2nd month of the 22nd year of Meiji

(Countersigned)

Count Kuroda Kiyotaka, Minister President of State

Count Ito Hirobumi, President of the Privy Council

Count Okuma Shigenobu, Minister of State for Foreign Affairs

Count Saigo Tsukumichi, Minister of State for the Navy

Count Inouye Kaoru, Minister of State for Agriculture and Commerce

Count Yamada Akiyoshi, Minister of State for Justice

Count Matsugata Masayoshi, Minister of State for Finance, and Minister of State for Home Affairs

Count Oyama Iwao, Minister of State for War

Viscount Mori Arimori, Minister of State for Education

Viscount Enomoto Takeaki, Minister of State for Communications

Chapter I: The Emperor

◆ **Article I**

The Empire of Japan shall be reigned over (and governed) by a line of Emperors unbroken for ages eternal.

◆ **Article II**

The Imperial Throne shall be succeeded to by Imperial male descendants, according to the provision of the Imperial House Law.

◆ **Article III**

The Emperor is sacred and inviolable.

◆ **Article IV**

The Emperor is the head of the Empire, combining in himself the rights of sovereignty, and exercises them, according to the provision of the present Constitution.

◆ **Article V**

The Emperor exercises the legislative power with the consent of the Imperial Diet.

◆ Article VI

The Emperor gives sanction to laws, and orders them to be promulgated and executed.

◆ Article VII

The Emperor convokes the Imperial Diet, opens, closes, and prorogues it, and dissolves the House of Representatives.

◆ Article VIII

The Emperor, in consequence of an urgent necessity to maintain public safety or to avert public calamities, issues, when the Imperial Diet is not sitting, Imperial Ordinances in the place of law.

Such Imperial Ordinances are to be laid before the Imperial Diet at its next session, and when the Diet does not approve the said Ordinance, the Government shall declare them to be invalid for the future.

◆ Article IX

The Emperor issues, or causes to be issued, the Ordinances necessary for the carrying out of the laws, or for the maintenance of the public peace and order, and for the promotion of the welfare of the subjects. But no Ordinance shall in any way alter any of the existing laws.

◆ Article X

The Emperor determines the organization of the different branches of the administration, and the salaries of all civil and military officers, and appoints and dismisses the same. Exceptions especially provided for in the present Constitution or in other laws, shall be in accordance with the respective provisions (bearing thereon).

◆ Article XI

The Emperor has the supreme command of the Army and Navy.

◆ Article XII

The Emperor determines the organization and peace standing of the Army and Navy.

◆ Article XIII

The Emperor declares war, makes peace, and concludes treaties.

◆ Article XIV

The Emperor proclaims the law of siege.

The conditions and effects of the law of siege shall be determined by law.

◆ Article XV

The Emperor confers titles of nobility, rank, orders, and other marks of honor.

◆ Article XVI

The Emperor orders amnesty, pardon, commutation of punishment, and rehabilitation.

◆ Article XVII

A Regency shall be instituted in conformity with the provisions of the Imperial House Law.

The Regent shall exercise the powers appertaining to the Emperor in His name.

Chapter II: Rights and Duties of Subjects

◆ Article XVIII

The condition necessary for being a Japanese subject shall be determined by law.

◆ Article XIX

Japanese subjects may, according to qualifications determined in law or ordinances, be appointed to civil or military offices equally, and may fill any other public offices.

◆ Article XX

Japanese subjects are amenable to service in the Army or Navy, according to the provisions of law.

◆ Article XXI

Japanese subjects are amenable to the duty of paying taxes, according to the provision of law.

◆ Article XXII

Japanese subjects shall have the liberty of abode and of changing the same within the limits of law.

◆ Article XXIII

No Japanese subjects shall be arrested, detained, tried, or punished, unless according to law.

◆ Article XXIV

No Japanese subject shall be deprived of his right of being tried by the judges determined by law.

◆ Article XXV

Except in the cases provided for in the law, the house of no Japanese subject shall be entered or searched without his consent.

◆ **Article XXVI**

Except in the cases mentioned in the law, the secrecy of the letters of every Japanese subject shall remain inviolate.

◆ **Article XXVII**

The right of property of every Japanese subject shall remain inviolate.

Measures necessary to be taken for the public benefit shall be provided for by law.

◆ **Article XXVIII**

Japanese subjects shall, within limits not prejudicial to peace and order, and not antagonistic to their duties as subjects, enjoy freedom of religious belief.

◆ **Article XXIX**

Japanese subjects shall, within the limits of law, enjoy the liberty of speech, writing, publication, public meetings, and associations.

◆ **Article XXX**

Japanese subjects may present petitions, by observing the proper forms of respect, and by complying with the rules specially provided for the same.

◆ **Article XXXI**

The provisions contained in the present Chapter shall not affect the exercise of the power appertaining to the Emperor, in times of war or in cases of a national emergency.

◆ **Article XXXII**

Each and every one of the provisions contained in the preceding Articles of the present Chapter, that are not in conflict with the laws or the rules and discipline of the Army and Navy, shall apply to the officers and men of the Army and of the Navy.

Chapter III: The Imperial Diet

◆ **Article XXXIII**

The Imperial Diet shall consist of two Houses, a House of Peers and a House of Representatives.

◆ **Article XXXIV**

The House of Peers shall, in accordance with the Ordinance concerning the House of Peers, be composed of the members of the Imperial Family, of the orders of nobility, and of those persons who have been nominated thereto by the Emperor.

◆ **Article XXXV**

The House of Representatives shall be composed of Members elected by the people, according to the provisions of the Law of Election.

◆ **Article XXXVI**

No one can at one and the same time be a member of both Houses.

◆ **Article XXXVII**

Every law requires the consent of the Imperial Diet.

◆ **Article XXXVIII**

Both Houses shall vote upon projects of law submitted to it by the Government, and may respectively initiate projects of law.

◆ **Article XXXIX**

A Bill, which has been rejected by either the one or the other of the two houses, shall not be again brought in during the same session.

◆ **Article XL**

Both Houses can make representations to the Government, as to laws or upon any other subject. When, however, such representations are not accepted, they cannot be made a second time during the same session.

◆ **Article XLI**

The Imperial Diet shall be convoked every year.

◆ **Article XLII**

A session of the Imperial Diet shall last during three months. In case of necessity, the duration of a session may be prolonged by Imperial Order.

◆ **Article XLIII**

When urgent necessity arises, an extraordinary session may be convoked, in addition to the ordinary one.

The duration of an extraordinary session shall be determined by Imperial Order.

◆ **Article XLIV**

The opening, closing, prolongation of session, and prorogation of the Imperial Diet, shall be effected simultaneously for both houses.

In case the House of Representatives has been ordered to dissolve, the House of Peers shall at the same time be prorogued.

◆ **Article XLV**

When the House of Representatives has been ordered to dissolve, Members shall be caused by Imperial Order to be newly elected, and the new House shall be convoked within five months from the day of dissolution.

◆ **Article XLVI**

No debate can be opened and no vote can be taken in either House of the Imperial Diet, unless not less than one-third of the whole number of the members thereof is present.

◆ **Article XLVII**

Votes shall be taken in both Houses by absolute majority. In the case of a tie vote, the President shall have the casting vote.

◆ **Article XLVIII**

The deliberations of both Houses shall be held in public. The deliberations may, however, upon demand of the Government or by resolution of the Houses, be held in secret sitting.

◆ **Article XLIX**

Both Houses of the Imperial Diet may respectively present addresses to the Emperor.

◆ **Article L**

Both Houses may receive petitions presented by subjects.

◆ **Article LI**

Both Houses may enact, besides what is provided for in the present Constitution and in the Law of the Houses, rules necessary for the management of their internal affairs.

◆ **Article LII**

No member of either House shall be held responsible outside the respective Houses, for any opinion uttered or for any vote given in the House. When, however, a Member himself has given publicity to his opinions by public speech, by documents in printing or in writing, or by any other similar means he shall, in the matter, be amenable to the general law.

◆ **Article LIII**

The members of both Houses shall, during the session, be free from arrest, unless with the consent of the House, except in cases of flagrant delicts, or of offences connected with a state of internal commotion or with a foreign trouble.

◆ **Article LIV**

The Ministers of State and the Delegates of the Government may, at any time, take seats and speak in either House.

Chapter IV: The Ministers of State and the Privy Council

◆ **Article LV**

The respective Ministers of State shall give their advice to the Emperor, and be responsible for it.

All Laws, Imperial Ordinances, and Imperial Rescripts of whatever kind, that relate to the affairs of the State, require the countersignature of a Minister of State.

◆ **Article LVI**

The Privy Council shall, in accordance with the provisions for the organization of the Privy Council, deliberate upon important matters of State, when they have been consulted by the Emperor.

Chapter V: The Judicature

◆ **Article LVII**

The Judicature shall be exercised by the Courts of Law according to law, in the name of the Emperor.

The organization of the Courts of Law shall be determined by law.

◆ **Article LVIII**

The judges shall be appointed from among those, who possess proper qualification according to law.

No judge shall be deprived of his position, unless by way of criminal sentence or disciplinary punishment.

Rules for disciplinary punishment shall be determined by law.

◆ **Article LIX**

Trials and judgment of a Court shall be conducted publicly. When, however, there exists any fear that such publicity may be prejudicial to peace and order, or to the maintenance of public morality, the public trial may be suspended by provision of law or by the decision of the Court of Law.

- **Article LX**

    All matters, that fall within the competency of a special Court, shall be specially provided for by law.

- **Article LXI**

    No suit at law, which relates to rights alleged to have been infringed by the legal measures of the executive authorities, and which shall come within the competency of the Court of Administrative Litigation specially established by law, shall be taken cognizance of by a Court of Law.

Chapter VI: Finance

- **Article LXII**

    The imposition of a new tax or the modification of the rates (of an existing one) shall be determined by law.

    However, all such administrative fees or other revenue having the nature of compensation shall not fall within the category of the above clause.

    The raising of national loans and the contracting of other liabilities to the charge of the National Treasury, except those that are provided in the Budget, shall require the consent of the Imperial Diet.

- **Article LXIII**

    The taxes levied at present shall, in so far as are not remodelled by new law, be collected according to the old system.

- **Article LXIV**

    The expenditure and revenue of the State require the consent of the Imperial Diet by means of an annual Budget.

    Any and all expenditures overpassing the appropriations set forth in the Titles and Paragraphs of the Budget, or that are not provided for in the Budget, shall subsequently require the approbation of the Imperial Diet.

- **Article LXV**

    The Budget shall be first laid before the House of Representatives.

- **Article LXVI**

    The expenditures of the Imperial House shall be defrayed every year out of the National Treasury, according to the present fixed amount for the same, and shall not require the consent thereto of the Imperial Diet, except in case an increase thereof is found necessary.

- **Article LXVII**

    Those already fixed expenditures based by the Constitution upon the powers appertaining to the Emperor, and such expenditures as may have arisen by the effect of law, or that appertain to the legal obligations of the Government, shall be neither rejected nor reduced by the Imperial Diet, without the concurrence of the Government.

- **Article LXVIII**

    In order to meet special requirements, the Government may ask the consent of the Imperial Diet to a certain amount as a Continuing Expenditure Fund, for a previously fixed number of years.

- **Article LXIX**

    In order to supply deficiencies, which are unavoidable, in the Budget, and to meet requirements unprovided for in the same, a Reserve Fund shall be provided in the Budget.

- **Article LXX**

    When the Imperial Diet cannot be convoked, owing to the external or internal condition of the country, in case of urgent need for the maintenance of public safety, the Government may take all necessary financial measures, by means of an Imperial Ordinance.

    In the case mentioned in the preceding clause, the matter shall be submitted to the Imperial Diet at its next session, and its approbation shall be obtained thereto.

- **Article LXXI**

    When the Imperial Diet has not voted on the Budget, or when the Budget has not been brought into actual existence, the Government shall carry out the Budget of the preceding year.

- **Article LXXII**

    The final account of the expenditures and revenue of the State shall be verified and confirmed by the Board of Audit, and it shall be submitted by the Government to the Imperial Diet, together with the report of verification of the said Board.

    The organization and competency of the Board of Audit shall be determined by law separately.

Chapter VII: Supplementary Rules

- **Article LXXIII**

    When it has become necessary in future to amend the provisions of the present Constitution, a project to that effect shall be submitted to the Imperial Diet by Imperial Order.

In the above case, neither House can open the debate, unless not less than two-thirds of the whole number of Members are present, and no amendment can be passed, unless a majority of not less than two-thirds of the Members present is obtained.

◆ Article LXXIV

No modification of the Imperial House Law shall be required to be submitted to the deliberation of the Imperial Diet.

No provision of the present Constitution can be modified by the Imperial House Law.

◆ Article LXXV

No modification can be introduced into the Constitution, or into the Imperial House Law, during the time of a Regency.

◆ Article LXXVI

Existing legal enactments, such as laws, regulations, Ordinances, or by whatever names they may be called, shall, so far as they do not conflict with the present Constitution, continue in force.

All existing contracts or orders, that entail obligations upon the Government, and that are connected with expenditure shall come within the scope of Art. LXVII.

THEODOR HERZL'S "A SOLUTION TO THE JEWISH QUESTION"

" In countries where we have lived for centuries we are still cried down as strangers. "

Overview

Theodor Herzl's essay "A Solution to the Jewish Question," which appeared in a London weekly newspaper, the *Jewish Chronicle*, in 1896, argued that the world's Jews needed a homeland and that the homeland should be Palestine—an ancient region on the eastern Mediterranean that encompasses the modern-day nation of Israel. At the time that Herzl wrote, Israel did not exist. Indeed, the Jewish population in what is today Israel numbered less than one hundred thousand people, who lived among their Muslim and Christian Arab neighbors as part of the Ottoman Empire. This state of affairs would abruptly change in the twentieth century, primarily because of the activities of European Jewish intellectuals and activists, including Herzl. While Herzl was not the only actor in creating a Jewish homeland in Palestine, he contributed significantly to the effort through a number of publications, including "A Solution to the Jewish Question."

Context

Israel is a young state, having come into existence only in 1948, though its foundations were laid in the late nineteenth century. Historically, Jews had been a minority population in Palestine after the Romans destroyed the Temple of Solomon in Jerusalem in 70 CE. This event led to the expulsion and dispersal of much of the Jewish population from the region, with the majority fleeing to other parts of the Middle East or Europe. Afterward, the remaining Jews were ruled as a minority by various Muslim powers. The last of these rulers were the Ottomans, after the Ottoman Turks conquered Syria and Palestine during the Ottoman-Mamluk War (1485–1491) and established the Ottoman Empire in 1516.

Most of the early Jewish immigration to Palestine came from Spain as part of the exodus resulting from the Reconquista, or the Christian reconquest of the Iberian Peninsula from Muslims. The Reconquista ended in 1492, when Spanish Muslims and Jews were given three choices: convert to Christianity, die, or leave. Needless to say, many left to seek

religious toleration elsewhere, and they found it in Muslim lands, where they were considered *dhimmis*, or "people of the Book"—those who, like Muslims, had received a revelation from God but, unlike Muslims, had not accepted the teachings of Muhammad. Thus, they had rights and were protected as citizens of the Ottoman Empire.

With the advent of the Industrial Revolution and European imperialism in the nineteenth century, the once fairly harmonious relationship between the Ottomans and their non-Turk subjects began to alter. As European merchants jockeyed to gain commercial advantages in the region, they often favored particular religious or ethnic groups—especially Christians and Jews. This new contact also led to fresh immigration of Jews to Palestine, where they hoped to avoid the persecution and prejudice they had encountered in Europe, particularly eastern countries of Europe. Thousands of Jews fled from the Russian Empire after the pogroms of 1881–1884 and 1903–1906; in Russia the government used the Jews as scapegoats for many of the nation's ills. This wave of immigration from 1882 to the early 1900s became known as the First Aliyah ("first ascent") to Israel. Most of these Jews entered the Ottoman Empire on religious visas used to allow pilgrims to visit holy sites, but they never returned home. Gradually they settled in Palestine and formed new villages and towns built on land purchased from wealthy Jews, such as Baron Edmond Benjamin James de Rothschild, the patriarch of the wealthy banking family, and sympathizers in western Europe. The majority, however, spoke Yiddish, Polish, or Russian and not the Arabic that most of the Jews who dwelled in Palestine spoke. The culture of the new Jews was different from that of those who already lived there. At the beginning of the nineteenth century, only five thousand Jews lived in Palestine, out of a population of approximately 300,000 people. By the end of the First Aliyah, twenty-eight settlements had been founded with twenty-five thousand to thirty thousand European Jews. Their arrival caused the Ottomans to vacillate on a consistent policy toward Jewish immigration as they attempted to balance European sympathy and pressure with the concerns of Palestinian Arabs.

The Ottoman Empire was not the only state to deal with large numbers of Jewish immigrants. Although the First Aliyah brought thousands to Palestine, many more Jews

1860

- **May 2**
  Theodor Herzl is born in Budapest, Hungary.

1881

- Pogroms against Jews in the Russian Empire begin, continuing until 1884.

1882

- The First Aliyah, or immigration to Palestine by European Jews, begins, continuing until the early 1900s.

1894

- Herzl publishes *The Ghetto*, a play that examines the Jewish question; he covers the conviction for treason of Alfred Dreyfus, a Jewish officer in the French army, for the *Neue Freie Presse*.

1896

- **January 17**
  Herzl publishes "A Solution to the Jewish Question," based on the pamphlet *Der Judenstaat* ("The Jewish State").

1897

- **August 29**
  The First World Zionist Congress is held in Basel, Switzerland.

came from eastern to western Europe. The sudden influx of immigrants thus prompted the "Jewish question," which was a series of questions that boiled down to one: How do the Jews fit into a Western secular society? Underlying this question were old prejudices in a secular, yet very Christian society that viewed Jews as outsiders who refused to assimilate into Western society. Indeed, with the influx of eastern European Jews, the differences between the Jews and Western society became more apparent. Although many western European Jews had become more assimilated, while retaining their religion as part of their identity, eastern European Jews were different. They had lived apart from their Christians neighbors in what were termed "ghettos," or Jewish quarters in cities. Although at times they could be poor, many ghettos were often affluent areas. This separation, once required by medieval law, helped keep alive prejudice dating back centuries.

The true turning point, however, came with the advent of Zionism, or what might be termed Jewish nationalism. This movement came as a reaction to the pogroms and persecution of the Jewish Diaspora throughout Europe. Although Jews received much better treatment in western Europe, many Jewish intellectuals and religious leaders became concerned that the secular environment of the industrialized West could lead to their absorption and loss of identity. Integration was not unacceptable, but the concern was that latent prejudice among Europeans would prevent Jews from ever fully becoming part of Western society. A Jewish minority would always be outsiders no matter how long their families had lived in a particular country.

As a result, some intellectuals, such as Theodor Herzl, began to consider the feasibility of establishing a Jewish state. This led to the creation of the World Zionist Congress, which promoted the creation of a Jewish state and sought support for it not only among the Diaspora but also from non-Jews. The First World Zionist Congress met in Basel, Switzerland, in 1897, with approximately two hundred delegates from fifteen countries. While enthusiasm for a Jewish state grew, widespread disagreement arose about where the state should be. Initially, Herzl had no strong preference. One suggestion, prompted by the British government, was Uganda, while others proposed that the Jews should follow the model of the Mormons and settle in the western United States, Canada, or Australia, where they could form a state within an existing country. In view of the already significant Jewish presence in the United States, it was a serious consideration. Thus when Herzl wrote his "Solution to the Jewish Question," he attempted to find an answer to deal with all of these conditions. In eastern Europe random and violent pogroms were a constant threat, while in western Europe Jews faced an underlying prejudice or risked assimilation into the larger population and thus the loss of their Jewish identity and religion. In Herzl's opinion, the only solution was to find a homeland. While others looked at more recent models, Herzl turned to an ancient biblical covenant made between God and the first Jews—the Hebrews.

Theodor Herzl was one of the founders of the Zionist movement and convened the first World Zionist Congress in 1897. The ideas of Zionism existed well before he came into prominence, but his influence became seminal. Herzl was born in 1860 in Budapest, in the Austro-Hungarian Empire, but he was raised and educated in a secular German world. While Judaism played a role in his background, for much of his life he possessed only a cursory understanding of it. In 1878 Herzl's family moved to the capital of the Austro-Hungarian Empire, Vienna, where Herzl attended the University of Vienna and obtain a doctorate in law in 1884.

After graduation, Herzl earned a living as a civil servant and a writer of plays, short stories, and articles. Eventually he secured a job as a journalist for the prestigious Viennese newspaper *Neue Freie Presse* ("New Free Press"), which stationed him in Paris as their correspondent. This was the transforming event of Herzl's life, as he would experience firsthand massive anti-Semitism when he covered the treason trial of Alfred Dreyfus, a Jewish officer in the French army, for his newspaper. Earlier, in 1894, he had published a drama titled *The Ghetto* that he hoped would serve as a vehicle for discussion and a step toward harmony between Christians and Jews. Prior to the Dreyfus affair, Herzl was fully committed to assimilation into the culture of secular Europe, but the widespread anti-Semitism he witnessed during the Dreyfus affair convinced him that the only solution was a Jewish state. Toward that end, in 1896 he published a pamphlet titled *Der Judenstaat* ("The Jewish State"), which was ridiculed by many Jewish leaders who could not conceive it as reality. "The Solution to the Jewish Question" (also published in 1896) is a modified version of *Der Judenstaat* intended for a British audience.

Herzl's ideas found rapid acceptance among the general Jewish public, but the leaders of the Jewish Diaspora were skeptical as to whether it was feasible. Herzl eventually found sufficient support to call for a meeting of Jewish leaders in Basel, Switzerland, in 1897. This was a significant step, for it was the first international meeting of major Jewish leaders. There the World Zionist Congress was formed with Herzl as its president.

As president, Herzl attempted to find a solution to the "Jewish question," and he even traveled to the Ottoman Empire in 1898 to pursue his dream. Ultimately, his visit was a failure. He did not meet the Ottoman sultan, Abdul Hamid II, at that time, though he did eventually meet with him in 1901. Still, Ottoman officials informed him that the Ottomans were opposed to autonomous regions or self-rule. He also timed his 1898 visit so that he could meet with the German emperor, Kaiser Wilhelm II, who was visiting the Middle East. He finally met with Kaiser Wilhelm, hoping to recruit him as an ally in the Zionist effort, but the kaiser was dismissive of the idea. A trip to Britain resulted in a modest proposal of Uganda as a potential autonomous homeland. The fact that Herzl considered this as a temporary solution undermined his support in the World Zionist Congress. His death in 1904 ensured that the Uganda plan was forgotten.

Time Line

1898
- **October**
Herzl travels to Palestine and meets Kaiser Wilhelm II of Germany.

1901
- **May**
Herzl meets Abdul Hamid II, sultan of the Ottoman Empire.

1903
- Pogroms against Jews in the Russian Empire begin, continuing until 1906.

1904
- **July 3**
Theodor Herzl dies.

1906
- **July 12**
Alfred Dreyfus is exonerated of charges of treason.

1917
- **November 2**
The British issue the Balfour Declaration in support of a Jewish homeland in Palestine.

1947
- **November 29**
The United Nations General Assembly approves the partition of Palestine.

1948
- **May 14**
Israel proclaims its independence.

Milestone Documents

The body of Theodore Herzl lies in state before reburial in Israel in 1949. (© Bettmann/CORBIS)

Explanation and Analysis of the Document

Herzl's essay "A Solution to the Jewish Question" was a radical proposal that sought to ameliorate the oppression and persecution of Jews throughout Europe. In it, Herzl is appealing not only to his fellow Jews but also to the governments of Europe. His work was crucial for laying the foundations of the modern state of Israel but also detrimental, in that it led to the oppression of another group, the Palestinians—an unintended consequence that Herzl did not imagine and probably could not have conceived.

◆ Paragraph 1

What exactly was the Jewish question? The readers of the *Jewish Chronicle* knew what Herzl meant: How do Jews fit into any country's society and culture? What is their role? It is not a single question but a series of questions that all countries and cultures ask themselves when they receive or possess a large minority who are considered outsiders by virtue of race, culture, or custom. Herzl speaks both about the abominable pogroms against Jews in the Russian Empire and other parts of eastern Europe and about the prejudice against Jews in western Europe. While the intellectual movement of the Enlightenment—the cultural shift coinciding with the eighteenth century in Europe, when reason replaced tradition as the source of authority—had alleviated most outright religious hostility, Jews remained a minority in a largely Christian, albeit secular, western Europe. Jews remained separate because they

lived in communities apart from non-Jews, and this contributed to a fear of the unknown.

A contributing factor to Herzl's publication of "A Solution to the Jewish Question" is also revealed when he makes a specific reference to France: "France itself is no exception." Herzl is referring to one of the major headlines of his day, the so-called Dreyfus affair. This incident concerned the trial of a Jewish French army officer, Alfred Dreyfus, who was convicted of treason by a military tribunal in 1894 on charges of spying for the Germans. Ultimately, the court reversed the conviction, and Dreyfus was proved innocent of all charges.

Nonetheless, the Dreyfus affair awakened anti-Semitism in French society—a society that since the French Revolution in 1789 had generally been regarded as a secular and tolerant country. At all levels of society, debates raged about the trial as well as the place of Jews in France: Could they be trusted? Did they owe their allegiance to France or to their religion? The trial immediately became a key event in the formation of Zionism, for Herzl covered the trial as a reporter. There he witnessed crowds chanting "Death to the Jews," and the now open anti-Semitism did not dissipate after Dreyfus was proclaimed to be innocent.

◆ Paragraph 2

In Herzl's eyes, Jews had to view themselves as a single group—not Russian Jews or French Jews but a single nation of Jews. He also laments here that no matter how loyal Jews are to the countries they live in, they are still outsiders. Even though they have died in battle or sacrificed for their respective countries, they remain unaccepted. Again he turns to France, using the Huguenots to illustrate his point that ultimately people's differences outweigh their loyalty. The Huguenots were French Protestants who followed the teachings of John Calvin during the Protestant Reformation of the sixteenth and seventeenth centuries. They suffered greatly in the religious wars that occurred throughout the Reformation, but eventually they achieved a degree of official tolerance by the French government with the Edict of Nantes in 1598. This toleration was fleeting, however, for King Louis XIV ignored the edict and then declared Protestantism illegal, despite Protestants' loyalty to France in time of war. Hundreds of thousands of Huguenots fled to other European countries and the New World. "Yet," Herzl concludes, "in spite of all, we are loyal subjects, loyal as the Huguenots, who were forced to emigrate." In other words, the situation of France's Jews is analogous to that of the French Huguenots.

◆ Paragraphs 3 and 4

Herzl then calls for the Jewish Diaspora—the term used to refer to Jews dispersed throughout the world—to unite together in the common goal of forming a state. In the fourth paragraph he asks for a nation to grant them territory and says that the Jewish community will manage the rest. Herzl may have been appealing to Great Britain. "The Solution to the Jewish Question" appeared in a British newspaper so it could gain the attention of the govern-

Captain Alfred Dreyfus with his wife and children (Library of Congress)

ment, which did have some Jewish members. Furthermore, as the world's most powerful nation, the British were in a position to exert their influence overseas on behalf of a Jewish homeland.

This section also reveals that Herzl was not simply an idealist, although naive idealism is not absent. He understands that many Jews and non-Jews would not comprehend what he is proposing. He illustrates his point by noting that new states had appeared in Europe, and these states had been created largely from the wreckage of older empires. Nevertheless, the new nations were populated by people who were linguistically and culturally unified; examples include Italy in 1870 and Germany in 1871. Jews, however, were united only in religion. Hebrew was a dead language, spoken only by rabbis during religious services. Russian Jews had little in common with those in Great Britain and France. In many of these western European countries, the bulk of the population was poorly educated with fewer economic resources, whereas the Jewish population tended to be largely middle class and well educated. Herzl also argues that granting sovereignty to a Jewish homeland would be beneficial to the state through the transfer of property. At the same time, land within other countries, such as Great Britain, would be freed up by the exodus of the Jews.

◆ **Paragraph 5**

Here Herzl ponders where the Jews should make their new homeland—Argentina or Palestine. He points out that Argentina is a rich and vast land with a sparse population, so there would be room. Herzl notes that some anti-Semitism already exists there—probably as a result of immigration from Europe in the second half of the nineteenth century. Many Europeans, including Jews, moved to Argentina to take advantage of Argentina's economic boom in the 1880s. Herzl's statement that Jews need to demonstrate "the intrinsic difference of our new movement" simply indicates that they hope to establish an independent state and not to be outsiders within an existing state. One might wonder how the Argentine government reacted to an offer by someone to take a portion of "unused" territory and create a new state.

◆ **Paragraph 6**

In the final paragraph Herzl turns to Palestine—the biblical Promised Land of the Jews. He notes that the ideal of a homeland there has tremendous appeal to the Jewish Diaspora. He also offers a proposal to the Ottoman sultan, Abdul Hamid II: In return for land, the Jews would manage the finances of the Turks. It is curious how at one point Herzl decries anti-Semitism based on stereotypes and yet, when it suits him, he plays it to his advantage. To be fair, the Ottomans in the late nineteenth century suffered from acute fiscal shortfalls, and thus Herzl assumed that the sultan would be eager to take whatever assistance was offered. Indeed, by making the offer that the World Zionist Congress would pay off the considerable Ottoman debt, Herzl demonstrates that he commanded extensive financial resources. Still, it is doubtful that Abdul Hamid would have been pleased with Herzl's remark that the Jewish presence

would then serve as a rampart of civilization against the barbarism of Asia. Thus, while Herzl denigrates European anti-Semitism, he himself is not above adopting European airs of superiority over the non-Europeans. It is thus not surprising that not long after Herzl's publications and visit, the Ottomans forbade the sale of land to foreign Jews and decreed that Jewish immigrants could settle in Syria and Iraq but not Palestine.

Herzl also proposes that the Jewish state would be neutral, thus suggesting that in return for managing the fiscal affairs of the Ottoman Empire, he expected full independence for his new state. To allay the fears of the Europeans, he grants extraterritorial status to the sanctuaries of Christendom—in other words, they would be protected and not officially incorporated into the state. He obviously recognized that in order to procure the support of European powers for this project, any settlement in Palestine must include protection for Christian holy sites.

What is most interesting about this paragraph is that Herzl never mentions what would happen to the people already dwelling in Palestine or the portion of Argentina that he hoped to claim. One supposes that in Argentina, he envisioned the Pampas, the great plains of Argentina that were largely empty except for vast cattle ranches and a Native American presence. Meanwhile, already living in Palestine were tens of thousands of Arab Christians and Muslims. Indeed, it is not clear what Herzl thought—whether there was plenty of room or that only Jews should live there. Like many Europeans, he may have held a simplistic view that the area was devoid of people. Herzl must have later realized, though, that a large population did live in the area, as he visited the region two years after he wrote his "Solution." Nonetheless, in the appeal for Palestine, this fact was often conveniently overlooked under the slogan that Zionists later adopted: "A land without a people for a people without a land."

Audience

Considering that "The Solution to the Jewish Question" appeared in the *Jewish Chronicle*, a paper printed in English, Herzl was attempting to reach two audiences. The first audience consisted of Jews living in Great Britain and the rest of the English-speaking world. Here he tried to build support among the Jewish community for the idea. The second audience was the British government. The British Empire dominated nearly a quarter of the planet and was in a position to influence other governments, such as those of the Ottomans and Argentina. By securing British support and influence, Herzl could make his "solution" a reality. Without British support, he would have to rely heavily on luck.

Impact

Herzl's article had an enormous impact. It planted the seed of the idea for a Jewish homeland among like-minded

"We have honestly striven everywhere to merge ourselves in the social life
of surrounding communities, and to preserve only the faith of our fathers.
It has not been permitted to us."

(Paragraph 2)

"In countries where we have lived for centuries we are still cried down as
strangers; and often by those whose ancestors were not yet domiciled in the
land where Jews had already made experience of suffering."

(Paragraph 2)

"Let the sovereignty be granted us over a portion of the globe large enough
to satisfy the requirements of the nation—the rest we shall manage for
ourselves."

(Paragraph 4)

"The creation of a new state has in it nothing ridiculous or impossible. We
have, in our day, witnessed the process in connection with nations which
were not in the bulk of the middle class, but poor, less educated, and
therefore weaker than ourselves."

(Paragraph 4)

"Supposing His Majesty the Sultan were to give us Palestine, we could in
return pledge ourselves to regulate the whole finances of Turkey. There we
should also form a portion of the rampart of Europe against Asia, an
outpost of civilisation as opposed to barbarism."

(Paragraph 6)

Zionists and other Jews and in the minds of others as well. If nothing else, he outlined a plan and its necessity. For Herzl, the article helped propel him to the forefront of the Zionist movement. He transformed from a bystander to one of the leaders of Zionism. His influence and charisma became most evident with his success in organizing the First World Zionist Congress in 1897 and his subsequent election as president of the organization.

Although Herzl failed to establish an independent state, in part because of his own lack of tact when dealing with world leaders, he laid the foundation for the future estab-lishment of a homeland in Palestine. Such a homeland was impossible during his lifetime simply because of the existence of the Ottoman Empire. His British friends could exert only so much pressure and influence on the Ottomans, who were concerned with not only waves of immigrants but also the increasing European influence within the empire—influence that undermined Ottoman authority within their own territories. Not until World War I did the opportunity manifest itself: Herzl's seed, first planted in the "The Solution to the Jewish Question," ulti-mately matured into a possibility through the 1917 Balfour

Declaration, in which Britain offered supported for a Jewish state in Palestine.

After World War I, Great Britain and France partitioned the Ottoman Empire, with Syria and Lebanon becoming a French Mandate and Palestine becoming a British Mandate. The intent of the League of Nations, the predecessor of the United Nations, was that Britain and France would develop their mandates so that they would eventually emerge as fully functioning independent states. Well-organized and well-funded Jewish immigration to Palestine, arranged by the Jewish Agency—a part of the World Zionist Organization—increased. The British government generally cooperated with the Jewish Agency in its efforts, although military commanders on the ground often opposed the agency and its work, for they saw the brewing hostility between Jews and Arabs. Eventually violence occurred, giving rise to the Haganah, a Jewish defense force. Also coming to the fore were Jewish terrorist groups such as the Irgun, which sought not only to create a Jewish homeland but also to drive the British out of Palestine. The Arabs, much to their detriment, were less well organized or funded. With the rise of Adolf Hitler in Nazi Germany, Jewish immigration increased. Although the British government attempted to limit it, sympathy for the Jewish plight made it impossible for the government to enact limits to immigration, leading to an Arab rebellion against the British. During World War II many Jews living in Palestine joined the British army to fight the Nazis, thus receiving valuable military training. After World War II, tensions between Jewish settlers, Arabs, and the British only heightened. With stunning revelations about the Holocaust, international pressure, led by the United States, for a Jewish homeland increased. In 1947 the United Nations approved a partition of Palestine into Jewish and Arab areas, and on May 14, 1948, Israel claimed its independence.

Further Reading

■ Articles

Friedman, Isaiah. "The Austro-Hungarian Government and Zionism: 1897–1918." *Jewish Social Studies* 27, no 3 (July 1965): 147–167.

Kornberg, Jacques. "Theodore Herzl: A Reevaluation." *Journal of Modern History* 52, no. 2 (June 1980): 226–252.

Rabinowicz, Oskar K. "Herzl and England." *Jewish Social Studies* 13, no. 1 (January 1951): 25–46.

Rubinstein, Elyakim. "Zionist Attitudes in the Arab-Jewish Dispute to 1936." *Jerusalem Quarterly File* 22 (1982): 120–144.

■ Books

Gelvin, James L. *The Israel-Palestine Conflict: One Hundred Years of War*. Cambridge, U.K.: Cambridge University Press, 2005.

Hertzberg, Arthur, ed. *The Zionist Idea: A Historical Analysis and Reader*. New York: Atheneum, 1981.

Questions for Further Study

1. Just a year after Herzl wrote "A Solution to the Jewish Question," Bernhard von Bülow spoke about Germany's "Place in the Sun." How do these two documents, read side by side, portend some of the major conflicts of the twentieth century?

2. Herzl offered a "solution" to the "Jewish question." So did Nazi Germany some four decades later. How did Herzl's solution differ from that of the Nazis as reflected in such documents as the Nuremberg Laws?

3. Trace the history of the Jews in the twentieth century, using this document, the Balfour Declaration, and the Declaration of the Establishment of the State of Israel.

4. Jewish settlement in Palestine has continued to be a source of controversy and violence. The Jewish state has had to defend itself, sometimes aggressively so, in the face of repeated attacks and acts of terrorism. Do you believe that Jewish settlement in Palestine is justified under the United Nations Declaration of Human Rights?

5. Over the centuries, many people have been troubled by what they have seen as Jewish refusal to assimilate into the larger culture of the countries in which they have lived. Assume for a moment that this was sometimes, perhaps frequently, true. Why do you suppose Jews were unable or unwilling to assimilate? To what extent might that have been the fault of the larger society? What other groups in modern history have resisted assimilation in the dominant culture and why?

Marcus, Amy Dockser. *Jerusalem 1913: The Origins of the Arab-Israeli Conflict*. New York: Viking, 2007.

Milton-Edwards, Beverley. *The Israeli-Palestinian Conflict: A People's War*. New York: Routledge, 2009.

■ **Web Sites**

"Herzl's 'The Jewish State.'" MidEastWeb Web site.
http://www.mideastweb.org/thejewishstate.htm.

"Theodor Herzl." Jewish Virtual Library Web site.
http://www.jewishvirtuallibrary.org/jsource/biography/Herzl
.html.

—Timothy May

THEODOR HERZL'S "A SOLUTION TO THE JEWISH QUESTION"

The Jewish Question still exists. It would be foolish to deny it. It exists wherever Jews live in perceptible numbers. Where it does not yet exist, it will be brought by Jews in the course of their migrations. We naturally move to those places where we are not persecuted, and there our presence soon produces persecution. This is true in every country, and will remain true even in those most highly civilised—France itself is no exception—till the Jewish Question finds a solution on a political basis. I believe that I understand antisemitism, which is in reality a highly complex movement. I consider it from a Jewish standpoint, yet without fear or hatred. I believe that I can see what elements there are in it of vulgar sport, of common trade, of jealousy, of inherited prejudice, of religious intolerance, and also of ligitimate self-defence....

We are one people—One People. We have honestly striven everywhere to merge ourselves in the social life of surrounding communities, and to preserve only the faith of our fathers. It has not been permitted to us. In vain are we loyal patriots, in some places our loyalty running to extremes; in vain do we make the same sacrifices of life and property as our fellow-citizens; in vain do we strive to increase the fame of our native land in science and art, or her Wealth by trade and commerce. In countries where we have lived for centuries we are still cried down as strangers; and often by those whose ancestors were not yet domiciled in the land where Jews had already made experience of suffering. Yet, in spite of all, we are loyal subjects, loyal as the Huguenots, who were forced to emigrate. If we could only be left in peace....

We are one people—our enemies have made us one in our despite, as repeatedly happens in history. Distress binds us together, and thus united, we suddenly discover our strength. Yes, we are strong enough to form a state, and a model state. We possess all human and material resources necessary for the purpose.... The whole matter is in its essence perfectly simple, as it must necessarily be, if it is to come within the comprehension of all.

Let the sovereignty be granted us over a portion of the globe large enough to satisfy the requirements of the nation—the rest we shall manage for ourselves. Of course, I fully expect that each word of this sentence, and each letter of each word, will be torn to tatters by scoffers and doubters. I advise them to do the thing cautiously, if they are themselves sensitive to ridicule. The creation of a new state has in it nothing ridiculous or impossible. We have, in our day, witnessed the process in connection with nations which were not in the bulk of the middle class, but poor, less educated, and therefore weaker than ourselves. The governments of all countries, scourged by antisemitism, will serve their own interests, in assisting us to obtain the sovereignty we want. These governments will be all the more willing to meet us half-way, seeing that the movement I suggest is not likely to bring about any economic crisis. Such crisis, as must follow everywhere as a natural consequence of Jew-baiting, will rather be prevented by the carrying out of my plan. For I propose an inner migration of Christians into the parts slowly and systematically evacuated by Jews. If we are not merely suffered to do what I ask, but are actually helped, we shall be able to effect a transfer of property from Jews to Christians in a manner so peaceable and on so extensive a scale as has never been known in the annals of history....

Shall we choose [the] Argentine [Republic] or Palestine? We will take what is given us and what is selected by Jewish public opinion. Argentina is one of the most fertile countries in the world, extends over a vast area, and has a sparse population. The Argentine Republic would derive considerable profit from the cession of a portion of its territory to us. The present infiltration of Jews has certainly produced some friction, and it would be necessary to enlighten the Republic on the intrinsic difference of our new movement.

Palestine is our ever-memorable historic home. The very name of Palestine would attract our people with a force of extraordinary potency. Supposing His Majesty the Sultan were to give us Palestine, we could in return pledge ourselves to regulate the whole finances of Turkey. There we should also form a portion of the rampart of Europe against Asia, an outpost of civilisation as opposed to barbarism. We should remain a neutral state in intimate connection with the whole of Europe, which would guarantee our continued existence. The sanctuaries of Christendom would be safeguarded by assigning to them an extra-territorial status, such as is well known to

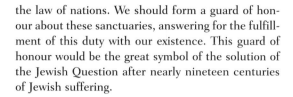

the law of nations. We should form a guard of honour about these sanctuaries, answering for the fulfillment of this duty with our existence. This guard of honour would be the great symbol of the solution of the Jewish Question after nearly nineteen centuries of Jewish suffering.

Bernhard von Bülow (Library of Congress)

BERNHARD VON BÜLOW ON GERMANY'S "PLACE IN THE SUN"

"We do not want to relegate anyone to the shadows, but we also demand our place in the sun."

Overview

Late in 1897 the young German Empire and its bellicose kaiser, Wilhelm II, were presented with the opportunity to exercise the tenets of Germany's *Weltpolitik*, or "world policy," in two international incidents. In the lesser of the two, a former German soldier, Emil Lüders, was arrested in Port-au-Prince, Haiti, for assault and battery; a German warship showed up in the harbor and threatened to bombard the city unless he was released and secured an indemnity. In the more momentous incident, a riot against foreign imperialists in the northern Chinese cities of Kiaochow (now known as Jiaozhou) and Tsingtao (now known as Qingdao) resulted in the murder of several German Catholic missionaries. In response, the barely nascent German navy sent battle cruisers to China, and German naval forces occupied the cities. They established a German "sphere of influence" on the Shandong Peninsula above Beijing and thus a German imperial presence in China.

The ensuing debate in the German parliament, the Reichstag, over these incidents coincided with the introduction of Germany's first Navy Bill, calling for the building of a larger German navy meant mostly to support similar ventures overseas in the future. During the debate, the kaiser's foreign minister, Bernhard von Bülow, asserted the German Empire's desire to find for itself a "place in the sun" in international affairs. The phrase was picked up and used in further speeches by the kaiser himself and became symbolic of his government's antagonistic attitudes in world and European diplomacy. Within a few short years, Germany would have its navy, the occupation of the Shandong Peninsula would spark the Boxer Rebellion in China, and Germany's "place in the sun" would be asserted at the expense of the goodwill of the rest of the world's imperial powers.

Context

In 1871, Germany became a united nation-state, formed around Prussia and by Prussian militarism. Over the course of a series of short wars with Denmark, Austria, and France, the Prussians united with several neighboring principalities to score a series of spectacular victories that instantly accorded the new nation status as the world's most formidable land-based military power. It also upset a balance of diplomatic power in Europe that had been in place since the Napoleonic Wars and reinforced by the stalemated Crimean War (1854–1856). To add to the anxiety, the new state punished the last of its military foes, France, by forcing it to pay an outrageous sum in reparations over the course of five years and annexing two border provinces, Alsace and Lorraine. It was an auspicious and audacious start.

From 1871 to 1890, nearly twenty years after the Franco-Prussian War (1870–1871), German power and ambitions were circumscribed by Germany's own wily Prussian chancellor, Prince Otto von Bismarck. Knowing that Germany's geographic position in the center of Europe made it vulnerable to attack from multiple borders and the North Sea, Bismarck pursued a series of defensive alliances with several European powers, the most permanent of which kept Germany allied with Austria-Hungary, the empire to its south. He also worked to maintain friendly relations with Britain and Russia and to keep the aggrieved France, implacably hostile to the new Germany, isolated from both those powers.

This policy kept Europe at a relative peace, but in 1890 Bismarck was dismissed by the new kaiser of Germany, Wilhelm II. In the late nineteenth century, Charles Darwin's ideas on evolution were circulating widely among intellectuals, and the kaiser was a "social Darwinist": He believed that there were biological distinctions between ethnic and national groups and that these groups were in the midst of a Darwinian "struggle for existence" with each other. Certain "races" were destined to dominate the planet, where other "races" were destined to be slaves. Wilhelm was thus a pan-Germanist, believing that the German "race" needed to compete with other "races" for dominance in European and world affairs and to assert its supremacy. Failure to do so would result in the long-term decline of the German "race" into miscegenation and insignificance. To that end, Germany needed to compete to build an empire, since Great Power status in Europe in the late nineteenth century was measured in colonies and Bismarck's policies of conciliation and defensiveness would simply not accom-

1871

■ **January**
Kaiser Wilhelm I
of Prussia is
named emperor
of Germany at
the Palace of
Versailles in
France, creating
a German
Empire.

1888

■ **June**
Kaiser Wilhelm
II accedes to the
throne of the
German Empire.

1890

■ **March**
Prince Otto von
Bismarck, who
has dominated
European
diplomacy for
nearly twenty
years, is forcibly
retired as
German
chancellor.

1897

■ **June**
Bernhard von
Bülow becomes
Kaiser Wilhelm's
secretary of
state for foreign
affairs.

■ **November**
After the murder of
two German
missionaries,
German naval
troops seize
Shandong
Peninsula in China,
including the cities
of Kiaochow and
Tsingtao.

■ **December 6**
A German gunboat
threatens the
Haitian government
over the
imprisonment of
Emil Lüders. Von
Bülow gives his
"place in the sun"
speech to the
German Reichstag.

plish this. Alsace and Lorraine were only the beginning of what was expected to be a huge European economic union under German control, in addition to a vast empire across the seas, which would replace British hegemony over the planet with that of Germany.

Thus, over the course of the 1890s, the kaiser's government—which according to the German constitution, answered to him in foreign and military affairs and not to the people—began looking to build an empire in Europe and beyond that was worthy of the legacy German *Kultur* (culture) had given to the advance of Western civilization. The problem was that there were few opportunities; most of the available colonies were taken. The British Empire dominated a quarter of the earth's surface and a quarter of its population; the French Empire in Africa connected across the Sahara, and France had a strong presence in Southeast Asia and the Caribbean. The Russian Empire, full of Slavic peoples that any pan-Germanist would find menacing to his racial designs, occupied most of Asia, and various other European empires stretched across the rest of the planet. All Bismarck had assembled during his time in office were four colonies in Africa and a meager assembly of islands in the Pacific. Furthermore, Germany lacked the kind of sizable navy that could be available at a moment's notice to snatch up further territorial conquests. Germany was behind in the race to assert world dominance, and the kaiser was determined to catch up.

One way was simply to throw around Germany's diplomatic weight and the weight of its meager navy; another was to find other places to colonize. The incident in Haiti represented the former; the incident in Kiaochow in China epitomized the latter. In Port-au-Prince, Wilhelm's major irritation was that a former German soldier had suffered an indignity, regardless of whether he had provoked it or not. With the threat of German bombardment, the Haitian government promptly paid Lüders $20,000, ran up a white flag of surrender over the National Palace, and issued an apology. In Shandong, German troops occupied the two major cities, Kiaochow and Tsingtao, and negotiated for a ninety-nine-year lease from China on the entire province, similar to that which the British had negotiated in Hong Kong fifty years earlier.

Above and beyond all else, however, a larger navy seemed necessary to assert future claims on colonization, and these two incidents seemed perfect proof as to why. Therefore, the Reichstag agreed four months after von Bülow's speech to fund a larger navy, a process that began a serious naval arms race in Europe after 1900. These were Germany's first real assertions of *Weltpolitik* under the kaiser, and because of von Bülow's phrasing, the kaiser's repetition, and the repeated seizing of opportunities in diplomacy, Germany's assertion of its "place in the sun" became a well-worn concept in European and world diplomacy in the early twentieth century.

About the Author

Bernhard von Bülow was born in 1849 in what at the time was the Danish-German duchy of Holstein; he was born into an aristocratic German family, but in the newly united Germany the family was not of the highest aristocratic order. Von Bülow graduated from law school at the University of Mainz in 1872, but he briefly left school in 1870 to fight in the Franco-Prussian War as an officer. Through his military pedigree, he achieved the highest social status in Germany, where he came into contact with the kaiser's social court. He was generally described as ingratiating, unprincipled, and fawning, which made his career possible. Although his diplomatic contemporaries referred to von Bülow as "the eel," Kaiser Wilhelm II liked the way von Bülow parroted his political and diplomatic opinions. In the beginning, he was made available for diplomatic postings; later, he occupied a series of embassy positions in the capitals of Europe for the new German Empire. A pan-Germanist like Wilhelm, he came to domestic political attention under Bismarck when he called for the forcible removal of Poles from eastern Germany. When Wilhelm II dismissed Bismarck as chancellor in 1890, men like von Bülow became advocates of the kaiser's aggressive foreign policy aims, which was often referred to as the "New Course." This led to few actual territorial acquisitions and more often to international disputes where German rhetoric threatened the use of German arms.

Von Bülow was a master of such rhetoric, which led him to the position of secretary of state for foreign affairs in 1897, when he made the famous "place in the sun" speech. He was made a count in 1900 when he succeeded to the office of the chancellery, where he served the kaiser for nine years. During his twelve years in consequential office, Germany acquired few colonies beyond Shandong Province but asserted its diplomatic preeminence and began the construction of a navy meant to rival that of the British Empire, which drove Britain into militarily based friendships with France and Russia by 1907.

Explanation and Analysis of the Document

Bernhard von Bülow delivered his "place in the sun" speech to the German Reichstag on December 6, 1897. The Navy Bill had just been introduced in the Reichstag, and the Reichstag was in charge of Germany's budget; therefore, several major figures in the kaiser's government were available for the debate, including Chancellor Chlodwig Fürst zu Hohenlohe-Schillingsfürst and Admiral Alfred von Tirpitz, who spoke in favor of building up the navy. Von Tirpitz claimed the navy would have only a defensive purpose. In opposition, the Social Democrat Bruno Schoenlank, editor of one of the nation's most powerful newspapers, forcefully denied that the navy could possibly be merely for defense, since, if it was, such a bill would have been introduced to the Reichstag far earlier. He claimed that the real purpose of the navy was to ensnare Germany in foreign adventures like that in China, which would only make for further conflict with Britain and Japan.

At the time, both the affairs in Port-au-Prince and Kiaochow were ongoing, so there was little von Bülow could say

about either of them directly. Yet, clearly, the possibility of establishing an economic toehold in China held great promise, and von Bülow was apparently excited over the possibility of expanding Germany's world role to a new sphere for the first time. What was perhaps most interesting was how he abandoned the careful wording of the previous speakers in addressing Schoenlank's assertions and instead verified that Germany did indeed seek to carve out a place for itself in the company of the great powers of the world. While he never addressed the actual Navy Bill itself, he undoubtedly seized the opportunity to give immediate, available instances as to why a larger navy was to the nation's advantage in becoming a world power.

It is important to note that von Bülow was not required to answer to the Reichstag about foreign affairs; according

Time Line

1897

- **December 7**
  The Haitian government bows to German might in the Lüders affair, running up a white flag over the capitol building and paying a $20,000 indemnity.

1898

- **March**
  The Navy Bill is passed by the German Reichstag, and expansion of the German navy begins.

1900

- **June**
  The German ambassador is murdered by Chinese rebels, which prompts European military involvement in the Boxer Rebellion.

- **June**
  A second Navy Bill is passed by the German Reichstag with the goal of achieving parity in battleships with the British Royal Navy.

German troops awaiting transport to China, to fight in the Boxer Rebellion (Library of Congress)

to the German constitution, he need only do the kaiser's bidding, as it was the kaiser who had appointed him. So his willingness to publicly discuss the affairs at all quite likely had a great deal to do with his desire to bring public opinion behind the kaiser's "New Course" and the desire for an expanded navy to implement it. Von Bülow opens by admitting that he could say little about the ongoing disputes in Haiti and China. He adds that he will inform the Reichstag more fully when events warrant, but for the moment, he states categorically that the German government will not be satisfied merely with Lüders's release from jail. Some form of compensation by way of apology would also be due from the Haitian government.

Von Bülow then addresses Schoenlank's attacks, not by denying Germany's intent to take territory in other parts of the world but by embracing it. He states that the pursuit of imperialism would not be a "futile enterprise" and that it is important to compete with other imperial powers from the very beginning in new parts of the world. The reign of "pure doctrine"—meaning the high-minded avoidance of imperial enterprise—he considers naive and long past its prime.

Then von Bülow addresses the Kiaochow occupation directly, explaining why it took place and asserting the benevolent intentions of the German occupation toward China. He considers it the righting of a serious wrong, since the murder of missionaries "who peacefully pursued their holy occupations" was an egregious breach of trust between Germany and China. He asserts that other expansionist-minded nations would have done the same thing, and, in fact, it was common for better-established European imperialist states to protect their missionaries in places like Africa. Plus, he asserts his expectation that other European powers would soon have to respect German interests in East

Asia as well. Effectively, Germany was about to move into its "place in the sun," as he famously refers to it, starting in Shandong Province. In the social Darwinist conception of racial competition on a world-ranging scale, Germany was about to "protect [its] rights and interests" by establishing a new colonial presence in China.

Audience

The Reichstag, the elected governing body of the German people, was the most important audience for von Bülow's speech. Like any national governing body, the Reichstag reflected the diversity of the German populace—there was a huge Socialist Party, of which Schoenlank was a powerful member, but also large conservative, Catholic, and nationalist parties that tended to side with whatever the kaiser's government planned to do. In the midst of the debate over the Navy Bill, von Bülow sought to provide the Reichstag's wide-ranging political members with a rationale for the creation of a stronger navy, and so he used the examples he had at hand.

Again, von Bülow, Chancellor Fürst zu Hohenlohe-Schillingsfürst, and Admiral von Tirpitz were not required to speak to the Reichstag about foreign policy or, for that matter, about the Navy Bill. But their presence in the chamber was a clear affirmation of the fact that the kaiser's government considered the Navy Bill important and that the Reichstag, with its power of the purse string, was required to support it. Moreover, encouraging the German people to support the patriotic effort to build a Germany navy, and a German empire, would give the kaiser's government the powerful weight of public opinion standing behind it. Through the Reichstag, then, von Bülow also expected to reach the German people, who would presumably read about the proceedings in the next day's newspapers.

Impact

One ramification of the assertion of Germany's "place in the sun" occurred in China. The German navy's intervention in Shandong Province came after China's humiliating loss to Japan in the Sino-Japanese War in 1894–1895; Germany and the other Western imperial powers discovered that the Qing Dynasty's treasury was as bankrupt as its army was ineffective. Therefore, it seemed clear to any number of imperialists that China could only benefit from European and American economic penetration. The Chinese peasant population, as usual, bore the burden of the Qing Empire's failures, paying massive taxes to make up for the treasury's losses in the war. Many Chinese blamed foreigners for their problems—the Europeans and the Qing themselves, who were Manchurian—thus prompting the murder of the German missionaries in 1897 and Germany's intervention.

As other Western powers asserted their own spheres of influence over Chinese ports, German capitalists bought farmland, mines, and railway rights-of-way and began to

Wilhelm II (Library of Congress)

"We do not at all feel the need to have our fingers in every pot. But we are of the opinion that it is not advisable to exclude Germany at the outset from competition with other peoples in countries that hold promise."

(Paragraph 4)

"The times are past when the Germans left to one of its neighbors the earth, to another the sea, and reserved the sky for itself—when pure doctrine reigned, these times are over. We regard it as one of our most important tasks to promote our shipping interests, particularly in East Asia, and to maintain our trade and our industry."

(Paragraph 5)

"In a word: we do not want to relegate anyone to the shadows, but we also demand our place in the sun."

(Paragraph 11)

import goods to compete with those produced in China, putting many peasants and businessmen out of work. As a result of their anger, an old Daoist cult returned to prominence in Shandong Province. The Yihetuan, or Society of the Harmonious and Righteous Fists, had arisen in the early eighteenth century in opposition to the Manchurian Qing emperors. In order to tap into the supernatural force of the Dao, or "way of the universe," its members practiced a martial art that looked to Europeans like boxing. Thus they acquired a European nickname, the "Boxers," by which they are better known to history. Long suppressed, in 1898 the Boxers became more popular in opposition to German penetration in Shandong, with their slogan of "annihilate the foreigner"; by the late nineteenth century "the foreigner" from Europe was clearly more dangerous than the Manchurian Qings, and the Boxers even had the tacit support of the Empress Dowager Cixi, who ran the Chinese empire as regent.

In early 1900 the Boxer movement had spread beyond Shandong Province to Beijing (known as Peking at the time) and escaped the control of the Qing armies, which were only half-hearted in their pursuit of the Boxers anyway. The Boxers focused on killing Christian converts and westernized Asians; one Japanese businessman had his heart torn out of his body, largely because he was wearing a European suit. In a series of riots the Boxers drove nearly all foreigners in Beijing back into the enclave where they lived, and for fifty-five days the Boxers laid siege to the embassy compounds. An international expedition was assembled from nearby forces representing Germany, Britain, France, Japan, the United States, Austria-Hungary, Russia, Italy, and an anti-Boxer Chinese contingent.

Fighting their way into Beijing three different times, troops finally lifted the siege when a company of Indian soldiers, led by the German commander of the entire expedition, Count Alfred von Waldersee, drove off the Boxers, and another force of German soldiers followed up by plundering, looting, and raping throughout Beijing and other cities sympathetic to the Boxers. Back in Germany, the kaiser crowed,

> Just as the Huns a thousand years ago, under the leadership of Attila, gained a reputation by virtue of which they still live in historical tradition, so may the name Germany become known in such a manner in China, that no Chinese will ever again dare to look askance at a German. (Zarrow, p. 4)

Germany's involvement in the Boxer Rebellion, among other events, clearly spurred the continued growth of the German navy as a major military force. Kaiser Wilhelm had summered as a boy on the Isle of Wight with his grandmother, Queen Victoria of Britain, and had admired the British navy as it conducted maneuvers in the English Channel. Now he would have his own navy to rival that of Britain, a nation-state that he seemed determined to provoke, despite all his assertions otherwise. Between 1899 and 1902 the

British fought a colonial war in South Africa against the so-called Afrikaaners, or Boers, Dutch Calvinists who had independently settled in South Africa and despised British rule. Because the kaiser was a racial nationalist and saw the Boers as a "racially similar" people, his government supplied them with Mauser rifles, which enraged the British government.

Worse, on the verge of the outbreak of the war, the kaiser ended a speech with the assertion, "Bitterly do we need a powerful German fleet" (Gauss, p. 150). In early 1900 another Navy Bill was introduced to the Reichstag, this time with the purpose of building a fleet to match the British Royal Navy in size. It passed in June 1900. In a speech to the North German Regatta Association a year later, Kaiser Wilhelm outlined his growing navy's purpose and, in the process, claimed von Bülow's phrasing as his own, stating: "In spite of the fact that we have no such fleet as we should have, we have conquered for ourselves a place in the sun" (Gauss, p. 181).

As von Bülow and his cohorts had hoped, the German people were solidly behind the kaiser's effort to build a larger navy by 1901. With the passage of the second Navy Bill in 1900, a popular program was attached to it, the German Navy League. Workers could contribute a portion of their weekly pay toward the state's purchase of a battleship, specifically with the goal of countering the popularity of the Socialist (and anti-kaiser) Social Democratic Party with an appeal to pride in the German military. By 1907 the Navy League had a million members. Patriotism became equated with the assertion of Germany's "place in the sun" in the early twentieth century, and the result would be an unstable and dangerous diplomatic situation in Europe.

With the growth of a massive and powerful German navy in the early twentieth century, Kaiser Wilhelm's government, with Count Bernhard von Bülow at its helm as chancellor from 1900 to 1909, managed to offend three out of four of the major powers in Europe with its demand for a "place in the sun." France was already an implacable enemy after losing Alsace and Lorraine in 1871. The Russian Empire, which Bismarck had carefully courted through the Reinsurance Treaty (1887), designed to keep either power neutral in the event of a European war, was made up of a subservient Slavic people with whom a superior race like the Germans should not be aligned, according to the pan-Germanist Wilhelm. He allowed the Reinsurance Treaty to lapse in 1892, and the French promptly locked the Russians into an anti-German alliance in 1894.

Finally, though every public utterance of the German government denied the reality, there was only one power against which a large German navy might be directed: Britain. Despite the kaiser's continual denial that his government harbored any ill intentions toward the British, it was obvious that any "place in the sun" to be acquired in a colonized world would be acquired at the expense of the world's largest colonial power and that any navy built to assert that "place in the sun" would likewise have to rival the world's largest naval power. The kaiser's public and military support for the Boers in 1899 only affirmed that fact.

Thus, despite Wilhelm's admiration for the British Royal Navy, the assembly of an imperial navy equal in size and firepower was calculated to drive the British government and people to distraction with a challenge to their island's security. In 1904 the British signed an entente with the French; in 1907 Britain followed up, signing an entente with the Russians. The British had thus assembled diplomatic defensive arrangements with the French and the Russians in the face of German aggression, and Europe was poised on the brink of war.

Questions for Further Study

1. What role did colonial competition play in Germany's attitude toward world affairs in the late nineteenth and early twentieth centuries?

2. How did the concept of Germany's "place in the sun" contribute to the alignment of powers in Europe that would eventually lead to World War I? What role did intangible factors such as suspicion, distrust, and prestige contribute to this alignment of powers?

3. Compare this document with the Nuremberg Laws. How did von Bülow's formulation eventually give rise to the Nuremberg Laws of Nazi Germany?

4. What effect did German aims and ambitions have on China at the turn of the twentieth century? For help, consult Articles Providing for the Favorable Treatment of the Great Ching Emperor after His Abdication (1912).

5. How might the events surrounding the Carlsbad Decrees of 1819 have helped lay the intellectual foundations for Bülow's assertion of Germany's "Place in the Sun"?

Further Reading

■ Articles

Hewitson, Mark. "The Kaiserreich in Question: Constitutional Crisis in Germany before the First World War." *Journal of Modern History* 73, no. 4 (December 2001): 725–780.

Kaiser, David E. "Germany and the Origins of the First World War." *Journal of Modern History* 55, no. 3 (September 1983): 442–474.

Mommsen, Wolfgang J. "Kaiser Wilhelm II and German Politics." *Journal of Contemporary History* 25, no. 2/3 (May–June 1990): 289–316.

■ Books

Beckett, Ian F. W. *The Great War: 1914–1918*. 2nd ed. Harlow, U.K.: Pearson/Longman, 2007.

Berghahn, Volker R. *Germany and the Approach of War in 1914*. New York: St. Martin's Press, 1973.

Clark, Christopher M. *Kaiser Wilhelm II*. New York: Longman, 2000.

Gauss, Christian, ed. *The German Emperor as Shown in His Public Utterances*. New York: Charles Scribner's Sons, 1915.

Lerman, Katharine Anne. *The Chancellor as Courtier: Bernhard von Bülow and the Governance of Germany, 1900–1909*. New York: Cambridge University Press, 1990.

Schrecker, John E. *Imperialism and Chinese Nationalism: Germany in Shantung*. Cambridge, Mass.: Harvard University Press, 1971.

Zarrow, Peter. *China in War and Revolution, 1895–1949*. New York: Routledge, 2005.

■ Web Sites

Chickering, Roger, and Steven Chase Gummer, eds. "Wilhelmine Germany and the First World War (1890–1918)." German History in Documents and Images Web site.
   http://germanhistorydocs.ghi-dc.org/section.cfm?section_id=11.

—David Simonelli

Bernhard von Bülow on Germany's "Place in the Sun"

Gentlemen, in the course of today's discussion, two overseas affairs of my government were brought to my attention: one being the affair in Port-au-Prince relating to the arrest and condemnation of the German national Emil Lüders, now being negotiated between the German Reich and Haiti, and the other being in Kiaochow [Jiaoxian] after our cruiser fleet had been sent to protect the German delegation there. Both affairs are ongoing, and for the moment I am required to show restraint in discussing them, though the desire for more information is understandable. As soon as the time comes, I will be glad and ready to give more information to this high house about what happened in both affairs from our point of view.

For today I would like to explain only the following about the incident in Haiti. We have not contented ourselves with the release of Lüders; on the contrary we regard it as inequitable, and it is our right and our obligation to demand appropriate satisfaction and compensation from the Haitian government, according to the rules of international law, for the lost rights of a German citizen.

I hope that the Haitian government will not hesitate to meet our requirements, which are moderate and well founded and to which we are entitled. I believe in all certainty that we have not only right on our side but also the will and the power to assert our validity.

Representative [Bruno] Schoenlank seemed to be afraid that we wanted to become entangled in adventures. Do not be afraid at all, gentlemen! The chancellor is not the man, and his workforce are not the people to possibly look to undertake a futile enterprise. Moreover, we do not at all feel the need to have our fingers in every pot. But we are of the opinion that it is not advisable to exclude Germany at the outset from competition with other peoples in countries that hold promise.

The times are past when the Germans left to one of its neighbors the earth, to another the sea, and reserved the sky for itself—when pure doctrine reigned, these times are over. We regard it as one of our most important tasks to promote our shipping interests, particularly in East Asia, and to maintain our trade and our industry.

Our cruiser division was sent to Kiaochow and occupied the bay in reparation for the murder of German and Catholic missionaries and to ensure enhanced security in the future against the recurrence of such events. Negotiations involving both sides are taking place, and consideration of the nature of diplomatic negotiations and business forces me to weigh my words very carefully. Nevertheless, I can say this much: with respect to China we are well meaning and have only friendly intentions. We want neither to snub nor to provoke China.

Despite the serious wrong done to us, the occupation of the port of Kiaochow was undertaken with the greatest care. We wish for the continuation of the friendship that has so long bound Germany with China and which so far has never been clouded. But the necessary condition for the continuation of this friendship is mutual respect of each other's rights. The massacre of our missionaries was the foremost compelling reason for our intervention, because we were not of the opinion that these pious people, who peacefully pursued their holy occupations, would be regarded as outlaws.

In addition, apart from this sad incident, we had a number of other complaints against China. We hope that we will be able to resolve these complaints civilly in the course of respectful negotiations. But we cannot allow the opinion to take hold in China that actions that would not be allowed against others can be presumed to be allowed with respect to us.

We require that German missionaries and German traders, German goods, the German flag, and German ships all be respected in the same way that China respects other powers.

Finally, we gladly stand ready to respect the interests of the other great powers in East Asia, knowing that our own interests will be entitled to their respect.

In a word: we do not want to relegate anyone to the shadows, but we also demand our place in the sun.

As in western India and true to the traditions of German policy, we will likewise be anxious to protect our rights and interests in East Asia—without unnecessary harshness but also without weakness.

Emperor Guangxu's Abolition of the Examination System

"We must establish elementary and high schools, colleges and universities, in accordance with those of foreign countries."

Overview

Emperor Guangxu's abolition of the examination system was part of the Hundred Days' Reform, an attempt he undertook from June 11 to September 21, 1898, to make China stronger and better able to stand up to the West. The Hundred Days' Reform—which more precisely spanned 104 days—brought several modernizations to Chinese society, including a reorganization of the Chinese army to more closely resemble Western armies, the provision of improved military arms and equipment, updates to the system of military education, a remodeling of the broader Chinese education system to be more like foreign (both Western and Japanese) education, and the abolition of the literary essay, which had been the basis of the Chinese examination system that had been in effect for over a thousand years. China felt that it needed to stand up to foreign powers because the West and also Japan had forced treaties upon China that set up leaseholds called "spheres of influence." While the foreign countries technically did not own Chinese land within these spheres of influence, under the terms of the leasehold they were allowed to operate as if they did, building factories, railroads, telegraph infrastructure, and mines. Under the system of spheres of influence, Germany essentially controlled the Shandong Peninsula, Russia leased Port Arthur (now Lüshun), Japan controlled Formosa (now Taiwan) after its victory in the Sino-Japanese War, Britain controlled Port Edward (now Weihai), and France had a leasehold near modern-day Guangzhou.

Japan had begun rapid modernization thirty years earlier, and Emperor Guangxu was determined that China could do the same. The Chinese state-sponsored examination system had remained important as the primary method of choosing bureaucratic officials for more than one thousand years, with various refinements and changes made to the examination system over time. It also played a vital role in the training and rewarding of members of the educated Chinese elite. Conservative members of the Manchu court proved extremely unhappy with all of the Hundred Days' Reform and with the emperor and his progressive advisers. (Manchus, an ethnic minority in modern China hailing from Manchuria, north of the Great Wall, established the Qing Dynasty to rule China from 1644 to 1912.) Owing to the conservative reaction against the Hundred Days' Reform, Emperor Guangxu was quietly put under house arrest on September 21, 1898, and his aunt, Empress Dowager Cixi, came out of retirement to rule China once again. Two of the emperor's closest advisers, Kang Youwei and Liang Qichao, fled China, while some of the other reformers were executed. September 21, 1898, thus marked the end of the Hundred Days' Reform, and conservative factions of the Manchu Qing Dynasty once more took control.

Context

The examination system as a method of selection of governmental officials was founded upon the study of the classics of Confucius, who lived in China from 551 to 479 BCE and is the philosopher credited as the original author of the Five Classics, a corpus of five books used by Confucianism as the basis of studies. Historians believe that his followers recorded these Five Classics in writing at later times in history, following his teachings. The Four Books, in turn, are texts that provide a guide to Confucianism. The Five Classics and Four Books were all written before 300 BCE. Under Confucian doctrine as embodied in these texts, a righteous (or upright and effective) ruler needs to provide moral guidance to his subjects. In accord with this line of thinking, the emperor needs to benefit from a group of advisers with moral integrity and wisdom. Among scholars, many years of studying the Confucian classics and reading and writing commentaries on them led to the formation of an elite group of educated men who were able to pass the rigorous examinations devised to distinguish them.

As in Europe during later eras, China was long dominated by aristocratic families that at times were more powerful than the Chinese emperor. In 196 BCE, when the Han Dynasty (206 BCE–220 CE) began to reorganize the empire, Emperor Gaozu issued an edict that local aristocrats were to look for talented men to come to the capital and potentially fill governmental posts. Under Emperor Wudi in 124 BCE, outstanding young men from all of the provinces came to the capital to study under Confucian classics scholar

Time Line

BEFORE 300 BCE

- The Confucian Four Books and Five Classics are written, outlining the doctrine that a righteous (upright and effective) ruler needs to provide moral guidance to his subjects.

196 BCE

- Emperor Gaozu issues an edict that local aristocrats are to look for talented men to come to the capital to fill governmental posts.

124 BCE

- Under Emperor Wudi, outstanding young men from all of the provinces travel to the capital to study under Confucian classics scholar-officials with the aim of earning government positions; this marks the first link between Confucian studies and the selection of officials.

EARLY 600s

- The modern examination system begins during the Sui Dynasty.

1700

- The quota system is established to ensure representation from all provinces of applicants sitting for the examinations.

officials; after one year they were examined and given official positions. The year 124 BCE thus marks the first time that Confucian studies and the selection of officials were linked. As power ebbed and flowed, the first attempts at an examination system faded, and powerful local families again controlled many government appointments. During the Sui Dynasty (581–618 CE), following several centuries of division within China among warring families, the examination system was again begun, as an effort to break up aristocratic power and institute a method to impartially choose governmental officials below the level of the emperor. During the Tang Dynasty (618–907) the examination system was refined such that examinations in different categories were conducted at the capital on a regular basis. The Song, Yuan, Ming, and Qing Dynasties (960–1912) relied heavily on the examination system to choose officials, with the emperor granting final approval, up until the discord and disruptions at the end of the Qing Dynasty, including Emperor Guangxu's abolition of the examination system in 1898.

Throughout the history of the examinations, the rate of passage of the state-sponsored tests was very low. Among scholars sitting for the examinations, only one or two out of every one hundred passed. However, scholars were allowed to keep attempting the examination in future years unless they were disqualified for an infraction such as cheating. Memorization and thorough understanding of the Confucian classics was always the main focus of study for the examinations, while at different times candidates were also required to demonstrate skillful calligraphy, to write poetry, or to discuss contemporary affairs, historic subjects, and politics. Sponsorship by influential Chinese men was still a requirement to be able to sit for an examination during the Sui Dynasty. During the succeeding Tang Dynasty, powerful men were still able to nominate their sons and heirs to official positions without their needing to pass any examinations, but tensions existed between appointed officials and officials who had passed the examination.

The Song Dynasty (960–1279) was when the examination system reached its height, and later changes, until it was abolished, were only minor. Any scholar-official who passed the examination and was approved by the emperor became prestigious, powerful, and in most cases, especially if he was willing to accept gifts, wealthy. His family also enjoyed many benefits as the result of his success. The examination system increasingly influenced culture and society as many thousands of men all across the nation studied and memorized the same materials. Some critics believe the examination system stifled originality. Other historians point to the high levels of scholastic achievement in China and believe that over one thousand years of such serious intellectual pursuit was beneficial in state building and in cultural aspects.

Some historians have compared seventeenth-century Europe, with its religious wars and philosophical struggles between Protestants and Catholics, with China during the same time period, when its Confucian spiritual center remained intact. As long as the examination system focused on the Five Classics, works attributed to Confucius, thousands of candidates were studying and memorizing the same body of knowledge. This may have enabled China to avoid the religious strife and unrest of Europe. The Jesuit Matteo Ricci witnessed the examinations of 1604 in Peking (now Beijing) and was very impressed. He wrote in his diary, "Another remarkable fact and quite worthy of note as marking a difference from the West, is that the entire kingdom is administered by the Order of the Learned, commonly known as The Philosophers. The responsibility for the orderly management of the entire realm is wholly and completely committed to their charge and care" (qtd. in Schrecker, p. 94). By the Song Dynasty, the local level "metropolitan" examinations did not require recommendations from powerful local men. Any candidate, as long as he was not in a prohibited class, could present himself for the examination. The prohibited classes included men who were slaves, prostitutes, or entertainers and those who worked in certain professions, such as butchers and tanners; women were never able to take examinations. At times during various dynasties, merchants and their family members were also prohibited from sitting for examinations. Although details of the examination system shifted over the years, in general the first level of the examination system, the provincial level, was held every year. For those who passed the first level, the next level was held every three years.

Song Dynasty literati (scholars) listed their occupation as *jinshi*, or preparing for the *jinshi* examination. During 1148 and 1246 the average ages of men taking the examinations were thirty-six and thirty-five, respectively, and the age range of candidates was from nineteen to sixty-six. A man who was able to pass the various levels of the examination system was considered a pinnacle of moral wisdom and had great advantages overall. He was exempt from corvée labor (forced labor demanded by the state, such as road building or public works) and the taxes that could replace it, and he was protected from lawsuits and punishment such as lashing for minor offenses. He could wear a special scholar's gown. For one to maintain his status as a member of the literati, regular examinations were required. Limited degrees were allowed to be purchased, however, and some officials were able to purchase part of the examination and pass part of the examination. Over the three centuries of the Song Dynasty, officials abolished various divisions of the examination system until only the *jinshi*, the most difficult level, remained. Officials tried to avoid favoritism by covering the names of candidates before the examinations were graded and hiring copyists to transcribe every examination under the theory that a grader thus would not know whose examination he was grading by the style of writing. A successful candidate still had to meet with the emperor and receive final recommendation.

Some scholars have studied printing in China in the late sixteenth and early seventeenth centuries, during the Ming Dynasty (1368–1644), and how it affected the examination system. Printed books, though beyond the financial ability of the very poor, were still much less expensive than hiring private tutors and allowed students to confidently learn on their

Time Line	
1761	■ Sui Chaodong submits a memorial to the Qianlong emperor, asking for the revival of "avoidance" examinations to help family and friends evade the examination system; the emperor condemns him to death and later abolishes the special examinations.
1898	■ **June 11** Emperor Guangxu begins the Hundred Days' Reform, which includes an edict ending the examination system.
	■ **September 21** Emperor Guangxu is deposed in a coup, and the Empress Dowager Cixi again takes control of the government.
1901	■ **September 7** The Boxer Protocol is signed following China's defeat during the Boxer Rebellion; under one of the provisions, civil service examinations are to be suspended for five years in all areas where foreigners were massacred or subjected to cruel treatment.
1904	■ The last metropolitan examinations are held.

Time Line

1905

- **September 2**
  Empress Dowager Cixi issues an order that the examination system is to be abolished in a year.

1908

- **November 14**
  Emperor Guangxu dies, prefiguring the end of the Qing Dynasty.

own. With thousands of men taking examinations each year, books to help candidates pass the examinations became very popular and profitable for printers. The Four Books and Five Classics of Confucius came to form the basis for what was called the "eight-legged" style of essay, one that was highly structured and had official style requirements. Dependence on this writing style, some historians believe, actually eroded the authority of the Confucian classics and turned a large number of Chinese literati into professional writers with less focus on scholarship and more focus on style. Further, when commercial printers published model essays, copying and cheating increased as some students merely memorized the model essays. In 1700 a quota system was established to ensure representation from all provinces of applicants sitting for the examinations. This had the unintended consequence of favoring those who were related to high officials when ministers assigned special quotas for relatives, whose examination papers were separated from the rest.

Despite certain inequities, since the examination system was open to all men with only a few exceptions, it was on the surface very equal. Also, belief in the possibility of social mobility helped stabilize society. However, the circumstances of the poor, whose families needed them to work in the fields and who were unable to afford years of study or the expense of hiring private tutors, gave the rich a tremendous advantage. With no public education system until near the end of the Qing Dynasty, students who could afford private tutors and had the resources of domestic libraries and educated fathers passed the examinations in overwhelming numbers compared to the few examples of those without such advantages. The Qianlong Emperor reacted angrily in 1761, when an official submitted a memorial requesting the revival of "avoidance" examinations to help officials' recommended family and friends evade the examination system in seeking recruitment. The Qianlong Emperor condemned the man who submitted the memorial, Sui Chaodong, to death and later abolished special examinations altogether. The examination system had

been crafted to diminish the power of important families, but the ruling houses of imperial China continued to witness power struggles among these families, the emperor, the families of the emperors' wives, and court eunuchs.

There were many less direct ways to gain advantages in the course of the examination system. Even though candidates' names were taken off the exam papers, sometimes candidates met as study groups before the examinations and asked potential graders to be their critics. When this happened, the examiners could recognize the students' style and wording and give them advantages, especially when bribes were involved. Sometimes open cheating, such as the bribing of both examiners and copyists, was used. Occasionally, copyists would change exams to improve them, and from time to time they rewrote entire papers, for a fee. Substitutes sometimes took the exams, and occasionally a candidate would write his own as well as several other examination papers. Candidates were caught with full examinations written on their undergarments, and candidates were known to illicitly smuggle books into the examinations. Other loopholes in the examination system included allegedly lax grading.

Some Chinese complained that focusing on Confucianism and memorization inhibited creative thinking. Some people believed that study for the examination took too many years, and some wanted more political questions and contemporary affairs to be stressed. Others wanted more practical categories, such as mathematics and foreign affairs, to be added. Throughout the nineteenth century the purchase system increased, and many more candidates became officials by buying the title instead of earning it through study. The Qing Dynasty, started by the Manchus from north of the Great Wall, ruled China from 1644 to 1912. Conservative opposition within the Manchu court made reform or changes very difficult until the last decade of the nineteenth century, after China lost the Sino-Japanese War in 1895. Kang Youwei and Liang Qichao, as well as other reformers, were able to influence Emperor Guangxu to initiate the Hundred Days' Reform on June 11, 1898. Among changes to Chinese military organization, training, and arms, his reform also included the Imperial Rescript on Education. This rescript attempted to modify the Chinese education system to be more like Japanese and Western education. Most significantly, it ended the literary essay, the thousand-year-old method of choosing bureaucrats called "mandarin scholars" who occupied high levels of the Qing Dynasty government. As a result of opposition by conservative members of the Manchu court, Emperor Guangxu was put under house arrest on September 21, 1898, ending the Hundred Days' Reform and allowing conservative factions to regain control of the government of Qing China.

About the Author

Emperor Guangxu is credited with the series of edicts constituting the Hundred Days' Reform, although most of the reforms were proposed by earlier political figures and a group of men in Beijing who were going to sit for the highest level of examinations in 1895. Emperor Guangxu was born in 1871 and became emperor at the age of four. When he assumed formal power, he began to formulate reforms that he believed would make China more politically and economically powerful. His advisers were more progressive than the Qing Dynasty conservatives, including his aunt, the Empress Dowager Cixi. When his reforms became too threatening to the existing power structure, his aunt had him deposed and imprisoned on September 21, 1898. He died on November 14, 1908, under suspicious circumstances, one day before his aunt died.

Two Confucian scholars, Kang Youwei and Liang Qichao, coordinated the reform movement. Both were seeking to pass the highest-level examination and attain the *jinshi* degree. Kang Youwei, born in 1858, believed in constitutional monarchy. He maintained that Confucius had not been averse to social change and that China could develop and progress under Confucianism. After Empress Dowager Cixi took control of China, he fled to Japan and remained in exile for sixteen years. On his return to China, he taught at a private academy in Shanghai and died there in 1927.

Kang Youwei's student Liang Qichao passed the first civil service examination at age eleven, in 1884. He passed the second level at the age of sixteen, the youngest successful scholar at the time. After he met Kang Youwei in 1890, he helped Kang organize almost thirteen hundred examination candidates in Beijing to protest the peace terms of the Sino-Japanese War. He fled to Japan along with Kang Youwei and other reformers when the conservatives ended the reform movement, living in exile for fourteen years. At the end of his life taught at a university in Tianjin, China.

Explanation and Analysis of the Document

The first sentence of the reform edict that abolished the examination system refers to Chinese scholars' lacking practical education. This assertion is made because Chinese scholars attempting to pass the three levels of examination were required to memorize the Four Books and Five Classics of Confucius, to understand and write about famous commentaries written on these Confucian classics, and to write in the "eight-legged" style, a highly structured official essay format. The Four Books and Five Classics of Confucius were the basis of China's education system for one thousand years, but the Guangxu Emperor did not consider this foundation to be practical knowledge. He refers to a lack of scientific instructors. Chinese scholars studied what would enable them to pass the three levels of examination; science was not one of the subjects, and Emperor Guangxu wanted this to change.

The emperor refers to how weak China has become. In 1895 China lost the Sino-Japanese War and, consequently, the territory of Formosa, while the incursion of European powers had long been a true threat to Chinese sovereignty. Through the eighteenth century, European maritime traders continued to sail into China's eastern seaboard and Southeast Asia, and Russia pushed across Siberia and threatened

Empress Dowager Cixi (© Hulton-Deutsch Collection/CORBIS)

China's northern border. In 1793 Great Britain's George Macartney attempted to set up an alliance with China but was rebuffed by Emperor Qianlong. The West still wanted to buy China's tea, silk, and porcelain but did not want to spend as much silver as it was spending, leading to the two Opium Wars of 1839–1842 and 1856–1860, with China losing the first to Great Britain and the second to Great Britain and France. The treaty ending the First Opium War allowed the West to have unrestricted access to certain Chinese ports, assessed reparations that China had to pay to Great Britain, and awarded Hong Kong to Great Britain. The treaty ending the Second Opium War opened more Chinese ports to the West and allowed Great Britain to navigate Chinese rivers. Other Western countries forced treaties upon China that set up leaseholds, or spheres of influence, and those countries with most-favored-nation clauses were allowed the same rights in China as Great Britain had.

Because of these Western incursions into China, Emperor Guangxu designed the 1898 edict to change China's education system to focus on practical items such as science and military training. By establishing elementary schools, high schools, colleges, and universities, China would be able to stand up to the West. According to Emperor Guangxu, China needed to end the old ways of doing things, which included abolishing the literary essay, the Chinese scholarly exam that had been in effect to choose Chinese officials for more than a thousand years. The emperor states his belief that the Chinese must study polit-

Boxer prisoners captured and brought in by the Sixth U.S. Cavalry in Tianjin, China (Library of Congress)

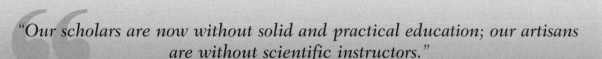

"Our scholars are now without solid and practical education; our artisans are without scientific instructors."

"We must establish elementary and high schools, colleges and universities, in accordance with those of foreign countries."

ical science, foreign affairs, and the arts, histories, and sciences of the West.

Audience

In Chinese history, memorials were orders written by the emperor to be obeyed by his subjects and officials as well as documents written to the emperor requesting action or explaining circumstances. In the case of the abolition of the examination system, a long memorial was written to Emperor Guangxu in 1895, and its influence inspired him to issue his series of edicts, the Hundred Days' Reform, which were directed to his officials to change major aspects of Chinese government, such as through the abolition of the examination system.

The abolition of the examination system would directly affect the Chinese gentry and scholars who had been educated by tutors and had studied for many years to earn the highest levels of employment available to Han Chinese under the Manchu Qing Dynasty. Since the thousand-year-old examination system would be replaced by public schools under the terms of the abolition, scholars and government officials were perhaps the most significant audience for the emperor's educational reforms. Public schools based on the education systems in Japan and the West would potentially alter the power structure that had been in place in China for generations.

Impact

All of Emperor Guangxu's reforms constituted threats to the conservative Qing Dynasty power structure. Every man employed at the higher levels by the dynasty had passed the required examinations; the emperor's embracing changes based on foreign models would potentially throw into disarray the existing power structure in China. The proposed educational system would shift the power away from the entrenched elite Chinese scholars who had worked for years and years to pass the examinations to allow for a more egalitarian education system that would not favor the rich, pow-

erful, and well connected. The potential for disruption of the power structure caused a backlash against the emperor and those men who encouraged him to seek change for China.

As such, the immediate impact of the Hundred Days' Reform and Emperor Guangxu's abolition of the examination system was his loss of power and forced retirement. He was disgraced by his aunt, Empress Dowager Cixi, who emerged from retirement herself to take power. Emperor Guangxu was placed under palace arrest and, it is believed, ultimately poisoned in 1908, dying the day before his aunt died. One successful result of the Hundred Days' Reform was the establishment in 1898 of the Imperial Capital University, which was renamed National Peking University in 1912. Its charter was drafted by the two intellectuals who influenced Emperor Guangxu, Kang Youwei and Liang Qichao.

The Boxer Rebellion, carried out by members of the Society of Righteous and Harmonious Fists (referred to as "Boxers" in English), started brewing in China's Shandong Peninsula in 1898. Boxers, who were primarily poor and uneducated Chinese peasants from the countryside, resented the presence of foreign missionaries and the European companies invested in mining, railroad building, and telegraph construction. In 1900 the Boxers began killing hundreds of foreign missionaries and thousands of Chinese Christian converts. When the Boxers made their way to Beijing, the foreigners and many Chinese Christians fled to the foreign legations and held out for fifty-five days, between June 20 and August 14, 1900. Empress Dowager Cixi declared war on foreigners in China on June 21 but then fled Peking when the international expedition sent to rescue the stranded Christians and foreigners reached the city. The expeditionary force, composed of troops from Japan, Britain, France, Germany, the United States, Austria-Hungary, Russia, and Italy, rescued the foreigners and Chinese converts in the Legation Quarter on August 14. The foreign troops plundered and looted and generally took revenge upon the Chinese for the Boxer killing of Christians.

China was forced to sign the Boxer Protocol on September 7, 1901. One of the provisions of the protocol suspended civil-service examinations for five years in all areas where foreigners were harmed. Conservative elements in the Qing court rethought some of their assumptions in light of the foreign response to the Boxer Rebellion and the Boxer Protocol. On August 29, 1901, the empress ordered that the eight-legged essay, which focused on the Four Books and Five Classics of Confucius, be abolished from all examinations and ordered that discussions on more current facts be valued equally with traditional subjects. Various edicts followed to begin the transition from the examination system to a school system patterned on the Japanese model. In 1904 the Committee on Education Draft of Regulations was established. On September 2, 1905, Empress Dowager Cixi issued an order that the examination system be abolished in a year. The degrees remained almost unchanged, but students now had to graduate from the new schools to receive them. The examination system has not been reinstituted in China since its demise, and Chinese leaders have since striven to modernize and update the country in various other ways, largely to be able to stand up with and potentially surpass the West.

Further Reading

■ Articles

Chow, Kai-wing. "Writing for Success: Printing, Examinations, and Intellectual Change in Late Ming China." *Late Imperial China* 17, no. 1 (June 1996): 120–157.

Crozier, Justin. "A Unique Experiment." *China in Focus* 12 (Summer 2002). Available online. Society for Anglo-Chinese Understanding Web site.
    http://www.sacu.org/examinations.html.

Elman, Benjamin A. "Imagining the Chinese Examination System: Historical Nature and Modern Usefulness." *China Review International* 13, no. 1 (Spring 2006): 21–32.

Man-Cheong, Iona D. "Fair Fraud & Fraudulent Fairness: The 1761 Examination Case." *Late Imperial China* 18, no. 2 (December 1997): 51–85.

■ Books

Brook, Timothy, and B. Michael Frolic, eds. *Civil Society in China.* Armonk, N.Y.: M. E. Sharpe, 1997.

Chaffee, John W. *The Thorny Gates of Learning in Sung China: A Social History of Examinations.* Cambridge, U.K.: Cambridge University Press, 1985.

Elman, Benjamin A. *A Cultural History of Civil Examinations in Late Imperial China.* Berkeley: University of California Press, 2000.

Gray, John Henry. *China: A History of the Laws, Manners, and Customs of the People.* 1878. Reprint. Mineola, N.Y.: Dover Publications, 2002.

Questions for Further Study

1. What factors influenced Emperor Guangxu and his advisers to attempt to abolish the examination system? Why did conservative elements in Chinese society oppose this change?

2. In contemporary America, examinations are often used to determine qualifications for certain kinds of occupations, including law, medicine, and such jobs as firefighter and police officer. Sometimes these exams are a source of controversy, leading to charges that they are racially biased or that they do not truly measure a candidate's potential effectiveness. Similarly, college entrance exams claim to measure college potential, though some critics disagree. What similarities do you see between these examinations and the kinds of examinations, and the problems associated with them, used in China?

3. Trace the history of Western involvement in Chinese affairs using this entry, "Qianlong's Letter to George III," "Lin Zexu's 'Moral Advice to Queen Victoria,'" and "Articles Providing for the Favorable Treatment of the Great Ching Emperor after his Abdication." Why were the Western powers so interested in China? How did they influence Chinese culture? How did the Chinese react to the presence of Western powers?

4. The field of education regularly wrestles with the question of the relative value of practical subjects and more theoretical, classical, or literary subjects. What arguments could be made in favor of the "impractical" examination system the emperor tried to abolish? What arguments could be made in opposition to the system?

5. What role did Confucianism play in Chinese culture and society? Do you believe that its effects overall were positive, negative, or a mix of both positive and negative? Explain.

Meskill, Johanna M. M., ed. *The Chinese Civil Service: Career Open to Talent?* Lexington, Mass.: D. C. Heath, 1963.

Miyazaki, Ichisada. *China's Examination Hell: The Civil Service Examinations of Imperial China*, trans. Conrad Schirokauer. New York: Weatherhill Publishing, 1976.

Schrecker, John E. *The Chinese Revolution in Historical Perspective*. Westport, Conn.: Praeger, 2004.

Spence, Jonathan D. *The Search for Modern China*. New York: W. W. Norton, 1990.

■ **Web Sites**

Buschini, J. "The Boxer Rebellion." Small Planet Communications Web site.
    http://www.smplanet.com/imperialism/fists.html.

Hooker, Richard. "Ch'ing, China: The Boxer Rebellion." World Civilizations, Washington State University Web site.
    http://www.wsu.edu/~dee/CHING/BOXER.HTM.

—Carole Schroeder

Milestone Documents

EMPEROR GUANGXU'S ABOLITION OF THE EXAMINATION SYSTEM

Our scholars are now without solid and practical education; our artisans are without scientific instructors; when compared with other countries we soon see how weak we are. Does any one think that our troops are as well drilled or as well led as those of the foreign armies? Or that we can successfully stand against them? Changes must be made to accord with the necessities of the times…. Keeping in mind the morals of the sages and wise men, we must make them the basis on which to build newer and better structures. We must substitute modern arms and western organization for our old regime; we must select our military officers according to western methods of military education; we must establish elementary and high schools, colleges and universities, in accordance with those of foreign countries; we must abolish the Wen-chang [literary essay] and obtain a knowledge of ancient and modern world history, a right conception of the present-day state of affairs, with special reference to the governments and institutions of the countries of the five great continents; and we must understand their arts and sciences.

D'ARCY CONCESSION

"[The Concessionaire] shall also pay the said Government annually a sum equal to 16 per cent of the annual net profits."

Overview

In 1901 the government of Persia (modern-day Iran) and the British entrepreneur William Knox D'Arcy signed an agreement known as the D'Arcy Concession. The agreement opened Persia's oil resources for exploration and ultimate exploitation. While large oil-drilling operations already existed, primarily in Russia and the United States, the explorations started as a result of the D'Arcy Concession would open up the entire Middle East to exploitation of its oil resources. Eventually, Middle Eastern nations would take back control of their resources and use them to influence economic and political events.

Since the end of the nineteenth century few commodities have affected economics, politics, war, and even ordinary life as much as oil. A smelly nuisance that occasionally seeped up from the earth with few possible uses that anyone could imagine, it has become the staple of life. Industrialized nations have become totally dependent on energy, in large part generated by petroleum products, principally oil. That oil was crucial to economic survival became a commonplace truth in the twentieth century and continues to be so into the twenty-first. The nineteenth-century German military theorist Carl von Clausewitz wrote that war is the extension of policy by other means. After the D'Arcy Concession was signed, war and policy became an extension of the efforts to secure the main supply of energy that exists: oil.

Context

By 1900, even though the world was less mechanized than it is now, the importance of petroleum was generally recognized. Although gasoline-powered automobiles were uncommon and heavier-than-air aircraft had yet to be flown, kerosene for lighting, gasoline, and oil for lubricating engines were fairly common. The need for oil would grow in the coming years, though the extent to which the world would become dependent upon it was far from clear.

What was realized, however, was that petroleum was becoming an increasingly valuable commodity. The first successful oil well was drilled in Pennsylvania in 1859, and just over ten years later the oil- and gas-refining industry had become so profitable that John D. Rockefeller created the Standard Oil Company of Ohio. In a few years other companies would be formed; while some of them were short-lived, others, such as Royal Dutch Shell, would survive into the twenty-first century. Oil wells and refineries were being built Baku, a territory in Azerbaijan that had once belonged to the kingdom of Persia, and expeditions for the exploration of oil were being conducted in ever-increasing numbers. The economic benefits of accessing and controlling oil sources were becoming obvious not only to those who wanted the oil but also to those who wanted revenues by making it accessible.

Precedent for the D'Arcy Concession had been established with the 1872 Reuter Concession, which granted Baron Julius de Reuter of Great Britain (remembered primarily for founding the Reuter News Agency) rights to mine for petroleum and other resources and to construct a railway in Persia. Then, in 1889, de Reuter received a second concession from the Persian government for mining rights, to include petroleum, for a period of sixty years, with Persia retaining 16 percent of the profits. The agreement would lapse after ten years if no discoveries were made, which is what happened.

In 1900 it was known that Persia had petroleum and natural gas resources, although Persia then imported most of its oil for commercial use from either Baku or the United States. Oil seeping to the surface provided petroleum that was used by the local population for caulking boats or as a fuel for lighting. Areas in northern Persia were said to be constantly burning, with flames fueled by natural gas. The commercial possibilities of selling rights to these resources were not lost on Persia's ruling class, especially its chief ruler, Mozaffar al-Din Shah Qajar, who spent a large amount of money on his personal amusement.

Because Persia did not have the technology to exploit the possibilities of extracting and selling oil, it looked to industrial nations to do so in return for financial consideration. The expectation that someone would pay a great deal for Persia's oil led officials in the Persian government to search for someone who would do so. In 1900 General Antoine Kitabgi, a high-ranking Persian official,

1846

- Oil is discovered in Baku, an area in Azerbaijan formerly under the control of Persia but now governed by Russia.

1859

- **August 27** In Titusville, Pennsylvania, Edwin Drake drills the first successful oil well in America.

1870

- **June** John D. Rockefeller founds Standard Oil of Ohio.

1872

- **July 25** The Persian government grants the Reuter Concession to Baron Julius de Reuter, but the concession is cancelled the following year.

1889

- **January** De Reuter receives a second concession from the Persian government for mining rights.

1900

- **October 27** General Antoine Kitabgi approaches the British diplomat Sir Henry Drummond Wolff to find an investor interested in searching for oil in Persia; Wolff informs Kitabgi of William Knox D'Arcy's interest.

approached the British diplomat Sir Henry Drummond Wolff (who had formerly been the British minister to Persia) to see if there was an investor interested in searching for oil in Persia. Within a month, Wolff notified Kitabgi that there was such a person, an investor who had made a fortune in Australian mines, William Knox D'Arcy. The successful effort to find someone who would find the oil and pay for it thus changed the history of Persia and the world.

About the Author

The concession bears D'Arcy's name, but like any negotiated business agreement or treaty, this one had several authors. Foremost among them was William Knox D'Arcy (1849–1917), an English businessman who moved with his family to Australia in the mid-1860s. D'Arcy formed a mining partnership with other individuals and succeeded so well that he became a multimillionaire. In the late 1880s he moved back to England. He knew little about the petroleum business, although having been involved in mining he was not totally ignorant. When he was approached in 1900 by Sir Henry Drummond Wolff, mostly on the basis of D'Arcy's extensive wealth and the knowledge that he was looking for new investments, he was interested in the idea of purchasing an oil concession in Persia. D'Arcy's efforts would extend from the negotiation of the concession to the actual discovery of oil in 1908. In that period the difficulties in finding oil nearly bankrupted him. However, from 1909, when he retired, to his death eight years later he not only recouped his investment but, in fact, increased his fortune substantially.

After D'Arcy had drawn up the initial draft, he sent his representative to conduct negotiations. The man he selected for this delicate task was Alfred L. Marriott, a cousin of one of D'Arcy's closest advisers. Marriott's counterpart and contributor to the final draft was a native Georgian, Antoine Kitabgi, one of several Europeans in the Persian government. Kitagbi had been the one to first approach Wolff in the search for an investor; he had held several important positions in the Persian government, including director-general of customs. He was extremely well connected, a fact that assisted negotiations, and as a result of the concession would be named commissioner to ensure that Persian interests were being served.

Explanation and Analysis of the Document

The D'Arcy Concession was negotiated and signed by representatives of the Persian government under Shah Mozaffar al-Din Shah Qajar and representatives of the English businessman William Knox D'Arcy. The document allowed D'Arcy, identified in the agreement as "the Concessionaire," to form a company (or companies) with the express purpose of searching for, drilling for, refining, and selling oil found almost anywhere in Persia, with some territorial exclusions. In return, the Persian government (meaning the shah himself) would receive fixed payments in cash and stock as well as subsequent payments based on the net profits of the enterprise. The concession guaranteed that the concessionaire (D'Arcy) and his company could take an unlimited amount of oil, refine it, and sell it domestically and overseas, as long as they adhered to the conditions contained in the concession. The parties to the agreement are identified in the document's opening paragraph.

◆ **Articles 1–3**

The first article stipulates that D'Arcy, as concessionaire for a period of sixty years, could search for, extract, prepare (that is, refine), transport out of the country, and sell natural gas, petroleum, asphalt, and ozokerite (a type of paraffin). Article 2 specifies that D'Arcy would receive the exclusive right to lay all of the necessary pipelines from wherever petroleum or natural gas was found to the Persian Gulf, where oil would be refined and then transported. He also had the right to construct any wells, reservoirs, holding facilities, factories, and other infrastructure necessary for his operation. Finally, the third article granted to D'Arcy (for free) any uncultivated land necessary to construct any of the facilities identified in Article 2. In instances where land was needed but under cultivation, he could have it but would have to purchase it at fair market value. D'Arcy could also purchase any other land or buildings needed. No construction would be allowed within "200 Persian archines" of any holy place; an archine (sometimes spelled arshin) was a unit of measurement equal to about twenty-eight inches, so two hundred archines is just over 460 feet.

◆ **Articles 4–7**

At the time of the agreement, three petroleum operations were already operating in Persia. D'Arcy, according to Article 4, could take these facilities but would be required to pay to the government an additional sum in tomans each year; the toman was Iran's unit of currency until 1932. While it is difficult to attach a modern value to the toman, its valued was pegged to the French franc at a rate of one toman to five francs, making it at the time worth very roughly twenty U.S. dollars.

Article 5 allows D'Arcy and his engineers to determine the routing and direction of all pipelines. However, Article 6 declares that provinces in northern Persia close to the border with Russia are off limits. The Persians did not want to alienate the Russians, who were exerting heavy influence in Persia because of their subsidies to the shah. Persia had lost the Baku region (at the time of the concession the world's major oil producer) some years previously The article specifies, however, that no one else, specifically the Russians, would be allowed to explore and drill and that the restriction on D'Arcy would apply only for as long as no one else was allowed in the region. Finally, Article 7 specifies that the concessionaire would be relieved of all import and export tax liabilities. He would not be taxed on any equipment brought into Persia.

◆ **Articles 8 and 9**

By Article 8, D'Arcy agreed to send out immediately, and at his own expense, a party of experts to survey the regions

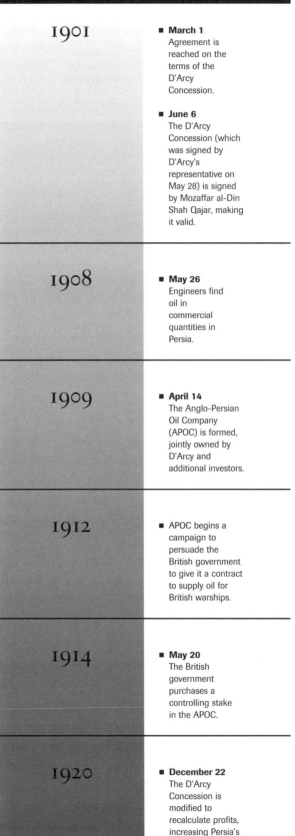

Time Line

1901

- **March 1**
  Agreement is reached on the terms of the D'Arcy Concession.

- **June 6**
  The D'Arcy Concession (which was signed by D'Arcy's representative on May 28) is signed by Mozaffar al-Din Shah Qajar, making it valid.

1908

- **May 26**
  Engineers find oil in commercial quantities in Persia.

1909

- **April 14**
  The Anglo-Persian Oil Company (APOC) is formed, jointly owned by D'Arcy and additional investors.

1912

- APOC begins a campaign to persuade the British government to give it a contract to supply oil for British warships.

1914

- **May 20**
  The British government purchases a controlling stake in the APOC.

1920

- **December 22**
  The D'Arcy Concession is modified to recalculate profits, increasing Persia's share.

1932

- **November 27**
  The Persian government announces it is cancelling the D'Arcy Concession.

1933

- **May 29**
  Shah Reza Shah Pahlavi approves a new agreement limiting the land area holdings of APOC.

1935

- APOC changes its name to the Anglo-Iranian Oil Company.

1951

- **April**
  The National Iranian Oil Company is founded.

1953

- **August 19**
  Iranian prime minister Mohammad Mossadeq, a supporter of nationalizing the oil industry, is overthrown in a coup sponsored by the British and U.S. governments.

1954

- The Anglo-Iranian Oil Company is renamed British Petroleum.

- **September**
  A consortium between the National Iranian Oil Company and British Petroleum is formed.

and search for oil. In the event of finding oil, he would immediately send the equipment and facilities (and required staff) to begin drilling wells. To this end, Article 9 authorizes D'Arcy to form one or several companies. The names of these companies and the regulations governing them would be determined by the concessionaire, who would also name the board of directors. He would inform the Persian government of the names and makeup of these companies, and the regulations governing them, through the imperial commissioner (whose duties are describe in Article 11). These companies would share in all of the privileges awarded to the concessionaire but would also have to meet all responsibilities levied on the concessionaire in this agreement.

◆ **Article 10**

Article 10, at least from the Persian point of view, is the heart of the agreement. It specifies that within a month of any contracts between the concessionaire and any company or companies, the Persian government would receive a payment of £20,000 in cash and a further £20,000 in stock (paid for by the company). At the time, the British pound was equivalent to just under five U.S. dollars. Further, the company would pay to the Persian government 16 percent of the annual net profits. The original amount offered had been 10 percent, but the shah refused to sign until the increase was agreed to. The amount of the percentage and even the definition of "profit" would be the subject of arguments and negotiations through the years. It would be a major sticking point in the early 1930s, when the Persian government demanded more revenues. The demand was triggered by two factors. First was the realization that 16 percent was not a fair return. Further, because of the effects of the Great Depression, oil revenues were not stable. In 1930 profits had been over £1,250,000; the following year profits had fallen to slightly over £303,000. It was this last drop in the payments that caused the shah to declare in 1932 that the agreement would be terminated. Through the years, the amount of payment percentages would increase in favor of the Persian and then the Iranian governments.

◆ **Articles 11–18**

The remaining articles of the concession address an assortment of important details. Article 11 states that the government of Persia would appoint an imperial commissioner to advise the concessionaire and his company. The company and it directors would be compelled to work with this person, whose major role would be to safeguard the Persian government's interests. The commissioner's salary was originally proposed to be £60 per year, but the agreement raised it to £1,000, to be paid by the concessionaire. The duties and powers of the commissioner would be specifically set forth in any regulations governing the companies. The first commissioner was General Antoine Kitabgi, who played a major role in the negotiations.

Article 12 specifies that with the exception of senior and technical staff such as engineers, managers, oil-drilling technicians, and foreman, all employees would be Persian subjects. Article 13 requires that in any area exploited for petroleum where the inhabitants were already acquiring and using it, the concessionaire would have to supply to them the amount they had received in the past for free. The amount to be provided would be determined by the people who had been acquiring it. Meanwhile, Article 14 obligated the Persian government to protect all facilities and the concessionaire's staff, although the concessionaire would have no rights to claim damages from the Persian government in the event of any harm. The concessionaire, in other words, was to bear the full risk and responsibility.

Article 15 states that at the end of the sixty-year term of the concession, all buildings and facilities would become the property of the Persian government, which would receive them without paying any costs. Article 16 requires D'Arcy to have established a company to search for and develop the petroleum within two years of the signing of the concession or it would be null and void. Article 17 sets the ground rules for settling disputes between the concessionaire and the Persian government. Arbitration of disputes would take place in Tehran. There would be two arbitrators, each party selecting one. The two arbitrators would appoint an umpire to make the final decision in the event that they could not agree. The decision by the arbitrators or, if necessary, the umpire would be final. Finally, Article 18 simply specifies that identical copies of the concession would exist in French and Persian. If there were a conflict between the two versions, however, the French version would take precedence.

Audience

The principals themselves were the chief audience for the concession. Other entities, however, formed part of a larger audience, and specific entries in the concession were addressed to them. Perhaps the most important audience was the Russian government. Because of the British presence in India, communications between the Asian subcontinent and Britain were essential. The British had installed a telegraph line through Persia that would allow India to keep in close contact with London. At the same time, Russia was also looking to expand its control in the area, and the competition between the two nations in the region—the "Great Game" described in Rudyard Kipling's novel *Kim*—was intensifying at the opening of the twentieth century. It was control over the region—or at least unlimited access to it—that was the major concern at this time, not the access to oil. The provision in the concession forbidding D'Arcy and his companies from entering the five northern provinces was meant to assure the Russians that the British would not be on their borders. At the same time, the article stipulating that D'Arcy could situate and build facilities himself was meant to inform the Russians (who had built several projects on behalf of the Persian government) that there would be limits on Russian influence. Even with the restrictions as to where oil exploration could take place, Britain was reassured that it would continue to have a presence in the Persian Gulf and that its lines of communication to and from India were safe.

Time Line

1979

■ The Iranian Revolution overthrows the shah and creates the Islamic Republic of Iran; the new government nationalizes British Petroleum assets.

Another audience, not anticipated at the time and not until D'Arcy was running dangerously low on funds, was investors who might underwrite some of the efforts. D'Arcy did not anticipate having this need, but as he ran through his fortune (over half a million pounds) in the years between the concession and the first oil strike, he needed support. The provisions of the concession were favorable enough to influence a private oil company, Burmah Oil, and eventually the British government to become major investors. Their subsequent investment would guarantee the exploration and drilling efforts until oil was found.

One group that was excluded was the Persian people themselves. While the concession, prior to signing by the shah, had to be formally ratified by the legislature, that was only a pro forma measure. The oil revenues did not in any way benefit the people of Persia (later Iran) until well into the twentieth century.

Impact

The D'Arcy Concession's influence on the history of the twentieth and twenty-first centuries cannot be overstated. It was, however, the concession itself that was significant, not D'Arcy. While he had the good luck to be the first major entrepreneur in the area, someone else very well could have been. In fact, D'Arcy was not the Persians' first choice; General Kitabgi offered the opportunity first to Royal Dutch Shell, but they turned the offer down.

After seven years of effort and at the cost of nearly all of D'Arcy's fortune, engineers finally found oil in commercial quantities in Persia on May 26, 1908. As a result of this discovery, the Anglo-Persian Oil Company (APOC) was formed on April 14, 1909; the company was jointly owned by D'Arcy and additional investors, for D'Arcy had been forced to seek investors to cover the costs of continued exploration and development. In 1912, APOC began a campaign to persuade the British government to give it a contract to supply oil for British warships, which were converting from coal-burning to oil-burning engines. Then, on May 20, 1914, the British government purchased a controlling stake in APOC, ensuring that Britain would have a reliable source of oil in the event of war; World War I broke out a month later. In

Reza Shah Pahlavi (AP/Wide World Photos)

1916, APOC completed a 120-mile pipeline from the oil fields to a new refinery at Ābādān, Persia.

In the years between the world wars, dissatisfaction with the original agreement led to changes in the original D'Arcy Concession and modifications of other contracts. The Persian government and APOC agreed to changes to the concession on December 22, 1920. The most significant change was a recalculation of the formula defining net profits, allowing Persia to receive a greater amount of money. Then, in 1928, the Persian government and APOC opened discussions for further major revisions to the concession. Although the Persian government was receiving a larger percentage, fluctuations in world demand caused significant variations from year to year. On November 27, 1932, the Persian government announced that it was cancelling the D'Arcy Concession, but on May 29, 1933, the shah, Reza Shah Pahlavi, approved a new agreement limiting the land area holdings of APOC. The agreement allowed the Persian government to grant new concessions, although APOC was allowed to select which holdings it would retain. The Persian government received 20 percent of the profits, with a guaranteed payment amount each year regardless of fluctuations in world demand. The agreement was to extend until 1993. In 1935, APOC changed its name from the Anglo-Persian Oil Company to the Anglo-Iranian Oil Company to conform to the state name change from Persia to Iran.

Dissatisfaction with the concession's original terms became even more intense in the years following World War II. The desire to take a larger share or all of the revenues, combined with a growing sense of nationalism and a distrust of the West, led to changes that left the oil companies more vulnerable to threats of nationalization, lost profits, and Western dependence on oil and the possibility that the flow of oil could be cut off. These fears grew in April 1951, when the National Iranian Oil Company was founded. This was a government-owned and -operated entity that nationalized facilities in Iran, taking control from the Anglo-Iranian Oil Company. The consequence of this event was the coup on August 19, 1953, against Mohammad Mossadeq, the Iranian prime minister, who supported nationalizing the oil industry. The British drew in the U.S. government, which was at first unwilling to assist in the process. But because the United States needed British support for the war in Korea, it found itself assisting in effecting the 1953 coup that placed the shah solidly on the throne and guaranteed British and American oil interests in Iran. From that step the United States became more and more heavily involved in the politics of the Middle East.

Fears were lessened after the coup. In 1954 the Anglo-Iranian Oil Company was renamed British Petroleum, and in September of that year a consortium between the National Iranian Oil Company and British Petroleum was formed to exploit oil reserves in Iran, with some lower-level participation by Shell and several American oil companies. A new payment schedule was agreed upon, with Iran receiving 50 percent of the profits. This period of stability was not to last. In 1979 the Iranian Revolution overthrew Mohammad Reza Shah Pahlavi (the son of the former

The Neftyanye Kamni oil field near Baku, Azerbaijan
(AP/Wide World Photos)

shah) and created the Islamic Republic of Iran. All British Petroleum assets were nationalized by the new Iranian government, ending a presence that had started with the signing of the D'Arcy Concession in 1901.

What happened as a result of that agreement profoundly affected Persia, the Middle East region, and the entire world in many ways. First, it helped solidify a British presence in the Persian Gulf region while at the same time counterbalancing Russian (and later Soviet) power. In 1919, after World War I, Britain would come to exercise control over the former Turkish territory of Iraq. That action was taken not so much for oil (for it was not discovered there until the late 1920s) but rather to ensure that British oil enterprises in Persia would be safe. The discovery of Iraqi oil and subsequent oil strikes throughout the Middle East only reinforced the importance of the first D'Arcy strike in 1908.

From a global perspective, the effects of the D'Arcy Concession and its success added a new dimension to economic, political, and military conflict. Oil conferred upon its possessor the ability to project military power over greater distances. Possessing control over this resource and the ability to use it militarily successfully secured econom-

"The Government of His Imperial Majesty the Shah grants to the Concessionaire by these presents a special and exclusive privilege to search for, obtain, exploit, develop, render suitable for trade, carry away and sell natural gas, petroleum, asphalt, and ozokerite throughout the whole extent of the Persian Empire for a term of 60 years as from the date of these presents."

(Article 1)

"The Imperial Persian Government authorizes the Concessionaire to found one or several companies for the working of the concession."

(Article 9)

"It [the Concessionaire] shall also pay the said Government annually a sum equal to 16 per cent of the annual net profits of any company or companies that may be formed in accordance with the said Article."

(Article 10)

"The said Government shall be free to appoint an Imperial Commissioner who shall be consulted by the Concessionaires and the directors of the companies to be formed. He shall supply all and any useful information at his disposal and he shall inform them of the best course to be adopted in the interest of the undertaking."

(Article 11)

"The workmen employed in the service of the Company shall be subjects of His Imperial Majesty the Shah, except the technical staff such as the managers, engineers, borers and foremen."

(Article 12)

"The Imperial Government binds itself to take all and any necessary measures to secure the safety and the carrying out of the object of this Concession, of the plant and of the apparatuses of which mention is made for the purpose of the undertaking of the Company and to protect the representatives, agents and servants of the Company."

(Article 14)

ic as well as political advantages. However, in the years after World War II, Middle Eastern nations began to exercise their own control over what had been exploited by outsiders, causing what seemed to larger powers a disconcerting change in power relationships.

In the 1970s the control of the oil supply exercised by the Organization of Petroleum Exporting Countries brought the new reality to the Western industrialized powers with a shock. Middle Eastern states were no longer compliant and could project their own power by withholding oil or charging more for it. The overthrow of the shah and the rise of the Islamic Republic of Iran resulted in intense hostility toward the United States. That hostility was in large part a consequence of the U.S. efforts to overthrow the Mossadeq government in 1953, all to preserve the security of the Anglo-Iranian Oil Company.

The presence of large oil reserves gave Venezuela an importance in world affairs it would not otherwise have. Russia in the post-Soviet world managed to regain much of its lost power and influence through the economic benefits of large oil reserves. A major portion of U.S. and Western foreign policy has been affected by the issue of oil availability and prices. Thus, far beyond what D'Arcy or any oil entrepreneurs might have imagined, petroleum came to exert an important influence in many aspects of life—and will continue to do so until the use of petroleum as a fuel decreases.

Further Reading

■ Articles

Beck, Peter J. "The Anglo-Persian Oil Dispute 1932–33." *Journal of Contemporary History* 9, no. 4 (October 1974): 123–151.

Carey, Jane Perry Clark. "Iran and Control of Its Oil Resources." *Political Science Quarterly* 89, no. 1 (March 1974): 147–174.

Hershey, Amos S. "The New Anglo-Persian Agreement." *American Journal of International Law* 13, no. 4 (October 1919): 749–754.

Jones, G. Gareth. "The British Government and the Oil Companies 1912–1924: The Search for an Oil Policy." *Historical Journal* 20, no. 3 (September 1977): 647–672.

Millspaugh, A. C. "The Persian-British Oil Dispute." *Foreign Affairs* 11, no. 3 (April 1933): 521–525.

Osborn, C. C. "The Future Oil Supply." *Journal of the American Statistical Association* 18, no. 144 (December 1923): 1004–1009.

■ Books

Ferrier, R. W., and J. H. Bamberg. *The History of the British Petroleum Company.* New York: Cambridge University Press, 1982.

Kinzer, Stephen. *All the Shah's Men: An American Coup and the Roots of Middle East Terror.* Hoboken, N.J.: John Wiley and Sons, 2008.

Longhurst, Henry. *Adventure in Oil: The Story of British Petroleum.* London: Sidgwick and Jackson, 1959.

McBeth, B. S. *British Oil Policy, 1919–1939.* London: F. Cass, 1985.

Yergin, Daniel. *The Prize: The Epic Quest for Oil, Money and Power.* New York: Free Press, 2008.

Questions for Further Study

1. Advanced nations have often been accused of exploiting other countries for their resources. Do you believe that the D'Arcy Concession was fair to Persia? Why or why not?

2. Oil politics is often thought of as a feature of the modern world, but to what extent did international politics play a role in the D'Arcy Concession and the events surrounding it?

3. How has the D'Arcy Concession continued to exert an effect on international relations in the twenty-first century?

4. Compare this document with Ayatollah Khomeini's *Islamic Government: Governance of the Jurist.* What do you think Khomeini's reaction would be to the terms of the D'Arcy Concession—and indeed to its very existence?

5. Do you believe that the D'Arcy Concession was an act of Western imperialism, similar to the Treaty of Nanjing between Britain and China, or what is simply a business transaction between a government and a private enterprise? Explain your reasoning.

▪ Web Sites

"The Centenary of the First Oil Well in the Middle East." Geo ExPro Web site.
   http://www.geoexpro.com/history/iran/

"History of BP: A Century of Searching." British Petroleum Web Site.
   http://www.bp.com/sectiongenericarticle.do?categoryId=2010123&contentId=7027817.

   —Robert Stacy

D'ARCY CONCESSION

Between the Government of His Imperial Majesty the Shah of Persia of the one part and William Knox D'Arcy of independent means residing in London at No 42 Grosvenor Square (hereinafter called "the Concessionaire") of the other part. The following has by these presents been agreed on and arranged, viz.:

◆ Article 1

The Government of His Imperial Majesty the Shah grants to the Concessionaire by these presents a special and exclusive privilege to search for, obtain, exploit, develop, render suitable for trade, carry away and sell natural gas, petroleum, asphalt, and ozokerite throughout the whole extent of the Persian Empire for a term of 60 years as from the date of these presents.

◆ Article 2

This privilege shall comprise the exclusive right of laying the pipelines necessary from the deposits where there may be found one or several of the said products up to the Persian Gulf, as also the necessary distributing branches. It shall also comprise the right of constructing and maintaining all and any wells, reservoirs, stations and pump services, accumulation services and distribution services, factories and other works and arrangements that may be deemed necessary.

◆ Article 3

The Imperial Persian Government grants gratuitously to the Concessionaire all uncultivated lands belonging to the State which the Concessionaire's engineers may deem necessary for the construction of the whole or any part of the above-mentioned works. As for cultivated lands belonging to the State, the Concessionaire must purchase them at the fair and current price of Province.

The Government also grants to the Concessionaire the right of acquiring all and any other lands or buildings necessary for the said purpose, with the consent of the proprietors, on such conditions as may be arranged between him and them without their being allowed to make demands of a nature to surcharge the prices ordinarily current for lands situate in their respective localities. Holy places with all their dependencies within a radius of 200 Persian archines are formally excluded.

◆ Article 4

As three petroleum mines situate at Schouster Kassre-Chirine in the Province of Kermanschahan and Daleki near Bouchir are at present let to private persons and produce an annual revenue of two thousand tomans for the benefit of the Government, it has been agreed that the three aforesaid mines shall be comprised in the Deed of Concession in conformity with Article 1, on condition that over and above the 16 per cent mentioned in Article 10 the Concessionaire shall pay every year the fixed sum of 2,000 (two thousand) tomans to the Imperial Government.

◆ Article 5

The course of the pipelines shall be fixed by the Concessionaire and his engineers.

◆ Article 6

Notwithstanding what is above set forth, the privilege granted by these presents shall not extend to the Provinces of Azerbadjan, Ghilan, Mazendaran, Asdrabad and Khorassan, but on the express condition that the Persian Imperial Government shall not grant to any other person the right of constructing a pipeline to the southern rivers or to the south coast of Persia.

◆ Article 7

All lands granted by these presents to the Concessionaire or that may be acquired by him in the manner provided for in Articles 3 and 4 of these presents, as also all products exported shall be free of all imposts and taxes during the term of the present Concession. All material and apparatuses necessary for the exploration, working and development of the pipeline shall enter Persia free of all taxes and custom-house duties.

◆ Article 8

The Concessionaire shall immediately send out to Persia and at his own cost one or several experts with a view to their exploring the region in which there exist, as he believes, the said products, and in the event of a satisfactory nature, the latter shall immediately send to Persia and at his own cost all the technical staff necessary with the working plant and machinery required for boring and sinking wells and ascertaining the value of the property.

◆ Article 9

The Imperial Persian Government authorizes the Concessionaire to found one or several companies for the working of the Concession.

The names, "statutes" and capital of the said companies shall be fixed by the Concessionaire, and the directors shall be chosen by him on the express condition that on the formation of each company the Concessionaire shall give official notice of such formation to the Imperial Government through the medium of the Imperial Commissioner and shall forward the "statutes" with information as to the places at which such company is to operate. Such company or companies shall enjoy all the rights and privileges granted to the Concessionaire, but they must assume all his engagements and responsibilities.

◆ Article 10

It shall be stipulated in the contract between the Concessionaire of the one part and the Company of the other part that the latter is within the term of one month as from the date of the formation of the first exploitation company to pay the Imperial Persian Government the sum of £20,000 sterling in cash and an additional sum of £20,000 sterling in paid-up shares of the first company founded by virtue of the foregoing Article. It shall also pay the said Government annually a sum equal to 16 per cent of the annual net profits of any company or companies that may be formed in accordance with the said Article.

◆ Article 11

The said Government shall be free to appoint an Imperial Commissioner who shall be consulted by the Concessionaire and the directors of the companies to be formed. He shall supply all and any useful information at his disposal and he shall inform them of the best course to be adopted in the interest of the undertaking. He shall establish by agreement with the Concessionaire such supervision as he may deem expedient to safeguard the interests of the Imperial Government.

The aforesaid powers of the Imperial Commissioner shall be set forth in the "statutes" of the companies to be created.

The Concessionaire shall pay the Commissioner thus appointed an annual sum of £1,000 sterling for his services as from the date of the formation of the first company.

◆ Article 12

The workmen employed in the service of the Company shall be subjects of His Imperial Majesty the Shah, except the technical staff such as the managers, engineers, borers and foremen.

◆ Article 13

At any place in which it may be proved that the inhabitants of the country now obtain petroleum for their own use, the Company must supply them gratuitously with the quantity of petroleum that they themselves got previously.

Such quantity shall be fixed according to their own declarations, subject to the supervision of the local authority.

◆ Article 14

The imperial Government binds itself to take all and any necessary measures to secure the safety and the carrying out of the object of this Concession, of the plant and of the apparatuses of which mention is made for the purpose of the undertaking of the Company and to protect the representatives, agents and servants of the Company. The Imperial Government having thus fulfilled its engagements, the Concessionaire and the companies created by him shall not have power under any pretext whatever to claim damages from the Persian Government.

◆ Article 15

On the expiration of the term of the present Concession, all materials, buildings and apparatuses then used by the Company for the exploitation of its industry shall become the property of the said Government, and the Company shall have no right to any indemnity in this connection.

◆ Article 16

If within the term of two years as from the present date the Concessionaire shall not have established the first of the said companies authorized by Article 9 of the present Agreement, the present Concession shall become null and void.

◆ Article 17

In the event of there arising between the parties to the present Concession any dispute or difference in respect of its interpretation or the rights or responsibilities of one or the other of the parties therefrom resulting, such dispute or difference shall be submitted to two arbitrators at Teheran, one of whom shall be named by each of the parties, and to an Umpire who shall be appointed by the arbitrators before they proceed to arbitrate. The decision of the arbitrators or, in the event of the latter disagreeing that of the umpire, shall be final.

◆ Article 18

This Act of Concession made in duplicate is written in the French language and translated into Persian with the same meaning.

But in the event of there being any dispute in relation to such meaning, the French text shall alone prevail. Teheran Sefer 1319 of the Hegine, that is to say May 1901.

(Signed) William Knox D'Arcy, by his Attorney,

(Signed) Alfred L. Marriott.

Certified that the above signatures were affixed in my presence at the British Consulate General at Gulaket near Teheran, on this 4th day of the month of June 1901 by Alfred Lyttelton Marriott, Attorney of William Knox D'Arcy, in accordance with the Notarial Act dated 21st March 1901, and seen by me.

(Signed) George Grahame,

Vice-Consul.

Thus far translation.

Here follows in English.

Certified that the writing in the Persian and French languages on this and the preceding seven pages were registered in the Archives (Register Book) of H.M.'s Legation, Tehran, on pages 117 to 124, on the 5th June 1901.

Dated at Gulaket near Tehran this 6th day of June 1901.

(Signed) George Grahame, Vice-Consul.

Vladimir Lenin (Library of Congress)

Vladimir Lenin's *What Is to Be Done?*

"No revolutionary organization can be durable without a stable organization of leaders to preserve continuity."

Overview

What Is to Be Done? is a political pamphlet written by Vladimir Ilich Lenin, the architect of the 1917 Bolshevik Revolution in Russia and one of the chief founders of the Soviet Union. Lenin's real last name was Ulyanov (sometimes spelled Ulianov). He began writing *What Is to Be Done?* in 1901, and it was published in 1902 under the name "N. Lenin." Although it is only a single document in the large corpus of Lenin's writings, it is often considered his most important. This is because it appears to provide a blueprint for the final form of the Bolshevik Party and therefore also for the revolutionary regime that the party established after seizing power in Russia on November 7–8, 1917 (October 25–26, according to the Russian calendar still in use at that time). Lenin focuses on questions of political agitation and proper revolutionary organization. In particular, he rejects open mass membership in the Russian Social Democratic Labor Party (RSDLP), also called the Russian Social Democratic Workers Party. The RSDLP had been founded in Minsk in 1898 to unite the movement for "social democracy," which at the time was represented by various Russian revolutionary Socialist organizations. Instead, he emphasizes the need for a highly organized, "centralized," "secret," and "conspiratorial" party composed of "professional revolutionaries" who would direct to a successful conclusion the much larger workers' movement in Russia.

Context

What Is to Be Done? appeared at a critical moment in the history of the Russian labor movement as well as in the history of the RSDLP. In the very early 1900s the conditions for social revolution in Russia were developing rapidly. Industrialization, although it was still nascent, had expanded significantly, especially under the influence of the Russian minister of finance, Count Sergey Yulyevich Witte, who had pursued a major expansion of railroads and other industries. Foreign investment capital had begun to pour into the country. The number of industrial workers, or urban proletarians, in Russia had reached two to three million (out of a total population of about160 million). Most of these workers were concentrated in the few large cities, including Moscow and Saint Petersburg, where conditions were particularly oppressive and exploitative. Worker unrest festered, and workers began to organize. The government responded only with minor concessions, such as an 1897 law that established a maximum 11½-hour workday in larger factories. Meanwhile, worker discontent and demands continued to rise.

Beginning in the 1880s, a growing number of Russian intellectuals had begun to look at these developments through the lens of Marxist philosophy, which initially had been expounded abroad. The explosive pamphlet *The Communist Manifesto*, by the German thinkers Karl Marx and Friedrich Engels, had been published in 1848. Marxism—soon dubbed "scientific Socialism"—viewed all history as a struggle between economic classes, primarily between those who owned the means of production and those who did not. Developed further in Marx's other writings, the theory offered a grand analysis of industrial capitalism and predicted its inevitable demise at the hands of class-conscious proletarians who would destroy the very foundation of the system that oppressed them.

Convinced that the march of history was on their side, Lenin and other members of the RSDLP sought to introduce into the broad workers' movement the concepts and ideals of Marxism, but they did not all agree on the appropriate methods for doing so. By far the largest and leading Socialist party in Europe at the time was the German Social Democratic Party, which in most respects provided a model for the much smaller Russian group. Matters were complicated, however, by the differences between the German and Russian political environments. German intellectual Socialists benefited from relatively advanced political freedoms that allowed the Social Democratic Party to participate openly in the political process. German industrial workers could legally unionize, demonstrate, and read and share ideas without necessarily bringing on government reprisal.

None of this was true in autocratic czarist Russia when Lenin wrote *What Is to Be Done?* All political power emanated from the czar. At least prior to 1905, Russia had neither a parliament nor a constitution. Political parties

1848

- **February**
  Karl Marx and Friedrich Engels publish *The Communist Manifesto*, which introduces "scientific Socialism" to the world.

1861

- **February 19**
  Czar Alexander II issues the Emancipation Act of 1861, which abolished serfdom in Russia.

1863

- Nikolay Gavrilovich Chernyshevsky's novel *What Is to Be Done?* is published; the book would later impress Lenin, who was to borrow the title for his own 1902 work.

1870

- **April 22**
  Vladimir Ilich Ulyanov is born in Simbirsk.

1874

- **Summer**
  The Populist (Narodist) movement peaks in the Russian countryside, but disillusionment over the Populists' failure to arouse revolutionary sentiments among the peasantry would soon help set the stage for the rise of Marxist ideology within Russian revolutionary circles.

were illegal, and their members faced harassment and arrest at every turn; moreover, the legal system did not recognize basic civil rights. Workers could not legally organize, demonstrate, or strike. Between 1898 and 1903, Russia experimented briefly with so-called "police unions," which were groups of workers authorized by the state and under police control. The intent behind allowing these unions was to undermine or control working-class movements rather than to achieve significant change, however. To Lenin, all of these circumstances meant that social democracy would have to work very differently in Russia than elsewhere. In particular, it would have to be differently organized, which is the main theme of *What Is to Be Done?*

The title of Lenin's work is borrowed from the identically titled 1863 novel by Nikolay Gavrilovich Chernyshevsky. A leading radical thinker in his own right, Chernyshevsky wrote in the immediate aftermath of the epochal 1861 emancipation of Russia's serfs by Czar Alexander II. This event—and the difficulties and discontent it engendered among the newly liberated peasants—provided the context within which a generation of pre-Marxist Russian radicals wrote and worked. Chernyshevsky was one of the founders of an unsuccessful Russian revolutionary movement known as Populism or Narodism, which advocated agitation among the peasants in order to weld them into a revolutionary force for the overthrow of the czarist regime and its replacement with a decentralized system based on peasant communes. The movement largely burned out in the summer of 1874. Although Lenin later criticized Narodism as utopian and unachievable, he was greatly impressed with Chernyshevsky's depiction of the revolutionary hero as a practical and utterly dedicated individual who through immense personal effort could affect the course of history.

About the Author

Like many champions of the working poor, Lenin was not of them. He was born into a prosperous family in Simbirsk (known as Ulyanovsk from 1924 to 1991) on the Volga River. His father was an inspector of schools and a ranking noble. Lenin was of mixed ancestry, including Russian, Swedish, German, Jewish, Kalmyk, and Mordvinian. Like most Russians, he was raised in the Orthodox Christian tradition. He was baptized as a sixteen-year-old in 1886. Lenin's "baptism" into the world of radical politics came the following year, when his older brother, Alexander, was arrested and executed for involvement in a plot to assassinate Alexander III, a very repressive czar. Lenin's sister was also implicated and sentenced to house arrest. Lenin soon enrolled in Kazan University but was subsequently expelled for his radical ideals. He studied independently for a time, focusing on Marxism, law, history, and languages, and he later enrolled in the University of Saint Petersburg, from which he graduated with a law degree in 1892.

After a short legal career, Lenin, already a convinced Marxist, turned increasingly to revolutionary propaganda and organization. He was arrested in late 1895 and sent to

Siberia, where he shared company with other exiled Marxists, including Nadezhda Konstantinovna Krupskaya, who became his wife in 1898. Lenin's first major publication, *The Development of Capitalism in Russia*, appeared in 1899. This began a prolific writing career. After his release in 1900, Lenin traveled widely in Western Europe. He came into contact with most of the leading left-wing thinkers and activists of the day, joined the RSDLP, and cofounded its official paper, *Iskra* ("The Spark"). It was at this time that Lenin began to regularly use his pseudonym—which means "man from the Lena river"—instead of his real name. (The Lena River actually is thousands of miles east of Lenin's birthplace.) Lenin's ideas on capitalism, revolution, and Communism had already begun to develop beyond their Marxist origins into a somewhat altered theory known subsequently as Marxism-Leninism (or just Leninism). Some of its most characteristic innovations, which focused on questions of organization, can be seen in *What Is to Be Done?*

Explanation and Analysis of the Document

The full Russian version of *What Is to Be Done?* runs to about 150 pages arranged in five sections, all of which treat in one way or another the question of how best to organize for a successful Socialist revolution in Russia (as opposed to in other countries). It was written in dialog with other Socialist pamphleteers of the time—that is, with other would-be leaders or spokespersons for working-class movements, both Russian and foreign. Writing in a fairly polemical style, and often naming names, Lenin takes his opponents to task for one or another fault in their basic approach and lays out what he believes is the one proper path forward. The excerpts presented here represent the heart of Lenin's arguments and are drawn from sections 2–4. Sections 1 and 5 deal, respectively, with trends in Marxist criticism and ideas for establishing an all-Russian political newspaper.

◆ II: "The Spontaneity of the Masses and the Consciousness of Social Democracy"

This section proposes and analyzes a critical distinction between two aspects of the overall struggle for worker liberation: "spontaneity" and "consciousness." Scholars have debated how best to translate and understand these and other key Russian terms—and by extension how best to understand Lenin himself. In general as well as in the context of Lenin's analysis, "spontaneity" connotes actions carried out without forethought or planning—emotional responses, gut reactions, and the like. They are often exhibited by crowds or unorganized groups. The reactions of masses of workers to everyday problems and oppressions are often spontaneous, as in a demonstration, riot, or act of sabotage carried out by workers against their employers and under the influence of anger and raised emotions. "Consciousness," on the other hand, connotes clarity and purposiveness, and it is accompanied and informed by a proper understanding of the whole structure of forces and circumstances at play. "Conscious" actions are carefully

Time Line

1881

- **March 13**
  Czar Alexander II is assassinated by revolutionary terrorists, an event that ushers in the successive reigns of Alexander III (1881–1894) and Nicholas II (1894–1917), both of whom would strive to preserve and strengthen autocratic rule.

1883

- In exile in Europe, the Russian revolutionary writer Georgy Valentinovich Plekhanov and others found the Emancipation of Labor Group, the first Russian Marxist organization, which introduces Marxist ideology into Russia largely through translations of Marx's works.

1887

- Lenin's older brother, Alexander, is arrested and executed for involvement in a plot to assassinate Czar Alexander III, and Lenin's involvement in revolutionary thought and activity begins in earnest.

1898

- **March**
  The Russian Social Democratic Labor Party is founded in Minsk, Belarus.

- *What Is to Be Done?* is published under the pseudonym N. Lenin.

1903
- **July 30–August 23** At its Second Congress in Brussels, Belgium, the Russian Social Democratic Labor Party splits into two factions, the Bolsheviks and the Mensheviks; the split would be officially formalized in 1912.

1917
- **November 7–8** Lenin's Bolshevik Party seizes power in Petrograd (Saint Petersburg), and the Communist era begins in Russia.

planned and done with a specific, achievable end result in mind. Lenin's twin goals in *What Is to Be Done?* are to define the two tendencies in all their details, varieties, and ramifications, and then to promote the idea that only through conscious action and proper organization could the goal of worker liberation be achieved. Spontaneity is presented more negatively. At times it is an indispensable but volatile force—something that, when properly controlled and directed, can achieve important results. More often, Lenin views spontaneity as a blind alley and critical weakness in the movement.

"THE BEGINNING OF THE SPONTANEOUS UPSURGE" Lenin begins with a few examples of "spontaneity" and "consciousness." He notes that workers' own actions are usually spontaneous, but at the same time he suggests that spontaneous actions can develop eventually into at least the "embryo" of conscious ones. Thus, workers might be expected eventually to achieve a level of consciousness themselves. However, Lenin also seems to reject this thought, stating instead that workers' actions ultimately remain spontaneous. For example, in the last paragraph of this section, Lenin asserts that true social democratic consciousness can be brought to the workers only "from outside"—that is, from dedicated revolutionary intellectuals—and that it can never develop out of workers' own experi-

ences. This ambiguity in Lenin's thinking provides material for those who see him as an elitist and would-be tyrant as well as for those who see him instead as genuine supporter of the interests of the working masses.

In this same section, Lenin makes the first of numerous contrasts between "trade unionist struggles" and "social democratic" ones. Shortly thereafter, he compares "trade union consciousness" with "social democratic consciousness." In each case, social democratic consciousness is presented as the higher form. Roughly speaking, trade union consciousness corresponds to spontaneous movements. Trade union consciousness focuses on the (spontaneous) short-term economic concerns of workers, such as pay and working conditions. The ultimate purpose of trade unions is to negotiate with—and within—the capitalist system, not to overthrow it. Trade union goals are thus inherently nonrevolutionary. They are also economic, not political. It was Lenin's conviction as a Marxist that true worker liberation required not only the economic adjustments that workers wanted (such as pay raises or shorter hours) but also a worldwide political revolution that would usher in a total transformation of the economic system by abolishing private ownership of the means of production.

Since Lenin viewed most workers as "capable only of working out trade union consciousness," he identified a compelling need for the input of revolutionary intellectuals. Around 1900 these men and women had typically come *not* from the working class but, like Lenin, from the property-owning class (the bourgeoisie). Lenin calls these revolutionary intellectuals the "social democrats," and he sees them as the only bearers of true political consciousness. Without them, the workers remain stuck forever either at trade union consciousness or mere "embryonic" forms of social democratic class consciousness. With them, however, real change is possible, even inevitable. The question remains, however, what is to be the form and organization of the merging of these two elements? Should the revolutionary social democrats lead the workers? Or was this to be a more equal partnership? What would the roles of each be? Lenin returns to these questions throughout *What Is to Be Done?*

BOWING DOWN TO SPONTANEITY: *RABOCHAIA MYSL'* *Rabochaia mysl'*, translated as *The Workers' Thought*, was the name of a radical newspaper of the time, and Lenin critiques its stance in this subsection. Lenin again shoots down any questions about the workers' developing an "independent ideology" for their own liberation. There are, he asserts, only two possible ideologies: bourgeois and Socialist. The first leads to oppression of the workers, the second to their liberation. Any effort by the workers to find their own "middle path" simply plays into the hands of autocracy and the employers. Statements like these have convinced many observers that from the start Lenin was completely dismissive of the workers and ready to use them as a means to his ends; that he was at heart undemocratic, paternalistic, and even dictatorial—characteristics that would later describe the Soviet regime.

Lenin defends himself from these charges at several points. In a lengthy footnote to this section (not repro-

Soldiers of the 1917 revolution seen at a barricade in Petrograd (Library of Congress)

duced), he argues that the workers *can and will* play a vital role in their liberation, but not *as* workers. Rather, he places his hopes on individual members of the working class who—through experience, hard work, and persistent study—will gain a sufficient level of education and themselves become revolutionary intellectuals and true social democrats. He cites as examples the French Socialist Pierre-Joseph Proudhon (a former print worker) and the German Socialist Wilhelm Weitling (a former tailor). Lenin returns to this theme later in the excerpts provided here.

◆ III: "Trade Unionist and Social Democratic Politics"

In this section Lenin again contrasts the two aspects of the workers' struggle. By "economists," Lenin does not mean what is now commonly understood by the term but rather a group of moderate Marxists, including Russian social democrats then living in exile in Europe. The term *economists* derives from the group's preference for focusing on precisely those same worker economic demands and concerns that Lenin criticizes as "spontaneous." Unlike Lenin, the "economists" believed that spontaneous worker action could grow into a genuine revolutionary movement that would sweep away the Russian autocracy and usher in a period of liberal bourgeois capitalism that would itself eventually sow the seeds of Socialist revolution. In comparison with Lenin, the economists generally took a longer-term view of the revolutionary movement and placed greater emphasis on following and supporting, rather than controlling and leading, the spontaneous

actions of the workers. Lenin too, like any Marxist, accepted that the coming of Socialism would have to be preceded by a period of capitalism. But to a greater degree than many of his contemporaries, he maintained that capitalism had already taken hold in Russia, and he had already argued that point in detail in *The Development of Capitalism in Russia.*

POLITICAL AGITATION AND ITS NARROWING BY THE ECONOMISTS In this subsection Lenin continues to distinguish between social democracy as he understands it and economism. Economism has a "narrow" viewpoint focused on workers' day-to-day economic struggles, while social democracy assumes a broader and more commanding perspective. Social democracy takes into account the full range and structure of class relations, and it emphasizes the importance of the political struggle against the Russian autocracy. Lenin urges social democrats not to lapse into economism. He calls for specific forms of propaganda and education aimed at opening workers' eyes to the larger issues and ideas of social democracy.

THE WORKING CLASS AS THE VANGUARD FIGHTER FOR DEMOCRACY By calling them the "vanguard," Lenin emphasizes the critical role the workers themselves will play in their own liberation. But then he restates that the workers cannot develop "class political consciousness" by themselves or from within the sphere of their own economic interests and struggles. They must see their struggle in the much larger context of class relations; that is, from the viewpoint of intellectual Marxists or social democrats.

◆ **IV: The Amateurishness of the Economists and the Organization of Revolutionaries**

ORGANIZATION OF WORKERS AND ORGANIZATION OF REVOLUTIONARIES In this critically important subsection, Lenin further pursues his division of revolutionary activity into two camps: the conscious "political struggle of social democracy" versus the spontaneous and trade unionist "economic struggle that pits the workers against their bosses and the authorities." Thereafter, he arrives at the heart of his argument, or at least the part that has attracted the greatest attention. This is the question of how best to *organize* revolutionary activity.

Lenin makes two points. First, he argues that both camps have an important role to play, although he clearly considers the "political struggle of social democracy" to be the primary one. Second, he argues that because the roles are *different*, each must be *differently organized*. Workers' organizations should be "by trade," "broad," and "un-conspiratorial," meaning that they should operate openly. But the organization of revolutionaries, he asserts, must be very different. It must "not be very broad," and it should be "as secret as possible." The organization must comprise "first and foremost people who are revolutionary activists by trade"—that is, persons engaged full-time in revolution. Later in the same section and then repeatedly throughout much of the document, Lenin refers to these persons as "professional revolutionaries." This term has become almost iconic in the literature about Lenin and *What Is to Be Done?*

"Professional revolutionaries," as Lenin explains, are more than mere full-time activists. They are also revolutionary intellectuals; they are men and women from any background, including the working masses, who have by experience and study made themselves experts in class theory and Socialist literature. Some scholars have argued that the word and concept of a "professional" does not translate perfectly from Russian to English and that this should be noted particularly in regard to Lenin's famous phrase. In English, the word generally refers to persons engaged in certain fields of work, such as law, medicine, or higher education. In Russian, it can sometimes be used more broadly in the sense of a trade or skill. An alternative translation, "revolutionary by trade," has recently been offered (Lih, p. 594).

For critics of Lenin and of the Soviet system more generally, the seeds of future tyranny may be found exactly here in Lenin's organizational blueprint for a small, compact, secretive party of "professional revolutionaries"—a party that is closed off to the broad mass of workers and certain of its own status as the correct and politically conscious leader of a wider spontaneous movement. Add to this Lenin's conviction that the spontaneous workers' movement, if left to its own devices, would head into defeat and disaster. In light of Lenin's biases, many of his critics have identified in *What Is to Be Done?* a formula destined to eventuate in a highly undemocratic system of leaders (the Bolsheviks) and followers (the workers).

Lenin does not see it this way, however. Much of the rest of *What Is to Be Done?* counters arguments of this sort, which had been leveled at him already from various quarters. In this section he takes on some of these criticisms. In the paragraph beginning "in countries with political freedom," Lenin argues that while an open party organization might be appropriate in other places, in the autocratic Russia of 1902 it is not. Openness would simply make it easier for the police to infiltrate and break up social democratic circles, dooming the movement to failure. Moreover, unlike the situation in western Europe, in Russia most public expressions of the workers' spontaneous and economic struggles (such as strikes and demonstrations) were illegal, as was also true for "conscious" political revolutionary activity. Thus, the two struggles tended to be easily confused with each other. Lenin maintains they need to be kept separate, both conceptually and organizationally. Leadership by conscious and conspiratorial social democrats is also necessary to thwart the drift into spontaneity, which Lenin asserts would "only be giving the masses over to trade unions of the Zubatov and Ozerov type."

After restating his convictions about party organization in five short statements of principle, Lenin attends to another criticism: that his plan to concentrate "all conspiratorial functions in the hands of the smallest possible number of professional revolutionaries" will mean that "these few 'will think for everyone'" and take over the entire movement. Lenin counters that without a stable and professional organization to guide it, the movement will inevitably fail. Moreover, the masses will, in fact, participate more, not less, because the "professional revolutionary" will provide a kind of highly respected role model that ever-increasing numbers of ordinary workers will emulate. He continues, however, to speak of the need for a barrier between the mass movement and the organization of professional social democrats.

"CONSPIRATORIAL" ORGANIZATION AND "DEMOCRATISM" Lenin here rejects two further criticisms. The first is that the organization he envisions—one that is "powerful and strictly secret" and "concentrates in its hands all the threads of conspiratorial activity" and "is highly centralized"—may ruin the revolution by acting before the masses of workers are sufficiently ready to back them up. The danger, he says, is the reverse. By acting without proper organizational leadership, the working masses themselves risk a devastating loss. He condemns the economists again and also "excitative" terrorists—groups who resort to spontaneous acts of violence and terror intended to bring about revolution before the objective conditions for it were ready.

Lenin then returns to charges that he is being antidemocratic. He expands on his ideas about the unsuitability of open and democratic practices in the context of the autocratic political climate of czarist Russia. How, he asks, can social democrats talk and vote openly, even among themselves, when everything they do is illegal and they must hide their very identities from the czarist authorities?

LOCAL AND ALL-RUSSIAN WORK In this subsection Lenin deflects the concern that centralization of social democratic organization will undermine local control and activity and thus place excessive power in the hands of professional revolutionaries. He answers that centralization will instead free up local activists for more productive work and improve the effectiveness of local agitation.

"The [main] strength of the current movement [for worker liberation] is the awakening of the masses (primarily the industrial proletariat), while its [main] weakness is the insufficiency of consciousness and initiative among revolutionary leaders."

(II: "The Spontaneity of the Masses and the Consciousness of Social Democracy")

"We have said there could not have been social democratic consciousness among the workers. It could be brought [to them] only from outside.... By its own efforts the working class is capable only of working out trade union consciousness—that is, the conviction that it is necessary to combine into unions [in order to] carry on a struggle with the owners, win from the authorities passage of this or that vital law, and so on."

(II: "The Spontaneity of the Masses and the Consciousness of Social Democracy"—"The Beginning of the Spontaneous Upsurge")

"The political struggle of social democracy is much broader and more complex than the economic struggle that pits the workers against their bosses and the authorities. In just the same way (indeed, because of this), the organization of the revolutionary social democratic party must also be of a different sort than the organization of workers."

(IV: "The Amateurishness of the Economists and the Organization of Revolutionaries"—"Organization of Workers and Organization of Revolutionaries")

"First of all, the workers must be organized by trade; second, their organizations must be as broad as possible; third, they must be as un-conspiratorial as possible.... In contrast, the organization of revolutionaries must encompass first and foremost people who are revolutionary-activists by trade."

(IV: "The Amateurishness of the Economists and the Organization of Revolutionaries"—"Organization of Workers and Organization of Revolutionaries")

"No revolutionary organization can be durable without a stable organization of leaders to preserve continuity.... Such an organization must consist chiefly of persons engaged in revolutionary activity as their profession."

(IV: "The Amateurishness of the Economists and the Organization of Revolutionaries"—"Organization of Workers and Organization of Revolutionaries")

Audience

Despite his view that social democrats must propagandize as widely as possible, Lenin wrote *What Is to Be Done?* with a narrow audience in mind. It was aimed first and foremost at certain Socialists and pro-worker groups then active in Russia or as émigrés (some of whom are explicitly named in the excerpts presented here). It was intended to convince as many of these people as possible of the correctness of Lenin's ideas— and of the wrongheadedness of alternatives—specifically on questions of party organization and activity in Russia at that time. More broadly, but certainly secondarily, it was written for the wider international Socialist movement of the day. The pamphlet was, of course, read somewhat beyond these circles as well, including by the czarist authorities. Lenin had only recently adopted his famous pseudonym at this point, and his identity was not well known.

The pamphlet's real rise to fame came after 1917, once Lenin had established himself as the founder of a new and hugely controversial state. Whereas in the Soviet Union the *whole body* of Lenin's work quickly became a kind of secular scripture (especially after his death in 1924), in the West only *What Is to Be Done?* began to attract particular attention. Beginning in the late 1920s, Stalin, Lenin's successor, took the Soviet Union off in bold and terrible new directions. His first Five-Year Plan (1928–1932) forced breakneck industrialization on the country, and agriculture was brutally collectivized with disastrous results. At the same time, Lenin's works became increasingly available in translation abroad. Of all his writings, *What Is to Be Done?* seemed to offer Western observers the clearest insights into the roots and real nature of the Soviet system that Lenin had created and Stalin later dominated. This opinion, although not unchallenged, is still largely accepted today.

Impact

The ideas put forth in *What Is To Be Done?* split the RSDLP into two factions (effectively in 1903 and finally and officially in 1912). Those who rejected Lenin's ideas— preferring instead a broader and more open movement and a more orthodox interpretation of Marxism—became known as Mensheviks ("minoritarians"), while Lenin's supporters became the Bolsheviks ("majoritarians"). *What Is to Be Done?* also helped shape the subsequent form and function of the Bolshevik Party itself, thus laying at least some of the groundwork for the Bolshevik seizure of power in 1917.

Beyond this effect, however, historians are not of one mind when assessing the document's overall importance and impact. While many argue that it remains the single clearest expression of Lenin's basic political ideology and also serves as a key for understanding the eventual Soviet system he founded, others have pointed out that Lenin himself rarely, if ever, referred back to this work after about 1907; that his thought underwent significant modifications thereafter; that many aspects of subsequent Bolshevik Party practice and organization are not covered here; and that the pamphlet in general should be seen as a specific

---

Questions for Further Study

1. According to Lenin, what was "to be done"?

2. What role did Karl Marx's *Communist Manifesto* play in laying the intellectual foundations for Leninism?

3. Compare the revolutionary movement in Russia with other revolutionary movements throughout the world as reflected, for instance, in Mao Zedong's "Report on an Investigation of the Peasant Movement in Hunan," Emiliano Zapata's Plan of Ayala, or Fidel Castro's *History Will Absolve Me*. Were there similarities in the impulses behind these revolutionary movements? How were they different?

4. In the twenty-first century, Lenin's name continues to be used almost as an insult in non-Communist, Western nations. For example, in much of the West, words and phrases such as *Marxist-Leninist* and *Bolshevik* are often used to denigrate the political philosophy of leaders and politicians with extreme liberal views. Do you believe that this characterization of Leninism is fair? Why have Lenin's views elicited fear from many people in capitalist countries over the past century?

5. Beginning in the 1990s numerous nations were formed out of the now dissolved Union of Soviet Socialist Republics, or Soviet Union. Did the ultimate dissolution of the Soviet Union, along with its bloc of Communist nations, mean that Lenin's views were incorrect? Explain.

response to particular debates and circumstances current only in 1901–1902 and not as a timeless and essential statement of Bolshevik ideology.

Further Reading

▪ Articles

Mayer, Robert. "Lenin and the Concept of the Professional Revolutionary." *History of Political Thought* 14, no. 2 (1993): 249–263.

▪ Books

Haimson, Leopold H. *The Russian Marxists and the Origins of Bolshevism*. Cambridge, Mass.: Harvard University Press, 1955.

———. "Russian Workers' Political and Social Identities: The Role of Social Representations in the Interaction between Members of the Labor Movement and the Social Democratic Intelligentsia." In *Workers and Intelligentsia in Late Imperial Russia: Realities, Representations, Reflections*, ed. Reginald Zelnik. Berkeley: University of California Press, 1999.

Harding, Neil. *Lenin's Political Thought: Theory and Practice in the Democratic Revolution*. London: Macmillan, 1977.

Lih, Lars T. *Lenin Rediscovered: What Is to Be Done? in Context*. Boston: Brill Academic Publishers, 2005.

Service, Robert. *Lenin: A Biography*. Cambridge, Mass.: Harvard University Press, 2000.

Schapiro, Leonard. "Lenin's Intellectual Formation and the Russian Revolutionary Background." In his *Russian Studies*. New York: Viking, 1987.

▪ Web Sites

"Vladimir Lenin Works Index." Lenin Internet Archive Web site. http://marxists.org/archive/lenin/works/index.htm.

"Marxism and Workers' Organisation: Writings of Marxists on Trade Unions, the General Strike, Soviets and Working Class Organisation." Marxists Internet Archive Web site. http://marxists.org/subject/workers/index.htm.

—Brian Bonhomme

VLADIMIR LENIN'S *WHAT IS TO BE DONE?*

II: The Spontaneity of the Masses and the Consciousness of Social Democracy

… The [main] strength of the current movement [for worker liberation] is the awakening of the masses (primarily the industrial proletariat), while its [main] weakness is the insufficiency of consciousness and initiative among revolutionary leaders.

… The relationship between consciousness and spontaneity is of enormous general interest and must be treated in detail.…

◆ The Beginning of the Spontaneous Upsurge

We noted in the previous chapter the [great] *general* interest shown by educated Russian youth in the theory of Marxism during the mid-1890s. At around the same time, the labor strikes that followed the famous Saint Petersburg industrial war of 1896 showed a similar general character. Their spread across all of Russia clearly testifies to the depth of the newly awakened popular movement, and if we are speaking of a "spontaneous element," then, of course, it is precisely this strike movement that must be recognized above all as spontaneous. But there are different levels of spontaneity. There were strikes in Russia during the seventies and sixties … accompanied by the "spontaneous" destruction of machinery and so on. Compared with these "riots" the strikes of the nineties could even be called "conscious"—so significant was the progress the workers' movement had made during that time. This shows that the "spontaneous element" is, in essence, nothing other than consciousness in *embryonic form*. Even primitive riots represent a certain degree of awakening of consciousness: the workers were beginning to lose their age-old faith in the permanence of the system of their oppression, and [they] began … I shan't say to understand, but to feel the need for collective resistance, and decisively broke from slavish submission toward the bosses. But this was still more a case of despair and revenge than of [genuine class] *struggle*. The strikes of the 1890s show us much more significant flashes of consciousness: specific demands were voiced; advance thought was given to picking the best moment [to act]; there was discussion of well-known events and examples from other places. If the riots [of the 1860s–1870s] were simply uprisings of oppressed people, then the systematic strikes [of the 1890s] represented class struggle in embryo, but only in embryo. In and of themselves these strikes were [only] trade unionist struggles, and not yet social democratic struggles; they marked the awakening of antagonism between the workers and owners, but the workers did not have—indeed they could not have—[true] consciousness of the irreconcilable opposition of their interests to the current political and social structure; in other words, [they did not have] social democratic consciousness. In this sense, the strikes of the 1890s, regardless of the great progress made in comparison with the "riots" [of the 1860s–1870s], remained purely an expression of spontaneity.

We have said there *could not have been* social democratic consciousness among the workers. It could be brought [to them] only from outside. The history of all countries demonstrates that exclusively by its own efforts the working class is capable only of working out trade union consciousness—that is, the conviction that it is necessary to combine into unions [in order to] carry on a struggle with the owners, win from the authorities passage of this or that vital law, and so on. The teachings of socialism grew out of philosophical, historical, and economic theories worked out by educated representatives of the propertied classes, [that is, by] intellectuals. The founders of modern scientific socialism, Marx and Engels, themselves belonged—by their social status—to the bourgeois intelligentsia. In just the same way, here in Russia the theoretical teachings of social democracy also arose as a natural and inevitable result of the development of thought among the revolutionary socialist intelligentsia—that is, completely independently of the spontaneous growth of the workers' movement.

◆ Bowing Down to Spontaneity: *Rabochaia mysl'*

… There can be no talk of an independent ideology worked out by the working masses themselves within the process of their own movement. There are only two choices: bourgeois ideology or socialist ideology. There is no middle path (for humankind has not worked out any 'third' ideology; moreover, in a society torn by class conflict there cannot be any kind of ideology that is non-class or above-class). Thus, *any* belittlement of socialist ideology, *any deviation* from it at all strengthens bourgeois ideology. People talk about spontaneity. But the *spontaneous* development of the workers' movement leads precisely toward its subordination to bourgeois ideology … for the spontaneous workers' movement is trade unionism … and trade unionism means the ideological enslavement of the workers to the bourgeoisie. Therefore, our task, the task of social democracy, is to *battle spontaneity*, to *divert* the workers' movement away from these spontaneous trade unionist strivings that lead it under the wing of the bourgeoisie, and to [instead] attract [the workers' movement] under the wing of revolutionary social democracy.…

But why—the reader asks—does the spontaneous movement, a movement along the line of least resistance, lead in fact to domination by bourgeois ideology? For the simple reason that bourgeois ideology … is much older than socialist ideology, because [therefore] it has been worked out from all angles, because it has at its disposal *immeasurably* greater resources for its dissemination. The younger the socialist movement is in any given country, the more energetically must the struggle be waged against all attempts to strengthen non-socialist ideology, the more necessary does it become to warn the workers against the bad counsel of those whose cry out against "the exaggerations of the conscious element."

III: Trade Unionist and Social Democratic Politics

… We have already demonstrated how the "economists," while they do not completely reject "politics," instead simply and consistently stray away from a social democratic conception of politics into a trade-unionist one.…

◆ Political Agitation and Its Narrowing by the Economists

… Social democracy leads the working class struggle not just for improvement of the conditions under which [the workers] sell their labor, but also for the destruction of the social conditions that force the have-nots to sell themselves to the rich. Social democracy conceives of the working class not just in terms of its relationship to a given group of entrepreneurs, but in its relationship to all classes of modern society and to the government—and as an organized political force. Thus, social democrats must not limit themselves only to the economic struggle; and they must not allow themselves to be dragged into an almost exclusive focus on exposing economic [exploitation of the workers]. We must actively take up the political education of the working class and the development of its political awareness.…

The question arises, what should the political education [of the masses] consist of? Is it enough to limit ourselves to propagandizing the idea of the hostility of the working class to the autocracy? Of course not. It is not sufficient merely to *explain* the political oppression of the workers (just as it is not sufficient merely to explain to the workers the irreconcilable nature of their interests and those of the owners). It is necessary [also] to carry out agitation in connection with every concrete example of [the workers'] oppression (just as we have begun to do with regard to concrete examples of economic oppression). Since *this* oppression [political rather than economic] falls upon the greatest diversity of social classes, and since it is apparent in the most varied areas of life and activity—professional, civic, private, family, religious, scientific, and so on—is it not evident that *we shall not be carrying out our mission* to develop the political consciousness of the workers if we do not *take upon ourselves* the organization of [efforts to] *expose all aspects of the political* [oppressiveness] of the autocracy? After all, in order to carry out agitation in response to concrete examples of oppression, it is necessary to [clearly] expose these examples (just as it was necessary to expose factory abuses in order to carry on economic agitation).…

◆ The Working Class as the Vanguard Fighter for Democracy

… Class political consciousness may be brought to the workers *only from outside*—that is, from outside the economic struggle, outside the sphere of relations between workers and owners. The only place from which this knowledge can come is from the sphere of relations of *all* classes and [social] layers to the state and government, [from] the nexus of interrelations among *all* classes. Therefore, when one is asked what is to be done in order to bring political knowledge to the workers, the answer cannot be … [simply] "Go among the workers." To bring political knowledge *to the workers* the social democrats must *go among all classes of the population*, must send detachments … to all *sides*.…

IV: The Amateurishness of the Economists and the Organization of Revolutionaries

◆ Organization of Workers and Organization of Revolutionaries

A social democrat who understands the political struggle as simply an "economic struggle with the owners and the government" will, naturally enough, conceive of the "organization of revolutionaries" as—more or less—an "organization of workers." And this is what actually happens, so that when speaking about [questions of] organization we are literally speaking different languages. In fact, I can recall a conversation with a reasonably consistent Economist whom I had not known previously. We were talking about a pamphlet entitled "Who Will Carry Out the Political Revolution? [*Kto sovershit politicheskuiu revoliutsiiu?*]." We quickly agreed that the pamphlet's main deficiency was that it ignored the question of organization. It seemed that we were firmly of one mind, but as the conversation progressed it became clear that we were talking about different things entirely. [The Economist started] accusing me of ignoring strike funds, mutual aid societies, and the like, but I had in mind the organization of revolutionaries—[which is] absolutely necessary for "accomplishing" the political revolution. And as soon as our differences became apparent I don't think there was a single thing at all about which I was in agreement with this "economist."

What was the source of our disagreement? It was precisely this: regardless of whether we are talking about organizational issues or political ones, the "economists" are always slipping away from social democracy and into trade unionism. The political struggle of social democracy is much broader and more complex than the economic struggle that pits the workers against their bosses and the authorities. In just the same way (indeed, because of this), the organization of the revolutionary Social Democratic Party must also be of a *different sort* than the organization of workers. First of all, the workers must be organized by trade; second, their organizations must be as broad as possible; third, they must be as unconspiratorial as possible (I am speaking here and elsewhere, of course, only about autocratic Russia). In contrast, the organization of revolutionaries must encompass first and foremost people who are revolutionary activists by trade (which is why I speak of an organization of *revolutionaries*, meaning revolutionary social democrats). Given that all members of the organization will share this general characteristic, *we*

must completely erase all distinction among them as to which is a worker and which an intellectual, not to mention distinctions of trade among them. This organization definitely must not be very broad, and it must be as secret as possible....

In countries with political freedom, the distinction between a trade organization and a political one is perfectly clear, as is the distinction between trade unionism and social democracy. Of course, the relationship of the latter to the former will inevitably take different forms in different countries, depending on [relevant] historical, legal, and other conditions. They might be more or less close or complex.... But in free countries there is never any conversation about them being basically the same thing. However, in Russia the oppressiveness of the autocracy immediately wipes out all distinctions between social democratic organization and labor unions, because any and all labor unions and any and all [organized] circles are forbidden, for the primary manifestation and weapon of the workers' economic struggle—the strike—is a criminal (and sometimes even a political) act! Thus, our circumstances, on the one hand, very much "push" those workers leading the economic struggle into political issues while, on the other hand, they "push" social democrats to mix trade unionism with social democratism....

The moral to be drawn here is simple: if we start by firmly establishing a strong organization of revolutionaries, then we can guarantee the stability of the movement overall and bring to fruition the goals both of social democracy and of the trade union movement. But if we start with a broader worker movement, one that is supposedly more "accessible" to the masses (but, in fact, just more accessible to the gendarmes, thereby making revolutionaries more accessible to the police), then we shall realize neither of these goals ... and, because of the fragmented nature [of our movement] we will only be giving the masses over to trade unions of the Zubatov and Ozerov type....

... I affirm: 1) That no revolutionary organization can be durable without a stable organization of leaders to preserve continuity; 2) That the greater the number of the masses who are attracted in spontaneous fashion to the struggle—who form the basis of the movement and who participate in it—then the more urgent does the need become for such an organization and the more solid must such an organization be (for it also becomes easier for the demagogues to attract the undeveloped stratum of the masses); 3) That such an organization must consist chiefly of persons engaged in revolutionary activity as their profession; 4) That in an autocratic country, the more we *narrow* the membership of such an organization to the participation only of persons for whom revolutionary activity is their profession and who have received professional training in the art of struggle against the political police, then the harder will it be [for the authorities] "to fish out" such an organization; and 5) The *broader* will the roster become of persons both from the working class and other social classes who are participating in the movement and actively working for it.

… If we rely on a broad organization we shall never be able to achieve the necessary level of conspiratorial work; and without this one cannot even talk about waging a solid and continuous struggle against the government. But the concentration of all conspiratorial functions in the hands of the smallest possible number of professional revolutionaries does not at all mean that these few will "think for everyone," or that the crowd will not take part in *the movement*. Quite the opposite, the crowd will itself produce these professional revolutionaries—and in ever-increasing numbers—because the crowd will realize that it is not sufficient to simply have a few students or working men—veterans of the economic struggle—come together in a "committee"; [they will understand instead] that it takes years to turn oneself into a professional revolutionary; and so the crowd will start to think not only of amateurish methods, but of this kind of training instead. The centralization of the conspiratorial functions *of the organization* does not at all mean the centralization of all functions *of the movement*. The active participation by the very widest number of the masses in illegal literature will not diminish, but will *increase* tenfold because a dozen or so professional revolutionaries will centralize the conspiratorial functions of this enterprise. Only in this way shall we get to a point where the reading of illegal literature, contributing to it, and even distributing it *will all cease to be conspiratorial work*, for the police will soon realize the absurdity and the impossibility of pursuing through legal and administrative channels every publication of which there will be thousands of copies. And this concerns not only the press, but every function of the movement, even demonstrations…. The centralization of the conspiratorial functions of the organization of revolutionaries will not weaken but will enrich the breadth and content of the activity of a whole mass of other organizations that are geared toward the general public and are therefore much less formalized and less conspiratorial: including workers' trade unions, workers' circles for self-education and

the reading of illegal literature, socialist circles, and also democratic circles in *all* other strata of the population, and so on. These kinds of circles, unions, and organizations are necessary everywhere and in the *absolute greatest* numbers, with the greatest diversity of functions; but it would be absurd and dangerous to *mingle* them with the organizations of revolutionaries, to destroy the barrier between them, to extinguish in the [minds of] the masses their already incredibly faint awareness that in order to "serve" the mass movement we need people who specially and wholly devote themselves to social democratic activity—and that to make a professional revolutionary of oneself takes patience and persistence.

Yes, this awareness is indeed incredibly faint. Our primary sin in terms of organization is that *with our amateurishness we have denigrated the prestige of the revolutionary* in [Russia]. Limp and shaky on questions of theory; with a narrow viewpoint; reliant on the spontaneity of the masses to justify his own apathy; more resembling a trade-union secretary than a tribune of the people; incapable of putting forward a broad and bold plan, one that would earn the respect even of our opponents; inexperienced and clumsy in practicing his trade—the struggle with the political police: Excuse me! Such a person is not a revolutionary, but just some kind of miserable amateur.

Nobody [within our movement] should take offense at my sharp comments, for when I speak of a lack of preparedness, I speak most of all about myself. I worked in a circle that undertook very broad, all-encompassing tasks—and all us, the members of this circle, suffered to the point of illness because we knew we were showing ourselves to be amateurs at that very historical moment when it could have been said—to adapt a well-known saying: give us an organization of revolutionaries and we will turn Russia upside down! And the more I have since thought about the burning shame I felt at that time, the angrier I have become with these pseudo social democrats who by their teachings bring disgrace to the rank of the revolutionary, who do not understand that our task is not to help lower the revolutionary to the rank of an amateur but to *elevate* the amateurs to [the rank of] revolutionaries….

◆ **"Conspiratorial" Organization and "Democratism"**

… The objection will be raised that such a powerful and strictly secret organization, one that concentrates in its hands all the threads of conspiratorial activity, one that is highly centralized … may too easily throw itself into a premature attack, may carelessly push the movement [to act] before [the necessary wider levels of] political discontent [have been reached], before the ferment and anger of the working class [has matured]. We reply: abstractly speaking, it cannot be denied, of course, that a militant organization *could* throw itself into an ill-conceived battle that *could* end in a defeat—one that might have been avoided in different circumstances. But we cannot limit ourselves to abstract reasoning when looking at this issue. It is possible, speaking abstractly, for any battle at all to end in defeat, and there is no way to *reduce* this possibility except through organized preparation for battle. If we [avoid abstractions and] deal instead with the concrete realities of the current Russian situation, then one has to come to the more optimistic conclusion that a solid revolutionary organization is absolutely indispensable [both] for giving stability to the movement and to *prevent* it from carrying out ill-conceived attacks. Precisely now, when there is no such organization, and when the revolutionary movement is growing rapidly and spontaneously *we already see* two opposite extremes (which, not surprisingly, "meet"). [These are] the completely ill-founded "economism" with its doctrine of moderation; and the equally ill-founded "excitative terror," which strives "to create artificially the symptoms of the end-stages of a [revolution] that is currently developing and becoming stronger, [but which is still] nearer its beginnings than its end" ([Vera Zasulich] in "Zaria")…. *Already there exist* social democrats who fail to resist these extremes. This is hardly surprising, because—among other reasons—the "economic struggle against the owners and the government" will *never* be enough for a revolutionary, and opposite extremes will always appear here and there. Only a centralized and militant organization—one that persistently follows social democratic policies and satisfies, so to speak, all revolutionary instincts and strivings—is capable of protecting the movement from wrong-headed attacks and also of preparing an attack that promises success.

We face yet another criticism—that our views on organization contradict "the democratic principle." … Let us look more closely at this "principle," put forward by the "economists." Everyone will agree, no doubt, that "the principle of broad democracy" requires the two following conditions: first, complete openness, and, second, that all [offices and] functions be decided by election. Without openness it would be silly to talk about democracy at all, and we mean openness that is not limited just to the members of the organization. We call the organization of the German Social Democratic Party democratic because everything in it is done openly, even the sessions of the Party Congress. But no one will call an organization democratic when it is [necessarily] sealed off from all non-members by a cloak of secrecy. So let us ask—what sense is there in promoting the "principle of broad democracy" when the basic condition underlying this principle [that of openness] *is impossible* for a secret organization *to fulfill?* The "principle of broad [democracy]" thus turns out to be simply a resonant but empty phrase….

Things are no better when we look at the second condition of democratism—elections. In countries with political freedom this condition makes perfect sense. "Everyone who accepts the principles of the Party program and supports the Party as best he can is considered a member" says the first paragraph of the organizational by-laws of the German Social Democratic Party. And since the whole political arena is open for all to see—just like the stage before a theater audience—so can everyone see how someone accepts, rejects, supports, or opposes [a given position]. All such things are well-known to all and sundry simply by reading the papers or by [attending] popular assemblies. Everyone knows that a given political figure started out from such-and-such a position, went through whatever changes, responded in this way or that to a difficult situation, and distinguishes himself by this or that set of qualities. And so it is only natural that *all* members of the Party may make an informed choice and elect or not elect a particular person to a particular post. [Similarly, the fact that] anyone … can oversee every step taken by a Party member … creates a self-mechanism akin to that which in biology is called "survival of the fittest." The "natural selection" provided by complete openness, the electoral process, and general public oversight guarantees that every activist finds his appropriate place in the end, gets the most suitable role based on his strengths and abilities, suffers all the consequences of his own mistakes, and demonstrates publicly his ability to realize these mistakes and to correct them in the future.

Now try putting this picture into the frame of our [Russian] autocracy! Is it conceivable that [here] everyone "who accepts the principles of the Party program and supports the Party as best he can" could remain informed about every step taken by a revolutionary conspirator? That they could all elect this or that revolutionary—when the revolutionary is *obliged* in the interests of work to hide his very identity from

90 percent of the people? Think for just a moment … and you will see that "broad democratism" of Party organization in the darkness of the autocracy, under the "[artificial] selection" of the gendarmes is nothing other than an *empty and dangerous toy*. I say "empty" because, in fact, no revolutionary organization of any sort has ever put this *broad* democratism into practice [under the conditions of autocracy] and never could, no matter how much it wished to. I say "dangerous" because any attempt to put "broad democratism" into practice would only help the police to expose [us]; would prolong indefinitely the current amateurishness [of the movement]; would distract … [revolutionary activists] from the serious, urgent work involved in transforming themselves into professional revolutionaries and [would burden them instead] with the "paperwork" involved in setting up elections. This "game of democratism" can develop only abroad—among people who are unable to find themselves real and vital work, in [their] various little groups.

… The single serious organizational principle for activists in our movement must be the strictest [level of] conspiracy, the strictest selection of members, [and] the preparation of professional revolutionaries. Once these qualities are achieved then we are assured of something greater than "democratism"—namely: complete comradely confidence among revolutionaries. And this is even more absolutely necessary among us [than in other countries] for in Russia there can be no question at all of replacing this [loyalty] with any general public oversight. But it would be a great mistake to assume that the impossibility of actual "democratic" oversight thereby renders the members of revolutionary organization beyond any accountability at all.… [On the contrary, these revolutionaries will] feel their *responsibility* vividly, knowing by their own experience that an organization of genuine revolutionaries will stop at nothing to rid itself of a substandard member. Moreover, there is a well-developed and time-honored system of thinking among Russian (and international) revolutionary circles that mercilessly punishes any and all slacking-off from the responsibilities of comradeship (indeed, "democratism"—real, not toy democratism—is a constituent part of this larger system of comradeship). Take all of this under consideration, and you will understand that all these conversations and resolutions about our [supposed] "anti-democratic tendencies" reek with the musty odor of outsiders playing at being generals.

◆ Local and All-Russian Work

… There is one more question that is frequently raised and deserves examining in detail. This concerns the relationship between local and all-Russian work. Some have voiced a worry that the formation of a centralized organization might shift the center of gravity towards all-Russian work in general, and away from local control; [and they worry] that this may threaten, in turn, to undermine the [the movement's] connection with the mass of workers and generally weaken the solidity of local agitation. We answer that our movement has suffered in recent years precisely because of the fact that local activists are totally swamped by local work and that it is therefore necessary to shift the center of gravity towards all-Russian work. Such a shift will not weaken but will strengthen our ties with [the working mass] as well as the stability of local agitation.

Glossary

Saint Petersburg industrial war of 1896	Lenin's name for a textile workers' strike that lasted more than three weeks and was suppressed by the government of Czar Nicholas II
Vera Zasulich	Russian revolutionary (1849–1919), who contributed to the publication "Zaria" (sunrise, or morning star; sometimes Mother Russia)

Emiliano Zapata (Library of Congress)

"We continue the revolution begun by [Madero], and will carry on until we defeat the dictatorial powers that exist."

Overview

On November 25, 1911, in the beginning stages of the Mexican Revolution (1910–1920), Emiliano Zapata, a mestizo of mixed Nahua Indian and Spanish ancestry from the southern state of Morelos, announced the Plan of Ayala, which some have referred to as the Mexican equivalent of the English Magna Carta. The Mexican president, Francisco Madero, tried to prevent Zapata from issuing this land reform manifesto with bribes of a hacienda and promises of future land reform, but Zapata proved unbribable, and his Plan of Ayala galvanized the support of peasants in southern Mexico (the state of Morelos) whose land had been appropriated by large landowners, the *hacendados*.

The Plan of Ayala caused an escalation in fighting and offered a chance for the peasants of southern Mexico to rally around a charismatic leader who was genuinely committed to resolving one of the long-standing problems in Mexican society, unequal land distribution. Additionally, the Plan of Ayala turned the tables on the *hacendados*. It encouraged peasants to seize land they believed the *hacendados* had unfairly appropriated and put the burden of proving land ownership on the *hacendados*, not on the peasants who had just taken the land. This was significant not only because many *hacendados* did not have titles to the land they appropriated from peasants but also because many of the peasants themselves lacked clear title to their own land. During the remaining eight years of his life Zapata's incorruptibility made him a hero to Mexico's peasants, mostly in southern Mexico but increasingly throughout the country. Zapata's assassination in 1919 by army officers loyal to then Mexican president Venustiano Carranza resonated throughout the twentieth century, as Zapata became a martyr adored by the peasantry for addressing the centuries-old grievances of Latin America's indigenous peoples.

Context

In colonial Mexico, or New Spain (1519–1821), a lack of infrastructure and the mountainous terrain meant that there was little movement of goods and people from region to region. Hence there was little sense of national unity among the people of southern, central, and northern Mexico. Further divisions in the population resulted from the origins of different groups. There were two kinds of Hispanics (those born in Spain, *peninsulares*, and those born in Mexico, creoles) and there were mestizos (of mixed Hispanic and Indian blood), members of indigenous tribes, and African Mexicans. In 1821 Agustín de Iturbide gained Mexican independence from Spain, but until 1876, when General Porfirio Díaz launched a coup d'état, Mexican politics was in almost constant turmoil. From a French invasion in 1838 to collect debts over stolen pastries (the Pastry War), through the state burial in 1842 of President Santa Anna's detached leg, through the disastrous war with the United States wherein Mexico lost half its territory in 1848, through the War of Reform (1858–1861), and finally through the installation of the French-backed Archduke Maximilian of Austria as Emperor Maximilian, Mexico's dizzying array of crises and leaders meant that little progress was made in nation building.

This changed when the Porfiriato—the name given to the era of Díaz's rule—ushered in thirty-five years of political stability and economic modernization from 1876 to 1910. On the positive side, the Porfiriato staked a claim to "order and progress." Order was true as far as politics went. Stating that his authority came from the people, Díaz believed that he was popular enough that his enemies were unwilling to identify themselves publicly. *Hacendados* were so anxious to curry favor with Díaz that when he visited the Yucatán, numerous sycophants spent $50,000 to entertain him and his entourage. As for progress, in the second half of the nineteenth century railroads were the hallmark of capitalist development, and during the Porfiriato approximately fifteen hundred miles of rail lines were built, the majority running north–south to facilitate the export of commodities to the United States. Mining, which had been the dominant source of wealth during the colonial era, revived with an infusion of foreign capital. Department stores opened in Mexico City, French food and fashion became popular, while the United States exported baseball and bicycle riding.

For all the accomplishments of the Porfiriato, there were negative consequences as well. Texas landowners, fin-

1876

■ **November 28**
Porfirio Díaz
becomes
president and
rules Mexico
(with two brief
interruptions)
for the next
thirty-six years.

1909

■ **September**
Emiliano Zapata, a
farmer and
muledriver from the
southern Mexican
state of Morelos,
becomes the village
chief of
Anenecuilco,
marking his
beginning in
politics.

1910

■ **April 16**
After Díaz recants
his intention to step
down from the
presidency, he
meets with the
presidential
candidate Francisco
Madero and
promises to hold a
free and honest
election.

■ **June 4**
The Mexican
government arrests
Madero while he is
campaigning.

■ **July 10**
Amid widespread
fraud, Díaz easily
wins the June
primary election
and the general
election and is
declared president.

■ **November 20**
From exile in San
Antonio, Texas,
Madero issues the
Plan of San Luis de
Potosí, which calls for
the Mexican people
to rise up at 6 pm
and overthrow Díaz
as a precursor to a
reinstitution of
democracy. The
Mexican Revolution
officially begins.

anciers, and railroad builders supported Díaz and invested in Mexico, thanks to legislation such as the law passed in 1833 that allowed the Mexican government to seize *baldíos* land—land it declared underutilized or unutilized. Mexicans with connections to Díaz and capitalists from the United States used the *baldíos* law to declare communal land fallow, bribe the appropriate officials, and increase the size of their export haciendas in southern Mexico. Exports of silver, copper, coffee, sugar, rubber, henequen (a fibrous plant), cotton, and mahogany boomed, yet failure to meet quotas often caused laborers in mahogany camps to be savagely beaten. Foreign investors and Mexico's elite prospered during the Porfiriato; rural peasants continued to suffer.

As railroad construction accelerated during the Porfiriato, so did land confiscation, and hacienda laborers and peasants began to fight back by seizing properties and filing petitions. Zapata's village of Anenecuilco became part of this process when it sent a delegation to protest the sugar *hacendados* who seized communal landholdings. Connections allowed the Anenecuilco delegation to meet with President Díaz, which was in itself a major coup. Still, the only outcome of the meeting for the villagers was the deportation of two of their spokesmen to a penal camp in Yucatán, where one of them died in captivity.

By 1907 the Mexican economy had entered a recession, and Zapata's revolutionary ideals had begun to solidify, largely as a result of the anarchist tracts he was reading, written by Pablo Torres Burgos and Pyotr Kropotkin. In Zapata's home state of Morelos, the violence between the large sugar *hacendados* and the land-poor peasants increased. Communal land was fenced in to prevent cultivation by the peasants, indigenous communities suffered as their inhabitants were forced to move in search for labor, and during elections in 1909 violence and hostage taking became commonplace. The lid was about to blow off the Porfiriato, and when it did, land reform would become the major issue in Morelos.

As in many land grievances in Mexican history, social class played a prominent role in the confrontation between the two protagonists. President Madero, who had assumed the presidency only nineteen days before Zapata issued the Plan of Ayala, was educated in France and at the University of California, Berkeley. Zapata, albeit not poor for a peasant, had little formal education. Zapata and Madero moved in different social circles and came to the land reform issue from different perspectives: Zapata witnessed land expropriations; Madero read about land expropriations. From the beginning, Madero was in an unwinnable situation. Had he enthusiastically embraced land reform, which he did not, Madero would have lost the support of the moderates. Madero also faced opposition from members of the Porfiriato who remained in power and had some support from the army. Madero wanted to delay land reform until the peasants disarmed and returned to their villages. Zapata, cognizant of the failed promises about land reform strewn through Mexican history, broke off negotiations with Madero. As a result of the Plan of Ayala, Zapata's followers were willing to go to war against the federal government.

Emiliano Zapata was born on August 8, 1879, in the southern Mexican state of Morelos. His parents could be considered "middle-class" peasants and were of mixed Hispanic and indigenous stock. In Zapata's village of Anenecuilco, his family was respected for having participated in both the Mexican independence movement of the 1810s and the fighting against the French in the 1860s. During his adolescence Zapata saw how the *hacendados* worked with the railroads to expropriate peasants' landholdings, how his father wept when a large landowner stole his orchards, and how the *rurales* (rural police forces) burned to the ground a neighboring village that resisted. As Zapata matured, various mentors encouraged him to read, especially anti-Díaz newspapers and socialist tracts. On the strength of his opposition to Díaz and to the governor of Morelos, Pablo Escandón, Zapata became village chief of Anenecuilco in September 1909. In less than two years Zapata consolidated his control of rebels and began his revolt on March 29, 1911, in the waning days of the Porfiriato. When negotiations with then President Madero broke down, Zapata and a local schoolteacher, Otilio E. Montaño, issued the Plan of Ayala on November 25, 1911.

Explanation and Analysis of the Document

At its core, the Plan of Ayala was an attempt to redress land grievances that went back to the colonial era. For Zapata, the Plan of Ayala served as a vehicle for his personal grudge against Madero, as he uses the Spanish word *traicíon* (treason or betrayal) five times in the document. Yet for all his emotional antipathy to Madero, Zapata's Plan of Ayala was realistic in its prescriptions. Zapata believed that in order to implement land reform successfully, or, more accurately, to redistribute land stolen from peasants, it would be necessary for him "to struggle against everything and everybody" (McLynn, p. 120).

◆ Clause 1

The three long paragraphs of the first clause are the most polemical of the entire Plan of Ayala and provide the reader with Zapata's list of personal grievances against Madero. Zapata slanders Madero with claims that the president caused "much bloodshed and many misfortunes to the fatherland in a cunning and ridiculous fashion, having no goals to satisfy apart from his own personal ambitions, [and] his boundless instincts for tyranny." Declaring Madero "more opprobrious and more terrible than Porfirio Díaz," the first clause of the Plan of Ayala characterizes Madero as betraying his earlier revolutionary principles and "pandering" to those who enslave the Mexican people.

In actuality, Madero had acted with restraint as fighting between the government and rebels had broken out in five areas of Mexico: the Gulf and Pacific Coasts, the southern and northern borders, and Morelos. Each region had its own agenda, and in contrast to the political slogan during

Milestone Documents

Time Line

1911

- **May 25**
  Porfirio Díaz steps down as president and goes into exile in France; Francisco León de la Barra assumes the presidency, with the understanding that he will step aside after a general election.

- **August 18–25**
  Negotiations take place between Madero and Zapata but fail because Zapata and his followers doubt the sincerity of Madero's promise to institute meaningful land reform in southern Mexico.

- **November 6**
  Madero assumes the presidency.

- **November 25**
  Emiliano Zapata issues the Plan of Ayala and revolts against the government of President Madero.

- **December**
  The Mexican Revolution spreads, and regional fighting against the federal government erupts in the south under Zapata and in the north under Francisco "Pancho" Villa.

1912

- Zapata's forces begin to take control of much of the countryside in southern Mexico and peasants begin to take back their land from *hacendados*.

1913

■ **February 22**
General Victoriano Huerta assassinates Madero while the former president is on his way into exile.

1914

■ Beginning this year, Zapatist forces fight numerous engagements with the Mexican army under Huerta and later Venustiano Carranza. Fighting continues sporadically until 1919, but the Zapatist forces are never decisively defeated.

1919

■ **April 10**
Pablo González, acting at the behest of President Carranza, lures Zapata into meeting with one of his aides and assassinates Zapata.

1994

■ **January 1**
The Zapatista Army of National Liberation, based in the southern Mexican state of Chiapas, uses Emiliano Zapata as a symbol and declares war on the Mexican government in order to redress centuries of repression against the Mayan population.

the Porfiriato era that offered the rural population either "bread or the stick," Madero attempted to offer both improved economic living standards and less governmental repression. He had to counter his relationship with Zapata and his men in Morelos with the legitimization of labor unions in Mexico City and an appeal for both working-class and middle-class support. The land issues in Morelos were different from those in the other four regions where fighting had begun, because the land disputes in Morelos did not involve foreigners (Americans). In this opening salvo against Madero, Zapata does not criticize the roll of foreign capital, a heated issue in all the other regions.

◆ **Clauses 2 and 3**

In the second and third clauses, Zapata lays out the identity of the true leaders of the revolution. In clause 2 he disavows Madero as the "Chief of the Revolution" and calls for his overthrow. In clause 3, Zapata puts forward the name of General Pascual Orozco as "Chief of the Liberating Revolution," and if Orozco refuses to accept the post Zapata states that he will take over himself. Zapata had credentials for the job. He had achieved success on the battlefield before he issued the Plan of Ayala, most notably six months previously when he led four thousand followers to the rail junction in the eastern Morelos town of Cuautla. When Zapata and the other revolutionaries cut the railroad between Mexico City and Veracruz, Zapata demonstrated that he possessed a fighting force potent enough to oppose both Díaz and, after November 1911, President Madero.

◆ **Clause 4**

The fourth clause declares that "the Revolutionary Junta of the State of Morelos manifests to the Nation, under formal protest, that it adopts the Plan of San Luis Potosí as its own, with the additions that shall be expressed below." Zapata had been involved in the framing of the Plan of San Luis Potosí, as he sent the anarchist author Torres Burgos (soon to be killed by federal troops) to confer with Madero in San Antonio, Texas. Madero intended the plan to be a *grito*, a rallying cry, and stated in it that the revolution was to commence on November 20, 1910.

The Plan of San Luis Potosí represented the high point in the collaboration between Madero and Zapata. The document sought to extricate the powers of the legislative and judicial branches of government from the executive branch, because a key component of the Porfiriato was Díaz's control of both the legislative and judicial branches (federal and state levels). In the aftermath of the Plan of San Luis Potosí, both Madero and Zapata faced their own pressure-packed circumstances. For Zapata, the peasants in Morelos were impatient to begin the revolution, while Madero struggled to build a national collation. Zapata, Montaño, and Torres Burgos met with Madero on March 10, 1911, in the village of Cuautla and shouted slogans that were bound to endear them to Madero ("Long Live Madero! Death to Díaz!") as well as antagonize him ("Down with the haciendas! Long live the villages!"). The Plan of San Luis Potosí did not specifically address land reform, but it did lay the groundwork to overturn the thirty-five-year Porfiriato.

◆ Clause 5

During the early days of the Mexican Revolution, Zapata and his Revolutionary Junta occupied the extreme left of the political spectrum, Madero took the center, and the *hacendados* held the extreme right. In this clause, Zapata is calling Madero a traitor for taking a cautionary, centrist approach to land reform. While Zapata wanted immediate land reform, Madero was trying to consolidate his power. The *hacendados* were being extorted by Zapata's men for funds to finance their revolution. Madero was under siege from both the left and the right.

◆ Clauses 6 and 7

The next two clauses contain the key provisions of land reform. Clause 6 calls for citizens to pick up weapons and take possession of all "lands, forests, and waters that have been usurped." This was especially pertinent in the state of Morelos, where seventeen *hacendados* produced roughly 114,600,000 pounds of sugar and where the heirs of the Spanish conquistador Hernán Cortés still held property. Throughout the land-grabbing Porfiriato, haciendas absorbed the villages of Acatlipa, Cuachichinola, Sayula, and San Pedro, while one particularly venal *hacendado* acquired the land belonging to the village of Tequesquitengo by flooding the surrounding countryside.

The Plan of Ayala called for the villagers whose land had been unjustly expropriated to rely on special tribunals. The tribunals would convene when the revolution had triumphed, but until then villagers were, "with weapon in hand," to retain what they felt was rightfully theirs. By November 1911, Zapata's reputation was as important as the words contained in the Plan of Ayala. Zapata's most famous quote—that it is better to die on your feet than to live on your knees—cemented his status as a dedicated revolutionary.

The seventh clause is the most radical clause in the Plan of Ayala. In this section, Zapata states that "only a few hands" have victimized the majority of the villages in Mexico. Again, Morelos was different from the other four regions that were rebelling in that the peasants' claims were against their fellow Mexicans, not against foreign (U.S.) landowners. Hence there is no vitriolic language directed at North Americans. The radical nature of this clause relates to the expropriation of the land held by the few. One third of the monopolies held by the *hacendados* are to be returned to the villages for the *ejidos* (communal landholdings). While historians have debated Zapata's commitment to Socialism, this clause, although it is Socialist in nature, more likely is expressing his nationalist sentiment by attempting to redress centuries of class and ethnic exploitation.

◆ Clauses 8 and 9

These clauses demonstrate the Socialist aspect of the Plan of Ayala. Zapata had witnessed the economic marriage of U.S. capitalists and Mexican sugar *hacendados* in the early 1900s, and his Socialist leanings are evident as he calls for retribution against those sectors that oppose the Plan of Ayala. Nationalization of agricultural property, which was to be known as land redistribution, would become one of the dominant leftist legacies of the Mexican Revolution, albeit after Zapata's death. In clause 9, Zapata draws on the example of five-term President Benito Juárez and the Law of Lerdo (1856). The Law of Lerdo, named after Secretary of the Treasury Miguel Lerdo de Tegada, reduced the power of the Catholic Church through appropriating church land that was not in daily use. In theory, this land was supposed to go to the peasants. In reality, the *hacendados* manipulated the financial and judicial system and acquired the bulk of the Church land. What Zapata terms as a positive—"laws put into effect by the immortal Juárez against ecclesiastical properties"—was actually a misguided reform effort.

◆ Clause 10

This clause sought to nationalize the disparate elements that had fought against Díaz and that in November 1911 were continuing to fight the federal army, albeit now under the direction of Madero. Zapata threatens the other insurgent military chiefs who would not drop their support of the Plan of San Luis Potosí and embrace his Plan of Ayala. He uses harsh language, calling those who do not support the Plan of Ayala "traitors … [that] placate the tyrants … for a fistful of coins." It is important to keep in mind, however, that only weeks before Zapata issued the Plan of Ayala he had escaped capture by a detachment of federal troops, possibly acting under the orders of the interim governor of Morelos, Ambrosio Figueroa, and that his life was continually in danger. With the Plan of Ayala, Zapata was for the first time stepping onto the national stage, although his priority would always be Morelos. Zapata was certainly aware of the fighting breaking out in other regions of Mexico; although a later alliance with his northern counterpart, Pancho Villa, would fail on a practical basis, Zapata was attempting to nationalize support for his land reform.

◆ Clauses 11–13

The dominant themes in these three clauses are the method of obtaining political power and a singular lack of political ambition on the part of Zapata. Having already addressed the nationalization of two-thirds of the property of those parties (*hacendados*, *científicos*, and *caciques*) that both opposed the Plan of Ayala, Zapata begins to address the future of the revolutionary government. Since the Spanish Conquest of 1519–1521, the dominant method of attaining political (or ecclesiastical) power in Mexico was through patronage. In one bold stroke, the Plan of Ayala was attempting to avoid "the forced appointments that brings misfortune to the people," such as one of Zapata's biggest enemies, Ambrosio Figueroa. Many of Zapata's followers had been clamoring for him to take a leadership role in a post-Madero government, yet Zapata would remain true to his ideals and reject all political appointments.

Mexicans aiming rifles from the mountains during Mexican Revolution (Library of Congress)

◆ **Clauses 14–15**

In the closing two clauses, the Plan of Ayala comes back to its original themes: the betrayal of Francisco Madero, and the call for his violent overthrow and for the Mexican people to unite. Although the focus on land reform was an issue that was especially pertinent to Morelos and southern Mexico, opposition to Madero was coming from all sides: Villa in the north, dissatisfied army generals, and the middle class in Mexico City. Zapata here reaches out to the Mexican people, irrespective of their social or geographic origins, and asks them to stand up for their principles instead of patronage. The Plan of Ayala ends on a truly principled message, seeking to reform a centuries-old system of corruption and repression.

Audience

The audience that watched the Mexican Revolution in general and the Plan of Ayala in particular was threefold: international, hemispheric, and national. The Mexican Revolution occurred when Western Europe, the United States, and Japan were extending their imperial interests throughout every part of the globe. The Plan of Ayala was

directed at the venality of rich Mexicans who were stealing land from poor Mexicans. In order for his plan to be successful, Zapata needed to break the link between the domestic elite and the Porfiriato. The other regions in Mexico also had to break this same bond, and in addition they needed to abrogate their subordination to American and British capitalists. Other contemporary revolutions in Iran (1905), China (1911), and Russia (1917) had these dual themes of control by a domestic elite and increasing foreign economic influence. Reactions from Europeans in Mexico toward Zapata were decidedly mixed. Rosa King, a British woman who owned a tea shop in the state of Morelos, compared Zapata to Caesar and found them to be equals. Conversely, Luise Böker, a German living in Mexico City, expressed concern for her family as Zapata and his troops (whom she called bandits) disrupted the food supply and threatened the safety of foreigners in the capital.

In the Western Hemisphere, Zapata's success lessened the respect that foreign dignitaries displayed to Madero. Central American leaders, fearful that land reform initiatives would spill over their own borders, adopted a suspicious attitude toward the Mexican Revolution. Throughout the administration of U.S. president Woodrow Wil-

"We declare Francisco I. Madero incapable of realizing the promises of the revolution of which he was the investigator, because he has betrayed all of his principles, mocking the will of the people in his rise to power.... Today we continue the revolution begun by [Madero], and will carry on until we defeat the dictatorial powers that exist."

(Clause 1)

"As an additional part of our plan, we make it known: that the lands, forests, and waters that have been usurped ... in the shadow of venal justice, will henceforth enter into the possession of the villages or of citizens who have titles corresponding to those properties, and who have been despoiled through the bad faith of our oppressors."

(Clause 6)

son, the United States consistently fought to protect U.S. economic interests and its seventy-five thousand citizens who lived in Mexico. The debate about how the United States should respond varied greatly. In California, Democrats formed the Mexican Property Owners Non-Interventionist League of Oakland, while another California Democrat, the publisher William Randolph Hearst, demanded the annexation of Mexico outright. Disputes with Mexico led the United States to invade twice, once in Veracruz in 1914 and again during the so-called Punitive Expedition (1916–1917).

From November 1910 until shortly after the death of Zapata, the Zapatists were the only faction that did not lay down their arms against the federal government, irrespective of whether the army was under the command of Díaz, Madero, Huerta, or Carranza. Hence, after his death, Zapata rightfully became the true hero-martyr of the Mexican Revolution, incorruptible and vigilant until the end. The post-Revolution muralist Diego Rivera portrayed Zapata in a mural at the National Palace, and David Alfaro Siqueiros depicted Zapata in *The Soldiers of Zapata*. During his lifetime, Zapata was a hero to the rural peasant, but the urban classes were less welcoming in their support, regardless of their socioeconomic status.

Impact

The Plan of Ayala bound together Zapata and his followers. Luis Cabrera, a man who wore many different professional hats (lawyer, schoolteacher, professor, and journal-

ist), wrote the Law of January 6, 1915, a competing land reform initiative to the Plan of Ayala. The Mexican Constitution of 1917 would incorporate many of Cabrera's recommendations. Cabrera's plan went further than the Plan of San Luis Potosí, calling for a reinvigoration of the *ejido*, yet unlike the Plan of Ayala it called for the judicial system to arbitrate disputes between *hacendados* and the peasantry. Cabrera recognized that if the large landowners did not limit their labor demands to a maximum of six months, the peasants would not put down their rifles or lessen their support for Zapata.

With Zapata assassinated in 1919 and Pancho Villa pensioned off (and then assassinated in 1923), the Mexican Revolution entered its institutional phase, in which the state tried to repair diplomatic relations with the United States, rebuild its damaged economy, and reestablish the support of the rural peasantry. As part of this process, from 1915 until 1940 every Mexican president acknowledged the need for land reform. By 1940 almost one-third of the rural population had received land from the federal government. President Lázaro Cárdenas (1934–1940) was the most enthusiastic, and during his presidency Mexico distributed approximately 49 million acres. From an economic perspective, land reform from 1915 to 1940 was not successful, as family-run farms were geared toward subsistence agriculture, not export agriculture. Even so, from a social perspective, millions of Mexico's peasants were able to reap benefits from the revolution and Zapata's work and feel grateful toward their government.

After World War II, Mexico's economy boomed in a process known as the "Mexican Miracle." The process had two components: The Green Revolution saw the application of a new generation of fertilizers, pesticides, and seedlings that dramatically increased the agricultural yield per acre. Import Substitution Industrialization allowed Mexico to produce rather than import many of its consumer productions. Both the Green Revolution and Import Substitution Industrialization led to a mass migration from the countryside to urban Mexico, which resulted in the breakdown of the *ejido* system and made Mexico City a megacity, with a population that approached (or even exceeded) 20 million people by the early 1990s.

Just as during the Porfiriato, many in Mexico did not reap the benefits of the Mexican Miracle. This was particularly true of the southern state of Chiapas, where in the mid-1990s approximately 40–55 percent of the population suffered from malnutrition. On January 1, 1994, a spokesperson with the nom de guerre of Subcomandante Marcos issued a declaration of war against the Mexican state. The name of his liberation movement, the Zapatista Army of National Liberation, was chosen to honor Emiliano Zapata and his campaign to bring land reform throughout Mexico. At the close of the twentieth century, Marcos's campaign was both different from and similar to Zapata's: Marcos railed against outside forces such as neoliberalism and global capitalism, where the state of Morelos in the time of Zapata was rebelling against colonization by the elite of Mexico. At their core, the two were similar, in that they sought greater indigenous autonomy over local resources, most of all land.

Further Reading

■ Articles

Brunk, Samuel. "Zapata and the City Boys: In Search of a Piece of the Revolution." *Hispanic American Historic Review* 73, no. 1 (February 1993): 33–65.

Knight, Alan. "Land and Society in Revolutionary Mexico: The Destruction of the Great Haciendas." *Mexican Studies/Estudios Mexicanos* 7, no. 1 (Winter 1991): 73–104.

McCaa, Robert. "Missing Millions: The Demographic Costs of the Mexican Revolution." *Mexican Studies/Estudios Mexicanos* 19, no. 2 (Summer 2003): 367–400.

Miller, Simon. "Land and Labour in Mexican Rural Insurrections." *Bulletin of Latin American Research* 10, no. 1 (1991): 55–79.

■ Books

Brunk, Samuel. *Emiliano Zapata: Revolution & Betrayal in Mexico.* Albuquerque: University of New Mexico Press, 1995.

Buchenau, Jürgen, ed. *Mexico Otherwise: Modern Mexico in the Eyes of Foreign Observers.* Albuquerque: University of New Mexico Press, 2005.

———. *Mexican Mosaic: A Brief History of Mexico.* Wheeling, Ill.: Harlan Davidson, 2008.

Questions for Further Study

1. The Plan of Ayala is considered by some to be the "Mexican equivalent of the English Magna Carta." Read the entry on the Magna Carta and compare the two documents. What do they have in common?

2. Land was a crucial factor in the Mexican Revolution and the Plan of Ayala. Why? What social factors gave rise to this concern with land and land distribution? In this regard, compare the Plan of Ayala with Mao Zedong's "Report on an Investigation of the Peasant Movement in Hunan" (1927). To what extent do the two documents address similar concerns? How do they address them differently?

3. The Plan of Ayala emerged from a stew of issues involving social class, economic development, agriculture and agricultural reform, trade unionism, governmental structure (for example, separation of powers in the branches of government), the position of the Catholic Church, capitalism as practiced in other countries such as the United States, and others. How did these issues coalesce to cause the Mexican Revolution and give rise to Zapata's Plan of Ayala?

4. What impact did foreign influences have on the Mexican Revolution and the Plan of Ayala? Why do you think Zapata and his followers were concerned about these influences? Were their concerns legitimate?

5. What short- and long-term impacts did the Plan of Ayala have? Is Mexico better off today than it was in, say, 1910 as a result of Zapata's efforts?

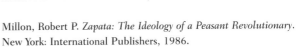

Gilly, Adolfo. *The Mexican Revolution*. New York: New Press, 2005.

Hart, John Mason. *Revolutionary Mexico: The Coming and Process of the Mexican Revolution*, 10th anniversary ed. Berkeley: University of California Press, 1997.

Joseph, Gilbert M., and Timothy J. Henderson, eds. *The Mexico Reader: History, Culture, Politics*. Durham, N.C.: Duke University Press, 2003.

LaFrance, David G. *Revolution in Mexico's Heartland: Politics, War, and State Building in Puebla, 1913–1920*. Wilmington, Del.: Scholarly Resources Books, 2003.

McLynn, Frank. *Villa and Zapata: A History of the Mexican Revolution*. New York: Carroll & Graf, 2001.

Millon, Robert P. *Zapata: The Ideology of a Peasant Revolutionary*. New York: International Publishers, 1986.

■ **Web Sites**

Zapatistas! Documents of the New Mexican Revolution. LANIC Web site.
   http://lanic.utexas.edu/project/Zapatistas/.

—David Conrad Johnson

EMILIANO ZAPATA'S PLAN OF AYALA

Liberating Plan of the sons of the State of Morelos, affiliated with the Insurgent Army which defends the fulfillment of the Plan of San Luis, with the reforms that it believes necessary to increase the welfare of the Mexican Fatherland.

The undersigned, constituted into a Revolutionary Junta to sustain and carry out the promises made to the country by the Revolution of 20 November 1910, solemnly declare before the civilized world which sits in judgment on us, and before the Nation to which we belong and which we love, the propositions we have formulated to do away with the tyranny that oppresses us and to redeem the Fatherland from the dictatorships that are imposed upon us, which are outlined in the following plan:

1. Taking into consideration that the Mexican people, led by don Francisco I. Madero, went out to shed their blood to reconquer liberties and vindicate their rights which had been trampled upon, and not so that one man could seize power, violating the sacred principles that he swore to defend with the slogan "Effective Suffrage and No Reelection," thereby insulting the faith, cause and liberties of the people; taking into consideration that the man to whom we refer is don Francisco I. Madero, the same who initiated the aforementioned revolution, who imposed his will and influence as a governmental norm upon the Provisional Government of the ex-president of the Republic, licenciado Francisco León de la Barra, causing with this deed much bloodshed and many misfortunes to the fatherland in a cunning and ridiculous fashion, having no goals to satisfy apart from his own personal ambitions, his boundless instincts for tyranny, and his profound disrespect for the fulfillment of the preexisting laws emanating from the immortal Constitution of 1857, written with the revolutionary blood of Ayutla.

Taking into account that the so-called chief of the Liberating Revolution of Mexico, don Francisco I. Madero, due to his great weakness and lack of integrity, did not bring to a happy conclusion the Revolution that he began with the help of God and of the people, since he left intact the majority of the governing powers and corrupt elements of oppression from the dictatorial Government of Porfirio Díaz, which are not and can never in any way be the representation of the National sovereignty, and that, being terrible enemies of ourselves and of the principles that we defend, are causing the ills of the country and opening new wounds in the breast of the Fatherland, making it drink its own blood, taking also into account that the aforementioned don Francisco I. Madero, current president of the Republic, tried to avoid fulfilling the promises he made to the Nation in the Plan of San Luis Potosí ... nullifying, persecuting, imprisoning, or killing the revolutionary elements who helped him to occupy the high post of president of the Republic, by means of false promises and numerous intrigues against the Nation.

Taking into consideration that the oft-mentioned Francisco I. Madero has tried to silence with the brute force of bayonets and to drown in blood the people who ask, solicit, or demand the fulfillment of the promises of the Revolution, calling them bandits and rebels, condemning them to a war of extermination, without conceding or granting any of the guarantees that reason, justice, and the law prescribe; taking equally into account that the president of the Republic, Francisco I. Madero, has made of Effective Suffrage a bloody mockery by imposing, against the will of the people, the licenciado José María Pino Suárez as Vice-President of the Republic, imposing also the governors of the States, designating such men as the so-called general Ambrosio Figueroa, cruel tyrant of the people of Morelos; and entering into collaboration with the científico party, feudal hacendados and oppressive caciques, enemies of the Revolution he proclaimed, with the aim of forging new chains and continuing the mould of a new dictatorship more opprobrious and more terrible than that of Porfirio Díaz; so it has become patently clear that he has undermined the sovereignty of the States, mocking the laws with no respect for life or interests, as has happened in the State of Morelos and other states, bringing us to the most horrific anarchy registered in contemporary history. Due to these considerations, we declare Francisco I. Madero incapable of realizing the promises of the revolution of which he was instigator, because he has betrayed all of his principles, mocking the will of the people in his rise to power; he is incapable of governing and because he has no respect for the law and for the justice of the people, and is a traitor to the Fatherland, humiliating the Mexicans by blood and fire because they wish for freedom and an end to the pandering to científicos, hacendados and caciques who enslave us; today we continue the Revolution begun by [Madero], and will carry on until we defeat the dictatorial powers that exist.

2. Francisco I. Madero is disavowed as Chief of the Revolution and as President of the Republic for the reasons expressed above. We shall bring about the overthrow of this functionary.

3. We recognize as Chief of the Liberating Revolution General Pascual Orozco, second of the caudillo don Francisco I. Madero, and in case he does not accept this delicate post, we shall recognize as chief of the Revolution General Emiliano Zapata.

4. The Revolutionary Junta of the State of Morelos manifests to the Nation, under formal protest, that it adopts the Plan of San Luis Potosí as its own, with the additions that shall be expressed below, for the benefit of the oppressed peoples, and it will make itself the defender of the principles that they defend until victory or death.

5. The Revolutionary Junta of the State of Morelos will not admit transactions or agreements until it has brought about the defeat of the dictatorial elements of Porfirio Díaz and of Francisco I. Madero, for the Nation is tired of false men and traitors who make promises like liberators, and upon attaining power forget those promises and become tyrants.

6. As an additional part of our plan, we make it known: that the lands, forests and waters that have been usurped by the hacendados, científicos or caciques in the shadow of venal justice, will henceforth enter into the possession of the villages or of citizens who have titles corresponding to those properties, and who have been despoiled through the bad faith of our oppressors, and they shall maintain that possession with weapon in hand, and the usurpers who believe they have rights to those lands will be heard by the special tribunals that will be established upon the triumph of the Revolution.

7. In view of the fact that the immense majority of Mexican villages and citizens own no more land than that which they tread upon, and are unable in any way to better their social condition or dedicate themselves to industry or agriculture, because the lands, forests, and waters are monopolized in only a few hands; for this reason, we expropriate without previous indemnization one-third of those monopolies from the powerful proprietors, to the end that the villages and citizens of Mexico should obtain ejidos, colonias, and rondos legales for the villages or fields for sowing or laboring, and this shall correct the lack of prosperity and increase the well-being of the Mexicans.

8. The hacendados, científicos or caciques who directly or indirectly oppose the present Plan, shall have their properties nationalized and two thirds of those properties shall be given as indemnizations of war, pensions to widows and orphans of the victims who are killed in the struggles surrounding the present Plan.

9. In order to execute the procedures respecting the aforementioned properties, the laws of disamortization and nationalization shall be applied, as convenient; for our norm and example shall be the laws put into effect by the immortal Juárez against ecclesiastical properties, which chastised the despots and conservatives who have always wanted to impose upon us the ignominious yoke of oppression and backwardness.

10. The insurgent military chiefs of the Republic who rose up in arms to the voice of don Francisco I. Madero in order to defend the Plan of San Luis Potosí, and who now forcefully oppose the present Plan, will be judged traitors to the cause that they defended and to the Fatherland, for presently many of them, in order to placate the tyrants, or for a fistful of coins, or owing to schemes or bribes, are shedding the blood of their brothers who demand the fulfillment of the promises that were made to the Nation by don Francisco I. Madero.

11. The expenses of war will be appropriated according to article XI of the Plan of San Luis Potosí, and all of the procedures employed in the Revolution that we undertake will be in accordance with the same instructions that are set out in the mentioned Plan.

12. Once the Revolution that we are making has triumphed, a junta of the principal revolutionary chiefs of the different States will name or designate an interim President of the Republic, who will convoke elections for the organization of federal powers.

13. The principal revolutionary chiefs of each State, in council, shall designate the governor of the State, and this high functionary will convoke the elections for the proper organization of public powers, with the aim of avoiding forced appointments that bring misfortune to the people, like the well-known appointment of Ambrosio Figueroa in the State of Morelos and others, who condemn us to the precipice of bloody conflicts sustained by the dictator Madero and the circle of científicos and hacendados who have suggested this to him.

14. If President Madero and the rest of the dictatorial elements of the current and old regime want to avoid the immense misfortunes that afflict the fatherland, and if they possess true sentiments of love for it, they must immediately renounce the posts they occupy, and by so doing they shall in some way stanch the grievous wounds that have opened in the breast of the Fatherland, and if they do not do so, upon their heads shall fall the blood and anathema of our brothers.

15. Mexicans: consider the deviousness and bad faith of a man who is shedding blood in a scandalous manner, because he is incapable of governing; consider that his system of Government is tying up the fatherland and trampling upon our institutions with the brute force of bayonets; so that the very weapons we took up to bring him to Power, we now turn against him for failing to keep his promises to the Mexican people and for having betrayed the Revolution he began; we are not personalists, we are partisans of principles and not of men!

Mexican people, support this Plan with weapons in your hands, and bring prosperity and welfare to the Fatherland.

Liberty, Justice, and Law. Ayala, State of Morelos, November 25, 1911

General in chief, Emiliano Zapata; signatures.

Glossary

Ayutla	a town that gave its name to the 1854 proclamation issued to overthrow Santa Anna
caciques	indigenous village chiefs
científicos	technocrats who advised Díaz
colonias	districts
ejidos	communal landholdings
hacendados	large landowners
licenciado	liberal arts graduate
rondos legales	government patrols

Three-year-old Puyi, emperor of China, with his father and younger brother (Library of Congress)

Articles Providing for the Favorable Treatment of the Great Ching Emperor after His Abdication

"The Republic of China will treat [the emperor] with the courtesy due to a foreign sovereign."

Overview

On February 12, 1912, Empress Dowager Longyu, acting on behalf of the five-year-old emperor of China, Puyi, announced the Articles Providing for the Favorable Treatment of the Great Ching Emperor after His Abdication (titled Youdai Tiaojian in Chinese). This document detailed what would happen to the emperor and his household when he renounced his power over the people of China. Along with other edicts she announced from the Forbidden City in Beijing, this document signaled the end of the monarchy's rule in China and the beginnings of a republic.

The abdication of the emperor came after years of uprisings against the ruling Manchu under the Qing (spelled "Ching" in the document) Dynasty (1644–1911). Always seen as outsiders to the predominantly ethnic Han majority, the Manchus had been the focus of anti-imperial protests and uprisings, the largest being the Taiping Rebellion, lasting from 1850 to 1864. On October 10, 1911, republican supporters, including the army, took the city of Wuchang. With this victory, other cites and provinces sided with the republicans and demanded the end of imperial rule in China. Unable to raise a defense because of financial woes and internal struggles, the Manchus of the Qing Dynasty, after 267 years, ended their rule with the abdication of the emperor.

Context

The Qing Dynasty was the last ruling dynasty of China. It was founded by the Manchu, an ethnic minority originally from northern China. The powerful family of Aisin-Gioro battled to become head of the clan, consolidated all the tribes of the north under them, and attacked the south of China, then ruled by the Ming emperors. They captured the capital, Beijing, in 1644 and declared they now held the "Mandate of Heaven," meaning they were given the right to rule by the heavens. The dominant Han Chinese were reluctant subjects under the Manchu and openly rebelled many times. By the mid-1800s these internal rebellions had weakened Manchu power in China.

One of the most devastating revolts was the Taiping Rebellion, which began in 1850. The leader of the rebels, Hong Xiuquan, belonged to the Hakka minority of southern China, as did many of his followers. Using a pseudo-Christian ideology, they were devoted to the overthrow of the Manchu. Large-scale fighting erupted in the lower Chang River in the southern region and continued until 1864, leaving forty million people dead. At the same time, Muslim groups in other parts of China were rioting over their treatment under the Qing. These riots were mostly suppressed by 1873. While these rebellions did affect the country, real political change came from reformers.

The cries for reform came from two areas. First, the Qing court itself had many who wanted change and called for the "self-strengthening" of China. The more liberal members of the court knew that the Western powers encroaching into China had to be met with modern political and military might in order to negotiate better treaties. Second, in an effort to modernize the governance of the country and bring about a constitutional monarchy, reformers such as the radical Kang Youwei worked with Emperor Guangxu to call for a national assembly, a constitution, and reform of all areas of Chinese cultural and intellectual life. This period, from June 11 to September 21, 1898, called the Hundred Days' Reform, was ambitious in its scope, but none of the reforms was implemented. Empress Dowager Cixi (who had twice ruled as regent for the emperor) knew her own power, and the status quo on which her whole life was built was being threatened. With the help of the top military commanders, she led a coup d'état and overthrew the emperor. He was placed under house arrest for the rest of his life. His advisers, among them, Kang Youwei, fled to Japan or were executed, and the reform movement ended. Now in power for the third time as regent, Cixi faced the advancement of the West into China.

Modernization was a necessity for China as the nation came into contact with other nations. Russia began to take over parts of northeastern Manchuria. The Chinese generals were able to push them back in 1878, indicating that while Qing China was weakened, it could still defend itself. Compounding these problems was that the European countries were attempting to carve up China as they had done in other parts of the world. This was the time of imperialist expansion, and Great Britain, France, Germany, and

1906

- Constitutional government is proclaimed in Beijing, and the National Assembly of provinces is created.

- **February 7**
  Puyi, last emperor of China, is born.

1908

- **November 15**
  Cixi dies, and Puyi is named emperor.

1910

- Northeastern China is divided into Russian and Japanese spheres of influence.

1911

- **October 10**
  Wuchang revolt of republican supporters spreads to surrounding areas.

- **November 8**
  Yuan Shikai is elected by National Assembly to be prime minister.

- **December 7**
  Both the imperial court and the republicans agree to a cease-fire, and negotiations begin on the abdication of the emperor and the creation of a Chinese democratic republic.

1912

- **January 1**
  Sun Yat-sen announces the creation of the Chinese Republic in Nanking.

- **January 3**
  Wu Tingfang presents the third revision of the abdication draft, but neither side agrees and it is rewritten.

Belgium were eager to cement their trading power in China. Forced to submit to unequal treaties, the Chinese government would refuse to obey them, resulting in more clashes with the technologically superior Western powers. These clashes cost money, and the government was struggling economically from past war costs.

More problematic than the rising debt were the revolts against the Manchus and the growing Western powers. A secret society called the I-ho chuan, which means "righteous and harmonious militia," formed from the populace. Because of their facility with the martial arts, members of the group were called "Boxers" by westerners. The Boxers wanted to overthrow the Manchus and remove Christian missionaries from the country. With cries to "expell the barbarian," the Boxer Rebellion began in 1900, leading to the deaths of thousands of missionaries and Chinese converts. When the Western communities were attacked, the foreign powers mounted a relief expedition. The Qing under Cixi saw this as an answer to many of their problems: Use the anti-Manchu Boxers on the westerners to push them out. The Qing Dynasty declared war on the westerners, who were living in concessions (sections of the city where only foreigners could live). Many court members opposed to this act knew that it could lead to a full-scale war with several nations. Beijing was besieged, and the court with Cixi had to flee into exile. On September 7, 1901, after months of tense negotiations, the war ended with many monetary concessions made by the Chinese to Western powers such as Germany. The reality that the Qing Dynasty was falling apart was hard to ignore.

In response, the court began to commit to some administrative reforms, such as reorganizing the ministries on Western models. The army too was reorganized, under General Yuan Shikai. Yuan, a member of the pro–empress dowager cadre, was named commander of the New Army in 1895. Yuan restructured the Chinese army in an effort to modernize it and to adopt Western military practices. Empress Dowager Cixi also issued guidelines to the ministries for a constitution and national assemblies in 1906. Whether or not she was serious is not known, for she died on November 15, 1908. Emperor Guangxu mysteriously died the day before she did. Their deaths left the conservative court and princes in power.

Cixi had named her two-year-old grandnephew, Puyi, as emperor, and his father, Zaifeng, was to act as prince regent. However, acting directly on behalf of the emperor was Empress Dowager Longyu, who had been married to Emperor Guangxu and was also Cixi's niece. After their deaths, she adopted Puyi as her son in 1908. When Longyu assumed the title of empress dowager, she was in a position to make all the most important decisions, but she let Zaifeng and Yuan Shikai dominate her. She did not have the presence that her aunt had had but still desired to maintain the supremacy of the Manchu in China. However, she and the conservative members of the court would be forced to agree to the abdication.

The end of the Qing and the Manchu rulers was sealed when the revolutionary movement became organized under leaders such as Sun Yat-sen, leader of the United League and the Nationalist Party (Guomindang; formerly, Kuomintang). They had new leadership, funding from Chinese people living overseas, and an ideology of republicanism that appealed to many people. Their calls for democratic government fueled revolutionary action. On October 10, 1911, soldiers in the New Army and local students in the city of Wuchang revolted. Despite the relatively small numbers of revolutionaries, the Manchu government fled the city. The Wuchang revolt was the tipping point: It showed that the Manchu could be overthrown. In the months that followed, Han Chinese attacked and killed thousands of Manchu. By December 1911 the southern, central, and northwestern provinces had declared independence. The Nationalists now controlled key provinces in China and called for a new provisional government to transition into a republic. Zaifeng, however, clashed with the new National Assembly, seeking to limit the assembly's power and maintain the supremacy of the court's Grand Council over it. The move failed, and the assembly impeached the Grand Council members and dissolved the council.

The pressure was mounting for Zaifeng to abandon the idea of a constitutional monarchy and step down from power as a prequel to the dissolution of Manchu rule. The republicans stressed that the imperial household would be treated well and that their actions were the only way to end the bloodshed between the southern Han and the northern Manchu. Zaifeng agreed, and on December 17, 1911, he and his advisers went to Shanghai to work with republican leaders such as Wu Tingfang (also called Ng Choy). Present at the meeting was also Wang Jingwei, who acted as adviser to the south. After weeks of negotiations, they presented their work to the court. As deliberations progressed, the real details were being worked out with Prime Minister Yuan Shikai and the republicans. Wu Tingfang submitted a draft of the settlement on January 18, 1912. After further edits and negotiations, the document was sent to Yuan Shikai to be presented to the court. The court argued and deliberated on what to do, as both republican and Qing supporters were present. Empress Dowager Longyu gave Yuan Shikai the authority to make a better deal with the republicans. He returned from these negotiations with the articles of abdication, which the court approved on February 2, 1912.

About the Author

Yuan Shikai (1859–1916) was a general in the Qing army. He had been involved in Korea in the 1890s as China's representative and fought in the First Sino-Japanese War. Yuan was named commander of the New Army in 1895. Yuan restructured the Chinese army in an effort to modernize it and to adopt Western military practices. He climbed through the bureaucratic ranks and gained favor with the court. He was in semiretirement when he was called back after the Wuchang uprising, as many of the troops were loyal to him. He was named prime minister by the court in 1911. At the same time, Sun Yat-sen returned from exile in America and was to be named the provisional prime minister of the new

republic. However, he named Yuan Shikai as provisional leader because Yuan supported the new order. Yuan would also be able to transition the country more smoothly because he understood the vast bureaucracy of the Qing Dynasty.

Wu Tingfang (1842–1922) was a diplomat and politician in both the Qing court and the republic. Trained as a barrister in England, he practiced law in Hong Kong until the Qing court called on him to serve as minister to the United States, Spain, and then Peru. Nonetheless, he was a supporter of the revolution and was useful to both sides as a lawyer. After the end of the Qing Dynasty, he served for a year as acting premier of the republic in 1917. Wu then backed Sun Yat-sen, becoming China's foreign minister when Sun became president.

Zhang Jian (1853–1926) was an educator and reformer. His career took off when he was a young man after he achieved the highest grade level on the imperial examinations to become a bureaucrat. After working as an instructor, he was named chairman of the Jiangsu provincial parliament in 1909. Zhang was respected by both republicans and conservative members of the court. As a result of this trust and his skills as an orator and writer, Zhang helped compose the articles of abdication in 1912. He continued as a civil servant in various positions, such as minister for industry and commerce. Additionally, he founded hundreds of schools in an effort to modernize China's education system.

Explanations and Analysis of the Document

The Articles Providing for the Favorable Treatment of the Great Ching Emperor after His Abdication was actually only one part of three edicts drafted by Wu Tingfang, Zhang Jian, and Yuan Shikai. The first edict states that the Qing had lost the Mandate of Heaven (the right to rule), and the emperor's sovereignty had transferred to the entire nation, thereby creating a republic. It also calls on northern and southern China (which had been at odds) and all ethnic groups to unify under the banner of the republic. The edict also names Yuan Shikai as temporary organizer of the provisional republican government. The second edict was a call to all officials to maintain peace and order during this critical transition period. The hope from both sides was that the transition would be as smooth as possible.

Christian missionary with eight Chinese converts in Fuzhou, China, in 1902 (Library of Congress)

The third edict was the sanction of the agreement of abdication, including the three sections detailing further the nature of the agreement. The first section is the Articles Providing for the Favorable Treatment of the Great Ching Emperor after His Abdication. The abdication edict itself directly states that the emperor's abdication was an absolute decision and that it would last forever. The agreement also allowed for the title of emperor to be inheritable and that subsequent emperors would be subject to the abdication agreement.

◆ **Article 1**

The edict of abdication of the emperor meant to the authors and proponents of the document that it was a full removal of the emperor from any part in the new state, its formation, or its continuance. However, he was not to be forcibly removed. Rather, his title would be retained, signifying that his status would be above that of a normal citizen. The authors of the articles stress that the emperor was to be treated with the same courtesy as a foreign sovereign: Because he was a Manchu, he would be treated as a foreigner but as an important one. This point is stressed throughout the document, in that he is never referred to as the emperor of China but as the "Great Ching Emperor."

◆ **Article 2**

This article deals with a vital area: money. The emperor could not work, because he was not a commoner, but he needed money to support himself and his court. The authors of the text believed that he should not keep up the lifestyle he was born into but should be given an annual allowance of four million taels, or $4 million. A tael was a monetary denomination attached to the weight of a precious metal, usually silver. Taels were still used in 1912, but they were being phased out as the republic printed its own money. Four million taels was not a large sum: It would keep the emperor and his court well, but it was not enough money to raise an army. The emperor would also then be beholden to the Nationalists for his livelihood and less inclined to oppose any changes.

◆ **Article 3**

To demonstrate to the emperor's supporters that he was being treated well, this article allowed for the emperor to gradually move out of the palace. The Imperial Palace was the seat of power, and the Forbidden City, where he lived, was attached to the grandeur and command of the emperor's being. The Summer Palace, however, was outside Beijing in an area removed from the center of power. This removal to the Summer Palace was a deliberate move to reduce the personal power of the emperor. Also, the new government wanted the emperor and his court to be located in a place where the government could monitor them and their actions. The other clause—that the emperor was to keep his bodyguard—may have been included to demonstrate the new government's concern for his safety. Many people still supported the emperor, and by showing concern for him the Nationalists could thwart any outcry regarding his treatment.

◆ Article 4

Taking care of an ancestor's tombs was a major responsibility that usually fell to the firstborn male in Chinese Confucian society. Emperors were culturally required to do the same, especially since they relied on the ancestor's assistance in difficult times. While the republicans despised a great deal of Confucian doctrine, they did not seek to destroy ancestral worship, for it was a popular practice. The Nationalists sought to preserve the dignity of past emperors but not to be held back by the past. Maintaining the emperor's ancestral temples and imperial tombs demonstrated this principle. Moreover, the status of the emperor's family as rulers of China would be preserved. Having guards present was a demonstration not only of the continued importance of the emperor's ancestors but also that the temples and tombs were part of the Chinese culture that had to be protected.

◆ Article 5

The promise of completion of the tomb of Guangxu was important to both the court and the republic. To the Qing court, he was an ancestor who should be praised and revered as a god. To the republicans, he was a fellow reformer. In 1898 he and his supporters had studied democracy in the West and looked at Japan as a possible model for China. Their efforts during the Hundred Days' Reform were stopped when Empress Dowager Cixi took control of the court and made Guangxu a prisoner in his home. He died in 1908, supposedly having been poisoned by Empress Dowager Cixi the day before she herself died. For his efforts, the Nationalist government, including Sun Yat-sen, praised him openly and agreed to finish his tomb.

◆ Article 6

Article 6 deals with two issues: the system of employment in the palace and the place of eunuchs. The work system was divided into grades or levels: Each person was given jobs and paid according to his or her grade, with the lowest grades being the highest number. Hence the first grade was the best paid. However, a provision was added that no eunuchs were to be engaged. Eunuchs were castrated men who had served as high-ranking civil servants in the court since the eighth century BCE. They enjoyed a great deal of political power, which was removed with the abdication of the emperor. By ceasing the creation of eunuchs, the republic was ending the use of them, for they were considered another talisman of the emperor's personal power. Nonetheless, a few eunuchs were secretly created after 1912.

◆ Article 7

The "private property" of the emperor of China was his whole household of goods, including the personal possessions of his family. Many members of the court believed that with the abdication they would have to flee with their possessions from rioters and looters. The republic agreed to protect these items. In the event, the process of abdication was peaceful, and there was no looting of the palace. This article did not cover the lands of the Forbidden City or even the Summer Palace, which fell under the ownership the Republic of China and were no longer considered imperial personal property.

◆ Article 8

The personal army of the emperor was the Palace Guards. Usually Manchu bannermen (heads of official households), they were loyal to the emperor alone and were the protectors of him and the Forbidden City. The government was deeply concerned that the Palace Guards might oppose the abdication and rebel. To make sure that this did not happen, Yuan Shikai and the princes gave them orders weeks before the abdication announcement. By making the guards part of the republic and paying them the same as others, the new government hoped to secure their loyalty. It worked: No mass protest against the emperor's abdication was staged by the Palace Guards.

Audience

The audience for the abdication articles spanned all areas. The emperor himself was one audience, for the articles detailed how he was to be treated as well as how he and the court were to act. The political supporters of the court were another audience, for it was made clear that the abdication was legal and not negotiable. Another audience consisted of the members of the new government of the Republic of China. The articles showed them that they had fully secured power over China. Finally, the articles announced to the people of China that the transference of power from the emperor to the republic was complete and that their emperor would be treated well.

Impact

The impact of the abdication articles was immediate. When the edicts were proclaimed, some of the royal family fled to the Legation Quarter, fearing that with the uprising the court would be raided or its members murdered. To ease the transition, Yuan Shikai was named provisional president of the Republic of China by the Nanjing Provisional Senate in 1912. However, the power vacuum resulting from the loss of the imperial system was an opportunity for many military leaders of the provinces. Yuan Shikai was no exception. He tried to destroy the Nationalist Party with bribes and assassinations, dissolved the parliament, and formed a cabinet that was responsible only to the prime minister, not to the parliament. In effect, Yuan spent the next four years as the dictator of China. While he was not popular, and his treaties with Japan provoked riots, Yuan began to campaign to be named emperor in 1915. This effort failed, for he died suddenly in June 1916.

Despite Yuan's turnabout as a dictator, the articles of abdication were not changed significantly. The Nationalists

The emperor's Dragon Throne, in the Forbidden City (Library of Congress)

> "*The Republic of China will treat [the emperor] with the courtesy due to a foreign sovereign.*"
>
> (Article 1)

> "*The sacrifices at his ancestral temples and the imperial tombs shall be maintained for ever.*"
>
> (Article 4)

> "*All the persons of various grades working in the palace may continue to be employed as before; with the provision that no further eunuchs be engaged.*"
>
> (Article 6)

and Yuan Shikai upheld all of the tenets, including the building of the emperor's tomb at great expense. The emperor was interred there in 1915. However, Yuan Shikai tried to have some changes made as part of the Reconstruction Plan of 1914, which modified the abdication articles, seeking to further minimize the powers of the emperor and move to a republican-style government. The first article of the plan stated clearly the position of the Court. The Qing imperial household was to remain loyal to the Republic of China and not disregard the laws of state. This meant that any attempt to undermine the government was unlawful. Article 2 required the court to stop using the lunar calendar and dynasty-reign dating and adopt the same system as the republic, the solar calendar and date from the year of the republic. Article 3 prohibited the court from bestowing posthumous titles and intangible honors on officials and citizens, but material rewards were still acceptable. Article 4 stated that the Ministry of Internal Affairs would protect the imperial tombs and the court's private property. Article 5 confirmed that the Imperial Household Department would oversee affairs of the court. Article 6 created a new palace guard, and article 7 reiterated that all court personnel were citizens and subject to the republic.

The long-term impact of the abdication edicts was a fractured government and country. The Chinese emperor had been the central figurehead, where he himself was the living embodiment of law and order. When there was no emperor with whom the people could bond, many military leaders decided to split from the Nationalist Party. They set up their own system for ruling their provinces: a rule by warlords. This was possible because the new republic splintered into multiple political parties that had no armies of their own to enforce their political authority and the parliament was filled

with factional fighting. Nonetheless, the government in Beijing tried to raise its own army and declared war on Germany in August 1917. To pay for the war and domestic battles, the government borrowed heavily from Japan. This was seen as an unpatriotic move, and Sun Yat-sen, the leader of the Nationalist Party, was forced to retire in 1918. The warlords continued their rule of China until 1928, taking very little direction from the central government in Beijing.

The direct impact on Emperor Puyi and his future was just as devastating. The emperor remained in the Forbidden City with his guard and lived there with the full amenities given to previous emperors. A year later, claiming that Beijing was in chaos, Wu Tingfang stated that the emperor could not be moved out of the city, probably to keep the court under the control of the government. Here the emperor and his court would remain until 1924, when the Nationalist Army removed him from the palace. He then traveled abroad and settled in the Japanese concession in Tianjin. By 1936 the Japanese had begun their attacks on China and controlled the northeastern Manchu homeland. Because Puyi had made alliances with the Japanese, they installed him as emperor of this area, renamed Manchukuo. When the Japanese lost the war in 1945, Puyi was captured by the Soviets and then returned to China in 1950. He was interned and then released, and he lived in Beijing as a normal citizen until his death in 1967.

Further Reading

■ Articles

Ch'en, Jerome. "The Last Emperor of China." *Bulletin of the School of Oriental and African Studies* 28, no. 2 (1965): 336–355.

▪ Books

Anderson, Mary M. *Hidden Power: The Palace Eunuchs of Imperial China*. Buffalo N.Y.: Prometheus, 1990.

Ch'en, Jerome. *Yuan Shih-k'ai*. Stanford, Calif.: Stanford University Press, 1972.

Crossley, Pamela Kyle. *The Manchus*. Cambridge, Mass.: Blackwell, 1997.

Fenby, Jonathan. *The Penguin History of Modern China: The Fall and Rise of a Great Power, 1850–2008*. New York: Allen Lane, 2008.

Hsu, Immanuel Chung-yueh. *The Rise of Modern China*. New York: Oxford University Press, 1990.

Pu Yi. *From Emperor to Citizen: The Autobiography of Aisin-Gioro Pu Yi*, 2 vols., trans. W. J. F. Jenner. Beijing: Foreign Language Press, 1964.

Rhoads, Edward J. M. *Manchus and Han: Ethnic Relations and Political Power in Late Qing and Early Republican China, 1861–1928*. Seattle: University of Washington Press, 2000.

Spence, Jonathan D. *The Gate of Heavenly Peace: The Chinese and Their Revolution, 1895–1980*. New York: Viking, 1981.

Wakeman, Frederic E. *The Fall of Imperial China*. New York: Free Press, 1975

—Tereasa Marie Maillie

Questions for Further Study

1. What historical events led to the abdication of the Chinese emperor and the end of the succession of imperial dynasties that had ruled China for thousands of years?

2. Why was it thought necessary to assure people that the emperor would receive "favorable treatment" after his abdication?

3. In the nineteenth and early twentieth centuries, China came into increasing contact with the outside world. What impact did these contacts have on Chinese society? How did they influence the course of Chinese politics?

4. Political turmoil often results from clashes between reformist elements who want to change government and society and more conservative elements who want to preserve existing traditions. To what extent did this clash between reform and conservatism lead to the emperor's abdication? To what extent did it continue to play a role in China after the abdication?

5. In modern times, most nations reject the notion of a monarch who has sweeping powers. Yet monarchies continue to exist in such countries as Great Britain, Sweden, Norway, and Spain and in various Middle Eastern countries and others around the world—some forty-four nations. Most, but not all, of these are "constitutional monarchies," meaning that the monarch is the head of state but power is vested in the hands of a parliament or similar body. What do you think is the continuing appeal of monarchies in modern life? Do you believe that monarchies should be entirely abolished—that all of the world's kings and queens should abdicate?

Articles Providing for the Favorable Treatment of the Great Ching Emperor after His Abdication

1. After the abdication of the Great Ching Emperor, his title of dignity is to be retained and not abolished. The Republic of China will treat him with the courtesy due to a foreign sovereign.

2. After the abdication of the Great Ching Emperor he shall receive an annual allowance of four million taels, or four million dollars after the minting of the new currency. This allowance shall be paid by the Republic of China.

3. After the abdication of the Great Ching Emperor he may live temporarily in the Imperial Palace; later he shall move to the Summer Palace. He may retain his usual bodyguard.

4. After the abdication of the Great Ching Emperor the sacrifices at his ancestral temples and the imperial tombs shall be maintained for ever. The Republic of China shall provide guards to ensure their protection.

5. The uncompleted tomb of Te Tsung [Emperor Guangxu] shall be finished according to the original plan. The funeral ceremonies shall be observed in accordance with the ancient rites. The actual expenses shall be borne by the Republic of China.

6. All the persons of various grades working in the palace may continue to be employed as before, with the provision that no further eunuchs be engaged.

7. After the abdication of the Great Ching Emperor his existing private property shall receive the special protection of the Republic of China.

8. The existing Palace Guard shall be incorporated into the Army of the Republic of China; its numbers and salary shall be continued as before.

Glossary

taels	a monetary denomination attached to the weight of a precious metal

"Ireland, through us, summons her children to her flag and strikes for her freedom."

Overview

On April 24, 1916, the Monday after Easter, a ragtag body of civilian soldiers led by members of the Irish Volunteers, a Catholic paramilitary organization, seized the General Post Office in Dublin in an attempt to make it the headquarters of a rebellion against the British Empire. The leaders of what came to be called the Easter Rising, or 1916 Rising, were romantics—poets, politicians, and professors mainly, as opposed to professionally trained soldiers. When they took the post office that morning, one of their leaders, Patrick Pearse, strode out the building's front entrance at noon to proclaim Ireland's independence from the British Empire.

The Republic of Ireland today dates its beginning to this moment in much the same way as the United States dates its birth to the Declaration of Independence in 1776. The similarities do not end there. Just as in the American colonies, there had been a viable alternative of home rule under the British Crown. There was a similar division of sentiment among the people whose independence was being declared. Certainly, the signatories to each declaration realized they had taken their lives in their hands, but there is a crucial difference. Unlike the American colonists, the writers and signatories to the Irish proclamation in 1916 expected to fail, to give their lives as a "blood sacrifice" to the cause of Irish independence. However, despite their correct assumption that they would all fail and die, or perhaps because of it, they launched Ireland on the path to rebellion against the British Empire that would finally end in their nation's freedom.

Context

The Easter Rising of 1916 was the product of long-term enmity between England and Ireland. The relationship of Ireland to what became the United Kingdom had been poorly defined ever since Henry II's Norman armies had successfully completed their conquest of the area surrounding Dublin in 1171. For centuries afterward, English rulers and Parliament never seemed able to appropriately define how Ireland fit into their realm. By the seventeenth century, Ireland was frequently considered an occupied European Catholic nation and potentially an enemy of Protestant England; it was also viewed as a sullen and often rebellious colony peopled by natives whose indigence, superstitions, and belligerent nature would not allow them to accept the "superiority" of English institutions. Yet, after the union of Great Britain and Ireland in 1801, Ireland was an integral part of the United Kingdom, and its security needed to be assured against European powers that in the past had threatened to occupy it and separate it from Great Britain. Nevertheless, as far as the Catholic Irish were concerned (and an increasing number of Protestant Irish, who often were the only people with the power, connections, and money to lead rebellions), there was only one status for the British in Ireland: hated occupiers, who had never followed through on their promises to equalize the status of the Irish people in the United Kingdom. The Irish— both Catholics and Protestants— always knew that the British considered them inferior; thus, they never fully accommodated themselves to British rule.

In the early twentieth century, several events came together to establish a real breaking point for Ireland and Great Britain. Among the most important were the growth of a proud and influential new Gaelic cultural movement, the imminent but never quite immediate success of the Home Rule movement to secure self-government for Ireland under the British Crown, the paramilitary efforts of Protestant Ulster to keep any effort at Irish separatism from succeeding, and the beginning of World War I and Ireland's contribution to the British war effort.

During the nineteenth century, famine, emigration, and a stagnant education system caused traditional Irish, or Gaelic, culture to go into steep decline. Meanwhile, political possibilities were developing abroad. In 1867, after the Austro-Prussian War, Hungary became a separate and self-governing entity under the Austrian Crown, and this provided a political model to which Irish patriots appealed. The Hungarian model became translated in the Irish context as the concept of Home Rule: the reestablishment of a separate Irish parliament, government, and state that was subject to the English Crown and its diplomatic and defense interests but otherwise remained independent.

In preparation for future Home Rule, members of the secret nationalist organization, the Irish Republican Broth-

1858

■ **March**
James Stephens founds the Irish Republican Brotherhood (IRB), a radical nationalist organization dedicated to Irish independence.

1893

■ **July**
Eoin MacNeill and others form the Gaelic League.

1905

■ **November**
The journalist Arthur Griffith founds the political arm of the umbrella organization Sinn Féin; most of its members also belong to the IRB, the Gaelic League, or both.

1908

■ **September**
Patrick Pearse founds Saint Enda's School; its faculty includes his brother, Willie Pearse, and the poet and activist Thomas MacDonagh.

1910

■ **December**
The Liberal Party retains power in Great Britain with a narrow two-seat majority and thus becomes reliant on the support of the Irish Parliamentary Party, which demands Home Rule for Ireland.

---

erhood (IRB), began to establish Gaelic cultural associations and institutions, intending to free themselves from the tyranny of the English language and culture. Thus, the Gaelic Athletic Association revived hurling and Gaelic football; it became a subsidiary of the Gaelic League, founded by Eoin MacNeill, which promoted the Gaelic language and culture. One of the league's executive directors was Patrick Pearse, a teacher of Gaelic who founded a pair of schools in the Dublin area. Another offshoot was the Abbey Theatre in Dublin, which put on plays by William Butler Yeats and John Millington Synge and later would premiere works by the Socialist and nationalist writer Seán O'Casey. All these organizations helped establish a political and economic union referred to by its founder, Arthur Griffith, as Sinn Féin, or "Ourselves Alone," in November 1905. The growth of a distinct Irish culture is central to understanding the authors of the Proclamation of the Irish Republic, since many of them were involved in these groups.

Although Sinn Féin called for the outright independence of Ireland, most Irish seemed content with the concept of Home Rule in the pre–World War I era. Most of Ireland's representatives in the British House of Commons had been working toward that goal since the 1870s and 1880s. In 1910 the Liberal Party maintained its hold on Parliament with a slim majority that had to rely in part on Irish support to stay in power. The price of power was a new Home Rule bill, the third attempt at such legislation in Britain's parliamentary history; owing to the leadership of John Redmond, the leader of Ireland's Home Rule Party in Parliament, the act finally passed the House of Commons in September 1912 and, after overcoming opposition in the House of Lords, was scheduled to be implemented on September 28, 1914.

Protestants in Ireland had always opposed Home Rule, especially those residing in the six predominantly Protestant counties in Ulster in northeastern Ireland. During past rebellions, Protestants had suffered displacement, torture, and murder at the hands of the Catholic majority. For most Protestants, Home Rule meant "Rome Rule," or rule by the Roman Catholic Church, and they fiercely opposed any separation from the British government. Their leader in Parliament was Sir Edward Carson, a well-known lawyer and leader of the Irish Unionist Parliamentary Party. Carson was likewise invited to lead the Ulster Unionists by James Craig, a member of Parliament. They, in turn, were supported by Andrew Bonar Law, whose ancestors had come from Ulster. Together in January 1913 they encouraged and supported the formation of a paramilitary organization, the Ulster Volunteer Force, which imported guns illegally and drilled in preparation for civil war should Home Rule finally be implemented. In opposition, the members of the Gaelic League, Sinn Féin, and the Irish Republican Brotherhood founded their own paramilitary group, the Irish Volunteers, in November 1913. The group's early members included Eoin MacNeill, one of the founders of the Gaelic League; Patrick Pearse, promoter of the Gaelic language at his school, Saint Enda's, in Dublin; Thomas MacDonagh, a poet and teacher at Saint Enda's and founder of the Irish Literary Theatre; and Joseph Mary

Plunkett, also a poet and playwright and editor of the *Irish Review*, an important literary magazine that connected the Irish nationalist community. The Irish Volunteers also staged a spectacular gun-smuggling operation in July 1914, and Ireland seemed on the verge of civil war just two months before Home Rule was to be implemented.

Then, to the surprise of all concerned, the focus swung away from events in Ireland. The Great War, now known as World War I, broke out, and Britain joined the side of France and Russia in early August 1914. The British and various Irish organizations all agreed to lay down their arms and conceded that Home Rule—set to be implemented in just a month —would be shelved until the end of the war, provided that special arrangements would be made for the concerns of the Ulster Unionists. Two hundred thousand Irishmen, Protestant and Catholic, joined Britain's war effort, including all the Ulster Volunteers and 170,000 of the Irish Volunteers, the vast majority, who renamed themselves the National Volunteers. About 13,500 Irish Volunteers refused to join the war to fight on the side of the British. They kept the name Irish Volunteers, and formed a Central Executive in Dublin, led by MacNeill, the members of which included Pearse, MacDonagh, and Plunkett.

The war was ostensibly fought against the imperialism of Germany, Austria-Hungary, and Turkey. The irony that Irish Catholics were fighting for the British Empire, which had suppressed their aspirations for independence for centuries, was not a small issue. Likewise, there seemed to be little recognition of Irish sacrifices in setting aside their national cause for that of London. As always, there was discrimination against Irish Catholic divisions in the British Army. Whereas members of the Ulster Volunteer Force were allowed to put orange badges on their uniforms to signify their national origin, the request of the former Irish Volunteers to have an Irish harp placed on their uniforms was rejected out of hand. Finally, the threat of conscription at home angered those who could not brook the hypocrisy of fighting and dying in the name of an empire whose sovereignty they opposed.

It was in light of this historical background that the Easter Rising of 1916 was organized. The Central Executive of the Irish Volunteers combined forces with a Socialist paramilitary group, the Irish Citizen Army, led by James Connolly and the future playwright Seán O'Casey. Through contacts in America, the rebels secured the aid of Sir Roger Casement, a prominent British diplomat and an Anglo-Irish sympathizer who negotiated with Germany to ship a boatload of weapons to the Irish coast. Casement also worked to recruit a brigade of Irish prisoners of war in Germany. Idealists all, the poets and playwrights in Dublin and the diplomat in Germany hoped that an organized uprising with German support would incite the Irish populace into general revolt. Ireland would force its independence in the middle of the war, and the new republic might even secure a place at the peace conference when the war ended.

All of this proved illusory, as was usual in Irish history. Casement could barely persuade fifty of two thousand prisoners to join his brigade; the rest despised him as a traitor.

Time Line

1912

- **September**
  A third Home Rule Bill passes the House of Commons; after two rejections by the House of Lords that are overridden by Commons, it is scheduled to become law in September 1914 as the Government of Ireland Act.

1913

- **January**
  The Protestant Ulster Volunteer Force is formed in preparation for civil war after the implementation of Home Rule.

- **November**
  The Socialist Irish Citizen Army and the mostly Catholic Irish Volunteers are formed to counter the Ulster Volunteer Force.

1914

- **August**
  Britain enters World War I on the side of France and Russia.

- **September**
  The Home Rule Act is suspended for the duration of the war; the Irish Volunteers split into the National Volunteers and the reorganized Irish Volunteers with IRB members Eoin MacNeill, Patrick Pearse, Thomas MacDonagh, and Joseph Mary Plunkett on its executive committee, which immediately begins to plan a rebellion against British rule.

1916

- **April 24**
  The Easter Rising in Dublin begins; the Proclamation of the Provisional Government of the Irish Republic is issued and read in public by Patrick Pearse.

- **April 30**
  The rebellion fails, and its leaders are arrested.

- **May 3–12**
  The leaders of the Easter Rising are hurriedly executed on the orders of the newly appointed military governor of Ireland, General Sir John Maxwell, according to the terms of a military court-martial.

1918

- **November**
  World War I ends in a British victory.

- **December**
  The British coalition government calls for a general election; Sinn Féin wins seventy-three Irish seats, but its members refuse to sit in Parliament in London.

1919

- **January**
  Sinn Féin's elected members instead sit in the first Dáil Éireann in Dublin. The Irish War of Independence begins.

The German government agreed to ship the guns but lost interest in fomenting rebellion, since it seemed clear that most of the Irish population was uninterested, if not hostile. The ship carrying the guns never met its contact on the Irish shore and was scuttled before the British navy captured it. Casement was brought to Ireland on a German U-boat and arrested just hours after he reached land. It was not even Easter Sunday, and the plot had already fallen apart. But people like Patrick Pearse, the most vocally supportive of the revolutionaries, were determined to go forward, because only "blood sacrifice" could rid Ireland of its servitude to the British Crown and dependence on English culture. The Easter rebels determined that the blood sacrifice would be their own, for their nation's good.

On Easter Monday, April 24, 1916, the rebels marched on the most imposing British government building in Dublin besides Dublin Castle, where the British authorities sat. Since the castle was considered too well defended, the rebels marched on the General Post Office (GPO) and seized it as their headquarters. With Pearse in the GPO were James Connolly, Joseph Mary Plunkett, and two of the main IRB military strategists for the Easter Rising, Thomas J. Clarke and Seán Mac Diarmida (also called Sean MacDermott). Also in the GPO was a young soldier who would rise to leadership in Sinn Féin and the Irish Republican Army when the Easter Rising was over, Michael Collins. Upon seizure of the GPO, a flag with the Irish tricolor was raised over the building, and Pearse walked outside to read the proclamation to a confused group of passersby.

Other strategic points were taken throughout the city over the course of the next twenty-four hours. The most important of these locations were the government's justice center, the Four Courts; a government workhouse for the poor, the South Dublin Union, where the rebels were commanded by one of the signers of the proclamation, Éamonn Ceannt; the W & R Jacob Biscuit factory, where Thomas MacDonagh was commander; the Royal College of Surgeons; and Boland's Flour Mill, where one of the leaders was a New York–born IRB member named Éamon De Valera. Outside Dublin, Irish Volunteers launched insurrections in Louth, Wexford, Galway, and Ashbourne. Two important cultural figures remained uninvolved: Eoin Mac-Neill, who called off most of the Irish Volunteers once he had heard about the failed landing of German arms and Roger Casement's arrest, and Arthur Griffith of Sinn Féin, who opposed using violence to achieve independence.

Despite being outnumbered three to one, the rebels held out for nearly a week, even as the GPO was being shelled from a British gunboat. When the rebels surrendered, British forces under Sir John Maxwell arrested 3,400 people, twice the number of actual participants in the Easter Rising. Nearly half were interned in Wales without trial. Under the rules of martial law, which had been declared by Lord Wimborne, the Lord Lieutenant of Ireland, Maxwell convened military courts-martial as if they were taking place on the battlefield in France. This meant there would be no jury and no defense witnesses. This procedure was controversial by British standards; according to the Defence of the Realm Act passed in August 1914, a court-martial was to have both a jury and a professional judge. In Ireland itself, 183 civilians were tried, and ninety of them received death sentences.

About the Author

The acknowledged author of the Proclamation of the Provisional Government of the Irish Republic was Patrick Pearse, whose name appears as "P. H. Pearse" among the document's signatories. Pearse was perhaps the most romantic of the rebels. Born in Dublin in 1879, he was an early exponent of Irish cultural nationalism; when he was only nineteen, he became a member of the executive committee of the Gaelic League because of his fascination with the Gaelic language. He had been university educated and was regularly published as a nationalist poet in both English and Gaelic. He later served as the editor of the Gaelic League's newspaper before founding Saint Enda's School in 1908 specifically to promote the cultural values he espoused. Many of his colleagues considered him an extremist. Eoin MacNeill, the nominal leader of the Gaelic League and the Irish Volunteers, even pulled his children out of Saint Enda's because he feared their exposure to the violent rhetoric of revolt. Fifteen of Pearse's teenage pupils, inspired by their teacher, joined the Easter Rising.

Pearse had few illusions about the potential success of the Easter Rising, yet he and his colleagues, thanks to their poetic mind-set, believed that their revolt would have an almost mystical effect on the Irish people. "Bloodshed is a cleansing and sanctifying thing, and the nation which regards it as the final horror has lost its manhood," wrote Pearse (qtd. in Fry and Fry, p. 279). With this statement, he echoed the feelings of thousands of modernist artists and intellectuals across Europe, nearly all of whom had greeted the Great War as a quasi-sacred bloodletting. But Pearse had a somewhat different vision; his death and that of other rebels would constitute a victory that would galvanize the Irish people into fighting for their freedom. It was certainly no mistake, then, that the rebellion and proclamation of a new Irish Republic was to take place over the Easter week. Pearse and the other rebels thought of themselves as almost Christ-like in their willingness to be sacrificed for the greater good of the Irish people.

Explanation and Analysis of the Document

The proclamation is titled "Poblacht na héireann," or "Republic of Ireland." In 1916 most people in Ireland would not have known Gaelic and thus what the title meant. The proclamation opens by calling on the Irish public—Ireland's "children"—to take up arms in the name of the "dead generations" that had established Ireland as a nation. Pearse then names all the revolt's supporters and actors: the IRB, the Irish Volunteers, the Irish Citizen Army, American supporters, and "gallant allies in Europe," meaning the Ger-

Time Line

1920

■ **November**
The British parliament passes the Government of Ireland Act, creating separate "Home Rule" parliaments for twenty-six predominantly Catholic southern Irish provinces and six predominantly Protestant provinces in Ulster, northern Ireland.

1921

■ **December**
The Articles of Agreement for a Treaty between Great Britain and Ireland, or the Anglo-Irish Treaty, is signed, ending the Anglo-Irish War; creating the Irish Free State, a self-governing dominion within the British Empire; and allowing the Home Rule government of Protestant northern Ireland to opt out of the Irish Free State and remain a part of the United Kingdom, an option it promptly exercises.

1921–1922

■ The Irish people fight a civil war over the acceptance of the partition of Ireland and the provisions of the Anglo-Irish Treaty; the signatories to the treaty and their allies win out, and Ireland remains divided.

1937

■ **December**
The Irish Free State establishes a new constitution, creating the independent republic of Eire and thus formally announcing Ireland's independence from the British Empire.

Irish prisoners being marched along a Dublin quay under British guard
during the bloody insurrection that began Easter Monday, 1916 (AP/Wide World Photos)

mans, who had already failed the Irish cause. Noticeably, one organization is not named: Sinn Féin, led by Arthur Griffith. Griffith had offered his support and been turned away, the rebels having known of his opposition to the use of violence. Yet throughout the country after the Easter Rising, it was immediately assumed, based on Griffith's support of independence and his rhetoric, that Sinn Féin must have been involved. For this reason, the Easter Rising was quickly and incorrectly termed the "Sinn Féin Rebellion."

Pearse then asserts the right of Irishmen to "ownership" of their island and their destinies, declaring that the Irish people would sooner disappear than submit that right to the British occupiers. He hearkens back to previous rebellions as proof and declares Ireland's independence, to which he pledges the lives of all the rebels. Considering his expectation of failure, this was a brave statement indeed. He then encourages "every Irishman and Irishwoman"—in a gesture of striking equality and lack of chauvinism for the time—to join the rebellion and promises that all citizens will be treated equally, including Protestants. Pearse chalks up hatred between Protestants and Catholics to the deliberate policies of the British government. This was an exceptionally biased reading of the history of the same six rebellions the proclamation invokes from Ireland's past. In all of them, Protestants had been slaughtered indiscriminately.

Pearse then reaffirms the provisional nature of the republic as constituted in the officers of the Easter Rising and calls upon God to protect the cause and keep it from devolving into the usual horrors of war and "cowardice, inhumanity, or rapine." He concludes by declaring that the Irish nation must be "worthy of the august destiny to which it is called." After he finished declaiming the proclamation that day, Pearse read off the names of the signatories. Then he turned and walked back into the GPO, and the Easter Rising continued.

Audience

Certainly, Pearse and his compatriots envisioned that their broader audience would include not only the British but also

Éamon De Valera (Library of Congress)

Sir Edward Carson (Library of Congress)

the world public. However, the proclamation's actual audience was targeted in its Gaelic title: "Poblacht na héireann." The people of Ireland were expected to read copies of the proclamation and join in the Easter Rising. But it said everything that a group of intellectuals would even consider putting the title of the document in Gaelic; they knew little, if anything, about their audience. From the beginning, the Irish populace rejected them. Like Casement's prisoners of war in Germany, the vast majority considered the insurgents to be traitors of the worst sort. As evidence, when the insurgents laid down their arms on April 30 and walked out of the GPO, they were spat upon and jeered at by surrounding crowds as British soldiers escorted them to jail. On the first day, the garrison near Boland's Flour Mill, commanded by Éamon De Valera, had fired on the unsuspecting and unarmed troops of the Georgius Rex Home Defence Force, a corps of proud old men in frumpy uniforms, many of them British military veterans, whom Dubliners had nicknamed the "Gorgeous Wrecks." Several of the Georgius Rex men were killed; the violence of the public reaction to the incident took the insurgents by surprise—and was probably instrumental in their harsh reception thereafter.

Impact

The leaders of the Easter Rising, as expected, received the opportunity to give their "blood sacrifice." They all

were executed by firing squad from May 3 to May 12. The methods and reasons behind the executions circulated widely soon after they had taken place. Patrick Pearse's little brother, Willie, was executed for no more reason than having worshiped his brother. Joseph Mary Plunkett was ill after having had an operation on the glands in his neck; just before his execution he married the sister of Thomas MacDonagh's wife, and thus both sisters were left widows. James Connolly had been so gravely wounded that the firing squad had to prop him up in a chair to shoot him. Roger Casement—a Protestant with a better social pedigree—would be executed months later in Pentonville Prison in London after a formal trial for treason. The fifteen executed in Dublin received no funerals; their bodies were covered in quicklime as if they were corpses left to rot after a battle.

During his court-martial, Pearse declared, "You cannot conquer Ireland. You cannot extinguish the Irish passion for freedom. If our deed has not been sufficient to win freedom, then our children will win it by a better deed" (Judd, p. 243). He was right. If the insurgents had been considered fools and traitors during the Easter Rising, they became martyrs immediately after they had died. Most of the rest of the death sentences were commuted to imprisonments as the British government tried to correct its mistake, but the damage was done. The summary nature of the executions, the speed with which they had taken place in comparison to the excruciatingly long number of days it had taken to perform them, and the clear embarrassment of the coalition government in London over the conduct of their defense forces turned Irish public opinion decidedly in favor of the Easter Rising. Masses were said in the names of the rebels, and numerous public demonstrations followed throughout the remainder of World War I.

Although Sinn Féin had not been involved, it was still widely believed to have been the organization behind the Easter Rising. This had the odd benefit of causing scores of members of the IRB, the Irish Volunteers, and other politically minded people to flock to Sinn Féin and transform it into a political party. The father of Joseph Mary Plunkett was elected in a by-election to the British Parliament, but he refused to take his seat. He asserted that there was a legitimate government established in Ireland by the proclamation and that was the only government he recognized. Other separatists, some of them in jail, were also elected to Parliament. One of them was Éamon De Valera, elected in July 1917, and he likewise refused to go to London. Three months later in October, De Valera was appointed head of both the Irish Volunteers and Sinn Féin.

In early 1918 the British government tried to introduce conscription in Ireland; this was the last straw for many who had not gone to war earlier at the behest of their colonial overlords. Certainly, they were not willing to do so after the Easter Rising. Nationwide resistance to the draft meant that it was never implemented. Furthermore, Catholic southern Ireland was by this point virtually united for independence, just as Pearse and the other leaders of the Easter Rising had hoped.

"*Irishmen and Irishwomen: In the name of God and of the dead generations from whom she receives her old tradition of nationhood, Ireland, through us, summons her children to her flag and strikes for her freedom.*"

"*We declare the right of the people of Ireland to the ownership of Ireland, and to the unfettered control of Irish destinies, to be sovereign and indefeasible.*"

"*The Irish Republic ... guarantees religious and civil liberty, equal rights and equal opportunities to all its citizens, and declares its resolve to pursue the happiness and prosperity of the whole nation and of all its parts, cherishing all the children of the nation equally, and oblivious of the differences carefully fostered by an alien government, which have divided a minority from the majority in the past.*"

In December 1918 the British coalition government held a general election, largely to cement its status as the nation assigned to broker the peace agreement with Germany. The election was also the first in Britain's history to be conducted on the basis of universal adult male suffrage. The election results solidified Sinn Féin's hold on aspirations for an independent Ireland. Sinn Féin collected seventy-three of 105 Irish seats in Parliament, swamping the Ulster Unionists as well as the Irish Parliamentary Party, which advocated Home Rule. Promptly, the elected Sinn Féin members of Parliament refused to accept their seats in London and instead stayed home in Dublin, where they formed the Dáil Éireann, their own Irish parliament, just as Arthur Griffith had always wanted.

What Griffith had hoped for, however, was that the separation of governments could be concluded peacefully. Such was not to be the case; more as Pearse and his colleagues had foreseen, the independence of Ireland was to be obtained through the shedding of blood. The Irish War of Independence began in January 1919. The Irish Volunteers, having renamed themselves the Irish Republican Army in October 1917, fought a bitter guerrilla war against the British and their Protestant Irish allies across the streets of Dublin and Belfast and the whole of Ireland under the leadership of Michael Collins. Two years later a truce was signed, the Anglo-Irish Treaty of 1921. Ireland received a status in the British Empire that was vaguely more independent than "Home Rule"—the new Irish government would be called a "Free State." However, six Protestant counties in Ulster were allowed to opt out of the Free State to remain a part of the United Kingdom, and Ireland was divided between north and south. By the end of 1922, Collins and Griffith were dead, De Valera resigned as the new president of the Irish Free State, and Ireland launched itself into civil war over the provisions of the treaty. Yet the promises of the Proclamation of the Irish Republic had largely been achieved. It would take another year of civil war to force acceptance of the geographic and religiously based split on the population of Ireland. The rebels' prediction in 1916 of "blood sacrifice" had come true with a vengeance.

Further Reading

■ Articles

Gerson, Gal. "Cultural Subversion and the Background of the Irish 'Easter Poets'." *Journal of Contemporary History* 30, no. 2 (April 1995): 333–347.

O'Brien, Conor Cruise. "The Embers of Easter." *Massachusetts Review* 7, no. 4 (Autumn 1966): 621–637.

■ **Books**

Coogan, Tim Pat. *Ireland in the 20th Century*. New York: Palgrave Macmillan, 2004.

Duffy, Seán. *The Illustrated History of Ireland*. Chicago: Contemporary Books, 2002.

Fry, Peter, and Fiona Somerset Fry. *A History of Ireland*. New York: Routledge, 1988.

Judd, Denis. *Empire: The British Imperial Experience from 1765 to the Present*. New York: HarperCollins, 1996.

O'Broin, Leon. *Dublin Castle and the 1916 Rising*. Rev. ed. New York: New York University Press, 1971.

Wills, Clair. *Dublin 1916: The Siege of the GPO*. Cambridge, Mass.: Harvard University Press, 2009.

■ **Web Sites**

"The 1916 Rising." Department of the Taoiseach, Government of Ireland, Web site.
     http://www.taoiseach.gov.ie/eng/Taoiseach_and_Government/History_of_Government/1916_Commemorations/The_1916_Rising.html.

"Wars & Conflict: 1916 Easter Rising." BBC Web site.
     http://www.bbc.co.uk/history/british/easterrising/.

—David Simonelli

Questions for Further Study

1. Many of the key events in world history have to do with nations' aspirations for independence. Compare the proclamation and the events surrounding it with one or more similar assertions of independence. Possible documents include the Cartagena Manifesto, the Treaty of Cordoba, the Dutch Declaration of Independence, the Korean Declaration of Independence, and the Constitution of Haiti.

2. England maintained colonies in the New World. One group of those colonies, which would form the nation of Canada, broke with England in a manner that was nearly entirely peaceful and succeeded in becoming an independent nation. Why was Canada's break, as reflected in the events surrounding the Constitution Act of Canada, so "clean," while that of Ireland was accompanied by turmoil and continued violence?

3. Define the concept of Home Rule. Why did some people in Ireland support Home Rule while others opposed it? How would the modern history of Ireland have been different if the dispute had not arisen and the Irish people had largely supported either Home Rule or complete independence?

4. For hundreds of years, religion had played a major role in political disputes throughout Europe, often leading to armed conflict. What role did religion play in the events before and after the proclamation?

5. Still in the twenty-first century, Ireland remains divided. Why?

PROCLAMATION OF THE PROVISIONAL GOVERNMENT OF THE IRISH REPUBLIC

The Provisional Government of the Irish Republic to the People of Ireland

Irishmen and Irishwomen: In the name of God and of the dead generations from whom she receives her old traditions of nationhood, Ireland, through us, summons her children to her flag and strikes for her freedom.

Having organized and trained her manhood through her secret revolutionary organization the Irish Republican Brotherhood, and through her open military organizations, the Irish Volunteers and the Irish Citizen Army, having patiently perfected her discipline, having resolutely waited for the right moment to reveal itself, she now seizes that moment, and, supported by her exiled children in America and her gallant allies in Europe, but relying in the first on her own strength, she strikes in full confidence of victory.

We declare the right of the people of Ireland to the ownership of Ireland, and to the unfettered control of Irish destinies, to be sovereign and indefeasible. The long usurpation of that right by a foreign people and government has not extinguished the right, nor can it ever be extinguished except by the destruction of the Irish people. In every generation the Irish people have asserted their right to national freedom and sovereignty: six times during the past three hundred years they have asserted it in arms. Standing on that fundamental right and again asserting it in arms in the face of the world, we hereby proclaim the Irish Republic as a Sovereign Independent State, and we pledge our lives and the lives of our comrades-in-arms to the cause of its freedom, of its welfare, and of its exaltation among the nations.

The Irish Republic is entitled to, and hereby claims, the allegiance of every Irishman and Irishwoman. The Republic guarantees religious and civil liberty, equal rights and equal opportunities to all its citizens, and declares its resolve to pursue the happiness and prosperity of the whole nation and of all its parts, cherishing all the children of the nation equally, and oblivious of the differences carefully fostered by an alien government, which have divided a minority from the majority in the past.

Until our arms have brought the opportune moment for the establishment of a permanent National Government, representative of the whole people of Ireland and elected by the suffrages of all her men and women, the Provisional Government, hereby constituted, will administer the civil and military affairs of the Republic in trust for the people.

We place the cause of the Irish Republic under the protection of the Most High God, Whose blessing we invoke upon our arms, and we pray that no one who serves that cause will dishonor it by cowardice, inhumanity or rapine. In this supreme hour the Irish nation must, by its valor and discipline and by the readiness of its children to sacrifice themselves for the common good, prove itself worthy of the august destiny to which it is called.

Signed on Behalf of the Provisional Government.

Thomas J. Clarke
Seán Mac Diarmada,
Thomas MacDonagh,
P. H. Pearse,
Éamonn Ceannt,
James Connolly,
Joseph Plunkett.

BALFOUR DECLARATION

"I have much pleasure in conveying to you ...
the following declaration of sympathy with Jewish Zionist aspirations...."

Overview

The Balfour Declaration was conveyed in a letter addressed by Arthur James Balfour, the British secretary of state for foreign affairs, to Lord Walter Rothschild, a prominent member of the British Jewish community. In the letter, Balfour proclaimed that Britain would support Zionist aspirations by facilitating in Palestine the establishment of "a national home for the Jewish people." By declaring Britain to be Zionism's patron, Balfour's signature completed a process begun twenty years earlier at the First Zionist Congress, held in 1897 in Basel, Switzerland. It was then that a small group of Jewish leaders acted on their conviction that anti-Semitism in Europe was too deeply embedded to ever be eliminated and started canvassing political leaders—in Britain and Germany especially, but also in the Ottoman Empire itself—for a "charter" granting Jews the right to develop Palestine as a state of their own.

Balfour's promise was one of a number of contradictory pledges made by Britain during the course of World War I regarding the future disposition of Ottoman territories. Vague and ambiguous, it nonetheless stood as official policy until World War II. Throughout the interwar period, Britain provided Zionism with the necessary protective umbrella without which Jewish immigration, settlement, and state building in Palestine could not have succeeded. At the time of World War I, the Jewish population of Palestine was only 10 percent of the population, the other 90 percent consisting of an Arab community whose rights and aspirations Balfour had effectively ignored. In what was "one of the most improbable political documents of all time," wrote Arthur Koestler, "one nation solemnly promised to a second nation the country of a third" (p. 4). Britain assumed that the problematic balancing act was one that could be upheld, but this was a gross misjudgment that would come back to haunt the nation.

Context

The outbreak of World War I in 1914 forced profound changes in Britain's Middle East policies. During the next three years the nation signed a number of controversial treaties and agreements with different partners. Prior to the war, Britain's long-standing concern in this strategic region was to protect the sea routes to India. Britain had been able to satisfy its own interests in the late nineteenth century by securing control over Egypt and the Suez Canal. Beyond that, the main aim of British diplomacy was to preserve the territorial integrity of the Ottoman Empire as a way to guard against Russian expansionism. However, with the Ottoman entry into the war as an ally of Germany, new policies had to be adopted. Often hesitant and ambiguous, British wartime policies resulted in a confusing array of declarations. Despite the best efforts of British diplomats in the postwar years to square the contradictions, the promises concerning that part of the Ottoman Empire known as Palestine—the future disposition of which Britain pledged to no fewer than three different allies—have remained the source of much controversy.

Prior to being presented in November 1917 to Zionist leaders, the fate of Palestine was the subject of two separate British agreements concluded with Arab and French negotiators. Britain was greatly concerned over the potential impact of war with the Ottoman sultan-caliph and so quickly directed its attention to establishing an alliance with Sharif Husayn ibn 'Alī, the Arab emir of the Muslim holy city of Mecca and head of the Hashemite family. In return for the launching of an Arab rebellion against the Ottomans by Husayn's son, Faisal, the British high commissioner in Egypt, Sir Henry McMahon, promised Husayn money, munitions, and the right to establish an independent Arab state. The negotiation was worked out in an exchange of letters between July 1915 and March 1916, in what later became known as the McMahon-Husayn correspondence. The ambiguity of territorial boundaries set out in this correspondence resulted in great confusion over whether Palestine was in fact promised to the Arabs, as part of Husayn's Arab state, or was deliberately excluded by Britain in order to accommodate the interests of France.

Even while negotiating with Husayn, the British were secretly carving up the Middle East into spoils of war to be shared with European allies. Through the secret 1916 Sykes-Picot Agreement, the Ottoman provinces of the

1896

- Theodor Herzl publishes *Der Judenstaat* (*Jewish State: An Attempt at a Modern Solution of the Jewish Question*), an influential pamphlet arguing that only the creation of a Jewish state could put an end to the prevailing anti-Semitism of Europe.

1897

- **August 29**
  The First Zionist Congress convenes in Basel, Switzerland, where delegates endorse Herzl's scheme to first gain the diplomatic support of a Great Power.

1915

- **July**
  During World War I, in correspondence that lasts through January 1916, British diplomats negotiate with Sharif Husayn ibn 'Alī, the emir of Mecca; in return for Husayn's mounting an Arab revolt against the Ottoman Empire, Britain conditionally agrees to support an independent Arab kingdom.

1916

- **May 16**
  Britain and France ratify the secret Sykes-Picot Agreement, recognizing France's claims to a zone stretching from Lebanon to the Syrian interior and Britain's claims to a zone stretching from Gaza to Iraq, with Palestine to be placed under international administration.

Hashemite's hoped-for Arab kingdom were divided into a number of successor states, each of them under some degree of control by Britain or France. The repercussions of this calculated yet arbitrary drawing of new state boundaries resonate to this day. As for Palestine specifically, Britain resisted the attempts of French negotiators to secure for themselves control over the whole of Syria down to the Egyptian border, and in the end the agreement placed Palestine under the control of an international administration.

By the end of the following year, however, Britain had recalculated its own strategic interests in Palestine. The region had become the site of important military operations, and government officials concluded that Palestine's value as a buffer to Egypt was too high to make tolerable any sort of foreign presence there after the war. These new calculations were emerging just as British forces were amassing on the Sinai Peninsula to push back the Ottoman forces and break through to Palestine. Most significantly, the new calculations were developed in tandem with efforts of the British Jewish community to persuade the country's leaders that Zionist interests in developing Palestine for themselves complemented British interests. In November 1917, Britain issued the Balfour Declaration, thus concluding in less than three years a third round of negotiations over the promised land. The following month, British imperial forces occupied Jerusalem, ending over four hundred years of Ottoman rule and initiating over thirty years of British rule.

About the Author

The Balfour Declaration underwent successive drafts between July and October 1917. The main responsibility for the phrasing and rephrasing of the declaration was shared by Arthur Balfour, Prime Minister David Lloyd George, Lord Alfred Milner, and Leopold Amery. Balfour, a former prime minister (1902–1905), had graduated from Cambridge University in 1869 and became a Conservative member of Parliament in 1874. In what is sometimes referred to as "the first Balfour declaration," he had, as prime minister in 1903, supported a proposal to build a Jewish national presence in Uganda.

David Lloyd George, a Liberal member of Parliament since 1890, was appointed secretary of state for war in mid-1916 and became prime minister by the end of the year. The succession was controversial, largely owing to the nature of his authority; describing the concentration of war strategy in the hands of Lloyd George and his streamlined war cabinet, D. K. Fieldhouse notes that "never in modern times had the decision-making process in Britain been concentrated in so few hands" (p. 132). For Lloyd George, support for Zionism was deeply rooted in his Christian faith, and he would refer to Palestine by its ancient name of Canaan. Like Balfour, Lloyd George viewed Jews as a separate race whose global influence could so benefit Britain that, as he wrote later, Britain had no real choice other than to "make a contract with Jewry" (Segev, p. 38).

Such racial perceptions of identity were also readily apparent in the thought of Lord Milner, who was brought into the war cabinet as a minister without portfolio in December 1916, largely because of his administrative capabilities. But Milner, who had graduated from Oxford University in 1877 imbued with notions of imperial service and had been appointed governor of the Cape Colony and high commissioner of southern Africa in 1897, also believed firmly in the primordial nature of racial bonds. Significantly, his protégé from the colonial administration of South Africa, Leopold Amery—a lifelong imperialist and Zionist, appointed in 1917 as assistant secretary to the war cabinet secretariat—proposed in one draft of the declaration that the term "the Jewish people" be replaced with "the Jewish race."

Explanation and Analysis of the Document

The history and purpose of the Balfour Declaration remains a controversial subject. There is no straightforward explanation as to the declaration's origins. Over the years, historians have set out a complex combination of motives that led to the final decision to issue the declaration.

The earliest narratives stressed the biblical romanticism of British officials' interest in the restoration of the Jewish nation in Palestine and their sympathy for the plight of Jews in Eastern Europe. The first scholarly accounts, such as the detailed description of the decision-making process provided by Leonard Stein, focused more on the political and diplomatic context in which British officials came to see Zionism as an ally. These early interpretations stressed the Balfour Declaration as a product of the activities of the Zionist Organization, or specifically of Dr. Chaim Weizmann, a prominent Zionist spokesman engaged during the war in biochemical research for Britain's Ministry of Munitions. Weizmann's influential contacts and skillful persistence were credited with convincing British officials of the wartime propaganda value that a gesture of support for Zionism would carry in the United States and Russia, where Jews were believed to wield great power. It was argued, for example, that Britain's support for Zionism would mitigate domestic opposition in the United States, which protested against entry into the war on the side of the anti-Semitic regime of czarist Russia.

As government sources became more widely available, historians shifted the focus away from the role played by Zionist leaders in drawing British officials' interest to Palestine. In a reversal of emphasis, greater stress was laid on the actions of those British officials who, in fact, searched out Zionist support in pursuit of their own interests. As Mayir Vereté has famously argued, "Had there been no Zionists in those days, the British would have had to invent them" (p. 4). Vereté downplayed the role of Zionist representatives such as Weizmann and elaborated on the strategic value of the Balfour Declaration in keeping the French out of Palestine. Within a year of having negotiated the

Time Line

1917

- **November 2**
  The Balfour Declaration is issued by the British.

- **December 11**
  General Edmund Allenby makes official entry into Jerusalem, marking the start of British rule in Palestine.

1918

- **January 8**
  The U.S. president Woodrow Wilson proclaims the Fourteen Points that become the basis for the terms of Germany's surrender.

1919

- **January 3**
  In the Faisal-Weizmann agreement, Chaim Weizmann commits the Zionists to providing economic assistance to Emir Faisal's state, and Faisal endorses the Balfour Declaration.

1920

- **April 4–8**
  Arab riots against Zionism take place in Jerusalem.

- **April 19–26**
  The Allied Supreme Council meets in San Remo, Italy, to allocate League of Nations mandate administrations for the Arab territories of the defeated Ottoman Empire.

- **July 1**
  The British civilian administration of Palestine is inaugurated by Sir Herbert Samuel, its first high commissioner.

1922

■ **July 24**
The Council of the League of Nations ratifies a draft of the Mandate for Palestine, incorporating the critical terms of the Balfour Declaration.

1923

■ **September 29**
The Mandate for Palestine is formally enacted by the Council of the League of Nations.

1929

■ **August 23–30**
In the wake of rioting at the Western Wall in Jerusalem, the high commissioner requests revision of the mandate, but the British Foreign Office refuses to consider breaching a contract arbitrated by the League of Nations.

1937

■ **July 7**
Britain's Palestine Royal Commission, known as the Peel Commission, publishes a plan for partition.

1939

■ **May 17**
Britain issues the White Paper of 1939, abandoning the idea of partition to curtail Jewish immigration and land purchase and call for an independent Arab-Jewish state within ten years.

terms of the 1916 Sykes-Picot Agreement, which called for the international administration of Palestine, Britain came round to fearing any foreign presence so close to the Suez Canal. Britain's policy now aimed at establishing a land bridge between the Mediterranean and the Persian Gulf, an extension of the defense of British interests in India, and Zionism was perceived as a legitimate bargaining counter in attempts to nullify previous negotiations with France. In Vereté's account, the British wanted Palestine for themselves and sought to mobilize the Zionists to work for a legitimate, but exclusive, alternative to the internationalization arrangements of the Sykes-Picot Agreement.

In more recent years, historians have again shifted their attention. From emphases on the presumed rationales that motivated the decision-making process, historians have come to analyze more fully the prejudices that belied British support for Zionism. These studies argue that in order for British officials to even consider using Zionism in any sort of strategic way, they had to draw upon a reserve of mistaken, even anti-Semitic, notions of Jewish power and money and of invented notions of an essentialized Jewish nation. Such precepts, according to Tom Segev and James Renton, for example, ignored the multitudinous strains of identity that constituted modern Jewish politics, in which Zionism at the time was only a small minority party. As early as 1905, Balfour spoke of England's Jewry as "a people apart" (qtd. in Renton, p. 18). In 1903, in what is sometimes referred to as "the first Balfour declaration," Balfour as prime minister supported a proposal to build a Jewish national presence in Uganda. He viewed Jewry as an immutably different ethnic group and wrote about "the agelong miseries created for Western civilisation by the presence in its midst of a Body which it too long regarded as alien and even hostile, but which it was equally unable to expel or absorb" (Renton, p. 18).

An equally fundamental precept underpinning the British decision to pursue a pro-Zionist policy with regard to the future disposition of Palestine was that the inhabitants themselves did not merit attention beyond an idealized consideration of the improvements that European colonization brought to supposedly backward areas. These cultural preconceptions are boldly captured in Balfour's famous justification of his declaration: "Zionism, be it right or wrong, good or bad," he wrote in 1922, was "of far profounder import than the desires and prejudices of the seven hundred thousand Arabs who now inhabit that ancient land" (qtd. in Segev, p. 45).

That the subject has remained so contentious is rather remarkable, given the careful thought that went into drafting and redrafting various versions of the brief text throughout the summer and fall of 1917. Yet the declaration itself was deliberately worded as tenuous, limited, and noncommittal. The ambiguities and contradictions should be understood as reflecting the negotiations between the Zionist leadership and the 1917 war cabinet, most of whom, like Amery, Milner, and Lloyd George, supported Zionism while others, like Edwin Montagu, the new secretary of state for India, and Lord George Curzon, questioned the long-term impact of the promise at home and abroad and raised various objections.

The Balfour Declaration begins with the muted promise on the part of Britain to "favour" and "use their best endeavours to facilitate" Jewish aspirations. There was never an agreed consensus on how exactly Britain would facilitate Zionism, and rather than promise "a Jewish state," the declaration refers to "a national home." That phrase was an invention of the Zionist leadership in London who worried about demanding too much too soon. Zionist leaders certainly envisioned a state as the ultimate objective, but they sought to disguise their true intentions in order to lessen opposition. The use of the indefinite article "a," as is often the case in diplomatic negotiations that actually aim for ambiguous interpretations that accommodate the widest number of supporters, is also noteworthy. An early draft submitted by Jewish leaders entailed Britain's recognizing Palestine "as the National Home for the Jewish people" (qtd. in Fieldhouse, p. 149). The unease expressed by some cabinet officials resulted in the definite article later being replaced by the indefinite—"the National Home" being replaced by "a national home"—implying a much more open-ended commitment on the part of the British.

Vague as this declaration was—to somehow foster somewhere in Palestine something called a home—further questions were raised by the need to reconcile the ambiguous promise with the considerable provisos added to it. The first proviso clearly states that "nothing shall be done which may prejudice the civil and religious rights of existing non-Jewish communities in Palestine." Dismissive as this phrasing was to the national and political rights of the overwhelming Arab majority, which the document fails to cite by name, it constituted an attempt to meet the concerns of those British officials, particularly military soldiers in the field, who were genuinely concerned about running the risk of antagonizing the Arab populations. The second proviso adds that nothing shall be done to prejudice "the rights and political status enjoyed by Jews in any other country." This met the objections from leading figures in the British Jewish community, most prominent among them being the only Jew in the cabinet, Edwin Montagu, secretary of state for India. In mid-1917, Montagu brought negotiations to a standstill when he made clear that he saw Zionism as a threat to his own position as a citizen of British society. In their non-Zionism, British Jewish leaders such as Montagu may in fact have been speaking for the majority when they rejected any implication that Palestine, and not Britain, was their proper nation. Montagu worried that the Balfour Declaration's emphasis on Jewish national distinctiveness would, in fact, exacerbate European anti-Semitism.

Audience

Signed on November 2, 1917, Balfour's letter to Lord Rothschild conveying the British government's support for a Jewish national home was not publicly announced until the following Friday, when it was published in the Novem-

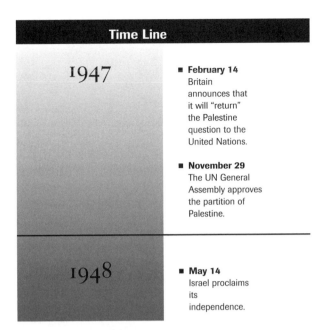

Time Line

1947

- **February 14**
  Britain announces that it will "return" the Palestine question to the United Nations.

- **November 29**
  The UN General Assembly approves the partition of Palestine.

1948

- **May 14**
  Israel proclaims its independence.

Milestone Documents

ber 9 edition of the weekly *Jewish Chronicle*. Following its publication, a celebration was organized by the British Zionist Federation at the Stoll Theatre (formerly the London Opera House), and this was reported on favorably by the London *Times* in December.

The main advocates of Zionism in the British government had clearly been convinced of its global propaganda value, as proven to them by the skillful initiatives adopted by Zionist leaders in the preceding months. As James Renton emphasizes, "The belief in Jewish influence, and the hold of Zionism on the Jewish imagination, meant that wherever there were Jews, there was a potential asset to help the Jewish cause" (p. 62). Accordingly, no time was lost in the manufacturing of propaganda to be distributed throughout the world. Special emphasis was placed on encouraging Jews in Russia and the United States to harness their energies to help ensure that the war would be fought through to a successful conclusion.

This propaganda also aimed at presenting Britain, particularly in American and French circles, as the champion of Jewish national self-determination. To French ears, the dissemination of the Balfour Declaration was aimed at justifying British control of Palestine and so extricating Britain from the international administration previously agreed to under the terms of the 1916 Sykes-Picot Agreement. To official circles in Washington, the attempt at camouflaging Britain's interest in controlling Palestine under the guise of the Balfour Declaration was perceived as a response to President Woodrow Wilson's "no annexation" wartime policy.

As for Middle Eastern audiences, the British did not evince interest in consulting Arab leaders before issuing the Balfour Declaration, nor did they appear worried about any adverse reaction from them. Regarding Palestinian Arabs, Prime Minster Lloyd George later caustically noted that he could not get in touch with them "as they were fighting against us" (qtd. in Fromkin, p. 297).

Arthur James Balfour (front) (Library of Congress)

Impact

For Zionist leaders the Balfour Declaration clearly represented, at long last, a triumph for their hard work. However, celebrations aside, the letter otherwise made very little impact in the short term. In Russia, the significance of the declaration was completely outweighed by the Bolshevik seizure of power. By the end of 1917, the new Bolshevik regime had not only withdrawn Russia from the war but had also proceeded to embarrass the Allies with the publication of secret wartime negotiations such as the Sykes-Picot Agreement. In the United States, there was no discernible change in official policy; in fact, the Zionist movement continued well into the interwar period to attract only a small minority of American Jews. As for the wartime fears that Germany might have preempted the entente with a declaration of its own, it was found that Germany had not been close to making such a decision. "The declaration was simply one more item in a long catalogue of wartime documents," Malcolm Yapp concludes, "and no sooner was it published than it was virtually forgotten by all except Zionists" (p. 291).

As for the Hashemites, the British initially encouraged Emir Faisal to cooperate with Zionism. Having established himself in Damascus (in modern-day Syria) during the war, Faisal's demands for independence came up against French imperial ambitions once the war ended. He thus had to rely increasingly on British goodwill. Whether or not Faisal had the authority to speak on behalf of the Palestinian Arabs, he did agree to meet with Weizmann, and they struck a deal on January 3, 1919, in which Weizmann committed the Zionists to providing economic assistance to Faisal's state and Faisal endorsed the Balfour Declaration. Faisal made his signature conditional, however, upon the fulfillment of his demand for Arab independence, a condition that was not fulfilled. He later renounced Zionist aspirations for a separate government.

In Palestine, British authorities did everything they could to tone down the effect of the pro-Zionist policy. Much to the chagrin of the Zionist leadership, no practical initiatives were allowed by the military administration, which was trying to restore order and stability to a destroyed landscape. But the rhetoric that had spread across Europe and North America made its way also to Palestine, and an increasingly wary Palestinian Arab population became as convinced as the Zionist leadership of the challenge Zionism posed to Arab patrimony of the country.

Edmund Allenby enters Jerusalem through the Jaffa Gate. (Library of Congress)

> "I have much pleasure in conveying to you, on behalf of His Majesty's Government, the following declaration of sympathy with Jewish Zionist aspirations which has been submitted to, and approved by, the Cabinet."
>
> (Paragraph 1)

On the first anniversary of the Balfour Declaration, which coincided with the end of the war and an opening up of political activity, Arab dignitaries and representatives petitioned the British denouncing the Balfour Day parade that was held in Jerusalem. From then on, Zionism became the chief oppositional factor in the articulation of a Palestinian Arab nationalist identity.

The hostility directed toward Zionism in Palestine did not deter the British government, which maintained its regard for Zionism into the immediate postwar period. This was especially important when the Allied Supreme Council awarded Britain the Mandate for Palestine at the 1920 San Remo conference. The genesis of the mandate lay in the wartime promises made by President Wilson to put an end to the secret diplomacy of imperialistically minded European leaders. The World War I slogan most often associated with Wilson—"the war to make the world safe for democracy"—both greatly bolstered the Allied war effort, by endowing it with a noble legacy, and gravely threatened Allied war aims, focused as they were on the expansion of European empire across the globe, especially into former Ottoman lands. The drafting of the mandate document, though it has not attracted as much attention as that of the Balfour Declaration, represented a crucial step: The mandate not only incorporated the entire text of the Balfour Declaration but also included several articles specifying the nature of the obligation of Britain, as mandatory power, to support the establishment of a national Jewish home in Palestine. These obligations included facilitating Jewish immigration and encouraging Jewish settlement on the land. Meanwhile, as was the case with the Balfour Declaration itself, not a single article of the mandate document referred specifically to the Palestinian Arab population. Palestine thus represented a striking anomaly among the League of Nations mandates, with the small Jewish minority, composing about 10 percent of the population, being placed in a uniquely privileged position.

The significance of the Palestinian mandate lay in the force attained by the Balfour Declaration once officially sanctioned by the newly formed League of Nations. In many ways, the mandate system originated as a way for Britain and France to disguise old-fashioned imperial acquisition as enlightened tutelage. In one important aspect, however, the mandate was more than just a fig leaf. Though Palestine in the interwar period walked and talked like a colony, the mandate system differed from prewar imperialism to the extent that Britain remained fettered by an institution that placed features of the administration of Palestine in the court of international public opinion. Once the Balfour Declaration was written into the terms of the League of Nations mandate sanctioning British rule in Palestine, one of several competing wartime promises was turned into a binding contract mediated by the League of Nations. Restrained in this way, British officials found it very difficult to even consider rescinding the promise of support for a Jewish national home, whatever the pressure being felt by British officials in Palestine caught in the simmering conflict between the nationalist demands of the Jewish and Arab communities. These pressures, which in the end Britain proved unable to contain, exploded in the bloody Arab revolt of 1936–1939.

The Arab revolt transformed British plans for Palestine. Facing the prospect of war with Germany, British officials accepted in 1939 that it was not possible to create "a national home" in Palestine if it meant Zionist domination over the Arab majority. Reinterpretations of the "singularly ambiguous" Balfour Declaration lay at the center of official debates at this time (Cohen, p. 40). Some officials stressed the provision for the protection of Arab interests; others argued that the obligation to help build "a national home" for the Jewish people had by 1939 been redeemed by the assistance given during the preceding two decades to the development of Jewish political, cultural, and economic institutions in Palestine. That the vague terms of the Balfour Declaration would in the end prove problematic had been foreseen by Lord Curzon back in 1917 when outlining his opposition to the whole idea: "We ought at least to consider," he had stressed, "whether we are encouraging a practicable idea, or preparing the way for disappointment and failure" (qtd. in Renton, p. 72).

Further Reading

■ Articles

Vereté, Mayir. "The Balfour Declaration and Its Makers." *Middle Eastern Studies* 6, no. 1 (January 1970): 48–76.

■ Books

Cohen, Michael J. *Palestine: Retreat from the Mandate; The Making of British Policy, 1936–45*. New York: Holmes & Meier, 1978.

Fieldhouse, D. K. *Western Imperialism in the Middle East, 1914–1958*. Oxford, U.K.: Oxford University Press, 2006.

Fromkin, David. *A Peace to End All Peace: Creating the Modern Middle East, 1914–1922*. New York: Henry Holt, 1989.

Koestler, Arthur. *Promise and Fulfilment: Palestine, 1917–1949*. London: Macmillan, 1949.

Monroe, Elizabeth. *Britain's Moment in the Middle East, 1914–1971*. London: Chatto & Windus, 1981.

Renton, James. *The Zionist Masquerade: The Birth of the Anglo-Zionist Alliance, 1914–1918*. New York: Palgrave Macmillan, 2007.

Segev, Tom. *One Palestine, Complete: Jews and Arabs under the Mandate*. New York: Metropolitan Books, 2000.

Shlaim, Avi. "The Balfour Declaration and Its Consequences." In *Yet More Adventures with Britannia: Personalities, Politics, and Culture in Britain*, ed. William Roger Louis. London: I. B. Tauris, 2005.

Stein, Leonard. *The Balfour Declaration*. London: Vallentine, Mitchell, 1961.

Tomes, Jason. *Balfour and Foreign Policy: The International Thought of a Conservative Statesman*. New York: Cambridge University Press, 1997.

Yapp, M. E. *The Making of the Modern Near East, 1792–1923*. London: Longman, 1987.

—Martin Bunton

Questions for Further Study

1. The Balfour Declaration was issued in the context of far-reaching changes in the makeup of Europe and the Middle East, as the great imperial powers jockeyed and vied for influence and advantage during (and after) World War I. Trace the power struggles that gave rise to the document and offer your opinion as to Great Britain's chief political motive for taking the position outlined in the declaration.

2. It is argued that the Balfour Declaration was part of a muddled, contradictory, and ambiguous Middle Eastern policy on the part of Great Britain. On what basis is this argument made? Do you think that the document reflected incompetence on the part of British diplomats, or do you think that those diplomats were deliberately pursuing an ambiguous policy?

3. To what extent was the Balfour Declaration an article of propaganda? Why?

4. In the twenty-first century the Jewish state of Israel and its Arab neighbors continue to live in a state of hostility and conflict. To what extent can the source of that hostility and conflict be traced to the Balfour Declaration?

5. Why did Great Britain in the 1910s agree to adopt a pro-Zionist position? Do you think that there was a single motive behind this decision or a mixture of motives? Were those motives noble, or were they selfish? Defend your position.

BALFOUR DECLARATION

Foreign Office
November 2nd, 1917
Dear Lord Rothschild,

I have much pleasure in conveying to you, on behalf of His Majesty's Government, the following declaration of sympathy with Jewish Zionist aspirations which has been submitted to, and approved by, the Cabinet:

"His Majesty's Government view with favour the establishment in Palestine of a national home for the Jewish people, and will use their best endeavours to facilitate the achievement of this object, it being clearly understood that nothing shall be done which may prejudice the civil and religious rights of existing non-Jewish communities in Palestine, or the rights and political status enjoyed by Jews in any other country."

I should be grateful if you would bring this declaration to the knowledge of the Zionist Federation.

Yours sincerely,
Arthur James Balfour

KOREAN DECLARATION OF INDEPENDENCE

*"For the first time in several thousand years,
we have suffered the agony of alien suppression for a decade."*

Overview

On March 1, 1919, at Pagoda Park in Seoul, Korea, a student nationalist read aloud to the crowd the Korean Declaration of Independence, giving rise to the nationwide March First Movement. In response to the unjust colonization of Korea by Japan in 1910, the Declaration proclaimed to the world that Korea had the right to exist as a free and independent nation. Among the thirty-three signers were sixteen Protestant Christians, fifteen leaders of Chondogyo (also called Cheondoism, the "religion of the Heavenly Way"), and two Buddhists.

The Chondogyo leaders Son Byonghui, O Sechang, Kwon Dongjin, and Choe Rin were most influential in producing the Declaration. They quietly arranged for Choe Namson, a pioneering poet and publisher-scholar, to draft it, and they collaboratively reached a consensus on its moderate tone and content, espousing the ideals of peace, humanity, and freedom. They then clandestinely printed it and disseminated it among the Korean people.

Since the early 1900s exiled nationalists such as Ahn Changho, the preeminent leader of the independence movement, had created myriad overseas organizations and transnational networks agitating for Korean independence. Foremost was the Korean National Association, which was founded in 1908 and served as the proto-provisional government, with more than a hundred branches in the United States, Manchuria, China, Russia, and Mexico, among other countries.

The movement for independence finally came home in 1919. Galvanizing Korean men and women of all ages and backgrounds, the March First Movement proved unprecedented in magnitude and scope, with more than two million participants joining over several months. The movement surprised the Japanese police, who reacted with violence against unarmed and peaceful Korean demonstrators, accounting for some 47,000 arrests, 7,500 deaths, and 16,000 injuries. The uprising against the Japanese inspired overseas revolutionaries to form the Provisional Government of the Republic of Korea in April 1919 in Shanghai, China.

Context

Following the First Sino-Japanese War (1894–1895) and the Russo-Japanese War (1904–1905), both of which were fought in part over control of Korean territory, Japan's takeover of Korea began in earnest with the forced signing of a protectorate treaty in 1905. After the Korean royal military was disbanded in 1907, the Korean "righteous army"—irregular militias—bitterly fought the Japanese throughout the country until 1910, when the nation was formally colonized by Japan, effectively ending the Choson Dynasty (1392–1910). According to Japanese statistics, over 2,800 clashes between Koreans and the Japanese army occurred during the period 1907–1910. By 1910 at least 17,600 Korean soldiers had died, though the numbers may have been higher.

When World War I ended, America emerged as a global leader, setting the agenda for international peace. President Woodrow Wilson expressed his vision for the postwar settlement in his Fourteen Points speech to the U.S. Congress on January 8, 1918. The Fourteen Points would later guide Wilson's approach to the Paris Peace Conference and the Treaty of Versailles, signed in 1919 to bring the war to an official close. The Fourteen Points advocated, among other ideals, international cooperation and respect for the right of self-determination of people. Koreans were not entirely persuaded that Wilson's statement would soon lead to Korean independence, but the nationalist leadership, both domestic and abroad, was quick to seize upon the statement as an opportunity to appeal for independence from Japan.

On January 21, 1919, King Kojong, the last king of the Choson Dynasty, died, possibly having been poisoned by the Japanese. Following Kojong's death, Korean nationalist activities accelerated. As anticolonial efforts intensified among exiled revolutionaries in China, Manchuria, Russia, the United States, and Japan, nationalists within Korea began to ponder the course of the independence movement. As most of the nationalist Korean leaders were either exiled or imprisoned, the domestic leadership was centered on religious communities such as Chondogyo and Protestant Christianity, which often served as shelters for covert nationalist activities. Chondogyo is an indigenous religion that teaches values of equality, justice, and brotherhood and incorporates

1876

- **February 27**
The Treaty of Ganghwa, or Japanese-Korea Treaty of Amity, is signed.

1894

- **July**
The First Sino-Japanese War begins.

1895

- **April 17**
The Treaty of Shimonoseki ends the First Sino-Japanese War.

1904

- **February 8**
The Russo-Japanese War begins.

1905

- **September 5**
The Portsmouth Treaty ends the Russo-Japanese War.

- **November 17**
The Japanese-Korean Protectorate Treaty is signed.

1910

- **August 22**
Japan annexes Korea after three years of fighting.

1918

- **January 8**
Woodrow Wilson delivers his Fourteen Points address to Congress, outlining his vision of the postwar order.

Christian and egalitarian values found within the Korean and Eastern traditions. Confucians did not participate in nationalist activities, because they had incurred severe losses during the fight against Japan before the annexation; the mainstream Buddhist establishment, in turn, declined to participate. With overwhelming numbers of Koreans expected to attend the funeral of Kojong, the nationalist leaders secretly planned demonstrations across the country for March 1. They also agreed to petition foreign representatives in Tokyo and send a message to President Wilson.

Meanwhile, Korean students in Tokyo were laying the foundations for the Korean Declaration of Independence. Choe Namson based the Declaration on an earlier version, the Tokyo declaration of Korean independence, which was drafted by Korean students and read before an assembled crowd in Tokyo in February 1919. In asserting Korean independence, the Tokyo declaration noted that Korea had a 4,300-year history of sovereignty and had been guaranteed independence in the aftermath of the Sino-Japanese War, but the Japanese had forcibly reduced Korea to a protectorate following the Russo-Japanese War. The Korean people had unsuccessfully resisted the Japanese protectorate, which was opposed to the wishes of the Korean people. Japan, this declaration asserted, had seen fit to exploit Korea, but the Japanese need for domination over Korea had passed, as Chinese and Russian influences no longer existed in Korea and were therefore no longer threats to Japanese security.

The Tokyo declaration pointed to the series of Japanese lies and deceits that had led to the annexation of Korea, dating back to the Treaty of Ganghwa, also called the Japanese-Korea Treaty of Amity—an unequal treaty signed by the two nations in 1876 that opened Korean ports and commerce to Japanese domination. The Tokyo declaration presented a long litany of political betrayals and deceptions committed by Japan against Korea and detailed the moral outrage and frustrations of Koreans. Whereas the Korean Declaration of Independence would prove tactful and emotionally detached, the Tokyo declaration displayed the raw emotions of a morally and physically wounded Korea. These emotions would erupt in conflagration in the March First Movement, as sparked by the initial reading of the Korean Declaration of Independence.

About the Author

Among the most influential leaders behind the Korean Declaration of Independence was Son Byonghui (1861–1922), the supreme leader of Chondogyo, who signed first on the document. A formidable character and charismatic leader, Son possessed the best-organized and best-financed network of followers within Korea. He had lived in exile in Japan in the early 1900s to avoid persecution—a fate that befell several Chondogyo leaders who opposed what they regarded as an oppressive government. Uprisings in 1894 had afforded a pretext for King Kojong to invite Chinese forces into the nation to quell the unrest, incidentally providing the Japanese with a pretext to invade Korea. These events initiated the First Sino-Japanese War, which in turn paved the way for the Japanese colonization of Korea. This sequence of events created the conditions that allowed Son to become the leader of the Chondogyo and, while still in exile, to spearhead an anti-Japanese movement in Korea.

O Sechang (1864–1953), also a Chondogyo leader, had served as a government interpreter and official and became a journalist after studying in Japan. Having been in charge of the printing and distribution of the Declaration, O Sechang was imprisoned for three years for his involvement in the March First Movement, as was Son Byonghui. Following his prison term, he prepared a series of biographical dictionaries about Korean art and calligraphy, based on the collected art in his family possession. In his later years, he came to be known as the foremost Korean calligrapher, a connoisseur-scholar of Korean paintings and calligraphy, and a seal engraver.

The Korean Declaration of Independence was drafted by Choe Namson (1890–1957), a leading Korean intellectual of his time who was knowledgeable about both traditional Chinese scholarship and new modern learning. He was persuaded to complete the draft by the Chondogyo leader Choe Rin. A poet whose work *From Sea to a Youth* introduced new Korean vernacular idioms, Choe Namson was a writer, journalist, and scholar. Although he did not sign the Declaration, he was jailed for two and a half years after the March First Movement for his overall involvement. Following his imprisonment, he wrote an encyclopedic multivolume history of ancient and premodern Korea. His works covered a wide range of topics, including Korean origins, folklore, language, culture, history, and ethnography.

The "Three Open Pledges" at the close of the Korean Declaration of Independence were added by Han Yong'un (1879–1944). Prior to Han's becoming an avid patriot, his father and brother were involved in anticolonial activities. A leading Buddhist reformer, he wrote a book of poetry, *Silence of Love*, which is one of the most representative and beloved works in Korean literature. At the heart of his poetic conception was the yet-to-be liberated Korea. Han Yong'un and Choe Namson disagreed over the Declaration's tone and content, as Han wanted it to be more ardent. In the end, a more moderate tone was adopted. Han was jailed for three years for his role in the March First Movement.

Explanation and Analysis of the Document

Simply titled "Declaration" (Seon-eon-seo), the Korean Declaration of Independence is written in poetic language. Although it is fresh and modern for 1919, the Sino-Korean literary form used for the Declaration manifests established Confucian educational traditions. It also reveals the authors' classical scholarship, intellectual resources and frame of reference, and literary aesthetics, as well as their moral outrage and political intuition. With majestic words that echo the emerging new world order of the postwar era, the Declara-

Milestone Documents

Time Line

1919

- **January 21**
  King Kojong, the last king of the Choson Dynasty, dies, perhaps having been assassinated with poison by the Japanese.

- **March 1**
  The Korean Declaration of Independence is read aloud in Seoul, Korea, launching the March First Movement.

- **March 17**
  The Korean National Council is created in Vladivostok, Russia, to represent Koreans in Manchuria and Siberia.

- **April 9**
  Korean nationalists in Shanghai, China, declare the formation of the Provisional Government of the Republic of Korea.

tion reads like a poem of self-determination, championing national freedom, equality, and justice. With idealism and optimism, it rests its case upon universal claims of humanitarian ethics and humanistic values in search of Korean freedom, independence, and self-determination.

◆ **Paragraph 1**
The opening of the Declaration announces to Koreans, the Japanese, and the world,

> We hereby declare that Korea is an independent state and that Koreans are a self-governing people. We proclaim it to the nations of the world in affirmation of the principle of the equality of all nations, and we proclaim it to our posterity, preserving in perpetuity the right of national survival.

In proclaiming independence and the right of national survival, Choe and the leaders of the March First Movement who drafted the Declaration were clearly deeply aware and proud of the long history, culture, and civilization of Korea—"the strength of five thousand years of history." The basis of the moral right to independence and democratic sovereignty of Koreans is thus understood to be

Japanese land pack ponies at Chemulpo for advance on Seoul during the Russo-Japanese War. (Library of Congress)

the principle of equality of nations and the historical authority of Korea's five thousand years of existence. The most spiritual phrase in the Declaration appears early: "This is the clear command of heaven, the course of our times, and a legitimate manifestation of the right of all nations to coexist and live in harmony." Certainly, the Chondogyo and Christian figures who comprised the March First leadership and led the drafting of the Declaration purposefully invoked the command of "heaven" or God in the inspirational beginning of the document. The Sino-Korean character *chon* can actually be translated as "heaven," "God," or "sky"; the Neoconfucian or Chondogyo notion of heaven is akin to the Christian notion of an omniscient and omnipresent moral God. Therefore, the phrase "command of Heaven" also implies the will of God.

◆ **Paragraph 2**

The main point of the second paragraph can be found in the first sentence: "For the first time in several thousand years, we have suffered the agony of alien suppression for a decade, becoming a victim of the policies of aggression and coercion, which are relics from a bygone era." Being a small nation surrounded by larger neighbors—China, Russia, and Japan—Korea had been repeatedly invaded in its long histo-

ry. Yet this was indeed the first time in "several thousand years" that it had been annexed or colonized by another country. For Koreans, it was infuriating and particularly humiliating to be colonized by Japan, which had long been considered a culturally inferior nation. Throughout history, the peninsular Korea had been a vital source of cultural and intellectual transmission to the islands of Japan, such as with Buddhism, a writing system, printing technology, and pottery-making methods, among other ideas and advances.

The original Korean language of the Declaration has both denotative and connotative aspects. For example, the Korean text uses the word *chimnyak*, which can be translated as "invasion" or "aggression," with a connotation of "territorial expansionism." The word *kanggeon* can be translated as "coercion" or "force," with connotations of "military force" or "brute might." The word *jui* means "principle" or also "ideology." The drafters wanted to express the awful reality of imperialism or colonialism for the colonized and highlight the associated aggressive, repressive, and coercive positionings as immoral and illegal strategies of a bygone era. That bygone era can be understood to be the sixteenth century, when Japan's invasion of Korea was repelled by Admiral Yi Sunshin's navy during the early Choson Dynasty.

◆ Paragraph 3

The third paragraph describes the tragic plight and suffering of the colonized, with which all Koreans could empathize. Myriad reasons for Koreans to struggle for independence are listed in a long, oratorical sentence. Directly addressing the Korean people, the second sentence builds up to the ultimate message: "The most urgent task is to firmly establish national independence." The highlight of the paragraph comes at the end in the reminder to Koreans that the collective conscience of humanity is now on their side. Adopting martial language, the Declaration affirms that Koreans are assisted by "the forces of justice and humanity" and that independence can be achieved if "every one of our twenty million people arms himself for battle."

◆ Paragraph 4

An intriguing part of the Korean Declaration of Independence, this paragraph is an artful rhetorical exercise. From the outset, the authors choose not to criticize or attack Japan directly for the annexation of Korea or the exploitation of Koreans; instead, they attempt to take the moral high ground by stating, "We do not intend to accuse Japan of infidelity for its violation of various solemn treaty obligations since the Treaty of Amity of 1876." They also include an admission of collective self-blame for the colonial predicament: "We shall not blame Japan; we must first blame ourselves before finding fault with others." However, the paragraph stresses that "Japan's scholars and officials, indulging in a conqueror's exuberance, have denigrated the accomplishments of our ancestors and treated our civilized people like barbarians." The concepts of civilization versus barbarism are juxtaposed to emphasize the barbarically debased and humiliated state of subjugated Koreans and to remind Koreans of the history and beauty of their civilization. Here, the Korean intelligentsia's acute awareness of the underlying political significance of scholarship and discourse on history and civilization is revealed. The writers of the Declaration observe that the sins of distorting history and truth by Japanese scholars and historians have consequences that are just as grave as the sins committed by Japanese officials, whether politicians or military officers.

◆ Paragraph 5

Shifting the focus to the Korean people as an audience, the authors state that the task at hand is "to build up our own strength, not to destroy others." A new beginning to shape a new destiny for the future of Korea is championed: "We must chart a new course for ourselves in accord with the solemn dictates of conscience, not malign and reject others for reasons of past enmity or momentary passion." Rather astutely, the Japanese leaders are described as actually being victims, as they are "chained to old ideas and old forces and victimized by their obsession with glory." A number of dichotomies appear in this paragraph: build versus destroy, conscience versus glory, natural versus unnatural, just versus unjust, and old versus new. Drawing on postwar optimism about a coming new world order and on perceptions of opportunity for change, the Declaration implies

that the constructive and future-oriented task for Koreans is not necessarily anticolonial but rather is prodemocratic. The foremost task of Koreans is to build a new order, new society, new culture, new civilization, and new democracy.

◆ Paragraph 6

From the outset, this paragraph intends to clarify the situation of the annexation of Korea by Japan, which clearly "did not emanate from the wishes of the people." As such, the outcome was "oppressive coercion, discriminatory injustice, and fabrication of statistical data," which in turn has deepened "the eternally irreconcilable chasm of ill will between the two nations." While the opening of the Declaration is addressed to all nations of the world, the text has thus far been directed to Koreans and Japanese. Here, the targeted audience is expanded to include the greater Far East, especially China, with whom Koreans have long shared historical ties. Japan's militarist ambitions extended not just to the Korean Peninsula but also to continental China and Southeast Asia, so the Declaration broadly calls for "peace in the East." The entwined historical destiny and political fate of Korea and China as well as their brotherhood and shared victimhood at the hands of Japan are narrated: "The enslavement of twenty million resentful people by force does not contribute to lasting peace in the East. It deepens the fear and suspicion of Japan by the four hundred million Chinese who constitute the main axis for stability in the East."

Essentially, the core message of the paragraph is an urging of Japan to "correct past mistakes and open a new phase of friendship based upon genuine understanding and sympathy," as a way to "avoid disaster and invite blessing." Perhaps the most forthright statement of moral and intellectual logic in the Declaration is found in the statement that independence will enable Koreans to lead normal lives and also will help Japan "leave its evil path" and bring stability to the East by freeing China from fear.

◆ Paragraph 7

In the most poetic and metaphorical of the paragraphs, the Declaration speaks of the arrival of the "new world" and a "new spring" in which the "days of force" are being replaced by the "days of morality." With March 1 being the date of the collective uprising, the double meaning of "spring" dominates the paragraph, lending heightened connotations to such phrases as "rays of new civilization," "myriad forms of life to come to life again," "breath of life," "mild breezes," "warm sunshine," and "reinvigorating the spirit." The rhythm of the poetic language reinforces the image of a "universal cycle" characterized by the "changing tide of the world" between good and evil and between right and wrong. The notion of the "universal cycle," in this sense, connotes not only the seasonal cycle but also historical cycles of morality and justice.

◆ Paragraph 8

The final paragraph of the Declaration reiterates the Korean will for independence: "We shall safeguard our

King Kojong (Library of Congress)

inherent right to freedom and enjoy a life of prosperity; we shall also make use of our creativity, enabling our national essence to blossom in the vernal warmth." The reference to an inherent right to a "life of prosperity" is reminiscent of the U.S. Declaration of Independence, with Thomas Jefferson's assertion of the rights to "life, liberty, and the pursuit of happiness." Through the metaphor of growth, on the other hand, what is evoked is the national culture rather than the more politicized concepts of democracy or national self-determination. This focus originates from the drafters' worldview and pride in Korea's long history and civilization as well as their conception of a new national culture as a new political order. Empowering the Korean people with words of moral strength, the Declaration pronounces, "Conscience is on our side, and truth guides our way." Then it calls for all people, of all ages, to "head for joyful resurrection together with the myriad living things." Incorporating the imagery of nature in springtime, "resurrection" is, of course, an allusion to Christ's miraculous rise after his sacrificial death on the cross. Announcing that "the spirits of thousands of generations of our ancestors protect us," the Declaration ends with assurances of success.

◆ **Three Open Pledges**

Appended to the Declaration are three pledges for the future. The first notes that the Declaration is a demand for freedom and dignity, not a document to create antiforeign feeling. In the second pledge the drafters assert their right to communicate the Declaration to the people of Korea. Finally, the drafters reject violence and urge their followers to maintain public order.

Audience

The Korean Declaration of Independence was written first and foremost for the Korean people, who had been suffering under Japanese colonial repression since 1910. It was also directed at Japan itself, whose military and police rule had become increasingly oppressive. Colonial Japan's exploitative economic, sociopolitical, and educational policies were systematically expanded to impoverish and denigrate Koreans. Initially, there was debate among the organizers of the March First Movement as to whether they would appeal to or petition the Japanese or, rather, declare Korea's independence outright. In the end it was decided that Koreans would proclaim their independence in the Declaration. Through their Declaration, Koreans also wished to inform the world of the unjust nature of their colonial plight and gain international attention and support.

Impact

As sparked by the Declaration, the March First Movement demonstrated Koreans' desire for independence and democracy. The demonstrators marched into the streets not only in Seoul but, indeed, in virtually every town, village, and county. People who had come to Seoul for the funeral of King Kojong joined the movement with shouts of "Long live Korea!" and "Long live Korean independence!" while waving forbidden Korean flags. The demonstrations were peaceful, for no armed revolt or violence had been planned by the organizers; in spearheading the movement, the Chondogyo leaders espoused three principles: popularization, unification, and nonviolence. The thirty-three signatories of the Declaration made no attempt to hide and allowed themselves to be arrested. The subsequent nationwide demonstrations lasted for months. Even by conservative estimates, the nation witnessed some fifteen hundred demonstrations in the first three months, with the participation of over two million people. Among those arrested, about ten thousand, including 186 women, were tried and convicted.

On March 17, 1919, the Korean National Council was created in Vladivostok, Russia, to represent more than half a million Koreans in Manchuria and Siberia. Although a provisional government could not be openly established within Korea, an underground meeting named a roster of leaders and adopted a constitution in Seoul in April. Korean nationalists also emerged one by one in Shanghai, and many committed revolutionaries from Korea, China, and Japan gathered there. During this time, collective efforts to unify the nationalists in China, Manchuria, Siberia, and America began. The nationalists in Shanghai declared the formation of the Provisional Government of the Republic of Korea on April 9, 1919. The next day, the Provisional Assembly was created by representatives from eight provinces in Korea and from Russia, China, and America. At the meeting of the Provisional Assembly on April 11, the formal name of the sovereign nation was proclaimed as Taehan Minguk (Republic of Korea), and the initial outline of the constitution was drafted. The constitution's preface included the Korean Declaration of Independence.

The March First Movement did not lead to Korean independence from Japanese colonialism, yet it was significant in that it exposed to the world the abuses of Japanese colonial rule. Rising publicity and criticism worldwide led to Japan's "cultural policy" of appeasement in the 1920s under a new governor-general. Nonetheless, during the late 1930s and throughout World War II, Japan essentially tried to exterminate Korean culture, forcing the people to adopt Japanese religious practices and Japanese names, forbidding the use of the Korean language in publications, and destroying or stealing Korean artifacts. One of the horrors of World War II was Japan's conscription of some two hundred thousand Korean women to serve as "comfort women," or sex slaves, for Japanese troops. Korea remained under Japanese control until the end of World War II and Japan's unconditional surrender to Allied forces on August 15, 1945. In the war's immediate aftermath, the country was divided into North Korea and South Korea, with the south under U.S. control and the north under the control of the Soviet Union. The arrangement was intended to be

“We hereby declare that Korea is an independent state and that Koreans are a self-governing people. We proclaim it to the nations of the world in affirmation of the principle of the equality of all nations, and we proclaim it to our posterity, preserving in perpetuity the right of national survival.”

(Paragraph 1)

“For the first time in several thousand years, we have suffered the agony of alien suppression for a decade, becoming a victim of the policies of aggression and coercion, which are relics from a bygone era.”

(Paragraph 2)

“The most urgent task is to firmly establish national independence.”

(Paragraph 3)

“In order to restore natural and just conditions, we must remedy the unnatural and unjust conditions brought about by the leaders of Japan, who are chained to old ideas and old forces and victimized by their obsession with glory.”

(Paragraph 5)

“We shall safeguard our inherent right to freedom and enjoy a life of prosperity; we shall also make use of our creativity, enabling our national essence to blossom in the vernal warmth. We have arisen now. Conscience is on our side, and truth guides our way.”

(Paragraph 8)

temporary, but cold war tensions between the Communists and the West led to the outbreak of war between North Korea and South Korea in 1950, with the south backed by the United States and the north eventually receiving support from China. The war ended in a stalemate in 1953 with the establishment of the two-mile-wide Korean Demilitarized Zone at latitude thirty-eight degrees north. The peninsula continues to be divided between the Democratic People’s Republic of Korea (Communist “North Korea”) and the Republic of Korea (“South Korea”) in the twenty-first century.

Further Reading

■ **Articles**

Allen, Chizuko T. “Northeast Asia Centered around Korea: Ch’oe Namson’s View of History.” *Journal of Asian Studies* 49, no. 4 (November 1990): 787–806.

■ **Books**

Buswell, Robert E., Jr., and Timothy S. Lee, eds. *Christianity in Korea.* Honolulu: University of Hawaii Press, 2006.

Han, Woo-keun. *The History of Korea*. Honolulu: University of Hawaii Press, 1971.

Kendall, C. W. *The Truth about Korea*, 2nd ed. San Francisco: Korean National Association, 1919.

Kim, C. I. Eugene, and Doretha E. Mortimore, eds. *Korea's Response to Japan: The Colonial Period, 1910–1945*. Kalamazoo: Center for Korean Studies, Western Michigan University, 1977.

Lee, Ki-baik. *A New History of Korea*, trans. Edward W. Wagner. Cambridge, Mass.: Harvard University Press, 1984.

Lee, Peter H., and Theodore de Bary, eds. *Sources of Korean Tradition*. 2 vols. New York: Columbia University Press, 1997.

Myers, Ramon H., and Mark R. Peattie. *The Japanese Colonial Empire, 1895–1945*. Princeton, N.J.: Princeton University Press, 1984.

Nahm, Andrew, ed. *Korea under Japanese Colonial Rule: Studies of the Policy and Techniques of Japanese Colonialism*. Kalamazoo: Center for Korean Studies, Western Michigan University, 1973.

■ Web Sites

Masayuki, Nishi. "March 1 and May 4, 1919 in Korea, China and Japan: Toward an International History of East Asian Independence Movements." Asia-Pacific Journal: Japan Focus Web site. http://www.japanfocus.org/-Nishi-Masayuki/2560.

—Jacqueline Pak

Questions for Further Study

1. The year 1919 could be regarded as pivotal year in world history. That year produced the Government of India Act, the Treaty of Versailles, the Covenant of the League of Nations, the Resolution of the General Syrian Congress, and the Korean Declaration of Independence. How did these documents, and the events surrounding them, reshape the world?

2. Declarations of independence were important "milestones" in the history of the world. Compare the Korean Declaration of Independence with another such declaration; possibilities include the Dutch Declaration of Independence, the Declaration of Independence of the State of Israel, and even such documents as the Declaration of the Rights of Man and of the Citizen and the Declaration of the Rights of Woman (France). How did these documents reflect similar—or differing—aspirations?

3. Students and young people have often been at the forefront of independence movements and resistance to oppressive rule, as they were in Korea. Why do you think this has been so?

4. Japanese militarism was a pressing international problem in the early decades of the twentieth century. Why do you suppose the nation developed in that direction, and what impact did Japanese militarism have on Korea?

5. Korea has played an unwitting role in several late-nineteenth- and twentieth-century conflicts, including the First Sino-Japanese War, the Russo-Japanese War, World War II, the Korean War, and the cold war between the West and the Soviet bloc. Why did this relatively small, peninsular nation loom so large in these conflicts?

KOREAN DECLARATION OF INDEPENDENCE

We hereby declare that Korea is an independent state and that Koreans are a self-governing people. We proclaim it to the nations of the world in affirmation of the principle of the equality of all nations, and we proclaim it to our posterity, preserving in perpetuity the right of national survival. We make this declaration on the strength of five thousand years of history as an expression of the devotion and loyalty of twenty million people. We claim independence in the interest of the eternal and free development of our people and in accordance with the great movement for world reform based upon the awakening conscience of mankind. This is the clear command of heaven, the course of our times, and a legitimate manifestation of the right of all nations to coexist and live in harmony. Nothing in the world can suppress or block it.

For the first time in several thousand years, we have suffered the agony of alien suppression for a decade, becoming a victim of the policies of aggression and coercion, which are relics from a bygone era. How long have we been deprived of our right to exist? How long has our spiritual development been hampered? How long have the opportunities to contribute our creative vitality to the development of world culture been denied us?

Alas! In order to rectify past grievances, free ourselves from present hardships, eliminate future threats, stimulate and enhance the weakened conscience of our people, eradicate the shame that befell our nation, ensure proper development of human dignity, avoid leaving humiliating legacies to our children, and usher in lasting and complete happiness for our posterity, the most urgent task is to firmly establish national independence. Today when human nature and conscience are placing the forces of justice and humanity on our side, if every one of our twenty million people arms himself for battle, whom could we not defeat and what could we not accomplish?

We do not intend to accuse Japan of infidelity for its violation of various solemn treaty obligations since the Treaty of Amity of 1876. Japan's scholars and officials, indulging in a conqueror's exuberance, have denigrated the accomplishments of our ancestors and treated our civilized people like barbarians. Despite their disregard for the ancient origins of our society and the brilliant spirit of our people, we shall not blame Japan; we must first blame ourselves before finding fault with others. Because of the urgent need for remedies for the problems of today, we cannot afford the time for recriminations over past wrongs.

Our task today is to build up our own strength, not to destroy others. We must chart a new course for ourselves in accord with the solemn dictates of conscience, not malign and reject others for reasons of past enmity or momentary passions. In order to restore natural and just conditions, we must remedy the unnatural and unjust conditions brought about by the leaders of Japan, who are chained to old ideas and old forces and victimized by their obsession with glory.

From the outset the union of the two countries did not emanate from the wishes of the people, and its outcome has been oppressive coercion, discriminatory injustice, and fabrication of statistical data, thereby deepening the eternally irreconcilable chasm of ill will between the two nations. To correct past mistakes and open a new phase of friendship based upon genuine understanding and sympathy—is this not the easiest way to avoid disaster and invite blessing? The enslavement of twenty million resentful people by force does not contribute to lasting peace in the East. It deepens the fear and suspicion of Japan by the four hundred million Chinese who constitute the main axis for stability in the East, and it will lead to the tragic downfall of all nations in our region. Independence for Korea today shall not only enable Koreans to lead a normal, prosperous life, as is their due; it will also guide Japan to leave its evil path and perform its great task of supporting the cause of the East, liberating China from a gnawing uneasiness and fear and helping the cause of world peace and happiness for mankind, which depends greatly on peace in the East. How can this be considered a trivial issue of mere sentiment?

Behold! A new world is before our eyes. The days of force are gone, and the days of morality are here. The spirit of humanity, nurtured throughout the past century, has begun casting its rays of new civilization upon human history. A new spring has arrived prompting the myriad forms of life to come to life again. The past was a time of freezing ice and snow, stifling the breath of life; the present is a time of mild breezes and warm sunshine, reinvigorating the spirit. Facing the return of the universal cycle, we set forth on the changing tide of the world. Nothing can make us hesitate or fear.

We shall safeguard our inherent right to freedom and enjoy a life of prosperity; we shall also make use of our creativity, enabling our national essence to blossom in the vernal warmth. We have arisen now. Conscience is on our side, and truth guides our way. All of us, men and women, young and old, have firmly left behind the old nest of darkness and gloom and head for joyful resurrection together with the myriad living things. The spirits of thousands of generations of our ancestors protect us; the rising tide of world

consciousness shall assist us. Once started, we shall surely succeed. With this hope we march forward.

◆ Three Open Pledges

1. Our action today represents the demand of our people for justice, humanity, survival, and dignity. It manifests our spirit of freedom and should not engender antiforeign feelings.

2. To the last one of us and to the last moment possible, we shall unhesitatingly publicize the views of our people, as is our right.

3. All our actions should scrupulously uphold public order, and our demands and our attitudes must be honorable and upright.

Jan Smuts (Library of Congress)

COVENANT OF THE LEAGUE OF NATIONS

" The League shall take any action that may be deemed wise and effectual to safeguard the peace of nations. "

Overview

The Covenant of the League of Nations was an integral part of the Treaty of Versailles concluding World War I. The Covenant is the first section of the treaty and differs markedly from the main treaty itself, which is distinguished by its unmitigated vengeance toward the defeated Germany. The Covenant's preamble and twenty-six articles define the scope, objectives, organization, and operations of a world body that would prevent future wars. The League, as described, would have representatives from all nations, though it at first excluded those nations that had lost the recent war. It was to be a permanent organization that would bring into practice the principles of negotiation, arbitration, respect for treaties, and international law.

With the signing of the Treaty of Versailles on June 28, 1919, both the treaty and the Covenant of the League of Nations went into effect. The first session of the League's Council (an executive body comprising four permanent and four rotating members) was held in 1920. The Assembly, made up of representatives from all member nations, met the same year. The League of Nations then began what was effectively its nineteen-year existence, ending for all purposes in 1939, though it would officially exist until 1946, when it was replaced by the United Nations. Its failure largely resulted from the lack of will to impose the rules and ideals of the Covenant. The Covenant was the product of conflicting national objectives, even among the victors of World War I, a situation that ultimately made it more difficult to enforce the League's role.

Context

World War I changed the world in many ways. Between 1914 and 1918 millions of people were killed or wounded in battle, and millions more died in a Spanish influenza outbreak that was exacerbated by the large transfers of soldiers and civilians. The winners, having suffered temporary but traumatic losses of territory and damage that can still be seen, were in a mood to exact revenge on the losing powers. Many of the old assumptions about the progress of humankind toward a better state through education, technical development, and a sense of culture and refinement had been destroyed. Empires that had existed for hundreds of years and that a short time before had seemed to be immortal had disintegrated. The falling apart and the accompanying turmoil and revolutions, particularly in eastern Europe, indicated that the old world order was dead.

However, the sense of bitterness and disillusion that would characterize the 1920s had not yet set in. While many senior statesmen did not hold great expectations for the League and doubted how effective it might be, the concept held enough merit in the eyes of many at least to warrant an attempt. The idea sprang directly from the Fourteen Points that U.S. president Woodrow Wilson had articulated in a speech delivered before a joint session of the U.S. Congress in 1918; these points outlined President Wilson's idea of what would need to be accomplished as a result of victory over Germany and its allies. Wilson's view was quite idealistic, and parts of the speech were in direct opposition to what he and many Americans had come to believe were the evils that had created the war. His Fourteen Points included freedom of the seas (a point with which his British allies did not agree), the end to secret treaties, and independence for such populations as the Poles and the nationalities that had been part of the Austro-Hungarian and Ottoman empires. The final point was a call to establish an international organization that would promote peace in the world.

The Fourteen Points were seen as an idealistic program that would benefit many of the peoples that had been part of prewar empires; nevertheless, the document was seen as a just peace. It did have an effect in Germany and, coupled with the fact that American soldiers were arriving in great numbers in Europe, influenced Germany's decision to surrender. It was the final point that Wilson considered to be the most important. At his insistence, discussions that would define the covenant of a new organization, the League of Nations, were conducted as the first discussions of the entire Treaty of Versailles, which ended the war with Germany. With the signing of the Treaty of Versailles on June 28, 1919, both the treaty and the Covenant of the League went into effect. The first session of the League's

Time Line

1914

- **August 1**
Germany declares war on Russia, and World War I begins.

1917

- **April 6**
The United States enters the war on the side of the Allies.

1918

- **January 8**
President Woodrow Wilson announces his Fourteen Points. The last point calls for the formation of "a general association of nations" using a mutual covenant to guarantee political independence and territorial integrity, regardless of the size of the nation.

- **November 11**
An armistice is declared, ending the war on the Western Front, to be followed by total cessation of hostilities.

1919

- **January 25**
The plenary session of the Paris Peace Conference accepts the proposals for the creation of a League of Nations.

- **April 18**
The Paris Peace Conference unanimously adopts the Covenant of the League of Nations, which was drafted by an elected committee during the preceding months.

About the Author

Although the Covenant was a compromise document, it basically had a single author, President Woodrow Wilson. Wilson was the leader of the discussions, and it was the last of his Fourteen Points that had called for an international peacekeeping organization. In addition, Wilson's stature as the leader of the United States, which had entered the war in 1917 and thus turned the balance against Germany, placed him in a position in which he could shape this organization and bring it into existence with the support of both greater and lesser allies. Formerly a president of Princeton University and a governor of New Jersey, Wilson was elected president of the United States in 1912. Reelected in 1916 on the basis of his ability to keep the United States out of the conflict, Wilson asked Congress to declare war against Germany within two months of his second inauguration. As the war progressed, Wilson sounded an idealistic note as he made statements concerning the just treatment of nations in the world after the war as well as calls for an international organization to maintain peace. He went to Paris in 1919 to help create the League of Nations and shape the Treaty of Versailles. Largely on the basis of his efforts to form the League, he was awarded the Nobel Peace Prize that year. He died in 1924.

Wilson's final draft leaned heavily on a book entitled *The League of Nations: A Practical Suggestion*, by General Jan Smuts of South Africa. During World War I, Smuts had led his forces against the Germans in Africa. In the last two years of the war he served British prime minister David Lloyd George as one of five members of the British government's Imperial War Cabinet. In World War II, he acted as a field marshal in the British army and joined Prime Minister Winston Churchill's War Cabinet. He was the only person to sign the peace treaties ending both world wars. Smuts was elected prime minister of South Africa twice; he served from 1919 until 1924 and then again from 1939 to 1948. In May 1945 he represented South Africa in San Francisco at the drafting of the UN charter. Smuts was the author of the preamble to the charter of the United Nations and was the only person to sign both the League Covenant and the UN Charter. He died in Pretoria, South Africa, in 1950.

Explanation and Analysis of the Document

The Covenant of the League of Nations brought that organization into being as an integral part of the Treaty of Versailles, signed in 1919 and ending World War I. It was the first part of the treaty to appear in the completed document and was also the first part to be written, before the specific clauses determining the conditions of the peace were drafted. The charter was purposely broad in many aspects. While laying down basic rules for conduct, membership, scope, and operations, it left many decisions about procedure to be determined by the League's Assembly and Council once they finally met in 1920. Despite the vagueness concerning procedures, there is a fair degree of specificity in the Covenant about the types of issues it would treat, which evidenced a strong desire to avoid what were considered to be the actions that had begun the war just ended. Another significant element is that in both practical and symbolic ways, there were concessions to the United States in several areas. It was believed that the League would not function successfully without U.S. participation. Thus, statements about sovereignty, immigration law, and regional influence were shaped with the idea of making it easier for Woodrow Wilson to persuade the U.S. Senate to approve the treaty and join the League. These concessions ultimately failed to persuade the American public in general or the Senate in particular.

◆ **Preamble**

The preamble to the Covenant identifies the League's objectives as an organization dedicated to maintaining peace and security in the world. The League would promote international law and the avoidance of war. It would ensure that all treaty obligations were honored. This last item was considered quite important. Before the start of World War I, Belgium's status as a neutral nation had been guaranteed by a treaty signed by several nations, including Germany. When, in August 1914, Germany invaded Belgium, it declared that the treaty safeguarding the smaller country had been only "a scrap of paper" (qtd. at http://www.firstworldwar.com/source/scrapofpaper1.htm). The preamble specifically included this mention of the inviolability of treaties as a direct response to Germany's actions.

Two proposals were raised but not accepted. France proposed that the preamble contain a specific condemnation of Germany as an aggressor in the last war, but this stipulation was rejected. The Japanese delegation attempted to add the phrase "by the endorsement of the principles of equality of nations and the just treatment of nationals," to follow the phrase "relations between nations." The proposal was voted down ostensibly because it would dictate domestic policy. The real reason was an objection from the United States based on its immigration policy. The proposal as written would have run counter to U.S. immigration quotas, which were being applied to significantly limit the numbers of Chinese and Japanese entering the country.

◆ **Articles 1–7**

The first seven articles of the Covenant describe the organization, where it would meet, the functions of the Council and the Assembly, and the general rules about how the League would conduct business and function. Article 1 defines the qualifications for membership for both original and subsequent League members. Because the League was originally comprised of the victorious Allies and neutral

Time Line

1919

■ **June 28**
The Treaty of Versailles is signed.

1920

■ **January 16**
The first session of the Council of the League of Nations is conducted in Paris.

■ **November 15**
The first Assembly of the League of Nations is convened, presided over by President Wilson; forty-one nations send representatives. None of the defeated powers is represented, as these nations have been specifically excluded from immediate membership in the League.

■ **December 1**
The League's Permanent Mandates Commission is appointed to advise on the administration of colonial possessions taken from the losing powers.

1921

■ **September 2**
The Permanent Court of International Justice comes into existence.

1930

■ **September 30**
The League creates the Nansen International Office for Refugees, which will eventually win the Nobel Peace Prize for its efforts.

1931

- **September 19**
Japan, a member of the League, invades Manchuria and seizes three provinces.

1935

- **October 3**
Italy, a member of the League, invades Ethiopia and eventually incorporates it into the Kingdom of Italy, in a conflict that will last until May 1936.

- **October 7**
Italy is declared to be the aggressor against Ethiopia, and the sanctions process described in the Covenant begins to go into effect. Sanctions are incomplete and applied halfheartedly.

1939

- **September 1**
Germany invades Poland, beginning World War II in Europe.

- **December 14**
The Assembly transfers its powers to the secretary-general. The League of Nations effectively ceases to exist.

1946

- **April 18**
In its last official act, the League transfers all of its assets to the United Nations.

nations, some provision for later membership had to be made for the defeated nations (Germany, Austria, and Hungary) as well as others that did not belong to the original body. The manner in which a member nation could withdraw was also defined, an action that would be taken in the 1920s principally by smaller nations, followed by the significant departures of Germany, Japan, Italy, and the Soviet Union in the 1930s. The second article states that the League would operate as an assembly of nations with a smaller council of members who would act as an executive body and a secretariat that would bear responsibility for daily operations.

Article 3 declares that each member nation was to have only one vote, thereby negating the influence that the larger nations would have gained on the basis of population, size, or wealth. Further, while a nation could have as large a staff as it wished, it would be restricted to only three official delegates. The League would meet regularly (though, like many provisions in the Covenant, the details were left to be worked out later), and the League's scope included anything that it considered relevant to maintaining the peace of the world.

The fourth article define the composition and activities of the League Council, a subset of the total membership that would provide leadership and direction. It would contain five permanent members, consisting of the war's major winning powers (the United States, Great Britain, France, Italy, and Japan). The United States never took its seat, but in the 1920s, when Germany was granted membership, that country became the fifth permanent member. The smaller powers were to be represented on the Council as well, with rotating memberships lasting three years. The number of temporary members was an issue from the beginning, and eventually their number would increase from four to eleven. The Council's scope of activities was purposely wide-ranging; the membership addressed any matter concerned with world peace or the operations of the League.

Article 5 declares that decisions adopted by the Council or the Assembly required unanimous approval. There were exceptions. Matters of procedure could be adopted by a simple majority, and amendments to the Covenant would be adopted by a majority vote. The first meeting of the Assembly would be called by the president of the United States, an honor recognizing Wilson's role in creating the League.

Article 6 concerns operations of the League and describes the role and responsibilities of the permanent secretary-general in conducting regular operations. As was the case in other portions of this document, detailed procedures were left to be settled by a future annex to the Covenant. The expenses of the secretariat were to be paid by the members in "accordance with the apportionment of the expenses of the Bureau of the Universal Postal Union." This bureau is an international organization that coordinates postal policies among member nations and thus the worldwide postal system. What is significant here is the adoption of standards already in use by an internationally recognized organization and the application of those rules to the League. Article 7 stipulates that the League headquarters were to be in Geneva, Switzerland, and that all positions would be open to both men or women. All League representatives and League buildings would have diplomatic privileges and immunity.

◆ Articles 8–12

Articles 8 through 12 describe in general terms the League's scope of activities in its major mission, which was to prevent war. This set of articles, while they are not as detailed as those that follow in Articles 13 through 17, address responsibilities incumbent on members to avoid war among themselves, in addition to other League peace initiatives.

The arms race between nations to build up military and naval forces, particularly navies, in the years before World War I was seen by many as a major precipitating cause of the war. Article 8 addresses the issue of arms control, such that each nation would have enough military strength to protect itself but not enough to wage aggressive war. The Council would form plans for disarmament, which would be reviewed and revised at least once every ten years. Based on a French proposal, the article states that the review would take into consideration the circumstances specific to each region and country, which essentially meant that because France feared another invasion by Germany, German forces would be restricted while the French government would be allowed to arm itself as it saw necessary.

In addition to government armament programs, there was before the war a very strong private arms industry, which made a wide range of weapons available to the highest bidder. These commercial concerns were seen as another danger to peace. In response, the Council would study and advise the best course of action to counter the effects of the private armaments manufacturers and merchants. Wilson had proposed abolishing all private arms companies, an idea opposed by smaller nations, such as Portugal and Romania, which did not have their own national arms manufacturers. Member nations would freely exchange information on their own military and naval and air and munitions industries. One effect of this last provision was an annually published listing, issued throughout the 1920s and 1930s, of detailed descriptions of the armies of the members.

Because military matters required the advice of experts, Article 9 established a permanent commission to advise the Council on how to perform the activities covered by articles 1 and 8 as well as on any questions concerning naval, air, and military matters. This commission would not act independently but rather solely on the Council's instructions. France attempted to amend this article so that the League could use military force—that is, form an international army to intervene in crisis situations—but that idea was rejected.

As part of the general revulsion toward war that informed so many postwar projects and plans, the issue of aggression, such as Germany's at the beginning of the war, was considered key. Article 10 states that the League would protect the territorial integrity of all members against external aggression. If such a case occurred, the Council would advise on what had to be done. The article is of great interest, because the eventual failure of the League was strongly signaled in 1935, when one member, Italy, invaded another member, Ethiopia.

While sanctions were implemented, they were ineffectively planned and indifferently enforced. Second, the use of the word *external* reflects the article's aim to exclude civil wars. That restriction was considered necessary to prevent a government from seeking League assistance in the event of a civil war (such as would occur in Spain from 1936 to 1939).

Article 11 declares that the League's scope of interest was anything that threatened world peace, specifically war or the threat of war. The League would take any action considered appropriate. Upon the request of any member nation, the secretary-general could summon a meeting of the Council. Further, any nation could bring to the attention of the Council or the Assembly anything that had the potential of disturbing international peace.

Article 12 stipulates that in the event of any disagreements between members, they would submit the issue for arbitration or inquiry by the Council. Further, they would not engage in any military activity for three months after the award by arbitration or report from the inquiry if they disagreed with the result. Decisions would be made in a reasonable time, and a report would be issued within six months. This particular insistence on time limits before a declaration of war could be made was proposed by France, based on the extraordinarily short time from the assassination of the Austrian archduke Franz Ferdinand on June 28, 1914, to the escalation to national mobilizations through July, followed almost immediately by ultimatums and invasions.

◆ Articles 13–17

While the previous five articles described general obligations, especially among members of the League, the following five articles provided detailed procedures for handling disputes that could not be resolved satisfactorily by the involved parties. According to Article 13, members having disputes that could not be resolved diplomatically would submit them for arbitration. These disputes could include, but were not restricted to, issues of international law or possible breaches of international obligations. The body to adjudicate these disputes would be a court mutually agreed upon by the parties involved in a dispute or whatever tribunal might be stipulated by a convention that existed between the parties. Article 14 established the authority and the responsibility of the League Council to bring to the Assembly plans to create and implement a Permanent Court of International Justice. The court would hear and adjudicate international disputes and would also provide legal opinions on any question raised by either the Council or the Assembly.

Article 15 expanded the possible number of parties that could be involved in bringing about peaceful solutions. If two members of the League engaged in a dispute that could lead to a breaking off of relations and they did not submit the dispute to arbitration as described in Article 13, the matter could be submitted to the Council by any concerned party. The secretary-general would publish the details and make arrangements for the case to be brought to the Council, which would provide a settlement. The Council would report on its findings and recommendations. If members of the Council unanimously agreed, excluding any nations

Woodrow Wilson on Armistice Day in 1922 (Library of Congress)

involved in the dispute, League members would not go to war with any party complying with the recommendations. The article also stipulates that in any dispute stemming from domestic policies and not international law for both parties, the Council would not become involved. The Council could refer the dispute to the Assembly.

Article 16 states that any League member declaring war on another member would be declaring war on all members. The League would impose sanctions against offending members. The Council would recommend whatever military or naval activity it deemed necessary. League members would mutually support one another to mitigate economic hardships resulting from the conflict. Finally, the offending member would be expelled from the League. Article 17 made the process for conflict resolution an option open to any nation. The article specifically states that nations engaged in disputes and not belonging to the League would be invited to join. After accepting, they would abide by the League's rules, starting with conflict resolution, and articles 12 though 16 of the Covenant would apply.

◆ **Articles 18–22**

Treaties and alliances, whether open or secret, were seen, along with the arms race, to have been a major cause of the war. While building alliances might have been a means of guaranteeing security, the obligations imposed on members to join their allies automatically in mobilizing and deploying their armies had led to a rapid and uncontrollable escalation that had brought about the recently ended war. Among Woodrow Wilson's Fourteen Points, one of which had specifically called for the formation of a League of Nations, was a point calling for treaties and covenants to be arrived at in a public fashion. The regulation and publicity of treaties and where previous treaties might or might not bind participants were addressed in these five articles.

Article 18 provided for a means of ensuring that treaties were made public. It states that no treaties entered into by any League member would be valid and binding until registered with the League's secretariat and formally published by the League. This stipulation affected only new treaties and did not apply to treaties formed before the existence of the League. In Article 19 the League declares its role to caution and advise members when they contemplate treaties that could present a danger to world peace. The League would request that members reconsider if a treaty seemed to pose that danger. The issue of the degree of power of the League over the rights and sovereignty of nations came up as a subject of debate. It was finally decided that the issue of sovereignty would not be a serious problem, as condemnation of a treaty by the League would require a unanimous vote. Further, it was declared that this article did not mean that the League had the right to refuse to register any treaties under the rules of Article 18.

While Article 19 discusses future treaties, Article 20 is concerned with past treaties in addition to future treaties that might create problems in maintaining world peace. By this article, the members of the League would cancel any past treaty obligations that would run counter to the Covenant and they would refrain from making any such agreements in the future. A nation wishing to join the League would have to repudiate any such treaties to which it had earlier agreed. While the League sought to provide advice and influence in the matter of treaties in the future, Article 21 states that nothing in the Covenant would negate any regional understandings that were not inconsistent with the Covenant. This article was inserted at the insistence of the United States, which had concerns that the Monroe Doctrine (the policy that opposed European interference in the Western Hemisphere) not be undermined in any fashion.

A direct effect of losing the war was that Germany and Turkey were to forfeit their colonies and other imperial possessions. The victorious nations were determined that these territories not be given back, but there had to be a mechanism to administer these territories until they were ready for independence. The winning powers (principally Britain, France, and Japan) would administer these territories as League mandates, report annually to the Council, and prepare the territories for eventual freedom. One of these mandates, the former Ottoman provinces combined to form Iraq, was administered by the British until 1932, when it became a fully independent nation. Most of the others, including Syria, Palestine (later to become Israel), and nations in Africa such as Tanganyika did not reach independence until after World War II.

◆ **Articles 23–25**

The League of Nations is commonly associated with grand failures, such as its ineffective methods to stop Italian aggression in Africa or to halt Japanese and German territorial advances. It is not so well understood, however, that the League was actually quite successful in implementing several initiatives beyond the prevention of war. Some of these initiatives made progress toward improving the lives of people in many countries, especially on health issues. These articles specify the League's interests in "social activities" as well as in supporting already existing organizations.

Article 23 defines the League's actions to resolve international problems that did not result from individual governmental actions but that adversely affected the well-being of all people. Specifically, the League would work on such issues as safe working conditions, fair treatment of native populations, international trafficking of women and children, and drug trafficking. These efforts attracted a great deal of support; even the United States, which never joined the League, participated in such endeavors as the antidrug-trafficking programs. Further, the League would monitor arms traffic and work to prevent and control disease.

Article 24 stipulates that the League would pay for the activities described in Article 23. If members agreed, it would take over existing international organizations and assume their expenses. The League would share any relevant information it had with organizations not affiliated with it. Under Article 25, League members would encourage and promote organizations to improve world health, prevent disease, or mitigate any form of suffering. The League pledged to support existing humanitarian organizations, such as the Red Cross.

> "The High Contracting Parties, In order to promote international co-operation and to achieve international peace and security by the acceptance of obligations not to resort to war, by the prescription of open, just and honorable relations between nations, by the firm establishment of the understandings of international law as the actual rule of conduct among Governments, and by the maintenance of justice and a scrupulous respect for all treaty obligations in the dealings of organized peoples with one another Agree to this Covenant of the League of Nations."
>
> (Preamble)

> "Any war or threat of war, whether immediately affecting any of the Members of the League or not, is hereby declared a matter of concern to the whole League, and the League shall take any action that may be deemed wise and effectual to safeguard the peace of nations. In case any such emergency should arise the Secretary-General shall on the request of any Member of the League forthwith summon a meeting of the Council."
>
> (Article 11)

> "Nothing in this Covenant shall be deemed to affect the validity of international engagements, such as treaties of arbitration or regional understandings like the Monroe doctrine, for securing the maintenance of peace."
>
> (Article 21)

◆ Article 26

The final article lays out the rules concerning amendments to the Covenant. Members would not have to abide by amendments, but if they chose not to do so, they forfeited their membership. Discussions centered on whether a simple majority or a three-fourths majority would be required. Those who favored a simple majority argued that a three-fourths majority might not be attainable and would give the impression that no changes could ever be made. The requirement of a simple majority carried the day.

Audience

In general, there was one huge audience for the Covenant, and that was the entire world, which had just gone through four years of war. There were other, specialized groups for which it was intended, however. Among them were the defeated nations that had allied themselves with Germany. While there is a conciliatory tone in the Covenant, its provisions that focus on the importance of international law and honoring obligations were a reminder that those nations had disregarded international law when they began the conflict in 1914. It was a signal that actions of that sort would not be tolerated by the League. The retribution contained in the Treaty of Versailles drove home the point. Another audience was the minor and especially the newer nations of Europe that had come into being as a result of the collapse of the Russian, German, and Austro-Hungarian empires. Their rights in their conflicts against one another and potential threats from larger nations were to be guaranteed by the League as described in the Covenant.

Yet another audience, one that was not receptive, was the U.S. Senate and the people of the United States. Wilson sought to convince them of the value of the League. That value was to be made clear by the antiwar provisions of the League's activities. At the same time, the Covenant guaranteed the validity of the Monroe Doctrine, which Americans felt to be essential to their security. Wilson was not successful; the Senate had to ratify the treaty for it to go into effect. It did not, and neither the Covenant nor the Treaty of Versailles was adopted. The Senate's opposition was based largely on the strengthening mood of isolationism in the United States. Isolationism did not mean that the United States cut itself off from the rest of the world, especially in the area of international trade. What it meant was that many Americans did not want to be drawn into political arrangements that would cause them to become involved in another war. Further, despite assurances that the Monroe Doctrine would be unaffected, membership in an international organization was seen as a sure means of limiting American sovereignty and independence of action. The United States would eventually conclude a separate peace with Germany and would not participate in the League of Nations.

Impact

The League of Nations described in the Covenant did, in fact, come into existence and for twenty years sought, with decreasing success, to contain the pressures leading to conflict between nations. The effects of the Covenant were immediate. In 1920 the first session of the League was held, and by the end of the 1920s it had begun to engage in several successful projects (such as halting Greece's invasion of Bulgaria in 1925, ending the Chaco War between Bolivia and Paraguay in the 1930s, and initiating the World Court). League programs to abolish drug trafficking were active and even benefited from the activities of the United States, a nonmember. The League did indeed function, despite the misgivings of many. (During negotiations for the Treaty of Versailles and the League Covenant, the French premier George Clemenceau was famously skeptical of its eventual success.) Part of the League's failure must be attributed to the lack of strength given the organization as well as the absence of some sort of military option. There was no provision for an armed force or any equivalent to the peacekeeping activities that would later be performed by the United Nations.

While the Covenant and the League can be seen as failures in their inability to exercise control over the activities of aggressive nations or to prevent the outbreak of war, both did exert a positive outcome even after their demise. During World War II, the Allies, especially the United States, saw the need for an international organization. Weaknesses in both structure and organization served as a model for how things could go wrong. The League, as defined by its Covenant, was an innovation. Nothing like it had been tried before. Despite its failure, the League that came out of the Covenant demonstrated that men emerging from an old world that had been thoroughly destroyed

Questions for Further Study

1. What impact, if any, did the formation of the League of Nations have on relationships between the European powers and other regions of the world? See, for example, the Government of India Act and the Resolution of the General Syrian Congress, both passed also in 1919.

2. Compare the Covenant of the League of Nations with the Treaty of Versailles. How do the two documents differ in tone and attitude? In what sense could the argument be made that the two documents, to some extent, canceled each other out by promoting different ends?

3. Do you believe that the history of the 1920s, 1930s, and 1940s might have been radically different if the powers defeated in World War I had been admitted to the League of Nations? For insights, see Hitler's Proclamation to the German People and, from Italy, Benito Mussolini's "The Doctrine of Fascism."

4. World War I and the postwar settlement, reflected in the Covenant and in the Treaty of Versailles, redrew the map of Europe. How did that map change? Did the changes tend toward good or ill? Why was the League of Nations unable to keep the peace?

5. Why did the U.S. Senate fail to ratify the document so that the United States was not a member of the League of Nations? Do you think that subsequent history might have been different if the United States had joined the League of Nations?

were capable of going beyond simple revenge and made an effort to create a system to preserve peace in a new world. That they made the effort and achieved some successes were significant achievements.

Further Reading

■ Articles

Eagleton, Clyde. "Reform of the Covenant of the League of Nations." *American Political Science Review* 31, no. 3 (June 1937): 455–472.

Myers, Denys P. "The League of Nations Covenant: 1939 Model." *American Political Science Review* 33, no. 2 (April 1939): 193–218.

———. "Liquidation of League of Nations Functions." *American Journal of International Law* 42, no. 2 (April 1948): 320–354.

Pell, Herbert C., Jr. "The League of Nations Covenant." *Proceedings of the Academy of Political Science in the City of New York* 8, no. 3 (July 1919): 46–49.

Pemberton, Jo-Anne. "New Worlds for Old: The League of Nations in the Age of Electricity." *Review of International Studies* 28, no. 2 (April 2002): 311–336.

Williams, John Fischer. "The Covenant of the League of Nations and War." *Cambridge Law Journal* 5, no. 1 (1935): 1–21.

Wright, Quincy. "Effects of the League of Nations Covenant." *American Political Science Review* 13, no. 4 (November 1919): 556–576.

■ Books

Kennedy, Sabe McClain. *The Monroe Doctrine Clause of the League of Nations Covenant*. Lubbock: Texas Tech Press, 1979.

Kuehl, Warren F., and Lynne K. Dunn. *Keeping the Covenant: American Internationalists and the League of Nations, 1920–1939*. Kent, Ohio: Kent State University Press, 1997.

MacMillan, Margaret. *Paris 1919: Six Months That Changed the World*. New York: Random House, 2002.

Miller, David Hunter. *The Drafting of the Covenant*. Buffalo, N.Y.: W. S. Hein, 2002.

Walters, F. P. *A History of the League of Nations*. Westport, Conn.: Greenwood Press, 1986.

Wilson, Florence A. *The Origins of the League Covenant: A Documentary History of Its Drafting*. London: Leonard and Virginia Woolf, 1928.

■ Web Sites

"Appeal to the League of Nations by Haile Selassie, June 1936." Mount Holyoke College Web site.
 http://www.mtholyoke.edu/acad/intrel/selassie.htm.

"Britain's Breaking Off of Diplomatic Relations with Germany, 4 August 1914." firstworldwar.com "Primary Documents" Web site.
 http://www.firstworldwar.com/source/scrapofpaper1.htm.

"President Wilson's Fourteen Points." The World War I Document Archive Web site.
 http://wwi.lib.byu.edu/index.php/President_Wilson's_Fourteen _Points.°

—Robert Stacy

COVENANT OF THE LEAGUE OF NATIONS

The High Contracting Parties,

In order to promote international co-operation and to achieve international peace and security

by the acceptance of obligations not to resort to war,

by the prescription of open, just and honorable relations between nations,

by the firm establishment of the understandings of international law as the actual rule of conduct among Governments, and

by the maintenance of justice and a scrupulous respect for all treaty obligations in the dealings of organized peoples with one another Agree to this Covenant of the League of Nations.

◆ Article 1.

The original Members of the League of Nations shall be those of the Signatories which are named in the Annex to this Covenant and also such of those other States named in the Annex as shall accede without reservation to this Covenant. Such accession shall be effected by a Declaration deposited with the Secretariat within two months of the coming into force of the Covenant. Notice thereof shall be sent to all other Members of the League.

Any fully self-governing State, Dominion or Colony not named in the Annex may become a Member of the League if its admission is agreed to by two-thirds of the Assembly, provided that it shall give effective guarantees of its sincere intention to observe its international obligations, and shall accept such regulations as may be prescribed by the League in regard to its military, naval and air forces and armaments.

Any Member of the League may, after two years' notice of its intention so to do, withdraw from the League, provided that all its international obligations and all its obligations under this Covenant shall have been fulfilled at the time of its withdrawal.

◆ Article 2.

The action of the League under this Covenant shall be effected through the instrumentality of an Assembly and of a Council, with a permanent Secretariat.

◆ Article 3.

The Assembly shall consist of Representatives of the Members of the League.

The Assembly shall meet at stated intervals and from time to time, as occasion may require, at the Seat of the League or at such other place as may be decided upon.

The Assembly may deal at its meetings with any matter within the sphere of action of the League or affecting the peace of the world.

At meetings of the Assembly each Member of the League shall have one vote, and may have not more than three Representatives.

◆ Article 4.

The Council shall consist of Representatives of the Principal Allied and Associated Powers (United States of America, the British Empire, France, Italy, and Japan), together with Representatives of four other Members of the League. These four Members of the League shall be selected by the Assembly from time to time in its discretion. Until the appointment of the Representatives of the four Members of the League first selected by the Assembly, Representatives of Belgium, Brazil, Greece and Spain shall be members of the Council.

With the approval of the majority of the Assembly, the Council may name additional Members of the League whose Representatives shall always be members of the Council; the Council, with like approval may increase the number of Members of the League to be selected by the Assembly for representation on the Council.

The Council shall meet from time to time as occasion may require, and at least once a year, at the Seat of the League, or at such other place as may be decided upon.

The Council may deal at its meetings with any matter within the sphere of action of the League or affecting the peace of the world.

Any Member of the League not represented on the Council shall be invited to send a Representative to sit as a member at any meeting of the Council during the consideration of matters specially affecting the interests of that Member of the League.

At meetings of the Council, each Member of the League represented on the Council shall have one vote, and may have not more than one Representative.

Article 5.

Except where otherwise expressly provided in this Covenant, or by the terms of the present Treaty, decisions at any meeting of the Assembly or of the Council shall require the agreement of all the Members of the League represented at the meeting.

All matters of procedure at meetings of the Assembly or of the Council, including the appointment of Committees to investigate particular matters, shall be regulated by the Assembly or by the Council and may be decided by a majority of the Members of the League represented at the meeting.

The first meeting of the Assembly and the first meeting of the Council shall be summoned by the President of the United States of America.

Article 6.

The permanent Secretariat shall be established at the Seat of the League. The Secretariat shall comprise a Secretary-General and such secretaries and staff as may be required.

The first Secretary-General shall be the person named in the Annex; thereafter the Secretary-General shall be appointed by the Council with the approval of the majority of the Assembly.

The secretaries and staff of the Secretariat shall be appointed by the Secretary-General with the approval of the Council.

The Secretary-General shall act in that capacity at all meetings of the Assembly and of the Council.

The expenses of the Secretariat shall be borne by the Members of the League in accordance with the apportionment of the expenses of the International Bureau of the Universal Postal Union.

Article 7.

The Seat of the League is established at Geneva. The Council may at any time decide that the Seat of the League shall be established elsewhere.

All positions under or in connection with the League, including the Secretariat, shall be open equally to men and women.

Representatives of the Members of the League and officials of the League when engaged on the business of the League shall enjoy diplomatic privileges and immunities.

The buildings and other property occupied by the League or its officials or by Representatives attending its meetings shall be inviolable.

Article 8.

The Members of the League recognize that the maintenance of peace requires the reduction of national armaments to the lowest point consistent with national safety and the enforcement by common action of international obligations.

The Council, taking account of the geographical situation and circumstances of each State, shall formulate plans for such reduction for the consideration and action of the several Governments.

Such plans shall be subject to reconsideration and revision at least every ten years.

After these plans shall have been adopted by the several Governments, the limits of armaments therein fixed shall not be exceeded without the concurrence of the Council.

The Members of the League agree that the manufacture by private enterprise of munitions and implements of war is open to grave objections. The Council shall advise how the evil effects attendant upon such manufacture can be prevented, due regard being had to the necessities of those Members of the League which are not able to manufacture the munitions and implements of war necessary for their safety.

The Members of the League undertake to interchange full and frank information as to the scale of their armaments, their military, naval and air programs and the condition of such of their industries as are adaptable to warlike purposes.

Article 9.

A permanent Commission shall be constituted to advise the Council on the execution of the provisions of Articles 1 and 8 and on military, naval and air questions generally.

Article 10.

The Members of the League undertake to respect and preserve as against external aggression the territorial integrity and existing political independence of all Members of the League. In case of any such aggression or in case of any threat or danger of such aggression the Council shall advise upon the means by which this obligation shall be fulfilled.

Article 11.

Any war or threat of war, whether immediately affecting any of the Members of the League or not, is hereby declared a matter of concern to the whole League, and the League shall take any action that may be deemed wise and effectual to safeguard the peace of nations. In case any such emergency should arise the Secretary-General shall on the request of any Member of the League forthwith summon a meeting of the Council.

It is also declared to be the friendly right of each Member of the League to bring to the attention of the Assembly or of the Council any circumstance whatever affecting international relations which threatens to disturb international peace or the good understanding between nations upon which peace depends.

◆ **Article 12.**

The Members of the League agree that if there should arise between them any dispute likely to lead to a rupture, they will submit the matter either to arbitration or to inquiry by the Council, and they agree in no case to resort to war until three months after the award by the arbitrators or the report by the Council.

In any case under this Article the award of the arbitrators shall be made within a reasonable time, and the report of the Council shall be made within six months after the submission of the dispute.

◆ **Article 13.**

The Members of the League agree that whenever any dispute shall arise between them which they recognize to be suitable for submission to arbitration or judicial settlement and which cannot be satisfactorily settled by diplomacy, they will submit the whole subject matter to arbitration or judicial settlement.

Disputes as to the interpretation of a treaty, as to any question of international law, as to the existence of any fact which if established would constitute a breach of any international obligation, or as to the extent and nature of the reparation to be made for any such breach, are declared to be among those which are generally suitable for submission to arbitration or judicial settlement.

For the consideration of any such dispute the court of arbitration to which the case is referred shall be the Court agreed on by the parties to the dispute or stipulated in any convention existing between them.

The Members of the League agree that they will carry out in full good faith any award or decision that may be rendered, and that they will not resort to war against a Member of the League which complies therewith. In the event of any failure to carry out such an award or decision, the Council shall propose what steps should be taken to give effect thereto.

◆ **Article 14.**

The Council shall formulate and submit to the Members of the League for adoption plans for the establishment of a Permanent Court of International Justice. The Court shall be competent to hear and determine any dispute of an international character which the parties thereto submit to it. The Court may also give an advisory opinion upon any dispute or question referred to it by the Council or by the Assembly.

◆ **Article 15.**

If there should arise between Members of the League any dispute likely to lead to a rupture, which is not submitted to arbitration in accordance with Article 13, the Members of the League agree that they will submit the matter to the Council. Any party to the dispute may effect such submission by giving notice of the existence of the dispute to the Secretary-General, who will make all necessary arrangements for a full investigation and consideration thereof.

For this purpose the parties to the dispute will communicate to the Secretary-General, as promptly as possible, statements of their case with all the relevant facts and papers, and the Council may forthwith direct the publication thereof.

The Council shall endeavor to effect a settlement of the dispute, and if such efforts are successful, a statement shall be made public giving such facts and explanations regarding the dispute and the terms of settlement thereof as the Council may deem appropriate.

If the dispute is not thus settled, the Council, either unanimously or by a majority vote, shall make and publish a report containing a statement of the facts of the dispute and the recommendations which are deemed just and proper in regard thereto.

Any Member of the League represented on the Council may make public a statement of the facts of the dispute and of its conclusions regarding the same.

If a report by the Council is unanimously agreed to by the members thereof other than the Representatives of one or more of the parties to the dispute, the Members of the League agree that they will not go to war with any party to the dispute which complies with the recommendations of the report.

If the Council fails to reach a report which is unanimously agreed to by the members thereof, other than the Representatives of one or more of the parties to the dispute, the Members of the League reserve to themselves the right to take such action as they shall consider necessary for the maintenance of right and justice.

If the dispute between the parties is claimed by one of them, and is found by the Council, to arise out of a matter which by international law is solely within the domestic jurisdiction of that party, the

Council shall so report, and shall make no recommendation as to its settlement.

The Council may in any case under this Article refer the dispute to the Assembly. The dispute shall be so referred at the request of either party to the dispute, provided that such request be made within fourteen days after the submission of the dispute to the Council.

In any case referred to the Assembly, all the provisions of this Article and of Article 12 relating to the action and powers of the Council shall apply to the action and powers of the Assembly, provided that a report made by the Assembly, if concurred in by the Representatives of those Members of the League represented on the Council and of a majority of the other Members of the League, exclusive in each case of the Representatives of the parties to the dispute, shall have the same force as a report by the Council concurred in by all the members thereof other than the Representatives of one or more of the parties to the dispute.

◆ Article 16.

Should any Member of the League resort to war in disregard of its covenants under Articles 12, 13, or 15, it shall *ipso facto* be deemed to have committed an act of war against all other Members of the League, which hereby undertake immediately to subject it to the severance of all trade or financial relations, the prohibition of all intercourse between their nationals and the nationals of the covenant-breaking State, and the prevention of all financial, commercial or personal intercourse between the nationals of the covenant-breaking State and the nationals of any other State, whether a Member of the League or not.

It shall be the duty of the Council in such case to recommend to the several Governments concerned what effective military, naval or air force the Members of the League shall severally contribute to the armed forces to be used to protect the covenants of the League.

The Members of the League agree, further, that they will mutually support one another in the financial and economic measures which are taken under this Article, in order to minimize the loss and inconvenience resulting from the above measures, and that they will mutually support one another in resisting any special measures aimed at one of their number by the covenant-breaking State, and that they will take the necessary steps to afford passage through their territory to the forces of any of the Members of the League which are co-operating to protect the covenants of the League.

Any Member of the League which has violated any covenant of the League may be declared to be no longer a Member of the League by a vote of the Council concurred in by the Representatives of all the other Members of the League represented thereon.

◆ Article 17.

In the event of a dispute between a Member of the League and a State which is not a Member of the League, or between States not Members of the League, the State or States not Members of the League shall be invited to accept the obligations of membership in the League for the purposes of such dispute, upon such conditions as the Council may deem just. If such invitation is accepted, the provisions of Articles 12 to 16, inclusive, shall be applied with such modifications as may be deemed necessary by the Council.

Upon such invitation being given the Council shall immediately institute an inquiry into the circumstances of the dispute and recommend such action as may seem best and most effectual in the circumstances.

If a State so invited shall refuse to accept the obligations of membership in the League for the purposes of such dispute, and shall resort to war against a Member of the League, the provisions of Article 16 shall be applicable as against the State taking such action.

If both parties to the dispute, when so invited, refuse to accept the obligations of membership in the League for the purposes of such dispute, the Council may take such measures and make such recommendations as will prevent hostilities and will result in the settlement of the dispute.

◆ Article 18.

Every treaty or international engagement entered into hereafter by any Member of the League shall be forthwith registered with the Secretariat and shall as soon as possible be published by it. No such treaty or international engagement shall be binding until so registered.

◆ Article 19.

The Assembly may from time to time advise the reconsideration by Members of the League of treaties which have become inapplicable and the consideration of international conditions whose continuance might endanger the peace of the world.

◆ Article 20.

The Members of the League severally agree that this Covenant is accepted as abrogating all obligations or understandings *inter se* which are inconsistent with the terms thereof, and solemnly undertake that they will not hereafter enter into any engagements inconsistent with the terms thereof.

In case any Member of the League shall, before becoming a Member of the League, have undertaken any obligations inconsistent with the terms of this Covenant, it shall be the duty of such Member to take immediate steps to procure its release from such obligations.

◆ Article 21.

Nothing in this Covenant shall be deemed to affect the validity of international engagements, such as treaties of arbitration or regional understandings like the Monroe doctrine, for securing the maintenance of peace.

◆ Article 22.

To those colonies and territories which as a consequence of the late war have ceased to be under the sovereignty of the States which formerly governed them and which are inhabited by peoples not yet able to stand by themselves under the strenuous conditions of the modern world, there should be applied the principle that the well-being and development of such peoples form a sacred trust of civilization and that securities for the performance of this trust should be embodied in this Covenant.

The best method of giving practical effect to this principle is that the tutelage of such peoples should be entrusted to advanced nations who by reason of their resources, their experience or their geographical position can best undertake this responsibility, and who are willing to accept it, and that this tutelage should be exercised by them as Mandatories on behalf of the League.

The character of the mandate must differ according to the stage of the development of the people, the geographical situation of the territory, its economic conditions and other similar circumstances.

Certain communities formerly belonging to the Turkish Empire have reached a stage of development where their existence as independent nations can be provisionally recognized subject to the rendering of administrative advice and assistance by a Mandatory until such time as they are able to stand alone. The wishes of these communities must be a principal consideration in the selection of the Mandatory.

Other peoples, especially those of Central Africa, are at such a stage that the Mandatory must be responsible for the administration of the territory under conditions which will guarantee freedom of conscience and religion, subject only to the maintenance of public order and morals, the prohibition of abuses such as the slave trade, the arms traffic and the liquor traffic, and the prevention of the establishment of fortifications or military and naval bases and of military training of the natives for other than police purposes and the defense of territory, and will also secure equal opportunities for the trade and commerce of other Members of the League.

There are territories, such as South-West Africa and certain of the South Pacific Islands, which, owing to the sparseness of their population, or their small size, or their remoteness from the centers of civilization, or their geographical contiguity to the territory of the Mandatory, and other circumstances, can be best administered under the laws of the Mandatory as integral portions of its territory, subject to the safeguards above mentioned in the interests of the indigenous population.

In every case of mandate, the Mandatory shall render to the Council an annual report in reference to the territory committed to its charge.

The degree of authority, control, or administration to be exercised by the Mandatory shall, if not previously agreed upon by the Members of the League, be explicitly defined in each case by the Council.

A permanent Commission shall be constituted to receive and examine the annual reports of the Mandatories and to advise the Council on all matters relating to the observance of the mandates.

◆ Article 23.

Subject to and in accordance with the provisions of international conventions existing or hereafter to be agreed upon, the Members of the League:

(a) Will endeavor to secure and maintain fair and humane conditions of labor for men, women, and children, both in their own countries and in all countries to which their commercial and industrial relations extend, and for that purpose will establish and maintain the necessary international organizations;

(b) Undertake to secure just treatment of the native inhabitants of territories under their control;

(c) Will entrust the League with the general supervision over the execution of agreements with regard to the traffic in women and children, and the traffic in opium and other dangerous drugs;

(d) Will entrust the League with the general supervision of the trade in arms and ammunition with the countries in which the control of this traffic is necessary in the common interest;

(e) Will make provision to secure and maintain freedom of communications and of transit and equitable treatment for the commerce of all Members of the League. In this connection, the special necessities of the regions devastated during the war of 1914–1918 shall be borne in mind;

(f) Will endeavor to take steps in matters of international concern for the prevention and control of disease.

◆ Article 24.

There shall be placed under the direction of the League all international bureaus already established by general treaties if the parties to such treaties consent. All such international bureaus and all commissions for the regulation of matters of international interest hereafter constituted shall be placed under the direction of the League.

In all matters of international interest which are regulated by general conventions but which are not placed under the control of international bureaus or commissions, the Secretariat of the League shall, subject to the consent of the Council and if desired by the parties, collect and distribute all relevant information and shall render any other assistance which may be necessary or desirable.

The Council may include as part of the expenses of the Secretariat the expenses of any bureau or commission which is placed under the direction of the League.

◆ Article 25.

The Members of the League agree to encourage and promote the establishment and co-operation of duly authorized voluntary national Red Cross organizations having as purposes the improvement of health, the prevention of disease and the mitigation of suffering throughout the world.

◆ Article 26.

Amendments to this Covenant will take effect when ratified by the Members of the League whose Representatives compose the Council and by a majority of the Members of the League whose Representatives compose the Assembly.

No such amendments shall bind any Member of the League which signifies its dissent therefrom, but in that case it shall cease to be a Member of the League.

Annex.

I. Original Members of the League of Nations Signatories of the Treaty of Peace—

United States of America
Belgium
Bolivia
Brazil
British Empire
—Canada
—Australia
—South Africa
—New Zealand
—India
China
Cuba
Ecuador
France
Greece
Guatemala
Haiti
Hedjaz
Honduras
Italy
Japan
Liberia
Nicaragua
Panama
Peru
Poland
Portugal
Rumania
Serb-Croat-Slovene State

Glossary

C.B.	Companion of the Most Honourable Order of the Bath, a class of member of a British order of chivalry that is typically made up of senior military advisers or civil servants
K.C.M.G.	Knight Commander of the Grand Cross (of the Order of Saint Michael and Saint George), an appointment bestowed on those who have rendered service on behalf of Britain in relation to the Commonwealth or foreign nations

Siam [Thailand]
Czecho-Slovakia
Uruguay

States Invited to Accede to the Covenant—
Argentine Republic
Chile
Colombia
Denmark
Netherlands
Norway

Paraguay
Persia
Salvador
Spain
Sweden
Switzerland
Venezuela

II. First Secretary-General of the League of Nations—

The Honorable Sir James Eric Drummond, K.C.M.G., C.B.

TREATY OF VERSAILLES

" Germany is forbidden to maintain or construct any fortifications either on the left bank of the Rhine or on the right bank...."

Overview

The Treaty of Versailles was the peace treaty signed between the defeated Germany and the Allied and Associated powers, most prominently Britain, France, Italy, and the United States, at the conclusion of World War I. It was presented to Germany's representatives for review on May 7, 1919, and signed on June 28, 1919.

The treaty was highly detailed, with more than four hundred articles and annexes that dealt in small part with the establishment of the League of Nations and in large part with the punishment of Germany. The German government, which had agreed to an armistice on November 11, 1918, was taken aback by the terms. The German negotiators expected the document to be based on U.S. president Woodrow Wilson's list of war aims, the Fourteen Points. However, the treaty not only seemed to ignore those points but also forced the Germans to take responsibility for the war's beginnings, prosecution, and conduct. As a result of this admission, the treaty forced the new German republic to pay an unprecedentedly high amount in war reparations, an amount meant to cripple Germany's economy permanently. The German negotiators signed only under duress, and resentment of the treaty's terms is widely accepted as having contributed to the German people's support of the National Socialist Party in the 1930s and thus to the eventual propagation of World War II.

Context

No continent's affairs were ever dictated entirely by one power at any time in world history, and Europe in the early twentieth century was no exception. On June 28, 1914, a Serbian terrorist assassinated the heir to the Austro-Hungarian throne, who was on a goodwill trip through Sarajevo. The Austro-Hungarian government declared war on Serbia a month later, which prompted Serbia's longtime ally, Russia, to declare war on Austria-Hungary. As various alliances were activated, all the major European powers ended up at war with one another—Austria-Hungary in alliance with Germany and in opposition to Russia, which was in alliance with Serbia, Britain, and France. The Great War, as Europeans came to know it, began in August 1914.

Seemingly, Serbian terrorists and the Serbian government that was alleged to support them were to blame for starting the war, but at the time politicians, intellectuals, diplomats, and soldiers on all sides debated which power was truly responsible for the war, and historians continue the debate to this day. Those on the side of the Allies held that Germany's determination to assert its military and diplomatic power in Europe created a climate in which war was likely. The German government of Kaiser Wilhelm II had built a massive navy to challenge Britain, had twice threatened war with France over colonial claims in Morocco, and had dismissed the Russians as an inferior people whose vast territory was a focus for German expansion. Such belligerence, coupled with the defensive alliances to which all the major powers belonged, provided the diplomatic context in which an all-out European war would be waged. On the other hand, it was the assassination in the Balkans that actually sparked the war, and the Germans declared war on Russia only when Russian troops began mobilizing on the German border.

The nature of the conflict was such that blame for the war's origins became central to its propagation, on both sides. The first two months of the war saw more casualties than all the major wars since the Napoleonic wars combined. Soldiers began to dig trenches on the Western Front to defend themselves against machine guns; for the next three years "battles" consisted of simply throwing more men and ammunition into the line than the other side had immediately available, in the hope that a breakthrough might be achieved. On the Eastern Front there was more movement, which meant there were more casualties; the Germans advanced over the bodies of Russian soldiers until they melted into the vast Russian steppes, unable to come up with the men or supplies to make a concerted march on Saint Petersburg or Moscow. The result in both cases was a bewildering stalemate that forced many thinking people to question not just the nature of the war but the very nature of Western civilization, capable as it was of such senseless murder. Critically, however, most soldiers found reasons to fight and found purpose in the war, par-

1914

■ **June**
The heir to the Austro-Hungarian throne, Archduke Franz Ferdinand, is assassinated in Sarajevo, capital of the predominantly Serbian province of Bosnia-Herzegovina, administered by the Austro-Hungarian Empire. The Austro-Hungarian government accuses the Serbian government of knowing about the assassination plot.

■ **July**
The Austro-Hungarian government declares war on Serbia.

■ **August**
Germany declares war on Russia and France and invades Belgium; Britain declares war on Germany and Austria-Hungary.

1916

■ **November**
Woodrow Wilson is reelected president of the United States.

1917

■ **April**
The United States declares war on Germany as an "Associated Power" not allied with France, Russia, or Britain but cooperating with them.

■ **November**
Georges Clemenceau is named prime minister of France.

---

ticularly on the side of the democratic states of Britain, France, and the United States. For most soldiers, victory over the expansionist and authoritarian German monarchy was important enough to merit continuing to risk their lives in what otherwise seemed to be senseless slaughter.

The threat against which they fought was likewise real. In September 1914, as the number of casualties mounted and the German offensive in France ground to a halt, the German political and military command sat down to write up a series of objectives to be attained, should they win the war. The so-called September Program called for the establishment of a Germanocentric economic bloc called Mitteleuropa; the annexation of Poland, Belgium, and the Netherlands; the crippling of the French economy; the expansion of the German peasantry into Russia; and unity with Austria, an ally that had no idea that winning the war would mean its own subservience to Germany. These war plans remained secret from the German public itself throughout the war for fear that the populace would turn on its leadership if they knew such slaughter was being conducted in the name of conquest as opposed to defense. Still, German military conduct of the war and its strategic aims, particularly on the Eastern Front, were aimed at fulfilling the terms of the September Program at all times. Effectively, the only difference between German war aims in the two world wars was the Holocaust—and the German leadership was hardly short on anti-Semitic feeling during World War I.

In sum, for the democratic allies and their soldiers the war was well worth fighting and winning. Even without knowing what the German government's true aims were, they sensed, correctly, that should they lose, they faced certain catastrophe, right down to the life of the lowliest private in any European army. As such, when the war finally turned in the allies' favor in 1918, its slow, bloody, painful but inexorable march toward victory was met with a powerful sense of satisfaction and a desire to punish the German aggressor. But there was also a desire to create a new world, one in which similar wars would not be possible. As the United States geared up to send troops to the continent, President Wilson made a speech to Congress on January 8, 1918, laying out a declaration of U.S. war aims known as the Fourteen Points. Among them was a call for a stop to arms races, an end to secret alliances, national self-determination, free trade, democracy, and a "general association of nations ... for the purpose of affording mutual guarantees of political independence and territorial integrity to great and small states alike" (http://avalon.law.yale.edu/20th _century/wilson14.asp). These war aims were openly declared and favorably received by people on both sides. When the German government agreed to an armistice on November 11, 1918, it was on the assumption that the terms of the peace treaty would be based on the Fourteen Points. This was already in sharp contrast to the terms of the armistice, which amounted to surrender and required German withdrawal from all occupied territories, the surrender of German arms, and the promise of reparation for damage done.

With the end of the war came the collapse of the German monarchy and empire, the atomization of the Austro-

Hungarian Empire, the birth of Turkey out of the Ottoman Empire, and the fear of further Bolshevik revolutions after the 1917 collapse of the Russian Empire. Italy, a victorious ally of the French and British, was wracked by leftist strikes, and the barely independent Hungary experienced a short Communist revolution in March 1919. Communist strikes took place in Glasgow, Scotland, and Chicago experienced race riots. Basically, the Western world lay not quite in ruins but ready for potential revolution and collapse.

The negotiations that took place in Paris thus had a dual nature. There was an air of hope and resolution, a determination to end the menace of the spread of Soviet Communism and to implement Wilson's Fourteen Points. Even so, the peace conference was also infused with an atmosphere of vengeance, blame, and recrimination for the destruction wrought on Europe by Germany's army. The eventual Treaty of Versailles reflected this desire to punish the German aggressor.

About the Author

The four main public negotiators of the Treaty of Versailles, referred to as the Council of Four, were the leaders of the Allied and Associated powers. Vittorio Orlando, the Italian prime minister, held a decidedly junior role among the negotiators. Italy did not share a border with Germany, had never been in the field against the German army alone, and had little interest in Germany's postwar fate, so the treaty's terms held little consequence for Orlando. The more important authors of the treaty were the leaders of the powers that had forced the Germans into an armistice based on the battles in France.

Georges Clemenceau was born in 1841 in the Vendée, in western France. He earned a degree as a medical doctor and worked as a journalist and as a teacher before entering politics in 1870, as France was losing the Franco-Prussian War. He became prime minister of France in November 1917, at a point when French morale was at its lowest. Famously, after becoming prime minister, he addressed the National Assembly of France (in March 1918) with the words: "Je fais la guerre!" (I make war!). Having guided France to victory in the war, he dictated many of the peace terms in the interest of destroying Germany as a threat to French security. As an author of the treaty, Clemenceau was relentless in his opposition to Wilson and was largely responsible for the vengeful tone of the treaty. Defeated in the presidential election of 1920, he gave up politics and retired from politics. He died in 1929.

David Lloyd George was born in 1863 and worked as a lawyer before entering politics. He rose from being minister of munitions and secretary of state for war to becoming prime minister of a multiparty coalition government in Britain in December 1916. He was the only Welshman ever to hold the office. Initially, Lloyd George was inclined to accept most of Woodrow Wilson's Fourteen Points as a basis for the peace. Britain had no claims on European territory and expected its colonial claims to met with no con-

Time Line

1918

- **January**
  President Wilson announces American war aims publicly in a speech to Congress that comes to be known as the "Fourteen Points."

- **November**
  Germany and Austria sue for peace. Kaiser Wilhelm II abdicates, and a new German republic is proclaimed.

1919

- **January**
  Peace negotiations begin at Versailles, outside Paris.

- **June**
  The Treaty of Versailles is signed by the German government.

testation, so a far-reaching European peace seemed worthy of pursuit. Just before the peace conference began, the British coalition government held an election to seal its pursuit of the peace terms. The coalition was overwhelmingly reelected, but everywhere he traveled on the campaign, Lloyd George was confronted with an electorate that demanded that he "hang the Kaiser." Disinclined to lead public opinion as opposed to appease it, Lloyd George found himself most often allied with Clemenceau in the effort to write a treaty that would punish the Germans. He continued to dominate British politics through the 1920s and in the 1930s promoted a program of economic reform along the lines of America's New Deal. He was still a member of Parliament when he died in 1945.

Before becoming president, Woodrow Wilson had served as president of Princeton University and governor of New Jersey. He was a leading intellectual of the day, holding a doctorate in politics and history from Johns Hopkins University. Wilson was first elected to the presidency in 1912 and was reelected in November 1916, on a platform that claimed he had kept the United States out of war. Within another five months, German sinkings of American ships led Wilson to call on Congress to declare war on Germany and join the side of Britain, France, and Italy. As the

David Lloyd George of Great Britain, Vittorio Orlando of Italy, Georges Clemenceau of France, and U.S. president Woodrow Wilson gather in Versailles to sign the treaty ending World War I. (AP/Wide World Photos)

United States built its tiny army into a formidable force capable of fighting in Europe, Wilson issued the Fourteen Points as a public list of American war aims, and it was well received. But implementation of war aims involves achieving victory, which led Wilson into some very confusing circumstances at the peace table. American troops did not reach the Continent until the summer of 1918, and their performance in the field amounted to little more than providing cannon fodder to the more experienced Germans. Yet the U.S. potential as a future source of men and material was so enormous for the future that the country's entry into the war was the key factor in forcing Germany to the peace table.

Upon arriving in Europe, Wilson toured Europe and was acclaimed a hero in both victorious and defeated nation-states for his presumed ability to dictate the terms of the peace according to the Fourteen Points. Still, his peoples' sacrifices were too negligible for him to have the same moral bearing on the writing of the treaty as men like Clemenceau and Lloyd George, whose peoples had lost a generation of young men to the war with Germany. Regardless, the Fourteen Points demanded an almost impossible magnanimity on the part of the victors toward the defeated

Germany, and Wilson did not prove to be a very successful negotiator for them as a result. After leaving the presidency in 1921, Wilson stayed on in Washington, D.C., and died in 1924.

The four major negotiators were supported by their foreign ministers, the French foreign minister Stephen Pichon, the British foreign secretary Arthur Balfour, the U.S. secretary of state Robert Lansing, and the Italian foreign minister Sidney Sonnino. There was also a rotating Japanese delegation of two ambassadors, but the power to dictate the really important terms of the treaty lay entirely in the hands of Clemenceau, Lloyd George, and Wilson. Counseling them were numerous lawyers, advisers, diplomats, and politicians, most notably André Tardieu, a French politician who helped write up the territorial concessions to which Germany would have to agree; Philip Kerr, Lloyd George's personal secretary, who seemed to play an outsized role in British decision making; Harold Nicolson of Britain, who kept a copious diary; John Maynard Keynes, a British economist who would soon after write a scathing review of the treaty's provisions; and Edward M. House of the United States, a close personal friend of Wilson's who acted as a sounding board for the president's lofty ambitions and became a go-between for the various negotiators.

Explanation and Analysis of the Document

The entire Treaty of Versailles amounted to fifteen parts and 440 articles. It was one of five treaties written up as a part of the Peace of Paris, dealing with each of the defeated powers—in 1919, besides Germany, the independent states of Bulgaria, Austria, Hungary, and Turkey. The Treaty of Versailles was by far the most important of these treaties, because it dealt with the fate of the most significant of the defeated powers and it established the League of Nations Covenant in its first section. In Part XIII, the new League established the International Labour Organization to counteract the appeal of Soviet Communism.

Those sections of the treaty excerpted here were the sections that caused the most offense to the new German republic and became the focus of contention in European diplomacy. In other sections, Germany's African, Chinese, and Pacific colonies were given away; its prisoners of war were sent home; financial and trade agreements were put into place or renewed; and German airspace and waterways were opened to international traffic. One interesting part of the full treaty was Part VII, in which the Allies made a confused and uncertain bid to put Kaiser Wilhelm II and several other German conductors of the war on trial for crimes against humanity. The language made it into the treaty, yet there was reluctance to define just what a war crime constituted, since it opened up the Allies to a number of charges of hypocrisy. In the end, the Dutch government's refusal to give up Wilhelm for trial once he settled there in exile scuttled the concept, to the relief of many of the treaty's authors.

◆ Part II

The borders that the treaty laid out for Germany meant that the German nation-state lost territory to Belgium and that the provinces of Alsace and Lorraine were returned to France, which were not unexpected revisions. In the south, three million German speakers in the Sudetenland aspired, like the new territory of Austria, to join postwar Germany, but the Allies insisted that Austria be an independent state and, in Article 27.6, that the Sudetenland remain a part of Bohemia in the new Czechoslovakia. The east saw the most devastating territorial restructuring. The new nation-state of Poland was given a "corridor" to the Baltic Sea, cutting off East Prussia from the rest of the German state. Three million people were removed from German sovereignty, though by the important standard of national self-determination that the conference emphasized, most of those three million people were not of German ethnicity. That hardly mattered to the German government and people, who were humiliated at having East Prussia —home of the Junker aristocracy that had been responsible for uniting the German nation between 1864 and 1871—cut off from the rest of Germany.

◆ Part III

The third part of the treaty gave the French the ability to access German territory in order to maintain French security. In Section III, the Rhineland, which ran between the French and Belgian borders and the Rhine River, was to remain without fortifications or troops, such that, should another war take place between France, Belgium, and Germany, the French and Belgians would be able to occupy German territory before any German army could invade. Section IV gave over the profits of the coal mines in the Rhineland's Saar basin to France for fifteen years.

◆ Part V

If Part III was meant to keep Germany from launching a surprise invasion of its western neighbors, Part V sought to make the German state all but indefensible. Article 160 reduced the size of the German army—numbering some three or four million men at its height during the war—to a mere hundred thousand men in seven divisions, allowed only to maintain Germany's internal order. Limits were placed on the production of armaments. The navy, built before the war to rival the British Royal Navy as the largest in the world and employing submarines effectively during the war, was reduced to six battleships, and submarines were forbidden. There would be no air force.

◆ Part VIII

The German government and people found the eighth part of the treaty the most objectionable. The prearmistice agreement had called for any reparations to be based on civilian damages, and the actual armistice called for "reparation for damage done." Yet any such amount would seem incalculable and understated considering that the conservative estimate had ten million people dead at the end of the war, with thirty million wounded. Eventually, the negotiators decided that the most important "damage done" was to the soldiers themselves and that any German reparations payments would go toward covering the amount of their pensions, as stated in the first annex. However, soldiers were not civilians; somehow, the prearmistice agreement had to be abrogated.

To that end, it was suggested by a young American negotiator, John Foster Dulles, that Germany should be made to acknowledge its responsibility for the propagation of the war and therefore for its culpability for all the war's damages. This notion was written into Article 231, the famous "war guilt clause." Article 232 acknowledged that it was beyond Germany's capacity to pay reparations for such an astronomical sum of damages, and in Article 233 it was determined that a fixed sum would be calculated by a reparations commission within the next two years. Effectively, Germany had to admit guilt for causing the war and had to agree to pay an undetermined amount for its damages. Eventually, in May 1921, the amount was set at 132 billion marks, or $31.5 billion, to be paid in 2 billion mark installments per year. Though Article 234 claimed that the Allies would periodically review Germany's ability to pay and adjust the yearly sum accordingly, at 2 billion marks per

German soldiers ready their machine gun as they stand in a trench watching enemy positions. (AP/Wide World Photos)

year, the German government would not finish paying for the war until 1987, at which point it was assumed that most veterans of the war would be dead.

◆ Part XIV

Article 428 of Part XIV placed Allied troops in the Rhineland for the next fifteen years, to guarantee that Germany upheld the terms of the treaty. No occupation of enemy territory had ever lasted so long after a major war, and the German people resented it. In Article 429 the Allies spelled out their slow evacuation of the Rhineland pursuant to Germany's demonstration of good faith, and the rest of Section I outlined ways in which Germany could see the troops removed sooner should the German government accept their culpability for the treaty's terms.

Audience

The German populace was the primary audience of the Treaty of Versailles. The most public political figure of the prewar German Empire, Kaiser Wilhelm II, had abdicated and been replaced by a democratic republic; though the treaty called for him to be placed on trial, no politician was willing to follow through on this demand. Thus, the punitive terms of the treaty were not about to fall on the man most associated with the war. In the social Darwinist climate of the early twentieth century, this made a certain indirect sense. It assumed that the German people were somehow biologically predisposed to be warlike—something the kaiser's bellicose rhetoric about the German people's racial destiny had encouraged them to think.

The people in the Allied countries comprised an only marginally less important secondary audience for the treaty. The French people, especially north of Paris, had suffered enormously during the war. The British people had already conceived of themselves as having lost an entire generation's worth of future leaders in the trenches. Americans had lost proportionately more casualties in the Great War than they had in the American Civil War and half as many dead in a mere four months as opposed to four years' worth of war. The civilian populations of the winners demanded that Germany be punished for the war. The politicians that represented them were all elected, and the main negotiators clearly felt pressure from their constituencies to punish the Germans, the Fourteen Points notwithstanding.

Perhaps more important was whom the treaty did not address: those who hoped for a more balanced consideration of the need to assure peace in Europe for future times. The French commander in chief Ferdinand Foch claimed that the treaty was really a twenty-year cease-fire, an uncannily accurate assessment.

Impact

On May 7, 1919, the draft text of the Treaty of Versailles was handed over to the German delegation for its perusal.

The German government's chief representative, Count Ulrich Graf von Brockdorff-Rantzau, made his displeasure known by remaining seated while making his speech accepting the treaty for revision, a major breach of diplomatic protocol. Over the next month and a half the new German republic fought the terms of the treaty by stalling, writing letters of observation that amounted to protest, and considering the possibility of renewing the war—all while a British naval blockade of their ports, in place since 1914, starved their people of trade in foodstuffs and thus applied intense pressure to Germany to sign the treaty. Finally, on June 28, 1919, the Treaty of Versailles was signed in a climate of icy tension in the Hall of Mirrors in the Palace of Versailles, where the unification of the German Empire had been declared in 1871.

Assessing the impact of the Treaty of Versailles after June 1919 is an exercise in defining the most critical events of the twentieth century in Europe. Four factors determined how the treaty's long-term implications played out in European politics and diplomacy: the Germans' hatred of the terms and effort to avoid meeting them, the French government's desire to force the Germans to uphold the terms, French politicians' increasing unwillingness to have the French military act unilaterally in enforcing the terms, and the British government's lack of desire to enforce the treaty from virtually its beginning.

From the start, the German government and military did everything possible to avoid disarmament and to evade making the reparations payments. In 1923, enforcing the required terms of the reparations payments, the French Army invaded the Ruhr Valley and occupied coal mines and timber yards to extract raw materials equivalent to the treaty-determined 2 billion marks per year. However, they were condemned by nearly every major Western power, including the United States and Great Britain, for overreacting to Germany's alleged inability to pay. The inflationary crisis that followed the occupation was largely due to the German government's policy of printing paper currency, without regard for whether there was gold to back it, in order to pay off the reparations. The policy and its consequences seem to confirm the idea that the German economy was artificially crippled, a notion most famously put forward by the British economist John Maynard Keynes in his book *The Economic Consequences of the Peace* (1919).

In late 1923 the German government stabilized behind a new chancellor, Gustav Stresemann, and Stresemann stayed on as foreign minister through 1929. Under his diplomatic leadership, a new plan was negotiated, the Dawes Plan, temporarily lowering the reparations payments and attaching them to the profits of the German railroad industry, which were considerable. Stresemann later guaranteed Germany's borders with Belgium and France in the Pact of Locarno in 1925, after which the punitive terms of the Versailles Treaty seemed outdated and mistaken to many politicians in all the Allied countries. A general air of relaxation of terms settled upon Europe.

This air of calm was based on the notion that Germany had moved on from the war and that its governments were willing to accept the treaty's provisions. Such was far from the

"*Germany is forbidden to maintain or construct any fortifications either on the left bank of the Rhine or on the right bank to the west of a line drawn 50 kilometres to the East of the Rhine.*"

(Article 42)

"*The Allied and Associated Governments affirm and Germany accepts the responsibility of Germany and her allies for causing all the loss and damage to which the Allied and Associated Governments and their nationals have been subjected as a consequence of the war imposed upon them by the aggression of Germany and her allies.*"

(Article 231)

"*As a guarantee for the execution of the present Treaty by Germany, the German territory situated to the west of the Rhine, together with the bridgeheads, will be occupied by Allied and Associated troops for a period of fifteen years from the coming into force of the present Treaty.*"

(Article 428)

case. The German army never completely demobilized and, under General Hans von Seeckt, continued to buy the latest weapons on the black market. By secret agreement, German officers were trained within the borders of Germany's only equal as an international pariah, the Soviet Union. Even the West's German hero, Stresemann, explained to colleagues that his negotiations in 1924 and 1925 were about "getting the wolf from our throat" so that disputes over the treaty could be negotiated in the future—or fought over—from a position of comparative strength. Meanwhile, numerous petty political parties of the left and right plotted the destruction of the government that had signed the treaty and dreamed of renouncing its terms in the future. One was the National Socialist German Workers' Party, the Nazis, and in 1933 their leader, Adolf Hitler, would accomplish just that. His repeated efforts to roll back the territorial terms of the treaty would launch World War II in 1939.

Ever since, historians, intellectuals, politicians, and others have argued over whether the Treaty of Versailles should have been written differently. Some say that it correctly punished the German people, not just their government, for creating the climate in which World War I became possible. Proponents of that position claim that if it had been enforced to the letter, there might never have been a second world war. Others argue that it would have

been better if the treaty had reflected the terms of Wilson's Fourteen Points, which were far more visionary and aimed at promoting peace above and beyond the notion of punishment. The integration of a new German democratic republic into the international system of nations as an equal—similar to the integration of the restored monarchy of France after the Napoleonic wars—might have promoted a genuine "peace in our time," to quote the phrase of Great Britain's prime minister Neville Chamberlain.

One thing seems certain. The treaty should not have included such draconian terms—deserved or otherwise—if the Allied politicians and their successors were not prepared to enforce those terms. Despite the warnings of a select few politicians in France and Britain, their governments clearly were not prepared to demand that the Treaty of Versailles be upheld to the letter by any German government. The result was, as predicted, a cease-fire of twenty years.

Further Reading

■ **Articles**

Lu, Catherine. "Justice and Moral Regeneration: Lessons from the Treaty of Versailles." *International Studies Review* 4, no. 3 (December 2002): 3–25.

Trachtenberg, Marc. "Versailles after Sixty Years." *Journal of Contemporary History* 17, no. 3 (July 1982): 487–506.

Sharp, Alan. *The Versailles Settlement: Peacemaking in Paris, 1919.* New York: St. Martin's Press, 1991.

■ **Books**

Adamthwaite, Anthony. *Grandeur and Misery: France's Bid for Power in Europe 1914–1940.* London: Arnold, 1995.

Fischer, Fritz. *Germany's Aims in the First World War.* New York: W. W. Norton, 1967.

Keynes, John Maynard. *The Economic Consequences of the Peace.* New York: Penguin, 1995.

Macmillan, Margaret. *Paris 1919: Six Months That Changed the World.* New York: Random House, 2001.

Prior, Robin, and Trevor Wilson. *The First World War.* London: Cassell, 1999.

■ **Web Sites**

"President Woodrow Wilson's Fourteen Points." Avalon Project Web site.

http://avalon.law.yale.edu/20th_century/wilson14.asp.

"Primary Documents: Allied Armistice Terms, 11 November 1918." First World War.com Web site.

http://firstworldwar.com/source/armisticeterms.htm.

—David Simonelli

Questions for Further Study

1. Why were the victorious Allies eager to punish Germany in the aftermath of World War I?

2. What short-term and long-term effects did the Treaty of Versailles have on Germany? What were its unintended consequences? For a possible answer, read the entry on Hitler's Proclamation to the German People.

3. How could a single assassination in Sarajevo be the fuse for such a widespread and lethal war?

4. What role did the emergence of Communism play in the terms of the Treaty of Versailles?

5. Do you believe that the Treaty of Versailles as written was justifiable (and should have been more rigorously enforced), or do you think World War II might have been avoided had the spirit of Woodrow Wilson's Fourteen Points prevailed in writing the treaty?

TREATY OF VERSAILLES

Part II. Boundaries of Germany.

Article 27

The boundaries of Germany will be determined as follows:

1. With Belgium: From the point common to the three frontiers of Belgium, Holland, and Germany and in a southerly direction: the north-eastern boundary of the former territory of neutral Moresnet, then the eastern boundary of the Kreis of Eupen, then the frontier between Belgium and the Kreis of Montjoie, then the northeastern and eastern boundary of the Kreis of Malmedy to its junction with the frontier of Luxemburg.

2. With Luxemburg: The frontier of August 3, 1914, to its junction with the frontier of France of the 18th July, 1870.

3. With France: The frontier of July 18, 1870, from Luxemburg to Switzerland with the reservations made in Article 48 of Section IV (Saar Basin) of Part III.

4. With Switzerland: The present frontier.

5. With Austria: The frontier of August 3, 1914, from Switzerland to CzechoSlovakia as hereinafter defined.

6. With Czecho-Slovakia: The frontier of August 3, 1914, between Germany and Austria from its junction with the old administrative boundary separating Bohemia and the province of Upper Austria to the point north of the salient of the old province of Austrian Silesia situated at about 8 kilometres east of Neustadt.

7. With Poland: From the point defined above to a point to be fixed on the ground about 2 kilometres east of Lorzendorf: the frontier as it will be fixed in accordance with Article 88 of the present Treaty; thence in a northerly direction to the point where the administrative boundary of Posnania crosses the river Bartsch: a line to be fixed on the ground leaving the following places in Poland: Skorischau, Reichthal, Trembatschau, Kunzendorf, Schleise, Gross Kosel, Schreibersdorf, Rippin, Furstlich-Niefken, Pawelau, Tscheschen, Konradau, Johallnisdorf, Modzenowe, Bogdaj, and in Germany: Lorzendorf, Kaulwitz, Glausche, Dalbersdorf, Reesewitz, Stradam, Gross Wartenberg, Kraschen, Neu Mittel-

walde, Domaslawitz, Wedelsdorf, Tscheschen Hammer; thence the administrative boundary of Posnania northwestwards to the point where it cuts the Rawitsch-Herrnstadt railway; thence to the point where the administrative boundary of Posnania cuts the Reisen-Tschirnau road: a line to be fixed on the ground passing west of Triebusch and Gabel and east of Saborwitz; thence the administrative boundary of Posnania to its junction with the eastern administrative boundary of the Kreis of Fraustadt; thence in a north-westerly direction to a point to be chosen on the road between the villages of Unruhstadt and Kopnitz: a line to be fixed on the ground passing west of Geyersdorf, Brenno, Fehlen, Altkloster, Klebel, and east of Ulbersdorf, Buchwald, Ilgen, Weine, Lupitze, Schwenten: thence in a northerly direction to the northernmost point of Lake Chlop: a line to be fixed on the ground following the median line of the lakes; the town and the station of Bentschen however (including the junction of the lines Schwiebus-Bentschen and Zullichau-Bentschen) remaining in Polish territory; thence in a north-easterly direction to the point of junction of the boundaries of the Kreise of Schwerin, Birnbaum, and Meseritz: a line to be fixed on the ground passing east of Betsche; thence in a northerly direction the boundary separating the Kreise of Schwerin and Birnbaum, then in an easterly direction the northern boundary of Posnania to the point where it cuts the river Netze; thence upstream to its confluence with the Kaddow: the course of the Netze; thence upstream to a point to be chosen about 6 kilometres southeast of Schneidemuhl: the course of the Kuddow; thence north-eastwards to the most southern point of the reentant of the northern boundary of Posnania about 5 kilometres west of Stahren: a line to be fixed on the ground leaving the Schneidemuhl-Konitz railway in this area entirely in German territory; thence the boundary of Posnania north-eastwards to the point of the salient it makes about 15 kilometres east of Flatow; thence north-eastwards to the point where the river Kamionka meets the southern boundary of the Kreis of Konitz about 3 kilometres north-east of Grunau: a line to be fixed on the ground leaving the following places to Poland: Jasdrowo, Gr. Lutau, Kl. Lutau, Wittkau, and to Germany: Gr. Butzig, Cziskowo, Battrow, Bock, Grunau; thence in a northerly direction the boundary between the Kreise of Konitz and Schlochau to the point where this boundary cuts the river Brahe; thence to a point on the boundary of Pomerania 15 kilometres east of Rummelsburg: a line to be fixed on the ground leaving the following places in Poland: Konarzin, Kelpin, Adl. Briesen, and in Germany: Sampohl, Neuguth, Steinfort, Gr. Peterkau; then the boundary of Pomerania in an easterly direction to its junction with the boundary between the Kreise of Konitz and Schlochau; thence northwards the boundary between Pomerania and West Prussia to the point on the river Rheda about 3 kilometres northwest of Gohra where that river is joined by a tributary from the north-west; thence to a point to be selected in the bend of the Piasnitz river about 1½ kilometres north-west of Warschkau: a line to be fixed on the ground; thence this river downstream, then the median line of Lake Zarnowitz, then the old boundary of West Prussia to the Baltic Sea.

8. With Denmark: The frontier as it will be fixed in accordance with Articles 109 to 111 of Part III, Section XII (Schleswig).

Article 28

The boundaries of East Prussia, with the reservations made in Section IX (East Prussia) of Part III, will be determined as follows: from a point on the coast of the Baltic Sea about 1½ kilometres north of Probbernau church in a direction of about 159° East from true North: a line to be fixed on the ground for about 2 kilometres; thence in a straight line to the light at the bend of the Elbing Channel in approximately latitude 54° 19½' North, longitude 19° 26' East of Greenwich; thence to the easternmost mouth of the Nogat River at a bearing of approximately 209° East from true North; thence up the course of the Nogat River to the point where the latter leaves the Vistula (Weichsel); thence up the principal channel of navigation of the Vistula, then the southern boundary of the Kreis of Marienwerder, then that of the Kreis of Rosenberg eastwards to the point where it meets the old boundary of East Prussia, thence the old boundary between East and West Prussia, then the boundary between the Kreise of Osterode and Neidenburg, then the course of the river Skottau downstream, then the course of the Neide upstream to a point situated about 5 kilometres west of Bialutten being the nearest point to the old frontier of Russia; thence in an easterly direction to a point immediately south of the intersection of the road Neidenburg-Mlava with the old frontier of Russia: a line to be fixed on the ground passing north of Bialutten;

thence the old frontier of Russia to a point east of Schmalleningken, then the principal channel of navigation of the Niemen (Memel) downstream, then the Skierwieth arm of the delta to the Kurisches Haff; thence a straight line to the point where the eastern shore of the Kurische Nehrung meets the administrative boundary about 4 kilometres southwest of Nidden; thence this administrative boundary to the western shore of the Kurische Nehrung.

Article 29

The boundaries as described above are drawn in red on a one-in-a-million map which is annexed to the present Treaty (Map No. 1). [See Introduction.] In the case of any discrepancies between the text of the Treaty and this map or any other map which may be annexed, the text will be final.

Article 30

In the case of boundaries which are defined by a waterway, the terms "course" and "channel" used in the present Treaty signify: in the case of non-navigable rivers, the median line of the waterway or of its principal arm, and, in the case of navigable rivers, the median line of the principal channel of navigation. It will rest with the Boundary Commissions provided by the present Treaty to specify in each case whether the frontier line shall follow any changes of the course or channel which may take place or whether it shall be definitely fixed by the position of the course or channel at the time when the present Treaty comes into force.

Part III....

◆ Section III. Left Bank of the Rhine.

Article 42

Germany is forbidden to maintain or construct any fortifications either on the left bank of the Rhine or on the right bank to the west of a line drawn 50 kilometres to the East of the Rhine.

Article 43

In the area defined above the maintenance and the assembly of armed forces, either permanently or temporarily, and military maneuvers of any kind, as well as the upkeep of all permanent works for mobilization, are in the same way forbidden.

Article 44

In case Germany violates in any manner whatever the provisions of Articles 42 and 43, she shall be regarded as committing a hostile act against the Powers signatory of the present Treaty and as calculated to disturb the peace of the world.

◆ **Section IV. Saar Basin.**
Article 45

As compensation for the destruction of the coalmines in the north of France and as part payment towards the total reparation due from Germany for the damage resulting from the war, Germany cedes to France in full and absolute possession, with exclusive rights of exploitation, unencumbered and free from all debts and charges of any kind, the coalmines situated in the Saar Basin....

Article 49

Germany renounces in favour of the League of Nations, in the capacity of trustee, the government of the territory defined above.

At the end of fifteen years from the coming into force of the present Treaty the inhabitants of the said territory shall be called upon to indicate the sovereignty under which they desire to be placed....

Part V. Military, Naval and Air Clauses.

In order to render possible the initiation of a general limitation of the armaments of all nations, Germany undertakes strictly to observe the military, naval and air clauses which follow.

◆ **Section I. Military Clauses.**
Chapter I—Effectives and Cadres of the German Army.
Article 159

The German military forces shall be demobilised and reduced as prescribed hereinafter.

Article 160

1. By a date which must not be later than March 31, 1920, the German Army must not comprise more than seven divisions of infantry and three divisions of cavalry.

After that date the total number of effectives in the Army of the States constituting Germany must not exceed one hundred thousand men, including officers and establishments of depots. The Army shall be devoted exclusively to the maintenance of order within the territory and to the control of the frontiers.

The total effective strength of officers, including the personnel of staffs, whatever their composition, must not exceed four thousand.

2. Divisions and Army Corps headquarters staffs shall be organised in accordance with Table No. 1 annexed to this Section.

The number and strengths of the units of infantry, artillery, engineers, technical services and troops laid down in the aforesaid Table constitute maxima which must not be exceeded.

The following units may each have their own depot: An Infantry regiment; A Cavalry regiment; A regiment of Field Artillery; A battalion of Pioneers.

3. The divisions must not be grouped under more than two army corps headquarters staffs.

The maintenance or formation of forces differently grouped or of other organisations for the command of troops or for preparation for war is forbidden.

The Great German General Staff and all similar organisations shall be dissolved and may not be reconstituted in any form.

The officers, or persons in the position of officers, in the Ministries of War in the different States in Germany and in the Administrations attached to them, must not exceed three hundred in number and are included in the maximum strength of four thousand laid down in the third sub-paragraph of paragraph (1) of this Article....

Chapter II—Armament, Munitions and Material.
Article 168

The manufacture of arms, munitions, or any war material, shall only be carried out in factories or works the location of which shall be communicated to and approved by the Governments of the Principal Allied and Associated Powers, and the number of which they retain the right to restrict.

Within three months from the coming into force of the present Treaty, all other establishments for the manufacture, preparation, storage or design of arms, munitions, or any war material whatever shall be closed down. The same applies to all arsenals except those used as depots for the authorised stocks of munitions. Within the same period the personnel of these arsenals will be dismissed.

Article 169

Within two months from the coming into force of the present Treaty German arms, munitions and war material, including anti-aircraft material, existing in Germany in excess of the quantities allowed, must be surrendered to the Governments of the Principal Allied and Associated Powers to be destroyed or rendered useless. This will also apply to any special plant intended for the manufacture of military material, except such as may be recognised as necessary for equipping the authorised strength of the German army.

The surrender in question will be effected at such points in German territory as may be selected by the said Governments.

Within the same period arms, munitions and war material, including anti-aircraft material, of origin other than German, in whatever state they may be, will be delivered to the said Governments, who will decide as to their disposal....

Chapter III—Recruiting and Military Training.

Article 173

Universal compulsory military service shall be abolished in Germany.

The German Army may only be constituted and recruited by means of voluntary enlistment....

Article 176

On the expiration of two months from the coming into force of the present Treaty there must only exist in Germany the number of military schools which is absolutely indispensable for the recruitment of the officers of the units allowed. These schools will be exclusively intended for the recruitment of officers of each arm, in the proportion of one school per arm....

Article 177

Educational establishments, the universities, societies of discharged soldiers, shooting or touring clubs and, generally speaking associations of every description, whatever be the age of their members, must not occupy themselves with any military matters.

In particular they will be forbidden to instruct or exercise their members or to allow them to be instructed or exercised, in the profession or use of arms.

These societies, associations, educational establishments and universities must have no connection with the Ministries of War or any other military authority....

Chapter IIV—Fortifications.

Article 180

All fortified works, fortresses and field works situated in German territory to the west of a line drawn fifty kilometres to the east of the Rhine shall be disarmed and dismantled....

◆ Section II. Naval Clauses.

Article 181

After the expiration of a period of two months from the coming into force of the present Treaty the German naval forces in commission must not exceed:

6 battleships of the Deutschland or Lothringen type, 6 light cruisers, 12 destroyers, 12 torpedo boats, or an equal number of ships constructed to replace them as provided in Article 190.

No submarines are to be included.

All other warships, except where there is provision to the contrary in the present Treaty, must be placed in reserve or devoted to commercial purposes....

Article 183

After the expiration of a period of two months from the coming into force of the present Treaty, the total personnel of the German Navy, including the manning of the fleet, coast defences, signal stations, administration and other land services, must not exceed fifteen thousand, including officers and men of all grades and corps.

The total strength of officers and warrant officers must not exceed fifteen hundred. Within two months from the coming into force of the present Treaty the personnel in excess of the above strength shall be demobilised....

Article 191

The construction or acquisition of any submarine, even for commercial purposes, shall be forbidden in Germany....

◆ Section III. Air Clauses.

Article 198

The armed forces of Germany must not include any military or naval air forces....

Article 200

Until the complete evacuation of German territory by the Allied and Associated troops, the aircraft of the Allied and Associated Powers shall enjoy in Germany freedom of passage through the air, freedom of transit and of landing....

◆ Section IV. Inter-Allied Commissions of Control.

Article 203

All the military, naval and air clauses contained in the present Treaty, for the execution of which a time-limit is prescribed, shall be executed by Germany under the control of Inter-Allied Commissions specially appointed for this purpose by the Principal Allied and Associated Powers....

Part VIII. Reparation.

◆ Section I. General Provisions.

Article 231

The Allied and Associated Governments affirm and Germany accepts the responsibility of Germany and her allies for causing all the loss and damage to which the Allied and Associated Governments and their nationals have been subjected as a consequence of the war imposed upon them by the aggression of Germany and her allies.

Article 232

The Allied and Associated Governments recognise that the resources of Germany are not adequate, after taking into account permanent diminutions of such resources which will result from other provisions of the present Treaty, to make complete reparation for all such loss and damage.

The Allied and Associated Governments, however, require, and Germany undertakes, that she will make compensation for all damage done to the civilian population of the Allied and Associated Powers and to their property during the period of the belligerency of each as an Allied or Associated Power against Germany by such aggression by land, by sea and from the air...

Article 233

The amount of the above damage for which compensation is to be made by Germany shall be determined by an Inter-Allied Commission, to be called the Reparation Commission....

This Commission shall consider the claims and give to the German Government a just opportunity to be heard.

The findings of the Commission as to the amount of damage defined as above shall be concluded and notified to the German Government on or before May 1, 1921, as representing the extent of that Government's obligations.

The Commission shall concurrently draw up a schedule of payments prescribing the time and manner for securing and discharging the entire obligation within a period of thirty years from May 1, 1921. If, however, within the period mentioned, Germany fails to discharge her obligations, any balance remaining unpaid may, within the discretion of the Commission, be postponed for settlement in subsequent years, or may be handled otherwise in such manner as the Allied and Associated Governments, acting in accordance with the procedure laid down in this Part of the present Treaty, shall determine.

Article 234

The Reparation Commission shall after May 1, 1921, from time to time, consider the resources and capacity of Germany, and, after giving her representatives a just opportunity to be heard, shall have discretion to extend the date, and to modify the form of payments, such as are to be provided for in accordance with Article 233; but not to cancel any part, except with the specific authority of the several Governments represented upon the Commission....

ANNEX I.

Compensation may be claimed from Germany under Article 232 above in respect of the total damage under the following categories:

1. Damage to injured persons and to surviving dependents by personal injury to or death of civilians caused by acts of war, including bombardments or other attacks on land, on sea, or from the air, and all the direct consequences thereof, and of all operations of war by the two groups of belligerents wherever arising.

2. Damage caused by Germany or her allies to civilian victims of acts of cruelty, violence or maltreatment (including injuries to life or health as a consequence of imprisonment, deportation, internment or evacuation, of exposure at sea or of being forced to labour), wherever arising, and to the surviving dependents of such victims.

3. Damage caused by Germany or her allies in their own territory or in occupied or invaded territory to civilian victims of all acts injurious to health or capacity to work, or to honour, as well as to the surviving dependents of such victims.

4. Damage caused by any kind of maltreatment of prisoners of war.

5. As damage caused to the peoples of the Allied and Associated Powers, all pensions and compensation in the nature of pensions to naval and military victims of war (including members of the air force), whether mutilated, wounded, sick or invalided, and to the dependents of such victims, the amount due to the Allied and Associated Governments being calculated for each of them as being the capitalised cost of such pensions and compensation at the date of the coming into force of the present Treaty on the basis of the scales in force in France at such date.

6. The cost of assistance by the Government of the Allied and Associated Powers to prisoners of war and to their families and dependents.

7. Allowances by the Governments of the Allied and Associated Powers to the families and dependents of mobilised persons or persons serving with the forces, the amount due to them for each calendar year in which hostilities occurred being calculated for each Government on the basis of the average scale for such payments in force in France during that year.

8. Damage caused to civilians by being forced by Germany or her allies to labour without just remuneration.

9. Damage in respect of all property wherever situated belonging to any of the Allied or Associated States or their nationals, with the exception of naval and military works or materials, which has been carried off, seized, injured or destroyed by the acts of Germany or her allies on land, on sea or from the air, or damage directly in consequence of hostilities or of any operations of war.

10. Damage in the form of levies, fines and other similar exactions imposed by Germany or her allies upon the civilian population....

Part XIV. Guarantees.

◆ Section I. Western Europe.

Article 428

As a guarantee for the execution of the present Treaty by Germany, the German territory situated to the west of the Rhine, together with the bridgeheads, will be occupied by Allied and Associated troops for a period of fifteen years from the coming into force of the present Treaty.

Article 429

If the conditions of the present Treaty are faithfully carried out by Germany, the occupation referred to in Article 428 will be successively restricted as follows:

1. At the expiration of five years there will be evacuated: the bridgehead of Cologne and the territories north of a line running along the Ruhr, then along the railway Julich, Duren, Euskirchen, Rheinbach, thence along the road Rheinbach to Sinzig, and reaching the Rhine at the confluence with the Ahr; the roads, railways and places mentioned above being excluded from the area evacuated.

2. At the expiration of ten years there will be evacuated: the bridgehead of Coblenz and the territories north of a line to be drawn from the intersection between the frontiers of Belgium, Germany and Holland, running about from 4 kilometres south of Aix-la-Chapelle, then to and following the crest of Forst Gemund, then east of the railway of the Urft valley,

then along Blankenheim, Valdorf, Dreis, Ulmen to and following the Moselle from Bremm to Nehren, then passing by Kappel and Simmern, then following the ridge of the heights between Simmern and the Rhine and reaching this river at Bacharach; all the places valleys, roads and railways mentioned above being excluded from the area evacuated.

3. At the expiration of fifteen years there will be evacuated: the bridgehead of Mainz, the bridgehead of Kehl and the remainder of the German territory under occupation. If at that date the guarantees against unprovoked aggression by Germany are not considered sufficient by the Allied and Associated Governments, the evacuation of the occupying troops may be delayed to the extent regarded as necessary for the purpose of obtaining the required guarantees.

Article 430

In case either during the occupation or after the expiration of the fifteen years referred to above the Reparation Commission finds that Germany refuses to observe the whole or part of her obligations under the present Treaty with regard to reparation, the whole or part of the areas specified in Article 429 will be reoccupied immediately by the Allied and Associated forces.

Article 431

If before the expiration of the period of fifteen years Germany complies with all the undertakings resulting from the present Treaty, the occupying forces will be withdrawn immediately.

Article 432

All matters relating to the occupation and not provided for by the present Treaty shall be regulated by subsequent agreements, which Germany hereby undertakes to observe.

Glossary

Gr.	*gross* (literally, great)
Great German General Staff	the official German organization for the ongoing study of all aspects of war and for developing both preparations for war and plans for active combat
Kl.	*klein* (literally, small)
neutral Moresnet	a small territory that had been, for about one hundred years, governed jointly by Belgium and Germany
Pioneers	the elite volunteer unit that operated the flamethrowers deployed against France in the war

King Faisal I (Library of Congress)

RESOLUTION OF THE GENERAL SYRIAN CONGRESS

"We do not acknowledge any right claimed by the French Government in any part whatever of our Syrian country."

Overview

In the aftermath of World War I, the disposition of territory formerly governed by the Ottoman Empire became an issue of concern, both to the inhabitants of that territory and to the victorious Entente powers meeting in Paris. At the suggestion of President Woodrow Wilson, who was the leader of the American delegation, the Big Four powers—Great Britain, France, the United States, and Italy—authorized a commission of inquiry to be sent to the former Asiatic Arab provinces of the empire to ascertain the wishes of their inhabitants with regard to their future political status. Soon thereafter the head of the provisional Arab government in Damascus, Emir Faisal, called for a General Syrian Congress to draft a document that would represent to the commission the political aspirations of a majority of those living in "Greater Syria"—the territory that now includes Syria, Lebanon, Israel-Palestine, and Jordan.

The resulting resolution reflected nationalist sentiments that were widely held at the time. It called on the Entente powers to honor their commitment to national self-determination, demanding complete and immediate independence for a united Syria. If Syria had to become a temporary ward (mandate) of any foreign power, that foreign power should be the United States or, if necessary, Great Britain. Finally, the resolution denounced French and Zionist ambitions in the region.

Context

During World War I the Ottoman Empire fought in alliance with Germany and the Austro-Hungarian Empire, among others, against the Entente powers, an alliance that included Great Britain, France, Russia, and, eventually, the United States. During the war Great Britain, France, and Russia signed secret agreements that arranged for the division of the territory of the Ottoman Empire among themselves after the war. Each of the powers viewed these agreements as a means to safeguard its interests and

enhance its strategic position in the Middle East. France, for example, claimed "historic rights" in "Syria"—an ambiguously defined geographic unit. The French based their claims on their historical relationship with Catholic and near-Catholic minorities (such as the Maronite Christians of Lebanon) who lived there and on French economic interests in the region, such as investments in railroads and silk production.

The British also made wartime pledges to a number of local warlords and nationalist groups, promising to support their goals if they allied themselves with the Entente. Two of these pledges were particularly important. In 1915 the British made contact with Sharif Husayn ibn 'Alī, an Arabian warlord based in Mecca. Husayn promised to delegate his son Faisal to launch a revolt against the Ottoman Empire to harass the empire from within—the famous Arab Revolt, guided by the British colonel T. E. Lawrence. In exchange, the British promised Husayn gold, guns, and, once the war ended, the right to establish an Arab "state or states" with ill-defined borders in the predominantly Arab territories of the empire. The second relevant pledge made by the British during the war was to the Zionist (Jewish nationalist) movement. In July 1917 the British foreign secretary Alfred Balfour placed a notice in the *Times* of London, stating that "His Majesty's Government view with favour the establishment in Palestine of a national home for the Jewish people" (Hurewitz, p. 106). The Balfour Declaration provided the first real diplomatic victory for the Zionist movement.

The postwar settlement was complicated by three factors. First, the various agreements and pledges made during the war were mutually contradictory. Second, Faisal's army had lodged itself in the territory of inland Syria (now labeled Occupied Enemy Territory–East, or OET-E), and with British cooperation Faisal established a rudimentary administration based in Damascus. Finally, in an address to the U.S. Congress, President Wilson announced his famous Fourteen Points—a summary of American (and later Entente) war aims. Point V implies the principle of the right of peoples to national self-determination; Point XII promised the non-Turkish portion of the Ottoman Empire "absolutely unmolested opportunity of autonomous development" (Link, p. 536).

1918

- **September 30**
  The British army, along with its Arab contingent, enters Damascus, ending four hundred years of Ottoman control.

- **October 22**
  The British establish OET-E (an administrative unit in inland Syria under joint British-Arab control) and OET-W (an administrative unit in coastal Syria under French control); Faisal is appointed Arab military commander and adviser to the British on Arab matters.

- **November 11**
  Husayn appoints Faisal "Asiatic Arab" representative to the peace negotiations in Paris.

1919

- **March 20**
  Great Britain, France, and the United States agree to send a commission of inquiry to Syria.

- **April 28**
  The Covenant of the League of Nations is presented to the delegates attending the Paris Peace Conference.

- **June**
  The General Syrian Congress convenes.

- **June 25**
  The King-Crane Commission, a commission of inquiry, arrives in Damascus.

To unravel their competing claims and arrange a final peace settlement, Entente leaders met in Paris. There they agreed to establish a League of Nations and initialed its charter. Article 22 of the charter deals directly with the Asiatic Arab provinces of the Ottoman Empire. Because the inhabitants of the region were not yet ready "to stand by themselves under the strenuous conditions of the modern world," the document states, they require assistance by a "mandatory" power until they are (Hurewitz, p. 179). Article 22 further stipulates that the wishes of the community were to be the principal concern in the choice of the mandatory power.

To determine those wishes, President Wilson proposed that a commission of inquiry be sent to the former Asiatic Arab provinces. Although both Great Britain and France acquiesced, neither country participated. Even the American government soon lost interest. Nevertheless, the announcement of the commission (named the King-Crane Commission after its two leaders) stirred great interest in Greater Syria. Faisal, who had been in Paris representing the interests of "Asiatic Arabs," returned home and called for an assembly to formulate a program expressing the wishes of a majority of the inhabitants. On July 2, 1919, the congress adopted the Damascus Program, also known as the Resolution of the General Syrian Congress. The announcement and site visits of the commission also stirred unprecedented and widespread nationalist agitation throughout inland Syria as the administration of Faisal attempted to win over the congress and the populace to his more conciliatory position, while various nationalist groups maneuvered to have their voices heard. In the end, the mobilization and the agitation of those nationalist groups outside the congress most influenced the resolution.

In the meantime, Great Britain and France worked out an understanding of their own. Having already ceded the coastal plain and the contiguous hinterland to the French (an area designated as Occupied Enemy Territory–West, or OET-W), the British withdrew their forces to Palestine from the interior. This decision, in effect, created three separate administrative units in Greater Syria and challenged the demand of the congress and most nationalist groups in the Arab administrative zone for a unified, independent Syria. In March 1920 the congress proclaimed Syria independent, with Faisal as its monarch. A little over a month later, the San Remo Conference awarded France the mandate for a truncated Syria. Tensions were rising between the French on the coast and nationalist guerrillas who were launching raids into French territory, and nationalist agitation was spreading throughout inland Syria. As a result, the French delivered an ultimatum to the newly proclaimed Arab government, invaded inland Syria, and assumed mandatory control over what would become Lebanon and Syria.

About the Author

The General Syrian Congress was made up of delegates from the Arab-, British-, and French-administered areas of

Greater Syria. Eighty-five representatives from the Arab-administered areas were elected in two stages: Voters first elected representatives to local assemblies; then those representatives chose the delegates. Faisal selected an additional thirty-five tribal and religious leaders as delegates. No elections took place in the British- and French-administered areas. Instead, local nationalist committees decided on the delegates. Seats were set aside for minority (Christian and Jewish) representation.

Two social groups were particularly well represented in the congress. One group consisted of urban notables, a stratum of society that had dominated local and provincial politics throughout the late Ottoman period. The other group included delegates who tended to be younger, more radical, and less socially prominent than the notables. Both groups contributed to the drafting of the resolution.

Explanation and Analysis of the Document

The General Syrian Congress was more of a bellwether than an architect of public opinion. While the deliberations that resulted in the drafting of the resolution remain unknown, it is evident that the resolution emerged as a compromise between the two main ideological blocs that dominated the politics of the Arab-administered area of Greater Syria.

The first bloc (which might be called the Arabist bloc) included the supporters of Faisal and his policies. Like most who had fought in the Arab Revolt, Faisal came from outside the territory of Greater Syria. As a result, he and his followers (many of whom also came to Syria from other areas) championed the eventual establishment of the *Arab* state that the British had promised his father. This state would include the Hejaz (the western region of Arabia from which Faisal came) and perhaps Iraq. Like Faisal, members of this bloc were also willing to bow to reality and accept a mandate, but only if France was not the mandatory power. Finally, while Zionist immigration into Palestine was not a central issue for this bloc, Faisal reached an accord with the Zionists that would have permitted continued Jewish immigration into Palestine.

The second bloc (which might be called the Syrianist bloc) included those who had belonged to or embraced ideas originally espoused by the Syrian Union, an organization formed by Syrian exiles in Egypt during the war. By the time the congress convened, this bloc had already begun to dominate the nationalist camp in the Syrian interior. Its members demanded complete independence for a unified Syria within clearly delineated borders, no connection to the Hejaz, separation from Iraq, no mandate, and an end to Zionist immigration. (In their view Palestine was southern Syria.) Because members distrusted Husayn and his son, they sought decentralization and limitations on the power of any government headed by Faisal. Because they also distrusted the British, who had sponsored Faisal's Arab Revolt and supported Zionist aspirations, they believed a British mandate to be no better than a French one.

Time Line

1919

- **July 2**
  The General Syrian Congress adopts the Damascus Program.

- **August 28**
  The King-Crane Commission Report is filed.

- **September 15**
  The British begin their evacuation of troops from Syria to Palestine.

1920

- **March 8**
  The General Syrian Congress declares Syrian independence.

- **April 25**
  The San Remo Conference assigns France the mandates for the territories that will become Lebanon and Syria.

- **July 24**
  France invades inland Syria and deposes the Arab government.

1946

- **April 17**
  The last French soldier leaves Syria.

- **December 31**
  The last French soldier leaves Lebanon.

The resolution begins with a prologue establishing the credentials of the General Syrian Congress and its right to represent to the commission of inquiry the wishes of the entire Syrian nation. That right rested on three grounds. First, the congress represented all regions of Greater Syria—OET-E, OET-W, and Occupied Enemy Territory–South, or OET-S (Palestine)—despite the fact that the French discouraged elections in the coastal zone and Palestine lacked the infrastructure for holding them. Second, delegates to the congress were authorized by the populations of their districts to act on their behalf. Finally, the congress included delegates who represented the three major religious communities living in Syria. Ensuring the representation of religious minorities was essential for both domestic and foreign reasons. The minority population of Greater Syria was not negligible, and its support was necessary for any government that wished to rule effectively. In addition, many from minority communities looked with suspicion on an emir who claimed descent from the prophet Muhammad and on an administration associated so closely with the Hejaz, the region of Arabia in which the two holy cities of Islam, Mecca and Medina, are located. By putting the issue of minority rights up front, the congress hoped to minimize foreign (particularly French) interference in the domestic affairs of Syria as well as to demonstrate to the Entente powers that the "religious fanaticism" about which those powers had frequently complained during the nineteenth century was a thing of the past. In other words, ensuring minority representation in the congress assured foreign observers that Syria had reached a "level of civilization" commensurate with independence. Ten articles follow the prologue.

◆ Article 1

The first article calls for the complete independence of Syria within a fixed set of boundaries. The wording is complex and allows for multiple interpretations. Nevertheless, it can be assumed that the boundaries of a future Syrian state stipulated by the resolution corresponded to the so-called "natural boundaries" of Syria found in other documents written at the same time. The northern boundary was demarcated by the Taurus Mountains in the southern part of contemporary Turkey. The eastern boundary followed the Euphrates and Khabur rivers in the north and then stretched from the town of Abu Kamal (on the borders of present-day Syria and Iraq), continued through the town of al-Jawf, and terminated around the town of Mada'in Salih. (Both al-Jawf and Mada'in Salih are located in the northwest of present-day Saudi Arabia.) The southern boundary followed a line stretching southeast from Rafah (on the present-day Gaza-Egypt border) through Aqaba (a port city in the south of present-day Jordan) until it met the eastern boundary in the proximity of Mada'in Salih.

Several aspects of Article 1 are significant. In its opening sentence, the article calls for "absolutely complete independence for Syria." Thus, in this article the General Syrian Congress rejected mandatory control. Moreover, by calling for "absolutely complete independence for Syria," this article rebuffed those, including Husayn and Faisal, who would have preferred an Arab state over a Syrian state. Indeed, the boundaries were deliberately drawn to sever the Syrian state from the Hejaz and from Iraq. In spite of the artificiality of Syria's "natural" boundaries, the victory of the Syrianist bloc over the Arabist bloc in the congress indicated that most delegates found a Syrian identity more compelling than an Arab one. While there were immediate political reasons for delegates to favor severing national

bonds with the Hejaz and Iraq (including resentment over the preeminent role played by Hejazis and Iraqis in the Damascus administration), a number of factors—migratory patterns, marriage alliances, economic exchange, and infrastructural development—had combined to make a Syrian identity plausible, while Syrian nationalists had acted to make it accepted.

◆ Article 2

Article 2 lays out the structure of the future Syrian state. It calls for the establishment of a decentralized constitutional monarchy that would safeguard the rights of minorities. It also nominated Faisal to serve as the first king of Syria, arguing that he merited the position because of his wartime service.

While the first article reflected a clear victory for the Syrianists over the Arabists, Article 2 represented a compromise between the two camps. On the one hand, it strongly limited the power of the monarch by compelling him to abide by constitutional strictures and by insisting upon local checks to decision making. These stipulations were undoubtedly the work of the Syrianist bloc, which distrusted the intentions of Faisal and his father. On the other hand, the Arabist bloc achieved its own success with the selection of Faisal as first king of Syria. Placing Syrian independence in the context of the Arab Revolt represented another victory for the Arabist bloc, integrating the Arab Revolt into the Syrian national narrative and proclaiming Faisal the liberator of Syria.

◆ Article 3

Article 3 protests the inclusion of Syria in the category of "Class A" mandates—that is, nations that were, according to the Covenant of the League of Nations, "inhabited by peoples not yet able to stand by themselves under the strenuous conditions of the modern world," whose independence could be "provisionally recognized" but whose complete independence had to be delayed to allow one or another "advanced nation" time to render them advice and assistance (Hurewitz, p. 179). Class A mandates occupied an intermediate space between nations worthy of independence and such territories as most of Africa and Micronesia, whose independence was indefinitely postponed. The article lists people of other nationalities—Bulgarians, Serbians, Greeks, and Romanians—who, like the Syrians, had once been subject peoples of the Ottoman Empire but who had been no more advanced at the time of their independence than Syrians were in 1919.

◆ Articles 4–6

Backtracking somewhat from the demand for complete and immediate independence for Syria articulated in Article 1, Articles 4–6 corresponded more closely to the more pragmatic views of the Arabist bloc than to those of the Syrianist bloc. Acknowledging that the League of Nations might not acquiesce to the demand for immediate independence, these articles sought to define the conditions under which mandate status would be acceptable and to

British army colonel T. E. Lawrence, who led the Arab revolt (AP/Wide World Photos)

identify a suitable mandatory power. Citing the position of President Wilson that the United States joined the war effort to end "conquest and colonization," Article 4 limited the role of any mandatory power to providing economic and technical assistance, which in no way would affect Syrian independence adversely.

That the General Syrian Congress would attempt to provide its own definition of the role of the mandatory power and the status of the mandate underscored the novelty of the mandates system. That system emerged as a compromise between the British and the French positions on the one hand and the American position on the other. The British and the French wanted the peace conference to put its imprimatur on imperial rule over less-developed areas; the Americans demanded an open door to those areas and the abolition of imperial trade preferences, a position that was inconsistent with British and French imperial policies. While the mandatory power would have enhanced access to and influence upon its mandates, the special access and influence were to be temporary, and all nations were to have equal rights in the mandates' markets.

Articles 4–6 also identify the United States and, if the United States refused, Great Britain as possible mandatory powers for Syria, rejecting the idea of a French mandate. While Article 4 cites the American reputation for anticolonialism, historians have attributed the appeal of an American mandate to a number of other causes as well, including President Wilson's renown in the region, the disinterest of the United States and its disinclination to project its power into a region that had been of little concern to it, and a misreading of the American colonial experience in the Philippines, which Syrians believed to have been more benign than it actually was. Even so, Article 4 limited an American mandate to twenty years. Great Britain was popular with the Arabist bloc because of its wartime support for the Arab Revolt (from whose ranks the Arab administration drew much of its personnel) and for a postwar Arab state or states. As opposed to the United States, Great Britain had a long history in the region and had periodically offered support to national movements seeking independence from the Ottoman Empire. France also had a long history in the region but had too close a relationship to Syria's Christians (particularly Maronite Christians) to satisfy many non-Christians in Syria, and France was sympathetic to the establishment of a separate Christian enclave on the Syrian coast. In addition, French missionary activity in the region had given France a reputation for being anti-Muslim. Finally, many Syrians feared that once it was established in Syria, France would never relinquish control because of its economic interests there.

◆ **Articles 7, 8, and 10**

Articles 7, 8, and 10 address threats to Syrian unity posed by Zionism (Articles 7 and 10) and by the possible detachment of the Syrian littoral (Lebanon) and southern Syria (Palestine) from Greater Syria (Articles 8 and 10). These articles once again enunciate a fundamental plank of the platform of the Syrianist bloc. Article 7 protests Zionist plans to establish a separate Jewish commonwealth in Palestine and Zionist immigration to any part of Syria, citing the national, economic, and political threat posed to Syria by Zionism. The article differentiates between Zionists, who were devoted to the partition of Syria, and Syrian Jews, who would enjoy the rights and obligations of citizenship in common with other Syrians after independence. By making this distinction, the article affirms that the opposition of the congress to Zionism rested on political, not religious, grounds.

Article 10 makes the argument against Zionism and partition from a different angle, citing President Wilson's oft-repeated condemnation of secret treaties secretly arrived at. While the British pledge to the Zionists had, in fact, been made publicly, the 1916 Sykes-Picot Agreement had been secret. This agreement would have divided Syria and much of the Middle East into zones of direct and indirect British and French control and would have established an international zone of Jerusalem. When the Bolsheviks took power in Russia in 1917, they published the secret treaties and agreements to which the czarist government had been party. Article 10 demands the annulment of those treaties and agreements.

◆ **Article 9**

Clearly the work of the Syrianist bloc, Article 9 requests that Mesopotamia also receive "complete independence" and that no economic barriers be established obstructing trade between Syria and Mesopotamia. During the war the British had occupied Mesopotamia, whose name originally referred to the territory between the Tigris and Euphrates rivers but subsequently referred to the larger territory roughly coincident with present-day Iraq. The Syrianist position of separating the two countries was supported by economic realities. During the nineteenth century the interregional caravan trade between Syria and Mesopotamia collapsed, though international trade increased as a result of the invention of steamships and the opening of the Suez Canal. Thereafter the international trade of Syria oriented west toward the Mediterranean, while that of Mesopotamia oriented south toward the Persian Gulf. Ironically, then, by the time this article was written, trade between the two regions had virtually disappeared. It is ironic as well that after the French established their mandate over Syria and Faisal was forced to flee Damascus, the British found a throne for him as the first king of Iraq.

The resolution concludes with three paragraphs. The first addresses what had become an American commission of inquiry and affirms the congress's confidence that its demands, rooted in Wilsonian principles, would be met and that President Wilson and the American people would demonstrate their compassion for weaker nations and the Arab world by assisting in their achievement. In the second paragraph, the congress reminded the representatives to the peace conference that Syrians had not rebelled against the Ottoman Empire because they had been denied civil, political, or representational rights in the empire; rather, they had rebelled because they were denied rights as a

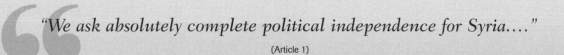

> *"We ask absolutely complete political independence for Syria...."*
>
> (Article 1)

> *"We ask that the Government of this Syrian country should be a democratic civil constitutional Monarchy on broad decentralization principles, safeguarding the rights of minorities, and that the King be the Emir Feisal, who carried on a glorious struggle in the cause of our liberation and merited our full confidence and entire reliance."*
>
> (Article 2)

> *"Considering the fact that the Arabs inhabiting the Syrian area are not naturally less gifted than other more advanced races and that they are by no means less developed than the Bulgarians, Serbians, Greeks, and Roumanians at the beginning of their independence, we protest against Article 22 of the Covenant of the League of Nations, placing as among the nations in their middle stage of development which stand in need of a mandatory power."*
>
> (Article 3)

> *"We do not acknowledge any right claimed by the French Government in any part whatever of our Syrian country and refuse that she should assist us or have a hand in our country under any circumstances and in any place."*
>
> (Article 6)

nation. The paragraph argues that after Syrians had shed so much blood for their independence, it was incumbent on the representatives to the peace conference not to leave them with fewer political rights than they had enjoyed before the war. The resolution concludes by requesting permission to send a delegation to the peace conference to ensure that Syrians rights would not be denied and to secure Syrian independence.

Audience

The General Syrian Congress directed the resolution at the commission of inquiry (the King-Crane Commission) that was visiting Greater Syria at the time of its drafting and, more broadly, at the Paris Peace Conference. By agreeing to the charter of the League of Nations, the representatives to that conference committed themselves to the proposition that the wishes of former subjects of empires defeated in the war would be paramount in determining the political future of those populations. The General Syrian Congress sought to hold the representatives to that proposition. After the congress adopted the resolution, the commission of inquiry received from Syrians 1,047 petitions that repeated the text of the resolution word for word. These petitions represented more than 56 percent of the total number of petitions submitted to the commission.

There was a second audience for the resolution as well. After the resolution was passed by the congress, a variety of nationalist organizations distributed copies of it throughout the territory of Greater Syria. For those associated with the Syrianist position in particular, the purpose of the resolution was not just to demonstrate the aspirations of Syrians but to shape those aspirations.

Impact

The resolution of the General Syrian Congress had no impact on the deliberations in Paris. Great Britain and France divided the territory of Greater Syria between them as mandates. As the mandatory power administering Palestine, Great Britain, for the time being, continued its support for the establishment of a Jewish national home there.

In Syria, however, the events leading up to the resolution had two effects. First, with the announcement of the commission of inquiry, the convening of the congress, and the debate over the resolution, nationalist groups successfully rallied the population that was politically engaged around the Syrianist position. Within several months, the slogan "We demand complete independence for Syria within its natural boundaries, no protection, no tutelage, no mandate" became virtually ubiquitous in nationalist rhetoric, while support for the promised "Arab state or states" evaporated. The second effect was the unprecedented mobilization of the population. This was first done by the Arab administration of Faisal, which brought the population of Damascus and other cities into the streets to display to the commission of inquiry the popular will in action and to create that popular will. Soon after, nationalist groups representing the Syrianist view also took to the streets and

began organizing mass-based political associations and popular militias. The mobilizing activities of these associations and militias led directly to the proclamation of Syrian independence in March 1920 and ultimately to the French invasion of inland Syria in July 1920.

Further Reading

■ **Books**

Fromkin, David. *A Peace to End All Peace: The Fall of the Ottoman Empire and the Creation of the Modern Middle East.* New York: Holt, 2009.

Gelvin, James L. *Divided Loyalties: Nationalism and Mass Politics in Syria at the Close of Empire.* Berkeley: University of California Press, 1998.

———. "The Ironic Legacy of the King-Crane Commission." In *The Middle East and the United States: A Historical and Political Reassessment*, 4th ed., ed. David W. Lesch. Boulder, Colo.: Westview Press, 2007.

Hurewitz, J. C. *The Middle East and North Africa in World Politics: A Documentary Record.* Vol. 2: *British-French Supremacy, 1914–1945.* New Haven, Conn.: Yale University Press, 1979.

Khoury, Philip S. *Syria and the French Mandate: The Politics of Arab Nationalism, 1920–1945.* Princeton, N.J.: Princeton University Press, 1987.

Questions for Further Study

1. What impact did World War I have on empires in Europe, central Asia, and the Middle East? How did the outcome of that war change the map of these areas? Why did the war have such an effect?

2. Read this entry and document in conjunction with the Balfour Declaration and Palestinian National Charter. How do these documents reflect similar aspirations on the part of countries in the Middle East? How do these documents articulate goals that have resulted in conflict and war?

3. How does the Syrian Congress Resolution represent the conflict between nationality and ethnicity? Which concern was the strongest and why?

4. Describe the "mandate" system that was in effect after World War I. What role did the mandate system play in the Middle East? What were the motives behind the mandate system? What arguments could be made in favor of the mandate system (under the conditions of the time), and what arguments could be made that it simply led to Western meddling in Middle Eastern affairs?

5. The Syrian Congress opposed both Zionism, or Jewish aspirations for a Middle East homeland, and the French because of their backing of Catholicism in the region. Why do you believe the Congress regarded these religions as a threat?

Link, Arthur S. *The Papers of Woodrow Wilson*. Vol. 45: *November 11, 1914–January 15, 1918*. Princeton, N.J.: Princeton University Press, 1984.

Russell, Malcolm B. *The First Modern Arab State: Syria under Faysal, 1918–1920*. Minneapolis, Minn.: Bibliotheca Islamica, 1985.

■ **Web Sites**

"The King-Crane Commission Report, August 28, 1919." Hellenic Resources Network Web site.
　　http://www.hri.org/docs/king-crane/.

United States Department of State. Papers Relating to the Foreign Relations of the United States: The Paris Peace Conference—1919. University of Wisconsin Digital Collections Web site.
　　http://digital.library.wisc.edu/1711.dl/FRUS.FRUS1919 Parisv01.

　　—James L. Gelvin

Milestone Documents

RESOLUTION OF THE GENERAL SYRIAN CONGRESS

We the undersigned members of the General Syrian Congress, meeting in Damascus on Wednesday, July 2nd, 1919, made up of representatives from the three Zones, viz., the Southern, Eastern, and Western, provided with credentials and authorizations by the inhabitants of our various districts, Moslems, Christians, and Jews have agreed upon the following statement of the desires of the people of the country who have elected us to present them to the American Section of the International Commission: the fifth article was passed by a very large majority; all the other articles were accepted unanimously.

1. We ask absolutely complete political independence for Syria within these boundaries. The Taurus System on the North; Rafah and a line running from Al Jauf to the south of the Syrian and the Hejazian line to Akaba on the south; the Euphrates and Khabur Rivers and a line extending east of Abu Kamal to the east of Al Jauf on the east; and the Mediterranean on the west.

2. We ask that the Government of this Syrian country should be a democratic civil constitutional Monarchy on broad decentralization principles, safeguarding the rights of minorities, and that the King be the Emir Feisal [Faisal], who carried on a glorious struggle in the cause of our liberation and merited our full confidence and entire reliance.

3. Considering the fact that the Arabs inhabiting the Syrian area are not naturally less gifted than other more advanced races and that they are by no means less developed than the Bulgarians, Serbians, Greeks, and Roumanians at the beginning of their independence, we protest against Article 22 of the Covenant of the League of Nations, placing us among the nations in their middle stage of development which stand in need of a mandatory power.

4. In the event of the rejection by the Peace Conference of this just protest for certain considerations that we may not understand, we, relying on the declarations of President Wilson that his object in waging war was to put an end to the ambition of conquest and colonization, can only regard the mandate mentioned in the Covenant of the League of Nations as equivalent to the rendering of economical and technical assistance that does not prejudice our complete independence. And desiring that our country should not fall a prey to colonization and believing that the American Nation is farthest from any thought of colonization and has no political ambition in our country, we will seek the technical and economical assistance from the United States of America, provided that such assistance does not exceed 20 years.

5. In the event of America not finding herself in a position to accept our desire for assistance, we will seek this assistance from Great Britain, also provided that such assistance does not infringe the complete independence and unity of our country and that the duration of such assistance does not exceed that mentioned in the previous article.

6. We do not acknowledge any right claimed by the French Government in any part whatever of our Syrian country and refuse that she should assist us or have a hand in our country under any circumstances and in any place.

7. We oppose the pretentions of the Zionists to create a Jewish commonwealth in the southern part of Syria, known as Palestine, and oppose Zionist migration to any part of our country; for we do not acknowledge their title but consider them a grave peril to our people from the national, economical, and political points of view. Our Jewish compatriots shall enjoy our common rights and assume the common responsibilities.

8. We ask that there should be no separation of the southern part of Syria, known as Palestine, nor of the littoral western zone, which includes Lebanon, from the Syrian country. We desire that the unity of the country should be guaranteed against partition under whatever circumstances.

9. We ask complete independence for emancipated Mesopotamia and that there should be no economical barriers between the two countries.

10. The fundamental principles laid down by President Wilson in condemnation of secret treaties impel us to protest most emphatically against any treaty that stipulates the partition of our Syria country and against any private engagement aiming at the establishment of Zionism in the southern part of Syria; therefore we ask the complete annulment of these conventions and agreements.

The noble principles enunciated by President Wilson strengthen our confidence that our desires emanating from the depths of our hearts, shall be the decisive factor in determining our future; and that President Wilson and the free American people will be our supporters for the realization of our hopes, thereby proving their sincerity and noble sympathy with the aspiration of the weaker nations in general and our Arab people in particular.

We also have the fullest confidence that the Peace Conference will realize that we would not have risen against the Turks, with whom we had partici-pated in all civil, political, and representative privileges, but for their violation of our national rights, and so will grant us our desires in full in order that our political rights may not be less after the war than they were before, since we have shed so much blood in the cause of our liberty and independence.

We request to the allowed to send a delegation to represent us at the Peace Conference to defend our rights and secure the realization of our aspirations.

Glossary

decentralization principles	conventions supporting the removal of power from a single national authority in favor of regional and local authorities
littoral	near a shore (here, the coast of the Mediterranean Sea)
mandatory power	power assumed by a country that had received a commission from the League of Nations to set up a government in a conquered territory

GOVERNMENT OF INDIA ACT

"The Governor-General may certify that the passage of [a] Bill is essential for the safety, tranquillity or interests of British India."

Overview

The Government of India Act of 1919 was the latest in a series of acts passed by the British parliament to define the structure of government and administration in Great Britain's chief colony, India. A total of sixteen other "Government of India" acts were passed by Parliament. The chief purpose of the 1919 act was to allow the people of India greater participation in their own government. Toward this end, it created a dyarchy, or a dual form of government, in India's provinces, with power shared by the Crown and local authorities. The act relinquished to provincial councils Britain's control of some areas of government, such as agriculture, education, and health, while other areas of government, such as foreign policy, justice, communications, and the military, remained under the authority of Great Britain through its appointed viceroy of India. The act also enlarged and reformed the Imperial Legislative Council, transforming it into a bicameral (two-house) legislature. Both the lower house, called the Legislative Assembly, and the upper house, called the Council of States, would consist of elected and appointed members. The 1919 legislation served to enact reforms that had been suggested by Edwin Montagu, the secretary of state for India, and Frederic Thesiger, Lord Chelmsford, the viceroy of India, in the wake of growing dissatisfaction with British rule and a blossoming independence movement in India.

Context

The context for the 1919 Government of India Act stretches back to the early years of the seventeenth century, when Queen Elizabeth I chartered the British East India Company and granted it perpetual trading rights in India. Throughout the seventeenth and eighteenth centuries, the East India Company drove out its French competitors, eclipsed its Dutch competitors, and defeated Bengalese forces that were allied with the French. When the dust settled, the East India Company had consolidated its hold on India and was the de facto ruler of some two-thirds of the nation. It carried on lucrative trade in such commodities as silk, cotton, indigo dye, tea, saltpeter, and opium, in large part by striking alliances with local rulers.

In the late eighteenth and early nineteenth centuries, however, charges of corruption, bribery, and abuse were leveled against the East India Company, causing Parliament to pass legislation designed to rein in the company's activities. Despite these attempts at reform, discontent with British rule in India simmered for years. It boiled over in 1857 when the sepoys, or Indian soldiers serving under the British, revolted in what is variously called the Sepoy Mutiny (or Sepoy Rebellion), the Great Rebellion, or, among Indians, the First War of Indian Independence. Indians believed that British rule was heavy-handed. If, for example, a landowner died without a male heir, his property reverted to the British Crown. Traditional customs, such as suttee, the act of a widow's immolating herself on her dead husband's grave, were forbidden. Local rulers had been eliminated, and Indians sensed that the British wanted to westernize them and convert them to Christianity. The revolt erupted on May 10, 1857, among sepoys stationed near Bengal, and soon sepoy garrisons at several other cities, notably Delhi and Kanpur, mutinied, in some instances with the backing of civilians. Over the following year, British forces regrouped, gained control of the cities where sepoys had revolted, and reasserted the authority of the East India Company, finally quashing the revolt on June 20, 1858. The conflict was bloody, and British forces felt justified in retaliating. Entire villages were wiped out, and mutineers were put to death.

In the aftermath of the Sepoy Rebellion, Britain abolished the East India Company and made efforts to create more of a cooperative relationship with Indians. The army was restructured to include more Indians, and no efforts were made to impose Christianity on Indians or to interfere further with traditional religious beliefs and social practices. The British created a complex governmental and administrative structure that came to be called the British Raj—a Hindustani word meaning "reign." A secretary of state for India and a Council of India oversaw the administration of the colony. India was governed by a viceroy, but other governmental officials oversaw affairs in India's various regions with the help of Indian officials who served in

1858

- **August 2**
  The British parliament passes the Government of India Act of 1858, which abolishes the East India Company.

1876

- **May 1**
  "Empress of India" is added to Queen Victoria's titles.

1885

- The Indian National Congress, a political party, is formed.

1892

- **June 20**
  The Indian Councils Act gives Indians more voice in government.

1904

- **March 21**
  The Indian Universities Act gives Britain control of India's institutions of higher education.

1905

- **October 16**
  The Indian province of Bengal is partitioned.

1909

- **February**
  The Indian Councils Act of 1909, based on reforms suggested by John Morley and the Earl of Minto, increases Indian political representation.

an advisory capacity. Additionally, a number of so-called princely states were recognized. These were smaller regions in India that remained under the rule of Indian princes, though the princes were answerable to the viceroy. Meanwhile, the Indian economy developed rapidly as the British built an economic infrastructure, including schools, irrigation projects, and roads. In 1876, England's Queen Victoria was given the title of empress of India.

Britain at this point had no intention of relinquishing control of India. The colony provided valuable raw materials and an export market for British-made goods. It also supplied manpower that enabled the newly industrialized Great Britain to project its power throughout Asia and to protect British access to Asia through the Middle East. Nevertheless, concessions were made. The Indian Councils Act of 1892 allowed Indians a voice in provincial legislation. Matters began to turn sour, though, in 1895, when the British imposed an excise tax on Indian cotton, enriching Britain at India's expense. Then in 1899, George Curzon became India's viceroy. Curzon would unwittingly foment growing dissatisfaction through two measures.

The first of these measures was the Indian Universities Act of 1904, which gave Britain control over all Indian colleges and universities. This step dismayed India's emerging middle class, which valued the nation's educational institutions and wished to leave them in Indian hands. The other measure was enacted in 1905, when Curzon partitioned Bengal into two provinces in an effort to curb the political activism—and acts of terrorism—there. The British regarded one of the new provinces, East Bengal, as more backward and less developed than the other new province, Assam. Because East Bengal was largely Muslim, it could function as a counterweight to Assam's political activism. The results of Curzon's arbitrary and heavy-handed decision were demonstrations and a boycott of goods manufactured in Britain, particularly in England's cotton mills. More significant, the viceroy's actions started to turn the Indian National Congress, a political party established in 1885, into a nationalist movement. One of the chief figures in that movement was a young Mohandas Karamchand Gandhi, who would become a worldwide symbol of nonviolent resistance to colonial rule.

In an effort to solve the crisis, the Crown replaced Curzon. After discussions in 1909 Parliament passed another Indian Councils Act, which is also referred to as the Morley-Minto reforms after its authors, John Morley, the secretary of state for India, and Gilbert Elliot-Murray-Kynynmond, Fourth Earl of Minto, India's governor-general. This act provided for Indian membership in provincial executive councils and enlarged the Imperial Legislative Council to give Indians greater political representation. In 1911 the partition of Bengal was reversed, and recommendations were made to increase Indians' participation in government and the military. World War I put issues of Anglo-Indian cooperation on hold, but the war also increased calls for greater independence. India made major contributions to the war effort, including monetary contributions of millions of pounds and the lives of some forty thousand soldiers who fought and died for Britain. Meanwhile, in 1917, the Indian people observed the overthrow of the monarchy in Russia with interest, and after the war's conclusion they saw the U.S. president Woodrow Wilson's Fourteen Points, outlined in January 1918, as holding out hope for self-government and an end to colonialism (particularly in the fifth point).

Throughout the war and afterward, political unrest in India grew. Militant activists in Bengal and Punjab backed insurrections and brought the provincial governments to a standstill. As conspiracies came to light, Britain passed the Defence of India Act in 1915 in an effort to curb revolutionary activities. In 1918 a sedition committee, chaired by Sydney Rowlatt, was formed to investigate possible links between Indian militants on the one hand and both German and Russian revolutionaries on the other; one such link came to be called the Hindu-German Conspiracy. Out of these investigations came the Rowlatt Act, passed in March 1919. The purpose of this repressive act was to strengthen and extend the Defence of India Act by exposing conspiracies and quelling civil unrest, which was being fomented by a combination of inflation, high taxes, a devastating flu epidemic, and disruption of trade because of the war. Unrest led to violence in the northern Indian city of Amritsar, which had been placed under martial law as a result of bombings, arson, and protest. On April 13, 1919, British troops opened fire on a religious gathering, according to official British estimates killing some 379 people and wounding 1,100 others in what has been called the Amritsar Massacre or, after the name of the park where it occurred, the Jallianwala Bagh Massacre. Indian authorities put the casualty figures much higher.

In light of these events, the new secretary of state for India, Edwin Montagu, acknowledged that Britain was in India's debt. Earlier, in August 1917, he had signaled a change in British policy in a declaration before the House of Commons:

> The policy of His Majesty's Government, with which the Government of India are in complete accord, is that of the increasing association of Indians in every branch of the administration and the gradual development of self-governing institutions with a view to the progressive realization of responsible government in India, as an integral part of the British Empire. (qtd. in Alam, p. 48)

He collaborated with India's viceroy, Lord Chelmsford, and in 1918 the two issued the Montagu-Chelmsford Report, which was submitted to Parliament in May 1918 and again in June of that year. Their recommendations formed the basis of the Government of India Act passed into law in December 1919.

About the Author

As with most legislation, identifying a particular author is difficult, for any bill is likely to be the work of numerous

Time Line

1915

- **March 18**
  The Defence of India Act is passed to curb revolutionary activity.

1917

- **August 20**
  Edwin Montagu makes a declaration in the House of Commons announcing a change in British policy in India.

1918

- **May 24**
  Cosponsored by Frederic Thesiger, Lord Chelmsford, viceroy of India, the Montagu-Chelmsford Report is submitted to Parliament; it is submitted again on June 7.

1919

- **April 13**
  Hundreds of Indians are killed and wounded in the Amritsar Massacre.

- **December 23**
  The Government of India Act of 1919 is passed to enact the Montagu-Chelmsford reforms.

1935

- **August**
  The Government of India Act of 1935 grants complete provincial authority to Indians.

1947

- **August 15**
  The independent Republic of India is created.

John Morley (Library of Congress)

legislators. Further, because the Government of India Act of 1919 was in large part an amendment of earlier acts of Parliament, it contains provisions written by the authors of those earlier acts. Nonetheless, two authors stand out, for the bill essentially enacted the reforms suggested by Edwin Montagu, the secretary of state for India, and Lord Chelmsford, India's viceroy at the time. Their conclusions were presented to the British Parliament as the Montagu-Chelmsford Report, which formed the core of the 1919 act.

Edwin Samuel Montagu, only the second Jew ever to serve in the British cabinet, was born in 1879. He entered politics in 1906, when he was elected to a seat in Parliament. In the years that followed he served in a variety of government posts, including undersecretary of state for India from 1910 to 1914. In 1917 he was appointed secretary of state for India, a post he held until 1922. Montagu died in 1924.

Lord Chelmsford was Frederic John Napier Thesiger, 3rd Baron Chelmsford; he was elevated to the position of 1st Viscount Chelmsford in 1921. He was born in 1868. After completing his education at Oxford University and succeeding his father as Baron Chelmsford, he was appointed governor first of Queensland, Australia, and then of neighboring New South Wales. During World War I he commanded a regiment in India, and he was appointed viceroy of India in 1916, a post he held until 1921. His service in India coincided with massive unrest and the Amritsar Massacre, and he returned to England amid

charges of incompetence. He spent the last years of his life retired from politics before his death in 1933.

Explanation and Analysis of the Document

In 1915 the British parliament passed yet another act called the Government of India Act. The purpose of the 1915 act was to consolidate into one set of laws all earlier legislation concerning the government of India. That set of laws was amended by the Government of India Act of 1916. The 1919 legislation, in turn, was in large part a further amendment to the 1915 act. Throughout the 1919 act, the 1915 act, as amended by the 1916 act, is referred to as the "principal Act."

◆ Preamble

The act's preamble seems almost grudgingly to acknowledge the need "for the increasing association of Indians in every branch of Indian administration, and for the gradual development of self-governing institutions." Despite this acknowledgment, the act states that Indian self-government can be achieved only in "successive stages" and asserts that "the welfare and advancement of the Indian peoples" lies with Parliament.

◆ Part I

Part I of the act amounts to the definition of terms. The chief point made in section 1 is the division between two types of concerns, central and provincial. "Central subjects" refers to those matters directly administered by the government of India whereby interests across the borders of provinces are predominant. "Provincial subjects" refers to matters in which individual provincial interests are predominant. Reference is also made to the governor-general, a title used in combination with viceroy to designate the Crown-appointed governor of India, and to the Council, meaning the governor-general's advisory Council of India. "Transferred subjects" are those matters being turned over to the provincial governments, while "reserved subjects" are those that would remain under the control of the governor-general. This division of provincial and central functions constituted the essence of the dyarchy formed by the act.

Section 1 goes on to specify legalities associated with the "devolution of authority" down to the provinces. In particular, it outlines how matters of taxation, funding, salaries, and the like are to be handled. But section 1 also makes clear that the act is in no wise turning India over to the Indians. It states that "the rules shall not authorise the revocation or suspension of the transfer of any subject except with the sanction of the Secretary of State in Council." It further states that "the Governor-General in Council shall be the sole judge as to whether the purpose of the exercise of such powers in any particular case comes within the purposes so specified." Section 3 specifies which provinces in India will remain under the control of British-appointed governors, called "governor's provinces." "United Provinces" refers to the United Provinces of Agra and Oudh, in northern India.

The shell-pocked Kashmir Gate in the northern wall of Delhi stands unrestored a hundred years after the end of the mutiny of the sepoys. (AP/Wide World Photos)

Section 4 goes on to state that "in relation to transferred subjects, the governor shall be guided by the advice of his ministers, unless he sees sufficient cause to dissent from their opinion, in which case he may require action to be taken otherwise than in accordance with that advice." Put simply, the power to devolve authority down to the provinces remained in the hands of British authorities.

Transfer of some authority is accomplished in section 10: "The local legislature of any province has power, subject to the provisions of this Act, to make laws for the peace and good government of the territories for the time being constituting that province." Later, in a table appended to the act, the memberships of the local legislative councils are established. The largest was the province of Bengal, with 125 members, followed by Madras and the United Provinces, each with 118, and Bombay, with 111. Additionally, Bihar and Orissa would have 98, Punjab 83, the Central Provinces 70, and Assam 53.

Section 10 continues by specifying those areas in which local legislators cannot make laws. Among such restricted areas are the bodies of law related to taxation, customs duties, the public debt, the military, and foreign affairs. Addi-

tionally, emergency powers are reserved to the governor-general. Provisions are then made for the procedures to be followed for the enactment of laws by Indian legislatures. Interestingly, section 15 notes that the act does not apply to any portion of India that the governor-general deems a "backward tract." This provision gave the governor-general broad powers to retain control over areas regarded as recalcitrant.

◆ **Part II**

Part II turns to the nuts and bolts of the national Indian government. It creates a bicameral legislature consisting of a Council of State and a Legislative Assembly. The Council of State is to consist of no more than sixty members, some of whom would be elected and some appointed. The Legislative Assembly is to consist of one hundred elected members and forty appointed members; the act outlines the duties of the assembly's president and deputy president and includes provisions relating to membership in the assembly. The governor-general would retain a hand in the deliberations and actions of the assembly, for, as noted in section 22, "every member of the Governor-General's Executive Council shall be nominated as a member of one chamber of the Indian legislature." Section 26 goes on to say that if either chamber of the Indian legislature refuses to introduce or pass bills in a form the governor-general recommends, "the Governor-General may certify that the passage of the Bill is essential for the safety, tranquillity or interests of British India." Finally, section 26 specifies that any bill passed by the Indian legislature must be submitted to the British parliament.

◆ Part III

Sections 31–35 of the act consist primarily of legalities as they pertain to the Council of India. Again, the 1919 act consists largely of amendments to the earlier "principal Act" of 1915 as amended in 1916. The 1919 act, then, specifies such matters as the terms of office of the Council of India, the members' salaries, eligibility for membership on the council, the powers of the council and of the secretary of state for India, and procedures to be followed by the council and Parliament for the enactment of the council's orders.

◆ Part IV

Part IV turns to the civil services. The civil service was already an important part of the Raj and would continue to be so after 1919. Attention had been paid to the civil service as early as 1886, when the Aitchison Commission was set up to address Indian demands for more extensive participation in the civil service at higher levels. Then, in 1912, the Royal Commission on the Public Services of India—often called the Islington Commission after the name of its chair, John Dickson-Poynder, Lord Islington—was formed to make further recommendations. In its report, issued in 1915, the commission called for appointments to high-level posts to be made in both England and India and recommended that a quarter of the highest posts should be filled by Indians. Because of World War I, however, no action was taken on the Islington Commission's report.

Section 36 begins by noting that any Indian who serves in the civil service does so "during His Majesty's pleasure" (the king of England at the time was George V—until that time the only British monarch who had ever visited India, in 1911). Again, this part of the act deals with legalities. It specifies conditions under which people could be dismissed from the civil service, but it also specifies how they could be reinstated. It vests in the secretary of state for India and the Council of India the power to determine the "rules for regulating the classification of the civil services in India, the methods of their recruitment, their conditions of service, pay and allowances, and discipline and conduct." Part IV goes on to address such issues as compensation and pensions.

Audience

The principal audience for the Government of India Act of 1919 was, of course, the Indian people. In the wake of growing civil unrest, agitation for independence, and outbreaks of violence, the law was intended to give Indians a greater role in their own governance with a view to India's eventually achieving dominion status. Such status would have made India similar to Canada and Australia, which were self-governing under the British monarch as head of state. This status was often referred to by the phrase "responsible government," referring to the principle of parliamentary accountability. It was hoped that the 1919 act would appease the nationalist movement and restore peace to the colony. In this respect, a major component of the audience was the Indian National Congress, a political party formed in 1885 whose goal was Indian independence.

Another audience was the British people, many of whom were appalled by events in India, particularly the Amritsar Massacre. The massacre was condemned worldwide, and in 1920 a commission that investigated the matter exposed the extraordinary callousness of the British commander, General Reginald Dyer. In the House of Commons, Winston Churchill stated, "It is an extraordinary event, a monstrous event, an event which stands in singular and sinister isolation" (qtd. in Farwell, p. 286). In this climate of unrest, the British public had to be reassured that their government had a handle on the situation in India and was willing to recognize Indian aspirations for self-rule.

Impact

The Indian National Congress expressed disappointment with the Government of India Act of 1919. Accordingly, under the leadership of Gandhi, agitation for independence continued. Gandhi was the leader of the "noncooperation movement," which urged Indians to refuse to pay taxes, to resign from government posts, to decline British honors and titles, and to boycott educational institutions and the court system. Throughout the 1920s numerous political parties calling for Indian independence emerged. Their activities culminated at a conference in Bombay in May 1928 that called for Indian resistance to British rule. Then in 1929, at a historic conference in Lahore, the Indian National Congress passed a resolution calling for complete independence from Britain.

The 1930s witnessed widespread civil disobedience. A key event was Gandhi's famous Salt March, which took place in March–April 1930 to protest British taxation on salt. Police and protesters clashed in Calcutta and Peshawar, and by the end of 1931 some one hundred thousand Indians had been arrested for various forms of civil disobedience. In 1935 Britain passed yet another Government of India Act, this one granting complete provincial authority to Indians. It was not enough, however. The nationalist "Quit India" movement continued to urge civil disobedience, and in 1946 the Royal Indian Navy mutinied. Finally, on August 15, 1947, the British colony was partitioned into India, primarily Hindu, and Pakistan, primarily Muslim, and both nations achieved complete independence.

The Government of India Act of 1919 was part of a mosaic of laws stretching back to the eighteenth century. The act was passed in the middle of an independence

"Concurrently with the gradual development of self-governing institutions in the Provinces of India it is expedient to give to those Provinces in provincial matters the largest measure of independence of the Government of India, which is compatible with the due discharge by the latter of its own responsibilities."

(Preamble)

"The powers of superintendence, direction, and control over local governments vested in the Governor-General in Council under the principal Act shall, in relation to transferred subjects, be exercised only for such purposes as may be specified in rules made under that Act, but the Governor-General in Council shall be the sole judge as to whether the purpose of the exercise of such powers in any particular case comes within the purposes so specified."

(Part I, Section 1)

"The local legislature of any province has power, subject to the provisions of this Act, to make laws for the peace and good government of the territories for the time being constituting that province."

(Part I, Section 10)

"Subject to the provisions of this Act, the Indian legislature shall consist of the Governor-General and two chambers, namely, the Council of State and the Legislative Assembly."

(Part II, Section 17)

"Where either chamber of the Indian legislature refuses leave to introduce, or fails to pass in a form recommended by the Governor-General, any Bill, the Governor-General may certify that the passage of the Bill is essential for the safety, tranquillity or interests of British India."

(Part II, Section 26)

movement that had its roots in the early to mid-nineteenth century, accelerated in the late nineteenth century, and crescendoed throughout the first half of the twentieth century. In one sense, the act had little impact. If it was designed to appease Indian nationalists, it failed signally, for true power remained vested in British hands, and that fact was obvious to Indian nationalist leaders. Nevertheless, the act served as a wedge, a crack in British authority.

It gave Indians a taste of government participation as well as forums in which they could express their aspirations. Less than three decades later, those aspirations would be realized. India today, with more than 1.1 billion people, remains the world's largest democratic nation.

Further Reading

■ Articles

Gallagher, John, and Anil Seal. "Britain and India between the Wars." *Modern Asian Studies* 15, no. 3 (1981): 387–414.

■ Books

Alam, Jawaid. *Government and Politics in Colonial Bihar, 1921–1937*. New Delhi: Mittal Publications, 2004.

Bayly, C. A. *Indian Society and the Making of the British Empire*. Cambridge, U.K.: Cambridge University Press, 1995.

Curtis, Lionel. *Papers Relating to the Application of the Principle of Dyarchy to the Government of India*. Oxford, U.K.: Clarendon Press, 1920.

Farwell, Byron. *Armies of the Raj: From the Mutiny to Independence, 1858–1947*. New York: Norton, 1991.

James, Lawrence. *Raj: The Making and Unmaking of British India*. New York: St. Martin's Press, 1998.

Kulke, Hermann, and Dietmar Rothermund. *A History of India*, 3rd ed. New York: Routledge, 1998.

Lawson, Philip. *The East India Company: A History*. London: Longman, 1993.

Metcalf, Thomas R. *The Aftermath of Revolt: India, 1857–1870*. Princeton, N.J.: Princeton University Press, 1964.

Moorhouse, Geoffrey. *India Britannica*. New York: Harper & Row, 1983.

Porter, Andrew, and Alaine M. Low, eds. *The Oxford History of the British Empire*, Vol. 3: *The Nineteenth Century*. Oxford, U.K.: Oxford University Press, 1999.

Ramunsack, Barbara. *The Indian Princes and Their States*. Cambridge, U.K.: Cambridge University Press, 2004.

Robb, Peter G. *The Government of India and Reform: Policies towards Politics and the Constitution, 1916–1921*. Oxford, U.K.: Oxford University Press, 1976.

Rothermund, Dietmar. *An Economic History of India: From Precolonial Times to 1986*. London: Croom Helm, 1988.

Wolpert, Stanley. *A New History of India*. 8th ed. New York: Oxford University Press, 2008.

—Michael J. O'Neal

Questions for Further Study

1. Using the British Regulating Act, Queen Victoria's Proclamation concerning India, and the Government of India Act, prepare a time line with the ten events you believe were most important in the evolution of India to an independent nation. Be prepared to justify your inclusion of each entry on the time line.

2. Why did the Government of India Act fail to satisfy the nationalist movement in India?

3. In the long term, did institutions such as those created by the Government of India Act contribute to a tradition of democratic government that survived in India? Explain.

4. Compare the independence movement in India with that of Algeria, which broke from France in 1954, as reflected in the events surrounding the Proclamation of the Algerian National Liberation Front. What were the motivations of the two countries' nationalists? How did the colonial powers—England and France—respond to independence movements in their colonies?

5. Another nation in England's sphere of influence, Ireland, fought for independence in the early twentieth century. Compare India's independence movement with Ireland's, as reflected in the Proclamation of the Provisional Government of the Irish Republic, which was issued just three years before the Government of India Act.

Government of India Act

Whereas it is the declared policy of Parliament to provide for the increasing association of Indians in every branch of Indian administration, and for the gradual development of self-governing institutions with a view to the progressive realisation of responsible government in British India as an integral part of the empire:

And whereas progress in giving effect to this policy can only be achieved by successive stages, and it is expedient that substantial steps in this direction should now be taken:

And whereas the time and manner of each advance can be determined only by Parliament, upon whom responsibility lies for the welfare and advancement of the Indian peoples:

And whereas the action of Parliament in such matters must be guided by the co-operation received from those on whom new opportunities of service will be conferred, and by the extent to which it is found that confidence can be reposed in their sense of responsibility:

And whereas concurrently with the gradual development of self-governing institutions in the Provinces of India it is expedient to give to those Provinces in provincial matters the largest measure of independence of the Government of India, which is compatible with the due discharge by the latter of its own responsibilities:

Be it therefore enacted by the King's most Excellent Majesty, by and with the advice and consent of the Lords Spiritual and Temporal, and Commons, in this present Parliament assembled, and by the authority of the same, as follows:—

Part I. Local Governments

1. (*1*) Provision may be made by rules under the Government of India Act, 1915, as amended by the Government of India (Amendment) Act, 1916 (which Act, as so amended, is in this Act referred to as "the principal Act")—

(*a*) for the classification of subjects, in relation to the functions of government, as central and provincial subjects, for the purpose of distinguishing the functions of local governments and local legislatures from the functions of the Governor-General in Council and the Indian legislature;

(*b*) for the devolution of authority in respect of provincial subjects to local governments, and for the allocation of revenues or other moneys to those governments;

(*c*) for the use under the authority of the Governor-General in Council of the agency of local governments in relation to central subjects, in so far as such agency may be found convenient, and for determining the financial conditions of such agency; and

(*d*) for the transfer from among the provincial subjects of subjects (in this Act referred to as "transferred subjects") to the administration of the governor acting with ministers appointed under this Act, and for the allocation of revenues or moneys for the purpose of such administration.

(2) Without prejudice to the generality of the foregoing powers, rules made for the abovementioned purposes may—

(*i*) regulate the extent and conditions of such devolution, allocation, and transfer;

(*ii*) provide for fixing the contributions payable by local governments to the Governor-General in Council, and making such contributions a first charge on allocated revenues or moneys;

(*iii*) provide for constituting a finance department in any province, and regulating the functions of that department;

(*iv*) provide for regulating the exercise of the authority vested in the local government of a province over members of the public services therein;

(*v*) provide for the settlement of doubts arising as to whether any matter does or does not relate to a provincial subject or a transferred subject, and for the treatment of matters which affect both a transferred subject and a subject which is not transferred; and

(*vi*) make such consequential and supplemental provisions as appear necessary or expedient:

Provided that, without prejudice to any general power of revoking or altering rules under the principal Act, the rules shall not authorise the revocation or suspension of the transfer of any subject except with the sanction of the Secretary of State in Council.

(3) The powers of superintendence, direction, and control over local governments vested in the Gover-

nor-General in Council under the principal Act shall, in relation to transferred subjects, be exercised only for such purposes as may be specified in rules made under that Act, but the Governor-General in Council shall be the sole judge as to whether the purpose of the exercise of such powers in any particular case comes within the purposes so specified.

(4) The expressions "central subjects" and "provincial subjects" as used in this Act mean subjects so classified under the rules.

Provincial subjects, other than transferred subjects, are in this Act referred to as "reserved subjects"...

3. (1) The presidencies of Fort William in Bengal, Fort St. George, and Bombay, and the provinces known as the United Provinces, the Punjab, Bihar and Orissa, the Central Provinces, and Assam, shall each be governed, in relation to reserved subjects, by a governor in council, and in relation to transferred subjects (save as otherwise provided by this Act) by the governor acting with ministers appointed under this Act.

The said presidencies and provinces are in this Act referred to as "governor's provinces" and the two first-named presidencies are in this Act referred to as the presidencies of Bengal and Madras.

(2) The provisions of section forty-six to fifty-one of the principal Act, as amended by this Act, shall apply to the United Provinces, the Punjab, Bihar and Orissa, the Central Provinces, and Assam, as they apply to the presidencies of Bengal, Madras, and Bombay: Provided that the governors of the said provinces shall be appointed after consultation with the Governor-General.

4. (1) The governor of a governor's province may, by notification, appoint ministers, not being members of his executive council or other officials, to administer transferred subjects and any ministers so appointed shall hold office during his pleasure.

There may be paid to any minister so appointed in any province the same salary as is payable to a member of the executive council in that province, unless a smaller salary is provided by vote of the legislative council of the province.

(2) No minister shall hold office for a longer period than six months, unless he is or becomes an elected member of the local legislature.

(3) In relation to transferred subjects, the governor shall be guided by the advice of his ministers, unless he sees sufficient cause to dissent from their opinion, in which case he may require action to be taken otherwise than in accordance with that advice:

Provided that rules may be made under the principal Act for the temporary administration of a transferred subject where, in cases of emergency, owing to a vacancy, there is no minister in charge of the subject, by such authority and in such manner as may be prescribed by the rules.

(4) The governor of a governor's province may at his discretion appoint from among the non-official members of the local legislature council secretaries who shall hold office during his pleasure, and discharge such duties in assisting members of the executive council and ministers, as he may assign to them.

There shall be paid to council secretaries so appointed such salary as may be provided by vote of the legislative council.

A council secretary shall cease to hold office if he ceases for more than six months to be a member of the legislative council....

10. (1) The local legislature of any province has power, subject to the provisions of this Act, to make laws for the peace and good government of the territories for the time being constituting that province.

(2) The local legislature of any province may, subject to the provisions of the sub-section next following, repeal or alter as to that province any law made either before or after the commencement of this Act by any authority in British India other than that local legislature.

(3) The local legislature of any province may not, without the previous sanction of the Governor-General, make or take into consideration any law—

(a) imposing or authorising the imposition of any new tax unless the tax is a tax scheduled as exempted from this provision by rules made under the principal Act; or

(b) affecting the public debt of India, or the customs duties, or any other tax or duty for the time being in force and imposed by the authority of the Governor-General in Council for the general purposes of the government of India, provided that the imposition or alteration of a tax scheduled as aforesaid shall not be deemed to affect any such tax or duty; or

(c) affecting the discipline or maintenance of any part of His Majesty's naval, military, or air forces; or

(d) affecting the relations of the government with foreign princes or states; or

(e) regulating any central subject; or

(f) regulating any provincial subject which has been declared by rules under the principal Act to be, either in whole or in part, subject to legislation by the Indian legislature, in respect of any matter to which such declaration applies; or (*g*) affecting any power expressly reserved to the Governor-General in Council by any law for the time being in force; or

(*h*) altering or repealing the provisions of any law which, having been made before the commencement of this Act by any authority in British India other than that local legislature, is declared by rules under the principal Act to be a law which cannot be repealed or altered by the local legislature without previous sanction; or

(*i*) altering or repealing any provision of an Act of the Indian legislature made after the commencement of this Act, which by the provisions of that Act may not be repealed or altered by the local legislature without previous sanction:

Provided that an Act or a provision of an Act made by a local legislature, and subsequently assented to by the Governor-General in pursuance of this Act, shall not be deemed invalid by reason only of its requiring the previous sanction of the Governor-General under this Act.

(*4*) The local legislature of any province has not power to make any law affecting any Act of Parliament....

13. (*1*) Where a governor's legislative council has refused leave to introduce, or has failed to pass in a form recommended by the governor, any Bill relating to a reserved subject the governor may certify that the passage of the Bill is essential for the discharge of his responsibility for the subject, and thereupon the Bill shall, notwithstanding that the council have not consented thereto, be deemed to have passed, and shall, on signature by the governor, become an Act of the local legislature in the form of the Bill as originally introduced or proposed to be introduced in the council or (as the case may be) in the form recommended to the council by the governor.

(*2*) Every such Act shall be expressed to be made by the governor, and the governor shall forthwith send an authentic copy thereof to the Governor-General, who shall reserve the Act for the signification of His Majesty's pleasure and upon the signification of such assent by His Majesty in Council, and the notification thereof by the Governor-General, the Act shall have the same force and effect as an Act passed by the local legislature and duly assented to:

Provided that where, in the opinion of the Governor-General a state of emergency exists which justifies such action, he may, instead of reserving such Act, signify his assent thereto, and thereupon the Act shall have such force and effect as aforesaid, subject however to disallowance by His Majesty in Council.

(*3*) An Act made under this section shall, as soon as practicable after being made, be laid before each House of Parliament, and an Act which is required to be presented for His Majesty's assent shall not be so presented until copies thereof have been laid before each House of Parliament for not less than eight days on which that House has sat....

15. (*1*) The Governor-General in Council may after obtaining an expression of opinion from the local government and the local legislature affected, by notification, with the sanction of His Majesty previously signified by the Secretary of State in Council, constitute a new governor's province, or place part of a governor's province under the administration of a deputy-governor to be appointed by the Governor-General, and may in any such case apply, with such modifications as appear necessary or desirable, all or any of the provisions of the principal Act or this Act relating to governors' provinces, or provinces under a lieutenant governor or chief commissioner, to any such new province or part of a province.

(*2*) The Governor-General in Council may declare any territory in British India to be a "backward tract," and may, by notification, with such sanction as aforesaid, direct that the principal Act and this Act shall apply to that territory subject to such exceptions and modifications as may be prescribed in the notification Where the Governor-General in Council has, by notification, directed as aforesaid, he may, by the same or subsequent notification, direct that any Act of the Indian legislature shall not apply to the territory in question or any part thereof, or shall apply to the territory or any part thereof subject to such exceptions or modifications as the Governor-General thinks fit, or may authorise the governor in council to give similar directions as respects any Act of the local legislature....

Part II. Government of India

17. Subject to the provisions of this Act, the Indian legislature shall consist of the Governor-General and two chambers, namely, the Council of State and the Legislative Assembly.

Except as otherwise provided by or under this Act, a Bill shall not be deemed to have been passed by the Indian legislature unless it has been agreed to by both chambers, either without amendment or with such amendments only as may be agreed to by both chambers.

18. (*1*) The Council of State shall consist of not more than sixty members nominated or elected in accordance with rules made under the principal Act, of whom not more than twenty shall be official members.

(2) The Governor-General shall have power to appoint, from among the members of the Council of State, a president and other persons to preside in such circumstances as he may direct.

(3) The Governor-General shall have the right of addressing the Council of State, and may for that purpose require the attendance of its members.

19. (*1*) The Legislative Assembly shall consist of members nominated or elected in accordance with rules made under the principal Act.

(2) The total number of members of the Legislative Assembly shall be one hundred and forty. The number of non-elected members shall be forty, of whom twenty-six shall be official members. The number of elected members shall be one hundred:

Provided that rules made under the principal Act may provide for increasing the number of members of the Legislative Assembly as fixed by this section, and may vary the proportion which the classes of members bear one to another, so, however, that at least five-sevenths of the members of the Legislative Assembly shall be elected members, and at least one-third of the other members shall be nonofficial members.

(3) The Governor-General shall have the right of addressing the Legislative Assembly, and may for that purpose require the attendance of its members.

20. (*1*) There shall be a president of the Legislative Assembly, who shall, until the expiration of four years from the first meeting thereof, be a person appointed by the Governor-General, and shall thereafter be a member of the Assembly elected by the Assembly and approved by the Governor-General:

Provided that, if at the expiration of such period of four years the Assembly is in session, the president then in office shall continue in office until the end of the current session, and the first election of a president shall take place at the commencement of the ensuing session.

(2) There shall be a deputy-president of the Legislative Assembly, who shall preside at meetings of the Assembly in the absence of the president, and who shall be a member of the Assembly elected by the Assembly and approved by the Governor-General.

(3) The appointed president shall hold office until the date of the election of a president under this section, but he may resign his office by writing under his hand addressed to the Governor-General, or may be removed from office by order of the Governor-General, and any vacancy occurring before the expiration of his term of office shall be filled by a similar appointment for the remainder of such term.

(4) An elected president and a deputy-president shall cease to hold office if they cease to be members of the Assembly. They may resign office by writing under their hands addressed to the Governor-General, and may be removed from office by a vote of the Assembly with the concurrence of the Governor-General.

(5) A president and deputy-president shall receive such salaries as may be determined, in the case of an appointed president by the Governor-General, and in the case of an elected president and a deputy-president by Act of the Indian legislature....

22. (*1*) An official shall not be qualified for election as member of either chamber of the Indian legislature, and if any non-official member of either chamber accepts office in the service of the Crown in India, his seat in that chamber shall become vacant.

(2) If an elected member of either chamber of the Indian legislature becomes a member of the other chamber, his seat in such first-mentioned chamber shall thereupon become vacant.

(3) If any person is elected a member of both chambers of the Indian legislature, he shall, before he takes his seat in either chamber, signify in writing the chamber of which he desires to be a member, and thereupon his seat in the other chamber shall become vacant.

(4) Every member of the Governor-General's Executive Council shall be nominated as a member of one chamber of the Indian legislature, and shall have the right of attending in and addressing the other chamber, but shall not be a member of both chambers....

26. (*1*) Where either chamber of the Indian legislature refuses leave to introduce, or fails to pass in a form recommended by the Governor-General, any Bill, the Governor-General may certify that the passage of the Bill is essential for the safety, tranquillity or interests of British India or any part thereof, and thereupon—

(*a*) if the Bill has already been passed by the other chamber, the Bill shall on signature by the Governor-General, notwithstanding that it has not been consented to by both chambers, forthwith become an Act of the Indian legislature in the form of the Bill as originally introduced or proposed to be introduced in the Indian legislature, or (as the case may be) in the form recommended by the Governor-General; and

Milestone Documents

(b) if the Bill has not already been so passed, the Bill shall be laid before the other chamber and, if consented to by that chamber in the form recommended by the Governor-General, shall become an Act as aforesaid on the signification of the Governor-General's assent, or, if not so consented to, shall, on signature by the Governor-General become an Act as aforesaid.

(2) Every such Act shall be expressed to be made by the Governor-General, and shall, as soon as practicable after being made, be laid before both Houses of Parliament, and shall not have effect until it has received His Majesty's assent, and shall not be presented for His Majesty's assent until copies thereof have been laid before each House of Parliament for not less than eight days on which that House has sat; and upon the signification of such assent by His Majesty in Council, and the notification thereof by the Governor-General, the Act shall have the same force and effect as an Act passed by the Indian legislature and duly assented to:

Provided that, where in the opinion of the Governor-General a state of emergency exists which justifies such action, the Governor-General may direct that any such Act shall come into operation forthwith, and thereupon the Act shall have such force and effect as aforesaid, subject, however, to disallowance by His Majesty in Council....

Part III. Secretary of State in Council...

31. The following amendments shall be made in section three of the principal Act in relation to the composition of the Council of India, the qualification, term of office, and remuneration of its members:—

(1) The provisions of sub-section (1) shall have effect as though "eight" and "twelve" were substituted for "ten" and "fourteen" respectively, as the minimum and maximum number of members, provided that the council as constituted at the time of the passing of this Act shall not be affected by this provision, but no fresh appointment or re-appointment thereto shall be made in excess of the maximum prescribed by this provision.

(2) The provisions of sub-section (3) shall have effect as if "one-half" were substituted for "nine" and "India" were substituted for "British India."

(3) In sub-section (4) "five years" shall be substituted for "seven years" as the term of office of members of the council, provided that the tenure of office of any person who is a member of the council at the

time of the passing of this Act shall not be affected by this provision.

(4) The provisions of sub-section (8) shall cease to have effect and in lieu thereof the following provisions shall be inserted:

"There shall be paid to each member of the Council of India the annual salary of twelve hundred pounds: provided that any member of the council who was at the time of his appointment domiciled in India shall receive, in addition to the salary hereby provided, an annual subsistence allowance of six hundred pounds.

Such salaries and allowances may be paid out of the revenues of India or out of moneys provided by Parliament."

(5) Notwithstanding anything in any Act or rules, where any person in the service of the Crown in India is appointed a member of the council before completion of the period of such service required to entitle him to a pension or annuity, his service as such member shall, for the purpose of any pension or annuity which would be payable to him on completion of such period, be reckoned as service under the Crown in India whilst resident in India.

32. (1) The provision in section six of the principal Act which prescribes the quorum for meeting of the Council of India shall cease to have effect, and the Secretary of State shall provide for a quorum by directions to be issued in this behalf.

(2) The provision in section eight of the principal Act relating to meetings of the Council of India shall have effect as though "month" were substituted for "week."

(3) Section ten of the principal Act shall have effect as though the words "all business of the council or committees thereof is to be transacted" were omitted, and the words "the business of the Secretary of State in Council or the Council of India shall be transacted, and any order made or act done in accordance with such direction shall, subject to the provisions of this Act, be treated as being an order of the Secretary of State in Council" were inserted in lieu thereof.

33. The Secretary of State in Council may, notwithstanding anything in the principal Act, by rule regulate and restrict the exercise of the powers of superintendence, direction, and control, vested in the Secretary of State and the Secretary of State in Council, by the principal Act, or otherwise, in such manner as may appear necessary or expedient in order to give effect to the purposes of this Act.

Before any rules are made under this section relating to subjects other than transferred subjects, the rules proposed to be made shall be laid in draft before both Houses of Parliament, and such rules shall not be made unless both Houses by resolution approve the draft either without modification or addition, or with modifications or additions to which both Houses agree, but upon such approval being given the Secretary of State in Council may make such rules in the form in which they have been approved, and such rules on being so made shall be of full force and effect.

Any rules relating to transferred subjects made under this section shall be laid before both Houses of Parliament as soon as may be after they are made, and, if an Address is presented to His Majesty by either House of Parliament within the next thirty days on which that House has sat after the rules are laid before it praying that the rules or any of them may be annulled, His Majesty in Council may annul the rules or any of them, and those rules shall thenceforth be void, but without prejudice to the validity of anything previously done thereunder.

34. So much of section five of the principal Act as relates to orders and communications sent to India from the United Kingdom and to orders made in the United Kingdom, and sections eleven, twelve, thirteen and fourteen of the principal Act, shall cease to have effect and the procedure for the sending of orders and communications to India and in general for correspondence between the Secretary of State and the Governor-General in Council or any local government shall be such as may be prescribed by order of the Secretary of State in Council.

35. His Majesty may by Order in Council make provision for the appointment of a High Commissioner for India in the United Kingdom and for the pay pension powers, duties, and conditions of employment of the High Commissioner and of his assistants; and the Order may further provide for delegating to the High Commissioner any of the powers previously exercised by the Secretary of State or the Secretary of State in Council whether under the principal Act or otherwise in relation to making contractor and may prescribe the conditions under which he shall act on behalf of the Governor-General in Council or any local government.

Part IV. The Civil Services in India

36. (*1*) Subject to the provisions of the principal Act and of rules made thereunder, every person in the civil service of the Crown in India holds office during His Majesty's pleasure, and may be employed in any manner required by a proper authority within the scope of his duty, but no person in that service may be dismissed by any authority subordinate to that by which he was appointed, and the Secretary of State in Council may (except so far as he may provide by rules to the contrary) reinstate any person in that service who has been dismissed.

If any such person appointed by the Secretary of State in Council thinks himself wronged by an order of an official superior in a governor's province, and on due application made to that superior does not receive the redress to which he may consider himself entitled, he may, without prejudice to any other right of redress, complain, to the governor of the province in order to obtain justice and the governor is hereby directed to examine such complaint and require such action to be taken thereon as may appear to him to be just and equitable.

(2) The Secretary of State in Council may make rules for regulating the classification of the civil services in India, the methods of their recruitment, their conditions of service, pay and allowances, and discipline and conduct. Such rules may, to such extent and in respect of such matters as may be prescribed, delegate the power of making rules to the Governor-General in Council or to local governments, or authorise the Indian legislature or local legislatures to make laws regulating the public services:

Provided that every person appointed before the commencement of this Act by the Secretary of State in Council to the civil service of the Crown in India shall retain all his existing or accruing rights, or shall receive such compensation for the loss of any of them as the Secretary of State in Council may consider just and equitable.

(3) The right to pensions and the scale and conditions of pensions of all persons in the civil service of the Crown in India appointed by the Secretary of State in Council shall be regulated in accordance with the rules in force at the time of the passing of this Act. Any such rules may be varied or added to by the Secretary of State in Council and shall have effect as so varied or added to, but any such variation or addition shall not adversely affect the pension of any member of the service appointed before the date thereof.

Nothing in this section or in any rule thereunder shall prejudice the rights to which any person may, or may have, become entitled under the provisions in relation to pensions contained in the East India Annuity Funds Act, 1874.

(4) For the removal of doubts it is hereby declared that all rules or other provisions in operation at the

time of the passing of this Act, whether made by the Secretary of State in Council or by any other authority, relating to the civil service of the Crown in India, were duly made in accordance with the powers in that behalf, and are confirmed, but any such rules or provisions may be revoked, varied, or added to by rules or laws made under this section.

37. (*1*) Notwithstanding anything in section ninety-seven of the principal Act the Secretary of State may make appointments to the Indian Civil Service of persons domiciled in India, in accordance with such rules as may be prescribed by the Secretary of State in Council with the concurrence of the majority of votes at a meeting of the Council of India.

Any rules made under this section shall not have force until they have been laid for thirty days before both Houses of Parliament.

(*2*) The Indian Civil Service (Temporary Provisions) Act, 1915 (which confers power during the war and for a period of two years thereafter to make appointments to the Indian Civil Service without examination), shall have effect as though "three years" were substituted for "two years."

Glossary

Bengal	today, the nation of Bangladesh and the Indian state of West Bengal
Bombay	today, Mumbai
Lords Spiritual and Temporal, and Commons	members of Parliament. At the time of the act, the lords spiritual were bishops and the lords temporal were members of the hereditary peerage; they comprised the House of Lords. "Commons," representatives of the towns and cities, sat in the House of Commons, as they do today.
Punjab	Today, the western part lies in the nation of Pakistan; East Punjab is an Indian state.

RESOLUTIONS OF THE NATIONAL CONGRESS OF BRITISH WEST AFRICA

" The time has come to open definitely to African practitioners of experience all Judicial appointments. "

Overview

Throughout the latter half of the nineteenth century, Britain's colonial policy of indirect rule in Africa relied on indigenous leaders who served as intermediaries between British governors, the cadre of elite missionary-educated Africans who worked directly for the government, and common Africans. At the beginning of the twentieth century, the British altered their policy by systematically withdrawing support from African elites, who were then replaced by whites. During this period new concepts about Africans' perceptions of themselves and Europeans arose across the continent, and Africans participated in congress movements that challenged European control. These movements were supported by the intercontinental Pan-African movement, through which African Americans encouraged African peoples to seek independence.

In 1920 the National Congress of British West Africa (NCBWA) sketched on the colonial canvas in some detail various Afrocentric ideas for reform that would restructure the relationship between Africans and the colonizers. Among these ideas was a proposal for a federated British West Africa that would join the colonies of Gambia, Gold Coast, Nigeria, and Sierra Leone. This proposal set the stage for later nationalist independence movements. Representatives from each of the colonies met in March 1920 in Accra, Gold Coast, and discussed eleven major issues, which were transformed into a set of resolutions. The NCBWA thus became the first West African organization to officially document the nationalist ideas being formulated by the African elite and to express political solidarity among Africans.

Six months after the conference, the NCBWA sent a deputation to the colonial government in London, whose members were not willing to accept the idea of federated African colonies and thus refused to see the deputies. While London's initial rejection meant failure for the NCBWA resolutions, the impact of the ideas reverberated throughout British West Africa, and each colony achieved many of the resolutions' goals by 1930. Later, as the importance of the NCBWA declined, other more radical organizations took its place, as did broad-based political parties that demanded

governmental changes based on the ideas articulated in the Resolutions of the National Congress of British West Africa.

Context

At the beginning of the colonial period, the British implemented a management style in Africa that reflected their way of thinking about colonial administration. The tropical environment rich in unfamiliar diseases had turned the African colonies into a "white man's grave," so hardly any whites were found there. Accordingly, British indirect rule reflected the view that Africans should retain their own culture and assimilate British culture only when it benefited their rule. The British used the indigenous leaders, legitimate heads of their own communities, to control the population at the local level, a practice considered good management because it allowed the colonized people to maintain local rule. Meanwhile, to ensure their unchallenged control, the British continued to apply a policy of "divide and conquer" so as to isolate each community.

The system of indirect colonial administration required junior administrators and civil servants, many of whom were drawn from the pool of educated Africans acculturated by the mission stations that had preceded the British conquest. Although missionaries specifically tried to educate the sons of indigenous leaders, many leaders resisted Western-style education. As a result, many of those Africans who gravitated to the mission schools were not part of the indigenous hierarchy but were instead those who sought opportunity by working for the Europeans. Western-trained students went on to study at British universities and return as models of a new type of African leader, the educated elite. These Africans thus became attorneys, doctors, merchants, teachers, civil servants, and highly trained workers whose education enabled them to work alongside the British, whereas the indigenous elite remained in rural areas and maintained their culture. From about 1840 to 1880 the educated elite rose to high administrative positions, including seats on colonial legislative councils. However, acculturation to a British lifestyle distanced the Western-educated Africans from their roots, their families, and their indigenous culture.

1913

- Joseph Ephraim Casely Hayford conceives of an independent federation of British colonies in West Africa.

1914

- **August 1**
Marcus Garvey founds the Universal Negro Improvement Association (UNIA), with branches established in Gold Coast, Gambia, Nigeria, and Sierra Leone.

1918

- William J. Davies organizes the first regional West African conference in Sierra Leone.

1919

- The African Progress Union is founded with the object of upholding the principle of equal treatment for all within the British Empire.

- Casely Hayford writes in favor of West African unity in a pamphlet entitled *United West Africa.*

1920

- **March 11–28**
The inaugural conference of the National Congress of British West Africa (NCBWA) is held in Accra, Gold Coast, producing eighty-three resolutions.

The British did not foresee the indigenous and Western-educated groups uniting to challenge their rule, but this is exactly what occurred in the Gold Coast colony (now part of the nation of Ghana) in 1897. The combined effort of the two classes led to the formation of the Aborigines' Rights Protection Society (ARPS). That year, the society's members successfully challenged the British Lands Bill, which had been written in 1894 to usurp African land. The ARPS had no intention of becoming independent from Britain, and neither did the subsequent National Congress of British West Africa; both wanted rather to restructure their association with England. Nevertheless, the British reacted by immediately reverting to its divide-and-conquer mentality, to thus stoke hostility between the two groups. The British government dissolved its partnership with the educated African elite at the turn of the twentieth century, recruiting whites to work as junior and senior colonial officials because advancements in tropical medicine allowed them to maintain their health. The British nonetheless expected the African elite to train the inexperienced whites to whom they would relinquish their own jobs. Africans vigorously challenged the change in British policy, which not only reduced their status in society but also affected them economically.

By 1914 a color bar had been placed between the colonial administrative positions reserved for whites and the less prestigious clerical positions reserved for educated Africans. British colonial policy in other parts of the world was very different from its West African policy. In their Indian and Ceylonese colonies, a competitive exam was used to select colonial administrators based on merit, not on race. British policy in West Africa, possibly based on reaction to the success of the ARPS in 1897, seemed short-sighted because it had the unintended consequence of creating discontent among the African elite, who began to support the emerging nationalist movements.

The rise of nationalism among Africans was seen first in the Gold Coast's political sector, where in 1897 the multiethnic ARPS used British law to win their case over the land issue. This small step in constitutional, political activity against British colonialism set a precedent for nationalism. During the 1880s and 1890s a broader multiethnic religious movement, sometimes referred to as the African breakaway church movement, evolved. Through this movement, Africans abandoned mainstream Christian congregations and formed independent African churches, in which they merged African culture and European Christianity. Members of this movement included William Wade Harris in West Africa and Simon Kimbangu in south-central Africa. Additionally, the Pan-African congress movement encouraged unity among Africans and people of African descent from the Americas. While most Africans called only for the reform of their colonial relationships, Americans offered a more radical call for African nations independent from Europe.

The first quarter of the twentieth century witnessed a rise in African national consciousness in a number of Pan-African congresses, beginning with the First Universal Races' Congress, held in London in 1911, and Booker T.

Washington's International Conference on the Negro, held at Tuskegee, Alabama, in 1912. Washington's conference entertained delegations from African countries led by leaders such as Joseph Ephraim Casely Hayford of the Gold Coast. In 1914 the Jamaican Marcus Garvey established the Universal Negro Improvement Association and African Communites League (UNIA-ACL; also referred to as UNIA), with African branches in Gambia, Gold Coast, Nigeria, and Sierra Leone. This association vocalized racial pride and the need to establish an independent black republic in Africa. In 1918 two Pan-African associations of peoples of African descent within the British Empire, the Union of African Peoples and the Society of Peoples of African Origin, joined together to form the African Progress Union, which advocated equal treatment for everyone within the empire. African student organizations in Britain were not as political but did have an impact on nationalist causes. The Union of Students of African Descent was founded in 1917, and the West African Students' Union would be founded in 1925. In 1919, W. E. B. Du Bois brought Africans and their American descendants together at the inaugural Pan-African Congress, held in Paris, where Americans encouraged their African brothers to seek independence from their colonizers.

Casely Hayford, a Gold Coast colony attorney, began advocating for a national congress on British West Africa in 1914. He envisioned the four English-speaking West African colonies as an independent federation operating as one colony. By 1918 Gold Coast elites proposed a congress to discuss greater African participation in the colonial government. That year, Sierra Leone hosted the first regional West African conference as a forerunner of the National Congress of British West Africa. When the NCBWA formed in 1920, each colony had a committee. Sierra Leone's committee was supported by an overlapping membership of local professional associations, such as the Sierra Leone Bar Association and the Sierra Leone branch of the UNIA. The African branches of the Universal Negro Improvement Association supported the NCBWA because they shared some of the same goals.

In preparing and planning the first convention of the NCBWA, Casely Hayford tried to reprise a degree of cooperation with the indigenous African leadership by enlisting the support of the ARPS leaders, but they wanted only to address rights in the Gold Coast colony, refusing to join the other colonies. Britain's policy change had effectively made rivals of the ARPS and Casely Hayford's elite. The ARPS was unwilling to acknowledge a common cause for the colonies or accept the wisdom of the collective power a federation might provide; the society was even displeased with Casely Hayford's initiative. Nevertheless, Casely Hayford and his allies proceeded to organize the joint West African congress. In going his own way, Casely Hayford abandoned the protocol of informing the indigenous and colonial leaderships of his plans, a serious error in judgment that cost the NCBWA support for its resolutions from very powerful segments of society close to the British government. In particular, Nana William Ofori Atta, a powerful paramount

Time Line

1920

■ **August 1–31**
The UNIA-sponsored International Convention of the Negro Peoples of the World is held in New York, with NCBWA members in attendance.

■ An NCBWA deputation travels to London to discuss the resolutions with the secretary of state.

1923

■ **January– February**
An NCBWA meeting held in Freetown, Sierra Leone, produces a constitution for the organization.

1930

■ **August 11**
Casely Hayford dies.

chief, took offense at the breach in protocol when he heard that the conference organizers had sent the resolutions directly to Britain's secretary of state and through him to the prime minister.

In March 1920, Casely Hayford and T. Hutton Mills convened the inaugural meeting of the National Congress of British West Africa in Accra, Gold Coast. Speaking for the assembled group, Casely Hayford insisted on the loyalty to the British Empire of all the participants and, speaking for African elites, he asserted that their education gave them the right to lead African people. Delegates attending the congress represented nearly the same socioeconomic class in each colony, including large contingents of attorneys, journalists, educators, clergy, doctors, and merchants as well as several indigenous leaders. The African elite's platform outlined their intentions to secure local self-government through constitutional means, to secure a voting franchise, to establish institutions of higher education, and to institute a civil-service employment process based on merit. Elected as officers were T. Hutton Mills as president, J. E. Casely Hayford as vice president, F. V. Nanka-Bruce and L. E. V. M'Carthy as joint secretaries, and A. B.

Quartey-Papafio and H. Van Hien as joint treasurers. The leadership was dominated by the Gold Coast contingent; however, the NCBWA added five regional vice presidents to be inclusive in broader representation. The congress lasted two weeks and addressed eleven major topics through a total of eighty-three resolutions.

The organizers brought the Resolutions of the National Congress of British West Africa to Frederick Gordon Guggisberg, the Gold Coast governor, who concluded that the document was a benign request to reform existing policies and to reopen administrative positions to elites. The bishop of Accra validated the resolutions, and one newspaper compared the NCBWA to the Indian National Congress. As an extension of the congress, a deputation was sent to London to discuss the resolutions in person with the British government. The delegation drafted two petitions to submit to the British government, a "Memorandum of the Case of the National Congress of British West Africa" and "The Humble Petition of the National Congress of British West Africa by Its Delegates Now in London."

About the Author

No individual representative can be identified as the author of the Resolutions of the National Congress of British West Africa. The resolutions were introduced, discussed, and voted on by the assembled representatives, who were primarily members of the British-educated African elite who in the past had worked hand in hand with both indigenous African leaders and the British colonizers. The resolutions that they passed expressed the grievances of colonial subjects who were looking for redress through constitutional means and sought to change the power structure, not break it.

Although he is not recognized as an author of the resolutions, Casely Hayford contributed to their conception more than any other individual. He had been the first to envision the unification of the four British colonies in 1913; in 1914 he brought the idea to other African nationalists; in 1919 he wrote the pamphlet *United West Africa*. Consequently, he was generally regarded as the founding father of the Congress and a mentor to the proceedings.

Casely Hayford was born into a wealthy family in Cape Coast (in modern-day Ghana) in 1866 and attended Fourah Bay College in Freetown, Sierra Leone. There he became an admirer and follower of Edward Wilmot Blyden, a leading Pan-African proponent, who edited *Negro*, the first overtly Pan-African journal in West Africa. After completing his education, he returned to Ghana, where he became a high school teacher and then principal at Wesleyan Boys' High School in Accra. He lost his job at the school as the result of his political activism and went to work as a newspaper editor. In 1893 he went to London, where he trained as a lawyer, returning to Africa in 1896 to practice law. In 1911 in his book *Ethiopia Unbound*, Casely Hayford advocated for an African university with African curricula, and his pursuit of this goal came to fruition in

1927 with the establishment of the Achimoto College in the Gold Coast. He entered politics in 1916, with his nomination to the Legislative Council. After forming the NCBWA, he represented the congress in London in 1920 to demand constitutional reforms from the colonial secretary. The NCBWA was dissolved shortly after Casely Hayford's death in 1930.

Casely Hayford's experiences as a journalist inspired the resolutions for a free press. His educational pursuits and his contribution to education in the Gold Coast are evident in the resolutions on education that include incorporating African identity into African education and establishing an African university. His participation with the ARPS in stopping the Lands Bill of 1897 can be seen in the resolutions concerning the land policy of the colonial government. He asserted the right of the educated elites to lead all of the African people, and he believed that the only way to challenge the colonial government with respect to all the issues was to do so constitutionally.

Explanation and Analysis of the Document

The NCBWA's resolutions, composed during the interwar years of the colonial period, constituted a vision of the African elite across British West Africa. The document is divided into eight sections, each listing a number of resolutions; the full text contains eighty-three resolutions.

◆ **"Legislative (Including Municipal) Reforms and the Granting of the Franchise and Administrative Reforms with Particular Reference to Equal Rights and Opportunities"**

Under British rule, African subjects were allowed to participate in their own governance only in a secondary capacity. The indigenous leaders were advisers, and some of the British-educated Africans participated in legislative councils that were purely advisory, while others worked as junior administrators and civil servants. While the British practiced democracy at home, they were more autocratic in their dealings with the colonies. Consequently, they established no institutions to instruct Africans in democratic principles. The first set of resolutions sought constitutional reform at all levels of government in each colony, including, in resolution 6, the creation of municipal corporations for towns in which four-fifths of the local leaders would be elected by the people.

This section introduced the democratic right of Africans to vote, a right that had been denied them. However, while resolution 3 allowed Africans the right to vote, it did not provide a structure for determining which citizens would vote, how they would be selected, or how they would be educated into the democratic process. Resolution 2 proposes a reorganization of representation in the Legislative Council. Previously, British administrators selected African elites to serve on advisory councils. With the voting franchise established, representatives to these councils were to be voted into office and invested with the right to share power with the British as equals in governmental decision making. Resolution 2 also proposes a new House of Assembly with special financial power, which would be composed of the Legislative Council and six elected financial representatives. The assembly would review the governor's budget and proposed taxes and then would approve or restrict financial matters of the colonies. This method would enable African residents to have some say over the budget and the expenditure of their taxes. In resolution 4, the congress addresses African discontent with the judicial system by objecting to the practices of the colonial judiciary under British administrative officers. While the congress does not here offer any suggestions for changes in the judiciary, it does reserve the right to make them at a later time. Resolution 5 condemns the practice of choosing administrative officers and civil servants based on race and forcefully recommended that these positions be filled based on merit demonstrated through a competitive exam.

◆ "Education with Particular Reference to a West African University"

There was no system of compulsory European-style education in Britain's West African colonies, and the European education that was available was not open to all children. A number of children did go to elementary schools in both rural and urban areas. Under the British system, students who completed the elementary level had to take an exam to proceed to the secondary level. Because secondary schools were located only in larger towns or cities, students in rural areas were required to leave home and move to the closest town with a secondary school. In many cases this was a hardship on rural parents, who often needed their children for labor, had no relatives in town with whom to board their children, or could not afford to support their children at a distance. For these reasons, more urban than rural students advanced to the secondary level. To institute compulsory education, the government needed to build more secondary schools closer to the homes of rural students. The gateway from secondary school to the university was another exam; however, to attend university, students were required to travel abroad, because in the colonies there were no universities that were equivalent to those in Britain. Many parents were unable to support their child's study in Britain unless the student won a scholarship. This set of resolutions calls for laws requiring compulsory education for all students and a funding system in each colony run through a National Educational Fund, which would be eligible for government subsidies. The government would be expected to provide elementary and secondary education of sufficient quality for all qualified students to be capable of proceeding to higher education.

While agreeing with the importance of British Western education, these resolutions also address the importance of preserving African culture through education. The African elite wanted to be consulted about incorporating a sense of African nationalism into the curricula. Resolution 3 recommends that boards of education in the colonies invite experienced educators and others with similar expertise to make suggestions concerning transforming a discriminatory educational system into one based on equality. With regard to higher education, resolution 2 seeks the establishment of a West African university that would provide a Western-style education while at the same time developing in students a sense of African identity. More secondary-level graduates would thus have an opportunity to earn a quality degree without having to leave the country.

◆ "Commercial Enterprise with Particular Reference to (A) The Scheme of the Empire Resources Development Committee; (B) Banking; (C) Shipping"

These resolutions generally charge that during the postwar period, Europeans benefited economically at the expense of their African colonies. In fact, the trade relationship between Britain and its colonies was based on imbalanced mercantilism; Britain bought raw materials from its colonies at low prices and then sold manufactured goods made from those raw materials back to the colonies at high prices. In this set of resolutions, the congress voices the need for the colonies to constitutionally regain control of their economies. The first resolution condemns the British government and government-sponsored companies for buying African resources at the lowest price possible and selling them to other European nations for a profit. It also states that the government should not sell African natural resources to pay off its World War I debt. Resolution 2 insists that the British allow the colonies free trade so that they would be able to trade with other colonies and nations.

Addressing inequitable practices against Africans, resolution 4 criticizes the Currency Board for discriminating against West Africa by creating different face values for West African currency than for the rest of the empire. Resolution 3 focuses on banking, urging the end of economic discrimination against Africans in favor of European business interests. Africans were credit starved because British banks would not give commercial loans to African entrepreneurs. Thus, the British government was challenged to form under the Companies Acts a West African corporation, British West Africa Co-operative Association, with the ability to found banks, cooperative stores, and buying centers. The African elite pledged to raise capital for the association and promote investment through a grassroots campaign educating the public. The establishment of an African bank would promote African-owned regional and international businesses. Finally, in resolutions 5 and 6 the African elite accuse British shippers of discriminating against African entrepreneurs' products, and they further condemn a specific passenger line for discriminating against West African passengers. Resolution 5 specifically advocates in favor of the UNIA's Black Star Line for long-distance transportation to and from the British West African colonies.

◆ "Judicial Reforms with Particular Reference to an Appellate Court"

These resolutions question discrimination in the court system in British West Africa. As citizens of the empire, citi-

Marcus Garvery, who founded the Universal Negro Improvement Association, with branches in West Africa
(Library of Congress)

zens of the colonies should be treated under the law no differently from citizens of Britain. Africans should have the same right to regulation by common law and statutes that applied in Britain. Resolution 5 condemns the colonial administration for taking away the African citizen's right to trial by jury in criminal cases. The congress recommends in resolution 6 that the citizens of the colonies benefit from the Criminal Appeal Act of 1908 just as did British citizens. In resolution 12 it denounces the flogging of African women for any reason, and while the flogging of men seems to have been an accepted practice, the congress asserts that it should be used only according to law. This resolution spoke to the issue of violence spawned by racial discrimination in the colonies. In the first several resolutions in this section, the congress challenges the methods of appointing judges in West Africa. The appointments of judges for the colonies should be conducted as in Britain. Only qualified and experienced attorneys should hold judicial appointments, and the pool of candidates should be expanded to include the cadre of African attorneys who met the qualifications. In resolution 4 the congress announces its dissatisfaction with the membership of the Appeal Court as well as its judgments and recommends that a mix of judges from outside British West Africa be appointed to form a new appellate court.

♦ **"West African Press Union"**

Many members of the press from British West Africa were involved in establishing and supporting the congress because they had a vested interest in preserving the freedom of the press. Resolution 3 calls for freedom of the press in the colonies equal to that experienced in Britain. News in the colonies was disseminated through newspapers, but the British government shut down any newspapers that published ideas that threatened it or criticized its actions. Since the press was critical to national development, the congress recommends the appointment of a committee of experienced journalists to find ways for the British West African Press to better cooperate. This being so, the congress asserts in resolution 4 that it should publish its own quarterly magazine, to be called the *British West African National Review.*

♦ **"The Policy of the Government in Relation to the Land Question"**

All delegates, indigenous and educated elite alike, unanimously opposed the British government's administration of African land and wanted to deal with the colonizers on their own terms. The indigenous leaders, in particular, wanted more control over the rights to the land for commercial purposes. Resolution 1 acknowledges the principle of trusteeship with respect to the land but insists that Africans are capable of land ownership and management and have the right to sell or lease land without government involvement. Resolution 2 softens the sting of this assertion of self-sufficiency by deferring to the colonizers' advisory role.

♦ **"The Right of the People to Self Determination"**

At end of World War I, the Western powers proclaimed the principle of self-determination; however, this was for

Europeans and was not applied to any of the colonies. The first resolution accuses Europeans of a sort of slavery, as the Europeans divided up the German colonies among themselves without consulting the people who lived in those colonies or considering the consequences of dividing ethnic groups with international borders. Resolution 3 requests that the British government give assurances to its West African colonies that organizational changes would not be made without the colonies' consent. In light of the fact that the congress was directly challenging the British administration, resolution 4 assures the British government of the loyalty of congress participants with citizenship in the empire.

♦ **"The Inauguration of the Congress of Africans of British West Africa"**

The resolution in this section proclaims the creation of the permanent organization called the National Congress of British West Africa. A final statement reassures the government that British West Africa considered itself a part of the empire and asserts that, therefore, as loyal subjects, residents of the colonies were entitled to rights as citizens as expected under the "principle that taxation goes with effective representation."

Audience

The resolutions were intended to be presented to the British government in London for redress of grievances. However, the British declined to give an audience to the delegates from the NCBWA. The representatives of all four colonies proceeded to share the resolutions with their constituencies, and in some cases they educated the populace further to impart fuller understanding of the resolutions.

Impact

With regard to the NCBWA's primary intentions, the resolutions proved a failure because the British government was unwilling to receive the delegation. The government challenged the congress's claim to being representative of all of the constituents of the four colonies, instead viewing it as representing only a small interest group. Behind the scenes, the government's rejection was based on advice from the colonial governors of the Gold Coast and Nigeria as well as advice from representatives of the indigenous leadership in the Gold Coast. The British government refused to treat the congress as legitimately representing the block of united colonies; each colony would be recognized only on an individual basis. Although the quest for reform of the colonial system by constitutional means was denied, at this time none of the groups vying for leadership was willing to resort to radical measures. Consequently, the British continued to apply their divide-and-conquer strategy, successfully fomenting conflict between indigenous leaders and the educated elites.

"*The time has arrived for a change in the Constitutions of the several British West African Colonies, so as to give the people an effective voice in their affairs both in the Legislative and Municipal Governments.*"

(Legislative [Including Municipal] Reforms and the Granting of the Franchise and Administrative Reforms with Particular Reference to Equal Rights and Opportunities)

"*Compulsory Education throughout the British West African Colonies be introduced by law.*"

(Education with Particular Reference to a West African University)

"*The time has come to open definitely to African practitioners of experience all Judicial appointments.*"

(Judicial Reforms with Particular Reference to an Appellate Court)

"*The liberty of the Press is the birthright of every Community within the British Empire.*"

(West African Press Union)

The resolutions nonetheless manifested themselves through the work of the NCBWA, which continued its activities throughout the 1920s with three meetings: in 1923 in Freetown, Sierra Leone, where it established its constitution; in 1925–1926 in Bathurst (now Banjul), Gambia; and in 1930 in Lagos, Nigeria. Although the resolutions had been rejected, the separate colonial committees of the NCBWA did accomplish some of them. For example, the individual local constitutions in Nigeria (1923), Sierra Leone (1924) and the Gold Coast (1925) were modified and elective representation was established in each nation; however, it is unclear that the Gambia benefited at this time. In turn, a feeling of unity developed among the colonies in acknowledgment of their common political destiny, foreshadowing the later independence movements. During this same period, some West Africans from the NCBWA supported the Universal Negro Improvement Association by disseminating its constitution and its newspaper, the *Negro World*, to other NCBWA members and many other residents of the British colonies. In 1921 a West African delegation participated in the second UNIA convention held in New York City, where NCBWA members were appointed to executive positions within the UNIA organization.

The death of Casely Hayford on August 11, 1930, caused the NCBWA to decline. However, its influence could be seen in the local movements that evolved. The youth league movement started as ethnic unions, youth associations, voluntary associations, societies, and clubs created during the 1920s and 1930s throughout British West Africa. Like the African elite represented in the congress, this younger group of missionary-educated elite desired to assume leadership roles and to replace older conservative congress leaders. However, around 1935 youth leagues took more radical political turns with the founding of I. T. A. Wallace Johnson's West African Youth League. This organization challenged colonial control by contesting for and winning the Gold Coast Legislative Council elections of 1935.

Meanwhile, the NCBWA's precedent for collective political action inspired the rise of political parties formed to agitate for reform. Herbert Macaulay's Nigerian National Democratic Party was established in 1923, winning elections in that year, 1928, and 1933. The party echoed the NCBWA resolutions in a program platform that called for the election of its members to the Lagos Legislative Council, the development of higher education, the introduction of compulsory education throughout Nigeria, increased African representation in the civil service, free trade in Nigeria, and equal treatment for Nigerian traders and producers. The British West African colonies ultimately achieved independence from Great Britain in the late 1950s and early 1960s.

Further Reading

■ Articles

Eluwa, G. I. C. "Background to the Emergence of the National Congress of British West Africa." *African Studies Review* 14, no. 2 (September 1971): 205–219.

Gershoni, Yekutiel. "Common Goals, Different Ways: The UNIA and the NCBWA in West Africa—1920–1930." *Journal of Third World Studies* 18, no. 2 (Fall 2001): 171–185.

Langley, J. Ayodele. "The Gambia Section of the National Congress of British West Africa." *Africa: Journal of the International African Institute* 39, no. 4 (October 1969): 382–395.

Okonkwo, R. L. "The Garvey Movement in British West Africa." *Journal of African History* 21, no. 1 (January 1980): 105–117.

Wyse, Akintola J. G. "The Sierra Leone Branch of the National Congress of British West Africa, 1918–1946." *International Journal of African Historical Studies* 18, no. 4 (1985): 675–698.

■ Books

Boahen, A. Adu. "Politics and Nationalism in West Africa, 1919–35." In *UNESCO General History of Africa*, Volume 7: *Africa under Colonial Domination, 1880–1935*, ed. A. A. Boahen. Berkeley: University of California Press, 1990.

Fage, J. D. *Ghana: A Historical Interpretation*. Madison: University of Wisconsin Press, 1959.

George, Claude. *The Rise of British West Africa: Comprising the Early History of the Colony of Sierra Leone, the Gambia, Lagos, Gold Coast, Etc., Etc.*. 1904. Reprint. Whitefish, Mont.: Kessinger Publishing, 2009.

Kilson, Martin. "The National Congress of British West Africa, 1918–1935." In *Protest and Power in Black Africa*, ed. Robert I. Rothberg and Ali A. Mazrui. New York: Oxford University Press, 1970.

Kimble, David. *A Political History of Ghana: The Rise of Gold Coast Nationalism, 1850–1928*. Oxford, U.K.: Clarendon Press, 1963.

Langley, J. Ayodele. *Ideologies of Liberation in Black Africa, 1856–1970: Documents on Modern African Political Thought from Colonial Times to the Present*. London: Rex Collings, 1979.

Webster, J. B. "African Political Activity in British West Africa, 1900–1940." In *History of West Africa*, vol. 2, ed. J. F. Ade Ajayi and Michael Crowder. London: Longman, 1974.

■ Web Sites

"Early Manifestations of Nationalism." Ghana, Country Studies Web site.
    http://countrystudies.us/ghana/12.htm.

Questions for Further Study

1. Trace the history of efforts in Africa to form cooperative federations, using this document alongside such documents as the Constitution of the Fante Confederacy and the Constitutive Act of the African Union.

2. Great Britain emerged as one of the great colonial powers in the nineteenth century. Trace the history of British colonialism, using this document along with such documents as the Treaty of Nanjing, the British Regulating Act, and the Government of India Act of 1919. Overall, how would you characterize British administration of its colonies?

3. How and to what extent did the Resolutions of the National Congress balance indigenous concerns with the recognition that Western, British institutions could be of benefit to British West Africa?

4. Were the resolutions, in your estimation, intended to benefit only a small interest group, or were they intended to benefit all West Africans? Explain.

5. The Resolutions of the National Congress of British West Africa have been accounted a failure in that the British government ignored them. Nevertheless, do you think that such documents had a long-term impact on colonialism in Africa? Explain.

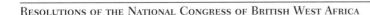

"The End of the British Empire in Africa." Learning Curve: British Empire, National Archives Web site.
   http://www.learningcurve.gov.uk/empire/g3/cs2/background.htm.

"History of Ghana." 50th Independence Anniversary Celebration of Ghana Web site.
   http://www.ghana50.gov.gh/history/index.php?op=independence.

—Dianne White Oyler

RESOLUTIONS OF THE NATIONAL CONGRESS OF BRITISH WEST AFRICA

Legislative (Including Municipal) Reforms and the Granting of the Franchise and Administrative Reforms with Particular Reference to Equal Rights and Opportunities

◆ **Resolutions**

1. That in the opinion of this Conference the time has arrived for a change in the Constitutions of the several British West African Colonies, so as to give the people an effective voice in their affairs both in the Legislative and Municipal Governments, and that the Conference pledges itself to submit proposals for such reforms.

2. That this Conference recommends a Constitution on the following lines: (1) An Executive Council as at present composed. (2) A Legislative Council composed of representatives of whom one-half shall be nominated by the Crown and the other half elected by the people, to deal with Legislation generally. (3) A House of Assembly, composed of the members of the Legislative Council together with six other financial representatives elected by the people, who shall have the power of imposing all taxes and of discussing freely and without reserve the items on the Annual Estimates of Revenue and Expenditure prepared by the Governor in the Executive Council and approving of them.

3. That each British West African Community shall have the power of electing members to both the Legislative Council and the House of Assembly through such local groups as may be found most convenient and expedient, and that where indigenous institutions do not provide a ready means of ascertaining the will of the people, other qualifying method for voting, such as a property or an Educational standard, shall be resorted to. In ascertaining groups, consideration shall be given to the most natural and scientific aggregations.

4. That this Conference is of the opinion that the exercise by the executive of Judicial functions in the West African Administrations is inimical to the best interests of the people, and pledges itself to submit representations at the proper quarter with a view to remedying the evil.

5. That this Conference desires to place on record its disapprobation of the invidious distinctions made in the present West African Civil Service by reason of colour, and is of the opinion that all future entries should be based on merit by competitive examinations, and pledges itself to submit proposals thereanent [sic] at the proper quarter.

6. That Municipal Corporations with full powers of local self-government be established in each principal town of the British West African Colonies, and that of the members of such Municipal Corporations four-fifths shall be elected by the rate-payers and one-fifth nominated by the Crown, and that such elected and nominated members have the power of electing the Mayor of the Corporation, who however must be an elected member.

Education with Particular Reference to a West African University

◆ **Resolutions**

1. That this Conference is of the opinion that the system of Education best suited to the needs and conditions of the various British West African peoples under British influence is one which, whilst enabling the students to attain the highest possible proficiency in the many departments of learning, will least interfere with the development by the student of a proper spirit of reverence for indigenous institutions and modes of life not opposed to equity and good conscience.

2. That in the opinion of this Conference the time has come to found a British West African University on such lines as would preserve in the students a sense of African Nationality, and therefore recommends that all existing Secondary Schools throughout West Africa, or those about to be formed, should promote a course of training that shall best attain the end in view.

3. That with this object in view it recommends that the different Boards of Education of each Colony should admit on them, African and other Educationists capable of contributing practical suggestions, and that in the submission of such suggestions they be guided by the experience of such communities as Japan which have encountered similar problems to that of West African Communities.

4. That besides existing Secondary Schools the Conference recommends each section of it to promote a scheme in each Colony whereby sound Secondary Education on national lines supported by the people may be promoted, and which shall form a further nucleus for the formation of the proposed British West African University.

5. That compulsory Education throughout the British West African Colonies be introduced by law, and that the standard of both the Primary and the Secondary Schools be uniformly raised to meet the Standard of the University.

6. That the Education Schemes of the Governments of the several British West African Dependencies be considered and incorporated in the Scheme and given as far as practicable a more national tone by cooperation between the Educationists controlling the working of the Scheme and such experienced educated Africans capable of suggesting lines of African National evolution.

7. That each British West African Colony promote a National Educational Fund so as to ensure the development of a national Educational Scheme, which fund, when the Scheme is in operation, may be supplemented by Government subsidies.

Commercial Enterprise with Particular Reference to (A) The Scheme of the Empire Resources Development Committee; (B) Banking; (C) Shipping

◆ Resolutions

1. That this Conference views with great disfavour the propaganda of the Empire Resources Development Committee with respect to the British West African Colonies, and is strongly of the opinion that the natural resources of the British West African Dependencies are not for the exploitation of Concessionaires under State control.

Further, that it condemns any policy which would make such resources available for the liquidation of the Imperial War Debt or any part of it, and pledges itself by constitutional means to oppose strenuously any such policy and directs that copies of this Resolution be forthwith transmitted to His Majesty's Principal Secretary of State for the Colonies and to each of the Governors of the Dependencies and all public bodies and societies whom it may concern.

2. That this Conference, being of the opinion that Trade competition in the British West African Dependencies should be free from restriction, views with great dissatisfaction the passing of the Palm Kernels Export Duty Ordinance in the various British West African Dependencies and pledges itself to make representations at the proper quarter with the object of securing their repeal.

3. That this Conference, being strongly convinced that the time has come for the co-operation of the peoples of the British West African Dependencies in promoting their economical development, recommends the consideration by the various Committees of the formation of a Corporation, to be known as the British West African Co-operative Association, under the Companies Acts, with powers, *inter alia*, to found Banks, promote shipping facilities, establish Co-operative Stores, and produce buying centres, in such wise as to inspire and maintain a British West African National Economical development.

Further, to ensure the object in view, this Conference pledges itself to educate the public opinion of the different communities, through their local Committees, as to the raising of a substantial capital in the British West African Co-operative Association and subject to the rules and conditions of the Companies Acts.

Further, that the collection and banking of such sums shall be under the direction and control of such Committee provided that the aggregate sum collected is to be treated as one fund and directs that this suggestion be referred to the different Committees for their consideration and report at the first sitting of the proposed Congress of Africans of British West Africa.

4. That this Conference disapproves of the issue by the Currency Board of coins and notes of a different face value from coins and notes outside British West Africa, and desires to place on record its opinion of the unfairness of such discrimination, and pledges itself to make representations at the proper quarter for the removal of such discrimination.

5. That, in view of the difficulties hereto experienced in the matter of space on British bottoms by legitimate African Traders and Shippers, this Conference welcomes competition in the shipping line with particular reference to the "Black Star Line."

6. That this Conference desires to draw the particular attention of the Directors of Messrs. Elder Dempster Line of Steamers to the indignities that British West African passengers suffer on their boats, and directs that representations be made at the proper quarter to correct the evil.

Judicial Reforms with Particular Reference to an Appellate Court

◆ **Resolutions**

1. That this Conference, having taken into its deep consideration the question of Judicial Reforms, is strongly of the opinion that further to enhance the integrity and independence of the Judges of the Supreme Courts of the British West African Dependencies, the source and conditions of their appointments should be the same as those of His Majesty's Judges in England.

2. That none but duly qualified and experienced legal men should hold Judicial appointments either as Judges of the Supreme Court, or as Magistrates, or as Commissioners, or exercise any functions whatsoever as such throughout British West Africa.

3. That the time has come to open definitely to African practitioners of experience all Judicial appointments.

4. That this Conference desires to place on record the widespread dissatisfaction throughout British West Africa as to the Constitution of the Appeal Court in which Judges sit on their Judgments, and recommends an early arrangement by which experienced Judges outside the British West African Judiciary might be appointed to form an Appellate Court for British West Africa.

5. That this Conference deplores the gradual modification in successive Ordinances throughout British West Africa of the right of citizens to trial by Jury in Criminal cases, and recommends that the right should be regulated in accordance with English Common and Statute Laws, all local Ordinances thereanent [sic] notwithstanding, and that the Assessors Ordinance should be abolished.

6. That the benefits of the Criminal Appeal Act in Criminal cases be preserved to citizens of West Africa in terms of the Criminal Appeal Act of 1908 and the same be extended to citizens of British West Africa....

12. That this Conference wholly condemns the barbarous practice of flogging African women for any offence whatsoever, notwithstanding any local Ordinance to the contrary, and also deprecates the resort to flogging in any other case save in suitable cases ordered by a sentence of a Judge or Magistrate of competent Jurisdiction.

West African Press Union

◆ **Resolutions**

1. That this Conference desires to record its deep sense of the important part the Press plays in National development, and directs that a Committee of experienced Journalists be appointed to investigate and report upon the best means of promoting greater co-operation in the British West African Press....

3. That this Conference is strongly of the opinion that the liberty of the Press is the birthright of every Community within the British Empire, and deprecates any Legislation that threatens such a right, recommends the immediate repeal of any such repressive laws wherever operating in the British West African Dependencies, and directs strong representations to be made upon the matter at the right quarter.

4. That, it being desirable that the projected Congress of Africans of British West Africa should own a quarterly Magazine to be known as the British West African National Review and the Official organ of the Congress, this Conference directs that such an organ be established, with Head office at Seccondee in the Gold Coast, under the editorship of the Honourable Casely Hayford, and that the same be maintained out of the Congress Inaugural Fund.

The Policy of the Government in Relation to the Land Question

◆ **Resolutions**

1. That in the opinion of this Conference the principle of Trusteeship with respect of the lands of the people of British West Africa by Government has been overdone, and that it is proper to declare that the average British West African is quite capable of controlling and looking after his own interests in the land.

2. That however welcome occasional advice on the part of Executive Officers may be, it is desirable that in Government dealings with the people in respect of their lands, no steps should be taken which might shake their confidence....

The Right of the People to Self Determination

◆ **Resolutions**

1. That the Conference views with alarm the right assumed by the European powers of exchanging or partitioning Countries between them, without refer-

ence to, or regard for, the wishes of the people, and records the opinion that such a course is tantamount to a species of slavery.

2. That this Conference condemns specifically the partitioning of Togo-land between the English and the French Governments and the handing over of the Cameroons to the French Government without consulting or regarding the wishes of the peoples in the matter.

3. That it respectfully desires an assurance from His Majesty's Government that under no circumstances whatsoever will it be a consenting part to the integrity of any of the four British West African Colonies being disturbed.

4. That this Conference desires to place on record the attachment of the peoples of British West Africa to the British connection and their unfeigned loyalty and devotion to the throne and person of His Majesty the King-Emperor, and directs that copies of these Resolutions be forwarded in due course to His Majesty's Principal Secretary of State for the Colonies and to each of the Governors of the several Dependencies.

The Inauguration of the Congress of Africans of British West Africa

◆ Resolutions

1. That this Conference being fully convinced of the importance of continuing and perpetuating its work, resolved itself into the National Congress of British West Africa.

◆ Policy

It is hereby resolved by this Congress that its policy is to maintain strictly and inviolate the connection of the British West African Dependencies with the British Empire, and to maintain unreservedly all and every right of free citizenship of the Empire and the fundamental principle that taxation goes with effective representation.

Glossary

British bottoms	in this context, British ships
His Majesty	King George V
propaganda of the Empire Resources Development Committee	that nongovernmental body's position that Africans should be assimilated into European society and that the inevitably accompanying breakdown of tribal organization was a proper goal
Togo-land	the territory that in 1920 was known as British Togoland; later integrated with Gold Coast, now part of independent Ghana

Sun Yat-sen (Library of Congress)

SUN YAT-SEN'S "THE THREE PRINCIPLES OF THE PEOPLE"

"There are 400 million Chinese: if they cannot organise a single nation, a united State, this is their disgrace."

Overview

On March 6, 1921, Sun Yat-sen, the founder of the Republic of China, delivered a speech at a meeting of the Executive Committee of the National People's Party in the southern Chinese city of Guangzhou (Canton). In this speech, titled "The Three Principles of the People" ("*Sanmin zhuyi*"), Sun elaborated on the three primary tenets of his political doctrine: the ethnic nation (*minzu*), the people's rights (*minquan*), and the well-being of the people (*minsheng*). In English, these principles have often been translated as nationalism, democracy, and Socialism. In Chinese, each of these principles contains the character *min*, which means "people." Sun likened his principles to U.S. president Abraham Lincoln's ideals of government "of the people" (nationalism), "by the people" (democracy), and "for the people" (Socialism).

As early as 1905, Sun had drafted the first version of "The Three Principles" in collaboration with some of his followers. Initially, the principles constituted a guideline for his revolutionary plan to overthrow the Qing (Manchu) Dynasty, which had ruled China since 1644. After the successful Chinese Revolution of 1911 and the proclamation of the Republic of China the following year, Sun transformed his Revolutionary Alliance into the National People's Party (also known as the Nationalist Party, or Guomindang in Chinese). Despite its victory in the first parliamentary election, the Guomindang was unable to extend influence over most of China. Instead, rivalries between factional military leaders dominated the first fifteen years of the young republic. In 1921 the Chinese Communist Party was founded in Shanghai, while Sun was in the process of reviving the Guomindang in its regional stronghold of Guangzhou. For several years during the 1920s, the Guomindang was allied with the Chinese Communist Party.

In a series of lectures given in Guangzhou in 1924 only months before his death, Sun issued his final version of "The Three Principles." Despite the existence of various versions of the principles, in essence they remained largely unaltered and undisputed from the first version of 1905 to the final version of 1924. However, Sun repeatedly refined his political program as reflected in "The Three Principles" and amended his thought on democratic and constitutional ideals in further writings. Sun envisioned China as a republic in which all Chinese people could exert their political rights and secure their material well-being. During the war against Japan (1937–1945), all of China's major political leaders followed Sun's principles but disagreed about how to interpret them. Today, Sun is revered as the founder of modern China not only by the Chinese Communist Party in the People's Republic of China on the mainland but also in the Republic of China on the island of Taiwan, where "The Three Principles" have become part of the constitution.

Context

Since the mid-seventeenth century, China had been ruled by the Qing, or Manchu, Dynasty, which was considered culturally and racially foreign by the majority of the Han Chinese. During the first 150 years of their rule, the Qing gradually expanded their influence over vast parts of today's China. In the nineteenth century, however, their rule was continually challenged by local and regional insurrections as well as the court's inability to deal with Western nations. After China's defeat by the British in the First Opium War (1840–1842), the country was forcefully opened to the West by treaties that were considered unequal by the Chinese, as they were not the result of negotiation but rather were imposed on China by the Western powers through threat of force. Although the treaties' direct impact was hardly felt beyond the capital (Beijing), Hong Kong, and the port cities in the southeast (Shanghai, Xiamen, Fuzhou, Ningbo, and Guangzhou), Qing rule was enormously weakened when religious sects and ethnic groups started rebellions throughout the country. In 1853 the Taiping, a Christian religious sect, even declared its own independent country in the former capital of Nanjing. The Qing Dynasty eventually managed to crush the Taiping Rebellion (1850–1864) and other insurrections; however, it never fully recovered from these challenges to its authority. In the 1890s the Qing court finally gave in to calls for political reform following China's defeat by France in the Sino-French War of 1883–1885, fought over economic and

1866

- **November 12**
  Sun Yat-sen is born in the village of Choy Hung (Guangdong Province).

1894

- Sun submits a reform proposal to Governor-General Li Hongzhang and founds his first revolutionary organization, the Revive China Society, while living abroad in Honolulu.

1898

- The Hundred Days' Reform movement in Beijing, led by the scholars Kang Youwei and Liang Qichao, fails.

1905

- Sun Yat-sen founds the Revolutionary Alliance (Tongmenghui) while living in exile in Tokyo.

- **November 26**
  The Tongmenghui newspaper *People's Paper* publishes the first version of "The Three Principles of the People."

1911

- **December 29**
  Following the overthrow of the Qing Dynasty, Sun Yat-sen is elected provisional president of the first Chinese Republic.

political dominance in Vietnam, and defeat by Japan in the first Sino-Japanese War of 1894–1895, fought over political supremacy in Korea. Initially, the Qing court and Emperor Guangxu encouraged the Hundred Days' Reform of 1898, which was led by Chinese scholars who had been educated in Japan and aimed at making comprehensive social and institutional changes within China. But the reform movement was soon suppressed at the behest of the Empress Dowager Cixi, who staged a coup and took over power in September. Foreign intervention to end the Boxer Rebellion, a violent anti-imperialist uprising of 1900–1901, further weakened Qing rule.

As early as 1894, Sun had submitted reform proposals to Li Hongzhang, the governor-general of the province of Zhili who was known as a reformer at court. When Sun was rebuffed, he called for the abolition of the monarchy. The Qing court's reintroduction of reform policies from 1902 onward failed to placate opposition groups such as Sun's Revive China Society, which he had founded in 1894 in Honolulu. Most members were Chinese living overseas (including Sun), and the goal was primarily to overthrow the Qing and set up a central, unified Han Chinese government. In 1905 the Revive China Society and other revolutionary groups met in Tokyo (where Sun was living in exile) to form the Revolutionary Alliance, known in Chinese as Tongmenghui, under Sun's leadership. The alliance stated its political goals as the expulsion of the Qing, revival of China, establishment of a republic, and equal land distribution. In his first version of "The Three Principles of the People," published in the Tongmenghui's *People's Paper* (*Min bao*) as early as 1905, Sun called for the Han Chinese ethnic majority to realize the principle of nationalism by overthrowing the Qing Dynasty and assuming political control of China. This anti-Qing ideology remained central until the successful Chinese Revolution of 1911, after which the cause of national unification in the form of a democratic republic and the integration of the various ethnic groups in China began to take priority.

The Qing Dynasty was finally overthrown in 1911, after which Sun returned to China and was elected provisional president of the first Chinese Republic. Following the establishment of the Chinese Republic in 1912, regional army leaders gained control of vast territories and undermined the ideals of Sun, despite his political prominence and his party's win of a majority of seats in the new National Assembly. Sun was compelled to resign as provisional president of the republic by the powerful General Yuan Shikai, who in 1915 established himself briefly as quasi-emperor, after having undermined the Guomindang and forced Sun into exile once more. From Yuan's death in 1916 to Chiang Kai-shek's establishment of a central government in Nanjing in 1928, China remained divided and ruled by regional warlords.

From 1916, when he returned to China, until his death in 1925, Sun undertook several attempts to extend his influence from his native base in Guangzhou to other parts of the country. His reiteration and reinterpretation of the "The Three Principles of the People" in 1921 must be seen against the background of continuing domestic power struggles. In view of popular calls for extending political rights and achieving national independence, Sun's combination of Socialist, democratic, and nationalist ideas appeared particularly promising. Although Sun was well known and respected abroad, he failed to gain international support for his campaign to establish central authority in China under his leadership. His last effort at national unity—the alliance of the reorganized Guomindang with the newly founded Chinese Communist Party in 1923—ended prematurely when he fell sick in late 1924 while on his way to Beijing to attend a conference on national reconstruction. He died weeks later, in March 1925.

About the Author

Sun Yat-sen was born in 1866 in southeastern China near Guangzhou in today's Guangdong Province. In 1879 he left China to study medicine in Hawaii and then moved to Hong Kong. In 1895, after China's defeat in the First Sino-Japanese War, he led his first insurrection against the Qing Dynasty. When it failed, Sun was banned from Hong Kong and went into exile in Japan. He also traveled widely and lived in other Asian and Western countries, where he sought support for his revolutionary cause. While he was in London in 1896, he was kidnapped by Chinese agents and detained by the Chinese legation. The event was well publicized and immediately elevated Sun to the ranks of a celebrity. In 1905 he brought several anti-Qing forces together and founded the Revolutionary Alliance (Tongmenghui) in Tokyo. Several of Sun's attempts to overthrow the Qing Dynasty and establish a Chinese republic failed before the successful Chinese Revolution of 1911.

Outside his native base in southern China, Sun lacked the support and means to unify the country. In 1912 he had to allow general Yuan Shikai to become president. After Yuan undermined the power of the Chinese National Assembly in 1913, Sun was forced into exile again. Upon his return to China in 1916, Sun attempted to reestablish his political power base in Guangzhou, where in 1919 he reorganized the Guomindang. Although he successfully recruited new allies, such as Chiang Kai-shek, who was then still an army officer, and gained the support of the newly founded Communist Party, he failed to expand his Guangzhou base of operations into a national government. In 1924 he accepted an invitation by northern militarists to a conference about national reconstruction. On his way there, Sun fell ill; he died in Beijing of liver cancer on March 12, 1925.

Explanation and Analysis of the Document

In March 1921 prominent members of the Guomindang assembled in Guangzhou for a meeting of the party's Executive Committee. In a speech given on March 6, Sun addressed the committee with the intent of strengthening the ideological unity of the Guomindang. His central mes-

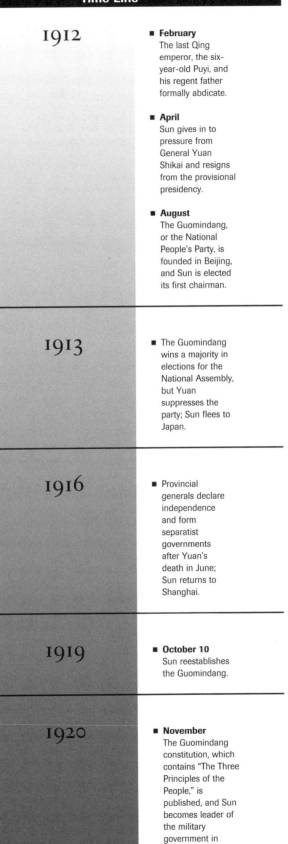

Time Line

1912

- **February**
  The last Qing emperor, the six-year-old Puyi, and his regent father formally abdicate.

- **April**
  Sun gives in to pressure from General Yuan Shikai and resigns from the provisional presidency.

- **August**
  The Guomindang, or the National People's Party, is founded in Beijing, and Sun is elected its first chairman.

1913

- The Guomindang wins a majority in elections for the National Assembly, but Yuan suppresses the party; Sun flees to Japan.

1916

- Provincial generals declare independence and form separatist governments after Yuan's death in June; Sun returns to Shanghai.

1919

- **October 10**
  Sun reestablishes the Guomindang.

1920

- **November**
  The Guomindang constitution, which contains "The Three Principles of the People," is published, and Sun becomes leader of the military government in Guangzhou.

1921

- **March 6**
  Sun addresses the Executive Committee of the Guomindang at a meeting in Guangzhou and reiterates the importance of "The Three Principles."

- **April**
  Sun is appointed extraordinary president of the Republic of China in Guangzhou.

- **July**
  The Chinese Communist Party is founded in Shanghai.

1924

- **January–August**
  Sun delivers a series of speeches in Guangzhou that contain the final version of "The Three Principles."

1925

- **March 12**
  Sun dies in Beijing of liver cancer.

1928

- Sun's successor, General Chiang Kai-shek, forms a national government in Nanjing after having unified most of China by means of successful military campaigns against remaining warlords.

sage was the necessity of awakening the Chinese people to the significance of "The Three Principles of the People." According to Sun, it was the party members' task to work toward the realization of these principles in order to unify China under his leadership.

◆ Paragraphs 1–6

The 1921 version of "The Three Principles" begins with a brief historical overview of the early days of the Guomindang. Sun then devotes most of his speech to elaborating on his principles, here translated as "nationalism," "democracy," and "Socialism." Against the rising influence of Marxist forces after the Russian Revolution, Sun calls his comrades to take seriously not only the principle of nationalism—which he viewed as partially realized after the overthrow of the Qing Dynasty (called "Tsing" and "the Manchus" in the text)—but also those of democracy and Socialism. Notwithstanding the nationalist and anti-imperialist political trends of the times, Sun emphasizes his openness to foreign ideas and makes numerous references to political and social conditions abroad from which the Chinese could learn.

In his opening paragraphs, Sun addresses the role of the Guomindang in the establishment of the Chinese republic and briefly introduces the main points of his speech. By likening the dissolution of the party to the political disorder in China, Sun implies that the country can be saved only if the party and its members work as a cohesive unit. Moving on to the "fundamental principles of our Party," Sun emphasizes that the party's mission had not been fulfilled simply with the overthrow of Qing rule and the implementation of the principle of nationalism. Rather, the principles of democracy and Socialism needed to be realized, too, in order to achieve national stability.

Sun then presents the United States as a model for China and compares his three principles to Abraham Lincoln's principles of government of, by, and for the people. Sun counters claims of cultural essentialists—and older versions of his own principles—that demanded an approach to modernization based on ancient Chinese virtues. Instead, Sun stresses the international trend of times, within which his Western-inspired teachings were strongly rooted.

◆ Paragraphs 7–14: "Nationalism"

Sun argues that the party has failed to bring "complete freedom" and "the blessings of liberty" to the people since the Chinese Revolution. Consequently, China must be characterized as "only semi-independent." Sun offers both internal and external reasons for this failure. Out of the five primary nationalities that he names (Han Chinese, Manchurians, Mongols, Tartars, and Tibetans), Sun observes that three were still under foreign control: Manchuria was controlled by the Japanese, Mongolia by Russia, and Tibet by Great Britain. Sun also attacks the failure of the Han Chinese majority to form a "single nation, a united State." As models of national unity, Sun lifts up the United States and Switzerland. Just as members of different ethnic groups consider themselves citizens of the United States or Switzerland, all ethnic groups in China should unite as one nation and stop identifying themselves primarily by ethnic background. They ought to commit themselves to the cause of *zhonghua* (called Chunhua in the document)—referring essentially to the Chinese nationality as a whole.

At the end of this section, Sun refers to the principle of "self-determination of nations," as expressed by U.S. president Woodrow Wilson in 1918 in his Fourteen Points. Sun employs this phrase to define his "positive," or voluntary, conception of nationalism, which assumes that an individual is free to become a citizen of the country of his or her choice. At the same time, however, Sun's statements reveal vestiges of Han centrism, which asserted the cultural superiority of the Han over all other ethnicities in China. This assumption has remained the cornerstone of China's policy toward minorities to this day. According to this reasoning, the Han's mission is one of "setting free" China's other ethnic groups and uniting them "under the banner of a single Chinese nation"—if necessary, against their will.

◆ Paragraphs 15–16: "Democracy"

The shortest section of Sun's speech is dedicated to the principle of the rights of the people, or democracy. Sun again mentions Switzerland and deems it the country in which democracy has reached "its highest point of development." However, he criticizes the Swiss form of representative government for having not fully provided for the rights of all citizens. He contends that this was also true in France, the United States, and the United Kingdom. Herein lies Sun's revolutionary approach to democracy. Instead of a representative democratic system, Sun advocates the implementation of direct and equal rights for all citizens. As the four cornerstones of this direct form of democracy, Sun names universal suffrage ("the franchise for all citizens"), the right to recall elected officials, the right to reject laws by referendum, and "the right of initiative," in which citizens may propose legislation to be "carried and adopted" by the legislative body.

This section does not represent a comprehensive summary of Sun's concept of a democratic political order. Rather, Sun here briefly explains his views on the rights of the people within the general framework of constitutional democracy. However, the Fivefold Constitution, to which Sun alludes in his introductory remarks, did not actually grant such broad rights to the people. The Fivefold Constitution provided for a highly structured Chinese government consisting of executive, legislative, judicial, examining, and supervisory branches. Moreover, Sun's three stages of the revolution—military dictatorship, political tutelage, and constitutional government, none of which are mentioned in this speech—placed considerable limitations on the rights to be enjoyed by the people.

◆ Paragraphs 17–32: "Socialism"

The longest section of the speech is dedicated to the principle of the well-being or livelihood of the people, usually translated as "Socialism." After a brief recapitulation of all three of his principles, Sun moves on to his explanation of "solving the problem of land and capital," which he identifies as underlying the inequality between rich and poor.

Sun first notes the disproportional distribution of land in China. As a solution to this problem, he proposes the socialization of land. By this, however, Sun does not mean the immediate and coercive nationalization of all land. Rather, he proposes a proportional distribution of land, that is, the equalization of land ownership by implementing a new taxation system. According to Sun's proposal, the state or a local authority such as a municipality would have the right to purchase land at a price fixed by the owner. In return, according to the system of graduated taxes, the landowner would pay taxes based on the self-declared value of the land. Thus, the state would have the right to buy any privately owned land at a price fixed by the owner. The state normally would not do so, so the land would remain privately owned and subject to taxation. This way, Sun thought, the state could make a fair deal with the land owner without losing money to the potentially corrupt tax collectors. However, the land would be taxed according to the price fixed by the land owner. If the landowner sought to betray the state (by naming too low a price in order to save annual taxes), he would have to fear that the state might actually buy the land at this low price. This system, according to Sun, would naturally eliminate dishonesty among tax collectors and landowners.

The last paragraphs of this section deal with "the problem of capital." Sun refers to his book *The International Development of China*, first published in 1920, and affirms that the party should be open to utilizing foreign capital for the development of China's key industries and infrastructure, such as mining and railways. Sun's openness to anything foreign—whether foreign ideas or foreign capital—is again well reflected in this section. His phrasing, however, remains more careful, as many Chinese feared that depending too much on foreign aid would obstruct China's struggle for independence and autarky, both economically and politically. This fear was particularly widespread with regard to financial aid from Japan, which, however, was Sun's favored source of help owing to his long-cultivated contacts there. On the other hand, Sun had little choice but to accept loans from any side, as his southern regime needed to raise huge sums not only to develop industry and infrastructure there but also to compete with the government in the north of China over the claim for central authority.

◆ Paragraphs 33–38

In his ending remarks, Sun addresses the role of the party in implementing his three fundamental principles. In Sun's view, the political revolution had been achieved in 1911, but the social revolution was yet to come. He calls on the party to work toward a social revolution in which his principles "will grow into reality." On one hand, Sun expresses his satisfaction with the strong position the party has regained in the province of Guangdong (called Kwantung in the speech). On the other, though, he warns his fellow party members not to stop at this stage. Rather, starting from Guangzhou, the party should strive to implement

Sun's principles all over the country and thus realize the true meaning of the word "republic," or *minguo*, which literally translates as "country of the people." Sun closes with an appeal to his comrades to use the Guomindang's return to power in Guangzhou as a springboard for propagating the party program, namely, the "great principles of nationalism, democracy, and Socialism."

Audience

The direct audience of Sun's speech were members of the Guomindang who had convened in Guangzhou for a meeting of the Executive Committee. Sun held high hopes for the party members' active role in the promotion of his trio of principles, which he regarded as fundamental to the prosperous future of a unified China. Because of the political struggle for power in China, Sun explicitly delegated the propagation of his ideas to his most immediate followers. Yet Sun's broader audience included all Chinese and also foreigners living in China. Additionally, Sun's careful and diplomatic choice of words indicated that he had an even larger international audience in mind, namely, potential allies abroad. Ever since he had started his political activities in the late nineteenth century, Sun had undertaken to gain the support of foreigners for his revolutionary cause. His internationalist outlook never wavered. In fact, the problematic situation in China had often made it necessary for Sun to look for support abroad, both political and financial.

"The Three Principles" had been a core component of Sun's agenda since before the Chinese Revolution. Various versions were published between 1905 and 1924, when Sun delivered his last series of lectures. The principles were also well known abroad, in particular in Japan, where Sun had spent many years in exile and had become a prominent political figure. Although the concrete political circumstances of 1921—the domestic power struggle and the revitalization of the Guomindang—were the immediate historical backdrop to Sun's speech, his words were not intended merely to reaffirm the validity of his long-held convictions. Rather, Sun's reiteration of his principles constituted an attempt to construct a theoretical continuity for establishing political authority, first in Guangzhou and then nationwide.

Impact

The most immediate impact of Sun's speech was the affirmation of his role as the theoretical and practical leader of the Guomindang and, potentially, the Chinese nation. This claim was affirmed one month later on April 7, 1921, when Sun was elected extraordinary president of the Republic of China. More significantly, the speech revealed that Sun had already largely formulated a blueprint for what would become his final version of "The Three Principles," which was set forth in his final series of lectures, given in Guangzhou between January and August 1924. This last version was transcribed from the lectures and

became canonical soon after Sun's death in 1925. It is unlikely, however, that most of Sun's followers ever read the entire 250-page text of the final version.

"The Three Principles of the People" became Sun's central political and ideological legacy, and his potential successors fought harshly over the interpretation of his fundamental tenets. Eventually, the traditionalist interpretation of the principles prevailed. This interpretation was put forth by so-called rightists within the Guomindang; two of the most prominent were Sun's disciple and translator, Dai Jitao (1890–1949), and Sun's son-in-law and eventual successor, Chiang Kai-shek (1887–1975). Chinese Communists, with whom the Guomindang were allied in the 1920s and during the war against Japan, and Soviet advisers to both parties attempted to place more emphasis on the Socialist, revolutionary, and anti-imperialistic character of the principles.

The issues Sun addressed in "The Three Principles" remained of central concern for China in the decades following his death. In accordance with Sun's principle of Socialism, the Communists emphasized fair treatment of common people, as opposed to the Guomindang's protection of the bourgeoisie and capitalists. Chiang Kai-shek gave priority to the cause of national unification and justified his authoritarian rule in the name of Sun's principle of nationalism. During the Japanese invasion of China, a third position emerged under Chiang's rival, Wang Jingwei, who had been a close follower of Sun since his earliest days. Wang argued for close cooperation with the Japanese in order to bring peace to China and allow for national reconstruction as a precondition to the fulfillment of Sun's ideology. Sun's legacy remained central to the political history of China until the civil war between Mao Zedong's Communists and Chiang Kai-shek's Nationalists, which divided China. While Sun's legacy on the mainland today is overshadowed by that of Mao Zedong, on Taiwan he is still referred to by his honorary title, "father of the country" (*guofu*), and the national anthem is named after "The Three Principles."

Further Reading

■ Articles
Gregor, A. James, and Maria Hsia Chang. "Nazionalfascismo and the Revolutionary Nationalism of Sun Yat-sen." *Journal of Asian Studies* 39, no. 1 (November 1979): 21–37.

■ Books
Bergère, Marie-Claire. *Sun Yat-sen*, trans. Janet Lloyd. Stanford, Calif.: Stanford University Press, 1998.

Etō, Shinkichi, and Harold Z. Schiffrin, eds. *China's Republican Revolution*. Tokyo: University of Tokyo Press, 1994.

Jansen, Marius B. *The Japanese and Sun Yat-sen*. Cambridge, Mass: Harvard University Press, 1954.

Schiffrin, Harold Z. *Sun Yat-sen, Reluctant Revolutionary*. Boston: Little, Brown, 1980.

"It is now clear that the reason for all that has happened is that our comrades despised—in the name of nationalism—the other two principles of democracy and Socialism.... We must firmly know and remember that, so long as all three principles have not been carried into real life..., there can be no stable conditions of existence."

(Paragraph 5)

"The principles of President Lincoln completely coincide with mine. He said: 'A government of the people, elected by the people and for the people.' These principles have served as the maximum of achievement for Europeans as well as Americans. Words which have the same sense can be found in China: I have translated them: 'nationalism, democracy and Socialism.'"

(Paragraph 6)

"There are 400 million Chinese: if they cannot organise a single nation, a united State, this is their disgrace.... We shall establish a united Chinese Republic in order that all the peoples—Manchus, Mongols, Tibetans, Tartars and Chinese—should constitute a single powerful nation.... Such a nationalism is possible, and we must pursue it."

(Paragraph 11)

"Although revolutions took place at various times in France, America and England, and resulted in the establishment of the existing representative system, nevertheless that system does not mean direct and equal rights for all citizens, such as we are fighting for to-day. The most essential of such rights are: the franchise for all citizens: the right of recall ... the right of referendum ... the right of initiative."

(Paragraph 15)

"Those who discuss the question of the brotherhood of peoples in America and Europe have in view only two problems—labours and capital.... In China there is general poverty, since there are no large capitalists.... Disproportion in the distribution of products, both in America and in Europe, are a bad example for us. Therefore I agitate for Socialism—the socialisation of land and capital."

(Paragraph 25)

Strand, David. "Community, Society, and History in Sun Yat-sen's Sanmin zhuyi." In *Culture & State in Chinese History: Conventions, Accommodations, and Critiques,* ed. Theodore Huters et al. Stanford, Calif.: Stanford University Press, 1997.

Sun, Yat-sen. *Kidnapped in London.* London: China Society, 1969.

———. *Prescriptions for Saving China: Selected Writings of Sun Yat-sen,* trans. and ed. Julie Lee Wei et al. Stanford, Calif.: Hoover Institution Press, 1994.

Zheng, Zhuyuan, ed. *Sun Yat-sen's Doctrine in the Modern World.* Boulder, Colo.: Westview Press, 1989.

■ **Web Sites**

Spence, Jonathan D. "Sun Yat-sen." Time Asia Web site. http://www.time.com/time/asia/asia/magazine/1999/990823/sun_yat_sen1.html.

—Torsten Weber

Questions for Further Study

1. In conjunction with Articles Providing for the Favorable Treatment of the Great Ching Emperor after His Abdication, Mao Zedong's "Report on an Investigation of the Peasant Movement in Hunan," and the Constitution of the People's Republic of China, create a time line of key events in modern Chinese history. Be prepared to explain why each entry in your time line is important and how each event paved the way for subsequent events.

2. Why is Sun Yat-sen "revered as the founder of modern China" both by the mainland Communists and the Nationalists on Taiwan—nations with deeply opposing political ideologies?

3. What forces made it difficult for Sun Yat-sen to unify China in the wake of the overthrowing of the Qing Dynasty?

4. Compare this document with the Meiji Constitution of Japan. What similarities—and differences—do the two documents have as Japan and China attempted to make the transition into the modern era? What similar cultural and economic factors played a role in this effort at modernization?

5. How do you think that U.S. president Abraham Lincoln would have reacted to Sun Yat-sen's use of his words in his formulation of a political ideology? Do you think that Lincoln would have regarded this appeal to his words as accurate and as fair?

SUN YAT-SEN'S "THE THREE PRINCIPLES OF THE PEOPLE"

Comrades,...

To-day, at the opening of our Executive session, the question involuntarily arises before me: what does our organisation represent? This in brief is its history, and the principles which guide it.

Our Party was formed after the overthrow of the Tsing (Manchu) dynasty and the establishment of a republican form of Government. It has to play a tremendous part in the future of our country. From the time this Party was dissolved, China has been constantly in a state of disorder. It is, of course, natural that the reason for the disturbances and sufferings of the Chinese people was the dissolution of our Party. For many years we have fought, and are still fighting, against the traitors to the people who live to this day in the northern provinces of China, where the influence of our Party is very small: nevertheless, sooner or later the northerners will join us. In the south of China, in the sphere of influence of the Party, there is only the single province of Kwantung.

Our Party is revolutionary. In the second year after the establishment of the republican order, many of its members went abroad, where they worked energetically for the development of the revolutionary movement in China. Hence the name of the Party. While it was working in Tokyo, the Party was known as the "National League": the difference of names, of course, does not alter the character and essence of the aims it pursues. Our Republic is already ten years old, but we still cannot look upon it as a fully perfected type, or consider that our aim has been achieved. Our work is not yet completed: we must continue the struggle.

Our Party is radically different from all the other parties of China, Thus, there was a Party which strove for the overthrow of the Tsing dynasty and the establishment of another dynasty, Ming. Of course, the principles of this party were opposed to ours. When in the last years of the Tsing dynasty, we were forced to establish ourselves in Tokyo, we determined the following as the fundamental principles of our Party: nationalism, democracy and Socialism.

At that time, power in China was still in the hands of the Manchus, and the Revolution had only arrived at its first stage, nationalism, passing over the other two principles."The Fivefold Constitution" has great importance for our country in the sense of establishing a firm and just form of government; but, before the overthrow of the Tsing dynasty, many thought that the overthrow of that dynasty was the ultimate aim of our Party, and that thereafter China would proceed along the road of universal development and success. But has that proved to be the case? It is now clear that the reason for all that has happened is that our comrades despised—in the name of nationalism—the other two principles of democracy and Socialism. This once again proves that our work did not conclude with the overthrow of the Tsing dynasty. We must firmly know and remember that, so long as all three principles have not been carried into real life (even if one of them had been completely realised), there can be no stable conditions of existence.

Furthermore, in fact, our nationalism has not yet been completely realised. The principles of President Lincoln completely coincide with mine. He said: "A government of the people, elected by the people and for the people." These principles have served as the maximum of achievement for Europeans as well as Americans. Words which have the same sense can be found in China: I have translated them: "nationalism, democracy and Socialism." Of course, there can be other interpretations. The wealth and power of the United States are a striking example of the results of great men's teachings in that country. I am glad to observe that my principles, too, are shared by the greatest political minds abroad and are not in contradiction to all the world's democratic schools of thought.

I now wish to speak of nationalism.

(1) Nationalism

What meaning do we impart to the word "nationalism"? With the establishment of the Manchu dynasty in China, the people remained under an incredible yoke for over two hundred years. Now that dynasty has been overthrown, and the people, it would seem, ought to enjoy complete freedom. But does the Chinese people enjoy all the blessings of liberty? No. Then what is the reason? Why, that our

Party has as yet far from fulfilled its appointed tasks, and has carried out only the negative part of its work, without doing anything of its positive work.

Since the end of the great European War, the world position has sharply changed: the eyes of the whole world are now turned to the Far East, particularly to China. Strictly speaking, amongst all the nations of the Far East only Siam and Japan are completely independent. China, vast territorially and exceeding dozens of times in population the independent countries, is yet in effect only semi-independent. What is the reason?

After the overthrow of the monarchy and the establishment of the republican system in the territory populated by the five nationalities (Chinese, Manchus, Mongols, Tartars and Tibetans), a vast number of reactionary and religious elements appeared. And here lies the root of the evil. Numerically, these nationalities stand as follows: there are several million Tibetans, less than a million Mongols, about ten million Tartars, and the most insignificant number of Manchus, Politically their distribution is as follows: Manchuria is in the sphere of Japanese influence, Mongolia, according to recent reports, is under the influence of Russia, and Tibet is the booty of Great Britain. These races have not sufficient strength for self-defence but they might unite with the Chinese to form single State.

There are 400 million Chinese: if they cannot organise a single nation, a united State, this is their disgrace, and moreover a proof that we have not given complete effect even to the first principle, and that we must fight for a long while yet to carry out our tasks to the full. We shall establish an united Chinese Republic in order that all the peoples—Manchus, Mongols, Tibetans, Tartars and Chinese—should constitute a single powerful nation. As an example of what I have described, I can refer to the people of the United States of America, constituting one great and terrible whole, but in reality consisting of many separate nationalities: Germans, Dutch, English, French, etc. The United States are an example of a united nation. Such a nationalism is possible, and we must pursue it.

The name "Republic of Five Nationalities" exists only because there exists a certain racial distinction which distorts the meaning of a single Republic. We must facilitate the dying out of all names of individual people inhabiting China, i.e. Manchus, Tibetans, etc. In this respect we must follow the example of the United States of America, i.e. satisfy the demands and requirements of all races and unite them in a single cultural and political whole, to constitute a single nation with such a name, for example, as "Chunhua" (China—in the widest application of the name). Organise the nation, the State.

Or take another case of a nation of mingled races—Switzerland. It is situated in the heart of Europe: on one side it borders on France, on another on Germany, on a third, Italy. Not all the parts of this State have a common tongue, yet they constitute one nation. And only the wise cultural and political life of Switzerland makes its people of many races united and strong. All this is the consequence of the citizens of this Republic enjoying equal and direct electoral rights. Regarding this country from the aspect of international policy, we see that it was the first to establish equal and direct electoral rights for all the population. This is an example of "nationalism."

But let us imagine that the work of uniting all the tribes who inhabit China has been completed, and one nation, "Chunhua," has been formed. Still the object has not been achieved. There are still many peoples suffering from unjust treatment: the Chinese people must assume the mission of setting free these people from their yoke, in the sense of direct aid for them or uniting them under the banner of a single Chinese nation. This would give them the opportunity to enjoy the feeling of equality of man and man, and of a just international attitude, i.e. that which was expressed in the declaration of the American President Wilson by the words "self-determination of nations." Up to the moment of reaching this political stage, our work cannot be considered as finished. Everyone who wishes to join China must be considered Chinese. This is the meaning of nationalism—but "positive" nationalism, and to this we must give special attention.

(2) Democracy

I have already said that in Switzerland democracy has reached its highest point of development: but at the same time the system of representation prevailing there does not constitute real democracy, and only the direct right of the citizen fully answers to the requirements of democracy. Although revolutions took place at various times in France, America and England, and resulted in the establishment of the existing representative system, nevertheless that system does not mean direct and equal rights for all citizens, such as we are fighting for to-day. The most essential of such rights are: the franchise for all citizens: the right of recall (the officials elected by the people can be dismissed by them at will): the right of referendum (if the legislative body passes a law contrary to the wishes of the citizens, the latter may reject the law): the right of initiative (the citizens may propose draft laws, to be carried and adopted by the legislative body).

These four fundamental clauses constitute the basis of what I call "direct electoral right."

(3) Socialism

The theory of Socialism has become known in China comparatively recently. Its chief advocates usually limit their knowledge of this tendency to a few empty words, without having any definite programme. By long study I have formed a concrete view of this question. The essence of Socialism amounts to solving the problem of land and capital.

Above I have set forth the general main idea of the "three principles." The efforts of the whole world, including the Chinese people, are directed to this aim, and I say that our Party must immediately set about carrying these principles into effect.

Summing up the above, I want also to make a few additional observations.

(1) *Nationalism.*—Since the overthrow of the Tsing dynasty, we have carried out only one part of our obligations: we have fulfilled only our passive duty, but have done nothing in the realm of positive work. We must raise the prestige of the Chinese people, and unite all the races inhabiting China to form one Chinese people in eastern Asia, a Chinese National State.

(2) *Democracy.*—To bring about this ideal we must first of all adopt all the four points of direct electoral rights: universal suffrage, the referendum, the initiative and the right of recall.

(3). *Socialism.*—Here I have my plan.

The first task of my plan is to bring about the proportional distribution of the land. During my stay at Nanking (as Provisional President), I tried to carry out this proposal, but my desire was not fulfilled, as I was not understood. Social questions arise from the inequality between rich and poor. What do we understand by inequality? In ancient times, although there was a distinction between rich and poor, it was not so sharp as to-day. Today the rich own all the land, while the poor have not even a little plot. The reason for this inequality is the difference in productive power. For example, in ancient times timber-cutters used axes, knives, etc., for their work, whereas to-day

industry is greatly developed, machines have replaced human labour, and the result is that a much greater quantity of products is secured at the expense of much less human energy.

Take another example, from the sphere of agriculture. In ancient times only human labour was employed in this sphere; but with the introduction of ploughing with horses and oxen, the process of tilling became more speedy and greatly reduced human effort. In Europe and America electrical energy is now used to till the soil, which affords the opportunity of ploughing in the best possible way more than a thousand acres a day, thus eliminating the use of horses and oxen. This has created a truly amazing difference, expressed by the ratio of a thousand to one. If we take the means of communication, however, we see that the introduction of steamships and railways has made communications more than a thousand times more rapid in comparison with human energy.

Those who discuss the question of the brotherhood of peoples in America and Europe have in view only two problems—labours and capital; but European conditions are very different from our own. The thing is that in Europe and America all their misfortunes arise from an extremely unfair distribution of products, whereas in China there is general poverty, since there are no large capitalists. But this, of course, should not serve as a reason for not advocating Socialism: this would be a great mistake. If we see mistakes in Europe and America, we are bound to correct them: disproportion in the distribution of products, both in America and in Europe, are a bad example for us. Therefore I agitate for Socialism—the socialisation of land and capital.

First we shall speak of the socialisation of land. The land systems of Europe and America are very different. In England up to this day the feudal system of land-holding has survived, whereas in the United States all the land is private property. But my social theory advocates the proportionalisation of the land, as a means of providing against future evils. We can see the latter beginning even at the present day. Take what is going on under our very eyes since the reorganisation of the Canton municipality: communications have improved, and in consequence the price of land along the embankment and in other most thickly populated districts has begun to increase daily, some estates selling for tens of thousands of dollars per mu. And all this belongs to private persons, living by the labour of others.

The old Chinese land system partially conforms to the principle of proportionalisaton of land. In the event of this principle being applied, the two following conditions must be observed: taxation according to the value of the land, and compensation according to declared value. In China up to this day the so-called three-grade system of collection of land taxes has been preserved, but, owing to the weak development of transport and industry, land values were not so high in the past as they are to-day. Well developed means of communication and developing industry have led, owing to the maintenance of the old system, to an extremely unequal rise in the value of the land. There are, for example, lands worth 2,000 dollars per mu, while there are also lands worth 20,000 dollars per mu, while between these two extremes of values there are a large number of the most varying values. But if taxes continue to be collected on the old system, both the tax collectors and taxpayers will be put in such a position that dishonest collectors and landowners can make easy profits thereby.

Therefore if we want to abolish this evil and introduce the graduation of taxes, we must adopt the following method: to collect one per cent of the value of the land. For example, if a given piece of land is worth 2,000 dollars its owner pays 20 dollars. The collection of further taxes will depend on an increase in the value of the land. The process of State purchase of the land must begin with the establishment of its definite value. In England, at one time, special offices for collection of land tax and purchase of land were set up, which fixed definite assessments: these methods are not suitable for introduction in China. In my opinion, it is much more profitable and certain to leave it to the landowner himself to determine and fix the value and the tax, and to inform accordingly the Government department in charge of these matters.

The question arises: will not the landowner communicate a smaller value for his land, and thus pay a smaller tax? But if we adopt the system of compensation for lands according to their value, all illegal activities must disappear of themselves. For example, there is a piece of land of one mu, worth 1,000 dollars, for which the owner must pay 10 dollars yearly in to the tax office. He may declare that the value of his land is only 100 dollars, and thus pay only one dollar; but the application of the principle whereby the Government can compulsorily purchase his land at its declared value obliges the owner to declare its real value, as otherwise he runs the risk of being left without his land. If these two methods are applied, the proportionalisation of land will achieve itself; we can leave other processes on one side for the time being.

Thus I have discussed the land question. There still remains the issue of how to settle the problem of capital.

Last year I published a book entitled: *The International Development of China*. In this book I discussed the question of utilising foreign capital for the purpose of developing Chinese industry and commerce. Look at the Pekin-Hankow and Pekin-Mukden railways, and also at the Tientsin-Pukow line, built by foreign capital and yielding enormous profits. At the present time the total length of the Chinese railways is 5000–6000 miles, and their profits amount to 70–80 millions—more even than the land tax. But if the total length is increased to 50 or 60 thousand miles, the profits will also increase considerably. My opinion about the application of foreign capital to our industry is the following: all branches of our industry, for example mining, which represent, with any management worth its salt, profitable undertakings, are awaiting foreign capital.

When I speak of a loan in this connection, I mean the procuring of various machines and other necessary appliances for our industry. For example, after the construction of the Pekin-Hankow railway, the profits of which were enormous, the foreigners would have given us the chance to acquire it, with its future profit-making possibilities. These were so great that we could have completed the Pekin-Kalgan line, which now reaches Sunyang. In brief, we can easily incur debt to foreign capital, but the question is—how shall we utilise it, productively or otherwise?

There are also other questions of which I must speak. The British and American diplomats are undoubtedly a skilful race, but still the spectre of social revolution is extremely menacing in these countries. Why? Because the principles of Socialism have not been fully realised there.

We must admit that the degree of sacrifice required for the social revolution will be higher than for the political. The Revolution of 1911 and the overthrow of the Manchus only partially realised the principle of nationalism, while neither the theory of democracy nor the theory of Socialism left any impression. But we must strive our utmost not only to secure the triumph of our first Party principle, but, in accordance with modern world ideas, to develop if possible the principles of democracy, which are also old principles of our Party. Although both England and America are politically developed, political authority there still remains in the hands, not of the people as a whole, but of a political party.

I remember that, on my return to Kwantung, a well-known Hong Kong paper stated the meaning of our return to be that Kwantung was governed, not by the people of the province, but by a "Party." There was a certain point in this declaration. At all events, I was pleased to hear a confirmation that it was governed by a "Party," as the same was true of England and America. If we succeed in achieving our Party ends, this will undoubtedly be a great achievement for the people of Kwantung. We must energetically set about organising, explaining our principles, spreading them far and wide. If we want to awaken others, we must first of all wake up ourselves.

Now there is a committee of the Kuomintang at Canton, where propaganda will be concentrated. In this respect there will be no limitations. We shall soon find that the province of Kwantung will not only be the soil on which our principles will grow into reality, but will be the birthplace of the idea of democracy and its practical realisation. From here these principles and their realisation will spread all over China. The people of the Yangtse and Yellow River valleys will follow our example. The haste of our action is explained by the fact that the people which has been actually living in the Republic set up by itself over ten years ago is quite ignorant of what the word means: the explanation of the significance of the Republic must be our task.

During the great European War, President Wilson put forward the watchword: "self-determination of peoples." This corresponds to our Party principle of "nationalism." After the Peace Conference at Versailles, a number of small but independent republics were formed, living without any common tie. This must clearly show you the principal tendency in the modern life of nations. Now the time is approaching to carry into effect our great principles of nationalism, democracy and Socialism. Only by the transformation of all three principles into reality can our people live and develop freely. But the explanation and application of these principles depends very largely on the display of your forces and the degree of energy shown in your propaganda.

We now have a favourable occasion for the propaganda of our ideas: the whole Kwantung Province, with its population of 30 millions, is in our hands. We must immediately tackle the work of explaining in detail to all citizens the essential principles of our Party programme.

Glossary

Canton	Guangzhou
great European War	World War I
Kuomintang	Guomindang
mu	666.66 square meters; 0.1647 acre
Nanking	Nanjing
Pekin-Hankow and Pekin-Mukden railways	Beijing-Wuhan and Beijing-Shenyang railways
Pekin-Kalgan line	Beijing-Xuanhua line
Our Party	the Guomindang (Kuomintang in the document)
Siam	Thailand
Tientsin-Pukow line	Tianjin-Pukow line
Tsing (Manchu)	Qing

Lord Curzon (Library of Congress)

TREATY OF LAUSANNE

"[Turkey] undertakes to assure full and complete protection of life and liberty to all inhabitants ... without distinction of birth, nationality, language, race or religion."

Overview

The Treaty of Lausanne is a peace treaty signed in 1923 at Lausanne, Switzerland, between Turkey and the British Empire, France, Italy, Japan, Greece, Romania, and the Serb-Croat-Slovene State. It was the final treaty that brought World War I (1914–1918) to a close. The treaty was based on respect for the independence and sovereignty of the states on both sides and reestablished friendly relations among them.

The Treaty of Lausanne was signed after the Turkish War of Independence came to a successful end. The Treaty of Sèvres of 1920 (between the Ottoman Empire and the Allies in World War I) then became an invalid document, and a new agreement was negotiated between the Allies of the West and Turkey. The negotiations started on November 20, 1922, and lasted about eight months—broken by Turkish protest on February 4, 1923, and restarted on April 23 and continuing until the final agreement was reached on July 24, 1923. The Turkish delegation was headed by the foreign minister Ismet Pasa (later named Ismet Inönü). The chief negotiator for the Allies was the British foreign secretary Lord George Curzon, while the statesman Eleuthérios Venizélos represented Greece. The treaty recognized the Grand National Assembly of Turkey, based in Ankara, as representative of the defunct Ottoman Empire. It also drew the boundaries of the new Turkish state, with Turkey making no claims to the former Ottoman territories. The terms of the treaty thus prepared the ground for the declaration of a new state in place of the Ottoman Empire—the Republic of Turkey, established on October 29, 1923.

Context

At the end of World War I, the Ottoman Empire collapsed and disintegrated into a number of nation-states on the Balkan Peninsula and in the Middle East. The empire was forced to sign first the Armistice of Moudros on October 30, 1918, and then the Treaty of Sèvres on August 10, 1920. The terms of the armistice and treaty were so burdensome that the two together ensured the demise of the Ottoman Empire. The Armistice of Moudros was signed between the Ottoman Empire and the Allies in the port of Moudros on the Greek island of Lemnos. World War I had ended in political turmoil and created a power vacuum in the former territories of the Ottoman Empire, which now passed to the British and their allies—who therefore had unique opportunities to shape the former territories. Under the terms of the armistice, the Ottomans surrendered their garrisons outside the region of Anatolia, while the Allies had the right to occupy the Bosporus and Dardanelles straits. They also had the right to seize any strategic points in case of threats to their security and to occupy the six provinces of eastern Anatolia in case of disorder. The Taurus tunnels, a system of train tunnels passing through the Taurus mountain range, and a strategic point on the railway linking the Ottoman Empire capital of Constantinople (now Istanbul) to Hejaz (part of modern-day Saudi Arabia) were to be occupied as well. The Ottoman army was demobilized, and ports, railways, and strategic points were to be used by the Allies. Soon after signing the armistice, the Allies occupied Constantinople and divided Anatolia among themselves in accordance with the terms of the Armistice of Moudros.

Constantinople, the Ottoman capital, was occupied by a joint army of British, French, Greeks, and Italians, while the key port of Izmir was occupied by the Greeks, on behalf of the Allies. The Ottoman government, meanwhile, exercised almost no authority, nor did it represent the Turkish people. During the two years between the Armistice of Moudros and Treaty of Sèvres, a nationalist movement came into existence. It became organized and was transformed into a new government in Ankara on April 23, 1920, as headed by Mustafa Kemal (who adopted the surname Atatürk in 1933). The occupation by the Greeks posed the most serious threat to the Ankara government, and the Greek army expanded its control of western Anatolia in a series of attacks. Initially, the Greek advance was checked by Ismet Pasa (who was to be the chief negotiator at the head of the Turkish delegation at the Conference of Lausanne); a renewed Greek offensive caused a retreat by Kemal. Military crisis caused political crisis, and the Grand National Assembly berated Kemal for the disaster. Kemal nonetheless persuaded the assembly to give him full power as commander in chief, and he drove out the invading

1922

■ **October 26**
The British government sends out invitations for a peace conference to be held at Lausanne, Switzerland, starting in November.

■ **October 29**
The Ankara government proposes that the conference take place in Constantinople but adds that Lausanne would be acceptable with secure communication lines; the Constantinople sultanate stipulates that it wants the Constantinople and Ankara governments to jointly represent Turkey at the conference.

■ **November 1**
The sultanate is abolished by Ankara's Grand National Assembly.

■ **November 2**
The Grand National Assembly elects representatives to the conference, including Foreign Minister Ismet Pasa, Riza Nour Bey, and Hassan Bey as delegates.

■ **November 5**
The sultan Mehmed VI rejects the decision of the Ankara government and refuses to abdicate as sultan and caliph; the Constantinople government is notified that the Ankara government is assuming control and is asking the Allies to leave Constantinople at once.

Greek army in a series of renewed attacks. The Greeks fled to the sea, and the Turkish troops entered Izmir on September 9, 1922. Anatolia was cleared of the Greeks, but there were still Greeks in Thrace, across the straits. A small number of British troops were guarding the straits, backed by naval units. Kemal's forces advanced up to the straits zone and stopped. Here, both sides agreed to negotiate.

The Armistice of Mudanya was signed on October 11, 1922, with the Allied powers agreeing to restore Turkish control in Constantinople, Thrace, and the Bosporus and Dardanelles straits and to convene a peace conference. Thus, the Turks were victorious in the Turkish War of Independence, and the Treaty of Sèvres became an invalid document, with a new treaty yet to be made. The Allies sent formal invitations to the Turkish governments in Ankara and in Constantinople for a peace conference to be held in Lausanne, Switzerland. The representation of the Turkish government by two delegations would injure Turkish prospects at the forthcoming negotiations. Therefore, after a long discussion, Ankara's Grand National Assembly abolished Constantinople's sultanate on November 1, 1922, and chose Abdülmecid II as the new caliph of the Ottoman line. The thirty-sixth and last sultan of the Ottoman Empire, Mehmed VI (Vahideddin), left Constantinople on November 17 on a British warship, to live in exile in San Remo, Italy, until his death. Thus, the Ankara government alone represented Turkey at the Lausanne conference, which began on November 20.

Lord Curzon, the British foreign secretary and head of the British delegation, was the chief negotiator on behalf of both his own nation and the Allies. Greece was represented by a separate negotiator. It was Lord Curzon who prepared and proposed the first draft of the agreement on behalf of Britain and the Allies. The Turkish delegation did not present its own draft agreement but instead prepared a document consisting of their points for consideration. Initial discussions were carried out based on Curzon's draft agreement, most of which was rejected by the Turkish delegation. Curzon refused to compromise on the draft agreement and insisted that it was the Turks who had to bend and accept the terms offered to them, while the Turkish delegation insisted that they should be treated on a basis of equality. Curzon's demands and Ismet Pasa's reactions and counterdemands remained contradictory throughout the negotiation process. In fact, almost all issues discussed at the conference were met by opposition on both sides.

Curzon presented a draft treaty on January 31, 1923, incorporating all the agreements reached in the three main committees and including the provisions that he wanted but that the Turkish delegation refused to accept. He demanded that Ismet Pasa accept the proposal as it was written, without negotiation or change, but Pasa communicated with Ankara and was instructed to refuse to sign the agreement. The French and Italian delegations attempted to arrange a compromise, and new meetings were held between February 1 and 5. However, the Turkish delegation was not ready to accept Curzon's demands, while the British refused to make any changes to Curzon's draft treaty. Therefore, the conference adjourned before any agreement was reached or a common document was produced. Historians from both sides agree that Curzon's arrogant and uncompromising approach was the main reason for the initial failure of the conference.

Ismet Pasa and the Turkish delegation returned to Turkey on February 16, 1923, and met with Mustafa Kemal to discuss the proceedings of the conference. Debate over the conference by the Grand National Assembly in a secret session started on February 21 and lasted two weeks. Pasa was criticized heavily on the ground that he had gone beyond the original instructions given to him, particularly on territorial matters. Meeting on March 7, the Ankara government revised Curzon's text, formulated its own treaty in about a hundred pages, and sent it to the Allied governments. On March 11, the British government called the Allies to London to discuss the Turkish proposal. The Allies at first suggested many changes to the Turkish proposal but then responded more favorably in the interest of resuming talks. With the conference resuming in Lausanne on April 23, 1923, Britain was represented by two new delegates, Horace Rumbold and Andrew Ryan. Curzon's absence proved an asset to negotiations. The British delegation sought to meet Ismet Pasa's objections, and most of the problems were handled through compromise. The final treaty was signed by all the states involved.

About the Author

The Treaty of Lausanne was authored by the delegates to the conference. Several delegates played major roles in composing the final treaty, including Lord Curzon, Horace Rumbold, Eleuthérios Venizélos, and Ismet Pasa. George Curzon was an educated British statesman from an aristocratic background. He became undersecretary of state for India in 1891 and undersecretary of state for foreign affairs in 1895. In 1899 he was appointed viceroy of India, where he introduced a series of reforms and became familiar with the affairs of the East. During World War I, he joined the war cabinet of Prime Minister David Lloyd George and became involved in Middle Eastern affairs. He opposed the Greek occupation of Anatolia and wanted to offer peace to Turkey. Because of his involvement and expertise in Eastern affairs, he became foreign secretary and represented Britain at the Lausanne conference. He was a tough negotiator, playing a major role in arbitrating population exchanges between Greece and Turkey, and uncompromising in his views. He served as foreign secretary from 1919 until his retirement in 1924.

Horace Rumbold was also an aristocratic British diplomat. He was fluent in Eastern languages, and between 1900 and 1913 he was appointed as an attaché in Cairo, Egypt; Tehran, Iran; Munich, Germany; and Vienna, Austria. Because of his knowledge and understanding of the Middle East, he was appointed ambassador to Constantinople, serving from 1920 to 1924. Joining the second phase of conference negotiations, he compromised on the terms of the final agreement and signed the treaty on Britain's behalf. He then served as an ambassador in Madrid and then in Berlin before retiring in 1933.

Time Line

1922

- **November 14**
  Lord George Curzon, the British foreign minister, sends proposals to the French and Italian governments for a settlement, essentially based on the Treaty of Sèvres with only minor changes.

- **November 20**
  The Conference of Lausanne officially opens.

1923

- **January 31**
  Curzon presents his draft treaty, which incorporates all the agreements reached in three main committees, focusing on territory, capitulations, and population and minorities.

- **February 1–5**
  New meetings are held to arrange a compromise.

- **February 5**
  The conference adjourns.

- **February 7**
  The Turkish delegation is instructed to refuse to sign the agreement.

- **March 11**
  The British government calls the Allies to London to discuss restarting the conference.

- **April 23**
  The conference resumes with a second phase of negotiations.

■ **May 26**
Turkey and
Greece agree on
war reparations.

■ **July 24**
The Treaty of
Lausanne is signed
by all delegates.

■ **August 24**
The Treaty of
Lausanne is ratified
by the newly
elected Grand
National Assembly
in Turkey.

Born as an Ottoman citizen in Crete in 1864, Eleuthérios Venizélos became a Greek statesman. He was the architect of the Megali Idea, the concept of expanding the Greek state to include all ethnic Greeks, and worked for the annexation of Anatolia to Greece. In 1910 he became prime minister of the military administration of Greece, which allied with Serbia, Bulgaria, and Montenegro against the Ottoman Empire during the Balkan Wars. He managed to keep his nation neutral during World War I but went to war with Turkey afterward, with the Turkish War of Independence being waged against the Greek occupation of Anatolia. Venizélos signed the Treaty of Sèvres, and he joined the Lausanne conference negotiations as head of the Greek delegation. He maintained peace with Turkey after 1928 but ultimately proved unsuccessful in his policies and resigned from the government in 1935. Venizélos died as a Greek citizen in Paris in 1936.

Ismet Pasa would adopt the name Ismet Inönü¸ and serve as prime minister of Turkey and as the country's second president, from 1938 to 1950. He graduated from the Turkish Military Academy in 1903 and from the Artillery War Academy in 1906 and joined the army the same year. He fought in the Balkan Wars, World War I, and the Turkish War of Independence. After the establishment of the Republic of Turkey, he became prime minister under Mustafa Kemal. Because of his success during the war for liberation, he was selected to defend the nation's interests at the Lausanne conference negotiations. After the death of Atatürk in 1938, Ismet Inönü¸ became president. During his administration, Turkey shifted to a multiparty system. He was a close follower of Atatürk's ideas on modernization of the Turkish Republic, development of parliamentary democracy, and foreign policy.

Explanation and Analysis of the Document

The Treaty of Lausanne was signed at Lausanne, Switzerland, on July 24, 1923, and deposited in the archives of the government of the French Republic. It was signed by Horace Rumbold, Maurice Pelle, Camillo Garroni, Giulio Cesare Montagna, Kentaro Otchiai, Eleuthérios K. Venizélos, Demetrios Caclamanos, Constantine Diamandy, Constantine Contzesco, Ismet Pasa, Riza Nour Bey, and Hassan Bey. The treaty consists of 143 articles divided into five parts, with each part divided into a number of sections. A number of conventions, agreements, and protocols are annexed to the treaty, including separate peace treaties with Greece, England, Italy, Japan, Romania, and France. The treaty opens with an expression of the desire to bring to a final close the state of war which has existed in the East since 1914. It continues with an expression of anxiety to reestablish relations of friendship and commerce and considers that these relations must be based on respect for the independence and sovereignty of the states involved. The expressions of the desire for peace, friendship, and respect for independence were very important for Turkey, as they show that Turkey has been treated as equal and that the terms of the treaty were negotiated among equals, not imposed.

◆ **Part I**

Part I of the treaty includes three sections, on territorial clauses, nationality, and the protection of minorities. Section I, concerning territorial issues, draws the boundaries of Turkey with the surrounding countries. The boundaries were essentially those demanded by the Turks, except that around Mosul. Turkey insisted that this region was included in the National Pact (a resolution, dated 1920, stating the goals of independence of Turkey and forming the basis of the negotiating position of Turkey) and was overwhelmingly inhabited by Turks; therefore, it should belong to Turkey. However, Britain was not ready to relinquish the oil-rich area. The problem of Mosul was not resolved during the conference negotiations and was left to further negotiations between Britain and Turkey, to be held within nine months of the signing of the treaty. Mosul eventually became a part of Iraq.

The border with Greece was resolved by acceptance of the Turkish proposal to draw the boundary at the deepest point in the middle of the Maritsa (or Maritza) River. In return, Turkey agreed that the island of Castellorizzo (Kastellórizon) would go to Italy. Western Thrace remained in Greece on the condition of respect for the rights and freedoms of the Turkish minority living there.

The border with Syria remained as described in the Franco-Turkish Agreement of October 20, 1921. Antakya (formerly Antioch) and Iskenderun (formerly Alexandretta), which were acquired by Turkey in 1938 after the withdrawal of France from Syria, would remain in Syria. The islands of Imbros (now Gökçeada) and Tenedos (now Bozcaada) and the Rabbit Islands would belong to Turkey, while the islands of Lemnos, Samothrace, Mytilene, Chios, Sámos, and Ikaria (or Nikaria) would belong to Greece. Turkey's complete control of the straits was recognized, but it had to demilitarize the zone around the straits and establish an international commission to supervise the transmission of ships. Thus, Soviet control of the straits was avoided.

As to population issues, to minimize minority problems in a nation state, the Turks and Greeks agreed to exchange the Greeks living in Anatolia with the Turks living in Greece. Only Greeks of Constantinople and the Turks of Western Thrace were excepted from the population exchange.

As to the protection of minorities, Turkish nationals belonging to non-Muslim minorities were not granted any privileges; they were to enjoy the same treatment and security as other Turkish nationals. They would have equal right to establish charitable, religious, and social institutions and schools for education. They would have the right to use their own languages and to exercise their own religions freely. The Allies did not ask for any war reparations. Greece did not pay any compensation but instead gave Karaagaç to Turkey.

◆ **Part II**

Part II of the treaty is concerned with financial issues and is divided into two sections, the first covering the Ottoman public debt and the second containing miscellaneous clauses. The Ottoman public debt was the main financial problem of the treaty negotiations. The Allies agreed that Turkey would have to pay only its portion of the debt; the former Ottoman territories would pay their shares as well. The Turks won the right to have their debt set in francs, regardless of its value in gold. Among the miscellaneous clauses, capitulations, which were the trade concessions given to European countries during the Ottoman Empire, were abolished completely. Another clause is concerned with the foreign concessions within Turkey awarded by the Ottoman Empire. The Allies insisted that these concessions had to be recognized by Turkey, too. It was finally agreed that some payment would be made for the loss of the concessions and that Turkey would award future concessions to whomever it wanted.

◆ **Part III**

Part III concerns economic issues, with Section I covering property, rights, and interests and Section II taking up contracts, prescriptions, and judgments. According to the treaty, all property, rights, and interests that still existed and could be identified in territories detached from the Ottoman Empire after the Balkan Wars as belonging to Turkish nationals were to be immediately restored to the owners. This part of the treaty also includes clauses concerning life, marine, fire, and other kinds of insurances; debt; industrial, literary, and artistic property rights; arbitral tribunals; and established treaties.

◆ **Part IV**

Part IV is divided into two sections, on communications and sanitary questions. According to the articles concerning communications, Turkey would adhere to the freedom of transit statute laid by the Conference of Barcelona, dated April 14, 1921. Turkey was also to adhere to the recommendations of that conference dated April 19, 1921, concerning ports and railways. In this part of the agreement, foreign post offices in Turkey were abolished. Concerning sanitary questions, the Superior Council of Health in Constantino-

Turkish troops march across the Galata Bridge into Constantinople, Turkey, in October of 1923. (AP/Wide World Photos)

ple was to be abolished, and Turkey was entrusted with the sanitary organization of the coasts and frontiers of Turkey. Pilgrimages to Jerusalem and Hejaz (or Hedjaz) were to be supervised by Turkey and the interested states, and appropriate measures were to be taken in accordance with the provisions of international sanitary conventions.

◆ **Part V**

Part V includes three sections, covering prisoners of war, graves, and general provisions. Both sides agreed to repatriate at once the prisoners of war and interned civilians still in their hands. The states would respect and maintain the cemeteries, graves, and memorials of soldiers and sailors killed in action since October 29, 1914, within their territories. The general provisions are concerned with the property, rights, and interests of the people concerned, as well as archives, registers, title deeds, and other documents and judicial matters.

Audience

The members of the Conference of Lausanne were the treaty's initial audience. The treaty was first introduced in the newly elected Grand National Assembly of Turkey and was ratified on August 23, 1923. Mustafa Kemal made a

Mehmed VI, the last sultan of the Ottoman Empire (Library of Congress)

"*Turkey hereby recognises the annexation of Cyprus proclaimed by the British Government on the 5th November, 1914.*"

(Article 20)

"*The High Contracting Parties are agreed to recognise and declare the principle of freedom of transit and of navigation, by sea and by air, in time of peace as in time of war, in the strait of the Dardanelles, the Sea of Marmora and the Bosphorus, as prescribed in the separate Convention signed this day, regarding the regime of the Straits.*"

(Article 23)

"*Each of the High Contracting Parties hereby accepts, in so far as it is concerned, the complete abolition of the Capitulations in Turkey in every respect.*"

(Article 28)

"*The Turkish Government undertakes to assure full and complete protection of life and liberty to all inhabitants of Turkey without distinction of birth, nationality, language, race or religion. All inhabitants of Turkey shall be entitled to free exercise, whether in public or private, of any creed, religion or belief, the observance of which shall not be incompatible with public order and good morals.*"

(Article 38)

speech in support of the terms of the treaty, and members of the assembly welcomed the treaty.

The third-most significant audience of the treaty was the Turkish population. Most of the Turkish people of the era considered the treaty a major Turkish victory, as it overturned the vindictive provisions of the Treaty of Sèvres, which was used as a means to destroy the national identity of Turkish people by the Allies. However, some people, from the time of the signing of the treaty until the present, have considered the treaty a defeat, behind the notion that if Ismet Pasa and the Ankara government had held out longer and even refused to sign the treaty, they could have gotten much more of the territories included in the National Pact, such as Western Thrace, Mosul, and the port of Batumi. These places had substantial Turkish populations that could well have justified their inclusion

in Turkey. Also, Turkey might have received considerable war reparations from all the Allies, particularly from Greece, for the monumental damage caused during their occupation. Detractors of the treaty also claim that negotiators should not have allowed the Greek Orthodox Ecumenical Patriarchate to remain in Constantinople and that Turkey should never have agreed to allow the international community to maintain a role in establishing regulations for passage through the straits. Kemal responded to these conservative critiques by asserting that after twelve years of war, the Turkish people had reached the limit of their endurance, and the Turkish army had gone as far as it could. Further efforts might have jeopardized all the achievements of the national movement. The arguments made by both sides have remained a matter of dispute in Turkey to the present day.

Impact

The conclusion of the treaty led to the recognition of the Republic of Turkey by the international community as the successor state of the Ottoman Empire. The genuine peace following the military victory gave Mustafa Kemal and the nationalist government sufficient prestige to take further steps. The Allied forces began to move out of Constantinople on August 23, 1923, and left the city on October 2; the Turkish army entered Constantinople on October 6. Ankara was named the capital of Turkey officially on October 13, while the Turkish Republic was proclaimed by the assembly on October 29. On the same day, Atatürk was elected president, and the next day Inönü, the hero of the Lausanne conference, became prime minister. A series of reforms were then undertaken to modernize the newly established republic.

A meeting was held between Turkey and Britain to negotiate the Mosul problem on May 19, 1924. However, no result was obtained, and the problem was transferred to the League of Nations. Turkey accepted the League of Nations' decision giving Mosul to Iraq on June 5, 1926. By the terms of the 1926 treaty, Turkey surrendered its right to a permanent share in the exploitation of Mosul oil in return for a single payment of £500,000 together with twenty-five years of annual payments of a 10 percent share in the oil revenues.

The agreement concerning the Bosporus and Dardanelles straits lasted only thirteen years, as a new agreement was signed in 1936 giving more control to Turkey. This became important in the 1990s when the international community demanded that Turkey continue to allow unrestricted passage by huge oil tankers, whose contents constituted a danger to the lives of the local people and the ecology of the region. Antakya and Iskenderun, which were left to Syria under French mandate, were acquired by Turkey in 1938 after the withdrawal of France from Syria. According to the population exchange agreement signed between Turkey and Greece on January 30, 1923 (prior to the signing of the Treaty of Lausanne), around two million Greeks living in Turkey and five hundred thousand Turks living in Greece were exchanged. This entailed the large-scale transfer of peoples out of their homelands, which caused a proportional degree of human misery.

Further Reading

■ **Articles**

Hatzivassiliou, Evanthis. "The Lausanne Treaty: Minorities in Greece and Turkey and the Cyprus Question, 1954–1959." *Balkan Studies* 32, no. 1 (1991): 145–161.

■ **Books**

Davison, Roderic. *Turkey.* Englewood Cliffs, N.J.: Prentice-Hall, 1968.

Demirci, Sevtap. *Strategies and Struggles: British Rethoric* [sic] *and Turkish Response; The Lausanne Conference (1922–1923)*. Istanbul, Turkey: Isis Press, 2005.

Questions for Further Study

1. Why were the various parts of the defunct Ottoman Empire of particular interest to the British and to Western Europe generally?

2. Initially, it appeared that negotiations preceding the Treaty of Lausanne would be a failure and that the treaty would never be signed. What factors may have motivated the British to take a more flexible approach to the negotiations and ultimately agree to the final document?

3. Compare the Treaty of Lausanne with the Treaty of Versailles. Both brought an official end to World War I, but with very different consequences. How did those consequences differ? Why?

4. The treaty states that "the Turkish Government undertakes to assure full and complete protection of life and liberty to all inhabitants of Turkey without distinction of birth, nationality, language, race or religion. All inhabitants of Turkey shall be entitled to free exercise, whether in public or private, of any creed, religion or belief." To what extent do you believe this provision has contributed to the development of a stable, relatively prosperous modern-day Turkey?

5. Some Turks continue to believe that the treaty represented a defeat. Why do they take this position? Based on what you know about the Ottoman Empire, World War I, and the aftermath of the war, do you agree or disagree with this position?

Montgomery, A. E. "Allied Policies in Turkey from the Armistice of Mudros, 30 October 1918, to the Treaty of Lausanne, 24 July 1923." PhD diss., Birkbeck College (London), 1969.

Shaw, Stanford. *From Empire to Republic: The Turkish War of National Liberation, 1918–1923; A Documentary Study.* Ankara, Turkey: Turkish Historical Association, 2000.

■ **Web Sites**

"The Demographic Consequences of Lausanne Treaty in Turkey." Forced Migration Online Web site. http://repository.forcedmigration.org/show_metadata.jsp?pid=fmo:1824.

—Fatma Acun

TREATY OF LAUSANNE

The Convention Respecting the Regime of the Straits and Other Instruments Signed at Lausanne

The British Empire, France, Italy, Japan, Greece, Roumania and the Serb-Croat-Slovene State, of the one part, and Turkey, of the other part; Being united in the desire to bring to a final close the state of war which has existed in the East since 1914,

Being anxious to re-establish the relations of friendship and commerce which are essential to the mutual well-being of their respective peoples,

And considering that these relations must be based on respect for the independence and sovereignty of States,

Have decided to conclude a Treaty for this purpose, and have appointed as their Plenipotentiaries:

His Majesty the King of the United Kingdom of Great Britain and Ireland and of the British Dominions Beyond the Seas, Emperor of India: The Right Honourable Sir Horace George Montagu Rumbold, Baronet, G.C.M.G., High Commissioner at Constantinople;

The President of the French Republic: General Maurice Pelle, Ambassador of France, High Commissioner of the Republic in the East, Grand Officer of the National Order of the Legion of Honour;

His Majesty the King of Italy: The Honourable Marquis Camillo Garroni, Senator of the Kingdom, Ambassador of Italy, High Commissioner at Constantinople, Grand Cross of the Orders of Saints Maurice and Lazarus, and of the Crown of Italy;

M. Giulio Cesare Montagna, Envoy Extraordinary and Minister Plenipotentiary at Athens, Commander of the Orders of Saints Maurice and Lazarus, Grand Officer of the Crown of Italy;

His Majesty the Emperor of Japan: Mr. Kentaro Otchiai, Jusammi, First Class of the Order of the Rising Sun, Ambassador Extraordinary and Plenipotentiary at Rome;

His Majesty the King of the Hellenes: M. Eleftherios K. Veniselos, formerly President of the Council of Ministers, Grand Cross of the Order of the Saviour;

M. Demetrios Caclamanos, Minister Plenipotentiary at London, Commander of the Order of the Saviour;

His Majesty the King of Roumania: M. Constantine I. Diamandy, Minister Plenipotentiary;

M. Constantine Contzesco, Minister Plenipotentiary;

His Majesty the King of the Serbs, the Croats and the Slovenes: Dr. Miloutine Yovanovitch, Envoy Extraordinary and Minister Plenipotentiary at Berne;

The Government of the Grand National Assembly of Turkey: Ismet Pasha, Minister for Foreign Affairs, Deputy for Adrianople; Dr. Riza Nour Bey, Minister for Health and for Public Assistance, Deputy for Sinope; Hassan Bey, formerly Minister, Deputy for Trebizond;

Who, having produced their full powers, found in good and due form, have agreed as follows:

Part I. Political Clauses

Article 1.

From the coming into force of the present Treaty, the state of peace will be definitely re-established between the British Empire, France, Italy, Japan, Greece, Roumania and the Serb-Croat-Slovene State of the one part, and Turkey of the other part, as well as between their respective nationals. Official relations will be resumed on both sides and, in the respective territories, diplomatic and consular representatives will receive, without prejudice to such agreements as may be concluded in the future, treatment in accordance with the general principles of international law.

◆ Section I

1. TERRITORIAL CLAUSES

Article 2.

From the Black Sea to the Aegean the frontier of Turkey is laid down as follows:

(1) With Bulgaria: From the mouth of the River Rezvaya, to the River Maritza, the point of junction of the three frontiers of Turkey, Bulgaria and Greece: the southern frontier of Bulgaria as at present demarcated;

(2) With Greece: Thence to the confluence of the Arda and the Maritza: the course of the Maritza; then upstream along the Arda, up to a point on that river

to be determined on the spot in the immediate neighbourhood of the village of Tchorek-Keuy: the course of the Arda; thence in a south-easterly direction up to a point on the Maritza, 1 kilom. below Bosna-Keuy: a roughly straight line leaving in Turkish territory the village of Bosna-Keuy. The village of Tchorek-Keuy shall be assigned to Greece or to Turkey according as the majority of the population shall be found to be Greek or Turkish by the Commission for which provision is made in Article 5, the population which has migrated into this village after the 11th October, 1922, not being taken into account; thence to the Aegean Sea: the course of the Maritza.

Article 3.

From the Mediterranean to the frontier of Persia, the frontier of Turkey is laid down as follows:

(1) With Syria: The frontier described in Article 8 of the Franco-Turkish Agreement of the 20th October, 1921

(2) With Iraq: The frontier between Turkey and Iraq shall be laid down in friendly arrangement to be concluded between Turkey and Great Britain within nine months.

In the event of no agreement being reached between the two Governments within the time mentioned, the dispute shall be referred to the Council of the League of Nations.

The Turkish and British Governments reciprocally undertake that, pending the decision to be reached on the subject of the frontier, no military or other movement shall take place which might modify in any way the present state of the territories of which the final fate will depend upon that decision....

Article 12.

The decision taken on the 13th February, 1914, by the Conference of London, in virtue of Articles 5 of the Treaty of London of the 17th–30th May, 1913, and 15 of the Treaty of Athens of the 1st–14th November, 1913, which decision was communicated to the Greek Government on the 13th February, 1914, regarding the sovereignty of Greece over the islands of the Eastern Mediterranean, other than the islands of Imbros, Tenedos and Rabbit Islands, particularly the islands of Lemnos, Samothrace, Mytilene, Chios, Samos and Nikaria, is confirmed, subject to the provisions of the present Treaty respecting the islands placed under the sovereignty of Italy which form the subject of Article 15.

Except where a provision to the contrary is contained in the present Treaty, the islands situated at less than three miles from the Asiatic coast remain under Turkish sovereignty.

Article 13.

With a view to ensuring the maintenance of peace, the Greek Government undertakes to observe the following restrictions in the islands of Mytilene, Chios, Samos and Nikaria:

(1) No naval base and no fortification will be established in the said islands.

(2) Greek military aircraft will be forbidden to fly over the territory of the Anatolian coast. Reciprocally, the Turkish Government will forbid their military aircraft to fly over the said islands.

(3) The Greek military forces in the said islands will be limited to the normal contingent called up for military service, which can be trained on the spot, as well as to a force of gendarmerie and police in proportion to the force of gendarmerie and police existing in the whole of the Greek territory.

Article 14.

The islands of Imbros and Tenedos, remaining under Turkish sovereignty, shall enjoy a special administrative organisation composed of local elements and furnishing every guarantee for the native non-Moslem population in so far as concerns local administration and the protection of persons and property. The maintenance of order will be assured therein by a police force recruited from amongst the local population by the local administration above provided for and placed under its orders.

The agreements which have been, or may be, concluded between Greece and Turkey relating to the exchange of the Greek and Turkish populations will not be applied to the inhabitants of the islands of Imbros and Tenedos.

Article 15.

Turkey renounces in favour of Italy all rights and title over the following islands: Stampalia (Astrapalia), Rhodes (Rhodos), Calki (Kharki), Scarpanto, Casos (Casso), Piscopis (Tilos), Misiros (Nisyros), Calimnos (Kalymnos), Leros, Patmos, Lipsos (Lipso), Simi (Symi), and Cos (Kos), which are now occupied by Italy, and the islets dependent thereon, and also over the island of Castellorizzo....

Article 17.

The renunciation by Turkey of all rights and titles over Egypt and over the Soudan will take effect as from the 5th November, 1914.

Article 18.

Turkey is released from all undertakings and obligations in regard to the Ottoman loans guaranteed on the Egyptian tribute, that is to say, the loans of 1855, 1891 and 1894. The annual payments made by Egypt for the service of these loans now forming part of the service of the Egyptian Public Debt, Egypt is freed from all other obligations relating to the Ottoman Public Debt.

Article 19.

Any questions arising from the recognition of the State of Egypt shall be settled by agreements to be negotiated subsequently in a manner to be determined later between the Powers concerned. The provisions of the present Treaty relating to territories detached from Turkey under the said Treaty will not apply to Egypt.

Article 20.

Turkey hereby recognises the annexation of Cyprus proclaimed by the British Government on the 5th November, 1914.

Article 21.

Turkish nationals ordinarily resident in Cyprus on the 5th November, 1914, will acquire British nationality subject to the conditions laid down in the local law, and will thereupon lose their Turkish nationality. They will, however, have the right to opt for Turkish nationality within two years from the coming into force of the present Treaty, provided that they leave Cyprus within twelve months after having so opted....

Article 22.

Without prejudice to the general stipulations of Article 27, Turkey hereby recognises the definite abolition of all rights and privileges whatsoever which she enjoyed in Libya under the Treaty of Lausanne of the 18th October, 1912, and the instruments connected therewith.

2. SPECIAL PROVISIONS

Article 23.

The High Contracting Parties are agreed to recognise and declare the principle of freedom of transit and of navigation, by sea and by air, in time of peace as in time of war, in the strait of the Dardanelles, the Sea of Marmora and the Bosphorus, as prescribed in the separate Convention signed this day, regarding the regime of the Straits. This Convention will have the same force and effect in so far as the present High Contracting Parties are concerned as if it formed part of the present Treaty....

Article 26.

Turkey hereby recognises and accepts the frontiers of Germany, Austria, Bulgaria, Greece, Hungary, Poland, Roumania, the Serb-Croat-Slovene State and the Czechoslovak State, as these frontiers have been or may be determined by the Treaties referred to in Article 25 or by any supplementary conventions.

Article 27.

No power or jurisdiction in political, legislative or administrative matters shall be exercised outside Turkish territory by the Turkish Government or authorities, for any reason whatsoever, over the nationals of a territory placed under the sovereignty or protectorate of the other Powers signatory of the present Treaty, or over the nationals of a territory detached from Turkey.

It is understood that the spiritual attributions of the Moslem religious authorities are in no way infringed.

Article 28.

Each of the High Contracting Parties hereby accepts, in so far as it is concerned, the complete abolition of the Capitulations in Turkey in every respect....

◆ **Section II**

NATIONALITY

Article 30.

Turkish subjects habitually resident in territory which in accordance with the provisions of the present Treaty is detached from Turkey will become ipso facto, in the conditions laid down by the local law, nationals of the State to which such territory is transferred....

◆ **Section III**

PROTECTION OF MINORITIES

Article 37.

Turkey undertakes that the stipulations contained in Articles 38 to 44 shall be recognised as fundamental laws, and that no law, no regulation, nor official action shall conflict or interfere with these stipulations, nor shall any law, regulation, nor official action prevail over them.

Article 38.

The Turkish Government undertakes to assure full and complete protection of life and liberty to all inhabitants of Turkey without distinction of birth, nationality, language, race or religion.

All inhabitants of Turkey shall be entitled to free exercise, whether in public or private, of any creed, religion or belief, the observance of which shall not be incompatible with public order and good morals.

Non-Moslem minorities will enjoy full freedom of movement and of emigration, subject to the measures applied, on the whole or on part of the territory, to all Turkish nationals, and which may be taken by the Turkish Government for national defence, or for the maintenance of public order.

Article 39.

Turkish nationals belonging to non-Moslem minorities will enjoy the same civil and political rights as Moslems.

All the inhabitants of Turkey, without distinction of religion, shall be equal before the law....

Article 40.

Turkish nationals belonging to non-Moslem minorities shall enjoy the same treatment and security in law and in fact as other Turkish nationals. In particular, they shall have an equal right to establish, manage and control at their own expense, any charitable, religious and social institutions, any schools and other establishments for instruction and education, with the right to use their own language and to exercise their own religion freely therein....

Article 44.

Turkey agrees that, in so far as the preceding Articles of this Section affect non-Moslem nationals of Turkey, these provisions constitute obligations of international concern and shall be placed under the guarantee of the League of Nations. They shall not be modified without the assent of the majority of the Council of the League of Nations. The British Empire, France, Italy and Japan hereby agree not to withhold their assent to any modification in these Articles which is in due form assented to by a majority of the Council of the League of Nations....

Article 45.

The rights conferred by the provisions of the present Section on the non-Moslem minorities of Turkey will be similarly conferred by Greece on the Moslem minority in her territory.

Part II. Financial Clauses

◆ **Section I**

OTTOMAN PUBLIC DEBT

Article 46.

The Ottoman Public Debt, as defined in the Table annexed to the present Section, shall be distributed under the conditions laid down in the present Section between Turkey, the States in favour of which territory has been detached from the Ottoman Empire after the Balkan wars of 1912–13, the States to which the islands referred to in Articles 12 and 15 of the present Treaty and the territory referred to in the last paragraph of the present Article have been attributed, and the States newly created in territories in Asia which are detached from the Ottoman Empire under the present Treaty. All the above States shall also participate, under the conditions laid down in the present Section, in the annual charges for the service of the Ottoman Public Debt from the dates referred to in Article 53.

From the dates laid down in Article 53, Turkey shall not be held in any way whatsoever responsible for the shares of the Debt for which other States are liable.

For the purpose of the distribution of the Ottoman Public Debt, that portion of the territory of Thrace which was under Turkish sovereignty on the 1st August, 1914, and lies outside the boundaries of Turkey as laid down by Article 2 of the present Treaty, shall be deemed to be detached from the Ottoman Empire under the said Treaty.

Article 47.

The Council of the Ottoman Public Debt shall, within three months from the coming into force of the present Treaty, determine, on the basis laid down by Articles 50 and 51, the amounts of the annuities for the loans referred to in Part A of the Table annexed to the present Section which are payable by each of the States concerned, and shall notify to them this amount.

These States shall be granted an opportunity to send to Constantinople delegates to check the calculations made for this purpose by the Council of the Ottoman Public Debt.

The Council of the Debt shall exercise the functions referred to in Article 134 of the Treaty of Peace with Bulgaria of the 27th November, 1919.

Any disputes which may arise between the parties concerned as to the application of the principles laid down in the present Article shall be referred, not more than one month after the notification referred to in the first paragraph, to an arbitrator whom the Council of the League of Nations will be asked to appoint; this arbitrator shall give his decision within a period of not more than three months. The remuneration of the arbitrator shall be determined by the Council of the League of Nations, and shall, together with the other expenses of the arbitration, be borne by the parties concerned. The decisions of the arbitrator shall be final. The payment of the annuities shall not be suspended by the reference of any disputes to the above-mentioned arbitrator.

Article 48.

The States, other than Turkey, among which the Ottoman Public Debt, as defined in Part A of the Table annexed to this Section is attributed, shall, within three months from the date on which they are notified, in accordance with Article 47, of their respective shares in the annual charges referred to in that Article, assign to the Council of the Debt adequate security for the payment of their share. If such security is not assigned within the above-mentioned period, or in the case of any disagreement as to the adequacy of the security assigned, any of the Governments signatory to the present Treaty shall be entitled to appeal to the Council of the League of Nations.

The Council of the League of Nations shall be empowered to entrust the collection of the revenues assigned as security to international financial organisations existing in the countries (other than Turkey) among which the Debt is distributed. The decisions of the Council of the League of Nations shall be final....

Article 50.

The distribution of the annual charges referred to in Article 47 and of the nominal capital of the Ottoman Public Debt mentioned in Article 49 shall be effected in the following manner:

(1) The loans prior to the 17th October, 1912, and the annuities of such loans shall be distributed between the Ottoman Empire as it existed after the Balkan wars of 1912–13, the Balkan States in favour of which territory was detached from the Ottoman Empire after those wars, and the States to which the islands referred to in Articles 12 and 15 of the present Treaty have been attributed; account shall be taken of the territorial changes which have taken place after the coming into force of the treaties which ended those wars or subsequent treaties.

(2) The residue of the loans for which the Ottoman Empire remained liable after this first distribution and the residue of the annuities of such loans, together with the loans contracted by that Empire between the 17th October, 1912, and the 1st November, 1914, and the annuities of such loans shall be distributed between Turkey, the newly created States in Asia in favour of which a territory has been detached from the Ottoman Empire under the present Treaty, and the State to which the territory referred to in the last paragraph of Article 46 of the said Treaty has been attributed....

Article 53.

The annuities for the service of the loans of the Ottoman Public Debt (as defined in Part A of the Table annexed to this Section) due by the States in favour of which a territory has been detached from the Ottoman Empire after the Balkan wars, shall be payable as from the coming into force of the treaties by which the respective territories were transferred to those States. In the case of the islands referred to in Article 12, the annuity shall be payable as from the 1st–14th November, 1913, and, in the case of the islands referred to in Article 15, as from the 17th October, 1912.

The annuities due by the States newly created in territories in Asia detached from the Ottoman Empire under the present Treaty, and by the State to which the territory referred to in the last paragraph of Article 46 has been attributed, shall be payable as from the 1st March, 1920.

Article 54.

The Treasury Bills of 1911, 1912 and 1913 included in Part A of the Table annexed to this Section shall be repaid, with interest at the agreed rate, within ten years from the dates fixed by the contracts....

Article 56.

The Council of the Administration of the Ottoman Public Debt shall no longer include delegates of the German, Austrian and Hungarian bondholders.

Article 57.

Limits of time fixed for the presentation of coupons of or claims for interest upon the loans and advances of the Ottoman Public Debt and the Turkish Loans of 1855, 1891 and 1894 secured on the Egyptian tribute, and the limits of time fixed for the presentation of securities of these loans drawn for repayment, shall, on the territory of the High Contracting Parties, be considered as having been suspended from the 29th October, 1914, until three months after the coming into force of the present Treaty....

◆ **Section II**

MISCELLANEOUS CLAUSES

Article 58.

Turkey, on the one hand, and the other Contracting Powers (except Greece) on the other hand, reciprocally renounce all pecuniary claims for the loss and damage suffered respectively by Turkey and the said Powers and by their nationals (including juridical persons) between the 1st August, 1914, and the coming into force of the present Treaty, as the result of acts of war or measures of requisition, sequestration, disposal or confiscation.

Nevertheless, the above provisions are without prejudice to the provisions of Part III (Economic Clauses) of the present Treaty.

Turkey renounces in favour of the other Contracting Parties (except Greece) any right in the sums in gold transferred by Germany and Austria under Article 259 (I) of the Treaty of Peace of the 28th June, 1919, with Germany, and under Article 210 (I) of the Treaty of Peace of the 10th September, 1919, with Austria....

Article 59.

Greece recognises her obligation to make reparation for the damage caused in Anatolia by the acts of the Greek army or administration which were contrary to the laws of war.

On the other hand, Turkey, in consideration of the financial situation of Greece resulting from the prolongation of the war and from its consequences, finally renounces all claims for reparation against the Greek Government.

Article 60.

The States in favour of which territory was or is detached from the Ottoman Empire after the Balkan wars or by the present Treaty shall acquire, without payment, all the property and possessions of the Ottoman Empire situated therein.

It is understood that the property and possessions of which the transfer from the Civil List to the State was laid down by the Irades of the 26th August, 1324 (8th September, 1908) and the 20th April, 1325 (2nd May, 1909), and also those which, on the 30th October, 1918, were administered by the Civil List for the benefit of a public service, are included among the property and possessions referred to in the preceding paragraph, the aforesaid States being subrogated to the Ottoman Empire in regard to the property and possessions in question. The Wakfs created on such property shall be maintained....

Part III. Economic Clauses

Article 64.

In this part, the expression "Allied Powers" means the Contracting Powers other than Turkey. The term "Allied nationals" includes physical persons, companies and associations of the Contracting Powers other than Turkey, or of a State or territory under the protection of one of the said Powers.

The provisions of this Part relating to "Allied nationals" shall benefit persons who without having the nationality of one of the Allied Powers, have, in consequence of the protection which they in fact enjoyed at the hands of these Powers, received from the Ottoman authorities the same treatment as Allied nationals and have, on this account, been prejudiced.

◆ Section I
PROPERTY, RIGHTS AND INTERESTS
Article 65.

Property, rights and interests which still exist and can be identified in territories remaining Turkish at the date of the coming into force of the present Treaty, and which belong to persons who on the 29th

October, 1914, were Allied nationals, shall be immediately restored to the owners in their existing state.

Reciprocally, property, rights and interests which still exist and can be identified in territories subject to the sovereignty or protectorate of the Allied Powers on the 29th October, 1914, or in territories detached from the Ottoman Empire after the Balkan wars and subject to-day to the sovereignty of any such Power, and which belong to Turkish nationals, shall be immediately restored to the owners in their existing state. The same provision shall apply to property, rights and interests which belong to Turkish nationals in territories detached from the Ottoman Empire under the present Treaty, and which may have been subjected to liquidation or any other exceptional measure whatever on the part of the authorities of the Allied Powers.

All property, rights and interests situated in territory detached from the Ottoman Empire under the present Treaty, which, after having been subjected by the Ottoman Government to an exceptional war measure, are now in the hands of the Contracting Power exercising authority over the said territory, and which can be identified, shall be restored to their legitimate owners, in their existing state. The same provision shall apply to immovable property which may have been liquidated by the Contracting Power exercising authority over the said territory. All other claims between individuals shall be submitted to the competent local courts.

All disputes relating to the identity or the restitution of property to which a claim is made shall be submitted to the Mixed Arbitral Tribunal provided for in Section V of this Part....

Article 67.

Greece, Roumania and the Serb-Croat-Slovene State on the one hand, and Turkey on the other hand undertake mutually to facilitate, both by appropriate administrative measures and by the delivery of all documents relating thereto, the search on their territory for, and the restitution of, movable property of every kind taken away, seized or sequestered by their armies or administrations in the territory of Turkey, or in the territory of Greece, Roumania or the Serb-Croat-Slovene State respectively, which are actually within the territories in question.

Such search and restitution will take place also as regards property of the nature referred to above seized or sequestered by German, Austro-Hungarian or Bulgarian armies or administrations in the territory of Greece, Roumania or the Serb-Croat-Slovene State, which has been assigned to Turkey or to her nationals, as well as to property seized or sequestered by the

Greek, Roumanian or Serbian armies in Turkish territory, which has been assigned to Greece, Roumania or the Serb-Croat-Slovene State or to their nationals.

Applications relating to such search and restitution must be made within six months from the coming into force of the present Treaty.

Article 68.

Debts arising out of contracts concluded, in districts in Turkey occupied by the Greek army, between the Greek authorities and administrations on the one hand and Turkish nationals on the other, shall be paid by the Greek Government in accordance with the provisions of the said contracts....

Article 72.

In the territories which remain Turkish by virtue of the present Treaty, property, rights and interests belonging to Germany, Austria, Hungary and Bulgaria or to their nationals, which before the coming into force of the present Treaty have been seized or occupied by the Allied Governments, shall remain in the possession of these Governments until the conclusion of arrangements between them and the German, Austrian, Hungarian and Bulgarian Governments or their nationals who are concerned. If the above-mentioned property, rights and interests have been liquidated, such liquidation is confirmed.

In the territories detached from Turkey under the present Treaty, the Governments exercising authority there shall have power, within one year from the coming into force of the present Treaty, to liquidate the property, rights and interests belonging to Germany, Austria, Hungary and Bulgaria or to their nationals.

The proceeds of liquidations, whether they have already been carried out or not, shall be paid to the Reparation Commission established by the Treaty of Peace concluded with the States concerned, if the property liquidated belongs to the German, Austrian, Hungarian or Bulgarian State. In the case of liquidation of private property, the proceeds of liquidation shall be paid to the owners direct.

The provisions of this Article do not apply to Ottoman limited Companies.

The Turkish Government shall be in no way responsible for the measures referred to in the present Article....

◆ **Section II**

CONTRACTS, PRESCRIPTIONS AND JUDGMENTS ...

Article 77.

Contracts between Allied and Turkish nationals concluded after the 30th October, 1918, remain in force and will be governed by the ordinary law.

Contracts duly concluded with the Constantinople Government between the 30th October, 1918, and the 16th March, 1920, also remain in force and will be governed by the ordinary law.

All contracts and arrangements duly concluded after the 16th March, 1920, with the Constantinople Government concerning territories which remained under the effective control of the said Government, shall be submitted to the Grand National Assembly of Turkey for approval, if the parties concerned make application within three months from the coming into force of the present Treaty. Payments made under such contracts shall be duly credited to the party who has made them.

If approval is not granted, the party concerned shall, if the circumstances demand it, be entitled to compensation corresponding to the direct loss which has been actually suffered; such compensation, in default of an amicable agreement, shall be fixed by the Mixed Arbitral Tribunal.

The provisions of this Article are not applicable either to concessionary contracts or to transfers of concessions....

Article 83.

The provisions of this Section do not apply between Japan and Turkey; matters dealt with in this Section shall, in both of these countries, be determined in accordance with the local law.

ANNEX -1. LIFE ASSURANCE

Paragraph 1.

Life assurance contracts entered into between an insurer and a person who subsequently became an enemy shall not be deemed to have been dissolved by the outbreak of war or by the fact of the person becoming an enemy....

◆ **Section III**

DEBTS

Article 84.

The High Contracting Parties are in agreement in recognising that debts which were payable before the war or which became payable during the war under contracts entered into before the war, and which remained unpaid owing to the war, must be settled and paid, in accordance with the provisions of the contracts, in the currency agreed upon, at the rate current in its country of origin....

Article 85.

The Ottoman Public Debt is by general agreement left outside the scope of this Section and of the other Sections of this Part (Economic Clauses).

◆ Section IV

INDUSTRIAL, LITERARY AND ARTISTIC PROPERTY

Article 86.

Subject to the stipulations of the present Treaty, rights of industrial, literary and artistic property as they existed on the 1st August, 1914, in accordance with the law of each of the contracting countries, shall be re-established or restored as from the coming into force of the present Treaty in the territories of the High Contracting Parties in favour of the persons entitled to the benefit of them at the moment when the state of war commenced, or of their legal representatives. Equally, rights which, but for the war, could have been acquired during the war, by means of an application legally made for the protection of industrial property or of the publication of a literary or artistic work, shall be recognised and established in favour of those persons who would have been entitled thereto, from the coming into force of the present Treaty.

Without prejudice to the rights which are required to be restored in accordance with the above provision, all acts (including the grant of licences) done by virtue of the special measures taken during the war by a legislative, executive or administrative authority of an Allied Power in regard to the rights of Turkish nationals in respect of industrial, literary or artistic property, shall remain in force and continue to have their full effect. This provision applies mutatis mutandis to corresponding measures taken by Turkish authorities in regard to the rights of the nationals of any Allied Power....

◆ Section V

MIXED ARBITRAL TRIBUNAL

Article 92.

Within three months from the date of the coming into force of the present Treaty, a Mixed Arbitral Tribunal shall be established between each of the Allied Powers, on the one hand, and Turkey, on the other hand.

Each of these Tribunals shall be composed of three members, two being appointed respectively by each of the Governments concerned, who shall be entitled to designate several persons from whom, according to the case in question, they will choose one to sit as a member of the Tribunal. The president shall be chosen by agreement between the two Governments concerned.

In case of failure to reach agreement within two months from the coming into force of the present Treaty, the president shall be appointed, upon the request of one of the Governments concerned, from among nationals of Powers which remained neutral during the war, by the President of the Permanent Court of International Justice at The Hague.

If within the said period of two months one of the Governments concerned does not appoint a member to represent it on the Tribunal, the .Council of the League of Nations will have power to proceed to the appointment of such member upon the request of the other Government concerned.

If a member of the Tribunal should die or resign or for any reason become unable to perform his duties, he shall be replaced by the method laid down for his appointment, the above period of two months running from the date of death, resignation or inability as duly verified....

◆ Section VI

TREATIES

Article 99.

From the coming into force of the present Treaty and subject to the provisions thereof, the multilateral treaties, conventions and agreements of an economic or technical character enumerated below shall enter again into force between Turkey and those of the other Contracting Powers party thereto:

(1) Conventions of March 14, 1884, of December 1, 1886, and of March 23, 1887, and Final Protocol of July 7, 1887, regarding the protection of submarine cables;

(2) Convention of July 5, 1890, regarding the publication of customs tariffs and the organisation of an International Union for the publication of customs tariffs;

(3) Arrangement of December 9, 1907, regarding the creation of the International Office of Public Hygiene at Paris;

(4) Convention of June 7, 1905, regarding the creation of an International Agricultural Institute at Rome;

(5) Convention of July 16, 1863, for the redemption of the toll dues on the Scheldt;

(6) Convention of October 29, 1888, regarding the establishment of a definite arrangement guaranteeing the free use of the Suez Canal, subject to the special stipulations provided for by Article 19 of the present Treaty;

(7) Conventions and Agreements of the Universal Postal Union, including the Conventions and Agreements signed at Madrid on November 30, 1920;

(8) International Telegraphic Conventions signed at St. Petersburgh on July 10–22, 1875; Regulations

and Tariffs drawn up by the International Telegraph Conference, Lisbon, June 11, 1908.

Article 100.

Turkey undertakes to adhere to the Conventions or Agreements enumerated below, or to ratify them:

(1) Convention of October 11, 1909, regarding the international circulation of motor cars;

(2) Agreement of May 15, 1886, regarding the sealing of railway trucks subject to customs inspection and Protocol of May 18, 1907;

(3) Convention of September 23, 1910, respecting the unification of certain regulations regarding collisions and salvage at sea;

(4) Convention of December 21, 1904, regarding exemption of hospital ships from dues and charges in ports;

(5) Conventions of May 18, 1904, of May 4, 1910, and of September 30, 1921, regarding the suppression of the White Slave Traffic;

(6) Conventions of May 4, 1910, regarding the suppression of obscene publications;

(7) Sanitary Convention of January 17, 1912, Articles 54, 88 and 90 being reserved;

(8) Conventions of November 3, 1881, and April 15, 1889, regarding precautionary measures against phylloxera;

(9) Opium Convention, signed at The Hague, January 23, 1912, and additional Protocol of 1914;

(10) International Radio-Telegraphic Convention of July 5, 1912;

(11) Convention regarding liquor traffic in Africa, signed at St. Germain-en-Laye, September 10, 1919;

(12) Convention revising the General Act of Berlin of February 26, 1885, and the General Act and Declaration of Brussels of July 2, 1890, signed at St. Germain-en-Laye, September 10, 1919;

(13) Convention of October 13, 1919, regulating aerial navigation, provided that Turkey obtains, under the Protocol of May 1, 1920, such derogations as her geographical situation may render necessary;

(14) Convention of September 26, 1906, signed at Berne, prohibiting the use of white phosphorus in the manufacture of matches.

Turkey further undertakes to take part in the elaboration of new international conventions relating to telegraphy and radio-telegraphy.

Part IV. Communications and Sanitary Questions

◆ **Section I**

COMMUNICATIONS

Article 101.

Turkey undertakes to adhere to the Convention and to the Statute respecting the Freedom of Transit adopted by the Conference of Barcelona on the 14th April, 1921, as well as to the Convention and the Statute respecting the regime for waterways of international interest adopted by the said Conference on the 19th April, 1921, and to the supplementary Protocol.

Turkey accordingly undertakes to bring into force the provisions of these Conventions, Statutes and Protocol as from the entry into force of the present Treaty....

Article 106.

When, as a result of the fixing of new frontiers, a railway connection between two parts of the same country crosses another country, or a branch line from one country has its terminus in another, the conditions of working, in so far as concerns the traffic between the two countries, shall, subject to any special arrangements, be laid down in an agreement to be concluded between the railway administrations concerned. If these administrations cannot come to an agreement as to the terms of such agreement, those conditions shall be decided by arbitration.

The establishment of all new frontier stations between Turkey and the neighbouring States, as well as the working of the lines between those stations, shall be settled by agreements similarly concluded.

Article 107.

Travellers and goods coming from or destined for Turkey or Greece, and making use in transit of the three sections of the Oriental Railways included between the Greco-Bulgarian frontier and the Greco-Turkish frontier near Kuleli-Burgas, shall not be subject, on account of such transit, to any duty or toll nor to any formality of examination in connection with passports or customs.

A Commissioner, who shall be selected by the Council of the League of Nations, shall ensure that the stipulations of this Article are carried out....

Article 108.

Subject to any special provisions concerning the transfer of ports and railways, whether owned by the Turkish Government or private companies, situated in the territories detached from Turkey under the present Treaty, and similarly subject to any agreements which have been, or may be, concluded between the Contracting Powers relating to the concessionaries and the pensioning of the personnel, the transfer of railways will take place under the following conditions:

(1) The works and installations of all the railroads shall be left complete and in as good condition as possible;

(2) When a railway system possessing its own rolling-stock is situated in its entirety in transferred territory, such stock shall be left complete with the railway, in accordance with the last inventory before the 30th October, 1918;

(3) As regards lines, the administration of which will in virtue of the present Treaty be divided, the distribution of the rolling-stock shall be made by friendly agreement between the administrations taking over the several sections thereof. This agreement shall have regard to the amount of the material registered on those lines in the last inventory before the 30th October, 1918, the length of the track (sidings included) and the nature and amount of the traffic. Failing agreement, the points in dispute shall be settled by arbitration. The arbitral decision shall also, if necessary, specify the locomotives, carriages and wagons to be left on each section, the conditions of their acceptance and such provisional arrangements as may be judged necessary to ensure for a limited period the current maintenance in existing workshops of the transferred stock;

(4) Stocks of stores, fittings and plant shall be left under the same conditions as the rolling-stock....

Article 110.

Roumania and Turkey will come to an agreement as to an equitable arrangement for the working conditions of the Constanza-Constantinople cable. Failing agreement, the matter shall be settled by arbitration....

◆ **Section II**
SANITARY QUESTIONS
Article 114.

The Superior Council of Health of Constantinople is abolished. The Turkish Administration is entrusted with the sanitary organisation of the coasts and frontiers of Turkey.

Article 115.

A single sanitary tariff, the dues and conditions of which shall be fair, shall be applied to all ships without distinction between the Turkish flag and foreign flags, and to nationals of foreign Powers under the same conditions as to nationals of Turkey....

Article 117.

Turkey and those Powers which are interested in the supervision of the pilgrimages to Jerusalem and to the Hedjaz and the Hedjaz railway shall take such measures as are appropriate in accordance with the provisions of international sanitary conventions. With a view to ensuring complete uniformity in the execution of these measures, these Powers and Turkey shall constitute a Sanitary Coordination Commission for pilgrimages, on which the sanitary service of Turkey and the Maritime Sanitary and Quarantine Council of Egypt shall be represented.

This Commission must obtain the previous consent of the State on whose territory it holds its meeting....

Part V. Miscellaneous Provisions

◆ **Section I**
PRISONERS OF WAR
Article 119.

The High Contracting Parties agree to repatriate at once the prisoners of war and interned civilians who are still in their hands.

The exchange of prisoners of war and interned civilians detained by Greece and Turkey respectively forms the subject of a separate agreement between those Powers signed at Lausanne on the 30th January, 1923.

Article 120.

Prisoners of war and interned civilians awaiting disposal or undergoing sentence for offences against discipline shall be repatriated irrespective of the completion of their sentence or of the proceedings pending against them.

Prisoners of war and interned civilians who are awaiting trial or undergoing sentence for offences other than those against discipline may be detained....

◆ **Section II**
GRAVES
Article 124.

Without prejudice to the special provisions of Article 126 of the present Treaty, the High Contracting Parties will cause to be respected and maintained within the territories under their authority the cemeteries, graves, ossuaries and memorials of soldiers and sailors who fell in action or died from wounds accident or disease since the 29th October, 1914, as well as of prisoners of war and interned civilians who died in captivity after that date....

Article 125.

The High Contracting Parties further undertake to furnish each other:

(1) A complete list of prisoners of war and interned civilians who have died in captivity, together with all information tending towards their identification.

(2) All information as to the number and position of the graves of all those who have been buried without identification.

Article 126.

The maintenance of the graves, cemeteries, ossuaries and memorials of Turkish soldiers, sailors and prisoners of war who may have died on Roumanian territory since the 27th August 1916, as well as all other obligations under Articles 124 and 125 regarding interned civilians, shall form the object of a special arrangement between the Roumanian and the Turkish Governments....

Article 128.

The Turkish Government undertakes to grant to the Governments of the British Empire, France and Italy respectively and in perpetuity the land within the Turkish territory in which are situated the graves, cemeteries, ossuaries or memorials of their soldiers and sailors who fell in action or died of wounds, accident or disease, as well as those of prisoners of war and interned civilians who died in captivity....

Article 129.

The land to be granted by the Turkish Government will include in particular, as regards the British Empire, the area in the region known as Anzac (Ari Burnu), which is shown on Map No. 3....

♦ **Section III**
GENERAL PROVISIONS
Article 137.

Subject to any agreements concluded between the High Contracting Parties, the decisions taken and orders issued since the 30th October, 1918, until the coming into force of the present Treaty, by or in agreement with the authorities of the Powers who have occupied Constantinople, and concerning the property, rights and interests of their nationals, of foreigners or of Turkish nationals, and the relations of such persons with the authorities of Turkey, shall be regarded as definitive and shall give rise to no claims against the Powers or their authority.

All other claims arising from injury suffered in consequence of any such decisions or orders shall be submitted to the Mixed Arbitral Tribunal....

Article 139.

Archives, registers, plans, title-deeds and other documents of every kind relating to the civil, judicial or financial administration, or the administration of Wakfs, which are at present in Turkey and are only of interest to the Government of a territory detached

Glossary

Balkan wars of 1912–13	wars over the possession of European territories of the Ottoman Empire
Capitulations in Turkey	agreements whereby Ottoman sultans granted rights and privileges to foreign nationals living or doing business in Ottoman territories
concessionary contracts	in this context, contracts entered into by foreign nationals who have been granted the right to engage in profitable activities in the described territories
gendarmerie and police	authorities responsible for security in the countryside and in the city, respectively
General Act of Berlin	an agreement made at Berlin Conference of 1884–1885 that regulated European colonization and trade in Africa
General Act and Declaration of Brussels	a bill enacted on July 2, 1890, at the Brussels Conference and signed by seventeen world powers, abolishing slave trafficking from Africa
Hedjaz	region bordering on the Red Sea that includes the sacred Muslim sites Mecca and Medina
phylloxera	any of several species of plant lice
Scheldt	a navigable river that flows through France, Belgium, and the Netherlands
spiritual attributions	rights accruing to Muslim authorities because Islam is a religion
Wakfs	property grants for religious or charitable purposes

from the Ottoman Empire, and reciprocally those in a territory detached from the Ottoman Empire which are only of interest to the Turkish Government, shall reciprocally be restored.

Archives, registers, plans, title-deeds and other documents mentioned above which are considered by the Government in whose possession they are as being also of interest to itself, may be retained by that Government, subject to its furnishing on request photographs or certified copies to the Government concerned.

Archives, registers, plans, title-deeds and other documents which have been taken away either from Turkey or from detached territories shall reciprocally be restored in original, in so far as they concern exclusively the territories from which they have been taken.

The expense entailed by these operations shall be paid by the Government applying therefor.

The above stipulations apply in the same manner to the registers relating to real estates or Wakfs in the districts of the former Ottoman Empire transferred to Greece after 1912....

Article 142.

The separate Convention concluded on the 30th January, 1923, between Greece and Turkey, relating to the exchange of the Greek and Turkish populations, will have as between these two High Contracting Parties the same force and effect as if it formed part of the present Treaty.

Article 143.

The present Treaty shall be ratified as soon as possible.

The ratifications shall be deposited at Paris.

The Japanese Government will be entitled merely to inform the Government of the French Republic through their diplomatic representative at Paris when their ratification has been given; in that case, they must transmit the instrument of ratification as soon as possible.

Each of the Signatory Powers will ratify by one single instrument the present Treaty and the other instruments signed by it and mentioned in the Final Act of the Conference of Lausanne, in so far as these require ratification....

In faith whereof the above-named Plenipotentiaries have signed the present Treaty.

Done at Lausanne, the 24th July, 1923, in a single copy, which will be deposited in the archives of the Government of the French Republlc, which will transmit a certified copy to each of the Contracting Powers.

Mao Zedong in 1936 (AP/Wide World Photos)

Mao Zedong's "Report on an Investigation of the Peasant Movement in Hunan"

"A revolution is not a dinner party."

Overview

When Mao Zedong published his "Report on an Investigation of the Peasant Movement in Hunan" in 1927, he was relatively unknown, and peasants played no role in the revolution being planned by the Chinese Communist Party (CCP). In subsequent decades, however, Mao would emerge as the indisputable leader of the CCP and the People's Republic of China, and the peasantry would rise up to overthrow the system that had oppressed them for centuries, just as Mao had predicted in his report. While history would fulfill Mao's vision of a rural revolution, later interpretations of the report would demonstrate the ways in which history could be rewritten.

As is often stated, history is written by the victors. That Mao's report, which was either ignored or criticized when it initially appeared in the 1920s, now enjoys a prominent place in contemporary Chinese political philosophy reflects Mao's meteoric rise from relative obscurity to almost godlike status at the time of his death in 1976. After Mao's political ascendancy, the 1927 report resurfaced. Its inclusion in the multivolume *Selected Works of Mao Tse-tung* (published in 1944 and 1947) canonized the report. The inclusion of excerpts from the report in the widely published *Quotations from Chairman Mao Tse-tung* (1967), more commonly referred to as the "Little Red Book," spread Mao's wisdom to the masses. The historical significance of the report, then, did not become apparent until years after its initial publication.

Context

At the turn of the twentieth century, China experienced and experimented with changes that would dramatically and irrevocably transform its political, cultural, social, and economic landscape. Ideas imported from abroad circulated relatively freely in the burgeoning press in the treaty ports and spread to other urban areas. Chinese intellectuals passionately debated such topics as republicanism, anarchism, and Marxism, searching for solutions that would save China from the external and internal forces tearing it apart, namely imperialism and warlordism. At the half-century point, they would find China's salvation in the ideology of Marxism-Leninism and under the leadership of Mao.

For most of the early twentieth century, chaos and war reigned. Revolution in 1911 toppled the weak Qing Dynasty and ended the imperial system. In its place emerged the Republic of China, which existed more in name than in fact. Initially headed by Sun Yat-sen, later honored as the father of modern China, the republic soon fell into the hands of regional warlords. The most powerful of the lot, the military general Yuan Shikai, successfully quashed Sun Yat-sen and his fledgling political party, the Guomindang (formerly, Kuomintang), and made an aborted attempt to establish his own dynasty. His death in 1916 led to a decade-long period of internecine fighting among the warlords. In 1923, under the guidance of the Soviet-sponsored Communist International (Comintern), the Guomindang and the CCP formed the First United Front to rid the country of warlordism. After Sun's death, Chiang Kai-shek (commonly known today as Jiang Jieshi), the military general who had led the Northern Expedition to eliminate the warlords, emerged as the leader of the Guomindang. Chiang held a deep-seated animosity toward the CCP and in April 1927 launched what became known as the Shanghai Massacre in an effort to wipe out the party.

Driven underground, the CCP relocated to the countryside. A month before the Shanghai Massacre, Mao had published his "Report on an Investigation of the Peasant Movement in Hunan," arguing for a rural revolution. Although the CCP Central Committee initially dismissed Mao's ideas, after the Shanghai Massacre it was forced to reconsider a rural strategy. Mao's efforts led to the establishment in 1931 of the Jiangxi Soviet, which lasted until 1934, when it was destroyed by the Guomindang, now firmly under the leadership of Chiang.

After the Long March—a six-thousand-mile, yearlong trek across the most treacherous terrain in western China—the CCP established a base in Yan'an. With Mao now at the head, the CCP organized the peasantry to resist the Japanese when they invaded in 1937 and to defeat the Guomindang in the civil war that followed. With the establishment of the People's Republic of China on October 1,

1893

- **December 26**
  Mao is born in Shaoshan, Hunan.

1911

- **October 10**
  An uprising in Wuhan starts the 1911 Revolution, which topples the Qing Dynasty.

1912

- **January 1**
  The Republic of China is formally declared.

- **August**
  The Guomindang, also known as the Nationalist Party, is established.

1921

- **July**
  The Chinese Communist Party is established in Shanghai, with Mao as a founding member.

1923

- **May**
  The First United Front between the Guomindang and the CCP is formed. Mao works in the Propaganda Department of the Guomindang and the Peasant Training Center.

- **June**
  Mao becomes a member of the CCP Central Committee.

1925

- Mao returns to Hunan to organize the peasantry.

1949, under the leadership of the CCP, Mao realized the vision he had first outlined in his 1927 report on the Hunan peasant movement.

About the Author

Born in Shaoshan village in the province of Hunan on December 26, 1893, Mao Zedong would rise to become China's preeminent leader in the twentieth century. Biographies of Mao often point to his peasant roots and rebellious youth as early signs of his potential as a revolutionary leader of the peasant masses. In 1910 he left the family farm for the neighboring township of Xiangxiang, where he enrolled in a school that offered classes in both Chinese and Western subjects. When the revolution that would topple the Qing Dynasty broke out in 1911, Mao joined the Republican forces. His political activism was short-lived, however; in the aftermath of the revolution, Mao withdrew into private study, eventually enrolling in the Hunan Provincial First Normal School, from which he graduated in June 1918. Later that fall, Mao ventured to Beijing, where he took a job as a library attendant at Beijing University. There Mao debated the new ideas imported from the West and met leading intellectuals, including Li Dazhao and Chen Duxiu, both of whom played vital roles in the founding of the Chinese Communist Party.

Although Mao joined the party when it was founded in 1921, he had little formal training in Socialist ideologies, much less Marxism. Within a year, however, Mao was well on his way to becoming a professional revolutionary, organizing workers and coordinating strikes in Hunan. Beginning in the mid-1920s, his attention turned to the rural situation. Impressed by the activism of the peasantry and convinced of their revolutionary potential, Mao redirected his activities to the countryside, establishing what would be formally declared as the Jiangxi Soviet in 1931. Although the Jiangxi Soviet eventually crumbled under the pressure of Guomindang forces in October 1934, forcing the CCP to flee on the famous Long March, Mao would rise up in the party ranks as a result of the defeat. The Zunyi Conference, held on January 15, 1935, in effect recognized Mao's military strategy of guerrilla warfare as superior to the positional warfare that had led to the collapse of the Jiangxi Soviet. From this point forward, Mao became the de facto leader of the CCP. During the War of Resistance against Japan and the civil war with the Guomindang, Mao consolidated his control of the CCP and expanded the reach of the CCP. Through such policies as land redistribution and rent and interest reduction, the CCP gained the support of the peasant masses.

To a great extent, the establishment of the People's Republic of China on October 1, 1949, marked the transformation of Mao from an astute leader dedicated to the people to a demagogue obsessed with maintaining his power and securing his legacy. Eager to see Communism realized during his lifetime, Mao pushed for the collectivization of agriculture, launching in 1958 the Great Leap Forward, a plan intended to create a Communist utopia and make China an industrial power but which instead resulted in widespread famine that led to an estimated twenty million deaths. A decade later, Mao unleashed the Cultural Revolution to rid China of those ideas, practices, and people that hindered the development of Communism. Anarchy and chaos ensued as the party—and society—attacked itself. With Mao's death on September 9, 1976, a semblance of normalcy began to be restored.

Arguably the most famous and influential political figure in twentieth-century China, Mao left behind a mixed legacy. As a revolutionary leader and military strategist, Mao led China to victory against seemingly insurmountable odds and founded the People's Republic of China. As an ideologue, he created Mao Zedong Thought, a political philosophy that adapted the ideas of Marxism-Leninism to Chinese conditions and that to this day represents the official ideology of the CCP. Nevertheless, as chairman of the CCP, he betrayed his comrades and almost destroyed the party to which he had dedicated his life. As the head of state, he implemented such policies the Great Leap Forward and the Cultural Revolution, which led to millions of deaths. In the last decade of his life, the ideas that had inspired earlier revolutionary successes would be manipulated to legitimize violence and anarchy.

Explanation and Analysis of the Document

Mao's "Report on an Investigation of the Peasant Movement in Hunan" reflected his recent experiences in the mid-1920s organizing the peasantry in Hunan. In 1923 Mao was appointed director of the Peasant Training Center, and two years later he traveled to Hunan to oversee the peasant movement personally. Mao was impressed with the revolutionary zeal of the peasants and became convinced that the proletarian revolution would occur in the countryside and not in the cities as the majority of Mao's comrades in the CCP had predicted. In his report Mao brought attention to the uprising of poor peasants in several counties in Hunan during the winter of 1926–1927 in an effort to persuade the party leadership to redirect the revolution to the countryside and marshal the revolutionary potential of the peasantry.

The report first appeared in a local party publication in March 1927. The complete text also included a section describing fourteen achievements of the peasant associations, which ranged from the destruction of traditional bases of authority to improvements in education and infrastructure. The purpose of this section was to document the specific accomplishments of the peasant associations and to substantiate the statements Mao makes in the first half of the report. Throughout the report Mao defends the violent actions and terror tactics of the peasants, suggesting that the CCP should take advantage of rather than curtail peasant violence.

◆ "The Importance of the Peasant Problem"

In this first section Mao makes his case for a rural revolution. Impressed by the fervor and energy of the peasants he had met during his monthlong stay in the villages of

Time Line

1926

- **July**
  The Northern Expedition, a military campaign to unify China under the Guomindang, is launched under the command of Chiang Kai-shek.

1927

- **March**
  Mao publishes the "Report on an Investigation of the Peasant Movement in Hunan."

- **April**
  The Guomindang, under the direction of Chiang, launches a campaign to eliminate the CCP. This incident, referred to as the Shanghai Massacre, drives the CCP underground.

- **August 1**
  The CCP launches an uprising in Nanchang. The resistance fails, but it leads to the creation of the Red Army.

1931

- **November**
  The Jiangxi Soviet is formally declared, and Mao rises to power as the chairman of the Jiangxi Soviet.

1934

- **October**
  The Guomindang destroys the Jiangxi Soviet, causing the CCP to flee on the famed Long March.

1935

- **January**
At the Zunyi
Conference
during the Long
March, Mao
assumes
leadership of
the CCP.

1936

- **December**
The Second
United Front
between the
Guomindang
and the CCP is
formed.

1937

- **July 7**
The War of
Resistance
against Japan,
which becomes
part of the
larger conflict of
World War II,
begins.

1945

- **August 15**
Japan
surrenders,
ending World
War II; civil war
between the
Guomindang
and the CCP
soon follows.

1949

- **October 1**
The People's
Republic of
China is formally
declared.

1966

- **August**
The Great
Proletarian
Cultural
Revolution
begins.

1976

- **September 9**
Mao dies.

Hunan, Mao grew convinced that the revolution should be redirected to the countryside. The majority of the CCP, however, subscribed to the Marxist view that the revolution would be centered in the cities and that the proletariat (the working class) would play a leading role. Like Marx, they held little regard for the peasantry and dismissed the revolutionary potential of the peasant movement. Here Mao vehemently argues against that view by describing the peasantry as "a mighty storm, like a hurricane, a force so swift and violent that no power, however great, will be able to hold it back." Mao's language reflects his confidence in the revolutionary potential of the peasantry to destroy the power structures that oppressed them and to pave "the road to liberation." Of the three choices Mao presents at the conclusion of this section (to lead, to criticize, or to oppose the peasants), it is clear which position he favors. Given the strength of the peasant movement, it would be in the party's best interest to mobilize the peasantry for the revolution.

This discussion also reflects Mao's empirical approach to knowledge. Mao arrived at his conclusion after conducting "a first-hand investigation" and convening "fact-finding conferences." Because his proposal to direct the revolution to the countryside is based on a careful and thorough evaluation of local conditions, Mao implies, it should hold greater weight than the abstract ideas of Marxism. In many of his writings, Mao privileges practical learning over book learning, describing the latter as "book worship" and "dogmatism."

◆ "Get Organized!"

Mao's periodization of the peasant movement highlights three important points. First, as the section title indicates, it draws attention to the mobilization of the peasants into peasant associations and the organization of the masses under the leadership of the associations. Second, it emphasizes the significant increase in the number of peasants involved in the movement. Third, it marks the shift to revolutionary activity.

Distinguishing between the two stages of the peasant movement enabled Mao to emphasize the dramatic changes in the movement in the past year and to show the peasantry's readiness to participate in the Communist Revolution. The last sentence, which credits the peasants for launching "a revolution without parallel in history," reaffirms Mao's ultimate goal—to convince party leaders that the peasantry should play a central role in the revolution.

◆ "Down with the Local Tyrants and Evil Gentry! All Power to the Peasant Associations!"

Mao here documents the complete overturning of traditional power structures and the emergence of the peasant associations as the supreme authority in village society. The "targets of attack" Mao identifies in the opening sentence are either power brokers (tyrants, gentry, landlords, and officials) or social norms (patriarchy and custom) that had long oppressed the peasantry in the old order. In late imperial China, the gentry consisted of those who had passed the state-sponsored civil service examination. Although the examination system was abolished in 1905, the status of the

Andy McEwan (left) and Ed Jocelyn (right) pose near a sign that reads "Red Army Snow Slope" in Sichuan, China, in August 2003. The British men spent more than a year retracing the route of the 1930s Long March. (AP/Wide World Photos)

gentry as the political, social, cultural, and economic elite persisted, and the gentry continued to assume positions of leadership in village governance. Landlords, many of whom were also part of the gentry, amassed their wealth by renting out land, hiring laborers, and making loans, often at usurious interest rates. Tyrants referred to local bullies who used intimidation and violence to rise to power. As representatives of the state, officials held great political authority, but their residence in the cities minimized the consequences of their abuses of power; for this reason Mao groups them with the secondary objects of attack. Mao also places in this second category patriarchy and village customs, reflecting the CCP's efforts to raise women's status and to eliminate superstitions.

This section also reflects recurring themes in Mao's writings. The classification of the villagers as landlords, rich peasants, middle peasants, and poor peasants would become a hallmark of CCP rural strategy after Mao's rise to power. (Although the text does not explicitly mention the poor peasants, they represent the membership of the peasant associations.) The assumption that one's class standing determined one's attitude toward the peasant associations and toward the revolution in general had been expressed in an earlier article titled "Analysis of the Classes in Chinese Society" (1926). For Mao it was imperative to identify and to silence the enemies to prevent them from undermining

the revolution. The statement that the "local tyrants, evil gentry and lawless landlords have been deprived of all right to speak" would be fully developed in Mao's 1949 essay on the people's democratic dictatorship.

◆ **"'It's Terrible!' or 'It's Fine!'"**

Mao here reinforces many of the ideas he introduced earlier. First, his discussion of the two attitudes toward the peasant uprising—"It's terrible" and "It's fine"—reflects his belief that one's class shapes one's view of the revolution. Second, by linking the peasant revolt with the 1911 "national revolution" begun by Sun Yat-sen and crediting the peasants with achieving what Sun had failed to do, Mao restates his case for a rural revolution. The 1911 Revolution failed, he argues, because it had not involved the peasantry.

In this section Mao makes explicit what had been only implied in the earlier discussion—that to oppose the peasant movement was to be against the revolution; he concludes at the end of the section: "Every revolutionary comrade must support it, or he will be taking the stand of counter-revolution." Whereas at the end of the first section, Mao offers three choices—to lead, to criticize, or to oppose the peasant movement—in this section he makes clear that the first alternative is the only option because "what the peasants are doing is absolutely right."

◆ "The Question of 'Going Too Far'"

Mao tries to sway middle-of-the-roaders to his way of thinking by explaining the necessity of the use of terror and violence to overturn the established order. Since those straddling the fence already recognized the importance of the peasant associations, Mao did not need to convince them of the rightness of the peasants' activities; he needed only to persuade them that the excesses about which they were concerned were justified, reasonable, and crucial to the success of the revolution. To this end, he correlates the degree of violence that the peasants unleash to the depth of their suffering at the hands of those they now targeted. The attacks were neither arbitrary nor random. Mao describes the peasants as "clear-sighted" and points out that they "keep clear accounts" of who has wronged them in the past. (The term *settling accounts* would later be used to describe peasants' struggles against their oppressors.) A revolution, according to Mao, is by nature violent and destructive. He concludes with the warning that following the path of moderation will only open the door for the counterrevolutionaries to undermine the revolution.

To a great extent, this section inspired many of the excesses during the Cultural Revolution in the mid-1960s. Mao's statement that "a revolution is not a dinner party" appeared in the "Little Red Book" and on propaganda posters and was regularly cited to justify the use of terror tactics. The practice of parading the accused in tall hats that resembled dunce caps also resurfaced during the Cultural Revolution.

◆ "The 'Movement of the Riffraff'"

Mao now responds to criticisms of those members of the Guomindang who, like the gentry, criticize the poor peasants who run the peasant associations. The concluding sentence succinctly sums up the main idea of this section: "Those who used to rank lowest now rank above everybody else; and so this is called 'turning things upside down.'" Such is the nature of revolution. Influenced by Marx's ideas on class struggle, Mao viewed the revolution as the overthrowing of the feudal order (represented by the gentry, the Guomindang, and the warlords) by those at the very bottom of the social ladder (represented by the peasantry). The criticisms levied by the Guomindang and the gentry against the peasant associations, Mao suggests, stemmed from their resentment toward the poor peasants for usurping their authority and replacing them as the power brokers in village society.

◆ "Vanguards of the Revolution"

The term *vanguard of the revolution* was first introduced by Vladimir Lenin, who argued that a group of professional revolutionaries trained for the specific and exclusive task of waging revolution should lead the masses. As he did with many ideas inherited from Marx and Lenin, Mao adapted their principles to the local conditions of the Chinese countryside. Although Mao's later usage of the term would more closely resemble Lenin's definition of a small, tight-knit, and disciplined political party, here Mao uses the plural form of the term to include the poor peasants as the vanguards of the revolution. This interpretation enabled

Mao to underscore the vital and leading role that the poor peasants would play in the revolution, a point central to his overarching argument for a rural revolution.

Mao offers a class analysis of village society that would become standard CCP policy in the years to come. His categorization of the peasantry into rich, middle, and poor was based on the amount of land owned and the degree of exploitation practiced or experienced. Those with surplus land were considered rich peasants; they either hired laborers to work the extra land or rented it out; both practices were considered forms of exploitation. What differentiated the rich peasant from the landlord was that the former also labored on his land; the landlord's wealth was based exclusively on the exploitation of others. The middle peasants owned just enough land to meet their needs; they neither exploited others nor were exploited themselves. The majority of the peasantry were poor peasants, who had either no land or not enough land to support themselves; hence they had to rent land or hire themselves out to make ends meet.

Mao elaborates on the point that he made earlier—that class standing determines revolutionary attitude. Not surprisingly, since the poor peasants had nothing to lose and the most to gain from turning things upside down, they were the strongest supporters of revolutionary change and hence, Mao suggests, the most loyal and reliable allies in the revolution. Given the comfortable lives of the middle peasants in the existing order, they would join the revolution only if doing so would improve their lot or if not doing so might negatively affect them. Mao favors the recruitment of the middle peasants and encourages the peasant associations to persuade those straddling the fence to side with the revolution. Finally, the rich peasants, who would most certainly be worse off if the revolution succeeded, expressed interest in the revolution after it became clear that the balance of power in the village had shifted to the poor peasants; the rich peasants sought membership in the peasant associations, Mao implies, as a form of self-protection and not as a genuine commitment to the revolution's goals.

Audience

When it was originally published in 1927, the report was directed to the membership of the CCP. Mao wrote the report to persuade the party leadership to redirect the revolution to the countryside or, at the very least, to give the peasantry a larger role in the revolution. However, leading figures in the party dismissed Mao's report at the Fifth Party Congress, which convened later that spring. Top-ranking officials, including Chen Duxiu, Qu Qiubai, Li Lisan, and Wang Ming, maintained that the revolution would be carried out by workers in the cities and rejected Mao's notion of a rural revolution. Mao was openly criticized by party leaders as well as Comintern agents in China.

After Mao emerged as the supreme leader of the CCP, the audience of the report broadened to include the people of the newly founded People's Republic of China. To the masses, who in the 1950s and 1960s revered Mao almost

"*In force and momentum the attack is tempestuous; those who bow before it survive and those who resist perish.*"

("Down with the Local Tyrants and Evil Gentry! All Power to the Peasant Associations!")

"*Every revolutionary comrade must support it, or he will be taking the stand of counter-revolution.*"

("'It's Terrible!' or 'It's Fine!'")

"*A revolution is not a dinner party, or writing an essay, or painting a picture, or doing embroidery; it cannot be so refined, so leisurely and gentle, so temperate, kind, courteous, restrained and magnanimous. A revolution is an insurrection, an act of violence by which one class overthrows another.*"

("The Question of 'Going Too Far'")

"*People with no place in society, people with no right to speak, have now audaciously lifted up their heads.*"

("The 'Movement of the Riffraff'")

to the point of worship, the report provided evidence of the prescience of their sage leader. Later publications of the report in collected volumes of Mao's writings included a footnote blaming Mao's critics for ignoring the recommendations in the report and erroneously leading the CCP toward its near extinction in the Shanghai Massacre. The information provided in the footnote should not be taken as historical fact but rather as Mao's version of events. Once in control of the CCP, Mao ensured that history would prove him right and his critics wrong. The footnote identifies Chen as the leader of the "Right opportunists," a label given to those who lag behind what the current conditions require. Chen and his followers are accused of betraying the peasants, who would play a critical role in the success of the Communist Revolution, and of appeasing the Guomindang, which would be vilified as an enemy of the people. In this way the footnote makes clear from the outset that Mao had been right all along.

Finally, the inclusion of the report in a translated collection of Mao's writings by the Foreign Languages Press (first printing in 1965) further expanded the audience to the international community. In the climate of the cold war, the global dissemination of Mao's writings was perhaps the

CCP's attempt to showcase the success of the Communist experiment in China under the leadership of Mao.

Impact

When it was first published, Mao's report had little impact. In the 1920s the CCP Central Committee, operating under the supervision of the Soviet-sponsored Comintern, focused exclusively on organizing workers in the cities and disregarded Mao's recommendations to include the peasantry in the revolution. In addition, at the time of Mao's report, the CCP was still in an alliance with the Guomindang; encouraging peasant violence against landlord interests, as Mao urged in his report, would have alienated the Guomindang and its supporters. Finally, Mao did not have enough political clout at the time to push his agenda as he would be able to do after assuming leadership of the party.

The effect of the report on the course of the revolution that would culminate in the founding of the People's Republic of China would not be felt until later. After the Shanghai Massacre in April 1927 drove the CCP underground, Mao mobilized the peasantry and implemented policies that reflected the ideas he had expressed in the report. The success of the revolution in 1949 was in many ways a vindication of Mao's defense of rural revolution.

During the Cultural Revolution in the 1960s, Mao's report would inspire another generation of eager revolutionaries, this time young rebels who referred to themselves as Red Guards. Invoking Mao's oft-quoted statement that "a revolution is not a dinner party [but] … an insurrection, an act of violence by which one class overthrows another," the Red Guards indiscriminately attacked established authority—from party leaders to their parents. Much like Mao's other writings, the 1927 report shaped the revolutionary movement in China, even long after many considered the revolution to be over.

Further Reading

■ Articles

Dittmer, Lowell. "The Legacy of Mao Zedong." *Asian Survey* 20, no. 5 (May 1980): 552–573.

Esherick, Joseph W. "Ten Theses on the Chinese Revolution." *Modern China* 21, no. 1 (January 1995): 45–76.

Scalapino, Robert A. "The Evolution of a Young Revolutionary—Mao Zedong in 1919–1921." *Journal of Asian Studies* 42, no. 1 (November 1982): 29–61.

■ Books

Cheek, Timothy. *Mao Zedong and China's Revolutions: A Brief History with Documents*. New York: Bedford/St. Martin's, 2002.

Hinton, William. *Fanshen: A Documentary of Revolution in a Chinese Village*. New York: Monthly Review Press, 2008.

Snow, Edgar. *Red Star over China: The Classic Account of the Birth of Chinese Communism*, rev. ed. New York: Grove Press, 1968.

Van de Ven, Hans J. *From Friend to Comrade: The Chinese Communist Party, 1920–1927*. Berkeley: University of California Press, 1991.

■ Web Sites

Mao Tse-tung (Zedong) Internet Library Web site. http://www.marx2mao.com/Mao/Index.html.

"Stefan Landsberger's Chinese Propaganda Poster Pages." http://www.iisg.nl/landsberger/.

—Lisa Tran

Questions for Further Study

1. What role did China's exposure to Western thought, in particular the theories of Karl Marx and Vladimir Lenin, play in the emergence of Mao Zedong as the leader of Communist China? Would Mao's revolution have occurred had China not been encroached on by the West in the early twentieth century?

2. The revolution that Mao led centered on the rural peasantry and such issues as rents and land reform. Why do you think that Mao was able to tap into the concerns of rural people and mobilize them for his revolution? Why did he choose to focus his revolution on the countryside rather than the cities?

3. Mao expresses fear of "counterrevolutionaries" and even moderates who spoke out against—or wanted to speak out against—elements of his plans. What action does Mao propose taking against these people? Why?

4. Mao's revolution against tyrants, gentry, landlords, and officials evolved into an oppressive regime that was closed to the outside world, deprived people of their rights, and led to the death of millions. Why do you think this occurred in China but not in some other nations, notably the United States, which was formed from a revolution against foreign oppression?

5. Within a period of less than fifty years, China was a monarchy, then a republic, and then a Communist state. What effect do you think these rapid and tumultuous changes had on the development of Chinese society?

Mao Zedong's "Report on an Investigation of the Peasant Movement in Hunan"

The Importance of the Peasant Problem

During my recent visit to Hunan I made a first-hand investigation of conditions in the five counties of Hsiangtan, Hsianghsiang, Hengshan, Liling and Changsha. In the thirty-two days from January 4 to February 5, I called together fact-finding conferences in villages and county towns, which were attended by experienced peasants and by comrades working in the peasant movement, and I listened attentively to their reports and collected a great deal of material. Many of the hows and whys of the peasant movement were the exact opposite of what the gentry in Hankow and Changsha are saying. I saw and heard of many strange things of which I had hitherto been unaware. I believe the same is true of many other places, too. All talk directed against the peasant movement must be speedily set right. All the wrong measures taken by the revolutionary authorities concerning the peasant movement must be speedily changed. Only thus can the future of the revolution be benefited. For the present upsurge of the peasant movement is a colossal event. In a very short time, in China's central, southern and northern provinces, several hundred million peasants will rise like a mighty storm, like a hurricane, a force so swift and violent that no power, however great, will be able to hold it back. They will smash all the trammels that bind them and rush forward along the road to liberation. They will sweep all the imperialists, warlords, corrupt officials, local tyrants and evil gentry into their graves. Every revolutionary party and every revolutionary comrade will be put to the test, to be accepted or rejected as they decide. There are three alternatives. To march at their head and lead them? To trail behind them, gesticulating and criticizing? Or to stand in their way and oppose them? Every Chinese is free to choose, but events will force you to make the choice quickly.

Get Organized!

The development of the peasant movement in Hunan may be divided roughly into two periods with respect to the counties in the province's central and southern parts where the movement has already made much headway. The first, from January to September of last year, was one of organization. In this period, January to June was a time of underground activity, and July to September, when the revolutionary army was driving out Chao Heng-ti, one of open activity. During this period, the membership of the peasant associations did not exceed 300,000-400,000, the masses directly under their leadership numbered little more than a million, there was as yet hardly any struggle in the rural areas, and consequently there was very little criticism of the associations in other circles. Since its members served as guides, scouts and carriers of the Northern Expeditionary Army, even some of the officers had a good word to say for the peasant associations. The second period, from last October to January of this year, was one of revolutionary action. The membership of the associations jumped to two million and the masses directly under their leadership increased to ten million. Since the peasants generally enter only one name for the whole family on joining a peasant association, a membership of two million means a mass following of about ten million. Almost half the peasants in Hunan are now organized. In counties like Hsiangtan, Hsianghsiang, Liuyang, Changsha, Liling, Ninghsiang, Pingkiang, Hsiangyin, Hengshan, Hengyang, Leiyang, Chenhsien and Anhua, nearly all the peasants have combined in the peasant associations or have come under their leadership. It was on the strength of their extensive organization that the peasants went into action and within four months brought about a great revolution in the countryside, a revolution without parallel in history.

Down with the Local Tyrants and Evil Gentry! All Power to the Peasant Associations!

The main targets of attack by the peasants are the local tyrants, the evil gentry and the lawless landlords, but in passing they also hit out against patriarchal ideas and institutions, against the corrupt officials in the cities and against bad practices and customs in the rural areas. In force and momentum the attack is tempestuous; those who bow before it survive and those who resist perish. As a result, the privileges which the feudal landlords enjoyed for thousands of years are being shattered to pieces. Every bit of the dignity and prestige built up by the landlords is being swept into the dust. With the collapse of the power of the landlords, the peasant associations have now become the sole organs of authority and the popular slogan "All power to the peasant associations" has become a reality. Even trifles such as a quarrel between husband and wife are brought to the peasant association. Nothing can be settled unless someone from the peasant association is present. The association actually dictates all rural affairs, and, quite literally, "whatever it says, goes." Those who are outside the associations can only speak well of them and cannot say anything against them. The local tyrants, evil gentry and lawless landlords have been deprived of all right to speak, and none of them dares even mutter dissent. In the face of the peasant associations' power and pressure, the top local tyrants and evil gentry have fled to Shanghai, those of the second rank to Hankow, those of the third to Changsha and those of the fourth to the county towns, while the fifth rank and the still lesser fry surrender to the peasant associations in the villages.

"Here's ten yuan. Please let me join the peasant association," one of the smaller of the evil gentry will say.

"Ugh! Who wants your filthy money?" the peasants reply.

Many middle and small landlords and rich peasants and even some middle peasants, who were all formerly opposed to the peasant associations, are now vainly seeking admission. Visiting various places, I often came across such people who pleaded with me, "Mr. Committeeman from the provincial capital, please be my sponsor!"

In the Ching [Qing] Dynasty, the household census compiled by the local authorities consisted of a regular register and "the other" register, the former for honest people and the latter for burglars, bandits and similar undesirables. In some places the peasants now use this method to scare those who formerly opposed the associations. They say, "Put their names down in the other register!"

Afraid of being entered in the other register, such people try various devices to gain admission into the peasant associations, on which their minds are so set that they do not feel safe until their names are entered. But more often than not they are turned down flat, and so they are always on tenterhooks; with the doors of the association barred to them, they are like tramps without a home or, in rural parlance, "mere trash." In short, what was looked down upon four months ago as a "gang of peasants" has now become a most honourable institution. Those who formerly prostrated themselves before the power of the gentry now bow before the power of the peasants. No matter what their identity, all admit that the world since last October is a different one.

"It's Terrible!" or "It's Fine!"

The peasants' revolt disturbed the gentry's sweet dreams. When the news from the countryside reached the cities, it caused immediate uproar among the gentry. Soon after my arrival in Changsha, I met all sorts of people and picked up a good deal of gossip. From the middle social strata upwards to the Kuomintang [Guomindang] right-wingers, there was not a single person who did not sum up the whole business in the phrase, "It's terrible!" Under the impact of the views of the "It's terrible!" school then flooding the city, even quite revolutionary minded people became downhearted as they pictured the events in the countryside in their mind's eye; and they were unable to deny the word "terrible". Even quite progressive people said, "Though terrible, it is inevitable in a revolution." In short, nobody could altogether deny the word "terrible". But, as already mentioned, the fact is that the great peasant masses have risen to fulfil their historic mission and that the forces of rural democracy have risen to overthrow the forces of rural feudalism. The patriarchal-feudal class of local tyrants, evil gentry and lawless landlords has formed the basis of autocratic government for thousands of years and is the cornerstone of imperialism, warlordism and corrupt officialdom. To over-throw these feudal forces is the real objective of the national revolution. In a few months the peasants have accomplished what Dr. Sun Yat-sen wanted, but failed, to accomplish in the forty years he devoted to the national revolution. This is a marvellous feat never before achieved, not just in forty, but in thousands of years. It's fine. It is not "terrible" at all. It is anything but "terrible". "It's terrible!" is obviously a theory for combating the rise of the peasants in the interests of the landlords; it is obviously a theory of the landlord class for preserving the old order of feudalism and obstructing the establishment of the new order of democracy, it is obviously a counter-revolutionary theory. No revolutionary comrade should echo this nonsense. If your revolutionary viewpoint is firmly established and if you have been to the villages and looked around, you will undoubtedly feel thrilled as never before. Countless thousands of the enslaved—the peasants—are striking down the enemies who battened on their flesh. What the peasants are doing is absolutely right; what they are doing is fine! "It's fine!" is the theory of the peasants and of all other revolutionaries. Every revolutionary comrade should know that the national revolution requires a great change in the countryside. The Revolution of 1911 did not bring about this change, hence its failure. This change is now taking place, and it is an important factor for the completion of the revolution. Every revolutionary comrade must support it, or he will be taking the stand of counter-revolution.

The Question of "Going Too Far"

Then there is another section of people who say, "Yes, peasant associations are necessary, but they are going rather too far." This is the opinion of the middle-of-the-roaders. But what is the actual situation? True, the peasants are in a sense "unruly" in the countryside. Supreme in authority, the peasant association allows the landlord no say and sweeps away his prestige. This amounts to striking the landlord down to the dust and keeping him there. The peasants threaten, "We will put you in the other register!" They fine the local tyrants and evil gentry, they demand contributions from them, and they smash their sedan-chairs. People swarm into the houses of local tyrants and evil gentry who are against the peasant association, slaughter their pigs and consume their grain. They even loll for a minute or two on the ivory-inlaid beds belonging to the young ladies in the households of the local tyrants and evil gentry. At the slightest provocation they make arrests, crown the arrested with tall paper hats, and parade them through the villages, saying, "You dirty landlords, now you know who we are!" Doing whatever they like and turning everything upside down, they have created a kind of terror in the countryside. This is what some people call "going too far", or "exceeding the proper limits in righting a wrong", or "really too much." Such talk may seem plausible, but in fact it is wrong. First, the local tyrants, evil gentry and lawless landlords have themselves driven the peasants to this. For ages they have used their power to tyrannize over the peasants and trample them underfoot; that is why the peasants have reacted so strongly. The most violent revolts and the most serious disorders have invariably occurred in places where the local tyrants, evil gentry and lawless landlords perpetrated the worst outrages. The peasants are clear-sighted. Who is bad and who is not, who is the worst and who is not quite so vicious, who deserves severe punishment and who deserves to be let off lightly—the peasants keep clear accounts, and very seldom has the punishment exceeded the crime. Secondly, a revolution is not a dinner party, or writing an essay, or painting a picture, or doing embroidery; it cannot be so refined, so leisurely and gentle, so temperate, kind, courteous, restrained and magnanimous. A revolution is an insurrection, an act of violence by which one class overthrows another. A rural revolution is a revolution by which the peasantry overthrows the power of the feudal landlord class. Without using the greatest force, the peasants cannot possibly overthrow the deep-rooted authority of the landlords which has lasted for thousands of years. The rural areas need a mighty revolutionary upsurge, for it alone can rouse the people in their millions to become a powerful force. All the actions mentioned here which have been labelled as "going too far" flow from the power of the peasants, which has been called forth by the mighty revolutionary upsurge in the countryside. It was highly necessary for such things to be done in the second period of the peasant movement, the period of revolutionary action. In this period it was necessary to establish the absolute authority of the peasants. It was necessary to forbid malicious criticism of the peasant associations. It was necessary to overthrow the whole authority of the gentry, to strike them to the ground and keep them there. There is revolutionary significance in all the actions which were labelled as "going too far" in this period. To put it bluntly, it is necessary to create terror for a while in every rural area, or otherwise it would be impossible to suppress the activities of the counter-revolutionaries in the countryside or overthrow the authority of the gentry. Proper limits have to be exceeded in order to right a wrong, or else the wrong cannot be righted. Those who talk about the peasants "going too far" seem at first sight to be different from those who say "It's terrible!" as mentioned earlier, but in essence they proceed from the same standpoint and likewise voice a landlord theory that upholds the interests of the privileged classes. Since this theory impedes the rise of the peasant movement and so disrupts the revolution, we must firmly oppose it.

The "Movement of the Riffraff"

The right-wing of the Kuomintang says, "The peasant movement is a movement of the riffraff, of the lazy peasants." This view is current in Changsha.

When I was in the countryside, I heard the gentry say, "It is all right to set up peasant associations, but the people now running them are no good. They ought to be replaced!" This opinion comes to the same thing as what the right-wingers are saying; according to both it is all right to have a peasant movement (the movement is already in being and no one dare say otherwise), but they say that the people running it are no good and they particularly hate those in charge of the associations at the lower levels, calling them "riffraff". In short, all those whom the gentry had despised, those whom they had trodden into the dirt, people with no place in society, people with no right to speak, have now audaciously lifted up their heads. They have not only lifted up their heads but taken power into their hands. They are now running the township peasant associations (at the lowest level), which they have turned into something fierce and formidable. They have raised their rough, work-soiled hands and laid them on the gentry. They tether the evil gentry with ropes, crown them with tall paper-hats and parade them through the villages. (In Hsiangtan and Hsianghsiang they call this "parading through the township" and in Liling "parading through the fields".) Not a day passes but they drum some harsh, pitiless words of denunciation into these gentry's ears. They are issuing orders and are running everything. Those who used to rank lowest now rank above everybody else; and so this is called "turning things upside down".

Vanguards of the Revolution

Where there are two opposite approaches to things and people, two opposite views emerge. "It's terrible!" and "It's fine!", "riffraff" and "vanguards of the revolution"—here are apt examples.

We said above that the peasants have accomplished a revolutionary task which had been left unaccomplished for many years and have done an important job for the national revolution. But has this great revolutionary task, this important revolutionary work, been performed by all the peasants? No. There are three kinds of peasants, the rich, the middle and the poor peasants. The three live in different circumstances and so have different views about the revolution. In the first period, what appealed to the rich peasants was the talk about the Northern Expeditionary Army's sustaining a crushing defeat in Kiangsi, about Chiang Kai-shek's being wounded in the leg and flying back to Kwangtung,

and about Wu Pei-fu's recapturing Yuehchow. The peasant associations would certainly not last and the Three People's Principles could never prevail, because they had never been heard of before. Thus an official of the township peasant association (generally one of the "riffraff" type) would walk into the house of a rich peasant, register in hand, and say, "Will you please join the peasant association?" How would the rich peasant answer? A tolerably well-behaved one would say, "Peasant association? I have lived here for decades, tilling my land. I never heard of such a thing before, yet I've managed to live all right. I advise you to give it up!" A really vicious rich peasant would say, "Peasant association! Nonsense! Association for getting your head chopped off! Don't get people into trouble!" Yet, surprisingly enough, the peasant associations have now been established several months, and have even dared to stand up to the gentry. The gentry of the neighbourhood who refused to surrender their opium pipes were arrested by the associations and paraded through the villages. In the county towns, moreover, some big landlords were put to death, like Yen Jung-chiu of Hsiangtan and Yang Chih-tse of Ninghsiang. On the anniversary of the October Revolution, at the time of the anti-British rally and of the great celebrations of the victory of the Northern Expedition, tens of thousands of peasants in every township, holding high their banners, big and small, along with their carrying-poles and hoes, demonstrated in massive, streaming columns. It was only then that the rich peasants began to get perplexed and alarmed. During the great victory celebrations of the Northern Expedition, they learned that Kiukiang had been taken, that Chiang Kai-shek had not been wounded in the leg and that Wu Pei-fu had been defeated after all. What is more, they saw such slogans as "Long live the Three People's Principles!" "Long live the peasant associations!" and "Long live the peasants!" clearly written on the "red and green proclamations". "What?" wondered the rich peasants, greatly perplexed and alarmed, "'Long live the peasants!' Are these people now to be regarded as emperors?" So the peasant associations are putting on grand airs. People from the associations say to the rich peasants, "We'll enter you in the other register," or, "In another month, the admission fee will be ten yuan a head!" Only under the impact of all this are the rich peasants tardily joining the associations, some paying fifty cents or a yuan for admission (the regular fee being a mere ten coppers), some securing admission only after asking other people to put in a good word for them. But there are quite a number of die-hards who have not joined to this day. When the rich peasants join the associations, they generally enter the name of some sixty or seventy year-old member of the family, for they are in constant dread of "conscription." After joining, the rich peasants are not keen on doing any work for the associations. They remain inactive throughout.

How about the middle peasants? Theirs is a vacillating attitude. They think that the revolution will not bring them much good. They have rice cooking in their pots and no creditors knocking on their doors at midnight. They, too, judging a thing by whether it ever existed before, knit their brows and think to themselves, "Can the peasant association really last?" "Can the Three People's Principles prevail?" Their conclusion is, "Afraid not!" They imagine it all depends on the will of Heaven and think, "A peasant association? Who knows if Heaven wills it or not?" In the first period, people from the association would call on a middle peasant, register in hand, and say, "Will you please join the peasant association?" The middle peasant would reply, "There's no hurry!" It was not until the second period, when the peasant associations were already exercising great power, that the middle peasants came in. They show up better in the associations than the rich peasants but are not as yet very enthusiastic; they still want to wait and see. It is essential for the peasant associations to get the middle peasants to join and to do a good deal more explanatory work among them.

The poor peasants have always been the main force in the bitter fight in the countryside. They have fought militantly through the two periods of underground work and of open activity. They are the most responsive to Communist Party leadership. They are deadly enemies of the camp of the local tyrants and evil gentry and attack it without the slightest hesitation. "We joined the peasant association long ago," they say to the rich peasants, "why are you still hesitating?" The rich peasants answer mockingly, "What is there to keep you from joining? You people have neither a tile over your heads nor a speck of land under your feet!" It is true the poor peasants are not afraid of losing anything. Many of them really have "neither a tile over their heads nor a speck of land under their feet". What, indeed, is there to keep them from joining the associations? According to the survey of Changsha County, the poor peasants comprise 70 per cent, the middle peasants 20 per cent, and the landlords and the rich peasants 10 per cent of the population in the rural areas. The 70 per cent, the poor peasants, may be sub-divided into two categories, the utterly desti-

tute and the less destitute. The utterly destitute, comprising 20 per cent, are the completely dispossessed, that is, people who have neither land nor money, are without any means of livelihood, and are forced to leave home and become mercenaries or hired labourers or wandering beggars. The less destitute, the other 50 per cent, are the partially dispossessed, that is, people with just a little land or a little money who eat up more than they earn and live in toil and distress the year round, such as the handicraftsmen, the tenant-peasants (not including the rich tenant-peasants) and the semi-owner-peasants. This great mass of poor peasants, or altogether 70 per cent of the rural population, are the backbone of the peasant associations, the vanguard in the overthrow of the feudal forces and the heroes who have performed the great revolutionary task which for long years was left undone. Without the poor peasant class (the "riffraff," as the gentry call them), it would have been impossible to bring about the present revolutionary situation in the countryside, or to overthrow the local tyrants and evil gentry and complete the democratic revolution. The poor peasants, being the most revolutionary group, have gained the leadership of the peasant associations. In both the first and second periods almost all the chairmen and committee members in the peasant associations at the lowest level were poor peasants (of the officials in the township associations in Hengshan County the utterly destitute comprise 50 per cent, the less destitute 40 per cent, and poverty-stricken intellectuals 10 per cent). Leadership by the poor peasants is absolutely necessary. Without the poor peasants there would be no revolution. To deny their role is to deny the revolution. To attack them is to attack the revolution. They have never been wrong on the general direction of the revolution. They have discredited the local tyrants and evil gentry. They have beaten down the local tyrants and evil gentry, big and small, and kept them underfoot. Many of their deeds in the period of revolutionary action, which were labelled as "going too far", were in fact the very things the revolution required. Some county governments, county headquarters of the Kuomintang and county peasant associations in Hunan have already made a number of mistakes; some have even sent soldiers to arrest officials of the lower level associations at the landlords' request. A good many chairmen and committee members of township associations in Hengshan and Hsianghsiang Counties have been thrown in jail. This mistake is very serious and feeds the arrogance of the reactionaries. To judge whether or not it is a mistake, you have only to see how joyful the lawless landlords become and how reactionary sentiments grow, wherever the chairmen or committee members of local peasant associations are arrested. We must combat the counter-revolutionary talk of a "movement of riffraff" and a "movement of lazy peasants" and must be especially careful not to commit the error of helping the local tyrants and evil gentry in their attacks on the poor peasant class. Though a few of the poor peasant leaders undoubtedly did have shortcomings, most of them have changed by now. They themselves are energetically prohibiting gambling and suppressing banditry. Where the peasant association is powerful, gambling has stopped altogether and banditry has vanished. In some places it is literally true that people do not take any articles left by the wayside and that doors are not bolted at night. According to the Hengshan survey, 85 per cent of the poor peasant leaders have made great progress and have proved themselves capable and hard-working. Only 15 per cent retain some bad habits. The most one can call these is "an unhealthy minority", and we must not echo the local tyrants and evil gentry in indiscriminatingly condemning them as "riffraff." This problem of the "unhealthy minority" can be tackled only under the peasant associations' own slogan of "strengthen discipline", by carrying on propaganda among the masses, by educating the "unhealthy minority", and by tightening the associations' discipline; in no circumstances should soldiers be arbitrarily sent to make such arrests as would damage the prestige of the poor peasants and feed the arrogance of the local tyrants and evil gentry. This point requires particular attention.

Glossary

battened	prospered at the expense of another
Chao Heng-ti	one-time governor of Hunan Province who became commander in chief of Hunan in 1920 but was expelled by revolutionary forces
comrades	members of the Chinese Communist Party
October Revolution	the act by which Mao, on October 1, 1949, declared the establishment of the People's Republic of China, having largely defeated the Nationalists under Chiang Kai-shek
Revolution of 1911	also the Xinhai Revolution, which ended in 1912 with the abdication of the last Qing emperor, Puyi
Three People's Principles	Sun Yat-sen's political philosophy, based on freedom of the people from imperialist domination and government by the people and for the people; Sun borrowed the second and third principles from Lincoln's Gettysburg Address
Wu Pei-fu	right-wing warlord, known as the Jade Marshal, who was defeated by Zhang Zuolin, an ally of Sun Yat-sen

A. B. Xuma's "Bridging the Gap between White and Black in South Africa"

"What we need most is a revolution of the people's thoughts, their ideas, their ideals, and their spirit."

Overview

On the evening of July 1, 1930, Alfred Bitini Xuma, a black South African, spoke to a multiracial audience at the South African Native College, in Fort Hare, South Africa. He presented his speech during an unusual event, the Bantu-European Student Christian Conference, which met between June 27 and July 3. Tracing historical developments in South Africa following the arrival in 1652 of about ninety European men employed by the Netherlands East India Company, Xuma highlighted white-black interaction and conflict and the discovery and exploitation of diamonds and gold in the later nineteenth century. This exploitation created enormous demand for cheap black labor, radically modernized the nation's economy, and seriously affected race relations in South Africa. Xuma ended his historical narrative with a reference to the creation of the Union of South Africa in 1910, wherein the constitution excluded the majority African population from participation in the national parliament, leaving all political power in the hands of the white minority.

Xuma then discussed the legal disabilities imposed by restrictive laws passed by the white government after independence was achieved on May 31, 1910. This legislation discriminated against and repressed the black population in various ways, seriously limiting black economic opportunity. Xuma urged his audience, especially the black students, to take the initiative to promote change and called upon all to work for justice and fair treatment for the black majority, who had no voice in South Africa's politics. Xuma's speech was significant because of the author's status as an American-trained physician, the multiracial audience of students and adults, the large number of women who attended, the Christian context, and the moderate message, urging the listeners to build bridges between the races for the greater good of all.

Context

The demography of South Africa reflects a history of migration and interaction over the course of many centuries. The majority African population—farmers and cattle herders speaking Bantu languages—slowly migrated into the eastern 40 percent of South Africa during a period of more than a thousand years. The indigenous Khoisan speakers, mainly hunters and gatherers (though some owned cattle as well), lived in the western and central zones of South Africa. When the European employees of the Netherlands East India Company arrived in 1652 to set up a refreshment station at Cape Town, they encountered the Khoisan speakers but had little or no contact with the Bantu speakers on the frontier until the 1770s. In the seventeenth and eighteenth centuries, European immigrants, mainly from the Netherlands, France, and parts of Germany, lived a frontier existence through which the three European groups intermarried, slowly migrated eastward, and began to identify themselves as a separate European group, Afrikaners, with an evolving language, Afrikaans. Sexual relations between European males (mainly company employees and sailors) and free Khoisan women and slave women (of Malay or tropical African origins) yielded a racially mixed population who still refer to themselves as "coloreds."

After the 1770s, the history of African-European contact became one of periodic conflict well into the nineteenth century, when important Bantu-speaking kingdoms with strong central governments emerged. South Africa came under British colonial rule early in the century. After 1836 a portion of the Afrikaner population migrated into the South African interior to live among Bantu speakers rather than on a frontier with them. With the discovery and concomitant exploitation of diamonds in 1867 and large quantities of gold in the mid-1880s, South Africa became a modern industrial country.

British colonial rule ended in South Africa on May 31, 1910. At that time, there were approximately four million Bantu-speaking South Africans, 1.2 million whites, and considerably smaller numbers of coloreds and Indians (who had arrived in the later nineteenth century). The whites were divided between the Afrikaans speakers (about 60 percent of whites) and the English speakers. Political power, economic control, and ownership of more than 90 percent of the land rested with the white minority. South Africa was divided into four provinces: Cape, Natal, Orange Free State, and Transvaal. Only in Cape Province were a small number of Africans and coloreds who met an economic qualification allowed to

CA. 1893
- Alfred Xuma is born in the village of Manzana in the Transkei region of the Cape Colony.

1910
- May 31
  The Union of South Africa is formed.

1913
- June 19
  The Natives Land Act is enacted.

1916
- May
  Xuma graduates from the Tuskegee Institute (now Tuskegee University) in Alabama.

1920
- June 17
  Xuma graduates from the University of Minnesota.

1926
- 1926
  Xuma earns an M.D. from Northwestern University Medical School.

1927
- December 4
  After taking advanced medical training in Hungary and Scotland, Xuma returns to South Africa.

vote (a privilege dating back to 1853). After 1910 many whites, including politicians, were asking what was to be done about the "native question." Very few whites believed in equality between the races; consequently, there was no satisfactory answer to the question. One possible solution, according to some whites, was to separate the races as much as possible, and the white parliament passed laws trying to implement a segregation policy. Segregation laws fell into several categories: workplace, urban, and rural. Certain historians refer to the time between 1910 and 1948, the year that apartheid began, as the "segregation era."

Black Africans faced endless humiliations in their daily interaction with whites. Workplace segregation included prohibitions against Africans entering apprenticeship programs to learn skilled trades, working in supervisory positions, or earning equal pay for equal work. Africans suffered from racial discrimination in trains, housing, and schools and before juries. They were also subjected to physical abuse, especially in rural areas, at the hands of white farmers. In theory, sharecropping on white farms was illegal in certain provinces; meanwhile, rural African land buyers could not borrow money from the semi-independent government Land Bank. Black Africans were prohibited from walking on the sidewalk in Pretoria, the administrative capital, during part of the 1920s; were denied drivers' licenses; and were given discriminatory criminal sentences compared with those for whites for similar infractions. Parliament declared sex between whites and blacks illegal in 1927.

Despite the oppression, an educated black population expanded during this period, mainly because segregated primary and secondary missionary schools did exist. Yet there were never enough such schools in South Africa, so completing primary and secondary school was a signal achievement for black Africans. Xuma attended Clarkebury, one of a number of excellent secondary schools. In 1916 the South African government opened the South African Native College at Fort Hare, in eastern Cape Province, for advanced training. Education abroad was possible only for a select few. The highly educated African elite, trained as physicians, lawyers, teachers, social workers, journalists, and editors, gained opportunities to voice their distress, disappointment, and opposition to discrimination in South African society, such as in meetings with government officials and multiracial public and private conferences. Thus, the Bantu-European Student Christian Conference, while unusual, was not unprecedented. Black African leaders also voiced their opinions at the annual meetings of political organizations like the African National Congress (ANC), founded in 1912, and in black-edited newspapers as well as white-owned newspapers.

About the Author

Alfred Xuma was born in the late nineteenth century (in 1893, it is thought) to a Xhosa family in the village of Manzana in the Transkei region of the Cape Colony. He left South Africa to achieve an advanced education in the United States, where he had to work to pay his tuition, fees, and life expenses as he studied to earn a bachelor's degree and a medical degree. He then studied in Europe to gain the proper British credentials in order to practice medicine in South Africa. Xuma returned to his country at the age of thirty-four, after a fourteen-year absence, and established his medical practice in Johannesburg, becoming the "first and only western-trained African physician" (Gish, p. 59) practicing in South Africa's most important city.

Within less than three years, Xuma had gained enough of a reputation beyond his medical competence to be invited to speak at the Bantu-European Student Christian Conference of 1930. His speech demonstrates that he had quickly learned about the extent of the discrimination against the majority African population, most of which had been imposed during his absence. But it took the government's final assault on suffrage in Cape Province in 1935–1936 to lead Xuma to become politically active. He strongly opposed the Representation of Natives in Parliament, which would deprive the Africans in Cape Province of the right to vote. Xuma was one of the organizers of the All African Convention of December 1935, which was attended by nearly four hundred Africans who discussed ways to oppose the constitutional amendment. The delegates sent a deputation to the prime minister, with whom they met twice in February 1936, but to no avail. Ever since 1910 African leaders had protested against legislation adversely affecting the interests and opportunities of the majority; they spoke out at meetings, railed against bills in the newspapers, and met with officials. They seem to have been listened to respectfully by government officials and others, but the result was always the same: The parliament passed the laws, and Africans suffered the consequences. Xuma's biographer, Steven Gish, emphasizes a facet of his character that emerged during the effort to preserve suffrage in Cape Province: "Xuma had shown that he was less willing to equivocate on African rights than some of his colleagues" (p. 87).

In December 1940 the ANC elected Xuma as its president, a post he would hold for nine years. During his presidency, Xuma traveled around the country tirelessly working to expand the membership of the organization and improve the finances of an almost bankrupt organization. He gave many speeches emphasizing the main goal of the ANC: to end segregation and eliminate discrimination from the country. Xuma stated in February 1941 that "South Africa is fighting for noble and high ideals—for Christianity and human decency" (Karis and Carter, vol. 2, p. 165). Later that year, he stated his belief that "South Africa stands for freedom, democracy, and Christianity" (Karis and Carter, vol. 2, p. 171). Under his leadership, a group of ANC leaders adapted a key World War II document, the Atlantic Charter (which had been signed by Franklin Roosevelt and Winston Churchill in 1941 and referred to Europe under Nazi German control), to the South African situation. Other themes that dominated Xuma's speeches included an end to legal disabilities, the restoration of the vote to all black South Africans, and a demand for social justice within South African society. Most important, he promoted ideas about individual and political self-reliance among Africans.

Time Line

1930

- **July 1**
  Xuma delivers a speech, "Bridging the Gap between White and Black in South Africa," to the Bantu-European Student Christian Conference at Fort Hare.

1935

- **December**
  The meeting of the All African Convention takes place.

1936

- **April 22**
  Parliament passes the Representation of Natives in Parliament Act.

- **August 31**
  The Native Trust and Land Act passed by the parliament takes effect.

1940

- **December 16**
  Xuma becomes president of the African National Congress, a post he holds until 1949.

1948

- **May 26**
  The National Party wins the parliamentary election, marking the beginning of apartheid policies.

1962

- **January 27**
  Xuma dies at his home in Johannesburg.

A. B. Xuma (© Bettmann/CORBIS)

As president, Xuma transformed the ANC into a more dynamic organization. During the 1940s black South Africans recognized the need to challenge the discriminatory system more vigorously, staging strikes and boycotts to emphasize their demands for better lives. Xuma also helped prepare the ANC for a "bold new role" (Gish, p. 164) in protests against a much more extreme threat to Africans that the Afrikaner National Party imposed after 1948: apartheid.

After he left the ANC presidency, Xuma did not play a substantial role in the African challenges to the increasingly harsh system of apartheid. As Gish writes, however, Xuma continued to call for "change peacefully, reasonably and eloquently" (p. 203). Although Xuma was viewed as an elder statesman among the black elite by the time of his death on January 27, 1962, his efforts—as well as those of all opponents of apartheid—to speak out against South Africa's racist policies made no impact.

Explanation and Analysis of the Document

At the beginning of his speech, Xuma dispassionately suggests that he intends to challenge, in an unbiased manner, his listeners to look for truth and facts and to act on the results of their search. He informs his audience that his focus is on "the ills of our race relations" but stresses that he has no real answers to the so-called native question because it is a "human problem" and no change can be achieved until

the African voice is included in the key branches of government, the current absence of which he deplores. Xuma juxtaposes white minority fears and uncertainty with African dissatisfaction, anxiety, and loss of confidence in white institutions. Eventually, he reminds his listeners of the prevailing racial doctrine in the Afrikaner republics that emerged in the South African interior after 1836: "There shall be no equality between Black and White either in Church or in State."

Xuma informs his audience about parts of the U.S. Constitution, especially the Fourteenth and Fifteenth amendments. As part of his U.S.–South Africa comparisons, he refers to a large number of black American landowners and a pre-1930 Supreme Court decision about residential segregation. But the figures he provides are exaggerated, and the Supreme Court did not begin to rule favorably on the subject of residential segregation until after World War II in the case of *Shelley v. Kramer* (1948). (The case struck down restrictive covenants, that is, agreements made by neighbors not to sell their homes to African Americans.) Because this was a Christian-sponsored conference, Xuma asks if Jesus would approve of the "Native Policy" of the "Christian country" of South Africa and whether the nation's racial practices conform to the conferees "profession of the Christian faith." Then he issues his challenge: "How are we going to bridge the gap between White and Black?"

Xuma's talk comes to focus on the racially discriminatory policies, which he periodically refers to as "colour bars," promoted by the South African government. The South Africa Act, passed by the British parliament in 1909, established the constitutional framework for the creation of the Union of South Africa on May 31, 1910. This act set the groundwork for political discrimination in that it excluded Africans from the Parliament of South Africa. Xuma then speaks of the restrictive, repressive, and discriminatory laws that Parliament passed after 1910. He discusses the disabilities, injustices, and reduced economic opportunities resulting from legislation. He is particularly concerned about two threats in 1930: a bill designed to remove Africans from the common voters' roll in Cape Province and legislation he interprets as potentially restricting freedom of speech. Eligible black Africans in Cape Province alone, provided they met economic qualifications in place since 1853, were allowed to exercise the franchise. But this right was threatened in 1930. Prime Minister J. B. M. Hertzog had formed a government in 1924 after his National Party won, along with its coalition ally, the Labor Party, a majority of seats in the parliament.

In 1926 Hertzog introduced the Representation of Natives in Parliament bill as part of a package of four bills that he contended would settle the "native question" for the foreseeable future. This bill was designed to end African voting in the Cape. Because suffrage for Africans was an entrenched clause in the South Africa Act, a two-thirds majority of Parliament had to approve such an amendment. Xuma voices particular worry about the threat to the vote in the Cape Province as he asks, "Has the African ever abused the privilege?" and emphasizes that Africans voted responsibly. He identifies a racial reason why whites opposed the vote for Africans: Africans might sway the outcome of an election because voters exercise their right "intelligently" and are "a factor to be reckoned with," terms implying a measure of equality, a notion that was anathema to many whites. Prime Minister Hertzog had been unable to muster that two-thirds majority, but Xuma rightly feared that this threat might become a reality in the near future. In fact, Cape Africans lost their right to vote in 1936.

Xuma identifies pertinent clauses of the Native Administration Act of 1927 and the 1930 Riotous Assemblies Act that could be used to curb the right to freedom of speech, of special concern to an African leader trying to change the discriminatory policies prevailing in his country. However, neither Xuma nor most other members of the educated African elite were inclined to speak or write about their opposition to segregation in South Africa, with the generally moderate tone of their statements owing to their unwillingness to promote industrial strikes or violent opposition to the government. In fact, most of the black elite spoke of their loyalty to South Africa (especially during World War I) and their admiration for Western civilization and democratic government. African demands, as evidenced in Xuma's speech, focused on economic opportunity, justice, a political voice through the franchise, and the repeal of racially discriminatory laws, most of which applied even to well-educated Africans. On occasion, members of Parliament debated whether educated Africans should be exempted from a particular law, such as the Natives Land Act (1913), but the majority voted against exemptions in every case.

Three specific discriminatory policies discussed by Xuma are the pass system, rural land distribution, and education inequalities. He is particularly indignant about passes, which were used by white society to control the movements of the African population, especially migration from rural areas to cities. Restricting mobility seriously limited African economic opportunity, and there were important implications to the enforcement of the pass laws: Even highly educated blacks like Xuma could be stopped at any time by white policemen demanding to see their passes. Indeed, Xuma, a well-dressed professional driving his own car, was once assaulted by a policeman because he had left his documents in another suit pocket. Any African's failure to produce the pass could lead to imprisonment for days or weeks. Xuma and other African leaders condemned such incarcerations for technical offenses as contributing to disrespect for the law and risking the creation of new criminals because the innocent were incarcerated together with hardened criminals.

Xuma emphasizes the great importance of land to the African, and, as did many of his African peers, condemns the 1913 Natives Land Act. This law prohibited Africans from buying land in two of the four provinces, Transvaal and Natal, but also included a clause allowing the government to make exceptions to this prohibition. Several thousand exceptions had been allowed by 1930, but Xuma and his peers rarely discussed them. In fact, the land act left Africans only 7 percent of the land in 1913 (with the percentage increasing only slightly by 1930), not the 20 percent to which Xuma erroneously refers. He is correct, however, in stating that many African areas, called reserves in South Africa (similar to American Indian reservations), were overcrowded. It is true that the Natives Land Act limited and slowed buying by Africans.

Xuma is concerned with the problem of wholly inadequate (and segregated) education facilities for Africans and with the equally insufficient (and discriminatory) government funding for African teachers and schools. African education was overwhelmingly left as a missionary responsibility, while the government assumed responsibility for white education. Xuma reminds his audience of how, despite these inequalities, a select few well-educated men became important leaders within black South Africa. He decries the government's refusal to accept funding from the Rockefeller Foundation to establish an African medical school. The training of black doctors and nurses was a matter of lengthy debate at this time, because educators seriously limited African entry to white-dominated medical schools. The Rockefeller Foundation's offer was never accepted.

Xuma was baptized in the Wesleyan Church and remained an active Christian during his life. His address demonstrates his Christian point of view and the sincerity of his appeal to Christianity and its values. He invokes God and refers to Christian ideals to urge his listeners to dedicate their lives to pursuing righteousness and justice (a word he uses at least six times). He states that "God speaks to our students in this Conference" and that "our students are summoned to apply the principles and the teachings of Jesus Christ … to rechristianise and humanise western civilisation." He asks, "What is our task as Christian man and woman?" And he thanks God for the increasing number of whites who are "fair minded" and show "a devotion to the cause of the African," especially as exemplified by the delegates to the present conference.

Two institutions that have earned the respect of Africans, Xuma notes with praise, are the judiciary and the newspapers, "the pillars by the aid of which and upon which we hope to build our bridges." In general, black South Africans often complained about the injustices of the judicial system, especially in cases where whites and blacks were opposed in court, such as when whites were accused of felonies against blacks and juries were determining guilt or innocence. Xuma's discussion of the uneven implementation of the 1927 Immorality Act offers examples. There may be two explanations for Xuma's praise of judges: First, he was differentiating between members of the independent judiciary, which included legally trained judges, those he was praising, and magistrates, who were government administrators assigned certain judicial powers by the Department of Justice. Second, he knew of judges who spoke out against injustices and freed Africans when insufficient evidence was presented to convict them. Xuma's strong praise of the press undoubtedly refers to the English-language press, most likely newspapers such as the *Rand Daily Mail* and the *Star* of Johannesburg and the *Cape Times* of Cape Town.

Some of Xuma's remarks were directed toward the black portion of the audience, where blacks equaled almost 58

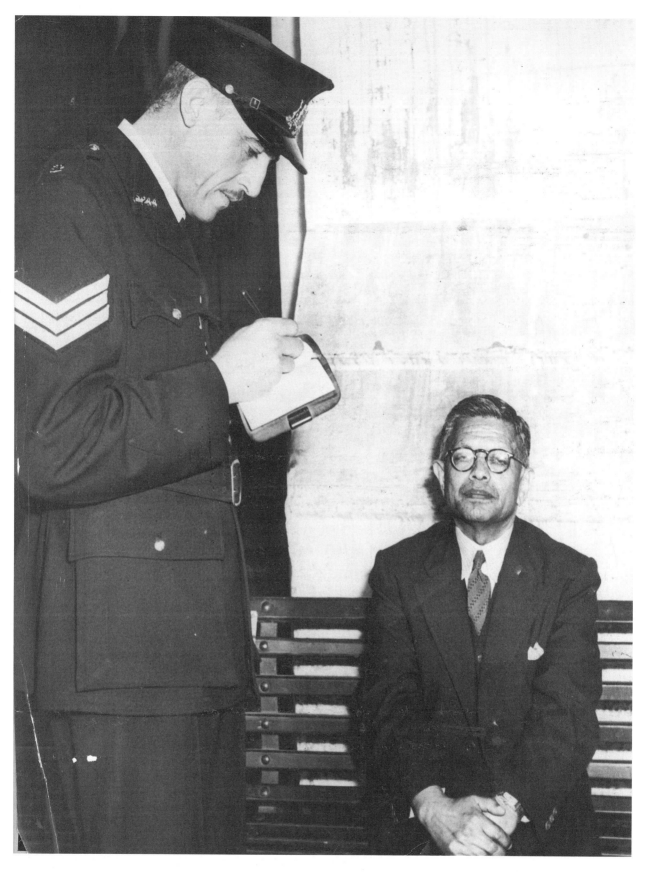

Manila L. Gandhi, second son of Mohandas Gandhi, is cited by a police sergeant for sitting on a bench reserved "For Europeans Only" at the main railway station in Durban, South Africa in 1951. (AP/Wide World Photos)

percent of attendees. To them he emphasizes self-reliance: Africans "must more and more organise themselves and do things for themselves." He still recognizes that cooperation with Europeans is helpful and should be encouraged, but ultimately Xuma tells the African students to assert themselves and avoid waiting "for some one to do things for them." He eloquently emphasizes the idea of a common humanity: "We must discover Africa's greatest wealth—the African himself. He transcends all; he excels all." Then, as if to counter the latent racism among whites attending the conference, he reminds his audience that the African "is a human being." For his white South African listeners, Xuma asserts that the "Native question" can be solved only by giving the African the rights of citizenship, including consent to legislation. He reminds whites that the demands of the majority are "moderate," that the African seeks not "preferential treatment" but only a "chance, a square deal.... All he wants is opportunity to work out his salvation." Xuma entreats whites to "leave the doors of opportunity wide open for all who may enter and provide the ladder to success for all who would climb." Referring to "partnership" and "co-operation," Xuma insists that whites must "hear from the African ... must more work *with* and less work *for* the African." He calls for a "revolution" of popular ideas and ideals, "to recognize the African as a human being with human desires and aspirations which must be satisfied."

The task at hand, then, "is to build our bridge between White and Black," following "the path of justice and fair dealing." The most important partners in that bridge-building effort will be educated Africans. Xuma wants his white audience to understand that

> the educated African is our hope, our bridge. He is an asset that ... White South Africa cannot afford either to ignore or to alienate without disastrous results.... It is he, and he alone, who can best interpret the European to the African, and the African to the European.

In a ringing conclusion, Xuma proclaims that "our aim, our motto, our ideal should be, therefore, 'Freedom, liberty, justice to all and privilege to none.'"

Audience

Some 344 men and women attended the 1930 Bantu-European Christian Student Conference, which Alan Paton identifies as the first sizable interracial meeting convened in South Africa. There were 130 African students and sixty European students who were enrolled in South African universities and secondary schools. More than 150 black and white South African, European, and American prominent personages were there, including speakers, educators, ministers, and others who were specially invited. Emphasizing the interracial nature of the conference, Paton writes that the white and black participants held a joint Communion service, probably the first large "ecumenical and interracial service" ever held in South Africa (p. 125).

Impact

The more important African leaders who attended the conference continued their protests against government policies, at least until 1948. D. D. T. Jabavu, a South African Native College professor, became a dominant figure in the 1935 All African Convention, while Z. K. Matthews, a lawyer who had earned a master's degree from Yale University, and Albert Luthuli became active in the African National Congress. Xuma continued promoting African-European cooperation and seemed to retain faith in the possible success of that cooperation in reducing discrimination in South African society. The loss of the vote in 1936 disillusioned him and contributed to his becoming a more forceful advocate for self-reliance. Xuma became an important leader in the 1940s, remaining relatively moderate but speaking out more forcefully against discrimination. One of the great ongoing frustrations for black South African leaders was that nothing they did made a difference: the white parliament continued to pass legislation against African interests through 1948, and the situation became much worse with the imposition of the apartheid system.

Sources discussing the 1930 conference do not identify the students who attended; consequently, historians are unable to determine in what ways the conference affected their lives and the degree to which they joined the antidiscrimination or antiapartheid struggles after graduation. The interracial nature of the conference probably affected the participants, but there is little evidence about a collective impact. Selected newspapers, such as *Umteteli wa Bantu*, reported on the conference, and the monthly publication *South African Outlook* included a day-to-day description of events and speeches. The entire proceedings were published as a book. Alexander Kerr, the chairman of the conference, notes in the introduction that it was the best example up to that time of an opportunity, "under Christian auspices, for ... discussion of the racial situation and its implications in South Africa." What was important to him was that this interracial conference actually occurred, and he lauds the "fervency of youth" as well as the "fellowship" and cooperative spirit—intangibles that have an impact on people's lives but are very difficult to measure(*Christian Students and Modern South Africa*, p. 7).

Further Reading

■ Articles

"The Bantu-European Students' Christian Conference, Fort Hare." *South African Outlook*, August 1, 1930: 146–163.

Digby, Anne. "Early Black Doctors in South Africa." *Journal of African History* 46, no. 3 (2005): 427–454.

Ralston, Richard D. "American Episodes in the Making of an African Leader: A Case Study of Alfred B. Xuma (1893–1962)." *International Journal of African Historical Studies* 6, no. 1 (1973): 72–93.

"*There is no such a thing as 'solving' the Native question once and for all even it if is on 'Nonparty lines.'* It does not stay fixed. *It is a* human problem *and like all other human problems, it is ever* changing. We must *recognise its changeability and legislate accordingly.*"

(Paragraph 5)

"*Where he [the African] has no vote he may be treated in any way or ignored because he has no means for redress or remedy for the wrongs committed against him.*"

(Paragraph 52)

"*By their impartiality, by their 'blind justice,' by their disregard for colour even in cases between White and Black, our Judges have kept faith with the African.*"

(Paragraph 63)

"*Most of our leading newspapers have elevated journalism in South Africa. They have shunned 'yellow-journalism' by refusing to play upon the African's weaknesses and foibles. They have steadied public opinion and kept it sane and civilised.*"

(Paragraph 64)

"*The task of reconstructing our South African public opinion along Christian lines is so great, so difficult, and impossible to accomplish unless we build our bridges by bringing together the coming leaders of all races into common understanding and sympathy.*"

(Paragraph 66)

"*What we need most is a revolution of the people's thoughts, their ideas, their ideals, and their spirit to recognize the African as a human being with human desires and aspirations which must be satisfied.*"

(Paragraph 73)

■ Books

Christian Students and Modern South Africa: A Report of the Bantu-European Student Christian Conference, Fort Hare, June 27–July 3, 1930. Fort Hare, Cape Province: Student Christian Association, 1930.

Gish, Steven. Alfred B. Xuma: African, American, South African. New York: New York University Press, 2000.

Karis, Thomas, and Gwendolen Carter, eds. From Protest to Challenge: A Documentary History of African Politics in South Africa, 1882–1990. Vol. 1: Protest and Hope, 1882–1934, by Sheridan Johns III. Stanford, Calif.: Hoover Institution Press, 1972; Vol. 2: Hope and Challenge, 1935–1952, by Thomas Karis. Stanford, Calif.: Hoover Institution Press, 1973.

Paton, Alan. South African Tragedy: The Life and Times of Jan Hofmeyr. New York: Scribner, 1965.

Xuma, Alfred B. Reconstituting the Union of South Africa; or, A More Rational Union Policy. Lovedale, South Africa: Lovedale Press, 1933.

—Harvey Feinberg

Questions for Further Study

1. In what ways did the colonization of South Africa, and the racial segregation and discrimination that resulted, parallel the history of slavery in the United States? What role did economics play in these developments?

2. The racial situation Xuma describes was in large part the historical result of a clash between two cultures that differed fundamentally in many ways, particularly in attitudes toward economics, land ownership, industrialization, wealth, social and political organization, and the like. Specify some of these differences in South Africa during the eighteenth, nineteenth, and early twentieth centuries and explain how they contributed to cultural clash.

3. Xuma spent a considerable portion of his young adulthood in the United States. He first attended Tuskegee Institute in the Deep South (Alabama), where racial discrimination was entrenched. He then attended the University of Minnesota and Northwestern University (near Chicago) in the North, where racial discrimination certainly existed but was perhaps somewhat less overt. To what extent might his experiences in the United States have affected his views on race relations and, more specifically, his views on how to improve race relations?

4. In the years following Xuma's speech, the racial situation in South Africa became worse, not better, culminating in the imposition of apartheid laws in 1948 and the years that followed. What factors in the years 1930–1948 might explain deteriorating race relations in South Africa?

5. In what respects might Alfred Xuma be regarded as the Martin Luther King, Jr., of South Africa? Based on what you know of King's life and activities, what parallels do you see between the two men and their way of confronting racial injustice? A place to start in investigating King is his famous "I Have a Dream" speech (1963).

A. B. Xuma's "Bridging the Gap between White and Black in South Africa"

On September 10th, 1840, at Bunkers Hill, Daniel Webster said:—

"When men pause from their ordinary occupations and assemble in great numbers, a proper respect for the judgment of the country and of the age requires that they should clearly set forth the *grave causes* which have brought them together, and the *purposes* which they seek to promote."

This evening, as I stand before you, I feel the force of this obligation. I shall in keeping with it endeavour, in my humble way, to place before you certain facts and suggestions which I believe are worthy of the study and consideration of all. I shall dictate to, and prescribe for, no man. The purpose of this paper is, not to convince or convert any one, but to stimulate in you a desire to seek the truth and facts and apply them. I shall state certain facts and interpret them according to what light I have as to their bearing upon the subject of our discussion. All are alike at liberty to reject or receive what opinions I shall express. I have neither desire nor design to offend the feelings of any, but I mean in perfect plainness to express my views.

I believe that a conference like this can be a success and justify its existence only if we can have the bare facts placed before us and bitter truths told us. We want facts, we want truth; we want a way out. Without the true facts, we have no way towards a just solution *of our* problem. Unless we know the truth, according to Paul the Apostle we are not free.

It must be clear to all that I have no pet prescriptions for the permanent cure of the ills of our race relations. I realise as well as any thinking person that there is no such a thing as "solving" the Native question once and for all even it if is on "Nonparty lines." It *does not stay fixed*. It is a *human problem* and like all other human problems, it is ever *changing*. We must recognise its changeability and legislate accordingly. Above all there can be no just solution of this question as long as the *chief factor* in the problem, the African with his interests and opinions, is excluded from the Councils of the State.

Throughout our country to-day, there seems to be a spirit of excitement, of fear, of unrest, and of uncertainty. Everywhere our European community seems to have a nightmare of the rising black masses encroaching upon their position of privilege, hence we have had the "Black Manifesto." The farmer presses upon the Government, to bind the Native down to the farms by restrictive legislation. The Mines are crying for more labour, more "Cheap Native labour." The Municipalities are clamouring for more powers to deal with the unemployed, "redundant" Native in the urban areas. The Government, without asking why is the African leaving the farms or where the "redundant" urban Native must be repatriated to, feverishly introduces more restrictive legislation to give effect to these cries. "Colour Bar" legislation appears on the Statute Book in one form or another at every session. The idea seems to be to legislate in haste and to think and discover the facts and mistakes at leisure.

In all this, the African, for whom the Government legislates, has no voice. His part is merely to obey the law without protest or expression of even his most legitimate grievance. If he expresses himself he is in danger of being charged for sedition either under Section 29 of the Native Administration Act 1925 or under the Riotous Assemblies Act 1930; because even his most legitimate claims may be in conflict with the interests of White voters of whom alone the lawmakers must think in connection with the next election.

The African is dissatisfied with his present lot, uncertain and anxious over his future. He is disgruntled, sullen and has largely lost confidence in the justice of the White. He is now becoming the *object* and *victim* of agitators—why? What is the reason for this? Is there any justification for this attitude on any or either side of the colour line?

As we intend to build bridges between White and Black, we can dismiss the case of the Coloured man by stating that the missionaries fought and secured some of the rights for the Hottentot until the Coloured man of to-day is, in *principle*, accepted as a White man politically, industrially, economically; and educationally.

The Indian in South Africa does not fall within the purview of our discussion, because, according to the Rt. Hon. S. Sastri, the Indian cannot make common cause with the African without alienating the right of intervention on their behalf on the part of the Government of India.

While the missionaries were fighting for the rights of the Hottentots and later of the Coloured man, the colonists had more or less a free hand with the African—the Bantu. Our legacy is a different policy for each Province reflecting the attitude of the earlier colonists towards their Native population.

As a conference of Christian students in a Christian country, we should ask ourselves whether the practices of our country between White and Black are in keeping with our profession of the Christian faith? Would Christ, whose followers and messengers we profess to be, approve of our Native Policy in practice? Has the Black man a real grievance? Has the White man been just to the Black man? Why did Mr. [Ernest] Jansen, present Minister of Native Affairs, say, to a deputation that waited upon him, "I shall do all in my power to make life more bearable for the Native?" What have we come here for? In short, what is our part and share in this great task? How are we going to bridge the gap between White and Black?

The stormy voyage of Bartholomew Diaz and the fitting name of his discovery which he called "Cape of Storms," which was later changed to Cape of Good Hope, presaged the conflicts and interracial "storms" which were to be almost the rule rather than the exception in South Africa. The Good Hope, like a rainbow, recedes as we move toward it.

It was however the arrival of Jan Van Riebeeck and his fleet on April 6th, 1652, which began the history of contact between Europeans and the then Natives—Hottentots and Bushmen. The introduction of slaves to supply the shortage of labour in 1658 complicated the problem of race relations. A new mentality was acquired by the free Burghers, and a new outlook and attitude toward manual labour and the Non-European developed in their minds.

It was not until 1686 that the Europeans came in contact with the Bantu when the crew of the wrecked "Stavenesse" tried to reach the Cape by land. A series of wars was to take place between the Europeans and Bantu beginning in 1779.

The British occupied the Cape Colony first in 1795 and again in 1806. The largest number of British Settlers arrived in 1820—5,000 strong.

By this time the pioneers or burghers had become accustomed to the institution of slavery. There was bound to be a conflict of attitude and outlook toward the people of colour between the pioneers, on the one hand, and the new settlers on the other.

The passing of Ordinance No. 50 in 1828 which gave legal and economic status to the people of colour was an unbearable boil on the neck of the free burghers. The boil burst when slaves were emancipated in 1833 and under the same ordinance acquired the status of free persons of colour. These two incidents combined had much to do with the initiation of the Great Dutch Trek of 1836. The Burghers marched northward giving the following reasons for their trek, according to Mrs. Anna Steenkamp, a daughter of Piet Retief.

First: "The continual depredations and robberies of the Kaffirs (with unfulfilled promises of compensation for stolen property).

Second: "The shameful and unjust proceedings with reference to the freedom of our slaves, and yet it is not so much their freedom that drove us to such lengths as their being placed on an equal footing with Christians, contrary to the laws of God and the natural distinctions of race and religion. So that, it was intolerable for any decent Christians to bow down beneath such a yoke, wherefore we rather withdrew in order thus to preserve our doctrine of purity."

This great people, determined to have their way and freedom, trekked Northward and in 1858 declared their articles of freedom in the Grondwet (Constitution of the Republics): "There shall be no equality between Black and White either in Church or in State."

Parallel to this, in the Cape Colony, the people of colour (Natives) were being granted the right of franchise with a property qualification—thus giving the non-European a political status.

Nominally the Native policy of Natal can be dismissed in a simple statement. "In the Letters Patent of 1848 by which Natal became a separate Colony, it was laid down that there shall be no interference with Native law and custom except in so far as these were repugnant to the principles of humanity, but Natal, though British in nationality, really developed the trekkers' attitude on the Native issue."

The tradition of segregation between Black and White more or less prevailed until the discovery of diamond and gold in 1867 and 1886. These discoveries were going to break down the barriers of segregation. Labour and cheap labour was necessary; and, consequently, Africans and Chinese were used.

The parallel but distinct policies on Native affairs continued to develop in each Province until after the Anglo-Boer war when one would think that the principle of the Grondwet would die a natural death. However, one finds, as the late Mr. Maurice Evans stated, that: "The Grondwet, which so clearly, concisely, and cynically laid down the relative positions of Black and White, disappeared as a defined policy at the close of the war in 1902, but the practice was not greatly changed."

As a matter of fact, a study of agreements and Compromises on "Native Policy" affecting Africans, from the Treaty of Vereeniging through the Act of the Union of South Africa to the Miners' Phthisis Act Further Amendment Act passed on May 27th, 1930, by our last session of Parliament, shows that one may safely say that though the Republicans lost the war physically they won it morally, because much of our legislation on Native Affairs is a series of colour bars and an expression of the principle of the Grondwet.

The Union of the White races in South Africa through the South Africa Act, 1909, has meant disunion and loss of liberty to the Black—especially in the Cape Province where he had attained citizenship rights. From the Act of the Union on, the negative and restrictive legislation has left the African in an inferior position.

The South Africa Act yields to the Republican principle in that in the former Republics the African by provision of the constitution shall neither exercise the right of franchise nor sit as representative in the Union Parliament even for the Cape Province. A Colour Bar in the legislature! Besides, though the Cape franchise seemed entrenched under section 35 of the South Africa Act 1909, yet, any day, it may be abolished "if the bill be passed by both Houses of Parliament sitting together and at the third reading be agreed to by not less than two-thirds of the total number of members of both Houses." Thus we see that the very Act of the Constitution of our country was conceived and born in an atmosphere charged with Colour Bars and prejudice. All hope for liberty and justice for the African was dimmed. This was his first grievance which was to be followed one after another, by a series of further disabilities and colour bars, thus making the African a promising and well prepared hotbed for the nurture of the seeds of agitation.

If we compare certain portions of the constitution of the Union of South Africa with that of the United States of America, we find that the Constitution of the latter country was based on a code of morals and ethics recognising liberties for all citizens of the country as expressed in the preamble, and the XIV and the XVth amendments.

The preamble recognises all the people in the United States, including the former slaves and their descendants, in the following words:—

"We, the people of the United States, in order to form a more perfect Union, establish justice, insure domestic tranquility, provide for the common defence, promote the general welfare, and secure the blessings of liberty to ourselves and our posterity, do ordain and establish this constitution for the United States."

Sections 1 of both 14th and 15th amendments respectively give full citizenship rights to all "persons" without regard to colour or any other distinction as follows:—

"All persons born or naturalised in the United States and subject to the jurisdiction thereof, are citizens of the United States and of the States wherein they reside. No State shall make or enforce any law which shall abridge the privileges or immunities of the citizens of the United States, nor shall any State deprive any person of life, liberty, or property without due process of law; nor deny to any person within its jurisdiction the *equal* protection of the laws."

"... The right of the citizens of the United States to vote shall not be denied or abridged by the United States or by any State on account of race or colour, or previous condition of servitude."

Thus we see that whatever may be the practice in certain sections of the United States, the principles of liberty and justice is the foundation stone in the law of the land. It gives hope and citizenship rights to all alike. Besides, in test cases of serious consequence the Supreme Court of the United States has, often, if not always, upheld the spirit and the letter of the Constitution.

Now coming back to South Africa, our land of colour bars and differential legislation and treatment, we find that following the South Africa Act 1909, the Land Act of 1913 is a constant, caustic irritant to the African. Through the provisions of this Act over 80 per cent of the land in the Union of South Africa went to the 1,500,000 Europeans and less than 20 per cent was left for the 5,000,000 Africans. The Beaumont Commission reported in 1917 that twice as much land was necessary for the immediate needs of the African community. It is now 13 years since this report but nothing has been done by the Government to relieve this tense situation. Through evictions of the Africans from European farms the Native reserves are crowded to overflowing. Many Natives have lost their stock; they are landless and poverty-stricken. Economic pressure is one of the many causes which drive the Natives into Urban areas.

Section 7 of the Native Administration Act of 1927 on "Land Registration and Tenure" makes land tenure for the individual African extremely insecure and yet, as Mr. A. G. Fraser has said, "Land is to the African (he might as well have said to every race of mankind) what the sea is to the fish; it is essential to his life. Without it he becomes detribalised. More harm has been done to African life and morals, except in West Africa, by European land hunger than by any drink trade."

If we look into the United States land policy, or practice, we again find no comparison but a striking contrast to South African land policy. Land in city or country can be bought by any citizen of the United States. For instance, there are today over 1,000,000 Negro farmers most of whom own their land; others rent or plough on shares. These people were, only 70 years ago, so poor as slaves that they did not even own themselves. Today, some are landlords owning millions of acres with full title deeds to the land in the same way as any other American citizens. In the cities, the Negroes buy and reside on their own property in any part of the city, notwithstanding the fact that in certain sections individual Whites had protested. In test cases on this principle of residential segregation, the Supreme Court of the United States has handed down its most considered and reasoned judgment that residential segregation cannot be upheld under the constitution of the United States. Thus we see the striking contrast between a country whose foundation is principle and the other whose structure is expediency.

Ejected from the farms, pressed by hunger or heavy taxation, the Black man enters one of the Northern cities (in the Transvaal or the Free State) and finds himself arrested for a new criminal offence; that is, failure to produce his *"past"* or "exemption" pass on demand by any constable and by even plain clothes men, anywhere and at any time. Every African, no matter what his standing may be, is not exempt from this indiscriminate stopping of African males on the street or "night raiding of Native dwellings and locations." If a professional African man or another African in independent business produces his business cards or any other personal papers for identification instead of the prescribed pass, he is under arrest and must pay a fine or be locked up. It is the question as to whether one has the particular pass the constable happens to demand—Poll Tax receipt? Night special? Service Contract Pass? Special to seek employment? Or any other. Failure to produce any of these there and then when demanded constitutes a criminal offence with a penalty of a fine or imprisonment. Thus many a man has been introduced into our prison system and initiated into a criminal career by such trivial and technical offences. Criminals are thus manufactured by many of our unnecessary restrictions.

The only probable but most irritating excuse for continuance of the pass system is that stated by a former member of the Native Affairs Commission on May 9th 1930, at Johannesburg. This gentleman admitted that the pass system was no longer serving the purpose for which it was intended. "But," said he, "I personally believe that where there is a highly civilised minority in the midst of a backward majority, the pass system is a necessary means of control by the civilised minority over the backward and less civilised masses." All one can say is

"He who is convinced against his will
Is of the same opinion still"

None of us would object very much if there was only a single "pass" which was demanded by a uniformed constable with a warrant for arrest, or when one was under suspicion of having committed a crime or disturbed public peace.

Let us now suppose that this Black man secures employment before he is arrested under the Pass laws, he then finds out that, under the Masters and Servants Act, "breach of contract is a criminal offence for him but not for the European employer." Under this same law, "a strike of Native workers is a criminal offence."

Because this African carries a "pass" which is required by law, he finds this a disability against him in that he cannot be legislated for under the Conciliation Act 1924. Besides, the pass system limits his freedom of movement and thereby destroys his bargaining power in a free labour market. He must therefore take such wages as are offered where he is.

Further, we find that any African over 18 years or "apparently" over 18 years of age with or without income must pay his annual Poll Tax of £1 or must suffer a term of imprisonment for failure to do so. A European, on the other hand, must not pay income-tax until he is *actually* 21 years of age with an annual income of £300, or £400 if he is married. Upon the strength of these facts, I ask you to draw your own conclusions.

The next question is a delicate case in social legislation—The Immorality Act of 1927. The object of this Act is "To prohibit illicit carnal intercourse between Europeans and Natives and other acts in relation thereto." The penalty is a term of imprisonment not to exceed five years for the offence. We do not intend to criticise the provisions of the Act; but, we are disturbed over the one-sided way in which it sometimes operates against the Native women and in favour of White men concerned. Cases have come to our notice where African women had been charged, sentenced and served terms of imprisonment under this law while the White man concerned in the case was acquitted by a jury or discharged by a Magistrate. The cases of Nogale Gwemba who was sentenced to nine months imprisonment at Grahamstown and that of Nellie Mofokeng who was sentenced to six months imprisonment in Johannesburg prove the truth of our statement. This is another colour bar and preferential treatment in favour of the White man.

I believe we all realise that no parliament can make people more moral by legislation. The sex impulse is stronger over the individual than social and racial loyalties. It knows no racial repugnance; it even challenges the law. It is a known fact that White men are strong advocates of race purity and are dead against intermarriage, but Black women and even slave Black women continue to give birth to children of mixed parentage. We protest strongly against the "double standards of morals in regard to race." We would urge that *all women* be protected and safeguarded irrespective of race or colour.

The last Bill on Native Policy was the Miners' Phthisis Act Further Amendment Act, passed on May 27th, 1930. "The amendment was designed to legalise the payment of compensation calculated on the basis of actual wages only." This is really legalising a wrong because when one complains that the Native wages in the mines are low, one is, at once, told that the Native miner receives more wages in kind, in the form of food, shelter and medical services. However, when the Native miner becomes a phthisis victim, the wages in kind are never included in the calculation of the compensation; consequently, the Native miner never receives his full compensation.

The compensation paid the Native is indeed small. "Since 1919 the compensation paid," according to Sir Robert Kotze, "had been £25 for the anteprimary, £55 for the primary stage and £72 for the secondary." It is well to remember that these small sums of money are often the last earnings of men, many of whom may have families of from one to ten children. These dependants get no further benefits of any kind should the breadwinner die after the full amount is received and spent. The statement made by Mr. MacMinamen showed the disparity between the compensation paid the European and that paid the African. He "pointed out that of the £10,000,000 paid in compensation the Natives had received £600,000 although they out-numbered the Whites by 20 to 1."

If we now turn to education, we find that in the Cape Colony the earlier educational curriculum was identical for both Europeans and Bantu. Lovedale Mission Institution was opened, with a class of 9 Europeans and of 11 Bantu students. From the time of the Rev. Mr. Govan through the period of Dr. Stewart, European and African students studied side by side. None seemed the worst for it. As a matter of fact, these generations of students produced some of the ablest and most prominent men in South Africa on both sides of the colour line. The Africans suffered no disabilities by this arrangement. The Europeans lost nothing in prestige by it. They were all being prepared and trained to play their part as citizens in their common country. It was in these generations that the best leaders among the Bantu were produced without any special system of education adapted to African mentality and for the African mind. (I often wonder if there is such a thing anyway.) No one would deny that men like the Rev. Tiyo Soga, pioneer missionary, Mr. John Tengo Jabavu, editor and journalist, the gifted Rev. Walter Benson Rubusana, and the versatile Rev. John Knox Bokwe, were leaders of thought of their day without regard to race or colour. They were educated to be full citizens, able to stand alone, as men, in church, in the school, in public affairs and not to be assistants to someone else. The point worthy of note is that these boys when they began their schooling were raw "Kaffir boys." They were primitive men so-called, not a day removed from savagery or from the life of barbarism, and yet side by side with White boys, they mastered the White man's education without special adaptation to Native mentality and needs and above all made the best use of their education for the good of their country.

Later on, however, the schools became separate and the change extended also into the quality and content of the curriculum as well as the qualifying certificates; so that to-day we have what are known as "N.P.L." and "N.P.H.," meaning "Native Primary Lower" and "Native Primary Higher," perhaps signifying that Africans in South Africa have a different mentality from that of other races.

It is, perhaps, from the point of view of finance that "Native Education" suffers most. In most civilised countries, the financing of education is the responsibility of the State. In South Africa, however, this is true only in so far as it affects the Europeans, Coloured, and Indians; because, under the Durban Agreement of 1923, the African in education was to be treated differently and exclusively. The Union Government spends over £8,000,000 for the education of the children of the 1,500,000 Europeans and only £500,000 for the education of the children of 5,000,000 Africans. Even this amount of £500,000 is taken from a direct tax imposed upon the Africans for the purpose, over and above what he pays indirectly, in customs duties and low wages. The consequence is that only less than one-third of Native children of school age (7–14 years) can attend the elementary schools, the other two-thirds are not and cannot be provided with any schooling under this arrangement. The funds are too small, and hence, no expansion or progress is possible in Native education.

Professional education for the African here at home is not provided for. Only in the last session the Union Parliament turned down an offer of £65,000 from the Rockefeller Foundation for the creation of a medical school for Africans. Why? We Africans, as in other things that concern us, are kept in the dark. For the present, we shall reserve our observations on the Government's decision to reject the proposed offer. We, however, venture to express the view that, until such time as the Government would deem it fit to make provision for the medical training of Africans here at home, the State would be making a friendly gesture as well as assuming its proper responsibility if a system of bursaries and loans were introduced to assist properly qualified African students to proceed overseas in order to complete their medical training.

Twenty-one years since the Union of South Africa was established, the Union Parliament created a Joint Select Committee to consider the so-called "Prime Minister's Native Bills." What are these Bills for? "To solve the Native problem once and for all," we are told. How? By taking away the Cape franchise for any substitute or nothing as the Joint Committee and joint sitting of both Houses may deem fit by two-thirds vote of all members of both Houses. Why is this necessary? Has the African ever abused the privilege? No, that is just the reason, he uses it so intelligently that he becomes a factor to be reckoned with in those constituencies where he exercises the right. Representatives of such constituencies must study his interests as well as those of the Europeans. Where he has no vote he may be treated in any way or ignored because he has no means for redress or remedy for the wrongs committed against him.

The Union Parliament would have a clear coast to establish a "White South Africa" if they could remove this last stumbling block, the "Cape Franchise," and thus consummate their unparalled and unexcelled series of colour bars. I still believe that our Parliament will soon discover its wrong course and rectify it.

The African protests strongly against this violation of the last vestige of his Cape citizenship. He knows all too well that without a vote he cannot maintain the ground he holds. He has no hope to gain new ground or even to regain lost ground. He is at the mercy of those who alone exercise this right. To use the words of Mr. J. H. Oldham, "Deprived of political influence an unfranchised class find themselves helpless to obtain redress or defend themselves against injustice. Without the franchise Natives of South Africa have no hope of obtaining a fairer share of the land. … A class excluded from all share in political power is condemned to permanent subordination. It becomes a servant of the interests of others, having no share or partnership in a common life."

Here and there the African begins to express himself. The pressure is getting too great. He must express his hopes and despair. Instead of finding out what his real grievance is, the Government has tried to muzzle him by Section 29 of the Native Administration Act 1927 and finally by the Riotous Assemblies Act 1930. Through this legislation freedom of speech and the airing of even the most legitimate grievances and expression are driven under ground after the ostrich philosophy. It were better that we suffered both fools and the wise to speak; because, as the Most Rev. Dr. Carter, Archbishop of Cape Town, has said," repression can only lead to reaction later on, and this is not so very much later on."

If anybody wishes to know whether justice is being done to the Native, I say to him "Study our Union Legislation." Who is the cause of agitation and unrest among the Natives? Is it the Communists? In reply, I would say in the laconic style of Colonel Denys Reitz in answer to Mr. Jansen, Minister of Native Affairs, "Your kind of legislation."

In Chapter X of the "Union of South Africa" entitled "The Natives," the author, the Hon. R. H. Brand, says:—"One may freely admit that a great deal of our South African opinion is ignorant, unintelligent, and crude. The man in the street and the man on the veld seldom realise even the elements of the stupendous problem with which they are faced. The policy which attracts them is often one of simple repression. Take away … from the Native the land which he possesses, and there will be more compulsion for him to work for the White man (hence Land Act 1913). Do not educate him, or else he will become too independent (hence no adequate budget for Native education). Keep him in his place. That is the simple creed of the average White man. He fails to see that in his own interest it is fatal. For, if the Black man sinks, he will inevitably drag the White man down. ... By raising in their breasts a sense of wrong the White man will merely be digging his own grave." This "simple creed of the average White man" is often the policy of "simple repression" of the man in the street and man on the veldt, and has become the approved policy and practice of our Parliament; because, under our Northern system of manhood franchise whose only qualification is that a man or woman must be 21 years of age with a White skin, it is the "man in the street" and "the man on the veldt" who elects and sends Parliamentary representatives. These representatives are responsible to them and they must carry out their policy, however crude it may seem, or else they are not again returned. In this connection the words of Schiller seem to be sound advice for my country when he said

"Majority—what does that mean? Sense has ever centred in the few. Votes should be *weighed* not counted. That state must soon or later go to ruin where numbers sway and ignorance decides."

When one studies and ponders over these legal disabilities of the African one is less inclined to blame him for little or no progress. His position is fixed by statutory bonds. One's feeling is expressed best in the words of John X. Merriman who said, writing from Kingwilliamstown;—

"What I regret most is the bitter feeling of race hatred which is being sown broadcast, and the terrible sacrifice of life which must take place before this wretched business is ended. Then what a task will be left for those who have to take up the reins of Government to evolve order out of chaos and by justice, honesty, and fair dealing try to remove some of the bitterness and animosity which will long survive the futile effort to establish the supremacy of the White man by might and not by right." Thus we have seen that the restrictive, repressive Union legislation has created more new problems than it has solved in our difficulties in race relations; because, this legislation has been based on the idea that the 1,500,000 Whites must for ever remain supreme over the 5,000,000 Blacks.

Although I emphasised the ascendency of Grondwetism in our Union legislation, I should not be understood to put the whole blame of race prejudice on the Dutch-speaking section. This section has no monopoly of colour prejudice. The Britons in South Africa, especially in Natal and in the former Republics share and fan the flame of these colour bars. To support this my conviction, I shall quote Mr. Maurice Evans who says in one of his books: "It is notorious that persons born and brought up in England, in the tradi-

tions of race equality are often more prejudiced when they come to live in a bi-racial country, than those brought up amongst a backward people. It is the rule and not the exception that those from Britain, who have been supporters of missions, and hold orthodox views on religious matters, who land in South Africa with these ideas undimmed, soon absorb the racial opinions current in the country of their adoption."

In spite of this conviction, I am not unmindful of the fact that there is a group, and thank God, an increasing group of fair minded, sympathetic and just people among both Boers and Britons. I, personally, have many friends in both sections. Some of these people will go any length to see that the scales of justice are held evenly between White and Black. Messrs. Fischer and Marquard, both Dutch-speaking Europeans, have, through their work as leaders of the Bloemfontein Joint Council of Europeans and Bantu (one of the best) and through their private night school for Africans, shown a devotion to the cause of the African which can hardly be excelled and is worthy of emulation by all. No more convincing evidence of this noble spirit can be found than the presence of, the interest and attitude of our delegates here. It is the hopeful sign of a better day between White and Black in South Africa.

I would not be fair, I would not be honest, I would not be just, if I did not mention two institutions which are a credit to South Africa and compare very favourably with the best of their kind anywhere in the world. I refer to our Bench of Judges and to the better class newspapers in South Africa.

By their impartiality, by their " blind justice," by their disregard for colour even in cases between White and Black, our Judges have kept faith with the African. To the African our Judges are the final hope and safety valve especially as they have more than once upset judgments of lower Courts and declared certain differential and preferential legislation ultra vires. May they always uphold the high standards and ethics of their esteemed profession for the preservation of the best in the world-civilisation namely, justice. So great is the African's faith in the justice of our Bench that I would not mind having to appeal against a judgment under the Liquor Law 1928 and appear before Mr. Justice Tielman Roos, its author, now one of our honoured Judges on the Bench. One can realise, therefore, how disturbed and agitated the African's mind is when the Riotous Assemblies Act 1930 eliminates our Bench as a Court of Appeal, in preference for one man, the Minister of Justice, with absolute power.

Besides, most of our leading newspapers have elevated journalism in South Africa. They have shunned "yellow-journalism" by refusing to play upon the African's weaknesses and foibles. They have steadied public opinion and kept it sane and civilised when political demagogues were undermining the foundation of the very civilisation they profess to build.

These two institutions are the pillars by the aid of which and upon which we hope to build our bridges. What then have we come here for? In answer to this question, may I quote and paraphrase the words of Dr. John R. Mott to our students' convention in Des Moines Iowa, U.SA.? "We have assembled here not only to take the wide view, the view and vision of a new world, but also to receive a new challenge—a fresh commission." God speaks to our students in this Conference and calls upon them to be leaders, and new types of leaders, who believe that true greatness is achieved by being servant of all and dedicating one's life of the service of God and man. Leaders who, by their lives and actions, will show the world that God values the souls of all human beings whatever their race or colour. Our students are summoned to apply the principles and the teachings of Jesus Christ in all our life activities and contacts—to rechristianise and humanise western civilisation. The call is to us as fellow students and friends to be "leaders of the forces of righteousness and unselfishness," to be "builders of a new order."

Boers, Britons, and Bantu, you are called upon to realise your unity in your diversity. This is all the more essential because the task of reconstructing our South African public opinion along Christian lines is so great, so difficult, and impossible to accomplish unless we build our bridges by bringing together the coming leaders of all races into common understanding and sympathy in order to devote themselves to a common programme.

What is our task as Christian man and woman? What are the purposes which we seek to promote? Our task then is not to change our Government from Nationalist to S. A. Party. That will get us nowhere. We must go deeper than that. First, we must discover Africa's greatest wealth—the African himself. He transcends all; he excels all. He is a human being with human limitations, desires and aspirations. He is not a mere tool of our economic order to be used and thrown away when worn out.

Boers and Britons, you cannot solve the so-called "Native question" as long as you leave your fellow-citizen, the Bantu, outside. Without him and his consent the question will *never* be settled *right*. The

Bantu stands outside bringing his gifts. Will you let him in? His demands are moderate. Where others ask for preferential treatment, he asks only for a man's chance, a square deal. Where others demand alms and Government aid, all he wants is opportunity to work out his salvation without let or hindrance. He says, to his European fellow-citizens, "Do not lower your standards for my sake; raise them as high as you will; but, leave the doors of opportunity wide open for all who may enter and provide the ladder to success for all who would climb."

The African must be trained to master and conquer his environment, to solve his own problem and manage his own affaire in the Church, in the school and in public affairs. Being trained for full citizenship he must enter into partnership and cooperate with the European for the welfare and prosperity of our common country.

The African wears the shoe. He alone can tell where the shoe pinches. The European must now be prepared to hear from the African and not merely about the African. As Professor Kelly Miller once put it, "The man who sustains the wound must give the groan." The European must more work *with* and less work *for* the African. The Africans, on the other hand, must not only co-operate with the European in European controlled activities but must more and more organise themselves and do things for themselves. They must not always wait for some one to do things for them.

Our Missionary friends, on the other hand, expose themselves to serious criticism when they sometimes refuse to support welfare work among the Africans only because such work is under no White supervision. Only recently a certain European Minister active in work among the Natives was handed a subscription list by a lady collecting for the A.M.E. Church Education Fund. He looked at the list and deplored that one of the teachers under him had already subscribed. Without subscribing a penny he handed the list back and rather emphatically told the lady not to come there again because the A.M.E. Church is under no European management. When I learned of this incident, I wondered then and wonder now whether the African's disability had become a new profession for some and a "closed trade union for Europeans only." This attitude must go. Time has come that the Missionaries should not only support but should encourage independent African enterprise wholeheartedly or else the African will be led to question their motive. If there is to be any progress in Missionary effort, leadership in "Native Affairs" and Native activities must gradually pass into the hands of trained African leaders in co-operation with their European friends. It must be a partnership.

Our task then, is to build our bridge between White and Black by pointing out and emphasizing the danger of a restrictive, repressive policy such as the "Union Native Policy." Such a policy leads to a spirit of discontent, sullenness, and suspicion on the part of its victim, instead of contentment, good-will, and co-operation, which only justice and due consideration can bring about. While South Africa must be persuaded to realize that only through the path of justice and fair dealing can it be hoped to establish and preserve the Western civilization, whose "true signs," according to Lord Russell, "are thought for the poor and the suffering, chivalrous regard and respect for woman, the frank recognition of human brotherhood, irrespective of race, or colour, or nation or religion, the narrowing of the domain of *mere force* as a governing factor in the world, the love of ordered freedom, abhorrence of what is mean and cruel and vile, ceaseless devotion to the claims of justice." Do our European friends, who talk so proudly of protecting "European Civilization," ever realize as Mr. G. P. Gooch has well said, that, "Civilization is a co-operative achievement. The civilization which we praise so highly is the result of the co-operative efforts of men and women known and unknown through all the ages belonging to all countries and all races and creeds. It is the most wonder-

A.M.E. Church	African Methodist-Episcopal Church
Anglo-Boer War	also known as the Boer War and the South African War, 1899–1902
Bartholomew Diaz	Portuguese explorer who sailed south following the east coast of Africa in 1488. When he passed the Cape of Good Hope, he realized that he had found the way around the continent.
Bushmen	nomadic hunters of the Kalahari Desert, a term used in derogatory fashion by some whites to apply to all black Africans
Colonel Denys Reitz	South African minister of lands in the early 1920s
colour bar	the laws, reflected in cultural and social conventions, that enforced racial discrimination by whites against blacks in South Africa
Daniel Webster	American politician of the first half of the nineteenth century who served in both houses of Congress and as secretary of state under two presidents
Dr. John R. Mott	American Protestant lay missionary who founded the World's Student Christian Federation and spent time in South Africa
A. G. Fraser	British specialist in Christian missionary education
G. P. Gooch	Lord Courtney; British scholar, elected vice president of Witwatersrand University of Johannesburg who opposed the Anglo-Boer War and disapproved of land grabs and capitalist expansion of British entrepreneurs
Great Dutch Trek of 1836	migration outward from the Cape Colony of white European settlers, also known as Voortrekkers, into the future Natal, Orange Free State, and Transvaal regions, motivated largely by dissatisfaction with newly imposed British rule, scarcity of good farmland in Cape Colony, and increasing population pressures
Grondwet	the constitution of the Boer community, begun in 1857
Hottentots	derogatory designation by whites of the pastoral, nomadic African people known as Khoikhoi, whose lands, in the early colonial period, the Dutch took over, killing great numbers of people

ful thing that the world has ever seen and it is the result of the common efforts of the human family."

What we need most is a revolution of the people's thoughts, their ideas, their ideals, and their spirit to recognize the African as a human being with human desires and aspirations which must be satisfied; to concede to the African "his reasonable demand to be considered a human being with full scope for human growth and human happiness."

The educated African is our hope, our bridge. He is an asset that responsible and thinking White South Africa cannot afford either to ignore or to alienate without disastrous results in the long run. He should be brought into close contact and co-operation with the thinking European. He must be consulted in all matters affecting the African community. It is he, and he alone, who can best interpret the European to the African, and the African to the European.

In our humble efforts to accomplish this task may we always remember the words of J. H. Oldham, who says, "Christians may help infuse the right spirit— the spirit which seeks the truth, is afraid of no facts, harbours no prejudices, condones no injustice, and sets the common good above all sectional and selfish interests."

May I, in conclusion, suggest that our aim, our motto, our ideal should be, therefore, "Freedom, liberty, justice to all and privilege to none." Then, and not until then are we justified in saying, "God our Father, Christ our Redeemer, and Man our Brother."

Benito Mussolini (Library of Congress)

"For Fascism the state is absolute; individuals and groups relative."

Overview

Italy's leader and head of the Fascist Party, Benito Mussolini, had always resisted attempts to codify Fascism. Yet when the *Enciclopedia italiana* ("Italian Encyclopedia") required an article defining Fascism, it became necessary to publish something that would give an appearance of thought and process behind what was essentially a constantly changing way of running the country. The result was his article, "The Doctrine of Fascism," published in 1932 and written with the help of Giovanni Gentile; in fact, it has been suggested that Gentile was the actual author of the document. The essay was in places misleading and in other places seemingly contradictory and actually differed from the way Fascism operated. But to those who did not read it critically, it at least supplied what seemed to be a logical basis for the political movement.

Context

By the early 1930s, when the encyclopedia version of Mussolini's essay on Fascism appeared, Italy had experienced more than sixty years of turbulent history. Italy as a culture was very old, but as a modern, unified nation it was quite new. The country had originally been unified under the Roman Empire, but from the fifth century on it had been invaded and governed in parts by the Normans, French, Spanish, North Africans, and Austrians until the middle of the nineteenth century. When not under foreign rule, cities such as Florence, Milan, and Venice were independent and separate city-states, some with their own colonies. Even the pope was a temporal ruler, with a domain that included a very large portion of the Italian peninsula and not merely Vatican City.

The unification of Italy, the Risorgimento, began with the end of the Napoleonic Wars in 1815 and continued to the early 1870s, when Italy became a unified and relatively cohesive entity. In 1915 Italy entered World War I, fighting costly and traumatic battles on the border with the Austro-Hungarian Empire. Italy's participation until late 1918 was marked by a string of defeats. Although Italy was on the side of the war's victors, it did not receive the territorial gains the Allies promised in 1915, specifically the cities of Fiume and Trieste. The Treaty of Versailles, which ended World War I, was signed in 1919. This treaty, confirmed by the subsequent treaties of Saint-Germain and Trianon, gave the promised cities to the newly formed Yugoslavia, leading to great bitterness toward the Allies. Italians felt as though they had suffered defeat and been betrayed.

Thus, the situation in post–World War I Italy was marked by the effects of war losses, severe economic difficulties, resentment toward the Allies, and fear of Socialism, workers' movements, and Bolshevism (Communism) from the newly born Soviet Union. The fact that a Communist government assumed power in Hungary in 1919 (albeit for only four months) did nothing to reassure Italians. Both domestic and international developments led many to desire stability and even a degree of authoritarianism to guarantee it.

Political activity on the part of both the left and right in postwar Europe increased dramatically. Many parties that came into being after the war eventually went out of existence for a variety of reasons. Some, however, became strikingly successful, including Italy's Fascist Party, founded in Milan by Mussolini in 1919. Mussolini's organization attracted attention and support from across the social and intellectual spectrum. His supporters and followers ranged from intellectuals such as Benedetto Croce and Giovanni Gentile to armed bands of thugs known as *squadristi* or "Blackshirts," who terrorized political opponents.

Within three years of founding the Fascist Party, Mussolini was Italy's prime minister. In just over two years—a period of street fights, parliamentary debate, and political maneuvering—he gained control of the press, consolidated his hold on power, and began both the militarization and the extensive public works projects that would characterize Italian Fascism.

Italy was the first but not the only country to have a Fascist government. It was not only the philosophy but also the term itself that originated there. The term *Fascism* has its origins in Roman history. In the time of the Roman Republic and later the Roman Empire, magistrates were accompanied by bodyguards known as lictors. The badge of office for these guards was an ax with several wooden rods (each known as a *fascis*). These rods, bound together, formed a symbol of strength and one that was considered quite appropriate as a symbol of Fascism in twentieth-century Italy.

1883

- **July 29**
  Benito Mussolini
  is born.

1914

- World War I
  begins.

1915

- Encouraged by
  promises of
  territory, Italy
  enters the war in
  1915 on the side
  of the Allies.

1919

- **March 23**
  Mussolini's Fascist
  Party is officially
  formed in
  Milan, Italy.

- **June 28**
  The Treaty of
  Versailles ending
  World War I is
  signed.

1922

- **October 27**
  Mussolini leads
  the March on
  Rome, essentially a
  coup in which King
  Victor Emmanuel
  names him prime
  minister; the
  march lasts until
  October 29.

1925

- **January**
  Mussolini
  establishes
  himself as the
  sole effective
  leader of Italy.

1932

- The article describing
  Fascism as a
  doctrine, authored
  by Giovanni Gentile
  and Benito Mussolini,
  is first published
  in the *Enciclopedia
  italiana*.

As a political phenomenon, Fascism dominated Europe in the period between the two world wars (1919–1939). It existed in some form in nearly every European country. Fascist parties (or parties that bore a great similarity to them) were found in Britain, France, Spain, Portugal, Belgium, Switzerland, Greece, Yugoslavia (particularly in Croatia), and Poland, among others. Fascism bore some similarities to the major rival ideology of the day, Communism. In both cases, individual liberty and options were subordinate to the needs of the state. Both used a form of ideology to provide a doctrinal background to justify policies. Freedom of expression in both was curtailed, and a significant degree of control was imposed on most aspects of life. While both enforced conformity, both also held themselves as a means of advancing and improving life.

The two ideologies, though, had significant differences. For Fascists, the ideology was more flexible (or more subject to changes in circumstances) and less important than was the case for Communists. For Fascists, the practical application of what was to be done to assert and maintain control took priority over doctrinal or ideological issues. Fascism's policy toward industry and commerce was quite different from that of either capitalism or Communism. Sometimes referred to as a "third way," the Fascist approach was to let private ownership stand but to regulate business to ensure that it met the needs of the state.

Further, Fascism was highly nationalistic, unlike Communism's international emphasis in the 1930s. While the Communist International—an international Communist organization founded in Moscow, Russia, in 1919 and sometimes called the Third International—was active in many countries and did not shy away from subversion or espionage, the Soviet Union by the late 1920s had abandoned the concept of world revolution. Instead, it concentrated on internal development. The nationalism that was so much a part of Fascism in different countries incorporated the goal of expanding national boundaries. The goal of that type of expansion was notably absent in the Soviet Union until it signed the Non-Aggression Pact with Germany in 1939.

The nationalist emphasis and national characteristics and culture contributed to making each type of Fascism different. Spanish Fascism was different from Polish or Greek or Italian Fascism. These differences were significantly greater than the differences between the Communist parties from the same countries. More significant may have been differences existing within individual Fascist movements. Because of a lesser dependence on dogma and a greater reliance on practical politics, individual Fascist organizations had internal organizational differences and, more commonly, inconsistent policies. That tendency was noted especially in Italy, where Fascism began.

About the Author

Although various Fascist officials seem to have reviewed and commented on drafts in development, two main authors wrote this essay. The credited author was Benito

Mussolini, certainly a key contributor, who approved the final draft. The other, and probably the greater contributor, was Giovanni Gentile (1875–1944), a major figure in Fascist intellectual and political circles. He founded the *Enciclopedia italiana* in the mid-1920s and directed the project, where this statement of Fascist doctrine was first published.

Gentile taught philosophy at several important Italian universities and was one of Italy's most prominent intellectuals. Originally he was a follower of Italy's famous philosopher Benedetto Croce, but the two eventually parted company. (Croce came to oppose Fascism.) Gentile joined the Fascist Party in 1923 and for the next six years held several significant positions in both the party and the government. These posts included his service as a senator and as a member of the Fascist Grand Council. His influence ended when he publicly opposed Mussolini's formal understanding with the Vatican, as confirmed in the Lateran Treaty of 1929. He then went into semiretirement from public office, though he was active in the development and publication of the encyclopedia. He reappeared in public in 1943 when he supported the new republic after the deposition of Mussolini that year. In April 1944 he was shot to death by anti-Fascist partisans. Gentile opposed the idea of individualism and believed in both nationalism and a strong corporate state. He referred to an "ethical state" (a term that appears in the essay on Fascism). That entity, as he described it, would be the basis of law. People should seek to fit themselves into the state instead of cultivating individualism.

Despite Gentile's prominent role in writing this essay, Mussolini's name appeared in the byline—the only article in the entire *Enciclopedia* that bore the name of an author. Benito Mussolini (1883–1945) was named after the Mexican revolutionary Benito Juárez. His father was active politically, and Mussolini himself showed an interest in politics, particularly agitation, at an early age. His early political beliefs seem to have contained elements of anarchism, Socialism, and Marxism in various mixtures at different times and in what appeared to be contradictory ways. Later commentators would remark that expressing inconsistent opinions on issues was a consistent characteristic of Mussolini in particular and Italian Fascism in general.

Before World War I, Mussolini worked at several occupations. He taught school in Italy, worked in construction in Switzerland, and for a very short time held a job as a newspaper reporter and eventually an editor for political journals. He served in the army during World War I and was severely wounded in 1917, after which he again became a political editor. In 1919, in Milan, Mussolini founded the Fascist Party. Three years later, as the result of a coup known as the March on Rome, King Victor Emmanuel named him prime minister. In 1940 Mussolini declared war on France, beginning the war that would end his government in 1943 when Italy surrendered. Captured by anti-Fascists in 1943, he was rescued by the Germans and set up as the ruler of a fictitious state comprising German-occupied Italy. He was then captured by partisans and executed on April 28, 1945.

Time Line

1935

- **October 3**
  Italy invades Ethiopia.

1940

- **June 10**
  Italy enters World War II on the side of the Axis, invading France. Italian troops will eventually fight in North Africa, Greece, Albania, Yugoslavia, Russia, and, of course, in the defense of Italy.

1943

- **July 25**
  The Fascist Grand Council deposes Mussolini.

- **September 3**
  The Italian government surrenders to the Allies; the new government enters the war on the side of the Allies against Germany.

- **September 12**
  Mussolini, who has been imprisoned, is rescued by German soldiers to become head of what is styled as the Italian Social Republic.

1944

- **April 15**
  Giovanni Gentile is shot and killed by Communist resistance fighters.

1945

- **April 28**
  Mussolini is captured by partisans and later executed, and his body is put on display in Milan.

Explanation and Analysis of the Document

Mussolini's statement of Fascist doctrine first appeared in the *Enciclopedia italiana* in 1932. The *Enciclopedia* was begun in the mid-1920s as a collection of articles on all aspects of human learning and culture with a decided emphasis on Italy's contributions. The first edition eventually numbered thirty-five volumes; Mussolini claimed to have read them all. This essay was later republished in an official publication, *Fascism: Doctrine and Institutions*, issued in 1935.

As printed in 1935, the essay has two main parts. The first, "Fundamental Ideas," is a series of introductory or basic philosophical tenets. This section presents the definition of Fascist principles. The second and longer section, entitled "Political and Social Doctrine," is more of a background piece. It is Mussolini's historical narrative of political and philosophical events in Europe, especially in Italy and, specifically, his role in them. It combines supplemental descriptions and definitions of the meaning of Fascism.

♦ "Fundamental Ideas"

The first section's opening paragraph describes Fascism as a combination of both action and thought. It is tied to historical forces and the here and now, the material world. Fascism is rooted in spiritual influences as well as in what is called "the transient and the specific reality" and the "permanent and universal reality." Here Mussolini also claims that while Fascists are men of action, they are not violent; among them are men who are restless but thoughtful. One other key point introduced here, which surfaces again in this essay, is the importance of dominating others.

In the second paragraph, the individual's role as a subordinate entity serving the state's larger goals is stressed. The devotion to the larger goal calls for avoiding "selfish momentary pleasure" and embracing self-sacrifice and duty, which would allow an individual to achieve a "spiritual existence." In other words, the ideal man—the Fascist—is not only a man of action but also one whose actions are in no way directed toward his own well-being but instead toward the good of the state. The following paragraph sets Fascism's spiritual conception in opposition to the previous century's materialism, which Mussolini sees as an effect of the era of the French Revolution in 1789. Here the essay uses the neither/nor type of opposition, often found in this piece. Fascist spirituality is described as "anti-positivistic but positive; neither skeptical nor agnostic; neither pessimistic nor supinely optimistic."

The fourth paragraph emphasizes action. To be active means to face difficulties. Constant struggle was a consistent tenet of Italian Fascism—as opposed to the democratic spirit, which Mussolini oddly characterizes as lacking in personal responsibility. Education is valued, as are all efforts to develop the self. Again, however, the individual does this for self but not for selfish ends. The objective is to become an "implement" for the state. The importance of work as the way to subjugate nature (draining marshes and agricultural projects were important Fascist programs until the mid-1930s) is emphasized.

The following paragraph discusses the positive conception of life embraced by the Fascist, with its ethical basis. It is described as "serious, austere, and religious." This particular phrase is interesting in that the medieval imagery of monks who were also knights fighting for a pure cause was found in more than one Fascist movement. In Germany, for example, the Teutonic knights, a religious order of warriors who had fought in eastern Europe in the thirteenth century, were seen as role models in their devotion to duty, self-sacrifice, and effectiveness as soldiers. The paragraph concludes that the Fascist disdains an "easy" life.

Next Mussolini proclaims that the Fascist concept of life is religious in nature in the context of a "higher law." The higher law, in this case the needs of the state, possesses an "objective will" (making any disagreement with the state a subjective disagreement with what is stated to be objective and therefore correct). The concept of Fascism as a religion means specifically that it can be regarded as a religious alternative to traditional Christian doctrine such as that taught by the Catholic Church. The paragraph closes with the comment that "Fascism is not only a system of government but also and above all a system of thought." This last statement has been vigorously questioned by both commentators of the time and subsequent historians.

The seventh paragraph provides more historical context, listing the movements of the past that Fascism opposes. The materialistic view of the eighteenth century (embodied specifically in the Enlightenment and the French Revolution), with its view of the human being's perfectibility, is dismissed. Perfectibility is seen as an individual pursuit that does nothing to help the state achieve its objectives. Also discredited is the religious notion that peace and rewards will come at the end of life, as the Fascist is a realist and knows there will always be problems to confront and solve.

The eighth paragraph declares that the individual can be accepted only on the basis of his usefulness and relationship to the state. Further, the liberty granted by the state, which is the set of values directed by the state, is the only liberty worth having. Here Mussolini contradicts the usual understanding of personal liberty, glorifying the liberty of the state to do as it will. He declares that Fascism is totalitarian and therefore interprets and develops the lives of all people, because the Fascist conception of the state is all-embracing. Nothing outside of what the state allows can even exist, "much less have value."

The next two paragraphs express opposition to other forms of political organization. There can be no organizations or individuals outside the state. Fascism is opposed to Socialism and trade unions but allows the existence of those trade unions that function in conformity with the policies of the state. Mussolini then declares Fascism's opposition to democracy as it is generally understood—a society in which the majority governs the will of the state. He provides his own definition of the purest form of democracy in terms that are contradictory to what is generally accepted as the real concept of democracy: The nation's will expressed and directed by the few is the most coherent and most ethical form of democracy. He offers a

*Armed group of Italian Fascists march along a street in Rome, Italy, on October 28, 1922,
following the March on Rome organized by Benito Mussolini.* (AP/Wide World Photos)

dramatic reversal of the concept of nationalism as it had developed in the preceding century. In the wake of the Napoleonic Wars and in empires containing many different nationalities, such as those found in Austria-Hungary, ethnic groups began to develop an identity based on language, literature, and culture. That gradually increasing awareness sparked movements resulting in new unified states, such as Germany and Italy, or new nations, such as Czechoslovakia and Poland. Mussolini refutes this process, stating that nations (that is, a group of people of the same nationality or using the same language) do not create states (that is, governments); indeed, the opposite is true.

In the eleventh and twelfth paragraphs, Mussolini declares that the state "creates the nation" and that "it is the state which, as the expression of a universal ethical will, creates the right to national independence." An inactive nation without will may sacrifice its independence to another, more active state. That provides a transition in the next paragraph to the discussion of the state, which is described as both a living and an ethical thing. It has the necessary right and duty to be active,

with the power to extend its will beyond its borders. By this time Italy had already shown its ambitions for projecting power. In 1923 it had seized the island of Corfu from Greece. Three years after this article first appeared, it would invade Ethiopia.

The closing paragraphs characterize the Fascist state as the summing up of "all the manifestations of the moral and intellectual life of man; indeed, it is the "soul of the soul." Its importance, especially in the context of what is described as an individual's "supposed rights," is here defined as a personality and force, although it is a "spiritual" one. As a basis for life, Fascism is the source of laws and institutions and is based on discipline and authority—the reason why the lictor's rod was chosen as the emblem for Fascism.

◆ "Political and Social Doctrine"

The second section's purpose is to define Fascism by spelling out its differences from other doctrines. The Fascist state is totalitarian, what Mussolini calls a "new departure in history." It is absolute, and individuals and groups are admissible and acceptable only to the extent to which they are willing to subordinate themselves to the new state. Fascism, he concludes, represents a moment in time.

In the narrative of this section, Mussolini asserts that in 1919 he had no doctrinal program and felt that existing doctrines were dead. Fascism was born of the need for action and answered this need because it was action. He emphasizes that Italy's situation before the 1922 March on Rome did not allow for the creation of an elaborate and detailed doctrine. Fascist doctrine, he goes on to say, was actually constructed in the ensuing years, as action was taken to change the Italian state. He admits that even in the early stages there were hints and forecasts of what would be the doctrine of Fascism, and in those early statements the careful reader can find doctrinal development.

In emphasizing action over the development of careful thought, Mussolini stresses the importance of not only action but also confrontation, with significant results. He states in paragraph 23 that "fighting was going on in the towns and villages. There were discussions, but there was something more sacred and more important: death. Fascists knew how to die." While the emphasis on action may seem to be constructive, encouraging people to fight and die for a cause that is not even well defined is a rather odd virtue. On the other hand, it is entirely consistent with Fascism's emphasis on the state over the individual.

Many of the points that Mussolini raises in the first part are raised again here, with additional detail. Peace and pacifism are cowardly and do not encourage self-sacrifice. War "keys up" human energy and is noble. Internationalism and international organizations (such as the League of Nations, which Italy would successfully defy in the coming years) are also undesirable. Mussolini identifies and then dismisses the various doctrines, movements, and schools of thought to which Fascism is opposed, including Marxism and Socialism, democracy, and what he calls "liberalism" with its emphasis on the individual. Yet Mussolini states that he does not want to return to feudalism. Further, in a rather strange claim, he declares that Fascist authority has nothing in common with a police state, a comment that political dissenters in Italy would have found ironic.

In the final paragraphs of this section Mussolini repeatedly emphasizes and expands on the theme that the state is the most important entity. The individual must be made secondary to what is good for the state. Mussolini claims that people have never desired an authoritarian government more than they do now and Fascism, the system of action and thought that makes the state the supreme entity, answers that need.

Audience

The audience for this essay was primarily the Italian public of the 1930s as well as posterity. Mussolini, though he was intelligent, was not a deep thinker. His calls to action and the primacy of action over thought were sincere. Because the real doctrine of Fascism was whatever results came from action, the idea of an unchanging or even rationally evolving platform did not exist. Mussolini would not have been concerned with the thoughts and opinions of his audience. His own best audience was perhaps himself. Writing an article for Italy's most significant cultural product of the time would have suited his conception of himself. Those who disagreed with the article's content would have placed themselves outside the Fascist conception of life, disqualifying them from participation in the state.

Impact

At first glance, Mussolini's essay could be seen as resembling Karl Marx's *Communist Manifesto* of 1848, which was a prophecy, a threat, and a description of a new political force. It could also be compared to Adolf Hitler's autobiographical *Mein Kampf* and Vladimir Lenin's *What Is to Be Done?* The works of Marx, Hitler, and Lenin, however, predated events. In contrast, the essay on Fascism was written after the system had taken root. Fascism as a means of governing and consolidating power predated this article by ten years, so it cannot be seen as a prediction of things to come or as a blueprint. As Fascism changed in what many saw as a mercurial fashion, the essay cannot be construed as a "snapshot" of a political system or philosophy undergoing a rational evolution.

The reasons for this lack of impact are important, however, and reveal a great deal about Mussolini and Italian Fascism. As Mussolini himself states here, Fascism in Italy was based on action, not doctrine. Action was taken to change events. After the action, one can find the doctrine in the results. Therefore, the article can be seen as a justification for what has been done as well as a general code of conduct and outlook required of individuals.

The essay's rhetoric and its calls to action are important, for once one reads it without trying to develop a rigorous intellectual picture and imagines it as a speech, it makes more sense and tells readers a great deal about Fascist Italy, its imagery and emotional content. The rousing tones and calls to action, the strong opposition to non-Fascists, and its promise of glory to those who subordinate themselves to the state are the main thrusts of the essay. The intent is to provide images of dedication and movement toward the state's goal. The word choices and the rhetoric create a dramatic performance that illustrates well what Fascism was. The essay gives readers an idea of the tone of Mussolini's speeches at highly charged political rallies in a way similar to the dramatic manipulation and frenzy generated at Hitler's Nazi Party rallies of the same decade.

As a practical phenomenon, Fascism had up to this point (1932) exerted a profound impact on Italy. Fascism in Italy came to dominate every aspect of life. The changes in government and eventual expansion of Italy's role in foreign policy along with economic, armaments, and public works projects were to be expected. What Fascism also did, however, was to permeate every aspect of life to include social and educational activities. The Fascist state was glorified, becoming a kind of religion, just as Mussolini stated it must. Ital-

"*Fascism sees in the world not only those superficial, material aspects in which man appears as an individual, standing by himself, self-centered, subject to natural law that instinctively urges him toward a life of selfish momentary pleasure. It sees not only the individual but also the nation and the country—individuals and generations bound together by a moral law.*"

(Paragraph 2)

"*Anti-individualistic, the Fascist conception of life stresses the importance of the state and accepts the individual only insofar as his interests coincide with those of the state, which stands for the conscience and the universal will of man as a historic entity.*"

(Paragraph 8)

"*Fascism, in short, is not only a law-giver and a founder of institutions but an educator and a promoter of spiritual life. It aims at refashioning not only the forms of life but also their content—man, his character, and his faith. To achieve this propose, it enforces discipline and uses authority, entering into the soul and ruling with undisputed sway.*"

(Paragraph 15)

"*Democratic regimes may be described as those under which the people are, from time to time, deluded into the belief that they exercise sovereignty, while all the time real sovereignty resides in and is exercised by other and sometimes irresponsible and secret forces. Democracy is a kingless regime infested by many kings who are sometimes more exclusive, tyrannical, and destructive than one king, even if he be a tyrant.*"

(Paragraph 28)

"*The keystone of the Fascist doctrine is its conception of the state, of its essence, its functions, and its aims. For Fascism the state is absolute; individuals and groups are relative. Individuals and groups are admissible insofar as they come within the state.*"

(Paragraph 37)

ians went along with Fascism, but not enthusiastically. There was not much choice, as political dissent was monitored and punished, though not as stringently as in Germany.

In the next thirteen years the effects would become far more dramatic not only for Italy but also for all of Europe. Italy became an active participant in European politics in the 1930s, regaining much of the status that it had lost after what it had considered betrayal by the other victorious allies at the end of World War I. In 1935, Mussolini ordered the Italian army to invade Ethiopia, which it then conquered and occupied until being driven out by the British in 1941. Although Italy was initially opposed to some of Hitler's foreign policy objectives, the country gradually came to match its objectives to those of Germany. In 1936 both nations became involved in the Spanish civil war, supporting the future winner, Francisco Franco. Mussolini became an ally to Hitler's successful attempt in 1938 to incorporate a portion of Czechoslovakia into Germany. Two years later Italy joined Hitler in declaring war on Britain and France. The active support for Fascism waned with the entry of Italy into World War II, and gradually—especially after Italy surrendered to the Allies in 1943—active military resistance commenced against the Fascist and German elements still fighting the Allies. Surrender did not bring an end to Italy's troubles, as it was now the scene of battles between the Allies and Germany in the south and between anti-Fascist partisans and Germans in the north. By the conclusion of the war in 1945, Italy was devastated. Mussolini, after having been rescued by the Germans from possible captivity under the Allies after his deposition, would be executed in May of that year. The destruction of Italy, perhaps the most significant impact of all, would take several years to repair.

Further Reading

■ Articles

Brustein, William. "The 'Red Menace' and the Rise of Italian Fascism." *American Sociological Review* 56, no. 5 (October 1991): 652–664.

Gentile, Emilio. "Fascism as Political Religion." *Journal of Contemporary History* 25, nos. 2/3 (May–June 1990): 229–251.

Gentile, Giovanni. "The Philosophic Basis of Fascism." *Foreign Affairs* 6, no. 2 (January 1928): 290–304.

Noether, Emiliana P. "Italian Intellectuals under Fascism." *Journal of Modern History* 43, no. 4 (December 1971): 630–648.

Roberts, David D. "How Not to Think about Fascism and Ideology, Intellectual Antecedents and Historical Meaning." *Journal of Contemporary History* 35, no. 2 (April 2000): 185–211.

Stewart, William Kilborne. "The Mentors of Mussolini." *American Political Science Review* 22, no. 4 (November 1928): 843–869.

Vivarelli, Roberto, "Interpretations of the Origins of Fascism." *Journal of Modern History* 63, no. 1 (March 1991): 29–43.

Questions for Further Study

1. The words *Fascist* and *Fascism* continue to be used in political discussions, often unthinkingly, to refer to laws, politicians, or viewpoints that are perceived to be repressive. Is this a fair and accurate use of the terms? Explain.

2. The terms of the 1919 Treaty of Versailles have been blamed for much of Europe's political unrest in the 1920s and 1930s, producing the conditions that sparked World War II. How did the Treaty of Versailles affect Italy? How did it contribute to Mussolini's rise to power? Compare this document with Adolf Hitler's Proclamation to the German People (1933). What viewpoints do the documents share with regard to recent history?

3. Fascism is generally regarded as a right-wing ideology, while Communism is regarded as a left-wing ideology—the two extremes of the political spectrum. How did these two ideologies compete in the 1930s in Italy and other European countries? As a point of comparison, see Vladimir Lenin's *What Is to Be Done?*

4. What was the relationship between the individual and the state under Fascism? Why was this definition of the relationship attractive to many Italians at that time?

5. Respond to the following statement: Fascism in Italy in the 1930s was not a clearly defined political ideology but an attitude or outlook.

■ Books

Ben-Ghiat, Ruth. *Fascist Modernities: Italy, 1922–1945*. Berkeley: University of California Press, 2001.

Blinkhorn, Martin. *Mussolini and Fascist Italy*, 3rd ed. London: Routledge, 2006.

Bosworth, R. J. B. *Mussolini's Italy: Life under the Dictatorship 1915–1945*. London: Allen Lane, 2005.

Gentile, Giovanni. *Origins and Doctrine of Fascism: With Selections from Other Works*. New Brunswick, N.J.: Transaction Publishers, 2002.

Gregor, A. James. *Giovanni Gentile: Philosopher of Fascism*. New Brunswick, N.J.: Transaction Publishers, 2001.

———. *Mussolini's Intellectuals: Fascist Social and Political Thought*. Princeton, N.J.: Princeton University Press, 2005.

Moss, M. E. *Mussolini's Fascist Philosopher: Giovanni Gentile Reconsidered*. New York: P. Lang, 2004.

Mussolini, Benito. *Fascism: Doctrine and Institutions*. New York: H. Fertig, 1968.

Passmore, Kevin. *Fascism: A Very Short Introduction*. New York: Oxford University Press, 2002.

■ Web Sites

"Totalitarianism: 1919–1939." TheCorner.org Web site. http://www.thecorner.org/hist/total/f-italy.htm.

—Robert Stacy

BENITO MUSSOLINI'S "THE DOCTRINE OF FASCISM"

Fundamental Ideas

Like all sound political conceptions, Fascism is action, and it is thought—action in which doctrine is immanent and doctrine arising from a given system of historical forces in which it is inserted and working on them from within. It has therefore a form correlated to contingencies of time and space, but it has also an ideal content which makes it an expression of truth in the higher region of the history of thought. There is no way of exercising a spiritual influence in the world as a human will dominating the will of others, unless one has a conception both of the transient and the specific reality on which that action is to be exercised and of the permanent and universal reality in which the transient dwells and has its being. To know men one must know man; to know man, one must be acquainted with reality and its laws. There can be no conception of the state which is not fundamentally a conception of life—philosophy or intuition, a system of ideas evolving within the framework of logic or concentrated in a vision or a faith, but always, at least potentially, an organic conception of the world.

Thus many of the practical expressions of Fascism, such as party organization, the system of education, and discipline, can be understood only when considered in relation to its general attitude toward life—a spiritual attitude. Fascism sees in the world not only those superficial, material aspects in which man appears as an individual, standing by himself, self-centered, subject to a natural law that instinctively urges him toward a life of selfish momentary pleasure. It sees not only the individual but also the nation and the country—individuals and generations bound together by a moral law, with common traditions and a mission that, suppressing the instinct for life closed in a brief circle of pleasure, builds up a higher life founded on duty, a life free from the limitations of time and space in which the individual, by self-sacrifice, by the renunciation of self-interest, by death itself, can achieve that purely spiritual existence in which his value as a man consists.

The conception is therefore a spiritual one, arising from the general reaction of the century against the materialistic positivism of the XIXth century.

Anti-positivistic but positive; neither skeptical nor agnostic; neither pessimistic nor supinely optimistic, as are, generally speaking, the doctrines (all negative) which place the center of life outside man—whereas, by the exercise of his free will man can and must create his own world.

Fascism wants man to be active and to engage in action with all his energies; it wants him to be manfully aware of the difficulties besetting him and ready to face them. It conceives of life as a struggle in which it behooves a man to win for himself a really worthy place, first of all by fitting himself (physically, morally, and intellectually) to become the implement required for winning it. As for the individual, so for the nation and so for mankind. Hence the high value of culture in all its forms (artistic, religious, and scientific) and the primary importance of education. Hence also the essential value of work, by which man subjugates nature and creates the human world (economic, political, ethical, and intellectual).

This positive conception of life is obviously an ethical one. It invests the whole field of reality as well as the human activities which master it. No action is exempt from moral judgment; no activity can be despoiled of the value which a moral purpose confers on all things. Therefore life, as conceived of by the Fascist, is serious, austere, and religious; all its manifestations are poised in a world sustained by moral forces and subject to spiritual responsibilities. The Fascist disdains an "easy" life.

The Fascist conception of life is a religious one, in which man is viewed in his immanent relation to a higher law, endowed with an objective will transcending the individual and raising him to conscious membership of a spiritual society. Those who perceive nothing beyond opportunistic considerations in the religious policy of the Fascist regime fail to realize that Fascism is not only a system of government but also and above all a system of thought.

In the Fascist conception of history, man is man only by virtue of the spiritual process to which he contributes as a member of the family, the social group, the nation, and a function of history to which all nations bring their contribution. Hence the great value of tradition in records, in language, in customs, in the rules of social life. Outside history, man is a nonentity. Fascism is therefore opposed to all individualistic abstractions based on eighteenth century materialism, and it is opposed to all Jacobinistic utopias and innovations. It does not believe in the possibility of "happiness" on earth as conceived by the economistic literature of the XVIIIth century, and it therefore rejects the theological notion that at some future time the human family will secure a final settlement of all its difficulties. This notion runs counter to experience which teaches that life is in continual flux and in process of evolution. In politics Fascism aims at realism; in practice it desires to deal only with those problems which are the spontaneous product of historic conditions and which find or suggest their own solutions. Only by entering into the process of reality and taking possession of the forces at work within it can man act on man and on nature.

Anti-individualistic, the Fascist conception of life stresses the importance of the state and accepts the individual only insofar as his interests coincide with those of the state, which stands for the conscience and the universal will of man as a historic entity. It is opposed to classical liberalism, which arose as a reaction to absolutism and exhausted its historical function when the state became the expression of the conscience and will of the people. Liberalism denied the state in the name of the individual; Fascism reasserts the rights of the state as expressing the real essence of the individual. And if liberty is to be the attribute of living men and not of abstract dummies invented by individualistic liberalism, then Fascism stands for liberty and for the only liberty worth having, the liberty of the state and of the individual within the state. The Fascist conception of the state is all embracing; outside of it no human or spiritual values can exist, much less have value. Thus understood, Fascism is totalitarian, and the Fascist state—a synthesis and a unit inclusive of all values—interprets, develops, and potentiates the whole life of a people.

No individuals or groups (political parties, cultural associations, economic unions, social classes) outside the state. Fascism is therefore opposed to socialism, to which unity within the state (which amalgamates classes into a single economic and ethical reality) is unknown and which sees in history nothing but the class struggle. Fascism is likewise opposed to trade unionism as a class weapon. But when brought within the orbit of the state, Fascism recognizes the real needs which gave rise to socialism and trade unionism, giving them due weight in the guild or corporative system in which divergent interests are coordinated and harmonized in the unity of the state.

Grouped according to their several interests, individuals form classes; they form trade unions when organized according to their several economic activities. But, first and foremost, they form the state, which is no mere matter of numbers, the sum of the individuals forming the majority. Fascism is therefore opposed to that form of democracy which equates a nation with the majority, lowering it to the level of the largest number. But it is the purest form of democracy if the nation be considered as it should be from the point of view of quality rather than quantity, as an idea—the mightiest because the most ethical, the most coherent, the truest, expressing itself in a people as the conscience and will of the few, if not, indeed, of one, and ending to express itself in the conscience and the will of the mass, of the whole group ethnically molded by natural and historical conditions into a nation, advancing, as one conscience and one will, along the self same line of development and spiritual formation. Not a race nor a geographically defined region, but a people, historically perpetuating itself. A multitude unified by an idea and imbued with the will to live, the will to power, self-consciousness, and personality.

Insofar as it is embodied in a state, this higher personality becomes a nation. It is not the nation which generates the state; that is an antiquated naturalistic concept which afforded a basis for XIXth century publicity in favor of national governments. Rather is it the state which creates the nation, conferring volition and therefore real life on a people made aware of their moral unity.

The right to national independence does not arise from any merely literary and idealistic form of self-consciousness and still less from a more or less passive and unconscious de facto situation, but from an active, self-conscious, political will expressing itself in action and ready to prove its rights. It arises, in short, from the existence, at least *in fieri*, of a state. Indeed, it is the state which, as the expression of a universal ethical will, creates the right to national independence.

A nation, as expressed in the state, is a living, ethical entity only insofar as it is progressive. Inactivity is death. Therefore the state is not only Authority, which governs and confers legal form and spiritual value on individual wills, but it is also Power, which makes its will felt and respected beyond its own frontiers, thus affording practical proof of the universal character of the decisions necessary to ensure its development. This implies organization and expansion, potential if not actual. Thus the state equates itself to the will of man, whose development cannot be checked by obstacles and which by achieving self-expression demonstrates its infinity.

The Fascist state, as a higher and more powerful expression of personality, is a force, but a spiritual one. It sums up all the manifestations of the moral and intellectual life of man. Its functions cannot therefore be limited to those of enforcing order and keeping the peace, as the liberal doctrine had it. It is no mere mechanical device for defining the sphere within which the individual may duly exercise his supposed rights. The Fascist state is an inwardly accepted standard and rule of conduct, a discipline of the whole person; it permeates the will no less than the intellect. It stands for a principle which becomes the central motive of man as a member of civilized society, sinking deep down into his personality; it dwells in the heart of the man of action and of the thinker, of the artist and of the man of science: soul of the soul.

Fascism, in short, is not only a law-giver and a founder of institutions but an educator and a promoter of spiritual life. It aims at refashioning not only the forms of life but also their content—man, his character, and his faith. To achieve this propose, it enforces discipline and uses authority, entering into the soul and ruling with undisputed sway. Therefore it has chosen as its emblem the Lictor's rods, the symbol of unity, strength, and justice.

Political and Social Doctrine

When in the now distant March of 1919, speaking through the columns of the *Popolo d'Italia*, I summoned to Milan the surviving interventionists who had followed me ever since the foundation of the Fasci of Revolutionary Action in January 1915, I had in mind no specific doctrinal program. The only doctrine of which I had practical experience was that of socialism, from 1903–1904 to the winter of 1914—a decade. My experience was that of a follower and a leader, but it was not doctrinal experience. My doctrine during that period was the doctrine of action. A uniform, universally accepted doctrine of socialism had not existed since 1905, when the revisionist movement, headed by Bernstein, arose in Germany, countered by the formation, in the seesaw of tendencies, of a leftist revolutionary movement which in Italy never quitted the field of slogans, whereas, in the case of Russian socialism, it became the prelude to Bolshevism.

Reformism, revolutionism, centrism—the very echo of that terminology is dead, while in the great river of Fascism one can trace currents which had their source in Sorel, Peguy, Lagardelle of the *Le Mouvement Socialiste*, and in the cohort of Italian syndicalists who from 1904 to 1914 brought a new note into the Italian socialist environment—previously emasculated and chloroformed by fornicating with Giolitti's party—a note sounded in Olivetti's *Pagine Libere*, Orano's *La Lupa*, Enrico Leone's *Divenire Sociale*.

When the war ended in 1919, socialism as a doctrine was already dead; it continued to exist only as a grudge, especially in Italy, where its only chance lay in inciting to reprisals against the men who had willed the war and who were to be made to pay for it.

Il Popolo d'Italia described itself in its subtitle as the daily organ of fighters and producers. The word *producer* was already the expression of a mental trend. Fascism was not the nursling of a doctrine previously drafted at a desk; it was born of the need of action and was action; it was not a party but, in the first two years, an anti-party and a movement. The name I gave the organization fixed its character.

Yet if anyone cares to reread the now crumpled sheets of those days giving an account of the meeting at which the Italian Fasci di Combattimento were founded, he will find not a doctrine but a series of pointers, forecasts, hints that when freed from the inevitable matrix of contingencies were to develop in a few years' time into a series of doctrinal positions entitling Fascism to rank as a political doctrine differing from all others, past or present.

At that time I said:

> If the bourgeoisie believe that they have found in us their lightning-conductors, they are mistaken. We must go toward the people.... We wish the working classes to accustom themselves to the responsibilities of management so that they may realize that it is no easy matter to run a business.... We will fight both technical and spiritual rear-guardism.... Now that the succession of the regime is open, we must not be fainthearted. We must rush forward; if the present regime is to be superseded, we must take its place. The right of succession is ours, for we urged the country to enter the war and we led it to victory.... The existing forms of political representation cannot satisfy us; we want direct representation of the several interests.... It may be objected that this program implies a return to the guilds (*corporazione*).

No matter! I therefore hope this assembly will accept the economic claims advanced by national syndicalism....

Is it not strange that from the very first day, at Piazza San Sepolcro, the word "guild" (*corporazione*) was pronounced, a word which, as the Revolution developed, was to express one of the basic legislative and social creations of the regime?

The years preceding the March on Rome cover a period during which the need of action forbade delay and careful doctrinal elaborations. Fighting was going on in the towns and villages. There were discussions, but there was something more sacred and more important: death. Fascists knew how to die. A doctrine, fully elaborated, divided up into chapters and paragraphs with annotations, may have been lacking, but it was replaced by something far more decisive: faith. All the same, if with the help of books, articles, resolutions passed at congresses, major and minor speeches anyone should care to revive the memory of those days, he will find, provided he knows how to seek and select, that the doctrinal foundations were laid while the battle was still raging. Indeed, it was during those years that Fascist thought armed and refined itself and proceeded ahead with its organization. The problems of the individual and the state; the problems of authority and liberty; political, social, and, more especially, national problems were discussed. The conflict with liberal, democratic, socialistic, Masonic doctrines and with those of the *Partito Popolare* was carried on at the same time as the punitive expeditions. Nevertheless, the lack of a formal system was used by disingenuous adversaries as an argument for proclaiming Fascism incapable of elaborating a doctrine at the very time when that doctrine was being formulated—no matter how tumultuously—first, as is the case with all new ideas, in the guise of violent dogmatic negations and, in the more positive guise of constructive theories, subsequently incorporated, in 1926, 1927, and 1928, in the laws and institutions of the regime.

Fascism is now clearly defined not only as a regime but as a doctrine. This means that Fascism, exercising its critical faculties on itself and on others, has studied from its own special standpoint and judged by its own standards all the problems affecting the material and intellectual interests now causing such grave anxiety to the nations of the world, and is ready to deal with them by its own policies.

First of all, as regards the future development of mankind, and quite apart from all present political considerations, Fascism does not, generally speaking, believe in the possibility or utility of perpetual peace. It therefore discards pacifism as a cloak for cowardly supine renunciation in contradistinction to self-sacrifice. War alone keys up all human energies to their maximum tension and sets the seal of nobility on those peoples who have the courage to face it. All other tests are substitutes which never place a man face to face with himself before the alternative of life or death. Therefore all doctrines which postulate peace at all costs are incompatible with Fascism. Equally foreign to the spirit of Fascism, even if accepted as useful in meeting special political situations—are all internationalistic or League superstructures which, as history shows, crumble to the ground whenever the heart of nations is deeply stirred by sentimental, idealistic or practical considerations. Fascism carries this anti-pacifistic attitude into the life of the individual. " I don't care a damn" [*me ne frego*]—the proud motto of the fighting squads scrawled by a wounded man on his bandages—is not only an act of philosophic stoicism, it sums up a doctrine which is not merely political. It is evidence of a fighting spirit which accepts all risks. It signifies a new style of Italian life. The Fascist accepts and loves life; he rejects and despises suicide as cowardly. Life as he understands it means duty, elevation, conquest; life must be lofty and full, it must be lived for oneself but above all for others, both nearby and far off, present and future.

The population policy of the regime is the consequence of these premises. The Fascist loves his neighbor, but the word *neighbor* does not stand for some vague and ungraspable conception. Love of one's neighbor does not exclude necessary educational severity; still less does it exclude differentiation and rank. Fascism will have nothing to do with universal embraces; as a member of the community of nations, it looks other peoples straight in the eye. It is vigilant and on its guard, it follows others in all their manifestations and notes any changes in their interests, and it does not allow itself to be deceived by mutable and fallacious appearances.

Such a conception of life makes Fascism the resolute negation of the doctrine underlying so-called scientific and Marxian socialism, the doctrine of historic materialism, which would explain the history of mankind in terms of the class struggle and by changes in the processes and instruments of production to the exclusion of all else. That the vicissitudes of economic life—discoveries of raw materials, new technical processes, and scientific inventions—have their importance, no one denies. But that they suffice to explain human history to the exclusion of other factors is absurd. Fascism believes now and always in sanctity and heroism, that is to say, in acts in which no economic motive—remote or immediate—is at work. Having denied historic materialism, which sees in men mere puppets on the surface of history, appearing and disappearing on the crest of the waves while in the depths the real directing forces move and work, Fascism also denies the immutable and irreparable character of the class struggle which is the natural outcome of this economic conception of history. Above all, it denies that the class struggle is the predominant agent in social transformations. Having thus struck a blow at socialism in the two main points of its doctrine, all that remains of it is the sentimental aspiration—old as humanity itself—toward social relations in which the sufferings and sorrows of the humbler folk will be alleviated. But here again Fascism rejects the economic interpretation of felicity as something to be secured socialistically, almost automatically, at a given stage of economic evolution when all will be assured a maximum of material comfort. Fascism denies the materialistic conception of happiness as a possibility, and abandons it to the economists of the mid-eighteenth century. This means that Fascism denies the equation that well-being equals happiness, which sees in men mere animals, content when they can feed and fatten, thus reducing them to a vegetative existence pure and simple.

After socialism, Fascism trains its guns on the whole block of democratic ideologies and rejects both their premises and their practical applications and implements. Fascism denies that numbers, as such, can be the determining factor in human society. It denies the right of numbers to govern by means of periodical consultations. It asserts the irremediable and fertile and beneficent inequality of men who cannot be leveled by any such mechanical and extrinsic device as universal suffrage. Democratic regimes may be described as those under which the people are, from time to time, deluded into the belief that they exercise sovereignty, while all the time real sovereignty resides in and is exercised by other and sometimes irresponsible and secret forces. Democracy is a kingless regime infested by many kings who are sometimes more exclusive, tyrannical, and destructive than one king, even if he be a tyrant. This explains why Fascism —though, for contingent reasons, it was republican in tendency prior to 1922—abandoned that stand before the March on Rome,

convinced that the form of government is no longer a matter of preeminent importance and because the study of past and present monarchies and past and present republics shows that neither monarchy nor republic can be judged *sub specie aeternitatis*, but that each stands for a form of government expressing the political evolution, the history, the traditions, and the psychology of a given country.

Fascism has outgrown the dilemma of monarchy versus republic, over which democratic regimes too long dallied, attributing all insufficiencies to the former and praising the latter as a regime of perfection, whereas experience teaches that some republics are inherently reactionary and absolutist while some monarchies accept the most daring political and social experiments.

In one of his philosophic meditations Renan—who had pre-Fascist intuitions—remarks,

> Reason and science are the products of mankind, but it is chimerical to seek reason directly for the people and through the people. It is not essential to the existence of reason that all should be familiar with it. Even if all had to be initiated, this could not be achieved through democracy, which seems fated to lead to the extinction of all arduous forms of culture and all highest forms of learning. The maxim that society exists only for the well-being and freedom of the individuals composing it does not seem to be in conformity with nature's plans, which care only for the species and seem ready to sacrifice the individual. It is much to be feared that the last word of democracy thus understood (and let me hasten to add that it is open to a different interpretation) would be a form of society in which a degenerate mass would have no thought beyond that of enjoying the ignoble pleasures of the vulgar.

So argues Renan. In rejecting democracy, Fascism rejects the absurd conventional lie of political equalitarianism, the habit of collective irresponsibility, the myth of felicity and indefinite progress. But if democracy be understood as meaning a regime in which the masses are not driven back to the margin of the state, and then the writer of these pages has already defined Fascism as an "organized, centralized, authoritarian democracy."

Fascism is definitely and absolutely opposed to the doctrines of liberalism, both in the political and in the economic sphere. The importance of liberalism in the XIXth century should not be exaggerated for present-day polemical purposes, nor should we make of one of the many doctrines which flourished in that century a religion for mankind for the present and for all time to come. Liberalism really flourished for fifteen years only. It arose in 1830 as a reaction to the Holy Alliance which tried to force Europe to recede further back than 1789; it touched its zenith in 1848 when even Pius IXth was a liberal. Its decline began immediately after that year. If 1848 was a year of light and poetry, 1849 was a year of darkness and tragedy. The Roman Republic was killed by a sister republic, that of France. In that same year Marx, in his famous *Communist Manifesto*, launched the gospel of socialism.

In 1851 Napoleon III made his illiberal coup d'état and ruled France until 1870, when he was turned out by a popular rising following one of the severest military defeats known to history. The victor was Bismarck, who never even knew the whereabouts of liberalism and its prophets. It is symptomatic that throughout the XIXth century the religion of liberalism was completely unknown to so highly civilized a people as the Germans but for one parenthesis, which has been described as the "ridiculous parliament of Frankfurt" which lasted just one season. Germany attained her national unity outside liberalism and in opposition to liberalism, a doctrine that seems foreign to the German temperament, essentially monarchical, whereas liberalism is the historic and logical anteroom to anarchy. The three stages in the making of German unity were the three wars of 1864, 1866, and 1870, led by such "liberals" as Moltke and Bismarck. And in the building up of Italian unity, liberalism played a very minor part when compared with the contribution made by Mazzini and Garibaldi, who were not liberals. But for the intervention of the illiberal Napoleon III we should not have had Lombardy, and without that of the illiberal Bismarck at Sadowa and at Sedan very probably we should not have had Venetia in 1866 and in 1870 we should not have entered Rome. The years going from 1870 to 1915 cover a period that marked, even in the opinion of the high priests of the new creed, the twilight of their religion, attacked by decadence in literature and by activism in practice. Activism, which is to say nationalism, futurism, Fascism.

The liberal century, after piling up innumerable Gordian knots, tried to cut them with the sword of the world war. Never has any religion claimed so cruel a sacrifice. Were the Gods of liberalism thirsting for blood? Now liberalism is preparing to close the doors of its temples, deserted by the peoples who feel that the agnosticism it professed in the sphere of economics and the indifference of which it has given proof in the sphere of politics and morals would lead the world to ruin in the future as they have done in the past. This explains why all the political experiments of our day are anti-liberal, and it is supremely ridiculous to endeavor on this account to put them outside the pale of history, as though history were a preserve set aside for liberalism and its adepts, as though liberalism were the last word in civilization beyond which no one can go.

The Fascist negation of socialism, democracy, and liberalism should not, however, be interpreted as implying a desire to drive the world backward to positions occupied prior to 1789, a year commonly referred to as that which opened the liberal-democratic century. History does not travel backward. The Fascist doctrine has not taken de Maistre as its prophet. Monarchical absolutism is of the past, and so is ecclesiolatry. Dead and done for are feudal privileges and the division of society into closed, noncommunicating castes. Neither has the Fascist conception of authority anything in common with that of a police state.

A party governing a nation in a totalitarian way is a new departure in history. There are no points of reference or of comparison. From beneath the ruins of liberal, socialist, and democratic doctrines, Fascism extracts those elements which are still vital. It preserves what may be described as "the acquired facts" of history; it rejects all else. That is to say, it rejects the idea of a doctrine suited to all times and to all people. Granted that the XIXth century was the century of socialism, liberalism, democracy, this does not mean that the XXth century must also be the century of socialism, liberalism, democracy. Political doctrines pass; nations remain. We are free to believe that this is the century of authority, a century tending to the "right," a Fascist century. If the XIXth century was the century of the individual (liberalism implies individualism), we are free to believe that this is the "collective" century and therefore the century of the state. It is quite logical for a new doctrine to make use of the still vital elements of other doctrines. No doctrine was ever born quite new and bright and unheard of. No doctrine can boast absolute originality. It is always connected, if only historically, with those which preceded it and those which will follow it. Thus the scientific socialism of Marx links up to the utopian socialism of the Fouriers, the Owens, the Saint-Simons; thus the liberalism of the XIXth century traces its origin back to the

Enlightenment of the XVIIIth and the doctrines of democracy to those of the Encyclopedists. All doctrines aim at directing the activities of men toward a given objective; but these activities in their turn react on the doctrine, modifying and adjusting it to new needs or outstripping it. A doctrine must therefore be a vital act and not a verbal display. Hence the pragmatic strain in Fascism, its will to power, its will to live, its attitude toward violence, and its value.

The keystone of the Fascist doctrine is its conception of the state, of its essence, its functions, and its aims. For Fascism the state is absolute; individuals and groups are relative. Individuals and groups are admissible insofar as they come within the state. Instead of directing the game and guiding the material and moral progress of the community, the liberal state restricts its activities to recording results. The Fascist state is wide awake and has a will of its own. For this reason it can be described as "ethical." At the first quinquennial assembly of the regime, in 1929, I said

> The Fascist state is not a night watchman, solicitous only of the personal safety of the citizens; nor is it organized exclusively for the purpose of guarantying a certain degree of material prosperity and relatively peaceful conditions of life, a board of directors would do as much. Neither is it exclusively political, divorced from practical realities and holding itself aloof from the multifarious activities of the citizens and the nation. The state, as conceived and realized by Fascism, is a spiritual and ethical entity for securing the political, juridical, and economic organization of the nation, an organization which in its origin and growth is a manifestation of the spirit. The state guarantees the internal and external safety of the country, but it also safeguards and transmits the spirit of the people, elaborated down the ages in its language, its customs, its faith. The state is not only the present; it is also the past and above all the future. Transcending the individual's brief spell of life, the state stands for the immanent conscience of the nation. The forms in which it finds expression change, but the need for it remains. The state educates the citizens to civic duty, makes them aware of their mission, urges them to unity. Its justice harmonizes their divergent interests. It transmits to future generations the conquests of the mind in the fields of science, art, law, human solidarity. It leads men up from primitive tribal life to that highest manifestation of human power, imperial rule. The state hands down to future generations the memory of those who laid down their lives to ensure its safety or to obey its laws. It sets up as examples and records for future ages the names of the captains who enlarged its territory and of the men of genius who have made it famous. Whenever respect for the state declines and the disintegrating and centrifugal tendencies of individuals and groups prevail, nations are headed for decay.

Since 1929 economic and political development has everywhere emphasized these truths. The importance of the state is rapidly growing. The so-called crisis can be settled only by state action and within the orbit of the state. Where are the shades of the Jules Simons, who in the early days of liberalism proclaimed that the "state should endeavor to render itself useless and prepare to hand in its resignation"? Or of the MacCullochs, who, in the second half of last century, urged that the state should desist from governing too much? And what of the English Bentham, who considered that all industry asked of government was to be left alone, and of the German Humbolt, who expressed the opinion that the best government was a "lazy" one? What would they say now to the unceasing, inevitable, and urgently requested interventions of government in business? It is true that the second generation of economists was less uncompromising in this respect than the first, and that even Adam Smith left the door ajar—however cautiously—for government intervention in business.

If liberalism spells individualism, Fascism spells government. The Fascist state is, however, a unique and original creation. It is not reactionary but revolutionary, for it anticipates the solution of certain universal problems which have been raised elsewhere, in the political field by the splitting up of parties, the usurpation of power by parliaments, the irresponsibility of assemblies; in the economic field by the increasingly numerous and important functions discharged by trade unions and trade associations with their disputes and ententes, affecting both capital and labor; in the ethical field by the need felt for order, discipline, obedience to the moral dictates of patriotism.

Fascism desires the state to be strong and organic, based on broad foundations of popular support. The Fascist state lays claim to rule in the economic field no less than in others; it makes its action felt throughout the length and breadth of the country by

Document Text

means of its corporative, social, and educational institutions, and all the political, economic, and spiritual forces of the nation, organized in their respective associations, circulate within the state.

A state based on millions of individuals who recognize its authority, feel its action, and are ready to serve its ends is not the tyrannical state of a medieval lord. It has nothing in common with the despotic states existing prior to or subsequent to 1789. Far from crushing the individual, the Fascist state multiplies his energies, just as in a regiment a soldier is not diminished but multiplied by the number of his fellow soldiers. The Fascist state organizes the nation, but it leaves the individual adequate elbow room. It has curtailed useless or harmful liberties while preserving those which are essential. In such matters the individual cannot be the judge, but the state only.

The Fascist state is not indifferent to religious phenomena in general, nor does it maintain an attitude of indifference to Roman Catholicism, the special, positive religion of the Italians. The state has no theology, but it has a moral code. The Fascist state sees in religion one of the deepest of spiritual manifestations, and for this reason it not only respects religion but defends and protects it. The Fascist state does not attempt, as did Robespierre at the height of the revolutionary delirium of the Convention, to set up a "god" of its own, and nor does it vainly seek, as does Bolshevism, to efface God from the soul of man. Fascism respects the God of ascetics, saints,

Glossary

Bernstein	the German Social Democrat Eduard Bernstein (1880–1932), who broke with the Marxists over whether a Socialist revolution could be achieved without violence
Convention	here, the French legislative assembly that was sitting during the Revolutionary year of 1793
de Maistre	Joseph-Marie, comte de Maistre (1753–1821); a highly conservative French philosopher
ecclesiolatry	an absolute insistence on the primacy of the church
Fasci di Combattimento	literally, fighting leagues; local Fascist groups, the first having been founded by Mussolini in 1919
Fasci of Revolutionary Action	umbrella organization of Italian Socialist groups that favored the country's entry into World War I
in fieri	in the process of becoming
Holy Alliance	coalition created in 1815 in which Russia, Austria, and Prussia sought to keep at bay the forces of democracy, revolution, and secularism
Olivetti's … , Orano's … , Leone's …	works Mussolini admired by the Italian syndicalists Angelo Olivetti, Paolo Orano, and Enrico Leone, though he came to later disagree to varying extents with the authors
Partito Popolare	a political party formed in 1919, with a Catholic-oriented agenda but with no support from the Vatican and which first opposed Socialists in general and later Mussolini
Piazza San Sepolcro	the location, in Milan, of the meeting Mussolini spoke to that has been called the founding moment of Fascism
Pius XI	the pope whose actions favoring Mussolini were rewarded by lenience on the part of the Fascist government toward Catholic education and institutions
[Il] Popolo d'Italia	[The] People of Italy, the newspaper Mussolini founded in 1914
prior to 1789	before the French Revolution

BENITO MUSSOLINI'S "THE DOCTRINE OF FASCISM"   1353

and heroes, and it also respects God as conceived by the ingenuous and primitive heart of the people, the God to whom their prayers are raised.

The Fascist state expresses the will to exercise power and to command. Here the Roman tradition is embodied in a conception of strength. Imperial power, as understood by the Fascist doctrine, is not only territorial, or military, or commercial; it is also spiritual and ethical. An imperial nation, that is to say, a nation which directly or indirectly is a leader of others, can exist without the need of conquering a single square mile of territory. Fascism sees in the imperialistic spirit—i.e. in the tendency of nations to expand—a manifestation of their vitality. In the opposite tendency, which would limit their interests to the home country, it sees a symptom of decadence. Peoples who rise and rise again are imperialistic; renunciation is characteristic of dying peoples. The Fascist doctrine is that best suited to the tendencies and feelings of a people which, like the Italians, after lying fallow during centuries of foreign servitude, are now reasserting themselves in the world.

But imperialism implies discipline, the coordination of efforts, a deep sense of duty and a spirit of self-sacrifice. This explains many aspects of the practical activity of the regime and the direction taken by many of the forces of the state, as also the severity which has to be exercised toward those who would oppose this spontaneous and inevitable movement of XXth century Italy by agitating outgrown ideologies of the XIXth century, ideologies rejected wherever great experiments in political and social transformations are being dared. Never before have the peoples thirsted for authority, direction, order as they do now. If each age has its doctrine, then innumerable symptoms indicate that the doctrine of our age is the Fascist. That it is vital is shown by the fact that it has aroused a faith; that this faith has conquered souls is shown by the fact that Fascism can point to its fallen heroes and its martyrs.

Fascism has now acquired throughout the world that universally which belongs to all doctrines which by achieving self-expression represent a moment in the history of human thought.

Adolf Hitler (Library of Congress)

ADOLF HITLER'S PROCLAMATION TO THE GERMAN PEOPLE

" Fourteen years of Marxism have ruined Germany."

Overview

At 10:00 on the evening of February 1, 1933, Adolf Hitler delivered his first address, by radio, to the German people as the nation's chancellor. He had taken the oath of office at about noon on January 30. The office of chancellor, called Reichskanzler in German, was (and still is) roughly equivalent to that of prime minister. At the time, the chancellor of Germany was appointed by the president and was responsible to the German parliament, the Reichstag. During the Weimar Republic, the name given to the German government from 1919 to 1933, the chancellor had been a weak figure, often functioning as little more than the head of the political party in power. Hitler, however, would use the office to seize absolute power in Germany, and historians generally regard his appointment as chancellor as the start of the Third Reich, which would remain in power as an absolute dictatorship until the end of World War II in 1945. The word *Reich* is generally translated as "empire" or "state." The First Reich was the period of the Holy Roman Empire, which united the Germanic lands and others in central Europe from 962 to 1806. The Second Reich refers to the period from 1871 to 1919 and to the polity that encompassed the regions of Prussia and Brandenburg.

In his proclamation to the German people, the *Volk*, Hitler enunciated themes that had obsessed him for more than a decade. He drew the nation's attention to the social and economic disarray and the humiliation it had suffered as a result of its defeat in World War I and the consequent Treaty of Versailles. He blamed the nation's ills on Communists and vowed that the government would work to improve the plight of the German farmer and the German industrial worker. He expressed his resolve to re-create a spirit of unity in the German people by sweeping away the political divisions of the Weimar Republic. His expressed goal was to revive the German nation and lead it back to the stature it had once enjoyed.

Context

Hitler's appointment as chancellor of Germany capped fourteen years of political agitation. After he returned from service in World War I, Hitler became active in the German Workers' Party, a nationalist party built around opposition to Jews and Communists that later changed its name to the National Socialist German Workers' Party, or the Nazi Party (a name derived from the German *Nationalsozialismus*, or "national socialism"). He quickly rose through the ranks until he was elected chairman of the party in 1921. He was already attracting a number of influential followers with his oratorical skills and nationalist sentiments, and he determined to use this backing to seize power in the German state of Bavaria in a coup attempt that began on November 8, 1923, called the Beer Hall Putsch. The coup failed, and Hitler was arrested, tried for treason, and sentenced to prison. During the year he spent in prison he wrote the first volume of *Mein Kampf*, or "My Struggle," which outlined his political beliefs.

After the Beer Hall Putsch, the Nazi Party was in disarray. Hitler devoted his efforts to rebuilding it, but in the national elections of 1924 and 1928 the party received few votes. The start of the Great Depression, though, made the party's message more attractive, so in the 1930 election the party claimed over 18 percent of the vote. This number rose to over 37 percent in the 1932 elections, giving the party 230 seats in the Reichstag. In 1932 Hitler ran for president against the incumbent president, Paul von Hindenburg; although he lost, he gained national stature. In the year that followed, despite Hindenburg's victory, his chancellors—first Franz von Papen and then Kurt von Schleicher—were unable to form workable coalitions (agreements among various political parties to work together). With German industrialists backing Hitler, Hindenburg reluctantly appointed him to the post of chancellor.

These events all took place in the context of political and social chaos in Germany after World War I. In 1918 members of the military, allied with industrial workers, staged a rebellion that appeared to the more conservative elements in Germany to resemble the Russian Revolution of a year before. The events that surrounded this effort deepened divisions between right-wing and left-wing parties; the conservative right wing wanted to see a return to a prewar imperial government, while the left wing called for a Communist government. In 1919 a new government

1889

- **April 20**
  Adolf Hitler is born in Austria.

1919

- **June 28**
  The Treaty of Versailles, the peace treaty at the end of World War I, is signed in Versailles, France.

1921

- **July 29**
  Hitler becomes chairman of the National Socialist German Workers' Party.

1923

- **November 8**
  Hitler leads the Beer Hall Putsch, an attempt to seize control of the government in Munich, Germany.

1932

- Hitler runs for president of Germany against the incumbent, Paul von Hindenburg, and loses.

1933

- **January 30**
  Hitler is appointed chancellor of Germany.

- **February 1**
  Hitler delivers his proclamation to the German people by radio.

- **February 28**
  Paul von Hindenburg signs the Reichstag Fire Decree, curtailing civil liberties.

was formed, and a new constitution was written in the German city of Weimar, giving the new parliamentary government the name Weimar Republic. But almost immediately, the government came under attack from both the right and the left. Uprisings occurred in numerous cities; rebels declared a Soviet-style republic in Munich and tried to do so in Berlin. Fighting in the streets became commonplace. Worsening the situation was the Treaty of Versailles, which officially ended World War I on June 28, 1919. At the conference in Versailles, France, the victorious Allies blamed Germany for the war. Germany was disarmed, required to pay reparations and make territorial concessions to the Allies, and forced to accept the "war guilt" clause of the treaty. Many Germans believed that their nation had been humiliated by the Allies. A once proud and prosperous people had been reduced to the status of a conquered nation.

In the aftermath of the treaty and the formation of the Weimar Republic, the chaos continued. Assassinations and bloody street fighting between paramilitary groups—the right-wing Freikorps and left-wing pro-Communist Red Guards—were frequent. Communists took over the government in the German state of Bavaria. The Freikorps tried to install a right-wing government in Berlin. By 1923 the government had concluded that it could no longer afford the reparations called for by the Treaty of Versailles and at the same time meet its obligations to pensioners, war veterans, and others. Accordingly, it simply began to print money, creating hyperinflation. A 50 million mark bill that twelve years earlier would have been worth about $12 million was worth $1 when it was printed, and people used bundles of German banknotes as notepads because the bills were so worthless. A common expression was that it took a wheelbarrow full of banknotes to buy a loaf of bread.

During the period from 1923 to 1929, conditions in Germany improved markedly. Hitler's Beer Hall Putsch had been put down. Inflation eased, and the United States agreed to provide loans to Germany to help it make its reparations payments. In 1926 Germany was admitted to the League of Nations, enhancing its international stature. But conditions took a turn for the worse in 1930 with the onset of the Great Depression. For three years the government was in disarray. Papen and Schleicher were unable to form coalitions. Hindenburg tried to rule by presidential decree rather than through the parliament. Meanwhile, the Nazi Party was rapidly expanding to include not just disaffected workers, farmers, and war veterans but also many members of the middle class. Faced with dissension and lack of support, Hindenburg made what proved to be a fatal appointment when he was persuaded to name Hitler as chancellor. Hindenburg and his supporters believed that they were co-opting the Nazis and that they would be able to control Hitler by surrounding him with more right-wing appointees. They failed to recognize Hitler's immense popularity. Later, Nazi propaganda would call Hitler's appointment the *Machtergreifung*, or "seizure of power." The Third Reich of Nazi Germany was under way.

Adolf Hitler, whose very name has become synonymous with evil, was born on April 20, 1889, in the small Austrian town of Braunau am Inn to a doting mother and an authoritarian father. In 1894 the family moved to Linz, Austria. After his father's death in 1903, Hitler lived on his own in Vienna, Austria, where he attempted to pursue a career as an artist and where he became a confirmed anti-Semite. He joined the army in World War I, attaining the rank of corporal, and on two occasions was decorated for bravery. After the war, he landed in Munich, Germany, and became involved in politics. His first appointment was as a police spy for the German military; his task was to infiltrate the German Workers' Party. Hitler, though, agreed with the party's nationalist, anti-Semitic, and anti-Communist message, so he joined the party and became a member of its executive committee. The party later changed its name to the National Socialist German Workers' Party—the Nazis—as a way of broadening its appeal.

In the years that followed, Hitler gained notoriety as a skilled orator who was able to tap into Germans' sense of humiliation as a result of defeat in World War I and the Treaty of Versailles. In 1921, Hitler threatened to resign from the party unless he was made chairman. The party's executive committee acceded to his demands because of his popularity. Hitler began attracting influential supporters, and based on that support, he led the so-called Beer Hall Putsch on November 8, 1923. Backed by the Sturmabteilung, a paramilitary group that protected party meetings and intimidated opponents, he and a group of supporters stormed a political meeting at a beer hall in Munich and declared that they were seizing the Bavarian government with a view to marching on Berlin and seizing the federal government. The next day, however, as the group marched on the Bavarian War Ministry, they were arrested. In his trial for treason, Hitler was given ample opportunity to speak; although he was convicted, he won widespread support for the views he expressed in his defense. He was sentenced to five years in prison but served only one year. During his year in prison, he was given preferential treatment by prison authorities, received volumes of fan mail, and wrote the first volume of his political manifesto, *Mein Kampf*.

In the years that followed, the party was in disarray and had to be rebuilt. Improvements in the German economy made the Nazi message less attractive to middle-of-the-road citizens. In the elections of 1924 (when Hitler was still in prison) and 1928, the party received little support. But in 1930 the worldwide Great Depression hit Germany. The administration of President Paul von Hindenburg met with opposition from both the left and the right. A series of chancellors were unable to form coalitions in Germany's parliamentary government. Unable to form majorities, the Reichstag was ineffective and powerless, forcing the president to rule by emergency decree. With violence, poverty, and unemployment soaring, the government seemed unable to meet the crisis. Hitler saw the economic crisis as an opportunity.

Time Line

1933

- **March 23**
  Paul von Hindenburg signs the Enabling Act, consolidating Hitler's power.

- **July 14**
  Law against the Establishment of Parties is promulgated.

1934

- **June 30**
  In the Night of the Long Knives, Hitler's rivals in the Nazi Party are killed in a purge that continues until July 2.

- **August 2**
  Paul von Hindenburg dies; his authority is transferred to Hitler as chancellor.

1939

- **September 1**
  Germany invades Poland, launching World War II.

1945

- **April 30**
  Hitler commits suicide in Berlin, Germany.

He declared his candidacy for president in the 1932 elections, running against Hindenburg and a Communist. He was perhaps the first politician to make use of the airplane in a political campaign, allowing him to speak in different cities on the same day. Although he lost the election, he attracted support from a broad cross-section of the public. More to the point, the party's candidates captured over a third of the vote. After the 1932 elections, it was the largest party in the Reichstag. Political infighting and intrigue left the governments of Franz von Papen and Kurt von Schleicher ineffective just as Hitler was gaining additional support from German industrialists. With great reluctance, and desperate to find a chancellor who could forge a parliamentary coalition, Hindenburg appointed Hitler chancellor.

Hitler moved quickly to consolidate his power through legislation such as the Reichstag Fire Decree and the Enabling Act and by the elimination of opponents in the Night of the Long Knives. In August 1934 Hindenburg died. The Reichstag decided to suspend the office of president and transfer the president's powers to the chancellor, Hitler. Throughout the 1930s Hitler assumed absolute control over Germany. During these years he and his supporters launched their persecution of the Jews, Communists, trade unionists, and political opponents. In defiance of the Treaty of Versailles, Hitler remilitarized Germany. He formed new alliances with the Soviet Union, Italy, and imperialist Japan. He merged German-speaking Austria with Germany (the "Anschluss") and grabbed the German-speaking Sudetenland region of Czechoslovakia. Few were surprised when he launched World War II in Europe with the invasion of Poland on September 1, 1939.

In the months and years that followed, the German military machine gobbled up large portions of Europe. Europe's Jews—along with Communists, the Roma ("Gypsies"), Jehovah's Witnesses, homosexuals, the mentally and physically disabled, and even severely wounded veterans—were systematically killed in what is generally called the Holocaust. As the war progressed and the Allies, led by the United States and England, fought back, Hitler became increasingly unstable. He insisted on directing military affairs himself, often against the advice of his generals. Perhaps his greatest blunder was his decision to attack his former ally to the east, the Soviet Union, forcing him to fight a war on two fronts. As the Allies from east and west converged on Berlin, Hitler holed up in a bunker beneath the chancellery building. On April 30, 1945, he and his longtime mistress, Eva Braun, whom he had married the day before, committed suicide. Various German military units throughout Europe surrendered in the days that followed; the formal surrender of all German forces was signed on May 7, 1945. In the end, Hitler's murderous regime massacred some six million people.

Explanation and Analysis of the Document

Hitler opens his proclamation by reminding his radio listeners of the Treaty of Versailles, which ended World War I. He does not mention the treaty by name, but he knows that every German will recognize his reference to "that ill-fated day when, blinded by promises at home and abroad, the German Volk lost sight of the most valuable assets of our past and of our Reich, its honor and its freedom." He deliberately uses two words that resonate with Germans: *Volk* and *Reich*. *Volk* would normally be translated simply as "people," yet the word tapped into a more elemental sense of the German people as a race apart, defined by their industry, achievements, traditions, and history. *Reich* is often translated as "kingdom," but of course Germany was not a monarchy, so the word carried implications more of "empire." It was this longing for empire—for *Lebensraum*, or "living space"—in central and western Europe that would

lead to World War II. He later uses the word *Vaterland*, or "fatherland," to similar effect, rallying the German people behind their sense of nationhood and history.

Hitler goes on to paint a picture of the disunity of Germany. The Treaty of Versailles had stripped the nation of its international standing, principally by imposing the "war guilt" clause that identified Germany as the aggressor and forced it to accept guilt for the war's devastation. Hitler, though, refuses to accept that guilt and briefly argues that Germany had been forced into the war from a need to defend itself against attack—a partial truth, for Russia had massed troops on the German border, and at the time, Europe was a powder keg of suspicions, distrust, alliances, and animosities that was waiting for an excuse to erupt in war.

Hitler then turns to the economic situation. Germany had been brought to its knees in the aftermath of World War I, and the German economy had been devastated. Although conditions had improved in the late 1920s, the onset of the worldwide Great Depression once again created economic turmoil. He refers to the "starving millions of unemployed proletarians in industry" and raises the specter of mass starvation when the economic crisis hits the agricultural sector.

Hitler traces the source of this turmoil and disunity to Communism. He argues that Communism "is attempting to poison and disrupt the Volk." Communism, he says, is a "negating, all-destroying dogma" that affects family and undermines morality and religious faith—an ironic statement, given that Hitler practiced no religion and was attracted to pagan mythologies and spiritualism. He suggests that the past fourteen years, coincident with the Weimar Republic, allowed Communists to gain power and influence. Hitler was in a sense correct. In 1920 only four members of the German Communist Party held seats in the Reichstag. That number steadily increased to sixty-two in 1924, seventy-seven in 1930, and a hundred in 1932. He refers to "Bolshevism," formed from the word *Bolshevik*, or the extremist party that advocated the violent overthrow of capitalism during the Russian Revolution of 1917. He also refers to Marxism, or the theories of Karl Marx, the nineteenth-century German political philosopher whose theories of class warfare formed the intellectual foundation of Communism. Communism, Hitler asserts, would render Germany a "heap of ruins."

Hitler then pays his respects to Paul von Hindenburg, the president who appointed Hitler as chancellor and who had come out of retirement from the Prussian army to lead the German military (along with Erich Ludendorff) during World War I. Hindenburg's victories over Russian forces had turned him into a national hero. Hitler then makes the transition to an inspirational message designed to rally the German people—peasants, workers, and the bourgeoisie (middle class)—to rebuild the empire by recapturing its "unity of spirit and will." This, says Hitler, will be the first task of the government. He appeals to concepts of family, Christianity, pride, and tradition to call for "national and political unity and its resultant duties," which is precisely the type of message that Germans wanted to hear, in light of the political and economic chaos of most of the postwar period. "Thus,"

SS bodyguards march past Hitler in Berlin in 1937. (AP/Wide World Photos)

Hitler says, the government "will declare a merciless war against spiritual, political and cultural nihilism," or absence of belief in any higher morality or higher good. The war, he says, will be against Communism. It should be noted that for all his anti-Semitism, Hitler hated Slavic peoples, including Russians, just as much, and one of his professed goals in World War II was to form a Western European empire that would turn and defeat the Slavic peoples to the east.

Hitler returns to the theme of economics and announces that the government will pursue two four-year plans. The goal of these plans is to ensure the "salvation" of the German peasantry and of German industrial workers. Both of these groups, he says, have been devastated by the "November parties," a reference to the parties that emerged in the wake of the 1918 military rebellion and the deepening divisions between right wing and left wing. One way of reconstituting the German peasantry was through a "settlement policy" that would remove non-German, non-Nordic elements from agricultural regions, thus allowing true Germans to reclaim their rightful place as productive agricultural workers. In foreign policy, Hitler offers soothing words about peace and the hope that the world could

reduce its supply of armaments so that Germany could avoid the need to increase its own.

Hitler argues that a precondition for restoring Germany's strength and greatness is to stop the "infiltration" of Communism into Germany. He goes on to note that over the past fourteen years, the Reichstag had been unable to restore order to the nation. Accordingly, says Hitler, it is up to the people to carry out programs of reform. In this way, Hitler signals, however subtly, his goal of stripping the Reichstag of its authority, for the nation "cannot make the work of reconstruction dependent upon the approval of those who are to blame for the collapse." In the months and years that followed, Hitler made good on his promise, rendering the Reichstag a purely symbolic institution. Hitler concludes by urging the people to give the new government just four years to accomplish its goals.

Audience

The audience for Hitler's proclamation was the German people. The address was broadcast by radio and

> "More than fourteen years have passed since that ill-fated day when, blinded by promises at home and abroad, the German Volk lost sight of the most valuable assets of our past and of our Reich, its honor and freedom, and thus lost everything."
>
> (Paragraph 1)

> "In a single gigantic offensive of willpower and violence, the Communist method of madness is attempting to poison and disrupt the Volk."
>
> (Paragraph 4)

> "Fourteen years of Marxism have ruined Germany."
>
> (Paragraph 5)

> "The National Government will therefore regard it as its first and foremost duty to reestablish the unity of spirit and will of our Volk."
>
> (Paragraph 9)

attracted a huge audience. Many members of the middle class had regarded Hitler as a bumbler and rabble-rouser, but they were impressed by the speech. Hitler's appointment as chancellor was an enormously popular decision. Large crowds had gathered outside the chancellery building in Berlin the previous day when he was appointed chancellor. The German people had grown weary of the Weimar Republic, regarding it as responsible for Germany's weakness and the economic ills that beset the nation. They had also grown tired of the political intrigue and infighting that characterized the administration of Hindenburg. They saw the appointment of Hitler as a new beginning, as a step toward a more effective government. Hitler's address was his first official effort to rally the German people to greatness.

Impact

As chancellor, Hitler no longer had to rely on putsches, or extralegal coups, to gain power; he could gain it through legislative decree. On February 27, 1933, the Reichstag building was the scene of a fire. To this day, the circumstances surrounding the fire remain a mystery, and it is possible that the fire was set under Hitler's direction or that of his supporters. Hitler and the Nazis seized on the event to foment a fear of Communism. In official statements, the government blamed Communists for the fire and suggested that it was the opening salvo in a civil war. The following day, Hindenburg issued the Order of the Reich's President for the Protection of People and State, informally called the Reichstag Fire Decree. The decree suspended civil liberties in Germany; the first article of the decree reads that various articles

of the Constitution of the German Reich are suspended until further notice. The following are therefore permitted: limits on personal freedom, freedom of opinion, including the freedom of the press, the freedom to organize and assemble, the privacy of postal, telegraphic and telephonic communications, and warrants for house searches, orders for confiscations of property as well as restrictions on property beyond the legal limits otherwise prescribed (http://www.southalabama.edu/history/faculty/rogers/348/reichstagfiredecree.html).

The decree was used as the legal basis for arresting Nazi opponents, primarily Communists, and suppressing publications critical of the Nazis.

The next step in Hitler's consolidation of power was the Enabling Act, more formally, Law to Remedy the Distress of the People and the Nation. The key provision of the act, passed in March 1933, was that it allowed the cabinet to pass legislation without the participation of the Reichstag. After considerable political maneuvering, Hitler was able to gain the two-thirds majority vote needed in the Reichstag to pass the law, a process made easier because many of the Communists who would have opposed it had been arrested as a result of the Reichstag Fire Decree. With the passage of the Enabling Act, the Reichstag was effectively stripped of all powers and played little to no role in German politics until after the end of World War II. Hitler went on to secure a July 14, 1933, law banning the formation of political parties, though by then most parties had either already been banned or had dissolved themselves. This law, the Law against the Establishment of Parties, stated simply: "The National Socialist German Workers Party constitutes the only political party in Germany" (Noakes and Pridham, eds., p. 200). Germany now was officially a one-party state; although the country was nominally ruled by the cabinet, power was effectively in the hands of Adolf Hitler.

At this point, Hitler's only real opponents were members of the Nazi Party and Nazi sympathizers who represented a threat to his hold on absolute power. To solve this problem, the Nazis carried out a purge that began on the night of June 30, 1934, which is generally referred to as the Night of the Long Knives. The purge targeted members of the Sturmabteilung, a paramilitary group usually called the Brownshirts under the leadership of Ernst Röhm. Röhm's ultimate goal was to merge with the German military under his command. The military, though, hated the Sturm-

abteilung, regarding its members as street thugs. Hitler was thus able to win the loyalty of the military by purging the group. It has been estimated that at least eighty-five people were killed in the purge, though it is likely that the number was much higher. At least a thousand were arrested. The forces that carried out the purge were the Schutzstaffel (more commonly known as the SS, Hitler's paramilitary guard unit) and the Geheime Staatspolizei (or Gestapo), the regime's feared secret police.

The final step in Hitler's consolidation of power was the effective elimination of the role of president. From Hitler's point of view, it was a convenience that Paul von Hindenburg died on August 2, 1934. Hindenburg had been ailing for some time and had largely withdrawn from governmental affairs. On his death, Hitler declared the office of president vacant and transferred the powers of the presidency to the office of chancellor. Hitler's assumption of absolute power in Germany, which began with his appointment as chancellor in 1933, was now complete.

Further Reading

■ Books

Abel, Theodore. *Why Hitler Came into Power*. Cambridge, Mass.: Harvard University Press, 1986.

Broszat, Martin. *Hitler and the Collapse of Weimar Germany*, trans V. R. Berghahn. Leamington Spa, N.Y.: Berg Publishers, 1987.

Halperin, S. William. *Germany Tried Democracy: A Political History of the Reich from 1918 to 1933*. New York: W. W. Norton, 1965.

Questions for Further Study

1. Adolf Hitler is not generally regarded as a champion of the common person, but in his proclamation he appealed directly to the "*Volk.*" On what did he base his appeal? Why do you think that appeal was effective?

2. Throughout the 1920s and up to the time Hitler was appointed chancellor, the fear of Communism was widespread among many Germans. Why do you think this was the case? What perceived threat did Communism hold, according to Hitler?

3. Specify the political, social, and economic conditions that allowed Hitler to rise to power and that he enumerates in his proclamation.

4. What steps did Hitler take to consolidate his power? Why do you think the Reichstag and the German people tolerated these steps?

5. Each year since 1927 the influential U.S. magazine *Time* has selected a "Man of the Year," now called "Person of the Year." Hitler was selected in 1938. Given what is now known about Hitler and his plans, why do you think this selection was made?

Kershaw, Ian. *Hitler: 1889–1936—Hubris.* New York: W. W. Norton, 1999.

Maracin, Paul R. *The Night of the Long Knives: Forty-Eight Hours That Changed the History of the World.* Guilford, Conn.: Globe Pequot, 2004.

McDonough, Frank. *Hitler and the Rise of the Nazi Party.* London: Pearson Longman, 2003.

Mommsen, Hans. *The Rise and Fall of Weimar Democracy,* trans. Elborg Forster and Larry Eugene Jones. Chapel Hill: University of North Carolina Press, 1996.

Noakes, Jeremy, and Geoffrey Pridham, eds. *Documents on Nazism, 1919–1945.* New York: Viking, 1975.

Silverman, Dan P. *Hitler's Economy: Nazi Work Creation Programs, 1933–1936.* Cambridge, Mass.: Harvard University Press, 1998.

Turner, Henry Ashby. *Hitler's Thirty Days to Power: January 1933.* Reading, Mass.: Addison-Wesley, 1996.

Zalampas, Michael. *Adolf Hitler and the Third Reich in American Magazines, 1923–1939.* Bowling Green, Ohio: Bowling Green State Univ. Popular Press, 1989.

■ **Web Sites**

"Decree of the Reich President for the Protection of the People and State."
http://www.southalabama.edu/history/faculty/rogers/348/reichstagfiredecree.html

"The Rise of Hitler—May to Dec. 1932 The Republic Collapses." The History Place Web site.
http://www.historyplace.com/worldwar2/riseofhitler/collapse.htm.

—Michael J. O'Neal

ADOLF HITLER'S PROCLAMATION TO THE GERMAN PEOPLE

More than fourteen years have passed since that ill-fated day when, blinded by promises at home and abroad, the German Volk lost sight of the most valuable assets of our past and of our Reich, its honor and its freedom, and thus lost everything. Since those days of treachery, the Almighty has withheld His blessing from our Volk. Dissension and hatred have made their way into our midst. In the profoundest distress, millions of the best German men and women from all walks of life watch as the unity of the nation vanishes and dissolves in a muddle of political and egotistical opinions, economic interests and differences in Weltanschauung.

As so often before in our history, Germany has presented a picture of heartbreaking disunity since that day of revolution. We were never given the promised equality and fraternity, and we have lost our liberty. The disintegration of the unity of spirit and will of our Volk at home was followed by the disintegration of its political standing in the world.

Imbued with burning conviction that the German Volk entered the great fight in 1914 without a thought to any guilt on its part and filled only with the burdensome care of having to defend the Reich from attack and preserve the freedom and the very existence of the German Volk, we see in the shattering fate which has plagued us since November 1918 merely the product of our disintegration at home. However, the rest of the world as well has been shaken no less by major crises since then. The historical balance of power, which once played no small part in bringing about an understanding of the necessity for internal solidarity of the nations, with all its positive economic consequences, has been done away with.

The insane conception of victors and vanquished destroys the confidence between nations and with it world economy. But the misery of our Volk is appalling! The starving millions of unemployed proletarians in industry are being followed by the impoverishment of the entire *Mittelstand* and artisan professions. When this disintegration ultimately reaches the German peasants, we will be confronted by a catastrophe of unfathomable dimensions. For not only will a Reich disintegrate at the same time, but also a two-thousand-year-old inheritance of valuable, the most valuable assets of human culture and civilization. The warning signs of this approaching disintegration are all about us. In a single gigantic offensive of willpower and violence, the Communist method of madness is attempting to poison and disrupt the Volk, which is shaken and uprooted to its innermost core, with the aim of driving it toward an age which would be even worse in relation to the promises of today's Communist spokesmen than the period we have now left behind us in relation to the promises of those same apostles in November 1918.

Beginning with the family and ranging through all of the concepts of honor and loyalty, *Volk und Vaterland*, culture and economy, all the way to the eternal foundation of our morality and our faith: nothing has been spared by this negating, all-destroying dogma. Fourteen years of Marxism have ruined Germany. One year of Bolshevism would destroy Germany. The richest and most beautiful cultural areas of the world today would be transformed into chaos and a heap of ruins. Even the suffering of the last decade and a half could not be compared to the misery of a Europe in whose heart the red flag of destruction had been hoisted. May the thousands of wounded, the innumerable dead which this war has already cost Germany serve as storm clouds warning against the coming tempest.

In these hours when we were overcome by a powerful anxiety as to the existence and the future of the German nation, the aged leader of the World War appealed to us men in the national parties and leagues to fight under him once more as we had at the front, this time at home, in unity and loyalty for the salvation of the Reich. The venerable Reich President has allied himself with us in this noble sense, and therefore we shall vow to God, our conscience and our Volk as national leaders that we may resolutely and steadfastly fulfill the task thus conferred upon us as the National Government.

The inheritance we have taken on is a terrible one.

The task which we must accomplish is the most difficult ever posed to German statesmen within the memory of mankind. But our confidence is unbounded, for we believe in our Volk and in its imperishable virtues. Peasants, workers, and bourgeoisie must all join together to provide the building blocks for the new Reich.

The National Government will therefore regard it as its first and foremost duty to reestablish the unity of spirit and will of our Volk. It will preserve and defend the foundations upon which the power of our nation rests. It will extend its strong, protecting hand over Christianity as the basis of our entire morality, and the family as the germ cell of the body of our Volk and State. It will reawaken in our Volk, beyond the borders of rank and class, its sense of national and political unity and its resultant duties. It will establish reverence for our great past and pride in our old traditions as the basis for the education of our German youth. Thus it will declare a merciless war against spiritual, political and cultural nihilism. Germany must not and will not drown in anarchistic Communism.

It will replace turbulent instincts with national discipline as the guiding rule of our life. In doing so, it will devote great care to those institutions which constitute the true guarantors of the power and strength of our nation.

The National Government will perform the immense task of reorganizing the economy of our Volk with two great four-year plans:

Salvation of the German peasant in order to maintain the food supply and thus the basis of life in our nation.

Salvation of the German worker in an enormous and all-embracing attack on unemployment.

In fourteen years, the November parties have ruined the German peasantry.

In fourteen years they have created an army of millions of unemployed.

The national government will, with iron determination and unshakeable persistence, implement the following plan:

Within four years the German peasant must be rescued from impoverishment.

Within four years unemployment must be finally overcome.

At the same time, this will lay the groundwork for the recovery of the rest of the economy.

The National Government will couple this gigantic task of reorganizing our economy with the task and accomplishment of reorganizing the Reich, the Länder, and the communities, both in administrative and fiscal terms.

Only then will the concept of a federal preservation of the Reich become a full-blooded, real-life certainty.

The concept of a compulsory labor service and the settlement policy number among the cornerstones of this program.

Securing daily bread, however, also includes the performance of social duties for the sick and the aged.

In economical administration, promoting employment, maintaining our peasantry, as well as exploiting individual initiative also lies the best guarantee for avoiding any experiments which would endanger our currency.

In terms of foreign policy, the National Government regards preserving the right to live and thus regaining the freedom of our Volk as its highest priority. By being resolute in bringing about an end to the chaotic state of affairs in Germany, it will assist in restoring to the community of nations a state of equal value and thus, however, also a state with equal rights. The Government is impregnated with the immensity of the duty of advocating, together with this free and equal Volk, the preservation and maintenance of a peace which the world needs today more than ever before.

May the understanding of all others assist us in fulfilling this, our most sincere wish, for the welfare of Europe, and more, for the welfare of the whole world. As great as is our love for our army as the bearer of our arms and the symbol of our great past, we would be happy if the world, by limiting its own armaments, would never again make it necessary for us to increase ours.

However, if Germany is to experience this political and economic revival and conscientiously fulfill its obligations to the other nations, one decisive step is required: overcoming the Communist infiltration of Germany.

We men of the Government feel that we are responsible to German history for reestablishing the great and orderly body politic and thus finally overcoming class madness and class struggle. It is not a certain class we see, but rather the German Volk, its millions of peasants, bourgeois and workers, who will together either overcome the problems of these times or succumb to them.

Resolved and true to our oath, we will thus—in view of the present Reichstag's inability to support this work—ask the German Volk itself to take on this task we call our own.

Reich President von Hindenburg has called upon us and given us the order to use our own unity to restore to the nation the chance for recovery.

Thus we now appeal to the German Volk to take part in signing this deed of reconciliation.

The Government of the National Uprising wants to work, and it will work.

It was not this government which led the German nation into ruin for fourteen years; this government wants to lead the nation to the top once more.

It is determined to pay the debt of fourteen years in four years.

But it cannot make the work of reconstruction dependent upon the approval of those who are to blame for the collapse.

The Marxist parties and their fellow travellers have had fourteen years to prove their prowess.

The result is a heap of ruins.

Now, German Volk, give us four years, and then pass judgment upon us!

True to the order of the Field Marshal, we shall begin. May Almighty God look mercifully upon our work, lead our will on the right path, bless our wisdom, and reward us with the confidence of our Volk. We are not fighting for ourselves, but for Germany!

Glossary

fellow travellers	Marxist sympathizers who were not members of any Communist Party
field marshal	another title of President Paul von Hindenburg
great fight of 1914	World War I
Länder	the constituent states of the Reich
Mittelstand	in this context, German entrepreneurs at the small- and midsized-business level; the bourgeoisie
November 1918	date of the signing of the armistice that ended World War I
Weltanschauung	literally, worldview; more narrowly, a specific framework for perceiving and interpreting global events as they occur

NUREMBERG LAWS

"Marriages between Jews and nationals of German or kindred blood are forbidden."

Overview

The Nuremberg Laws were two anti-Semitic (anti-Jewish) laws promulgated in 1935 by the Reichstag (the German parliament) in Nazi Germany. The laws were so named because they were passed in connection with a Nazi Party rally in the German city of Nuremberg, where that year the Reichstag met for the first time since 1543. The first of the laws, dated September 15, 1935, was the Law for the Protection of German Blood and German Honor. The second, with the same date, was the Reich Citizenship Law. A third piece of legislation, called the First Supplementary Decree, was dated November 14, 1935. The purpose of these laws was to address on a national level the so-called Jewish problem in Germany. Although Jews made up only about 1 percent of the German population, they had long been targeted as scapegoats for the economic and social problems that devastated Germany in the wake of World War I. Indeed, Europe as a whole had a long history of anti-Semitism, dating back at least to Spain's expulsion of the Jews in 1492. The effect of the Nuremberg Laws was to forbid "pure" Germans from intermarrying with Jews. The laws also excluded Jews from public office and denied them citizenship in the German Reich, or state. These laws were an early step toward the concentration camps of World War II, where millions of Europe's Jews died in a systematic genocide generally referred to as the Holocaust.

Context

The Nuremberg Laws represented an early culmination of Nazi racist ideology. This ideology, however, did not originate in Germany or with the Nazi (National Socialist) Party but rather had its roots in the nineteenth century, particularly in England. Under the influence of Darwinism, which advanced the concepts of natural selection and the survival of the fittest in the natural order, many anthropologists and pseudoscientists were attracted to the belief that there was a natural hierarchy of races. One of the earliest proponents of this view was Sir Francis Galton, who became interested

in the science of eugenics in the late nineteenth century. Those who advocated eugenics believed that it was possible to improve the human race by encouraging the birth of children to genetically fit parents and conversely by discouraging reproduction by those who were less genetically fit. Numerous other scientists in Europe took a similar line, extending eugenics to the study of human populations and racial groups. In 1853, for example, the French scientist Arthur de Gobineau published *The Inequality of Human Races*. In 1916 Madison Grant published *The Passing of the Great Race; or, The Racial Basis of European History*, and in 1920 Lothrop Stoddard published *The Rising Tide of Color against White World Supremacy*. Grant's book, which the German chancellor Adolf Hitler highly praised, was the first non-German book translated and published by the Nazis. These and numerous other books and lectures created fear that the white race was in danger of being overrun by so-called inferior races, particularly those from Africa and Asia. The texts provided intuitive justification for empire building in Africa and Asia; the alleged superiority of Europeans made their hegemony over "lesser" peoples part of the natural order of things.

Another branch of the eugenics movement was *Rassenhygiene* (racial hygiene), a term coined by Alfred Ploetz in 1895. Ploetz was less concerned with Jews and other "undesirables" than he was with a decline in the German birthrate and what he saw as an increasing number of mentally unfit people who were becoming a burden on the German state. He was not alone in his belief that, if necessary, the state should take coercive measures, such as involuntary sterilization of the "unfit," to improve the physical, mental, and moral qualities of future generations; such views were also held by British prime minister Winston Churchill and the U.S. presidents Theodore Roosevelt and Calvin Coolidge, among many others. By defining eugenics as a public health problem, Nazi ideologists moved toward condemning miscegenation (racial mixing) and promoting Aryan ethnic purity.

By the 1930s the myth of the superiority of the Nordic, or Aryan, races had become almost mainstream. One of the most influential documents reflecting this view was Alfred Rosenberg's book *The Myth of the Twentieth Century* (1930). Rosenberg went on to become one of the chief architects of

1895

- Alfred Ploetz coins the term *Rassenhygiene*, or "racial hygiene."

1918

- **November 11** An armistice is signed, ending World War I.

1919

- **June 28** The Treaty of Versailles, requiring Germany to pay reparations to the Allies, is signed in Versailles, France.

1930

- Alfred Rosenberg's *Myth of the Twentieth Century*, which asserts the superiority of the Nordic race, is published.

1933

- **January 30** Adolf Hitler is appointed chancellor of Germany.

- **April 1** A nationwide boycott of Jewish doctors, lawyers, and shops is called in Germany.

- **April 7** The Law for the Restoration of the Professional Civil Service, excluding Jews and other non-Aryans from civil service jobs, is enacted.

Nazi racist ideology. In his book he argues that the Nordic race originated on a now-lost landmass north and west of Europe. The Nordic peoples migrated south and east, settling the countries of Scandinavia and Germany. In time, however, these peoples intermingled with inferior peoples, causing the Nordic peoples to lose their dynamic spirit—in effect, to degenerate. The purpose of Nordic ideology in the German state was to restore the German people to purity by eliminating the elements that led to degeneration. These elements included Jews and Gypsies as well as homosexuals, Slavs, and anyone who was mentally ill or physically imperfect.

For the Nazis and their sympathizers, evidence of degeneration was provided by World War I and its aftermath. At the beginning of the twentieth century, Germany was the most technologically advanced nation on earth. At the Paris Peace Conference after the war, however, the victorious Allies blamed German aggression for the war, with its massive destruction and loss of life. Under the terms of the peace accord, Germany was stripped of its arms and was required to pay reparations to the Allies. These reparations proved to be ruinous to the German economy. To settle its massive debts, the German government simply printed money, causing a devaluation of the German currency. The devaluation was extreme, and it was said that a person needed a wheelbarrow full of currency to buy a loaf of bread. In the social and economic turmoil that followed the war, numerous groups tried to fill the power vacuum. Labor unrest was common, and fears arose that Communists would seize power, as they had in Russia in 1917. Chaos reigned in the streets. Bankruptcies, poverty, unemployment, and crime were commonplace. Germans lived in fear that their country was disintegrating, and a succession of weak governments seemed unable to resolve any of the nation's problems. In a period of just a few years, Germany had fallen from its preeminent position in Europe, becoming a defeated and demoralized country.

It was in this environment that Adolf Hitler rose to power, winning appointment as chancellor of Germany in 1933. He quickly moved to consolidate his power and remained the nation's dictator until his death in 1945. History remembers Hitler as the embodiment of evil, but at the time he was an extremely gifted orator whom the German people perceived to be the only person able to restore Germany to stability and strength. He adopted a strong nationalist policy and was able to direct all of Germany's energy and resources to the reestablishment of German superiority. One of the ways in which he accomplished this goal was to promote the view that Germans were racially superior to others. This superiority extended not only over Jews and other "undesirable" racial categories but over other European populations as well, all based on an elaborate scheme for classifying of European peoples as Nordics, "Alpines," and other groups. Ironically he regarded the British as his natural racial allies, and one of his goals was to subdue England, convert it into a military ally, and then use the combined might of Germany and England to defeat the inferior Slavic races to the east. Hitler's goal was to restore the purity of European blood, a view that was expressed, somewhat

---

inarticulately, by Heinrich Himmler, the head of Nazi Germany's feared secret police, the Schutzstaffel (SS):

> The ultimate aim … has been invariably the same: To create an order of good blood which is able to serve Germany…. To create an order which will spread the idea of Nordic blood so far that we will attract all Nordic blood in the world, take away the blood from our adversaries, absorb it so that never again, looking at it from the viewpoint of grand policy, Nordic blood … will fight against us…. The SS also is only a means to an end, always the Reich, the ideology, created by the Fuehrer, the Reich, created by him, the Reich of all Teutons (http://www.ess.uwe.ac.uk/genocide/SS1.htm).

The ideology for the anti-Semitic Nuremberg Laws was in place, but as of 1935 the German government had taken few steps to convert that ideology into law. The Nuremberg Laws were, in effect, a solution to a political problem that Hitler and the government faced. Beginning in 1933 assaults, boycotts, and vandalism against Jews were becoming commonplace; a major boycott of Jewish doctors, lawyers, and stores was called for April 1 of that year. Days later, the Law for the Restoration of the Professional Civil Service was passed to prevent Jews and others of "non-Aryan descent" from filling government posts, and in May legislation was passed to bar Jews from the German military. The perpetrators of the violence against Jews were largely those Nazis who had joined the party prior to 1930, the so-called Alte Kämpfer, or "Old Fighters." These rank-and-file Nazis were among the most strident anti-Semites in the party, and they were disappointed that Hitler had not taken firmer steps to solve the so-called Jewish problem. The government, however, was hesitant to take extreme steps against Jews. The economics minister Hjalmar Schacht, for example, recognized that the Jewish community, however much it was despised, had skills that could be used to help Germany in its rebuilding effort. Further, the German public was troubled by violence against Jews. On August 8, 1935, Hitler actually ordered that violence against Jews stop, and the government threatened harsher punishments against party members who ignored the order. Hitler, however, sympathized with those who were committing violence against Jews, and he knew that he had to take concrete action with regard to the Jewish problem. At the Nazi Party rally in Nuremberg, the Nuremberg Laws were hastily drafted by officials in the Interior Ministry; in an odd footnote, the officials were unable to find paper, so they drafted the laws on the backs of menus. Hitler announced the laws in a speech to the assembled multitude.

About the Author

The authorship of the Nuremberg Laws is unclear. The names that are listed under the Law for the Protection of German Blood and German Honor are not those of the

Time Line	
1935	■ **August 8** Hitler orders that violence against Jews stop until the government can officially deal with the "Jewish problem."
	■ **September 10–16** The Seventh Party Congress, the official title of the Nazi Party rally, is held in Nuremberg, Germany.
	■ **September 15** The Nuremberg Laws, including the Law for the Protection of German Blood and German Honor and the Reich Citizenship Law, are enacted.
	■ **November 14** The First Supplementary Decree to the Nuremberg Laws is enacted.
1936	■ Jews are banned from all professional jobs in Germany.
1938	■ **March 31** By law, government contracts can no longer be awarded to Jewish businesses.
	■ **September 30** By law, "Aryan" doctors can no longer treat "non-Aryan" patients.
	■ **November 9–10** Thousands of Jewish businesses are vandalized, some two hundred synagogues are burned or ransacked, and thirty thousand Jews are deported to concentration camps as a result of Kristallnacht, or the Night of Broken Glass.

1942

■ The "Final Solution" for the eradication of Jews in concentration camps (for forced labor) and death or extermination camps is under way as a result of the Wannsee Conference. Nearly six million Jews lose their lives in the Holocaust.

authors but rather those of the officials over whose names the laws were promulgated. Generally, the actual authorship of the laws is attributed to two individuals, Hans Globke and Wilhelm Stuckart, although three other men—Bernhard Lösener, Franz Albrecht Medicus, and Julius Streicher—are often mentioned. The drafting of the laws, which took place in haste on September 14–15, 1935, was likely accomplished by committee.

Globke, born in Düsseldorf, Germany, was a lawyer and a jurist in Aachen, Germany. He is perhaps best known for drafting the emergency legislation that gave Hitler unlimited powers after he was appointed chancellor. Ironically, Globke was never a member of the Nazi Party because of his staunch Catholicism, so he was never affected by the de-Nazification program that followed World War II. He went on to a career as a jurist and a close aide to Chancellor Konrad Adenauer in postwar West Germany.

Stuckart was a lawyer for the Nazi Party and was state secretary for the Interior Ministry. He was convicted of war crimes after World War II but was released from prison in 1949; a mitigating factor in his sentence was his effort to ensure that the Nuremberg Laws and other anti-Semitic laws were applied to as narrow a range of citizens as possible. Stuckart died following a car accident, but some people believe that he was, in effect, assassinated by Nazi hunters.

Lösener, born in Fürstenberg, Germany, was a lawyer and an Interior Ministry official who drafted anti-Semitic laws. In 1937 he and Globke coauthored a legal commentary on German racial laws. In 1942 Lösener was a participant in the Wannsee Conference, where the "Final Solution" for eliminating Jews was formulated.

Medicus was born in Strasbourg, Germany. After studying law, he became a member of the SS and then rose to the position of counselor in the Interior Ministry. He did not join the Nazi Party until 1937, after which he was the editor of the *Reich Law Gazette*. After the war he was a lawyer in the West German federal court system.

Streicher was a virulent anti-Semite and founder and editor of the anti-Semitic newspaper *Der Stürmer* (literally

"the Stormer," often translated as "the Militant"). Streicher was convicted of war crimes and was hanged on October 16, 1946.

Explanation and Analysis of the Document

Three documents are reproduced. The first is the Law for the Protection of German Blood and German Honor. The second is the Reich Citizenship Law. Both were promulgated on September 15, 1935, at the Seventh Party Congress, the Nazi Party rally held in Nuremberg, Germany. Taken together, they institutionalized the Nazi Party's racist ideology. The third document, enacted on November 14, 1935, was the First Supplementary Decree to the Nuremberg Laws. Its purpose was to clarify the earlier Nuremberg Laws and to make clear that a Jew could not be regarded as a citizen of Germany's Third Reich.

◆ Law for the Protection of German Blood and German Honor

The introduction to this law asserts the superiority of "German blood" and the need for Germans to preserve the purity of their racial heritage to ensure the continued existence of the German state. This emphasis on blood was an obsession of Nazi ideologues, who used theories of eugenics and racial categorization to rally the German people behind the nation's effort to rebuild and reassert its strength after World War I and the turmoil that followed the war.

Section 1 makes clear that the target of the law is Jews. The first part of this section outlawed marriages between people of German blood and Jews, even if those marriages were entered into in other nations. The second part of the section takes up the issue of the annulment of such marriages, stating that such annulments fell under the authority of the state prosecutor. Section 2 made it illegal for Germans to have sexual relations with Jews outside of marriage. Clearly, if such marriages were illegal, then having sexual relations with a Jew under any circumstances was also illegal.

As a result of Section 3, Jews were prohibited from hiring as a domestic servant any German woman under the age of forty-five. It was commonplace for affluent Jewish families to employ German women as servants, cooks, and housekeepers. To Nazi ideologists, such employment was regarded as undignified and as beneath German citizens. The law did, however, acknowledge that some older women, perhaps having been in domestic service for their entire adult lives, had no other employment opportunities because of their age. Thus the law allowed older women to continue to work in Jewish homes.

According to Section 4, Jews were no longer permitted to fly the German flag or to display the colors of the Reich. This action seems counterintuitive, for one might expect that German authorities would want anyone living within the nation's borders to engage in patriotic displays. Jews, however, were regarded as lesser humans—among many

Nazis, they were viewed as not even human but as vermin who had to be exterminated—so it was logical to them to exclude Jews from patriotic displays. Nevertheless, Jews were allowed to display Jewish colors—that is, a yellow Star of David. Colors played an important role in Nazi Germany. In the concentration camps, for instance, the categories to which prisoners belonged were identifiable by the colors of their badges. Red was reserved for Communists, anarchists, and enemies of the state; green was used for criminals, brown for Gypsies, pink for homosexuals, and so on. That the article grants Jews the "right" to wear Jewish colors was perverse, for this "right" soon became an obligation.

Sections 5–7 address legal procedures. Section 5 specifies the punishment that a German citizen would face for violating any of the earlier articles of the law. Section 6 notes that procedures for implementing the law would be promulgated by the Reich minister of the interior (Wilhelm Frick), in coordination with the deputy of the Führer (Rudolph Hess) and the Reich minister of justice (Franz Gürtner). (Führer, the German word for "leader," was the title generally given to Hitler.) Section 7 indicates when the laws would take effect.

◆ **Reich Citizenship Law**

The Reich Citizenship Law, announced on the same day in connection with the Law for the Protection of German Blood and German Honor, circularly defines a German citizen as anyone who is granted citizenship under the law. Article 1 of the law notes that a citizen enjoys the protection of the state, but it also points out that a citizen has obligations to the state. Article 2 reiterates the importance of blood; a person could be a citizen of the state only if he or she was of German blood. Additionally, to be a citizen, a person had to be "both desirous and personally fit to serve loyally the German people and the Reich." The Nazi regime had no patience with anyone who, in its view, was unable to serve the interests of the state. Although Jews figured most prominently in the horrors of the concentration camps, also shipped off to the camps were Communists, anarchists, labor unionists, homosexuals, foreign workers, alcoholics, vagrants, and anyone who had no fixed address—in short, anyone whom the Nazi regime regarded as unable or unwilling to make a contribution to Nazism and to Germany. Article 3 of the law again states that the Reich minister of the interior, in coordination with the deputy of the Führer, would issue procedures for implementing the citizenship law.

◆ **First Supplementary Decree**

In the months that followed the Nuremberg rally, the Nazi regime issued several supplementary decrees for the purpose of implementing the two Nuremberg Laws. The first of these decrees specifically defines who was a Jew. In general, the Nazis were not particularly interested in Judaism as a religion; rather, Judaism was a matter of ethnicity, of blood, so it did not matter to the Nazis whether a person was a practicing Jew. In the years that followed the Nuremberg Laws, many Europeans who were ethnic Jews

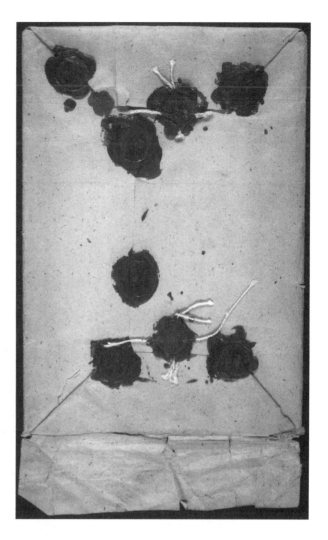

*A **paper package containing the Nuremberg Laws, marked with the wax seals of the Third Reich*** (AP/Wide World Photos)

but who had not practiced Judaism became victims of Nazism. Some of these ethnic Jews had even converted to Christianity, possibly in order to marry Christians, but religious practices did not influence the Nazis. Judaism was a matter of blood, and Jewish blood was regarded as a corruption, as part of the degeneration and defilement of pure German blood. Thus a person's beliefs did not matter. All that mattered was the person's race.

The practical problem, though, was clearly defining who was a Jew. Anyone whose parents were both Jews was a Jew. The question arose, however, as to what to do with so-called *Mischlings*, or people of mixed blood. What if just one of a person's parents was a Jew? What if a person's grandparents on one side, say the father's, were Jews, but the grandparents on the other side were not? Or what if just one of a person's four grandparents was a Jew? The First Supplementary Decree was designed to answer these questions. It begins with Article 1, which states that "all subjects of German or kindred blood who possessed the

Members of the National Socialist Party listen to speeches during a rally at the Seventh Party Congress in Nuremberg on September 10, 1935. (AP/Wide World Photos)

right to vote in the Reichstag elections when the Citizenship Law came into effect, shall, for the present, possess the rights of Reich citizens." Again, the law is circular, essentially defining citizenship by saying that a German citizen is one who has been granted citizenship.

Article 2 of the decree states that an "individual of mixed Jewish blood is one who is descended from one or two grandparents who, racially, were full Jews." Article 3 then states that only those who have voting rights and the right to hold public office can be considered citizens of the Reich, again a kind of circular statement that says, in effect, that a person is a citizen if that person has the rights of citizenship. The decree then takes up a different topic by stating in Article 4 that "a Jew cannot be a citizen of the Reich" and therefore cannot vote or hold public office—this despite the fact that Jews had lived in Germany for hundreds of years and had established schools, synagogues, businesses, cemeteries, and other institutions. Any Jew who served in an official capacity would be retired as of the end of the year. Jews who had served in World War I were receiving pensions, and this section outlines how future pensions would be computed. The remainder of Article 4

exempts religious organizations from the law, though the meaning of this statement is unclear, for the law does not state any sense in which religious organizations could be affected by the law. The article then mentions that issues involving teachers in Jewish schools would be taken up in future legislation. In the event, many Jewish children were expelled from state schools, and Jewish teachers were fired. The result was the establishment of numerous schools where Jewish children were taught by Jewish teachers.

Article 5 is the core of the Nuremberg Laws insofar as they applied to Jews. In this section the law specifies who precisely was a Jew. A person was automatically considered a Jew if three of his or her grandparents were Jews. Additionally, a person was considered a Jew if two of his or her grandparents were Jews, but only under certain conditions. The first of these conditions was that the person in question was a member of the Jewish religious community. The second was that the person in question was married to a Jew. The third was that the person in question was the son or daughter of a Jew as defined earlier, if the marriage that produced the child took place after the Nuremberg Laws were passed. Finally, a person was automatically a Jew if he

A man sweeps up broken glass from in front of a Jewish-owned shop in Berlin on the morning after Kristallnacht.
(AP/Wide World Photos)

> *"Marriages between Jews and nationals of German or kindred blood are forbidden."*
>
> (Law for the Protection of German Blood and German Honor, Section 1)

> *"A citizen of the Reich may be only one who is of German or kindred blood, and who, through his behavior, shows that he is both desirous and personally fit to serve loyally the German people and the Reich."*
>
> (Reich Citizenship Law, Article 2)

> *"Only citizens of the Reich, as bearers of full political rights, can exercise the right of voting in political matters, and have the right to hold public office."*
>
> (First Supplementary Decree, Article 3)

or she was born of an extramarital relationship with a Jew, provided that the person was born after July 31, 1936. Many Germans found the provisions of these laws confusing. In particular, many Jews were uncertain as to whether the regime would regard them as Jews. As a result, in promulgating the laws, German officials devised a chart, rather like a genealogical chart, that showed visually who exactly was a Jew and who was not. Further, the decree embodies a colossal irony. Jews, too, regarded Jewishness as a matter of blood, in a sense. For complicated religious reasons, Jewishness was matrilineal, meaning that it was established through the mother's line. Thus, to Jews, a person was a Jew if his or her mother was a Jew. It was characteristic of the Nazis, though, to complicate the matter to gather within the Jewish net anyone who, in the regime's estimation, was "tainted" by Judaism.

Article 6 makes clear that if any other laws existed to define German blood that went beyond Article 5 of the First Supplementary Decree, those laws would remain untouched—perhaps a tacit recognition that the Nazi regime was writing and passing these laws without much thought or consistency. Article 7 gave Hitler the authority to exempt any individual from the laws and decrees, allowing him to contradict his own ideology for his own ends for expediency's sake.

Audience

The audience for the Nuremberg Laws was twofold. First, the laws and supplemental decrees were directed at Jews. The laws represented a first official step on the part of the Nazi regime to deal with the "Jewish problem." By stripping Jews of their political rights, the Nazis began to move toward the Jews' eradication. The other, larger audience was the German people. The laws represented a concrete application of the Nazi ideology that asserted the superiority of German blood to that of other, inferior groups. As such, it was a key part of the Nazi propaganda program designed to unite Germans in the belief that Germans were a race of *übermenschen*, or "supermen," who could assert Germany's rightful place in the world order. By declaring war on the Jews, Hitler in effect began his assault on Europe, an assault that would lead to World War II.

Impact

The impact of the Nuremberg Laws was far-reaching. It was the first concrete step that led to the Final Solution—that is, to the Holocaust against the Jews. In the months and years that followed, further legislation restricted the rights and activities of Jews. In 1936 Jews were banned from all professional jobs in Germany. Jews, then, could not become lawyers or doctors, nor could they attend universities. On March 31, 1938, a law was passed stipulating that government contracts could no longer be awarded to Jewish businesses. On September 30, 1938, a law was passed to prevent "Aryan" doctors from treating "non-Aryan" patients, and since Jews could not legally be doctors, Jews were effectively denied medical care unless they obtained it illegally and clandestinely. Throughout these years violence against Jews increased. It culminated on the night of November 9–10, 1938. That night thousands of Jewish businesses were vandalized. Some two hundred synagogues were burned or ransacked, and thirty thousand Jews were deported to concentration camps. Because so many windows of Jewish businesses were broken, scattering glass on the sidewalks and streets, that night was called Kristallnacht, meaning "crystal night"—the Night of Broken Glass.

The logical conclusion of the denial of civil rights to Jews was the plan for their annihilation. This plan was formulated at the infamous Wannsee Conference on January 20, 1942, held in the Berlin suburb of Wannsee. There it was announced to senior Nazi officials that Reinhard Heydrich was Hitler's appointee to deal with the "final solution to the Jewish question." The plan called for the deportation of Jews to Nazi-occupied Eastern Europe. There they would work on road-building projects, during which many would die. The remainder would then be put to death in concentration camps. The exact plan was never implemented because the German military lost ground to the Soviet Union as the war progressed. As a result, Jews were either sent immediately to concentration camps or killed in their homes or communities.

Further Reading

■ Books

Browning, Christopher R., and Jürgen Matthäus. *The Origins of the Final Solution: The Evolution of Nazi Jewish Policy, September 1939–March 1942.* Lincoln: University of Nebraska Press, 2007.

Elon, Amos. *The Pity of It All: A History of Jews in Germany, 1743–1933.* New York: Metropolitan Books, 2002.

Kaplan, Marion A., ed. *Jewish Daily Life in Germany, 1618–1945.* New York: Oxford University Press, 2005.

Meyer, Michael A., ed. *German-Jewish History in Modern Times.* Vol. 4: *Renewal and Destruction, 1918–1945.* New York: Columbia University Press, 1998.

Office of U.S. Chief of Counsel for Prosecution of Axis Criminality. "Adolf Hitler." In *Nazi Conspiracy and Aggression*, vol. 4. Washington, D.C.: U.S. Government Printing Office, 1946. Available online. Web Genocide Documentation Web site. http://www.ess.uwe.ac.uk/genocide/SS1.htm.

—Michael J. O'Neal

Questions for Further Study

1. How did the Nuremberg Laws represent the culmination of European thought about racial differences dating back to the nineteenth century?

2. From the Nazi perspective, what was the logic behind the passage of the Nuremberg Laws? Why did the Nazis believe that such laws were necessary?

3. How did the Nuremberg Laws ultimately lead to the so-called Final Solution for dealing with the "Jewish problem"? What was that "final" solution?

4. Why do you think that many German people were so accepting of the Nazi Party's racist ideology? Alternatively, do you think that many Germans did not accept this ideology but were frightened to speak out? Explain.

5. To what extent did the terms of the Treaty of Versailles ending World War I contribute to the climate of opinion that made the Nuremberg Laws possible?

NUREMBERG LAWS

Thoroughly convinced by the knowledge that the purity of German blood is essential for the further existence of the German people and animated by the inflexible will to safeguard the German nation for the entire future, the Reichstag has resolved upon the following law unanimously, which is promulgated herewith:

Section 1

(1) Marriages between Jews and nationals of German or kindred blood are forbidden. Marriages concluded in defiance of this law are void, even if, for the purpose of evading this law, they are concluded abroad.

(2) Proceedings for annulment may be initiated only by the Public Prosecutor.

Section 2

Relations outside marriage between Jews and nationals for German or kindred blood are forbidden.

Section 3

Jews will not be permitted to employ female nationals of German or kindred blood in their households.

Section 4

(1) Jews are forbidden to hoist the Reich and national flag and to present the colors of the Reich.

(2) On the other hand they are permitted to present the Jewish colors. The exercise of this authority is protected by the State.

Section 5

(1) A person who acts contrary to the prohibition of section 1 will be punished with hard labor.

(2) A person who acts contrary to the prohibition of section 2 will be punished with imprisonment or with hard labor.

(3) A person who acts contrary to the provisions of section 3 or 4 will be punished with imprisonment up to a year and with a fine or with one of these penalties.

Section 6

The Reich Minister of the Interior in agreement with the Deputy of the Fuehrer will issue the legal and administrative regulations which are required for the implementation and supplementation of this law.

Section 7

The law will become effective on the day after the promulgation, section 3 however only on 1 January 1936.

Nuremberg, the 15th day of September 1935 at the Reich Party Rally of Freedom.

The Fuehrer and Reich Chancellor Adolph Hitler
The Reich Minister of the Interior Frick
The Reich Minister of Justice Dr. Goertner
The Deputy of the Fuehrer R. Hess

Reich Citizenship Law of September 15, 1935

The Reichstag has adopted by unanimous vote the following law which is herewith promulgated.

◆ Article 1

(1) A subject of the state is one who belongs to the protective union of the German Reich, and who, therefore, has specific obligations to the Reich.

(2) The status of subject is to be acquired in accordance with the provisions of the Reich and the state Citizenship Law.

◆ Article 2

(1) A citizen of the Reich may be only one who is of German or kindred blood, and who, through his behavior, shows that he is both desirous and personally fit to serve loyally the German people and the Reich.

(2) The right to citizenship is obtained by the grant of Reich citizenship papers.

(3) Only the citizen of the Reich may enjoy full political rights in consonance with the provisions of the laws.

◆ **Article 3**

The Reich Minister of the Interior, in conjunction with the Deputy to the Fuehrer, will issue the required legal and administrative decrees for the implementation and amplification of this law.

Promulgated: September 16, 1935. In force: September 30, 1935.

First Supplementary Decree of November 14, 1935

On the basis of Article 3 of the Reich Citizenship Law of September 15, 1935, the following is hereby decreed:

◆ **Article 1**

(1) Until further provisions concerning citizenship papers, all subjects of German or kindred blood who possessed the right to vote in the Reichstag elections when the Citizenship Law came into effect, shall, for the present, possess the rights of Reich citizens. The same shall be true of those upon whom the Reich Minister of the Interior, in conjunction with the Deputy to the Fuehrer shall confer citizenship.

(2) The Reich Minister of the Interior, in conjunction with the Deputy to the Fuehrer, may revoke citizenship.

◆ **Article 2**

(1) The provisions of Article I shall apply also to subjects who are of mixed Jewish blood.

(2) An individual of mixed Jewish blood is one who is descended from one or two grandparents who, racially, were full Jews, insofar that he is not a Jew according to Section 2 of Article 5. Full-blooded Jewish grandparents are those who belonged to the Jewish religious community.

◆ **Article 3**

Only citizens of the Reich, as bearers of full political rights, can exercise the right of voting in political matters, and have the right to hold public office. The Reich Minister of the Interior, or any agency he empowers, can make exceptions during the transition period on the matter of holding public office. The measures do not apply to matters concerning religious organizations.

◆ **Article 4**

(1) A Jew cannot be a citizen of the Reich. He cannot exercise the right to vote; he cannot hold public office.

(2) Jewish officials will be retired as of December 31, 1935. In the event that such officials served at the front in the World War either for Germany or her allies, they shall receive as pension, until they reach the age limit, the full salary last received, on the basis of which their pension would have been computed. They shall not, however, be promoted according to their seniority in rank. When they reach the age limit, their pension will be computed again, according to the salary last received on which their pension was to be calculated.

(3) These provisions do not concern the affairs of religious organizations.

(4) The conditions regarding service of teachers in public Jewish schools remains unchanged until the promulgation of new laws on the Jewish school system.

◆ **Article 5**

(1) A Jew is an individual who is descended from at least three grandparents who were, racially, full Jews....

(2) A Jew is also an individual who is descended from two full-Jewish grandparents if: (a) he was a member of the Jewish religious community when this law was issued, or joined the community later; (b) when the law was issued, he was married to a person who was a Jew, or was subsequently married to a Jew; (c) he is the issue from a marriage with a Jew, in the sense of Section I, which was contracted after the coming into effect of the Law for the Protection of German Blood and Honor of September 15, 1935; (d) he is the issue of an extramarital relationship with a Jew, in the sense of Section I, and was born out of wedlock after July 31, 1936.

◆ **Article 6**

(1) Insofar as there are, in the laws of the Reich or in the decrees of the National Socialist German Workers' Party and its affiliates, certain requirements for the purity of German blood which extend beyond Article 5, the same remain untouched....

◆ **Article 7**

The Fuehrer and Chancellor of the Reich is empowered to release anyone from the provisions of these administrative decrees.

Mohammed Ali Jinnah sits on his dais during ceremonies following his swearing-in as governor-general of Pakistan in 1947. (AP/Wide World Photos)

"[The] federation embodied in the Government of India Act 1935 ...
is altogether unacceptable to Muslim India."

Overview

On March 23, 1940, Abdul Kashem Fazlul Huq, a well-known politician and the premier of Bengal, presented a resolution in the twenty-seventh annual session of the All India Muslim League held in Lahore. The resolution was drafted by the then premier of Punjab, Sikandar Hayat Khan, and was seconded by Chaudhry Khaliquzzaman, a prominent leader from the United Provinces (Uttar Pradesh). Conceptualized as a bargaining device for the Muslim League with its two opponents—the Indian National Congress (INC), also called the Congress Party, and the British government—the resolution was composed in clumsy language, keeping the meaning amorphous and hence open to interpretation. The scheme of federation embodied in the Government of India Act of 1935 was rejected, and a demand was made for adequate, effective, and mandatory safeguards to protect religious, cultural, economic, political, administrative, and other rights and interests of the Muslim community and other minorities. To achieve this aim, the Working Committee, the executive body of the All India Muslim League, was also authorized to frame a constitution, keeping in mind issues related to defense, external affairs, communications, customs, and other such matters.

Each of the five paragraphs of the Lahore Resolution is linked to a core concern: the eagerness of Muslim communities to represent their aspirations for autonomous and sovereign regions constituting "independent states." These ambitions played a crucial role in defining the politics of South Asia in the 1940s, culminating in the formation of Pakistan in 1947. The document continued to reshape the political contours of the Indian Subcontinent in the second half of the twentieth century. The Awami League, formed to challenge the domination of the Muslim League and to champion the rights of the Bengali population, drew its theoretical justifications along similar lines, emphasizing the nature of sovereignty and the use of plurality mentioned in the Lahore Resolution while articulating demands for Bangladesh, which would achieve independence in 1971. In this way, the Lahore Resolution was a significant milestone in the creation of Muslim homelands in South Asia.

Context

The Lahore Resolution was drafted following a meeting between the viceroy of India, Victor Alexander John Hope, 2nd Marquis of Linlithgow, and Mohammed Ali Jinnah, the most significant leader of the Muslim community and the architect of the future Pakistan. On February 6, 1940, Linlithgow told Jinnah that British sympathy for the Muslim League should not be expected for "a party whose policy was one of sheer negation," making it essential to produce a "constructive policy" (Sarkar, p. 379). The British government wanted to counter the Congress Party's claim to represent all communities of the nation, including the Muslim League. The Congress Party, the largest nationalist party in India, had performed extremely well in the 1937 elections, winning 711 of 1,585 provincial assembly seats; by 1938 it had come to power in eight provinces of British India. Compared with the Congress Party's results, the Muslim League's performance was dismal.

Just as the British government wanted to counter the power of the INC, the Muslim League under Jinnah was striving to consolidate its authority over the Muslim community. In Bengal the Muslim League supported the Krishak Praja Party, headed by Fazlul Huq, and formed the only ministry after the 1937 election. The Congress Party formed the government in the North-West Frontier Province and in Punjab; another crucial Muslim majority province that included a large part of the future Pakistan was won by the Unionist Party under the leadership of Sikandar Hayat Khan. The Muslim League, however, had a formidable presence among Muslim minorities in the United Provinces, Bombay, and Madras, but the leadership was fragmented and rife with factional feuding. Its politicians lacked a clear program.

During the period of 1937–1940, oppression of Muslim minorities continued in the provinces ruled by the INC. This situation necessitated that Muslims consolidate their grievances and demands and voice their concerns for specific constitutional arrangements for the Muslim community. Jinnah, through his mass contact program and by bringing together religion and politics (something he had always opposed in earlier decades), improved the Muslim League's image and successfully championed it as a victim of Congress Party politics. Communal dissensions took center

1880s

■ Syed Ahmed Khan propagates the "two-nation theory," demanding safeguards for the Muslim community for administrative and political benefits.

1930

■ **December 29**
The poet Muhammad Iqbal, in a speech at the twenty-first session of the All India Muslim League, argues for the creation of a specified Muslim territory.

1940

■ **March 23**
The Lahore Resolution is moved in the annual session of the All India Muslim League at Lahore, demanding the territorial readjustments of Muslim-majority areas to constitute autonomous and sovereign independent states.

■ **August 8**
Viceroy Linlithgow makes a statement known as the August Offer, rejecting dominion status for India.

1944

■ Talks between Jinnah and the Indian leader Mohandas Gandhi fail to produce a plan for a unified India.

stage, and right-wing majoritarian politics cast a dark shadow over the secular Congress Party's provincial administration. The growing anxieties among the Muslim community gave way to the demand that future constitutional considerations should focus on meeting community demands.

In this situation, on September 3, 1939, Viceroy Linlithgow, without consulting the provincial ministries or Indian leaders, announced India's assistance to Britain in World War II. The Congress Party's hostility to Fascism was well known, but the INC also wanted assurance of a postwar constituent assembly to determine the political structure of a free India and the immediate formation of a genuine, responsible government. Instead of providing any concrete promise, the viceroy reiterated his old offer of dominion status, with an indefinite future and a vague modification of the 1935 Government of India Act but no plan for a democratically elected constituent assembly. On October 17, 1939, Linlithgow reiterated that the British government would not hand over the country "to any system of government whose authority is directly denied by large and powerful elements in India's national life" (Sarkar, p. 377). Linlithgow's statement provided the much-awaited opportunity for Jinnah and the Muslim League to represent the Muslim community and to demand equal status in future constitutional processes.

At this historical juncture different schemes were already in circulation articulating the Muslim community's aspirations, and the Lahore Resolution may be viewed as a crystallization of such grievances. In 1930, in his presidential address to the twenty-first session of the Muslim League, the famous poet Muhammad Iqbal had emphasized the need to carve out a "North West Indian Muslim state" on the presumption that "the life of Islam as a cultural force" and "development of the Shariat" (the body of doctrines that regulate the lives of those who profess Islam) depended upon the formation of "one or more Muslim states with absolute majorities" (Hasan, p. 91). However, the context of his speech leaves little doubt that this legendry Urdu poet and patriot was not visualizing a partition but merely a reorganization of Muslim-majority areas in the northwest into an autonomous unit within a weak Indian federation. Three years later the Muslim nationalist Choudhary Rahmat Ali and his group of Punjabi students in Cambridge launched the idea of a separate Muslim federation to be coequal with the federation of India. This federation he saw as a precondition for the preservation of an Islamic way of life. In two pamphlets published in 1933 and 1935, in which Rahmat Ali wrote about the formation of a Muslim nation, he coined the name *Pakistan*, picking up letters and phonetic threads from the names of five northern units of India: Punjab, Afghania (the North-West Frontier Province), Kashmir, Sind, and Baluchistan. The idea of Rahmat Ali's Pakistan was dismissed, however, as impractical. It was revived after 1937 when the Muslim League was searching for a way to consolidate and to articulate the demand for a weak center, as a 1937 Congress Party victory led to the real fear of a strong, Hindu-dominated central government.

Several proposals were floated in 1938–1939, suggesting different models of alignments of Muslim-majority and Muslim-minority provinces. The Aligarh scheme of the philosophers Syed Zafarul Hasan and Afzal Hussain Qadri advocated four independent states of Pakistan, Bengal, Hyderabad, and Hindustan. Sikandar Hayat Khan, a British Indian politician from the Punjab, had argued for a three-tier formula with autonomous provinces clubbed into seven regions armed with their own regional legislatures and linked through a loose confederation with a center responsible only for defense, external affairs, customs, and currency.

In 1939 the British government, in an effort to curtail Congress Party power, was toying with the idea of reviving the scheme of Rahmat Ali. However, earlier plans of the 1930s lacked broad vision, an openness to accommodate varied interpretations to cater to different political interests within the Muslim community, the backing of a consolidated Muslim League, and, most significantly, patronage by a British government eager to gain internal support in the context of World War II. These specific political developments of the 1930s had a longer historical context of separatism and communalism, the roots of which went back to revivalist and reformist initiatives among the Muslim and Hindu communities in the late nineteenth century. Since then the idea of a two-nation theory had gained currency among people. The theory was based on a presumption that Hindus and Muslims constitute two distinct social and cultural categories. The two-nation theory is attributed to the Indian educator and Islamic reformist Syed Ahmed Khan, who in the 1880s had asked Muslims to dissociate themselves from the INC and claimed recognition for the Muslim community on the basis of their political importance rather than their numbers. Hence the British government saw the need to safeguard Muslims as a minority community.

The Lahore Resolution is based on a brief given to the constitutional subcommittee by the Muslim League Working Committee following a marathon four-day meeting on February 3–6, 1940. Earlier, in March 1939, following Linlithgow's positive indications to Jinnah, the Muslim League had appointed a special committee to explore various circulating schemes with a common thread—an assertion that Indian Muslims, despite their differences, constituted a nation in themselves. Sikandar Hayat Khan was appointed as a prominent member of this committee. He had also advocated his scheme of federations linked loosely together. In his groupings of provinces armed with regional legislatures responding to common subjects, Punjab was to dominate the northwestern bloc (which would include Sind, the North-West Frontier Province, and Baluchistan). In this plan Muslim-majority provinces were to form two independent dominions in direct association with Great Britain. Components of each zone were to be autonomous units. This Punjab thesis was perhaps the most powerful influence in the making of the Lahore Resolution. However, Sikandar Hayat Khan later denied that the resolution was based on his draft.

In the 1937 election Sikandar Hayat Khan had vociferously opposed Jinnah and kept him away from Punjab. Even in the postelection phase, when Sikandar Hayat Khan agreed to join hands with the struggling Jinnah, the terms of collaboration were determined by Khan and not by Jinnah. However,

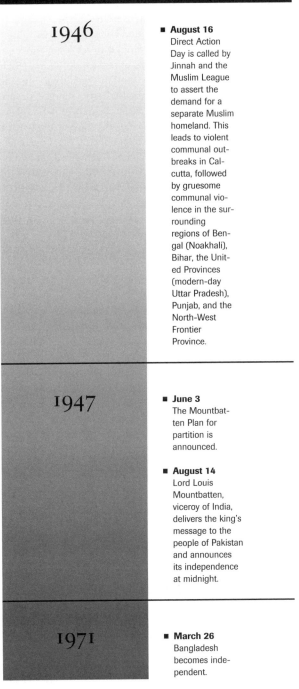

Time Line

1946

■ **August 16**
Direct Action Day is called by Jinnah and the Muslim League to assert the demand for a separate Muslim homeland. This leads to violent communal outbreaks in Calcutta, followed by gruesome communal violence in the surrounding regions of Bengal (Noakhali), Bihar, the United Provinces (modern-day Uttar Pradesh), Punjab, and the North-West Frontier Province.

1947

■ **June 3**
The Mountbatten Plan for partition is announced.

■ **August 14**
Lord Louis Mountbatten, viceroy of India, delivers the king's message to the people of Pakistan and announces its independence at midnight.

1971

■ **March 26**
Bangladesh becomes independent.

two and half years of Congress Party rule and a need to voice Muslim anxieties empowered Jinnah to set the terms for the Working Committee's brief for the Lahore Resolution and also led to Jinnah's growth as the future sole architect of Pakistan.

About the Author

Sikander Hayat Khan (1892–1942) was born to a wealthy landed family. After receiving his education in London, he served in the British military and then became a prominent finance expert in British India. Eventually, in 1933, he was knighted for his service to the Crown. In 1936 he became the leader of the Unionist Party, a Punjab political party that had been formed to represent the concerns of India's Muslims. He entered politics in 1921, when he was elected to the Punjab legislative council. Under his leadership, the Unionist Party emerged victorious in the 1937 election, and he became the chief minister of Punjab. Kahn was a supporter of the Allies during World War II and later became an opponent of the Quit India Movement, a mass struggle of nonviolent resistance and civil disobedience against British rule, instigated by Mohandas Gandhi. Wanting to cooperate with the British, and fearing the partitioning of Punjab, he resisted Jinnah and the Pakistan Movement. He did, however, join with Jinnah in supporting the Lahore Resolution.

Muhammad Ali Jinnah (1876–1948) was the most significant leader of the Muslim community that the Indian Subcontinent ever produced, and although the Lahore Resolution was drafted by Khan, Jinnah's name is the one most closely associated with the formation of Pakistan, and he is considered the architect of that nation. Born in Sind, Jinnah was a lawyer by profession and an advocate of Hindu-Muslim unity in his early life. In 1896 he joined the Indian National Congress and was instrumental in bringing together the Muslim League and the Congress in the Lucknow Pact of 1916—an agreement that established more cordial relations between the two organizations and that urged Britain to adopt a more liberal stance toward India. However, in 1920 he resigned from the Congress in disapproval of the political and spiritual leader Mohandas Gandhi and his noncooperation movement. He quickly emerged as the most prolific and able voice of the Muslim community and eventually its sole spokesman in 1930s and 1940s. He died in 1948, a year after the formation of Pakistan.

Explanation and Analysis of the Document

The Lahore Resolution is considered a watershed in the growth of the idea of Pakistan. Indeed, March 23, the day in 1940 when the resolution was put forward, is celebrated as Pakistan Day. Still, neither Pakistan nor partition is mentioned in the text of the resolution. Historians are divided in their opinions about this omission. For the orthodox school, the Lahore Resolution was the first formal pronouncement of the idea of Pakistan. This declaration was the basis on which Muslim-majority areas in the northwestern and eastern regions of the Indian Subcontinent were separated as sovereign and independent states, and it formed the foundation of the demand for a separate Pakistan. On the other hand, from the revisionist perspective, the Lahore Resolution was meant to be a tactical move and a bargaining chip; thus the emergence of Pakistan, in this view, was an outcome of the developments of the 1940s, and the Lahore Resolution did not reflect any ideo-

logical or religious transformation on the part of Jinnah but merely a significant shift in terms of his strategies.

◆ Paragraph 1

The first paragraph of the resolution clearly and unambiguously rejects the federal scheme of the Government of India Act of 1935. The act was a constitutional measure that provided for the establishment of a federation of India that consisted of both British-ruled provinces and princely states (areas directly governed by native rulers under the auspices of the British Crown), introduced direct elections, and established a provincial diarchy with certain areas placed under provincially elected ministers. The act expanded the franchise from seven million to nearly thirty-five million and gave a large measure of self-government to the provinces; some amount of decision-making power was provided to Indians in various departments. However, the democratic potential of the act was severely blunted by safeguards enabling the British government to intervene in the functioning of ministries through provincial governors and the viceroy.

There is no mention of dominion status for India; the document rejects "the scheme of federation embodied in the Government of India Act 1935." Provinces were to gain autonomy after the election, but the federation was to come into effect only after one-half of the Indian states, on the basis of population, agreed to accede. To safeguard Muslim interests, in this scheme, it was important that either the British should provide some privilege to Muslims or the Muslim community should demonstrate cohesiveness and unity. The results of the 1937 election enhanced the fear of a numerically powerful Congress Party and fractured representation from the Muslim community. In this context a weak Muslim community implied that Muslims would be unable to dominate in the Muslim majority provinces such as Punjab, Sind, and the North-Western Frontier Province. This perceived threat of non-Muslim domination, casting a shadow over Muslim majority provinces, led to the emergence of various plans and finally to the Lahore Resolution. The sense of fear was further augmented by the propaganda machinery of the Muslim League, which equated Congress rule with Hindu majoritarian rule.

◆ Paragraph 2

The second paragraph asserts the desire of the Muslim community for reconsideration of the whole constitutional plan afresh after due consultation with the Muslim community and with their approval and consent. By asserting this aspiration, the Muslim League and Jinnah successfully argued for the Muslim League to be accepted as the sole representative of Muslims. Linlithgow and the British government equally supported Jinnah in achieving this status by recognizing the Muslim League as a crucial player in all subsequent talks regarding the future of the Indian Subcontinent. The August Offer of 1940 marked a move in this direction; the key component of this proposal from the British government was that no constitutional change would be made in India without the support and agreement of both the provinces and the nation's social elements—that is, Muslims. Although a wartime government did not make any fresh commitment to Indian leaders, it suggested that the transfer of power would not be made to a government that important elements of India's national life did not support.

This effectively meant that any future negotiation for dominion status for India or for the transfer of power from Britain to Indian subjects required approval of the Muslim League. The Muslim League was in the complete control of Jinnah. Hence Jinnah's consent became a prerequisite for the success of any dialogue between India and Britain. Jinnah quite tactfully used this enhanced power to create deadlocks at crucial junctures throughout the decade of 1940s. For example, he was an opponent of the outcome of the Shimla Conference of 1945, an agreement between Britain and India's major political leaders for Indian self-governance. Likewise, he opposed the Cabinet Mission Plan of 1946, which laid the foundation for transference of power from Britain to India.

◆ Paragraph 3

The core of the resolution stipulates territorial autonomy. The units are visualized as autonomous and sovereign independent states. It was this section of the resolution, in particular, that inflamed the popular aspiration of the Muslim community for a Muslim homeland not dominated by non-Muslims. This demand for sovereign and independent states along with a constitution (as pointed out in paragraphs 2 and 4) was a response to Viceroy Linlithgow's insistence that the Muslim League should not embrace a policy of mere negation but that it should also come up with a constructive alternative. This was also a ploy for the Muslim League to win the popular sentiments of the Muslim-majority provinces, particularly in Punjab and Bengal, where the league's position was quite weak.

◆ Paragraph 4

The question of Muslims from minority provinces is addressed only in the fourth paragraph. This was the group that had most felt the brunt of communalism. The status of Muslims in Muslim-majority provinces (West Punjab, Sind, North-West Frontier Province, and East Bengal) was quite different from that in provinces where Muslims formed the minority. Most of the Lahore Resolution was concerned with the rights of the Muslim community where they constituted the majority. The fourth paragraph is crucial in that it not only talks about safeguarding the rights of Muslims in provinces where they were in the minority but also broadened the discussion by addressing the rights of minorities within Muslim-majority provinces. In this sense, the resolution theoretically made space to champion the rights of minorities across the Indian Subcontinent.

Articulated in the spirit of vagueness, a constitution not merely for the Muslims but for "other minorities" was proposed in consultation with them. A whole range of rights and interests (religious, cultural, economic, political, and

Men sell drinking water in front of the monument in Lahore honoring the resolution to create Pakistan.
(AP/Wide World Photos)

administrative) are called out for protection. Like the category of "other minorities," a reference to "other rights and interests" is included, leaving fertile ground for popular imagination and diplomatic maneuverings in the future. Also of note is that as in paragraph 3 (which refers to "states" rather than a "state") paragraph 4 (which refers to "other minorities") has a clearly pluralist dimension, an element that was downplayed by the Muslim League and Jinnah in later years.

◆ Paragraph 5

The concluding paragraph proposes the framing of a constitution to achieve the sovereign character referred to in earlier paragraphs. It authorized the Working Committee to frame this constitution. The final words enlist such departments as defense, external affairs, communications, and customs. These were kept by the British in the Government of India Act of 1935, leaving little doubt about the ambitious demands that the resolution made on the British government. These unrealistic demands were likely included to enhance the image of the Muslim League among Muslims as well as to provide elbow room for Jinnah in dealing with British government, an opportunity that he utilized in a manner unheard of for any single person in the history of the Muslim community.

Audience

The Lahore Resolution was aimed at addressing three different collectivities: the Muslim League, the INC, and the wartime British government. Under Jinnah's leadership the Muslim League's membership increased from a few thousand to several hundred thousand in 1937–1938. However, the leadership of the league was fractured along provincial lines. Many influential leaders, including Jinnah, were collaborating with the INC on the implementation of the 1935 Government of India Act. When Raja Mahmudabad from the United Provinces, an important voice from the community, joined the INC in 1936, he stated that the party and the league "were like two parts of the same army fighting a common enemy [the British government] on two fronts" (Hasan, p. 9). However, the Congress Party's success in the 1937 election had alarmed Jinnah. In the election of 1937 the popular mandate was either in favor of the Congress Party or in favor of provincial parties representing Muslim interests in Muslim-majority provinces. The Muslim League had obtained only 4.8 percent of the Muslim vote and won only forty-three of 272 Muslim seats in the Muslim-majority areas. In this situation, the Muslim League adopted the Lahore Resolution, hoping to unite the Muslim community by crystallizing already circulating ideas of Pakistan as a panacea for all social and personal ills.

The second target audience was the INC. The INC had always claimed to be representative of all the communities of India—majority and minorities alike. A sizable portion of the Muslim leadership and the Muslim masses was in the Congress Party's fold. It had consistently refuted the two-nation theory by rejecting the idea that Muslims formed a homogeneous social group. Instead, it emphasized the strength and historical realities of a composite Indian culture. The Muslim League challenged this claim of the INC, branding it an organization of Hindus that championed majoritarian agendas and ideas.

The third audience was the British government. The viceroy wanted Jinnah to come up with a constructive alternative to the 1935 act. A belligerent government needed support from the Indian corner and was willing to give some promises to the Muslim League in order to thwart the threat of a strong Congress Party. In this context, Jinnah found ample opportunity to present himself to the British government as the sole voice of a numerically small but formidable social community of Muslims. Jinnah, though, had little backing in the Muslim-majority provinces, but Muslims of other states (where they held minority status) were looking to the Muslim League and its leader to protect and represent their political concerns. The provincial leadership in Muslim-majority provinces, such as Bengal and Punjab, also saw in Jinnah a leader who could represent

provincial demands at a central level. In this way, though the 1940 resolution voiced the demands of Muslims from majoritarian provinces, it aimed at addressing a pan-Indian Muslim community.

Impact

In February 1941 Jinnah emphasized among the public and the media that the word *Pakistan* was synonymous with the Lahore Resolution. Very cleverly, without confirming this equation, he said that he had no objection to it. Similarly, the obscure nature of the demarcation of territories, their mutual relationship, and future constitutional arrangements were ambitiously meant to satisfy different schemes of the idea of Pakistan that were floated at the time of the Lahore Resolution. Any precise resolution would have fallen short of the popular imagination of the Muslim community and might have led to fissures within the league instead of consolidating it from within. However, the resolution acquired enormous popularity in a short time, and in this sense it not only provided the Muslim League Working Committee with a framework for future activities but also gave clear direction to secessionist tendencies prevalent within the Muslim community. Many Muslim politicians were unhappy about the Lahore Resolution. For Allah Bakhsh Gabol, the erstwhile premier of Sind, it was "harmful and fanatic." Sikandar Hayat Khan quickly distanced himself from the resolution and disputed that it was based on his scheme. Fazlul Huq also soon attacked Jinnah for preaching separatism and was ousted from the league in December 1941. The line between communal aspirations and the separatist agenda among Muslims of South Asia became clearer and finally led to the partition and the creation of Pakistan.

The Lahore Resolution permanently altered the political complexion of the Indian Subcontinent. Its impact can be assessed broadly in two interrelated matters: impetus in the growth of political power of the Muslim League and, more specifically, of Jinnah and the development of a separatist consciousness among Muslims at a national level, leading to the formation of Pakistan. In the rapid progression of provincial politics, Jinnah and the Muslim League acquired a strong foothold in Muslim-majority provinces, in both Punjab and Bengal. In its June 1940 Working Committee Resolution, the Muslim League authorized Jinnah alone to negotiate with the viceroy or the INC, and his consent became necessary for league members to accept membership on war committees. This power was utilized by Jinnah to strengthen his stature in the organization. In August 1940 he received another boost when the viceroy in his August Offer gave Muslims a veto on any constitutional scheme of the future. This affirmation provided political validity to the two-nation theory that Jinnah had quite effectively used throughout the 1940s.

In February 1944 Jinnah demanded the framing of a new constitution and the division of India into two sovereign nations, Pakistan and Hindustan, with the British managing defense and foreign affairs during a transitional phase of

> "This session of the All India Muslim League emphatically reiterates that the scheme of federation embodied in the Government of India Act 1935 is totally unsuited to and unworkable in the peculiar conditions of this country and is altogether unacceptable to Muslim India."
>
> (Paragraph 1)

> "Geographically contiguous units are demarcated into regions which should be constituted with such territorial readjustments as may be necessary, that the areas in which the Muslims are numerically in a majority as in the North Western and Eastern Zones of (British) India should be grouped to constitute 'independent states' in which the constituent units should be autonomous and sovereign."
>
> (Paragraph 3)

adjustment. In September 1944 talks between Jinnah and Gandhi failed, shattering the hope of a unified future. At the Shimla Conference in June 1945, Jinnah called for parity among Hindus and Muslims in the viceroy's executive council and was adamant that all Muslim members be Muslim League nominees, thereby rejecting the INC's claim to be a party of all social communities of the nation. Through these diplomatic standoffs, the Muslim League successfully transformed itself as a national voice of Muslims, and the dividend came in the form of its spectacular success in the 1946 election, in which the league garnered 86.6 percent of the Muslim vote and 442 of 509 Muslim seats in the provinces. This success gave Jinnah additional confidence, and he rejected the Cabinet Mission Plan of 1946 for the transfer of power from British to Indian subjects. On August 16, 1946, he urged Muslims to take direct action to create a Pakistani state. The day started a prolonged and bloody conflict on the Indian Subcontinent. Finally, by a plan termed the Mountbatten Plan (after the viceroy Lord Louis Mountbatten, who proposed it), which was announced on June 3, 1947, and implemented at midnight on August 15, 1947, two central governments, India and Pakistan, gained independence.

Further Reading

■ Articles

Jalal, Ayesha, and Anil Seal. "Alternative to Partition: Muslim Politics between the Wars." *Modern Asian Studies* 15, no. 3 (July 1981): 415–454.

Moore, R. J. "Jinnah and the Pakistan Demand." *Modern Asian Studies* 17, no. 4 (October 1983): 529–561.

Roy, Asim. "The High Politics of India's Partition: The Revisionist Perspective." *Modern Asian Studies* 24, no. 2 (May 1990): 385–408.

■ Books

Aziz, Kursheed K. *A History of the Idea of Pakistan*. Lahore: Vanguard Books, 1987.

Bose, Sugata, and Ayesha Jalal. *Modern South Asia: History, Culture, Political Economy*, 2nd ed. New York: Routledge, 2004.

Hasan, Mushirul, ed. *India's Partition: Process, Strategy, and Mobilization*. Delhi, India: Oxford University Press, 1993.

Jalal, Ayesha. *The Sole Spokesman: Jinnah, the Muslim League, and the Demand for Pakistan*. Cambridge, U.K.: Cambridge University Press, 1985.

Sarkar, Sumit. *Modern India, 1885–1947*. New York: St. Martin's Press, 1989.

Singh, Anita Inder. *The Origins of the Partition of India, 1936–1947*. Oxford, U.K.: Oxford University Press, 1990.

Talbot, Ian. *Pakistan: A Modern History*. New York: Palgrave Macmillan, 2005.

■ **Web Sites**

Hussain, M. T. "Lahore Resolution Outlined Bangladesh's Separate Entity." New Nation Web site.
　http://nation.ittefaq.com/issues/2008/03/23/news0835.htm.

"The Pakistan Movement: 1940–1947." Story of Pakistan Web site.
　http://www.storyofpakistan.com/timeline06.htm.

"Pakistan Resolution Day." Jang Group Online Editions Web site.
　http://www.jang.com.pk/thenews/spedition/23march2007/index.html.

Pania, Pravan. "The Lahore Resolution." South Asia Analysis Group Web site.
　http://www.southasiaanalysis.org/%5Cpapers15%5Cpaper1497.html.

—Sadan Jha

Questions for Further Study

1. How sympathetic do you believe the Muslim League and its representatives would have been to Osama bin Laden's Declaration of Jihad against Americans? Explain your reasoning.

2. In many, if not most, nations throughout the world any particular religious group could be a "minority" group within the nation. Why, though, was minority status so particularly troublesome to Indian Muslims during this period?

3. Using this document and the events surrounding the Indian Declaration of Independence, prepare a time line of the ten most important events giving rise to the nation of Pakistan. Be prepared to justify your choices.

4. Explain the source of the tension between Mohammed Ali Jinnah and Sikandar Hayat Khan. How did this tension play out? Specifically, how did it contribute to the course of events that led to the creation of Pakistan?

5. Do you believe that the separatism of Indian Muslims during this era contributed in any way to the development of Islamic extremism, such as that reflected in Osama bin Laden's Declaration of Jihad against Americans or the Palestinian National Charter? Why or why not?

LAHORE RESOLUTION

While approving and endorsing the action taken by the Council and the Working Committee of the All India Muslim League, as indicated in their resolutions dated the 27th of August, 17th & 18th of September and 22nd of October, 1939, and the 3rd of February, 1940 on the constitutional issue, this session of the All India Muslim League emphatically reiterates that the scheme of federation embodied in the Government of India Act 1935 is totally unsuited to and unworkable in the peculiar conditions of this country and is altogether unacceptable to Muslim India.

It further records its emphatic view that while the declaration dated the 18th of October, 1939 made by the Viceroy on behalf of His Majesty's Government is reassuring in so far as it declares that the policy and plan on which the Government of India Act, 1935, is based will be reconsidered in consultation with various parties, interests and communities in India, Muslims in India will not be satisfied unless the whole constitutional plan is reconsidered de novo and that no revised plan would be acceptable to Muslims unless it is framed with their approval and consent.

Resolved that it is the considered view of this Session of the All India Muslim League that no constitutional plan would be workable in this country or acceptable to the Muslims unless it is designed on the following basic principles, viz., that geographically contiguous units are demarcated into regions which should be constituted with such territorial readjustments as may be necessary, that the areas in which the Muslims are numerically in a majority as in the North Western and Eastern Zones of (British) India should be grouped to constitute "independent state" in which the constituent units should be autonomous and sovereign.

That adequate, effective and mandatory safeguards should be specifically provided in the constitution for minorities in these units and in the regions for the protection of their religious, cultural, economic, political, administrative and other rights and interests in consultation with them and in other parts of India where the Muslims are in a minority adequate, effective and mandatory safeguards shall be specifically provided in the constitution for them and other minorities for the protection of their religious, cultural, economic, political, administrative and other rights and interests in consultation with them.

The Session further authorizes the Working Committee to frame a scheme of constitution in accordance with these basic principles, providing for the assumption finally by the respective regions of all powers such as defense, external affairs, communications, customs, and such other matters as may be necessary.

Hideki Tōjō (AP/Wide World Photos)

"The Japanese Government has ... consistently exerted its best efforts to prevent the extension of war-like disturbances."

Overview

The Fourteen-part Message sent by the Japanese government to the United States on December 7, 1941, is rare, if not unique, among historical documents in that it owes its significance to the fact that it was *not* promulgated or published—at least not in a timely fashion. This memo was the means by which Japan broke off negotiations with the United States just as the attack on Pearl Harbor was taking place. Previously, in the summer of 1941, the United States had imposed a series of economic sanctions against Japan in response to the expansion of Japanese aggression in Asia. As a result of these sanctions, Japan's supplies of oil, steel, and aviation fuel had begun to run dangerously low; meanwhile, its financial assets in the United States had been frozen. Consequently, the Japanese cabinet took steps to implement a plan to attack the U.S. naval base at Pearl Harbor, Hawaii, in the belief that this move would allow Japan to seize oil and mineral assets in the Dutch East Indies without interference from American forces.

While it was intended as a prelude to war, the Fourteen-part Message was technically neither a declaration of war nor even a formal cessation of all diplomatic relations. It was notification that the Japanese imperial government felt that "it was impossible to reach an agreement" on peace in the Pacific through further talks. Embarrassingly, the message was delivered by the Japanese ambassador Kichisaburō Nomura to U.S. Secretary of State Cordell Hull an hour after the attack had begun. Moreover, the full content of the message was already known to Secretary Hull, since the U.S. government, thanks to the "Magic" cryptanalysis project, had long been able to intercept, decode, translate, and read Japanese diplomatic correspondence even before the Japanese diplomats themselves. The term *fourteen-part* refers not to the organization of the memo's content but rather to the number of separate telegrams by which the entire message was transmitted. Thus, even as Japanese embassy personnel were copying and translating the fourteen separate pieces of this message, American officials already knew that Japan had terminated diplomatic negotiations and would soon launch an attack—somewhere. The Fourteen-part Message brought an end to months of fruitless diplomacy and marked the escalation of the so-called "China Affair" into a multifront world war.

Context

The road to Pearl Harbor began in 1931, the year Japan initiated a fourteen-year war on the Asian continent and saw its relations with Western powers in the Pacific turn irreparably sour. On September 18, 1931, soldiers attached to Japan's Manchuria-based Kwantung Army staged an explosion on the Southern Manchurian railway and blamed it on Chinese saboteurs. In response to this fabricated emergency situation, Japanese troops occupied major cities along the railway, turning Manchuria into a Japanese possession virtually overnight. China protested the so-called Manchurian Incident, or Mukden Incident, but little was done by the international community to redress the assault on Chinese sovereignty. The League of Nations ordered a commission headed by Lord Victor Bulwer-Lytton of Great Britain to investigate and report on the situation. Not surprisingly, the Lytton Commission condemned Japan's actions and insisted that Japan withdraw its forces from the newly occupied territories. Ignoring both world opinion and the Lytton Commission, Japan created a puppet kingdom in Manchuria and withdrew its delegation from the League of Nations. The success of these operations brought the Japanese military great prestige at home. By the mid-1930s, militarists had taken control of the government and were using the rhetoric of expansion as a means of defining Japanese patriotism.

In July 1937 another crisis involving the Kwantung Army erupted when a Japanese soldier went missing during an exercise near Beijing's Marco Polo Bridge. Believing that the man had been killed or captured by the Chinese, Japanese officers ordered an armed search of the area. When local Chinese troops resisted, the Japanese responded by sending in combat units, and within several weeks Japan had occupied the cities of Beijing and Tianjin. Abandoning the existing policy of nonconfrontation, General Chiang Kai-shek of the Nationalist Chinese government ordered a general army mobilization that included attacks on Japan-

1931

■ **September**
The Japanese Kwantung Army stages an explosion on the Southern Manchurian railway and blames it on the Chinese—an act that becomes known as the "Manchurian Incident," which leads directly to Japanese seizure of Manchuria.

1932

■ **March**
The Japanese puppet state of Manchukuo is formed in Manchuria.

1933

■ **March**
After formal condemnation of its actions in Manchuria, the Japanese delegation withdraws from the League of Nations.

1936

■ **February**
A group of Japanese army officers attempt to take over the government. Although the insurrectionists are killed, the influence of the military in Japanese politics continues to grow.

1937

■ **July**
Japanese troops skirmish with Chinese troops near Beijing in what becomes known as the Marco Polo Bridge Incident. The Nationalist Chinese government responds with a nationwide mobilization.

ese forces near Shanghai. Infuriated by these counterattacks, Japan retaliated by sending a punitive force of nearly 200,000 men into China.

In August 1937 Japanese aircraft bombed Shanghai, while amphibious forces launched an assault that would deliver the city into Japanese hands three months later. From Shanghai, Japanese troops marched up the Chang River (also known as the Yangtze River) and ravaged the capital of Nanjing in one of the greatest atrocities in military history. The "Rape of Nanjing" in December 1937 resulted in 260,000 civilian casualties and over 20,000 rapes. From 1938 on, the China Affair became a quagmire for the Japanese army. In pursuit of the vague goal of pacifying a defiant Chinese population, the Japanese government poured more troops and resources into the unwinnable conflict. Then, in an effort to manage the expanding war, the Japanese cabinet took steps toward total mobilization, establishing new policies of state control at home and abroad. The Greater East Asia Co-Prosperity Sphere, officially announced by Foreign Minister Yōsuke Matsuoka in 1940, was a political and economic organization that sought to draw the economies of Taiwan, Manchuria, Korea, and the Japanese-controlled parts of China into an integrated commonwealth. The "New Domestic Order" was a quasi-Fascist program that channeled Japan's productive and "spiritual" capacity toward the elusive goal of victory in China. As resources evaporated, military planners abandoned their long-term strategy of expansion through northern Asia and shifted their focus to the south. The new thinking, promoted mostly by the navy, held that a strike on the oil-rich Dutch East Indies (Indonesia) would have a decisive impact on the war and bring the China Affair to a quicker close.

Growing ever-more alienated from the United States and Great Britain, Japan entered into an alliance, known as the Tripartite Pact or Tripartite Axis, with Nazi Germany and Fascist Italy in 1940. Membership in the Tripartite Axis provided Japan with the opportunity to establish bases in the northern part of French Indochina (Vietnam), which after May 1940 was controlled by the pro-Nazi Vichy French government. One year later, Japanese troops occupied the southern part of Indochina, a move that drew an especially angry response from the United States. The U.S. government had long been opposed to Japanese expansion in Asia and despite its neutrality had provided limited support to the Chinese government.

In the so-called Quarantine Speech of 1937, President Franklin Delano Roosevelt referred to "an epidemic of world lawlessness" and called for the world's peace-loving nations to contain the nations that were practicing "international aggression" (http://millercenter.org/scripps/archive/speeches/detail/3310). In 1938 the State Department urged U.S. arms and aircraft manufacturers to impose a "moral embargo" against Japan (U.S. Department of State, p. 89). In 1939 the United States abrogated its 1911 commercial treaty with Japan, a move followed in 1940 by restrictions on exports of aviation fuel, scrap iron, and steel. Finally, in 1941, after Japan's occupation of southern Indochina, the U.S. government froze Japanese assets in America and canceled all shipments of oil. In coordination with these steps, the United States entered into the ABCD (American, Britain, Chinese, and Dutch) Agreement, a pledge of mutual military support that could be invoked by any member in response to Japanese aggression.

Throughout the summer of 1941, Prime Minister Fumimaro Konoe pledged to keep Japan out of war with the United States and tried to arrange a personal meeting with President Roosevelt. In September a select group of Japanese cabinet members met with the emperor and decided that Japan would go to war if negotiations with the United States were to break down. In October, after his request for a presidential conference had been refused, Konoe resigned and was succeeded as prime minister by General Hideki Tōjō.

The month of November 1941 witnessed the final unraveling of negotiations prior to Pearl Harbor. Perhaps diplomats on both sides had still actually wanted peace, but given the inflexibility of both nations' positions, further talks were doomed. The Japanese position was that the China Affair had to be resolved. The war in China had to be won before any new agreements could be made, and therefore Japan needed the resources that would have allowed closure in that conflict. The Japanese maintained that America's sanctions and support of China stood in the way of this goal. The American position was that Japan needed to pull out of China immediately and renounce the Tripartite Pact before any trade could be resumed.

To break the deadlock, Japan offered two proposals: Plan A, which suggested that Japan keep forces in China for a "certain required period of time" (Iriye, p. 39), and Plan B, which suggested that Japan remove its troops from southern Indochina. Both plans additionally called for free trade in the Pacific and mutual efforts for the preservation of peace, which directly implied that the United States should stop assisting China and help Japan acquire oil. In response to these proposals, the United States considered a modus vivendi, a provisional agreement designed to preserve peace in the short term. The core of the modus vivendi was limited resumption of oil shipments to Japan in order to avert hostilities. Officials at the War Department believed that America should offer the modus vivendi, if only to buy preparation time. What blocked the modus vivendi was British Prime Minister Winston Churchill's suggestion to President Roosevelt that China had been ignored in the deliberations and its interests should not be sacrificed for the convenience of the United States.

To the shock of Ambassador Kichisaburō Nomura and Special Envoy Saburō Kurusu, the Japanese diplomats in Washington, D.C., Secretary Hull responded to Japan's proposals on November 26, 1941, with the most uncompromising American statement yet. The so-called Hull note demanded the removal of all Japanese military forces not only from Indochina but also from China. Hull also called for Japan to repudiate its alliance with Germany and Italy. This insistence, essentially, on a return to the status quo before 1937 was practically impossible for Japan, since it would have completely nullified the Greater East Asia Co-

Time Line

1937

- **August**
  Japanese forces conquer Shanghai after subjecting the city to aerial bombardment.

- **October**
  President Franklin Delano Roosevelt delivers the famous Quarantine Speech.

- **December**
  Japanese forces perpetrate the "Rape of Nanjing," in which more than 200,000 Chinese civilians are slaughtered; Japanese aircraft sink the USS *Panay* in the Chang (Yangtze) River.

1938

- **November**
  Prime Minister Fumimaro Konoe announces the creation of a New Domestic Order in East Asia.

1939

- **January**
  The United States restricts the sale of aircraft to Japan.

1940

- **September**
  The Tripartite Pact brings Japan into alliance with Germany and Italy; Japan sends its troops into northern Indochina.

1941

- **April**
  Foreign Minister Yōsuke Matsuoka visits Berlin and Moscow; Japan and the Soviet Union sign a treaty of neutrality.

1941

- **July**
  Japanese troops occupy southern Indochina, and the United States responds by freezing Japanese assets.

- **August**
  The United States restricts sales of oil to Japan.

- **September**
  An imperial conference convenes in Tokyo to make plans for going to war with the United States if an agreement on peace in the Pacific cannot be reached.

- **October**
  After having failed to secure peace with the United States, Konoe resigns as prime minister and is replaced by General Hideki Tōjō.

- **November**
  Japanese Plan A and Plan B are presented to the U.S. State Department by Ambassador Kichisaburō Nomura and Special Envoy Saburō Kurusu. A modus vivendi that would have allowed the resumption of oil shipments to Japan is scrapped by the State Department in favor of the proposals set forth in the Hull note.

- **December**
  An imperial conference decides to proceed with plans to attack Pearl Harbor. The Fourteen-part Message announcing Japan's intentions to break off negotiations is sent to the United States but is not delivered until after the attack on Pearl Harbor has commenced.

Prosperity Sphere and the Tripartite Axis and rendered meaningless Japan's operations in China for the previous four years. The Hull note led directly to Japan's implementation of strike plans, which were finalized at another imperial conference on December 1. The plans were communicated only indirectly to Nomura and Kurusu in a series of cryptic telegrams. Completely unknown to the Japanese embassy in Washington was that American cryptanalysts had broken Japan's diplomatic code, and all message traffic between Tokyo and Washington was being intercepted. Through these communications, the State Department gathered that a heightened sense of urgency had taken over the Japanese Foreign Ministry and that if some agreement were not reached by November 29, certain preplanned operations would proceed automatically. The United States would learn only later that these operations consisted of orders for a carrier task force to steam toward Hawaii and launch an attack on Pearl Harbor. The last transmission decoded prior to the attack was the Fourteen-part Message.

About the Author

The Fourteen-part Message was prepared in Tokyo by the Japanese Foreign Ministry and delivered by Ambassador Kichisaburō Nomura and Special Envoy Saburō Kurusu. Nomura was a retired admiral who had been serving as ambassador to the United States since late 1940. Kurusu was sent to join him in November 1941 in a last-ditch effort to break through the stalled talks with the United States. Unfortunately, Nomura's grasp of English was not up to the task of handling the delicate negotiations, and the more fluent Kurusu arrived too late to have any significant effect on the outcome. Both men claimed ignorance of the Tokyo government's decision for war and thus found themselves in the unenviable position of learning about the attack after it was already known to the White House.

The foreign minister at the time was Shigenori Togo, a career diplomat who had served in Berlin and Moscow. A strident nationalist, Togo was nevertheless apprehensive about the idea of going to war with the United States. By the time he took office in October 1941, prospects for peace were vanishing, and he was powerless to affect the diplomatic situation in any way. As a member of the Supreme Council for the Direction of the War (an inner group of advisers that included the prime minister, foreign minister, ministers of the army and navy, and chiefs of staff of the army and navy), Togo had expressed his hopes for peace. However, in the final weeks before the Pearl Harbor attack, he came to concur with the council that the United States was attempting to thwart the Greater East Asia Co-Prosperity Sphere and that compliance with the Hull note's demands would be impossible. Togo resigned from the cabinet in 1942 but was brought back into service near the end of the war in the hope that he could help secure favorable terms from the Allies. Because he was considered a perpetrator of the Pearl Harbor attack, he was sentenced to prison as a Class-A war criminal. He died in prison in 1950.

Explanation and Analysis of the Document

Perhaps the most the striking feature of the Fourteen-part Message is that it conceals its purpose until the very last line. As already noted, it is not really a fourteen-*part* message with respect to content, but rather a fourteen-*piece* message with respect to the mechanics of encoding and transmission. The message actually contains seven major parts, the third and fourth of which each have five sections.

◆ Parts I and II

Part I is unremarkable, consisting of diplomatic verbiage in which the Japanese government summarizes the negotiations of the previous eight months and asserts its sincerity in having tried to preserve peace in the Pacific. Part II addresses Japan's long-range geopolitical goal, the enabling of "all nations to find each its proper place in the world," as well as the more immediate concern of resolving the China Affair. Japan evades responsibility for the affair, asserting that hostilities broke out only because of China's "failure … to comprehend Japan's true intentions." Although these intentions are not specified, the reader is to understand that they relate to the preservation of peace. Japan indicates that it entered into the Tripartite Pact with Germany and Italy only for the purpose of preserving peace. Japan accuses the United States and Great Britain of interfering with national self-determination in Asia and threatening peace in China by "menacing" Indochina and unduly pressuring the Dutch East Indies. The tension in the Pacific is thus blamed on the Western powers for "encircling" Japan with military threats. Japan reminds the United States that its government, in the interest of defusing tensions in the region, had proposed a meeting between Prime Minister Konoe and President Roosevelt, which the United States had refused to consider until certain conditions had been met. These conditions meant Japan's compliance with the four principles that Secretary Hull had articulated as central to any diplomatic discussion: respect for territorial integrity, noninterference with the affairs of any state, equal commercial opportunity, and the use of peaceful rather than military means to change the balance of power in the Pacific.

◆ Part III

In Part III, Japan charges the United States with having "failed to display in the slightest degree a spirit of conciliation" when it had received Japan's proposals to address U.S. demands. This statement refers to Prime Minister Konoe's late-inning offer in September 1941 to consider some troop withdrawals from China. Moreover, this paragraph claims that the United States also rejected the more specific proposals, Plans A and B, which Japan had provided in November. The substance of Plans A and B are condensed into Sections 1 through 5 of Part III.

Section 1 enjoins both nations not to send armed forces into any Pacific region except Indochina. While this would have constituted a pledge to keep the region demilitarized, it still would have allowed Japan the right to keep troops in Indochina. Section 2 asks the United States not thwart

Cordell Hull (Library of Congress)

Japan's ability to obtain oil from the Dutch East Indies. Had the United States agreed to this request, it would have had to repudiate the ABCD Agreement, which had placed the United States, Great Britain, and the Netherlands in military alliance with the Chinese Nationalist government. Section 3 insists that the United States lift the freeze on Japanese assets. Section 4 is a catch-all demand exhorting the United States to mind its own business, especially with respect to China. As long as America supported China, Japan's ability to resolve the China Affair was frustrated.

In Section 5, Japan offers to withdraw troops from southern Indochina immediately as well as to withdraw from Indochina entirely once the China Affair was settled. While the offer promises to move troops out of Indochina and pledges not to deploy any more troops in Asia, no concrete proposals concerning the withdrawal of troops from China are put forth. This would continue to be the sticking point for the United States. The message then clearly refers to the Hull note of November 26, stating that the United States had all but ignored Japan's proposals before responding with what the imperial government regarded as an ultimatum to vacate China.

◆ Part IV

Part IV, aside from beginning with the assertion that Japan has "maintained an attitude of fairness and moderation" in negotiations, deals with the complex matter of international commerce. Japan takes the United States to task for having professed to promote "non-discrimination

*The USS Shaw **explodes after being hit by bombs during the Japanese surprise attack on Pearl Harbor.*** (AP/Wide World Photos)

in international commerce," even as it engaged in openly discriminatory trade practices. What was really at issue was U.S. opposition to the Greater East Asia Co-Prosperity Sphere, which would have excluded Western traders from Japan's colonies. Japan argues that America's own trade agreements, to say nothing of its tacit support for British and Dutch imperialism in the Pacific, violated those principles of free trade that it claimed to honor. The desire to abolish Western imperialism in the Pacific, especially in relation to unfair trade practices, may have been Japan's only legitimate rationale for opposing the Western powers that had signed the ABCD Agreement. Unfortunately, that point failed to stand out against the rest of Japanese rhetoric justifying open aggression in China.

The final paragraph of Part IV introduces a litany of grievances against the United States. Japan blames America in general for a lack of good faith in the negotiating process and specifically for its adherence to old notions of "collective security" and failure to understand new diplomatic realities in East Asia; its assistance of a third party, Great Britain, in a war against Germany, while at the same time condemning Japan for its alliance with a third party, namely Germany; its use of economic pressure as a substitute for military action; its support of outdated imperialist

practices that denied each nation "its proper place in the world"; and its pretense of desiring peace in China even as it worked to thwart Japan's efforts to restore peace. All but the last of these grievances may have had some validity. The United States had embraced the modern ideal of regional security through treaty diplomacy. It had declared its support for the British, it had been using economic sanctions against Japan, and it had continued to openly support the historical infrastructure of Western imperialism. This Japanese argument against Western imperialism might have gained some traction if its validity had not been undermined by the fact that Japanese colonial administration was as oppressive as its Western counterparts—and in almost every case much more so.

◆ Parts V–VII

Part V raises the real concern that an immediate withdrawal from China would have been an acute blow to Japanese prestige and would have negated the struggles of the previous four years. Secretary Hull's demand for complete withdrawal from China was simply impossible to accept. Part VI recognizes that the other ABCD powers were in agreement with the United States, which gave the appearance of a military alliance. Part VII brings us to the

"*Ever since the China Affair broke out owing to the failure on the part of China to comprehend Japan's true intentions, the Japanese Government has striven for the restoration of peace and it has consistently exerted its best efforts to prevent the extension of war-like disturbances.*"

(Part II)

"*The American Government, obsessed with its own views and opinions, may be said to be scheming for the extension of the war.*"

(Part IV, Section 2)

"*It is impossible not to reach the conclusion that the American Government desires to maintain and strengthen, in coalition with Great Britain and other Powers, its dominant position it has hitherto occupied not only in China but in other areas of East Asia.*"

(Part IV, Section 4)

"*The Japanese Government regrets to have to notify hereby the American Government that in view of the attitude of the American Government it cannot but consider that it is impossible to reach an agreement through future negotiations.*"

(Part VII)

crux of this long message: the summation that all hope of preserving peace in the Pacific "has finally been lost."

Audience

Secretary of State Cordell Hull, acting on behalf of President Roosevelt, was the personal recipient of the message. It goes without saying that Roosevelt's cabinet, Congress, and the American people made up the secondary audience. The message was a systematic defense and justification for an action that changed the course of history. Therefore, it is safe to assume that the Japanese Foreign Ministry must have composed the message with posterity in mind and must have believed that history would judge its actions and its logic favorably. In terms of the reputation of Japan's wartime government, history has been no kinder to this message than the American public was after the attack

on Pearl Harbor. Had the message not been the only warning of a devastating attack that had already been launched, its summary of the international scene and its recapitulation of a tragically failed diplomatic process might have gained a sympathetic audience in some quarters. The Fourteen-part Message was not only vague but late, and as such it has come to stand as the emblematic document of what President Roosevelt called in his Address to Congress Requesting a Declaration of War "a date which will live in infamy" (http://millercenter.org/scripps/archive/speeches/detail/3324).

Impact

The first documented response to the Fourteen-part Message was uttered by Secretary Hull to Ambassador Nomura and Special Envoy Kurusu only moments after he had read the message. "I have never seen," Hull said, "a document that was more crowded with infamous falsehoods and distortions" (http://www.mtholyoke.edu/acad/intrel/WorldWar2/memo.htm). The poor timing of the message convinced the American people that they had been the victims of a sneak attack, and this perception galvanized support for war, notwithstanding that only weeks prior to the attack a majority of Americans had opposed any kind of military action against Germany or Japan. On December 8, as young men stormed armed-forces recruiting offices around the country, President Roosevelt made a stirring (and easy) pitch to Congress for a declaration of war. It is probably safe to say that if Japan had given the United States several days to ponder the Fourteen-part Message, or even if Japan had formally declared war subsequent to that message, it would not have lessened the surprise or mitigated the fury of Americans after the attack on Pearl Harbor. America's subsequent goal of achieving total destruction of Japan's military forces and its stubborn imperative of unconditional Japanese surrender would be directly linked to the warning, or lack of warning, given by the Japanese government on December 7, 1941.

Further Reading

▪ Articles

Butow, R. J. C. "Marching Off to War on the Wrong Foot: The Final Note Tokyo Did Not Send to Washington." *Pacific Historical Journal* 63, no. 1 (February 1995): 67–79.

Conroy, Hilary, and Harry Wray. "Pearl Harbor Reexamined: Prologue to the Pacific War." *Monumenta Nipponica* 45, no. 3 (1990): 381–384.

McKechney, John. "The Pearl Harbor Controversy: A Debate among Historians." *Monumenta Nipponica* 18, no. 1 (1963): 45–88.

▪ Books

Boyle, John Hunter. *Modern Japan: The American Nexus*. Fort Worth, Tex.: Harcourt Brace Jovanovich, 1993.

Iriye, Akira. *Pearl Harbor and the Coming of the Pacific War: A Brief History with Documents and Essays*. Boston: Bedford/Saint Martin's, 1999.

McClain, James L. *Japan: A Modern History*. New York: W. W. Norton, 2002.

Prange, Gordon W., et al. *At Dawn We Slept: The Untold Story of Pearl Harbor*. New York: McGraw-Hill, 1981.

Toland, John. *Infamy: Pearl Harbor and Its Aftermath*. Garden City, N.Y.: Doubleday, 1982.

U.S. Department of State, *Peace and War: United States Foreign Policy, 1931–1941*. Washington, D.C.: U.S. Government Printing Office, 1943.

▪ Web Sites

"Address to Congress Requesting a Declaration of War (December 8, 1941)." Miller Center of Public Affairs Web site. http://millercenter.org/scripps/archive/speeches/detail/3324.

Questions for Further Study

1. Most Americans believe that World War II in the Pacific began with the Japanese attack on Pearl Harbor on December 7, 1941. Make the case that the war in the Pacific *really* began as far back as 1931, or perhaps 1937.

2. To what extent does the assertion in the message that one of Japan's goals is for "all nations to find each its proper place in the world" resemble the message contained in the entry Bernhard von Bülow on Germany's "Place in the Sun"? What do these messages tell you about the state of world politics in the first half of the twentieth century?

3. Using Japan's Fourteen-part Message and Hitler's Proclamation to the German People, make an argument that rabid nationalism was the underlying source of World War II.

4. Imagine that the surprise attack on Pearl Harbor had not taken place and that Japan and the United States either had not gone to war or went to war some months, perhaps a year, later. On what basis might the Japanese claims made in the Fourteen-part Message have gained some validity?

5. Draw a distinction, if any is to be made, between Japan's behavior in Asia during the 1930s and Great Britain's behavior in Egypt as reflected in the entry Gamal Abdel Nasser on the Nationalization of the Suez Canal. How did similar economic and strategic goals influence the behaviors of the two powers?

Fleming, Thomas. "Pearl Harbor Hype." History News Network Web site.
    http://hnn.us/articles/89.html.

Greenberg, David. "Who Lost Pearl Harbor?" Slate Magazine Web site.
    http://www.slate.com/id/94663/.

Lutton, Charles. "Pearl Harbor: Fifty Years of Controversy." Institute for Historical Review Web site.
    http://www.ihr.org/jhr/v11/v11p431_Lutton.html.

"Memorandum [95] Regarding a Conversation, between the Secretary of State, the Japanese Ambassador (Nomura), and Mr. Kurusu, 7 December 1941." Mount Holyoke College International Relations Web site.
    http://www.mtholyoke.edu/acad/intrel/WorldWar2/memo.htm.

"Quarantine Speech (October 5, 1937)." Miller Center of Public Affairs Web site.
    http://millercenter.org/scripps/archive/speeches/detail/3310.

"Text of the Document Handed by Secretary of State Hull to the Japanese Ambassador." Pearl Harbor History Associates Web site.
    http://www.ibiblio.org/pha/timeline/411002bwp.html.

"United States Note to Japan, November 26, 1941." UCLA Center for East Asian Studies Web site.
    http://www.international.ucla.edu/eas/documents/usnote411126.htm.

—Eric Cunningham

Japan's Fourteen-part Message

I. The government of Japan, prompted by a genuine desire to come to an amicable understanding with the Government of the United States in order that the two countries by their joint efforts may secure the peace of the Pacific Area and thereby contribute toward the realization of world peace, has continued negotiations with the utmost sincerity since April last with the Government of the United States regarding the adjustment and advancement of Japanese-American relations and the stabilization of the Pacific Area.

The Japanese Government has the honor to state frankly its views concerning the claims the American Government has persistently maintained as well as the measure the United States and Great Britain have taken toward Japan during these eight months.

II. It is the immutable policy of the Japanese Government to insure the stability of East Asia and to promote world peace and thereby to enable all nations to find each its proper place in the world.

Ever since China Affair broke out owing to the failure on the part of China to comprehend Japan's true intentions, the Japanese Government has striven for the restoration of peace and it has consistently exerted its best efforts to prevent the extension of war-like disturbances. It was also to that end that in September last year Japan concluded the Tripartite Pact with Germany and Italy.

However, both the United States and Great Britain have resorted to every possible measure to assist the Chungking regime so as to obstruct the establishment of a general peace between Japan and China, interfering with Japan's constructive endeavours toward the stabilization of East Asia. Exerting pressure on the Netherlands East Indies, or menacing French Indo-China, they have attempted to frustrate Japan's aspiration to the ideal of common prosperity in cooperation with these regimes. Furthermore, when Japan in accordance with its protocol with France took measures of joint defense of French Indo-China, both American and British Governments, willfully misinterpreting it as a threat to their own possessions, and inducing the Netherlands Government to follow suit, they enforced the assets-freezing order, thus severing economic relations with Japan. While manifesting thus an obviously hostile attitude, these countries have strengthened their military preparations perfecting an encirclement of Japan, and have brought about a situation which endangers the very existence of the Empire.

Nevertheless, to facilitate a speedy settlement, the Premier of Japan proposed, in August last, to meet the President of the United States for a discussion of important problems between the two countries covering the entire Pacific area. However, the American Government, while accepting in principle the Japanese proposal, insisted that the meeting should take place after an agreement of view had been reached on fundamental and essential questions.

III. Subsequently, on September 25th the Japanese Government submitted a proposal based on the formula proposed by the American Government, taking fully into consideration past American claims and also incorporating Japanese views. Repeated discussions proved of no avail in producing readily an agreement of view. The present cabinet, therefore, submitted a revised proposal, moderating still further the Japanese claims regarding the principal points of difficulty in the negotiation and endeavoured strenuously to reach a settlement. But the American Government, adhering steadfastly to its original assertions, failed to display in the slightest degree a spirit of conciliation. The negotiation made no progress.

Therefore, the Japanese Government, with a view to doing its utmost for averting a crisis in Japanese-American relations, submitted on November 20th still another proposal in order to arrive at an equitable solution of the more essential and urgent questions which, simplifying its previous proposal, stipulated the following points:

(1) The Government of Japan and the United States undertake not to dispatch armed forces into any of the regions, excepting French Indo-China, in the Southeastern Asia and the Southern Pacific area.

(2) Both Governments shall cooperate with the view to securing the acquisition in the Netherlands East Indies of those goods and commodities of which the two countries are in need.

(3) Both Governments mutually undertake to restore commercial relations to those prevailing prior to the freezing of assets.

The Government of the United States shall supply Japan the required quantity of oil.

(4) The Government of the United States undertakes not to resort to measures and actions prejudicial to the endeavours for the restoration of general peace between Japan and China.

(5) The Japanese Government undertakes to withdraw troops now stationed in French Indo-China upon either the restoration of peace between Japan and China or establishment of an equitable peace in the Pacific Area; and it is prepared to remove the Japanese troops in the southern part of French Indo-China to the northern part upon the conclusion of the present agreement.

As regards China, the Japanese Government, while expressing its readiness to accept the offer of the President of the United States to act as "introducer" of peace between Japan and China as was previously suggested, asked for an undertaking on the part of the United States to do nothing prejudicial to the restoration of Sino-Japanese peace when the two parties have commenced direct negotiations.

The American Government not only rejected the above-mentioned new proposal, but made known its intention to continue its aid to Chiang Kai-shek; and in spite of its suggestion mentioned above, withdrew the offer of the President to act as so-called 'introducer' of peace between Japan and China, pleading that time was not yet ripe for it. Finally on November 26th, in an attitude to impose upon the Japanese Government those principles it has persistently maintained, the American Government made a proposal totally ignoring Japanese claims, which is a source of profound regret to the Japanese Government.

IV. From the beginning of the present negotiation the Japanese Government has always maintained an attitude of fairness and moderation, and did its best to reach a settlement, for which it made all possible concessions often in spite of great difficulties. As for the China question which constitutes an important subject of the negotiation, the Japanese Government showed a most conciliatory attitude. As for the principle of non-discrimination in international commerce, advocated by the American Government, the Japanese Government expressed its desire to see the said principle applied throughout the world, and declared that along with the actual practice of this principle in the world, the Japanese Government would endeavour to apply the same in the Pacific area including China, and made it clear that Japan had no intention of excluding from China economic activities of third powers pursued on an equitable basis. Furthermore, as regards the question of withdrawing troops from French Indo-China, the Japanese Government even volunteered, as mentioned above, to carry out an immediate evacuation of troops from Southern French Indo-China as a measure of easing the situation.

It is presumed that the spirit of conciliation exhibited to the utmost degree by the Japanese Government in all these matters is fully appreciated by the American Government.

On the other hand, the American Government, always holding fast to theories in disregard of realities, and refusing to yield an inch on its impractical principles, cause undue delay in the negotiation. It is difficult to understand this attitude of the American Government and the Japanese Government desires to call the attention of the American Government especially to the following points:

1. The American Government advocates in the name of world peace those principles favorable to it and urges upon the Japanese Government the acceptance thereof. The peace of the world may be brought about only by discovering a mutually acceptable formula through recognition of the reality of the situation and mutual appreciation of one another's position. An attitude such as ignores realities and impose [sic] one's selfish views upon others will scarcely serve the purpose of facilitating the consummation of negotiations.

Of the various principles put forward by the American Government as a basis of the Japanese-American Agreement, there are some which the Japanese Government is ready to accept in principle, but in view of the world's actual condition it seems only a utopian ideal on the part of the American Government to attempt to force their immediate adoption.

Again, the proposal to conclude a multilateral non-aggression pact between Japan, United States, Great Britain, China, the Soviet Union, the Netherlands and Thailand, which is patterned after the old concept of collective security, is far removed from the realities of East Asia.

2. The American proposal contained a stipulation which states—"Both Governments will agree that no agreement, which either has concluded with any third power or powers, shall be interpreted by it in such a way as to conflict with the fundamental purpose of this agreement, the establishment and preservation of peace throughout the Pacific area." It is presumed that the above provision has been proposed with a view to restrain Japan from fulfilling its obligations under the Tripartite Pact when the United States participates in the war in Europe, and, as such, it cannot be accepted by the Japanese Government.

The American Government, obsessed with its own views and opinions, may be said to be scheming for the extension of the war. While it seeks, on the one hand, to secure its rear by stabilizing the Pacific Area, it is engaged, on the other hand, in aiding Great Britain and preparing to attack, in the name of self-defense, Germany and Italy, two Powers that are striving to establish a new order in Europe. Such a policy is totally at variance with the many principles upon which the American Government proposes to found the stability of the Pacific Area through peaceful means.

3. Whereas the American Government, under the principles it rigidly upholds, objects to settle international issues through military pressure, it is exercising in conjunction with Great Britain and other nations pressure by economic power. Recourse to such pressure as a means of dealing with international relations should be condemned as it is at times more inhumane [than] military pressure.

4. It is impossible not to reach the conclusion that the American Government desires to maintain and strengthen, in coalition with Great Britain and other Powers, its dominant position it has hitherto occupied not only in China but in other areas of East Asia. It is a fact of history that the countries of East Asia for the past two hundred years or more have been compelled to observe the status quo under the Anglo-American policy of imperialistic exploitation and to sacrifice themselves to the prosperity of the two nations. The Japanese Government cannot tolerate the perpetuation of such a situation, since it directly runs counter to Japan's fundamental policy to enable all nations to enjoy each its proper place in the world.

The stipulation proposed by the American Government relative to French Indo-China is a good exemplification of the above-mentioned American policy. Thus the six countries,—Japan, the United States, Great Britain, the Netherlands, China,, and Thailand,—excepting France, should undertake among themselves to respect the territorial integrity and sovereignty of French Indo-China and equality of treatment in trade and commerce would be tantamount to placing that territory under the joint guarantee of the Governments of those six countries. Apart from the fact that such a proposal totally ignores the position of France, it is unacceptable to the Japanese Government in that such an arrangement cannot but be considered as an extension to French Indo-China of a system similar to the Nine Power Treaty structure which is the chief factor responsible for the present predicament of East Asia.

5. All the items demanded of Japan by the American Government regarding China, such as wholesale evacuation of troops or unconditional application of the principle of non-discrimination in international commerce, ignored the actual conditions of China and are calculated to destroy Japan's position as the stabilizing factor of East Asia. The attitude of the American Government in demanding Japan not to support militarily, politically or economically any regime other than the regime at Chungking, disregarding thereby the existence of the Nanking Government, shatters the very basis of the present negotiations. This demand of the American Government falling, as it does, in line with its above-mentioned refusal to cease from aiding the Chungking regime, demonstrates clearly the intention of the American Government to obstruct the restoration of normal relations between Japan and China and the return of peace to East Asia.

V. In brief, the American proposal contains certain acceptable items such as those concerning commerce, including the conclusion of a trade agreement, mutual removal of the freezing restrictions, and stabilization of yen and dollar exchange, or the abolition of extra-territorial rights in China. On the other hand, however, the proposal in question ignores Japan's sacrifices in the four years of the China Affair, menaces the Empire's existence itself and disparages its honour and prestige. Therefore, viewed in its entirety, the Japanese Government regrets it cannot accept the proposal as a basis of negotiation.

VI. The Japanese Government, in its desire for an early conclusion of the negotiation, proposed simultaneously with the conclusion of the Japanese-American negotiation, agreements to be signed with Great Britain and other interested countries. The proposal was accepted by the American Government. However, since the American Government has made the proposal of November 26th as a result of frequent consultation with Great Britain, Australia, the Netherlands and Chungking, and presumably by catering to the wishes of the Chungking regime in the questions of China, it must be concluded that all these countries are at one with the United States in ignoring Japan's position.

VII. Obviously it is the intention of the American Government to conspire with Great Britain and other countries to obstruct Japan's effort toward the establishment of peace through the creation of a new order in East Asia, and especially to preserve Anglo-American rights and interest by keeping Japan and China at war. This intention has been revealed clearly during the course of the present negotiation.

Thus, the earnest hope of the Japanese Government to adjust Japanese-American relations and to preserve and promote the peace of the Pacific through cooperation with the American Government has finally been lost.

The Japanese Government regrets to have to notify hereby the American Government that in view of the attitude of the American Government it cannot but consider that it is impossible to reach an agreement through further negotiations.

December 7, 1941

Glossary

Chungking regime	the Chinese Nationalist government, with its seat at Chongqing (formerly, Chungking)
Nanking Government	the Japanese-sponsored puppet Chinese Nationalist government, with its seat at Nanjing (formerly, Nanking)